ENCYCLOPEDIA OF COMPUTER SCIENCE AND TECHNOLOGY

VOLUME 38

ENCYCLOPEDIA OF COMPUTER SCIENCE AND TECHNOLOGY

EXECUTIVE EDITORS

Allen Kent   *James G. Williams*

UNIVERSITY OF PITTSBURGH
PITTSBURGH, PENNSYLVANIA

ADMINISTRATIVE EDITOR

Carolyn M. Hall

ARLINGTON, TEXAS

VOLUME 38

SUPPLEMENT 23

CRC Press
Taylor & Francis Group
Boca Raton London New York

CRC Press is an imprint of the
Taylor & Francis Group, an **informa** business

CONTENTS OF VOLUME 38

CONTRIBUTORS TO VOLUME 38

ELISA BERTINO   Full Professor, Department of Computer Science, University of Milano, Milan, Italy: *Transaction Models and Architectures*

LEON BUN, Ir.   Faculty of Information Technology and Systems, Delft University of Technology, Delft, The Netherlands: *Formal Software Development Methods: An Engineering Perspective*

BARBARA CATANIA, Ph.D.   Department of Computer Science, University of Milano, Milan, Italy: *Transaction Models and Architectures*

S. M. CLARK   Lutchi Research Centre, Loughborough University, Loughborough, Leicestershire, England: *The LookingGlass Distributed Shared Workspace*

AL DAVIS   Department of Computer Science, University of Utah, Salt Lake City, Utah: *An Introduction to Asynchronous Circuit Design*

VASANT DHAR   Associate Professor, Information Systems Department, Leonard N. Stern School of Business, New York University, New York, New York: *A Practical Methodology for Applying Neural Networks to Business Decision Problems*

DROR G. FEITELSON, Ph.D.   Institute of Computer Science, The Hebrew University of Jerusalem, Jerusalem, Israel: *Job Scheduling for Parallel Supercomputers*

MICHAEL HADJIMICHAEL, Ph.D.   NRC Research Associate, Naval Research Laboratory, Marine Meteorology Division, Monterey, California: *Interactive Inductive Machine Learning and the Conditional Probabilistic Learning Algorithm*

PAUL HUDAK   Department of Computer Science, Yale University, New Haven, Connecticut: *Functional Programming*

N. KEEN Lutchi Research Centre, Loughborough University, Loughborough, Leicestershire, England: *The LookingGlass Distributed Shared Workspace*

MING C. LIN   Associate Professor, Department of Computer Science, University of North Carolina, Chapel Hill, North Carolina: *Applied Computational Geometry*

DINESH MANOCHA Associate Professor, Department of Computer Science, University of North Carolina, Chapel Hill, North Carolina: *Applied Computational Geometry*

ROBERT G. MAYS   Senior Programmer, Networking Software Division, International Business Machines Corporation, Research Triangle Park, North Carolina: *Defect Prevention*

STEVEN M. NOWICK   Department of Computer Science, Columbia University, New York, New York: *An Introduction to Asynchronous Circuit Design*

NICO PLAT, Dr. Ir.   Cap Gemini, Utrecht, The Netherlands: *Formal Software Development Methods: An Engineering Perspective*

WOLFGANG PÖLZLEITNER, Ph.D.   sensotech GmbH, and University of Technology, Graz, Austria: *Image Analysis and Synthesis*

LARRY RUDOLPH, Ph.D.   Institute of Computer Science, The Hebrew University of Jerusalem, Jerusalem, Israel: *Job Scheduling for Parallel Supercomputers*

SHIMON SCHOCKEN   Professor and Dean, School of Computer & Media Sciences, The Interdisciplinary Center, Herzliya, Israel: *A Practical Methodology for Applying Neural Networks to Business Decision Problems*

STEPHEN A. R. SCRIVENER   Design Research Centre, University of Derby, Derby, England: *The LookingGlass Distributed Shared Workspace*

RONALD LUTJE SPELBERG, Ir. Faculty of Information Technology and Systems, Delft University of Technology, Delft, The Netherlands: *Formal Software Development Methods: An Engineering Perspective*

ROGER M. STEIN   Vice President, Quantitative Analytics, Moody's Investors Service and Information Systems Department; Leonard N. Stern School of Business, New York University, New York, New York: *A Practical Methodology for Applying Neural Networks to Business Decision Problems*

HANS TOETENEL, Dr. Ir. Associate Professor of Programming, Programming Languages and Programming Language Implementation, Faculty of Information Technology and Systems, Delft University of Technology, Delft, The Netherlands: *Formal Software Development Methods: An Engineering Perspective*

JAN VAN KATWIJK, Dr. Ir. Full Professor, Software Engineering, Faculty of Information Technology and Systems, Delft University of Technology, Delft, The Netherlands: *Formal Software Development Methods: An Engineering Perspective*

HARRICK M. VIN, Ph.D. Assistant Professor and Director, Distributed Multimedia Computing Laboratory, Department of Computer Sciences, The University of Texas, Austin, Texas: *Algorithms for Designing Multimedia Storage Servers*

ALESSIA VINAI Pride, Milan, Italy: *Transaction Models and Architectures*

WOLFGANG L. ZAGLER, Dr. Institut fuer Allgemeine Elektrotechnik, Vienna University of Technology, Vienna, Austria: *Computer Applications for Persons with Special Needs*

YANCHING Q. ZHANG, Ph.D. Lockheed Martin, U.S. EPA Scientific Visualization Center, Research Triangle Park, North Carolina: *Environmental Visualization: Scientific Visualization in Environmental Research*

ENCYCLOPEDIA OF COMPUTER SCIENCE AND TECHNOLOGY

VOLUME 38

ALGORITHMS FOR DESIGNING MULTIMEDIA STORAGE SERVERS

INTRODUCTION

Recent advances in computing and communication technologies have made it feasible and economically viable to provide on-line access to a variety of information sources such as books, periodicals, images, video clips, and scientific data. The architecture of such services consists of *multimedia storage servers* that are connected to client sites via high-speed networks (1). Clients of such a service are permitted to retrieve multimedia objects from the server for real-time playback at their respective sites. Furthermore, the retrieval may be interactive in the sense that clients may stop, pause, resume, and even record and edit the media information if they have permission to do so.

The design of such multimedia servers differs significantly from traditional text/numeric storage servers due to two fundamental characteristics of digital audio and video:

- *Large data transfer rate* and *storage space requirement*: Playback of digital video and audio consumes data at a very high rate (see Table 1). Thus, a multimedia service must provide efficient mechanisms for storing, retrieving, and manipulating data in large quantities at high speeds.
- *Real-time storage and retrieval:* Digital audio and video (often referred to as "continuous" media) consist of a sequence of media quanta (such as video frames or audio samples) which convey meaning only when presented continuously in time. This is in contrast to a textual object, for which spatial continuity is sufficient. Furthermore, a multimedia object, in general, may consist of several media components whose playback is required to be temporally coordinated.

The main goal of this article is to provide an overview of the various issues involved in designing a digital multimedia storage server and to present algorithms for addressing the specific storage and retrieval requirements of digital multimedia. Specifically, to manage the large storage space requirements of multimedia data, we examine techniques for efficient placement of media information on individual disks, large disk arrays, as well as hierarchies of storage devices (third section). To address the real-time recording and playback requirements, we discuss a set of admission control algorithms which a multimedia server may employ to determine whether a new client can be admitted without violating the real-time requirements of the clients already being serviced (fourth section). We will then briefly describe some of the existing commercial multimedia servers, and then present some concluding remarks.

TABLE 1   Storage Space Requirements for Uncompressed Digital
Multimedia Data

Media type (specifications)	Data rate
Voice quality audio (1 channel, 8-bit samples at 8 kHz)	64 Kbits/s
MPEG-encoded audio (equivalent to CD quality)	384 Kbits/s
CD-quality audio (2 channels, 16-bit samples at 44.1 kHz)	1.4 Mbits/s
MPEG 2-encoded video	0.42 MBytes/s
NTSC-quality video (640 × 480 pixels, 24 bits/pixel)	27 MBytes/s
HDTV-quality video (1280 × 720 pixels/frame, 24 bits/pixel)	81 MBytes/s

MULTIMEDIA STORAGE SERVERS

Digitization of video yields a sequence of frames and that of audio yields a sequence of samples. We refer to a sequence of continuously recorded video frames or audio samples as a *stream*. Because media quanta, such as video frames or audio samples, convey meaning only when presented continuously in time, a multimedia server must ensure that the recording and playback of each media stream proceeds at its real-time rate. Specifically, during recording, a multimedia server must continuously store the data produced by an input device (e.g., microphone, camera, etc.) so as to prevent buffer overruns at the device. During playback, on the other hand, the server must retrieve data from the disk at a rate which ensures that an output device (e.g., speaker, video display) consuming the data does not starve. Although semantically different, both of these operations have been shown to be mathematically equivalent with respect to their real-time performance requirements (2). Consequently, for the sake of clarity, we will only discuss techniques for retrieving media information from disk for real-time playback. Analysis for real-time recording can be carried out similarly.

Continuous playback of a media stream consists of a sequence of periodic tasks with deadlines, where tasks correspond to retrievals of media blocks from disk, and deadlines correspond to the scheduled playback times. Although it is possible to conceive of systems that would fetch media quanta from the storage system just in time to be played, in practice the retrieval is likely to be bursty. Consequently, information retrieved from the disk may have to be buffered prior to playback.

Therefore, the challenge for the server is to keep enough data in stream buffers at all times so as to ensure that the playback processes do not starve (3). In the simplest case, as the data transfer rates of disks are significantly higher than the real-time data rate of single stream (e.g., the maximum throughput of modern disks is of the order of 3–4 MBytes/s, whereas that of an MPEG-2-encoded video stream is 0.42 MBytes/s, and uncompressed CD-quality stereo audio is about 0.2 MBytes/s), employing a modest amount of buffering will enable conventional file and operating systems to support continuous storage and retrieval of isolated media streams.

In practice, however, a multimedia server has to process requests from several clients simultaneously. In the best scenario, all the clients will request the retrieval of the same media stream, in which case, the multimedia server needs only to retrieve the stream once from the disk and then multicast it to all the clients. However, more often than not, different clients will request the retrieval of different streams; even when the same stream is being requested by multiple clients (such as a popular movie), requests may arrive at arbitrary intervals while the stream is already being serviced. Thus, each client may be viewing a different part of the movie at the same time.

A simple mechanism to guarantee that the real-time requirements of all the clients are met is to dedicate a disk head to each stream, and then treat each disk head as a single stream system. This, however, limits the total number of streams to the number of disk heads. In general, because the data transfer rate of disks are significantly higher than the real-time data rate of a single stream, the number of streams that can be serviced simultaneously can be significantly increased by multiplexing a disk head among several streams. However, in doing so, the server must ensure that the continuous playback requirements of all the streams are met. The number of clients that can be simultaneously serviced by a multimedia server is dependent on the placement of multimedia streams on disk as well as the servicing algorithm. In what follows, we first outline methods for managing the storage space requirements of digital multimedia, and then present algorithms for servicing a large number of clients simultaneously.

MANAGING THE STORAGE SPACE REQUIREMENT OF DIGITAL MULTIMEDIA

A storage server must divide video and audio streams into *blocks* while storing them on disks. Because media quanta, such as video frames or audio samples, convey meaning only when presented continuously in time, a multimedia server must organize their storage on disk so as to ensure that the playback of each media stream proceeds at its real-time rate. Moreover, due to the large storage space requirements of digital audio and video, an interactive, read–write storage server must employ flexible placement strategies that minimize copying of media information during editing.

In order to explore the viability of various placement models for storing digital continuous media on conventional magnetic disks, let us first briefly review some of the fundamental characteristics of magnetic disks. Generally, magnetic disks consist of a collection of platters, each of which is composed of a number of circular recording tracks (see Fig. 1). Platters spin at a constant rate. Moreover, the amount of data recorded on tracks may increase from the innermost track to the outermost track (e.g., zoned disks). The storage space of each track is divided into several disk blocks, each consisting of a sequence of physically contiguous sectors. Each platter is associated with a read–write head that is attached to a common actuator. A cylinder is a stack of tracks at one actuator position.

In such an environment, the access time of a disk block consists of three

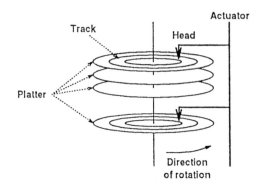

FIGURE 1   Architectural model of a conventional magnetic disk.

components: *seek time, rotational latency,* and *data transfer* time. Seek time is the time needed to position the disk head on the track containing the desired data and is a function of the initial start-up cost to accelerate the disk head as well as the number of tracks that must be traversed. Rotational latency, on the other hand, is the time for the desired data to rotate under the head before it can be read or written and is a function of the angular distance between the current position of the disk head and the location of the desired data, as well as the rate at which platters spin. Once the disk head is positioned at the desired disk block, the time to retrieve its contents is referred to as the data transfer time and is a function of the disk block size and data transfer rate of the disk.

Assuming a multimedia server consisting of such magnetic disks, in this section, we will first describe models for storing digital continuous media on individual disks, and then discuss the effects of utilizing disk arrays as well as storage hierarchies.

Placement of Data Blocks on Individual Disks

The placement of data blocks on disks in storage servers is generally governed by either contiguous, random, or constrained placement policy. Traditionally, high-performance storage servers have employed contiguous placement of media blocks on disk (4). In this case, once the disk head is positioned at the beginning of a stream, all the media blocks constituting the stream can be retrieved without incurring any seek or rotational latency, thereby defining a lower bound on the retrieval time of a media stream from disk. However, in highly interactive, read–write file system environments, contiguous placement of blocks of a stream is fraught with inherent problems of fragmentation and can entail enormous copying overheads during insertions and deletions for maintaining the contiguous nature of media streams on disk. Thus, the contiguous placement model, although suitable for read-only systems (such as compact discs, CLVs, etc.), is not viable for flexible, read–write storage systems.

Storage servers for read–write systems have traditionally employed random placement of blocks on disk (5,6). Because this placement model does not impose any restrictions on the separation between successive media blocks, editing operations do not incur any overhead for restructuring the storage of media streams on disk. However, the fundamental limitation of such a random placement policy, from the perspective of designing a multimedia storage server, is the overhead (seek time and rotational latency) incurred while accessing successive blocks of a stream. Although the effect of a higher separation between successive media blocks on disk can be circumvented by increasing the size of media blocks, the seek time and rotational latency resulting from the random separation between successive media blocks on disk may yield very low effective data transfer rates, thereby limiting the number of clients that can be serviced simultaneously.

Clearly, the contiguous and random placement models represent two ends of a spectrum: Whereas the former does not permit any separation between successive media blocks of a stream on disk, the latter does not impose any constraints at all. Recently, an efficient generalization of these two extremes, referred to as the constrained placement policy, has also been proposed (7). The main objective of the constrained placement policy is to ensure continuity of retrieval, as well as reduce the average seek time and rotational latency incurred while accessing successive media blocks of a stream by bounding the size of each media block as well as the separation between successive media blocks on disk. Such a placement policy is particularly attractive when the block size must be small (e.g., when utilizing a conventional file system with block sizes tailored for text). However, implementation of such a system may require elaborate algorithms to ensure that the separation between blocks conforms to the required constraints. Furthermore, for constrained latency to yield its full benefits, the scheduling algorithm must retrieve all the blocks for a given stream at once before switching to any other stream.

Efficient Placement in Multidisk Multimedia Servers

Due to the immensity of the sizes and the data transfer requirements of multimedia objects, multimedia servers will undeniably be founded on *large disk arrays*. Disk arrays achieve high performance by servicing multiple I/O requests concurrently, as well as by utilizing several disks to service a single request in parallel. The performance of a disk array, however, is critically dependent on the distribution of the workload (i.e., the number of blocks to be retrieved from the array) among the disks. The higher the imbalance in the workload distribution, the lower is the throughput of the disk array.

To effectively utilize a disk array, a multimedia server must interleave the storage of each media stream among the disks in the array. The unit of data interleaving, referred to as a *media block*, denotes the maximum amount of logically contiguous data that is stored on a single disk [this has also been referred to as the *striping unit* in the literature (8)]. Successive media blocks of a stream are placed on consecutive disks using a round-robin allocation algorithm.

Each media block may contain either a fixed number of media units or a fixed number of storage units (e.g., bytes) (9–11). If each media stream stored on the array is encoded using a variable bit rate (VBR) compression technique, the storage space requirement may vary from one media unit to another. Hence, a server that composes a media block by accumulating a fixed number of media units will be required to store variable-size media blocks on the array. On the other hand, if media blocks are assumed to be of fixed size, they may contain a varying number of media units. Thus, depending on the placement policy, accessing a fixed number of media units may require the server to retrieve either a fixed number of variable-size blocks or a variable number of fixed-size blocks from the array.

The most appealing feature of the variable-size block placement policy is that, regardless of the playback rate requirements, if we assume that a server services clients by proceeding in terms of periodic rounds during which it accesses a fixed number of media units for each client, then the retrieval of each individual video stream from disk proceeds in *lock-step*; that is, each client accesses exactly one disk during each round, and consecutive disks in the array are accessed by the same set of clients during successive rounds. In such a scenario, the server can partition the set of clients into D logical groups (where D is the number of disks in the array) and then admit a new client by assigning it to the most lightly loaded group. Such a simple policy balances the load across the disks in the array, thereby maximizing the number of clients that can be serviced simultaneously by the server. However, the key limitations of the variable-size block placement policy include (1) the inherent complexity of allocating and deallocating variable-size media blocks and (2) the higher implementation overheads. Thus, although the variable-size block placement policy is highly attractive for designing multimedia storage servers for predominantly read-only environments (e.g., video on-demand), it may not be viable for the design of integrated multimedia file systems (in which multimedia documents are created, edited, and destroyed very frequently).

In the fixed-size block placement policy, on the other hand, a multimedia server partitions video streams into fixed-size blocks for storing them on the array. Thus, to access a fixed number of frames of VBR-encoded video streams during each round, the server will be required to access varying number of blocks for each client. As the set of disks accessed by a client may be unrelated to those accessed by other clients, the number of media blocks to be accessed during a round may vary from one disk to another. Due to this variation, the time spent in accessing the required blocks from the most heavily loaded disk may occasionally exceed the duration of a round, resulting in playback discontinuities for clients. To reduce the occurrence of such discontinuities, the server must select a media block size that minimizes the expected service time of the most heavily loaded disk (11). Additionally, the server may be required to exploit the sequential nature of video and audio playback to precompute the set of blocks to be accessed from disks during future rounds and prefetch a subset of them on detecting an overflow in the future round. Although such dynamic load-balancing schemes yield improved quality of service for the clients being serviced simultaneously, it is at the expense of increase in buffer space requirement. By judiciously choosing the set of blocks to be read-ahead in underflow rounds, the increase in the buffer space requirement can be minimized (12).

Utilizing Storage Hierarchies

The preceding discussion has focused on utilizing fixed disks as the storage medium for the multimedia server. Although sufficient for providing efficient access to a small number of video streams (e.g., 25–50 most popular titles maintained by a video rental store), the high cost per gigabyte of storage makes such magnetic disk-based server architectures ineffective for large-scale servers. In fact, the desire for sharing and providing on-line access to a wide variety of video sequences indicates that large-scale multimedia servers must utilize very large tertiary storage devices (e.g., tape and optical jukeboxes—see Table 2). These devices are highly cost-effective and provide very large storage capacities by utilizing robotic arms to serve a large number of removable tapes or disks to a small number of reading

TABLE 2   Tertiary Storage Devices

	Magnetic disk	Optical disk	Low-end tape	High-end tape
Capacity	9 GB	200 GB	500 GB	10 TB
Mount time	0 s	20 s	60 s	90 s
Transfer rate	2 MB/s	300 KB/s	100 KB/s	1000 KB/s
Cost/GB	$555/GB	$125/GB	$100/GB	$50/GB

devices. Because of these long seek-and-swap times, they are poor at performing random access within a video stream. Moreover, they can support only a single playback at a time on each reader. Consequently, they are inappropriate for direct video playback. Thus, a large-scale, cost-effective multimedia server will be required to utilize tertiary storage devices (such as tape jukeboxes) to maintain a large number of video streams, and then achieve high performance and scalability through magnetic-disk-based servers.

In the simplest case, such a hierarchical storage manager may utilize fast magnetic disks to cache frequently accessed data. In such a scenario, there are several alternatives for managing the disk system. It may be used as a staging area (cache) for the tertiary storage devices, with entire media streams being moved from the tertiary storage to the disks when they need to be played back. On the other hand, it is also possible to use the disks only to provide storage for the beginning segments of the multimedia streams. These segments may be used to reduce the start-up latency and to ensure smooth transitions in the playback (13).

A distributed hierarchical storage management extends this idea by allowing multiple magnetic-disk-based caches to be distributed across a network. In such a scenario, if a high percentage of clients access data stored in a local (or nearby) cache, the perceived performance will be sufficient to meet the demands of continuous media. On the other hand, if the user accesses are unpredictable or have poor reference locality, then most accesses will require retrieval of information from tertiary storage devices, thereby significantly degrading the performance (14–16).

Having discussed the techniques for efficient placement of multimedia objects on disk arrays and tertiary storage devices, we will now describe the techniques for meeting the real-time playback requirements of multimedia streams from a disk-based server.

EFFICIENT RETRIEVAL OF MULTIMEDIA OBJECTS

Due to the periodic nature of multimedia playback, a multimedia server can service multiple clients simultaneously by proceeding in terms of rounds. During each round, the multimedia server retrieves a sequence of media blocks for each stream, and the rounds are repeatedly executed until the completion of all the requests. The number of blocks of a media stream retrieved during a round is dependent on its playback rate requirement, as well as the buffer space availability at the client (17). Ensuring continuous retrieval of each stream requires that the *service time* (i.e., the total time spent in retrieving media blocks during a round) does not exceed the minimum of the playback durations of the blocks retrieved for each stream during a round. Hence, before admitting a new client, a multimedia server must employ admission control algorithms to decide whether a new client can be admitted without violating the continuous playback requirements of the clients already being serviced.

To precisely formulate the admission control criteria, consider a multimedia server that is servicing n clients, each retrieving a different media stream (say, S_1, $S_2, \ldots, S_n$, respectively). Let $f_1, f_2, \ldots, f_n$ denote the number of frames of streams $S_1, S_2, \ldots, S_n$ retrieved during each round. Then, assuming that $\Re_{pl}^i$ denotes the playback rate (expressed in terms of frames/s) of stream S_i, the duration of a round, defined as the minimum of the playback durations of the frames accessed during a round, is given by

$$\Re = \min_{i \in [1, n]} \left(\frac{f_i}{\Re_{pl}^i} \right).$$

Additionally, let us assume that media blocks of each stream are placed on disk using a random placement policy and that the multimedia server is employing the SCAN disk scheduling policy, in which the disk head moves back and forth across the platter and retrieves media blocks in either increasing or decreasing order of their track numbers.

Deterministic Admission Control Algorithm

To ensure that the continuous playback requirements of all the clients are strictly met throughout the duration of service (i.e., to provide deterministic service guarantees), the server must ensure that the playback rate requirements of all the clients are met even in the worst case. Specifically, if $k_1, k_2, \ldots, k_n$ denote the maximum number of blocks of streams $S_1, S_2, \ldots, S_n$ that may need to retrieved during a round, then, in the worst case, each of the $(k_1 + k_2 + \cdots + k_n)$ blocks may be stored on separate tracks. Thus, the disk head may have to be repositioned onto a new track at most $(k_1 + k_2 + \cdots + k_n)$ times during each round. Hence, using the symbols for disk parameters presented in Table 3, the total seek time incurred during each round can be computed as $(a \sum_{i=1}^{n} k_i + b C)$. Similarly, retrieval of each media block may, in the worst case, incur a rotational latency of l_{rot}^{max} yielding that the total rotational latency incurred during each round is bounded by $(l_{rot}^{max} \sum_{i=1}^{n} k_i)$. Hence, the total service time for each round is bounded by

$$\tau = bC + (a + l_{rot}^{max}) \sum_{i=1}^{n} k_i. \tag{1}$$

TABLE 3   Summary of Disk Parameters Used

Symbol	Explanation	Units
C	Number of cylinders on disk	—
a, b	Constants (seek time parameters)	sec
$l_{seek}(c_1, c_2)$	Seek time $(a + b\lvert c_1 - c_2 \rvert)$	sec
l_{rot}^{max}	Maximum rotational latency	sec

Ensuring continuous retrieval of each stream requires that the total service time per round does not exceed the minimum of the playback durations of $k_1, k_2, \ldots,$ or k_n blocks (2,3,6,17–19). We refer to this as the *deterministic admission control principle*, which can be formally stated:

$$bC + (a + l_{\text{rot}}^{\text{max}}) \sum_{i=1}^{n} k_i \leq \Re. \tag{2}$$

Note, however, that due to the human perceptual tolerances as well as the inherent redundancy in continuous media streams, most clients of a multimedia server are tolerant to brief distortions in playback continuity as well as occasional loss of media information. Therefore, providing deterministic service guarantees to all the clients is superfluous. Furthermore, the worst-case assumptions that characterize deterministic admission control algorithms needlessly constrain the number of clients that can be serviced simultaneously, and hence, lead to severe underutilization of server resources.

Statistical Admission Control Algorithm

To exploit the human perceptual tolerances and the differences between the average and the worst-case performance characteristics of the multimedia server, a *statistical* admission control algorithm has also been proposed in the literature (20). This algorithm utilizes precise *distributions* of access times and playback rates, rather than their corresponding worst-case values, and provides *statistical* service guarantees to each client (i.e., the continuity requirements of at least a fixed percentage of media units is ensured to be met).

To clearly explain this algorithm, let us assume that the service requirements of client i be specified as a percentage p_i of the total number of frames that must be retrieved on time. Moreover, let us assume that each media stream may be encoded using a variable bit rate compression technique (e.g., JPEG, MPEG, etc.). In such a scenario, the number of media blocks that contain f_i frames of stream S_i may vary from one round to another. This difference, when coupled with the variation in the relative separation between blocks, yields different service times across rounds. In fact, while servicing a large number of clients, the service time may occasionally exceed the round duration (i.e., $\tau > \Re$). We refer to such rounds as *overflow* rounds. Given that each client may have requested a different quality of service (i.e., different values of p_i), meeting all of their service requirements will require the server to delay the retrieval of or discard (i.e., not retrieve) media blocks of some of the more tolerant clients during overflow rounds.* Consequently, to ensure that the statistical quality of service requirements of clients are not violated, a multimedia server must employ admission control algorithms that restrict the occurrence of such overflow rounds by limiting the number of clients admitted for service.

To precisely derive an admission control criterion that meets the above requirement, observe that for rounds in which $\tau \leq \Re$, none of the media blocks need to be discarded. Therefore, the total number of frames retrieved during such rounds

---

*The choice between delaying or discarding media blocks during overflow rounds is application dependent. As both of these policies are mathematically equivalent, in this article, we will analyze only the discarding policy.

is given by $\sum_{i=1}^{n} f_i$. During overflow rounds, however, because a few media blocks may have to be discarded or delayed to yield $\tau \leq \Re$, the total number of frames retrieved will be smaller than $\sum_{i=1}^{n} f_i$. Given that p_i denotes the percentage of frames of stream S_i that must be retrieved on time to satisfy the service requirements of client i, the *average* number of frames that must be retrieved during each round is given by $p_i f_i$. Hence, assuming that q denotes the overflow probability [i.e., $P(\tau > \Re) = q$], the service requirements of the clients will be satisfied if

$$q \, \mathfrak{F}_o + (1 - q) \sum_{i=1}^{n} f_i \geq \sum_{i=1}^{n} p_i f_i, \tag{3}$$

where $\mathfrak{F}_o$ denotes the number of frames that are guaranteed to be retrieved during overflow rounds. The left-hand side of Eq. (3) represents the lower bound on the expected number of frames retrieved during a round and the right-hand side denotes the average number of frames that must be accessed during each round so as to meet the service requirements of all clients. Clearly, the effectiveness of this admission control criteria, measured in terms of the number of clients that can be admitted, is dependent on the values of q and $\mathfrak{F}_o$. In what follows, we present techniques for accurately determining their values.

Computing the Overflow Probability

While servicing multiple clients simultaneously, an overflow is said to occur when the service time exceeds the playback duration of a round. Whereas the playback duration $\Re$ of a round is fixed (because the server is accessing a fixed number of frames for each client), the service time varies from round to round. Let the random variable τ_k denote the service time for accessing k media blocks from disk. Then overflow probability q can be computed as

$$q = P(\tau > \Re) = \sum_{k=k_{min}}^{k_{max}} P(\tau > \Re | \mathfrak{B} = k) P(\mathfrak{B} = k)$$

$$= \sum_{k=k_{min}}^{k_{max}} P(\tau_k > \Re) P(\mathfrak{B} = k), \tag{4}$$

where $\mathfrak{B}$ is the random variable representing the number of blocks to be retrieved in a round, and k_{min} and k_{max} denote its minimum and maximum values, respectively. Hence, computing the overflow probability q requires the determination of probability distribution functions for τ_k and $\mathfrak{B}$, as well as the values of k_{min} and k_{max}, techniques for which are described below.

- **Service time characterization**: Given the number of blocks to be accessed during a round, as the service time is dependent only on the relative placement of media blocks on disk and the disk scheduling algorithm and is completely independent of the client characteristics, service time distributions are required to be computed only *once* during the lifetime of a multimedia server, possibly at the time of its installation.

    The server can derive a distribution function for τ_k by empirically measuring the variation in service times yielded by different placements of k blocks on disk. The larger the number of such measurements, the greater is the accuracy of the distribution function. Starting with the minimum number of blocks that are guaranteed to be accessed during a round (i.e., the value of k_d derived earlier), the procedure for determining the distribution function for τ_k should be repeated for $k = k_d, k_d + 1, \ldots, k_{end}$, where k_{end} is the minimum value of k for which $P(\tau_{k_{end}} > \Re) \simeq 1$. Using these empirically derived distribution functions, the probability $P(\tau_k > \Re)$, for various values of k, can be easily computed.

- **Client load characterization**: Because f_i frames of stream S_i are retrieved during each round, the total number of blocks $\mathcal{B}$ required to be accessed is dependent on the frame size distributions for each stream. Specifically, if the random variable $\mathcal{B}_i$ denotes the number of media blocks that contain f_i frames of stream S_i, then the total number of blocks to be accessed during each round is given by

$$\mathcal{B} = \sum_{i=1}^{n} \mathcal{B}_i$$

Because $\mathcal{B}_i$ is only dependent on the frame size variations within stream S_i, $\mathcal{B}_i$'s denote a set of n *independent* random variables. Therefore, using the *central limit theorem*, we conclude that the distribution function $\mathcal{G}_{\mathcal{B}}(b)$ of $\mathcal{B}$ approaches a normal distribution (21). Furthermore, if $\eta_{\mathcal{B}_i}$ and $\sigma_{\mathcal{B}_i}$ denote the mean and standard deviation, respectively, of random variable $\mathcal{B}_i$, then the mean and standard deviation for $\mathcal{B}$ are given by

$$\eta_{\mathcal{B}} = \sum_{i=1}^{n} \eta_{\mathcal{B}_i}, \; \sigma_{\mathcal{B}}^2 = \sum_{i=1}^{n} \sigma_{\mathcal{B}_i}^2 \tag{5}$$

Consequently,

$$\mathcal{G}_{\mathcal{B}}(b) \simeq \Re \left(\frac{b - \eta_{\mathcal{B}}}{\sigma_{\mathcal{B}}} \right), \tag{6}$$

where $\Re$ is the standard normal distribution function. Additionally, as $\mathcal{B}_i$'s denote discrete random variables that take only integral values, they can be categorized as *lattice-type* random variables (21). Hence, using the central limit theorem, the point probabilities $P(\mathcal{B} = k)$ can be derived as

$$P(\mathcal{B} = k) \simeq \frac{1}{\sigma_{\mathcal{B}}\sqrt{2\pi}} \exp \left(- \frac{(k - \eta_{\mathcal{B}})^2}{2\sigma_{\mathcal{B}}^2} \right). \tag{7}$$

Finally, computing the overflow probability q using Eq. (4) requires the values of k_{min} and k_{max}. If b_i^{min} and b_i^{max} denote the minimum and the maximum number of media blocks, respectively, that may contain f_i frames of stream S_i, then the values of k_{min} and k_{max} can be derived as

$$k_{min} = \sum_{i=1}^{n} b_i^{min}; \quad k_{max} = \sum_{i=1}^{n} b_i^{max}. \tag{8}$$

Thus, by substituting the values of k_{min}, k_{max}, $P(\tau_k > \Re)$, and $P(\mathcal{B} = k)$ in Eq. (4), the overflow probability q can be computed.

Determination of $\mathfrak{F}_o$

The maximum number of frames $\mathfrak{F}_o$ that are guaranteed to be retrieved during an overflow round is dependent on (1) the number of media blocks that are guaranteed to be accessed from disk within the round duration $\mathfrak{R}$ and (2) the relationship between the media block size and the maximum frame sizes.

To compute the number of media blocks that are guaranteed to be accessed during each round, worst-case assumptions (similar to those employed by deterministic admission control algorithms) regarding the access times of media blocks from disk may need to be employed. Specifically, if k denotes the number of media blocks that are to be retrieved during a round, and if the server employs the SCAN disk scheduling algorithm, then as per Eq. (1), the worst-case service time can be computed as

$$\tau = bC + (a + l_{\text{rot}}^{\text{max}}) \, k.$$

Because $\tau \leq \mathfrak{R}$, the number of media blocks, k_d, that are guaranteed to be retrieved during each round is bounded by

$$k_d \leq \frac{\mathfrak{R} - bC}{(a + l_{\text{rot}}^{\text{max}})}. \tag{9}$$

Now, assuming that $f(S_i)$ denotes the minimum number of frames that may be contained in a block of stream S_i, the lower bound on the number of frames accessed during an overflow round is given by

$$\mathfrak{F}_o = k_d \min_{i \in [1,n]} f(S_i). \tag{10}$$

Admitting a New Client

Consider the scenario that a multimedia server receives a new client request for the retrieval of stream S_{n+1}. In order to validate that the admission of the new client will not violate the service requirements of the clients already being serviced, the server must first compute the overflow probability assuming that the new client has been admitted. In order to do so, the server must determine the following:

1.   The mean and the standard deviation of the number of media blocks that may contain f_{n+1} frames of stream S_{n+1} (denoted by $\eta_{(\mathfrak{B}n+1}$ and $\sigma_{(\mathfrak{B}n+1}$, respectively) to be used in Eqs. (5) and (6)
2.   The minimum and the maximum of media blocks that may contain f_{n+1} frames of stream S_{n+1} (denoted by b_{n+1}^{min} and b_{n+1}^{max}, respectively), to be used in Eq. (8)
3.   The minimum number of frames contained in a media block of stream S_{n+1} [denoted by $f(S_{n+1})$] to be used in Eq. (10)

As all of these parameters are dependent on the distribution of frame sizes in stream S_{n+1}, the server can simplify the processing requirements at the time of admission by precomputing these parameters while storing the media stream on disk.

These values, when coupled with the corresponding values for all the clients already being serviced as well as the predetermined service time distributions will yield new values for q and $\mathfrak{F}_o$. The new client is then admitted for service if the newly derived values for q and $\mathfrak{F}_o$ satisfy the admission control criteria:

$$q\,\mathfrak{F}_o + (1 - q) \sum_{i=1}^{n+1} f_i \geq \sum_{i=1}^{n+1} p_i f_i.$$

Discussion

In addition to the deterministic algorithms (which provide strict performance guarantees by making worst-case assumptions regarding the performance requirements) and the statistical admission control algorithms (that utilize precise distributions of access times and playback rates), other admission control algorithms have been proposed in the literature. One such algorithm is the *adaptive* admission control algorithm proposed in Refs. 12 and 22. As per this algorithm, a new client is admitted for service only if the prediction from the status quo measurements of the server performance characteristics indicate that the service requirements of all the clients can be met satisfactorily. It is based on the assumption that the average amount of time spent for the retrieval of each media block (denoted by η) does not change significantly even after a new client is admitted by the server. In fact, to enable the multimedia server to accurately predict the amount of time expected to be spent retrieving media blocks during a future round, a history of the values of η observed during the most recent W rounds (referred to as the *averaging window*) may be maintained. If η_{avg} and σ denote the average and the standard deviation of η over W rounds, respectively, then the time required to retrieve a block in future rounds ($\hat{\eta}$) can be estimated as

$$\hat{\eta} = \eta_{avg} + \epsilon\,\sigma, \tag{11}$$

where ϵ is an empirically determined constant. Clearly, a positive value of ϵ enables the estimation process to take into account the second moment of the random variable η and, hence, make the estimate reasonably conservative. Thus, if $\hat{k}_i$ and $\hat{\alpha}_i$ denote the average number of blocks accessed during a round for stream S_i, and the percentage of frames of stream S_i that must be retrieved on time so as to meet the requirements of client i, respectively, then the average number of blocks of stream S_i that must be retrieved by the multimedia server during each round can be approximated by $\hat{k}_i\hat{\alpha}_i$. Consequently, given the empirically estimated average access time of a media block from disk, the requirements of tolerant clients will not be violated if

$$\hat{\eta}\left(\sum_{i=1}^{n} \hat{k}_i\hat{\alpha}_i\right) \leq \mathfrak{R}. \tag{12}$$

This is referred to as the *adaptive admission control criterion*. Note that because estimation of the service time of a round is based on the measured characteristics of the current load on the server, rather than on theoretically derived values, the key function of such an admission control algorithm is to accept enough clients to utilize the server resources efficiently, and not to accept clients whose admission may lead to the violation of the service requirements.

COMMERCIAL VIDEO SERVERS

There has been significant work in developing multimedia servers for a wide variety of commercial applications. These products range from low-end PC-based multimedia servers designed to serve small work groups to high-end large-scale servers that can serve thousands of video-on-demand users.

The low-end servers are targeted for a local-area network (LAN) environment and their clients are personal computers, equipped with video-processing hardware, connected on a LAN. They are designed for applications such as on-site training, information kiosks, and so forth; the multimedia files generally consist of short video clips. An example of such a low-end server is the IBM LANServer Ultramedia product, which can serve 40 clients at MPEG-1 rates (23). Other systems in this class include FluentLinks, ProtoComm, and Starworks (6). As the computing power of personal computers increases, the number of clients that these servers can support will also increase.

High-end servers are targeted for applications such as video-on-demand, in which the number of simultaneous streams is expected to be in the 1000s, and the distribution system is expected to be cable based, or telephone-wire based. Because the distribution area is large, network connectivity is an important aspect of these systems. In order to provide a large collection of videos in a cost-effective solution, such servers employ a hierarchy of storage devices. Additionally, admission control mechanisms are extended to the distribution network, including allocation of bandwidth on the backbone network and TV "channels" on the cable plant. Finally, in such servers, the control mechanisms must also interact with large transaction processing systems to handle bookkeeping operations such as authorization and customer billing.

High-end video servers are based on collections of powerful workstations (IBM, DEC, Silicon Graphics, Oracle/NCube) or mainframe computers. For instance, the SHARK multimedia server is implemented on IBM RS/6000 and uses its own file system to ensure continuous throughput from the disk subsystem (24). Microsoft's TIGER video server uses a collection of PCs to construct a scalable server (25). It uses striping to distribute segments of a movie across the collection of servers to balance the access load across the servers. It also uses replication at the segment level as a mechanism for fault tolerance. Oracle's Media Server is based on the NCube massively parallel computer. It exploits the large I/O capability of the NCube and is slated to deliver approximately 25,000 video streams.

CONCLUDING REMARKS

Multimedia storage servers differ from conventional storage servers to the extent that significant changes in design must be effected. These changes are wide in scope, influencing everything from the selection of storage hardware to the choice of disk scheduling algorithms. This article provides an overview of the problems involved in multimedia storage server design and of the various approaches for solving these problems.

REFERENCES

1. G. Miller, G. Baber, and M. Gilliland, "News On-Demand for Multimedia Networks," in *Proceedings of ACM Multimedia '93*, August 1993, pp. 383–392.

2. D. Anderson, Y. Osawa, and R. Govindan, "A File System for Continuous Media," *ACM Trans. Computer Syst., 10*(4), 311–337 (1992).

3. J. Gemmell and S. Christodoulakis, "Principles of Delay Sensitive Multimedia Data Storage and Retrieval," *ACM Trans. Inform. Syst., 10*(1), 51–90 (1992).

4. R. Van Renesse, A. Tanenbaum, and A. Wilschut, "The Design of a High-Performance File Server," *IEEE Trans. Knowledge Data Eng., KDE-1*(2), 22–27 (1989).

5. M. K. McKusick, W. N. Joy, S. J. Leffler, and R. S. Fabry, "A Fast File System for UNIX," *ACM Trans. Computer Syst., 2*(3), 181–197 (1984).

6. F. A. Tobagi, J. Pang, R. Baird, and M. Gang, "Streaming RAID: A Disk Storage System for Video and Audio Files," in *Proceedings of ACM Multimedia '93*, August 1993, pp. 393–400.

7. P. Venkat Rangan and H. M. Vin, "Designing File Systems for Digital Video and Audio," *Operating Syst. Rev., 25*(5), 81–94 (1991).

8. H. Garcia-Molina and K. Salem, "Disk Stripping," in *International Conference on Data Engineering*, February 1986, pp. 336–342.

9. E. Chang and A. Zakhor, "Scalable Video Placement on Parallel Disk Arrays," in *Proceedings of IS&T/SPIE International Symposium on Electronic Imaging: Science and Technology*, February 1994.

10. K. Keeton and R. Katz, "The Evaluation of Video Layout Strategies on a High-Bandwidth File Server," in *Proceedings of International Workshop on Network and Operating System Support for Digital Audio and Video (NOSSDAV'93)*, November 1993.

11. H. M. Vin, S. S. Rao, and P. Goyal, "Optimizing the Placement of Multimedia Objects on Disk Arrays," in *Proceedings of the Second IEEE International Conference on Multimedia Computing and Systems*, May 1995, pp. 158–165.

12. H. M. Vin, A. Goyal, and P. Goyal, "Algorithms for Designing Large-Scale Multimedia Servers," *Computer Commun., 18*(3), 192–203 (1995).

13. T. Mori, K. Nishimura, H. Nakano, and Y. Ishibashi, "Video-on-Demand System Using Optical Mass Storage System," *Jpn. J. Appl. Phys., 1*(11B), 5433–5438 (1993).

14. C. Federighi and L. A. Rowe, "The Design and Implementation of the UCB Distributed Video On-Demand System," in *Proceedings of the IS&T/SPIE 1994 International Symposium on Electronic Imaging: Science and Technology*, February 1994, pp. 185–197.

15. T. D. C. Little, G. Ahanger, R. J. Folz, J. F. Gibbon, F. W. Reeves, D. H. Schelleng, and D. Venkatesh, "A Digital On-Demand Video Service Supporting Content-Based Queries," in *Proceedings of the ACM Multimedia '93*, October 1993, pp. 427–436.

16. L. A. Rowe, J. Boreczky, and C. Eads, "Indexes for User Access to Large Video Databases," in *Proceedings of the IS&T/SPIE 1994 International Symposium on Electronic Imaging: Science and Technology*, February 1994, pp. 150–161.

17. H. M. Vin and P. Venkat Rangan, "Designing a Multimedia-User HDTV Storage Server," *IEEE J. Selected Areas Commun., 11*(1), 153–164 (1993).

18. A. L. Narasimha Reddy and J. Wyllie, "Disk Scheduling in Multimedia I/O System," in *Proceedings of ACM Multimedia '93*, August 1993, pp. 225–234.

19. P. Yu, M. S. Chen, and D. D. Kandlur, "Design and Analysis of a Grouped Sweeping Scheme for Multimedia Storage Management," in *Proceedings of Third International Workshop on Network and Operating System Support for Digital Audio and Video*, November 1992, pp. 38–49.

20. H. M. Vin, P. Goyal, A. Goyal, and A. Goyal, "A Statistical Admission Control Algorithm for Multimedia Servers," in *Proceedings of the ACM Multimedia '94*, October 1994.

21. A. Papoulis, *Probability, Random Variables, and Stochastic Processes*, McGraw-Hill, New York, 1991.

22. H. M. Vin, A. Goyal, A. Goyal, and P. Goyal, "An Observation-Based Admission Control Algorithm for Multimedia Servers," in *Proceedings of the IEEE International Conference on Multimedia Computing and Systems* (*ICMCS'94*), May 1994.
23. M. Baugher et al., "A Multimedia Client to the IBM LAN Server," in *ACM Multimedia '93*, August 1993, pp. 105–112.
24. R. Haskin, "The SHARK Continuous Media File Server," in *Proc. CompCon,* 1993, pp. 12–15.
25. "Microsoft Unveils Video Software," *AP News*, May 17, 1994.

HARRICK M. VIN

APPLIED COMPUTATIONAL GEOMETRY

INTRODUCTION

Computational geometry, as a discipline, has been intended to provide algorithmic foundations and analytic tools for geometric problems encountered in many fields of sciences and engineering. These include computer graphics, solid modeling, manufacturing, robotics, computer vision, geographical information systems, fluid dynamics, computational biology, astrophysics, and so forth. As a research area, computational geometry has been gaining importance since the 1970s with influences from computer-aided design, theoretical computer science, mathematical programming, and other areas. Over the years, it has matured considerably as a discipline. Currently, a number of journals are specifically devoted to it and each year a number of workshops and conferences are held. However, most of the literature in computational geometry has emphasized the study of the computational complexity of geometric objects and well-defined geometric problems — such as data structures, analysis of lower/upper bound on running time and storage, algorithms, geometric operations, and combinatorial complexity of linear geometric structures (e.g., points, lines, polygons, and polyhedra). Some of the well-studied problems include computing convex hulls, Voronoi regions, triangulation, point location, interference detection, linear programming, arrangements, convex decomposition, and randomized algorithms. More information about these problems and algorithms can be found in Refs. 1–4.

Despite the wealth and abundance of literature and research in computational geometry, the intended technology transfer to the application areas has been slow and limited. The core of computational geometry can be enriched by the infusion of problems from application domains, thus making it more directly relevant. Today, computational geometry is at a crossroad — standing between the tradition which continues to pursue the theoretical investigations and the new path toward geometric engineering motivated by practical applications. To narrow the gap between theory and practice, several workshops have been organized in the last few years, and in terms of redefining the role of geometric computing, "applied computational geometry" has emerged.

Applied computational geometry emphasizes on good empirical performance of geometric algorithms instead of worst-case analysis. It focuses on new and improved methods for geometric problems which may require practical speedups and re-engineering of naive assumptions instead of investigating asymptotic complexity. Furthermore, it deals with issues in implementation of geometric algorithms on computers with finite precision arithmetic and developing tools to solve challenging problems. Most of all, applied computational geometry serves as the bridge between computational geometry and applied sciences, by considering ill-conditioned problems arising from the imperfection of physical world, coping with the limitations of computing machines and addressing tedious but important issues of model complexity and geometric degeneracies in practical applications.

With solid theoretical foundation and rigorous development of formal analysis, computational geometry offers an impressive wealth of results on algorithms and their analysis for fundamental geometric problems. Applied computational geometry, on the other hand, complements this research trend by attacking the robustness issues in geometric computing, by emphasizing development of geometric software and libraries with increasing focus on empirical results and benchmarking, and by designing and implementing practical geometric algorithms for specific applications.

In the following sections, we will address issues related to geometric robustness, implementation of geometric algorithms, and development of software libraries. Then, we highlight several applications of computational geometry in computer graphics, modeling, robotics, vision, molecular modeling, and manufacturing. Finally, we present three case studies of applied computational geometry. More details on these topics can be found in Refs. 5 and 6.

ROBUST COMPUTING

Most of the geometric algorithms assume that the input data are in a general position and that the existing computing machinery provides reliable exact real-number arithmetic. Unfortunately, such innocent assumptions often lead to inconsistent results or incorrect solutions, as the existing machines have finite precision arithmetic, and in many practical applications, geometric inputs are degenerate. This scenario is well known as the "robustness" problem in geometric computation and is increasingly becoming an important issue for scientific computing and engineering applications.

Finite Precision and Exact Arithmetic

Most of the existing implementation of geometric algorithms and operations use finite precision arithmetic (e.g. IEEE floating-point arithmetic) for geometric computation. However, such implementations can produce ambiguous results. If the ambiguity is not properly addressed, the resulting algorithm becomes unreliable. To circumvent these problems, a number of approaches based on tolerances and exact arithmetic have been proposed. Tolerance-based approaches have been successfully used in a few applications, like boundary computation. However, they are not guaranteed to be robust. Algorithms based on exact arithmetic are relatively slow. In particular, exact algorithms for linear primitives like lines and planes involve the use of rational arithmetic. Most implementations utilize software libraries for exact rational arithmetic. However, in the curved domain, exact arithmetic involves computations on algebraic or transcendental numbers which are very slow in practice. For instance, algebraic numbers are represented as roots of polynomial equations. Most computer algebra systems like Maple and Mathematica have utilities for exact computation on algebraic numbers. In practice, exact arithmetic has shown good potential for designing unambiguous algorithms for computing convex hulls, constructing Voronoi regions, performing boolean operations, and so forth. Another strategy that compromises the trade-off between speed and accuracy is *adaptive precision arithmetic*.

Geometric Degeneracies

Degeneracies arise from the special position of geometric objects. For example, four generic points in 3-space should not lie on the same plane. However, in many real-world applications, four points may correspond to vertices of a rectangle and are, therefore, degenerate. Consequently, real-world data can often be degenerate. Due to geometric degeneracies, it is necessary to consider all special cases in a given algorithm to obtain robust implementation. In general, it is nontrivial to enumerate all degeneracies. As a result, it is difficult to prove that a given implementation is robust and would work on all input configurations of geometric objects. In the last few years, techniques based on symbolic perturbations have been proposed to handle degeneracies. Combined with exact arithmetic, symbolic perturbation has achieved limited success in developing robust algorithms and implementations for computing convex hull of points and boundary computation on boolean combinations of polyhedral models.

Open Research Issues

Although robustness issues have received considerable attention in the past few years, the field is not yet mature enough to offer efficient and consistent techniques to various application domains. Study on generalization and extension of existing methodologies applied to a variety of problem domains will enhance the understanding of the problem nature and the limitations of different approaches. Further investigation of robust and effective solutions is especially needed to address issues related to nonlinear geometry and other geometric primitives.

SOFTWARE AND LIBRARIES

Computational geometry as a theoretical field has matured considerably in the last two decades. It is now possible to create robust, efficient, and portable implementations of many geometric algorithms as well as specializing them to various applications. One of the many focuses in applied computational geometry is to achieve this goal by providing software tools that enable technology transfer by offering basic building blocks and geometric modules commonly used in various applied fields. A number of critical issues that relate to the design and implementation of geometric software are as follows:

- **Correctness:** This is one of the most important criteria in the development of geometric software libraries. Programs must be correct at all times. This involves handling of geometric degeneracies and numerical problems due to finite precision arithmetic. Many libraries like LEDA (7) achieve this goal by developing a robust kernel using exact arithmetic. The kernel consists of underlying geometric routines for line intersections, convex hulls, Voronoi regions, triangulations, boolean operations, and so forth. The rest of geometric routines can be implemented on top of such a kernel.

- **Efficiency:** The other imperative concern of building geometric software and libraries is *efficiency* — both in terms of speed and storage. In contrast to the tradition of pursuing better asymptotic bounds, the current emphasis is now on expected run-time performance and actual memory requirements. Frequently, a software developer has to choose between correctness of the program and its speed. For example, one may use exact arithmetic to circumvent numerical problems. At the same time, it is slower as compared to finite precision arithmetic. In a few cases, researchers have shown that clever use of IEEE floating-point arithmetic available in machine hardware can yield not only efficient but also correct implementation of some basic geometric algorithms. However, it is not clear whether such an approach can be generalized to all geometric algorithms.
- **Modularity, portability, and ease of use:** It is essential that geometric software be developed in a modular fashion. One such example is the use of kernels to implement underlying geometric primitives. Not only does it help in developing robust and efficient algorithms, but it also makes it simple for other developers to extend the libraries. An object-oriented design, which hides the implementation details of a kernel, makes it easier for the user to interface it with numerous applications and make it possible to port the code across different computing platforms.

There has been considerable progress on this front and a number of researchers worldwide have developed libraries as well as efficient and robust implementations of certain geometric algorithms (e.g., convex hulls and triangulation). Several geometric software packages are available in the public domain. A few like XYZ-GeoBench (8) have also been used for educational purposes besides research and development.

APPLICATIONS

Computational geometry has been successfully used in designing efficient algorithms for many problems in different application areas. In this section, we briefly highlight several problems in some of these application areas. At the end of this section, we present three case studies from computer graphics, geometric modeling, and virtual prototyping.

Computer Graphics

A major goal in computer graphics is to generate realistic images of geometric models. It involves geometric representation of surfaces, modeling of light, media, and rendering. Given a viewer's position, any rendering algorithm involves computing the correct visibility of the model and scene from that viewpoint. A number of geometric algorithms have been developed based on hierarchical data structures, hidden surface removal, and global visibility to compute visible portions of the model. Other graphics applications include model simplification, where one reduces the geometric complexity of a model (in terms of number of polygons or primitives), thereby preserving its shape using surface approximation algorithms.

Geometric and Solid Modeling

The fields of geometric and solid modeling deal with representations of curves, surfaces, and solids and their manipulation based on geometric operations (9). A number of geometric techniques have been successfully employed for intersection computations, converting from one representation to another, boolean operations (e.g., set-union, intersection, and difference), generating linear approximations for higher-order primitives, and surface fitting.

Robotics

Computational geometry techniques have been successfully applied to collision-free path planning in robotics. For instance, given an environment composed of obstacles, an initial and final position of the robot, geometric algorithms for visibility graphs, Voronoi regions, and convex hulls have been used to compute a path along which the robot does not collide with any obstacle. Other applications of geometry in robotics include grasping, fixturing, and stable pose computation.

Computer Vision

A fundamental problem in computer vision is to reconstruct a three-dimensional (3D) model from a sequence of two-dimensional images. Geometric algorithms have been used for computing the geometric transformation that maps the model into the coordinate system of a camera. Many model-based recognition algorithms represent the object by a set of two-dimensional projections and have used geometric techniques to bound the number of combinatorially distinct projections. Geometric algorithms have also been used for matching image features to 3D objects.

Manufacturing

A major goal is to make manufacturing systems flexible and automated from design to prototyping to process planning. The problems of structural design and virtual prototyping are geometric in nature, and many algorithms for computer-aided design, tool-path generation, numerically controlled (NC) machining, and casting have utilized geometric algorithms. Geometric techniques have also been used for mesh generation in finite-element analysis.

Molecular Modeling and Drug Design

Geometric algorithms have been utilized for 3D manipulation of molecular chains for conformational analysis and docking applications. Conformational analysis deals with computation of minimal energy configurations of deformable molecules, and docking involves matching one molecular structure to a receptor site of a second molecule and computing the most energetically favorable 3D conformation. Furthermore, techniques based on convex hulls, Voronoi regions, and α-hulls have been used for computing the boundary of solvent-accessible molecules.

Case Studies

In this section, we present three case studies of applied computational geometry to problems in computer graphics, modeling, and simulation. In each case, we first present the problem, briefly describe the techniques used, and illustrate their performance. These include interactive display of curved geometry, model simplification, and interactive collision detection.

Case Study I: Interactive Display of Spline Models

In many fields like geometric modeling, computer-aided design/manufacturing (CAD/CAM), animation, and biomedical engineering, object models are often designed using spline surfaces. These include non-uniform rational B-spline (NURBS) surfaces and Bézier patches. The boundaries of many large-scaled models of automobiles, submarines, and airplanes are composed of tens of thousands of such high-order patches (see Fig. 1). Many applications like design, model evaluation, and walk-throughs demand interactive visualization of such models on current graphics systems. The exact representation of geometry makes it possible to render images at high resolution. On the other hand, current high-end graphics hardware systems are optimized to display triangles as opposed to higher-order surfaces. Fast generation of high-fidelity images from Bézier representation requires that we approximate the surfaces with an appropriate number of triangles, based on the viewer's current position. This places a high demand on computational resources. Recently, Kumar et al. have utilized techniques from Computational Geometry for dynamic tessellation and interactive display of tens of thousands of parametric spline surfaces on current graphics systems (10,11). The main components of the algorithm are as follows:

- **Visibility computations:** Use bounds on surface coordinates and normals to determine if a given patch is not visible from the given viewpoint. These

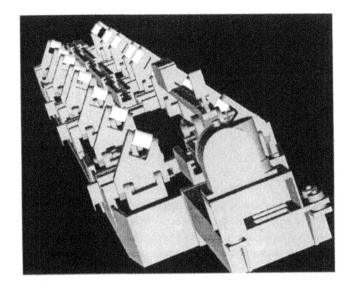

FIGURE 1   Part of a notional submarine torpedo room. The boundary of this part is composed of more than 4400 spline patches. It is approximated with triangles in real time as a function of viewing parameters and rendered on current graphics systems. The torpedo room model was supplied by Electric Boat, a subsidiary of General Dynamics.

algorithms make use of hierarchical data structures like octrees, k–D trees, and Gauss maps for visibility computations.

- **Surface approximation:** Utilize techniques from algebraic geometry, differential geometry, and approximation theory to compute an appropriate number of triangles from a given viewpoint.
- **Trimmed surfaces:** Many patches are defined using trimmed boundaries in the domain. These boundaries are specified using piecewise linear or higher-order trimming curves. Using computational geometric methods, it computes the triangulation of trimmed domains. This involves generation and triangulation of general nonconvex polygons with holes. One such triangulation is shown in Figure 2. Furthermore, the algorithm guarantees that there are no cracks in the surface triangulation.
- **Incremental triangulation:** The change in the viewer's position between two consecutive frames of an interactive rendering session is typically small. Exploiting coherence, the algorithm is able to incrementally update the surface triangulation at each frame.
- **Parallelization:** The algorithm can be parallelized for large models on shared-memory or distributed architectures.

The resulting algorithm has been implemented on different high-end graphics systems. Due to these geometric techniques, it is able to render large models at interactive frame rates (i.e., more than 15 frames/sec.). It is more than one order of magnitude faster than earlier algorithms.

Case Study II: Model Simplification

High-quality 3D models are of primary importance for a realistic-looking simulated world. They may be created by CAD tools for manufacturing automobiles, airplanes, submarines, or other machines which require parts made to exact specifications; or they may be created by closely approximating data gathered for scientific or medical purposes. In either case, the original model must be extremely precise for

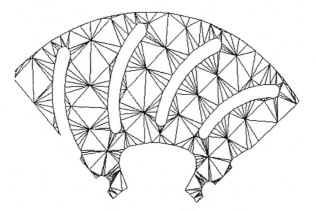

FIGURE 2 Triangulation of a trimmed Bézier patch. The algorithm incrementally computes a triangulation as a function of the viewing parameters.

its original application, but visualization at interactive rates requires one or more simpler approximations to the model. It is not uncommon to find CAD models composed of tens of thousands to millions of triangles. These models can be viewed interactively when taken alone, but not as part of a more complex scene. The *model simplification* problem is to reduce the polygonal complexity of the original model to allow visualization at interactive rates. This may include the creation of several models at different *levels of detail* to allow a trade-off between quality and speed as the importance of a model in the overall scene changes.

In the last few years, there have been several proposed solutions to the simplification problem for polygonal models. Most of these solutions neither guarantee preservation of global topology nor restrict the approximation to be within some error bound of the original solution.

Recently, Cohen et al. have utilized techniques from Computational Geometry and proposed the idea of *simplification envelopes* as a solution to this problem (12). A simplification envelope is a modified version of the well-known offset surfaces in geometric modeling. Given some constant, ϵ, the algorithms generate a simplification envelope by displacing every vertex of the input surface in the direction of its normal vector by a distance less than or equal to ϵ. The displacement is less than ϵ for certain vertices to prevent self-intersections in the envelope surface. Different pairs of simplification envelopes for a bunny model are shown in Figure 3.

By generating a *pair* of envelope surfaces to contain the input surface, they define the *envelope volume*, within which all simplification should take place. The simplification itself takes the form of local mesh operations, such as vertex removal

FIGURE 3   Three pairs of simplification envelopes for a bunny model (provided by the Stanford Computer Graphics Laboratory). The percentages represent the ϵ approximation distance in terms of the model's bounding box diagonal length.

or edge collapse and retriangulating the resulting mesh. If none of these new triangles intersect the envelope surfaces, then they are fully contained in the envelope volume. This implies that they are all within the distance ϵ of the original surface. Different levels of detail for a rotor from a break assembly are shown in Figure 4.

Such a metric is useful for determining the appropriate distance at which to view a particular level of detail. By projecting the approximation distance, ϵ, into screen-space, it is possible to bound the number of pixels of deviation that may be apparent in a model's silhouette.

Cohen et al. have created a robust implementation of this approach and applied it to the auxiliary machine room of a notional submarine (shown in Fig. 5), fully automating the process of simplifying the model and switching between levels of detail during an interactive visualization.

Case Study III: Collision Detection

Collision or interference detection is a fundamental problem in robotics, computer animation, physically based modeling, molecular modeling, and computer-simulated environments. In these applications, an object's motion is determined by collisions with other objects and by other dynamic constraints. The geometric models used in these applications are represented using a large number of polygons, curved surfaces (e.g., parametric splines and algebraic surfaces), or deformable models. The goal is to develop efficient and accurate algorithms to compute all contacts between moving objects composed of a large number of primitives. Recently, Lin and co-workers (13–15) have used techniques from Computational Ge-

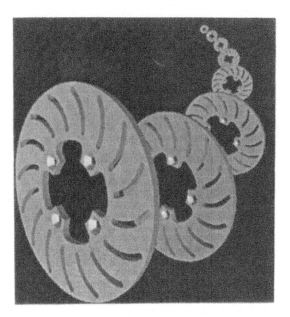

FIGURE 4   A levels-of-detail hierarchy for the rotor from a brake assembly (provided by the *Alpha__*1 Group at the University of Utah). The levels of detail contain 4735, 2146, 1514, 1266, 850, 716, 688, and 674 triangles.

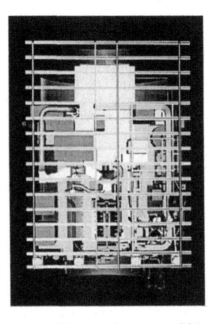

FIGURE 5   A top view of the auxiliary machine room model (provided by the Electric Boat division of General Dynamics). This original model contains over half a million triangles; the simplest level of detail generated contains about 150,000 triangles.

FIGURE 6   Threaded screw insertion. The collision detection algorithm is used for simulation of a threaded screw insertion. In manufacturing, the insertion and tightening of threaded fasteners is one of the 12 most commonly assembled tasks. The collision detection algorithm utilizes the dynamic simulation model presented by Nicolson and Fearing (16) and models the screws using thousands of polygons in close proximity. It is able to accurately compute all the contacts interactively.

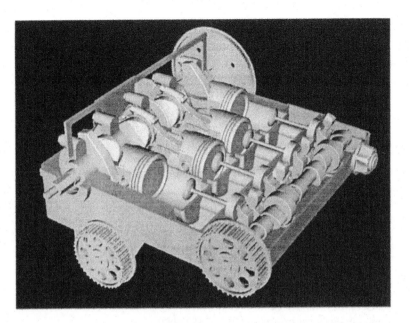

FIGURE 7 Engine simulation. The collision detection algorithm has been used to accurately and interactively compute all the contacts between the pistons and the fixed parts of the engine. The overall model is composed of more than 400,000 triangles. (Courtesy of Engineering Animation Inc.)

ometry to develop fast algorithms and systems to accurately compute the contacts between polygonal models in large environments.

Given the geometric models, the algorithms precompute convex hulls, external Voronoi region, and a hierarchical representation of each model in terms of oriented bounding boxes. Efficient and robust algorithms for convex hulls and tight bounding volumes are well known in Computational Geometry. As the objects undergo motion, the algorithms compute tight-fitting axis-aligned bounding boxes about each object. It checks the axis-aligned bounding boxes for overlap to reduce the number of object-pair interactions to only those pairs within *close proximity* of each other (13). The resulting algorithm exploits spatial and temporal coherence. Its run time is linear in terms of the number of objects and the number of object pairs in close proximity. For each pair of objects whose bounding boxes overlap, the algorithm verifies whether their convex hulls are overlapping based on the closest feature pairs. The closest feature pairs are updated using external Voronoi regions. Finally, for each object pair whose convex hulls overlap, it makes use of oriented bounding box hierarchy (OBBTree) to check for actual contact. The resulting algorithm traverse the OBBTree and check the oriented bounding boxes for overlap based on a new geometric algorithm which computes *separating axes* for a pair of boxes.

The resulting algorithms have been used to develop two collision detection systems: I-COLLIDE and RAPID. They are public-domain systems used by thousands of researchers worldwide for a variety of applications. Some of the applications include manufacturing and virtual prototyping, as shown in Figures 6 and 7. These algorithms have been used in commercial systems as well.

ACKNOWLEDGMENTS

We like to acknowledge the useful input and constructive suggestions provided by Jonathan Cohen and Subodh Kumar. The authors are grateful to the Army Research Office, National Science Foundation, Office of Naval Research, Sloan Foundation, and the University of North Carolina at Chapel Hill for their support.

REFERENCES

1. F. P. Preparata and M. I. Shamos, *Computational Geometry*, Springer-Verlag, New York, 1985.
2. H. Edelsbrunner, *Algorithms in Combinatorial Geometry*, Springer-Verlag, Heidelberg, 1987.
3. K. Mulmuley, *Computational Geometry: An Introduction Through Randomized Algorithms*, Prentice-Hall, Englewood Cliffs, NJ, 1994.
4. J. O'Rourke, *Computational Geometry in C*, Cambridge University Press, Cambridge, 1994.
5. B. Chazelle et al., "Application Challenges to Computational Geometry: Computational Geometry Impact Task Force Report," Technical Report TR-521-96, Department of Computer Science, Princeton University (1996).
6. M. C. Lin and D. Manocha, *Applied Computational Geometry: Towards Geometric Engineering*, Springer-Verlag, Heidelberg, 1996.
7. K. Mehlhorn and S. Näher, "LEDA: A Platform for Combinatorial and Geometric Computing," *Commun. ACM, 38*, 96–102 (1995).
8. Peter Schorn, "Implementing the XYZ GeoBench: A Programming Environment for Geometric Algorithms," in *Computational Geometry—Methods, Algorithms and Applications: Proc. Internat. Workshop Comput. Geom. CG '91*, Springer-Verlag, New York, 1991, pp. 187–202.
9. C. M. Hoffmann, *Geometric and Solid Modeling*, Morgan Kaufmann, San Mateo, CA, 1989.
10. S. Kumar, "Interactive Rendering of Parametric Spline Surfaces," Ph.D. thesis, Department of Computer Science, University of North Carolina at Chapel Hill (1996).
11. S. Kumar, D. Manocha, and A. Lastra, "Interactive Display of Large Scale Nurbs Models," in *Proc. of ACM Interactive 3D Graphics Conference*, 1995, pp. 51–58.
12. J. Cohen, A. Varshney, D. Manocha, G. Turk et al., "Simplification Envelopes," in *Proc. of ACM Siggraph '96*, 1996, pp. 119–128.
13. J. Cohen, M. Lin, D. Manocha, and M. Ponamgi, I-COLLIDE: "An Interactive and Exact Collision Detection System for Large-Scale Environments," in *Proc. of ACM Interactive 3D Graphics Conference*, 1995, pp. 189–196.
14. S. Gottschalk, M. Lin, and D. Manocha, "Obb-tree: A Hierarchical Structure for Rapid Interference Detection," in *Proc. of ACM Siggraph '96*, 1996, pp. 171–180.
15. M. C. Lin, "Efficient Collision Detection for Animation and Robotics," Ph.D. thesis, Department of Electrical Engineering and Computer Science, University of California, Berkeley (December 1993).
16. E. Nicolson and R. Fearing, "Dynamic Simulation of a Part-Mating Problem: Threaded Fastener Insertion," in *Proceedings, IEEE/RSJ International Conference on Intelligent Robots and Systems*, 1991, pp. 30–37.

MING C. LIN

DINESH MANOCHA

COMPUTER APPLICATIONS FOR PERSONS
WITH SPECIAL NEEDS

This article describes the state-of-the-art in applying standard and dedicated computer hardware and software to meet special needs of disabled persons and to overcome handicap induced barriers.

Following a suggestion of the TRACE Center at the University of Wisconsin (1), the description of the devices and programs will not be given with respect to specific disabilities but with reference to the function which is fulfilled by the device or program. This approach will avoid the danger of thinking only in categories of different disabilities or handicaps and will promote a solution-oriented way of thinking.

Nevertheless, after some terminology, statistical information, and an introduction into the principles of rehabilitation technology, at least a coarse and typical correlation table between impairment (the functional restriction or loss) and the possible technical support will be given in the Introduction.

The second section of this article deals with hardware and software components designed to create access to computers in order to use them in the same or a similar way and for the same reasons as nondisabled persons would do.

The third section will focus on such applications where the computer or other microprocessor equipped devices are used to allow the disabled person the performance of very common tasks (activities of daily living = ADL) for which a nondisabled user would not necessarily use a computer.

INTRODUCTION

Terminology

According to a proposal issued by the WHO (World Health Organization) in 1980 (2), there are three clearly separated definitions in the area of disability:

Impairment: Any loss or abnormality of a psychological or anatomical structure or function

Disability: Any restriction or inability (resulting from an impairment) to perform an activity in the manner or within the range considered normal for a human being

Handicap: Any disadvantage for a given individual, resulting from an impairment or a disability, that limits or prevents the fulfillment of a role that is normal (depending on age, sex, and social and cultural factors*) for that individual

---

*It has to be admitted that it is not always easy to determine what is normal for a given age, sex, or cultural or social role; for example, the aging of a person never should be used as an excuse for not being admitted to certain activities.

From these three basic definitions, two other important terms can be derived:

Disabled person: Person with one or more impairments, one or more disabilities, one or more handicaps, or a combination of impairment, disability, and/or handicap.

Technical aid: (for a disabled person): Any product, instrument, equipment, or technical system used by a disabled person, especially produced or generally available, preventing, compensating, relieving, or neutralizing the impairment, disability, or handicap.

These definitions form the basis of the International Standard on "Technical Aids for Disabled Persons — Classification" — ISO 9999 (1992) (3). See the subsection The ISO Classification Scheme for some examples.

The discipline behind the development of technical aids is commonly called rehabilitation engineering and should not be confused with medical engineering. The main goal of medical engineering is to provide the technology and the equipment which add to the restoration of health. In this category, we can find tools the physician will use for prophylactics, diagnosis, and therapy. Rehabilitation engineering plays a role where healing is not possible. In this sense, technical aids do not have a curative potential but act by compensating a given impairment, disability, or handicap. Apart from this definition, there are devices which cannot be assigned clearly to one of the two categories: An implanted cardiac pacemaker doubtless is a medical device. A hearing aid certainly is a technical aid to overcome hearing loss. But a cochlea implant, stimulating the hearing nerve? Is it just another form of hearing aid or is it more related to the pacemaker?

Some Statistical Remarks

Publications of the EU (European Union) state that some 25–30 million disabled people ($\sim$ 9% of the total population) are living in the EU member countries today (4). The incidence of disability rises steeply with advancing age. Approximately 70% of the people with disabilities are over 60 years old.

Demographic trends and improvements in medical care in all Western countries will cause a rise in the percentage of elderly people with respect to the total population, leading to increasing numbers of disabled persons and rising expenses for health care. For this simple economic reason, many industrialized countries have recognized the important role of rehabilitation technology (RT) and technical aids for disabled and elderly people in order to keep as many disabled persons in the mainstream of occupational and social life as possible and to maintain an aging person's autonomy as long as possible.

What Computers Can Do

The motivation for computer use by persons with disabilities can be clustered into two categories. The users of the first group employ the computer for exactly the same reasons as their nondisabled peers — for text processing, calculation, data retrieval, telecommunication, and so forth. The way of accessing the computer, however, will make the difference, and rehabilitation technology offers a vast number of special input and output devices which are the theme of the second section.

In the second category, computers are used by persons with disabilities for activities of daily living (ADL) for which nondisabled people would not (necessarily) use a computer. These applications are dealt with in the third section.

The description of assistive technology in this article will mainly focus on such applications where computers in the usual sense (say PCs, laptops, or terminals connected to host computers) are used. Nevertheless, some dedicated devices using microprocessors or other programmable components will not be excluded, as they also resemble information technology.

The ISO Classification Scheme

The International Standard ISO 9999, "Technical Aids for Disabled Persons – Classification" (3) – seeks to cover and to group all existing devices of rehabilitation technology. The main classes of this scheme are as follows:

03 Aids for therapy and training
06 Orthoses and prostheses
09 Aids for personal care and protection
12 Aids for personal mobility
15 Aids for housekeeping
18 Furnishings and adaptations to homes and other premises
21 Aids for communication, information, and signaling
24 Aids for handling products and goods
27 Aids and equipment for environmental improvements, tools, and machines
30 Aids for recreation

(Please note that ISO is presently using only every third classification number in order to have space for later expansion of the scheme.)

Systematic Glossary

For a better understanding of the details in the second and third sections, it is necessary to introduce and explain several general terms, techniques, and procedures used in rehabilitation technology.

Special Techniques of Communication

There are several impairments which affect a person's abilities for communication (person-to-person or telecommunication, written or oral) in such a way that it becomes impossible to use those communication conventions which are applied by the population at large.

Alternative and augmentative communication (AAC) is the global term for all ways and means of communication especially developed to overcome certain communication barriers imposed by any kind of impairment affecting the usual human capability of communication. Commonly, such techniques will become necessary if the function of a human sense or organ is affected by a disability to such a degree that all methods of amplification (e.g., the enhancement of size or contrast of an image, amplification of sounds, and increasing the size of an input device) will not be adequate to stimulate the residual sense or to cope with the reduced mechanical functionality of limbs.

(a) Severely *hearing impaired and profoundly deaf persons* are mainly using three alternatives to listening to another person's voice: lipreading, sign language, or written text. For telecommunication, therefore, the audio channel has to be replaced by displaying written text or by providing moving pictures of the partner in conversation.*

Lipreading is a method to recognize spoken language by carefully observing the lip and tongue movements of the speaker. Much training plus the proper distance and sufficient illumination is necessary to use this technique successfully. Nevertheless, only less than half of a spoken message really is recognized by lipreading. The remaining part has to be guessed from the context.

Finger-spelling (finger alphabet) is a method of optical communication with deaf (or also by speech impaired) persons, where the single characters of a spoken message are resembled by certain easy-to-distinguish patterns of finger and hand movements. Obviously, the conversation speed is far less than in a spoken dialogue.

Sign language tries to overcome the speed barrier of finger-spelling. As already expressed by the name, sign language is not just a sequence of single characters; it is a genuine language with its own grammar and syntax. Depending on the context, certain movements of arms, hands, and fingers and their relative position to the head and part of the chest can express entire phrases. Even if a lot of elements are common in the sign languages used in different countries, there is nothing like a universal or global sign language. The reason for this is that sign languages not only have developed from different spoken languages but that also a lot of cultural and ethnic aspects had to be taken into consideration.

Text telephone or telecommunication device for the deaf (TDD) is a device to transmit typed-in messages via telephone lines. The sender is using a keyboard connected to a modem generating a specific code for the transmission via the telephone lines. The receiver part also consists of a modem connected to a display or hardcopy unit. As a matter of fact, communication can only be established if both sides are using a text telephone operating according to the same standard. The usage of PCs with software emulating a text telephone is increasing. Presently, a number of different text telephone codes are in use worldwide (5). Thus, international communication by text telephones is restricted. Therefore, the ITU (formerly CCITT) Study Group 14 is preparing the V.18 standard, a new international modem protocol for text telephony (simultaneous transmission of text and voice) (6).

(b) Whenever *speech impairment on the level of articulation* is impeding vocal communication (person to person or telecommunication), methods of transforming a typed text into spoken language have to be applied. As typing is always much slower than speaking (especially in those frequent cases where a speech-impaired person is additionally affected by some

---

*Some of these techniques can also be used by those speech-impaired persons who are able to formulate a sentence in the mind but cannot utter this sentence by using the vocal tract.

restriction of the motor functions), techniques to save keystrokes can be very useful.

Computer programs for so-called **predictive typing** try to guess the rest of a word after the first character(s) of a word have been entered. If the intended word already appears among the suggestions the computer has made, the user will have to make a one keystroke selection to complete the word. If the proper word does not yet show up, the typing has to be continued. Predictive typing is using dynamic statistics of word occurrence for a certain person and sometimes even considers the previously typed words or the context (7–10).

Semantic compaction tries to go one step further, shifting the prediction from the word level to the semantic level. To generate a phrase, the user has to make a few selections from a given set of symbols.

(c) *The inability to speak* can also have its *reasons in the mind* of a person. In other words, it is not caused by a mere dysfunction of the vocal tract but by the disability of the person to think in terms of words, syntax, and grammar. For this reason, this disability is referred to as *language impairment*.

Symbolic language or **picture communication:** Instead of communicating by means of written or spoken words, alternative communication is established by a set of basic symbols (pictures, icons). By pointing at single symbols or a sequence of symbols displayed (e.g., on a board or a computer screen), the disabled person can express his or her needs. By grouping the picture symbols into hierarchical levels, it is possible to access large numbers of symbols (expressions) by only a few selections.

Bliss* symbols are a widely used and standardized set of simple but powerful graphical symbols. By combining Bliss symbols into sequences, complicated and abstract sentences can be formed (11).

(d) The term *visual impairment* covers the entire spectrum of reduced visual capability. In the context of this article, all visual impairments which can be compensated satisfactorily by optical means (glasses, contact lenses) like myopia, hypermetropia, and astigmatism will not be discussed. All visual impairments which reach a degree where the visual sense, even by using technical aids, cannot be used for tasks like reading and orientation, are addressed as blindness. In these cases, alternatives for the visual sense have to be used.

Braille† is a tactile alphabet comprised of raised dots that can be recognized through the fingertips in a tactile way. Standard Braille uses a 2 (columns) by 3 (rows) scheme of 6 raised dots which can be embossed in heavy paper or plastic film or displayed by a mechanical device (Braille display, refreshable or volatile Braille). The spacing between the dots is about 2.5 mm or 0.1 in., the height for smooth reading should be between 0.4 and 0.6 mm.

By using 6 dots, 63 different characters and a "space" can be repre-

---

*Charles Bliss, 1897–1985.

†Louis Braille, 1809–1862.

sented. Due to the necessary size of the Braille characters (or Braille cells), hardcopy Braille material is rather voluminous. Therefore, different grades of abbreviation were introduced.

Grade I Braille uses only a few contractions. The numerals (1 to 9 and 0) are represented by the first 10 characters of the alphabet (A to J) preceded by a number sign. Capital letters have to be indicated by a prefix.

Grade II Braille uses contractions on the syllable and word level utilizing abbreviation rules which are similar to shorthand.

As neither Grade I nor Grade II Braille is a character-to-character representation of a text, another code, so-called **computer Braille**, was introduced. Here, no contractions are used and all numerals are assigned to separate Braille characters.

The 6-dot Braille with its 63 different characters cannot display the entire ASCII character set. Especially for computer interaction and computer programming, the 6-dot scheme was expanded by two more dots beneath the standard Braille cell. These two extra dots are mainly used to express capital letters and control characters. With the 255 different symbols of 8-dot Braille, all characters of the ASCII and PC character sets can be displayed (12). It has to be mentioned that there are also special Braille notations for mathematics, chemistry, and music.

It is evident that reading Braille requires training, experience, and skill. Especially elderly persons, who represent the majority of the blind population, very seldom succeed in learning to read Braille. Mainly in Great Britain, another tactile alphabet called **Moon*** is in use. Moon characters are not represented by raised dots but consist of raised lines which have shapes very similar to the respective printed characters. Due to their size and familiar shape, Moon characters can be read by elderly persons more easily. The disadvantage of Moon is, that up to now, no Moon display could be developed, and hardcopy printing is much more complicated than it is for Braille.

Special Input and Output Devices

Computers can do the same for disabled people as for nondisabled ones, provided that they can have equal access to the input and output facilities. In this context, "equal" does not necessarily mean that the disabled person will use the same I/O channels in an adapted way, but very often this implies the change from one medium to another, like listening to a synthetic speech output instead of reading from a computer screen. The essential part of equal access is that the same information can be exchanged between user and computer. However, in most cases, using alternative I/O methods and devices will be more time-consuming than working with the usual peripherals. Much effort has been spent to keep these disadvantages as low as possible.

---

*William Moon, 1818–1894.

(a) Persons with *restricted mobility of fingers, hands, or arms* encounter severe problems when it comes to operating a computer in the usual way by a standard keyboard or a mouse. For this reason, alternative input devices are necessary.

Standard keyboards have several keys which have to be depressed simultaneously with another key. Normally these are the Shift, the Control, and the Alternate keys. Persons who are able to use only one hand, one finger, or even have to use a **mouth-stick** or a **pointer** fixed to the forehead need a keyboard modification which converts these **momentary-contact keys** into **latching keys** (toggle action) (13).

A **membrane keyboard (concept keyboard)** is a keyboard whose keys are located under a flexible, hermetically sealed surface. Some types offer a touch-sensitive surface which can be programmed to different keyboard layouts in order to tailor the size and position of the individual keys exactly to the personal needs and abilities of the user.

A **touch pad** is a pressure-sensitive device for generating input to a computer. The area can be divided into specific fields for making discrete selections or act as a pointing device for moving the cursor by sliding the fingertip over the touch pad surface in the desired direction.

A **touch screen** is operated in the same way as a touch pad but is transparent and fits over the standard computer screen. Symbols displayed on the screen can easily be selected by just touching them.

The term **keypad** usually refers to any keyboard having significantly less keys than an ordinary computer keyboard. Often the term *numeric keypad* is used for the array of numeric keys in the right-hand part of the PC keyboard.

If the residual dexterity of fingers, hands, and arms, the motor functions of the head using, for example, a mouth-stick or the feet do not permit the use of a keyboard (standard or special size), the input device must be reduced to a few **switches** or even to one switch. Apart from mechanical switches (often equipped with a large and easy to hit operating area) [e.g., pneumatic switches activated by a suck (sip) and/or puff operation], sensor switches or even light-operated switches are used.

If many different operations (like operating the various functions of a keyboard) have to be accomplished by one or only a few switches, so-called **selection or scanning techniques** are employed. **Scanning** involves moving sequentially through a given set of choices and making a selection when the desired position is reached by pressing a single key.

A **pointing device** is any peripheral device by which the cursor can be moved to the desired position. As a mouse or a trackball often is unsuitable for motor-impaired persons, other movements (e.g., of the head or the eyes) can be detected and converted into cursor movements.

(b) For working with a computer, *blind persons* must get access to all information displayed on the computer's screen. Special programs to solve this problem are referred to as **screen review software, talking screen** or **Screen Reader**™.* In combination with a **Braille display** and/or a **text-to-**

---

*Screen Reader is a registered trademark of IBM.

speech synthesizer, these software packages not only allow one to navigate across the screen and to bring the desired portion of information to the Braille display or speech synthesizer, but they can also be programmed to react immediately to changes on the screen, to automatically react to system messages, or to communicate text attributes (like bold print, underlined characters, colors, or other means of emphasis) to the blind user.

As long as computers were restricted to displaying alphanumerical characters on their screens, few problems arose with representing the contents by Braille or synthetic speech. Today, in a world of **graphic user interfaces (GUI)** like those first used by Xerox, Apple, and Atari and later introduced to the MS-DOS domain by MS-Windows, it has become much more difficult for blind computer users. By and by, screen review software which can handle GUIs is emerging. Nevertheless, research and development into better ways of nonvisual interaction with graphic computer screens will certainly go on for some years (14–16).

In addition to textual information for blind persons, there is an increasing need for **tactile graphic representation** of maps, drawings, and diagrams. Whereas it is technologically quite easy to manufacture hardcopy tactile graphics by thermoforming (deep drawing of thermoplastic sheets) or swell-paper (a specially coated copying paper, where all black lines or areas will raise when the sheet is exposed to infrared heating), the construction of a **refreshable tactile graphic display** is still at its beginning. Existing devices are either prototypes or very expensive arrays of conventional Braille displays.

Optical character recognition (OCR) denotes all techniques by means of which printed (or handwritten) characters are converted into computer data by scanning the document and recognizing the characters by pattern recognition techniques.

The term **synthetic speech** is often used for all kinds of computer-generated speech output. More precisely, one has to distinguish between **digitized speech** and **text-to-speech conversion.** For digitized speech, the voice of a human speaker is sampled and converted into a stream of digital information which can be stored in a computer and retrieved on demand. The vocabulary is restricted to what has been previously recorded. Text-to-speech conversion generates speech output from any text by applying phonetic rules and generating sound in analogy to the human vocal tract.

A Systematic Approach to Functional Restoration

Following a suggestion of the TRACE Center at the University of Wisconsin (1), this article presents the description of any computer application for people with special needs not with reference to a specific impairment or disability but only with respect to the (assistive or restorative) function which is addressed by the device or program. This approach will avoid thinking only in categories of impairments and disabilities and thus promote a practical and solution-oriented way of thinking.

Nevertheless, this introduction contains two very coarse and pragmatic cross-reference tables showing the typical relations between impairment (i.e., the abnormality or loss of a specific function) versus the common technical methods of providing support. It can be seen from these tabulated overviews that certain impairments can (but not necessarily must) lead to more than one functional restriction. A motor disorder which is affecting the ability to keep the head in a desired position will also affect the ability to keep the eyes fixed on a certain object. In other words, a motor disability could influence a person's ability to read small fonts from a computer screen.

It has, therefore, to be noted that very specific assistive devices (e.g., screen enlargement software, which has been developed to assist persons with low vision) can readily serve individuals suffering from a very different kind of disability.

The following abbreviations for impairments/disabilities are used in Tables 1 and 2:

Hearing:	HH	= Hearing impairment, hard of hearing
	PD	= Deafness (profound deafness)
Speech:	SI	= Speech impairment (on the articulation level)
	LI	= Language impairment (on the mental level)
Vision:	LV	= Low vision, visual impairment
	BL	= Blindness (both eyes, visual sense without practical function)
	CB	= Color blindness
Movement:	MF	= Motor impairment of fingers and hands
	MU	= Motor impairment of upper extremities
	ML	= Motor impairment of lower extremities
Mental:	MD	= Mental (cognition, learning) disability
Aging:	AG	= Disabilities typically connected with the process of aging, fragility, and dementia

Note that multiple disabilities are not taken into account separately. Tables 1 and 2 can only be a coarse guide for orientation. Discussing the various personal implications of impairments and disabilities in a one-page schematic would not be feasible.

As Tables 1 and 2 follow the same sequence as the detailed descriptions given

TABLE 1   Enabling or Enhancing Access to Computers, Special Peripheral Devices

II	Device or software function	HH	PD	SI	LI	LV	BL	CB	MF	MU	ML	MD	AG
A	Screen enlargement					x				o			o
B	Print enlargement					x				o			o
C	Displaying Braille					o	x						
D	Printing Braille					o	x						
E	Digitized speech output					o	x					o	o
F	Text-to-speech synthesis					o	x					o	o
G	Code translation				x		x						
H	Sign language robot		(x)				(x)						
I	Enhanced manual input					o	o		x	x		o	o
J	Alternative mechanical input								x	x			o
K	Alternatives for mech. input								o	x	o	o	o

TABLE 2   Using Computers and Microprocessor Devices to Perform ADL Tasks

III	Device or software function	HH	PD	SI	LI	LV	BL	CB	MF	MU	ML	MD	AG
A	Remote controlling								o	x	x		o
B	Text communication	o	x	x								o	
C	Speech communication			x	o							o	
D	Enhanced telecommunication	x		x									o
E	Alternative telecommunication	o	x	x	x								o
F	Picture communication	o	o	o	x							x	o
G	Calling and alarm systems			o	o						x	o	x
H	Alerting systems	o	x			o	o					o	o
I	Manipulators and robots								o	x	x		o
J	Speech recognition	o	x	o					o	x		o	o
K	Gesture recognition		x	x					o	o		o	
L	Optical character recognition					o	x					o	
M	Color recognition					o	x	x					
N	Image processing					x	x						
O	Navigation and Orientation					o	x				o	o	o

Note: x indicates a necessary assistive function; o indicates a function which could prove helpful in some cases. (x) true only for the combination of the marked impairments

in the second and third sections, respectively, they can also be used as quick reference index.

ACCESS TO COMPUTERS

Screen Enlargement

Computer screens commonly use rather small fonts to be able to display an entire line of edited text. Even if large monitors (19–21 in.) are used, this can prove insufficient for persons with reduced vision. Using just a large screen font of a text processor is not a viable solution, as this would result in a different layout of the page.

The way out is called screen enlargement, accomplished by special software or hardware, providing large print on the computer screen. Hardware solutions—a large print display processor plugged into the PC or hooked between the monitor connector of the PC and the monitor—will guarantee faultless operation with any user program running on the PC. Software solutions—terminate and stay resident (TSR) programs running in the background—are, of course, cheaper but have to be carefully selected to avoid conflicts with the user programs. Especially, the compatibility with GUIs has to be ensured as not all products can handle graphic screens.

Common screen enlargement offers magnifications between 2 and 16 times (sometimes up to 64 times). Therefore, only a small portion of the real screen will be visible, making it necessary to scroll the screen using the cursor keys or the mouse. Sometimes, automatic scrolling and cursor tracking functions are available.

Usually, the magnification can be switched on and off by "hot keys," thus offering the possibility of rapidly changing between standard and enlarged presentations. Simple screen magnifiers just will blow up the characters as they are, which will result in rather rugged character outlines. More advanced systems utilize their own large print fonts, thus producing smooth, easy-to-read characters.

Sometimes, users not only want the computer output to be displayed with large letters, but they have also to cope with printed material on their desk at the same time. Instead of using a second magnification system (optical or electronic magnifier) for the documents, it is possible to use one split screen. Half of the screen will present the enlarged computer output; the other half will show the magnified image of the document monitored by a CCTV camera.

Comfortable screen magnifiers should not only offer a variety of magnification factors and smooth scrolling but also a switch for positive and negative character representation, selectable colors, and split screens for an enlarged and not-enlarged portion.

There are also pure optical solutions using Fresnel lenses for screen magnification. Here, magnification factors range between 2 and 4.

Print Enlargement

For the same reasons as screen magnification, large print can be necessary for hardcopy material as well. Today, no special tools are necessary, as present text-processing programs in combination with state-of-the-art printers can generate printed characters of almost any size. Laser and inkjet printers are ideal for the production of high-contrast large print.

Common font sizes for large-print material are 18 points or more. Sans serif fonts which show sufficient differences between easily confused characters should be preferred. A line spacing of 5 points is recommended (17).

Displaying Braille

Braille has been described earlier as a tactile readable alphabet where single characters are represented by one or more raised dots out of a matrix of 6 or 8 dots. Braille displays are the tactile analogy to a computer screen — displaying the output of a computer in a volatile manner.

As Braille represents the characters of the alphabet, only textual information can be displayed. Using 8-dot Braille, capable of forming 255 different characters plus the space sign, all characters of the extended ASCII code can be displayed. Therefore, not only letters, figures, and punctuation marks but also control characters and semigraphic symbols can be represented.

Mechanical Braille displays consist of a plate with a hole for each Braille dot in which a cylindrical pin can be moved up and down. In the upward position, the pin will protrude 0.4–0.6 mm and thus form a Braille dot which can be recognized with the fingertip. In the lower position, the pin is hidden in the hole; pin and hole provide no tactile stimulus.

Various principles of driving the single pins have been developed. Former displays were driven by tiny electromagnets (solenoids), some utilizing sophisticated latching mechanisms in order to restrict power consumption to the moments when the pin actually is moved.

State-of-the-art Braille displays use stripes of two-layer piezoceramic material which will bend if high voltage is applied. These stripes which carry the pin at their moving end are mounted horizontally (stacked in several layers according to the number of dots of the Braille cell) beneath the Braille cell. As the size of a single Braille character is only 6–8 mm wide and 12–15 mm high, additional space is required for the driving mechanism. For this reason, using the piezoceramic technology, it is difficult to construct Braille displays with more than two lines, as the driving mechanisms need space in front and behind these two lines (18).

Experiments were also made with alternative driving mechanisms using bimetals, vaporization, shape memory alloys, pneumatics, and hydraulics, but until now, none of them found its way from laboratory into production (19–26).

Printing Braille

Braille printing is the mechanical production of hardcopy Braille material using thin cardboard (160–180 g/m^2). Before the computer age, this printing was accomplished either by hand (using slate and stylus or a Braille typewriter) or with a printing press.

In the same way as conventional printers serve as peripheral output devices of computers, Braille printers were developed for different speeds and quantities of Braille production. Braille printers for personal use usually employ an embossing head which is moved along the lines to be printed in the same manner as dot-matrix printers do. By this technology, printing speeds of between 20 and 40 characters per second are achieved. Printers designed for larger production quantities are able to emboss an entire line of Braille dots at a time, reaching printing speeds up to 400 characters per second.

In order to save paper and volume, it is possible to use both sides of the Braille paper. This so-called interpoint Braille is possible, as the fingertips will only recognize the protruding dots but not the holes of the reverse side. Some recently developed Braille printers are able to produce interpoint Braille.

For several reasons, it might be necessary or beneficial to have both, inkprint and Braille characters on one single sheet of paper. Consider a Brailled bank statement for a blind person which should also be readable for the sighted personnel. Textbooks and other study material for blind pupils and students should also be usable by the sighted teacher and the sighted peers. These are only two examples which call for possibilities to have the inkprint transcription beneath each line of Braille (interlinear Braille). At least one commercially available Braille printer offers this feature within a single device. A second possibility is to feed fanfold Braille paper through a combination of a standard (dot matrix) printer and a Braille printer. This system is used for the production of bank statements, for example. It has to be admitted that up until now, interlinear Braille is very rare.

Producing tactile graphic with a Braille printer is restricted due to mechanical reasons. Even if some modern Braille printers offer variable horizontal and vertical dot spacing, the production of smooth lines is not satisfactory compared with techniques like thermoforming. To overcome this drawback of mechanical Braille printers, a thermojet color printer has been modified to produce Braille, print, and tactile graphics on the same page. Plastic material which melts inside the unit is spattered to the paper, where it solidifies again. Although this technology would offer many advantages, it has not reached widespread usage (27,28).

Digitized Speech Output

For many reasons, auditory messages are helpful or necessary to provide computer access for disabled persons. Whenever the vocabulary of such messages can be limited to a predefined set of words or sentences, digitized (prerecorded) speech will be preferred. The technical effort is small (using readily available integrated circuits or sound boards for the PC) and the quality of speech is high. As present computers usually offer sufficient memory, the former drawback of prerecorded speech to be too much memory consuming is no longer true.

Typical applications of this technology are status or warning messages from the computer or a peripheral device. A Braille printer, for example, can echo all system settings to the blind user; a cognitive-impaired person might prefer spoken menu choices to pull-down menus on the computer screen.

Text-to-Speech Synthesis (as PC Output)

Text-to-speech conversion can be necessary for two reasons:

(a) To have the computer talk to a disabled person
(b) To give a voice to a speech- or language-impaired person

In this section, only the first application will be dealt with. For the second one, see the subsection Speech Communication.

As a device for accessing the computer, speech synthesis is needed as a replacement for or a supplement to the computer monitor. The goal should be to present the entire contents of the screen in an acoustic way. As long as the screen contents consist only of more or less unformatted lines of plain text, the task is quite simple. Especially today, this is the exception from common practice. In order to structure information presented on the screen, various additional elements are added, like underlining, bold print, italics, capitalizing, subscript and superscript, color, blinking, indentations, paragraphs, different font styles and sizes, and graphic elements. This long list should make it clear that conveying a screen containing these elements by using speech only is either impossible or rather time-consuming.

Therefore, using a text-to-speech synthesizer for accessing a computer screen is much more than just reading a list of words. Additional possibilities to navigate around the screen and to explore all these possible attributes must be provided in an interactive manner. The user must have the choice to select the depth of this screen investigation.

The demands on synthesizers used for this purpose are not necessarily high speech quality but short response time to commands, good differentiation of similar sounding characters or words, wide range of possible reading speed, and pitch. Usually, it takes only a short time to get acquainted with a synthesizer, which does not sound natural. Possibilities to spell a word and to speak punctuation marks must be provided.

As text-to-speech conversion is language dependent, synthesizers were developed for all major languages in the world. There are several products offering more than one language in one device with the possibility of rapidly switching between languages just by a software command (29,30).

Code Translation

As described earlier, not all Braille notations used by blind persons resemble a one-to- one equivalent of the printed text. Grade I Braille and Grade II Braille use abbreviations on the syllable and word levels which are context sensitive. Depending on the language, the translation rules between ASCII text and Braille are rather complex.

Especially for the production of Braille books, translation and text-formatting software was developed to automatically convert ASCII (or standard text processor) texts into Braille Grade I or Grade II. Because the standard translation rules cannot be applied to proper names or foreign words, it is necessary to manually mark these words prior to translation or to carefully proofread the Braille text.

The translation from Grade II Braille into ASCII is necessary for all applications where Braille writers want to exploit the benefits of abbreviated Braille when entering text into a computer or note-taking device. As long as input and output is in the same Braille notation, no translation would be necessary. The conversion, however, is necessary to produce inkprint outputs for sighted persons or to generate input data for a text-to-speech synthesizer (31,32).

For the tactile representation of mathematical expressions, various national Braille notations were developed. The main drawback of these schemes is that experts are necessary for converting mathematical inkprint into Braille and vice versa. To overcome this disadvantage, several text-coding systems like LaTeX or SGML (Standard General Markup Language) were analyzed for their suitability to act as a bidirectional link between mathematical Braille notation and inkprint (33–35).

Similar approaches are used for the conversion of music scores into their corresponding Braille notation in order to assist blind performers. One of the meta-codes used for this purpose is the MIDI (Musical Instruments Digital Interface) format. For assisting blind composers writing (typing) their artworks in Braille, several attempts for automatic production of inkprint scores are reported (36,37).

Translating a simple text file into Braille is one thing; passing on all the layout information of a well-formatted document like the beginning of a new paragraph, headers, titles, indents, and footnotes plus all the style information such as different character size, bold print, italics, and underline to a blind reader is a different thing. Sighted readers depend heavily on text formatting to recognize the structure of a document and to quickly browse large amounts of text. Structuring Braille texts follows rather different rules, as most of the layout parameters of the inkprint version will have no equivalent in Braille. Using document description languages like SGML (Standard General Markup Language), ODA (Open Document Architecture), or HTML (Hypertext Markup Language) offer a viable method for the automatic conversion of layout information (38–40).

Similar code-translation programs were developed for nonspeaking persons using Bliss or another symbolic language for communication (see the subsection Special Techniques of Communication). Here, the translation program will convert a sequence of picture symbols generated by the language-impaired person into a semantically and grammatically correct sentence which can be shown on a display or spoken by a speech synthesizer (41,42).

Sign Language Robot—Displaying the Finger Alphabet in a Tactile Way

For deaf–blind persons, the only remaining communication channel is the tactile sense, whereas persons acquiring deafness after blindness will continue using Braille and, therefore, when working with computers, Braille displays and Braille printers.

Persons who become deaf in early life usually use sign language for person-to-person communication and the monitor when working with the computer. If later on they become blind, the chances to learn Braille are rather limited. For this reason, a device has been developed by which a computer can output finger-spelling, which can be read in a tactile way by the deaf–blind user. This device is a **mechanical hand** with five computer-controlled fingers covered by a glove and mounted on top of a box. For each character, the computer issues the hand forms the corresponding finger position of the finger alphabet. By touching the mechanical hand, the deaf-blind person will read the computer output character by character (43).

Enhanced Manual Input

Today, the keyboard and mouse are the standard input devices for computer operation. It goes without saying that these devices call for a great amount of motor skills and dexterity. Persons who can use only one hand, one finger, their feet, or a head-stick are encountering problems in handling standard input devices. They all can benefit from one or more of the following assistive devices:

> **Mechanical keyguards:** A plate with a hole for every key of the keyboard is mounted on top of the keyboard. Because the fingers or the head-stick can reach the keys only through these holes, it becomes impossible to unintentionally hit one of the neighboring keys.
> **Special keyboard drivers** offer a wide range of parameter settings to make typing easier for physically handicapped persons. A keystroke will only be accepted if one single key is pressed long enough. Autorepeat functions can be switched off if necessary. Persons using only one hand or a head-stick can select a mode where the shift, alt and ctrl keys need not be pressed simultaneously with another key but can be operated in a sequential manner (13).
> **Large keyboards:** Persons having problems with fine movements or wanting to operate the keyboard with their feet or elbows will prefer keyboards with a larger size and greater robustness.
> **Small keyboards:** Vice versa there are persons who are not able to cover the area of a standard-sized keyboard with their restricted movements. If, for example, there is no arm movement but sufficient mobility in the wrist, a miniaturized keyboard can be the solution for typing.
> **Membrane keyboards:** For most users, it is convenient that the keys of the keyboard move mechanically, thus giving a tactile feedback when they are operated. However, sometimes a completely plane and hermetically sealed

keyboard with a touch-sensitive surface can be the better choice. Some types can be programmed to user-specific keyboard layouts. Size and position of the individual keys can be tailored to meet exactly the personal needs and abilities of the user (44).

Vision or motor impairment can make it difficult to use a standard mouse. Commercially available trackballs and joysticks can provide alternatives (45). To facilitate pointing to a screen object, a mouse with tactile feedback has been developed. The mouse button varies its vertical position and springload depending on the object to which is pointed (46).

Alternative Mechanically Operated Input Devices

In this subsection, a selection of more or less mechanical switches will be described which are used by persons who cannot use standard input and pointing devices like keyboards and computer mice but have the capability to at least perform some voluntary movements with any part of their body. Typical switch configurations consist of one, two, or five switches (four switches for moving the cursor into four directions and one switch for selecting). For entering commands or text by switches special scanning procedures are used as described in the subsection Special Input and Output Devices (47).

Mechanical switches with different sizes of the operation area and for a variety of operation forces are offered. These switches can be controlled by any movement of the hand, the arm, or the foot. They can also be activated by moving the shoulders or the chest, by tilting or turning the head, or by inflating the cheeks (1).

Suck–puff switches (sip–puff switches) are breath-activated pneumatic switches. A small tube like a drinking straw is placed between the lips of the user. Suck–puff switches are usually two-way switches. Some models can discern between two levels of pressure and vacuum, thus offering two times two output signals (1).

Eye lid control. Many severely paralyzed persons are still capable of controlling their eye and lid movements, as the nerves controlling these movements are directly connected to the brain and are not affected even by highly placed spinal cord lesions. The eye lid switch uses a beam of infrared light which is reflected differently if the lid is covering the eye. Involuntary eye blinks are rather short (< 100 ms) and can easily be discerned from voluntary blinks with a duration greater than 250 ms (48).

The **palatal tongue controller** is a set of (e.g., 11) sensor switches mounted on an intraorally worn thin plate which covers the hard palate and a part of the vestibule of the upper jaw. The use of a wireless signal transfer frees the user from cables between his/her lips (49,50).

For persons unable to use a mouse or a trackball, alternative pointer systems can be provided. These pointers are either for the same purpose as a mouse (i.e., for moving the cursor) or to operate an alternative keyboard displayed on a part of the computer screen. Using the latter technique, all keyboard and mouse functions of a computer can be accessed by pointing to objects on the screen. The following two-dimensional movements are suitable for pointing purposes:

> **Head movement.** Systems for converting head movements into cursor move-ments use either light or laser pointers attached to the head and a suitable detector mounted opposite of the user, or a mirror worn on the forehead whose deflections are monitored by a cameralike device usually mounted above the computer screen. Ultrasound, inertia, gravity, and magnetic field sensors have also been successfully used for measuring head movements (51).

> **Eye movement.** One possibility for eye tracking is using a complete image processing system composed of a camera, an infrared light source, and a dedicated computer. The entire image of the user's head is analyzed in order to determine the direction the eyes are pointing (52). As these systems are rather complicated and expensive, researchers also tried to exploit the so-called EOG (electrooculogram) for pointing purposes. The eye has an elec-tric potential which moves when the eyeball rotates within the eye socket. This potential can be detected by skin electrodes placed around the eye. After some conditioning (low-pass filter and isolation amplifier), the EOG can be used as a signal which is proportional to the eye movements (53,54).

Head pointers as well as eye pointers need calibration before and, due to drift problems, also during operation.

As the pointing operation is only moving the cursor to the desired place on the screen, a second activity is necessary for triggering the selection. This can be done by any additional switch (having the same function as the left mouse button) pro-vided that the disabled person has another movement at his or her disposal. If not, acoustic triggering by voice or by clicking the teeth together can provide an alterna-tive (55). Finally, the selection can also be done by keeping the cursor mark on the desired object for a defined period of time. This affords undisturbed fine motor control and a neutral area on the screen on which the cursor mark can rest without activating any command. It goes without saying that this technique is the most time-consuming one.

Alternatives for Mechanically Operated Input Devices

Speech Input

Voice control provides an alternative input method for persons without any motor abilities in the common sense. Due to the steadily increasing power of PCs, reliable and fast speech recognition can be offered at reasonable costs. For the purpose of computer input by disabled persons, it is not necessary to have speaker-independent speech recognition. On the contrary, it can be beneficial if the system responds only to the voice of the user and will not be disturbed by other voices or ambient noise.

When selecting a speech recognition (dictation) system for a handicapped user, one has to take care that not only text entry but all functions of the computer operation can be effected via speech control. This includes starting and terminating different applications (programs), handling menus, moving the cursor, correcting entries, and recovering from errors.

For using speech recognition for performing control tasks (in contrast to computer input) see the subsection Speech Recognition.

Brain-Computer Interface

There are disabilities (lesions of the cervical spine, hemiplegia, quadriplegia) which deprive a person not only of all motor functions but also all vocal utterances, leaving him or her in the so-called locked-in syndrome. As there is not the slightest possibility to interact with the environment or to react to stimuli, until a few years ago (1991) it was not possible even to find out whether such a person can recognize or understand anything from the world around.

As the EEG (electroencephalogram) of these patients show normal brain activities, a way out from the locked-in situation could be found by directly accessing the brain functions. Even if researchers are still far from directly reading thoughts from a person's mind, some intentional brain activities can be decoded to at least control the movement of a cursor.

The locked-in individual can be asked to move an arm or a leg. Due to the lesion of the spinal cord, there will be no physical movement at all, but the brain is still producing an EEG pattern which corresponds to the intended movement. By classification of certain signals of the EEG by artificial neural networks, it is possible to detect some signals which can serve for communication purposes (56–59).

USING COMPUTERS FOR DAILY LIVING TASKS

Remote Control

Remote control, in general, is used whenever an activity has to be performed at a place which is out of the user's reach. For motor-impaired persons, the term "out of reach" has to be defined very individually. For a bedridden person, for example, the other end of the room is out of reach. A completely paralyzed person would extend the term "out of reach" to the entire physical environment. "Out of reach," in a wider sense, does not only deal with the distance between user and object to be handled but also with questions of muscle strength, dexterity, fatigue, and pain. In other words, even near objects can become inaccessible due to individual reasons.

These examples not only show the great importance of remote control systems but also underline the necessity of flexible and individual adaptability. In the context of disability, remote control systems are very often called environmental control systems (ECS) (60–63).

An ECS can be considered to consist of three main components (hardware and software):

- The **user interface,** comprised of the following:
  - (a) The **user-interface controller** (matching the general features of the ECS with the specific needs of the disabled user). It interacts with
  - (b) The **sensors** (input devices), which can be a switch or a pointing device, a keyboard, or a speech recognizer and
  - (c) The **feedback units** (output devices) (e.g., a display, a CRT screen, a speaker)
- The **application interface** constitutes the link to the social and material environment.

(a) The **application-interface controller** (interpreting the user commands and matching the general features of the ECS to the existing environmental situation)

(b) The **communication channels** for transporting the various commands from the ECS to the target application. This can be accomplished by one of the following means: Wire bound (separate wires or bus systems; carrier frequency systems using existing power lines) or wireless (infrared, radio)

- The **application** (end effectors, peripheral devices); for example,
  (a) Using existing remote controls (like in video or hi-fi components)
  (b) Adding supplementary controls (by inserting a radio-controlled switch into the power line of a lamp)
  (c) Installing entirely new actuators (mounting an electrically powered window opener)

The applications for which disabled persons use remote control can be divided into the following areas:

- **Communication, safety, and security**

  Controlling a hands-free telephone (phone book management, off-hook, dialing)
  Attendance call (summoning a carer, triggering a pager)
  Controlling the door intercom and the door opener
  Alarm call in case of an emergency or a system break-down

- **Household appliances**

  Lights
  Air conditioning, ventilator, heating
  Windows, doors, curtains, and blinds
  Alarm clock

- **Medical appliances**

  Controlling the adjustable bed
  Controlling a manipulator or robot
  Controlling a "dead-man's" device ("watchdog," medical sensors, etc.)

- **Computer and network access**

  Accessing the PC by emulation of keyboard and mouse
  Editing of documents, taking notes
  Sending and receiving faxes
  Sending and receiving electronic mail
  Retrieving information from databases and computer networks (Internet, WWW)
  Reading newspapers and books stored on electronic media (CD-ROM, network)

- **Entertainment**

   Controlling hi-fi and video equipment
   Playing video and computer games
   Controlling electric toys

Text Communication

There can be two reasons making it impossible for a subject to conduct a spoken person-to-person dialogue: speech impairment (not to be confused with language impairment—see the subsection Picture Communication) and severe hearing impairment (which cannot be compensated by conventional hearing aids or cochlea implants). A way to overcome these communication barriers is to shift the entire conversation from the vocal level to text communication. Speaking will be replaced by writing (typing), and hearing will be replaced by reading.

Speech Impairment

In principle, a simple cardboard chart displaying all characters of the alphabet would serve the purpose. The speech-disabled person would spell a message by sequentially pointing at the characters and the other party would try to remember the characters and form words and sentences in his or her mind. As this basic method is slow, requires full attention and concentration, and makes correction rather difficult, electronic substitutes have been developed.

One of the first devices for composing text messages for speech-disabled persons was the Canon "Communicator," a cigarette-box-sized miniature typewriter to be carried on one's wrist like a large watch. Messages typed on the keyboard are printed on a slip of paper which can be torn off and handed to the conversation partner. Often-used phrases and standard answers can be stored and recalled on demand.

Users of the "Communicator" sometimes complained about the fact that the output is on a permanent medium. In other words, a device that is used to substitute speech, which is transitory, should also have a nonpermanent output. Devices using an alphanumeric display instead of the printer fulfill this requirement and have less mechanical parts.

The main bottleneck of all devices of this kind is the low communication speed, as typing always is much slower than speech. (The average speaking rate is about 160 words per minute). Using phrase catalogs and/or predictive typing can lower the speed barrier but will make handling more difficult and increase the size and weight of the device (7–9).

Severe Hearing Impairment and Deafness

Deaf people seldom use text communication devices for person-to-person communication. The reason may be that lipreading at least offers some real-time communication link even if usually not more than 30% of a spoken message can be retrieved by this method. However, when it comes to lectures or public events, the translation of the spoken message into displayed text is sometimes used (real-time captioning). Presently, this translation still has to be performed by a human typist, as voice recognition systems are not yet powerful enough. Machine shorthand—like the CAT (computer-aided transcription) system in the United States—can be considered as a prerequisite for efficient and successful real-time captioning, reaching 200 words per minute and more. Conventional typing will reach only 30–80 words per minute (64,65).

Speech Communication

A more natural method of restoring the ability to talk is the use of text-to-speech synthesizers as prosthetic devices. The input is the same as described in the previous section, but instead of printing or displaying, the typed text is fed into a speech synthesizer.

It goes without saying that in contrast to computer speech output applications (e.g., for blind users, see the subsection Text-to-Speech Synthesis), here much higher quality standards have to be set for the speech synthesizer, for the following reasons:

- The assistive device is much likely addressing a person who never worked with synthetic speech and is not trained to understand it. Therefore, the sound must be as natural as possible.
- The assistive device is the prosthetic replacement for a person's own voice. Thus, the synthesizer must be able to approach the (imaginary) voice of the user as close as possible. In other words, the synthetic speech must take into account sex, personality, age, and nationality of the user. It can be an awful experience if the synthesizer is speaking a dialect different to the user's home country.

Another problem is that common vocal prostheses are unable to express emotional feelings. For the nonspeaking user, it is essential also to communicate feelings like anger, happiness, sadness, fear, or disgust. By studying the vocal characteristics of emotions, researchers could find out their influence on the prosody, the pitch contour, and the time duration of single phonemes. Using these parameters, prototypes of vocal prostheses capable of expressing emotion could be designed (66,67).

Standard vocal prostheses require the skill of entering more or less correct messages (words, sentences with correct grammar and syntax). Recently, some progress could be achieved to assist persons with specific language impairments. The technical aid in these cases assists the user in remembering the correct terms and in putting together a natural sentence even if the input does not follow the correct syntactical rules (68).

Until now, we have considered persons who completely lack speech and who need a total substitute for their own voices. For persons with distorted and unintelligible speech, the combination of speech recognition and speech synthesis can hold some promises in the future. At first glance, using speech recognition for a person with speech disorders "may seem somewhat bizarre" (69). However, if the utterances of the speech-impaired person are reproducible, a (speaker dependent) speech recognizer can be trained to understand the person's speech. The recognized text, in turn, can be input to a speech synthesizer and the outcome of the procedure would be a voice that is easier to understand (70).

Enhanced Telecommunication

The present technical aids to facilitate vocal telecommunication for hard-of-hearing and speech-impaired persons are restricted to the amplification of the outgoing and incoming audio signal. For the near future, it can be expected that research and development of special speech-processing units will improve the usability of the (voice) telephone for disabled users. Speech intelligibility can be increased by the following:

- Plosive enhancement
- Second formant enhancement
- Transforming of the usually inaudible "s" fricative into an audible replacement sound

The European research project SICONA (Signal Conditioning Communication Aids for the Hearing-Impaired) tries to implement these features on a speech-processing ASIC. Applications in the field of voice telephony are envisaged (71).

Alternative Telecommunication

Voice telephony is still the most important means of telecommunication in our society. Voice telephony, strictly spoken, is nothing else than a spin-off product of Alexander Graham Bell's endeavors to develop an aid for hard-of-hearing persons. Ironically, severely hard-of-hearing, deaf, and speech-impaired persons are those who now are excluded from using Bell's invention. Two alternatives to voice telephony can be used by deaf and speech-impaired persons: text telephones and videophones.

Text Telephones

The text telephone can best be compared with a teletype (telex machine) offering the possibility of typing a text which will appear displayed or printed on the other party's unit. In contrast to teletypes, text telephones are connected to the PSTN (Public Switched Telephone Network) and offer a real-time two-way conversation almost equivalent to voice telephony. The major disadvantage of text telephones is that without special provisions (see later) the second party must also utilize a text telephone working according to the same communication standard.

A survey on presently used text telephone standards carried out by COST 219 (Future Telecommunications and Teleinformatics Facilities for Disabled People and Elderly, a program of the EU) revealed the list of incompatible methods (6) presented in Table 3.

Older text telephone units or standards require taking turns (i.e., the displays do not differentiate between the sent and the received text). The text messages of

TABLE 3   Text Telephone Standards

V.23 (1200/75 bit/s)	France	Minitel standard, videotex
EDT (110 bit/s)	Germany, Switzerland, Austria, Italy, Spain, Malta	one channel, carrier only while sending
V.21 - Nordic (300 bit/s)	Sweden, Norway, Finland	full duplex, 7 bit, even parity
V.21 - British (300 bit/s)	United Kingdom	full duplex
DTMF (touch tone signals)	Denmark, Netherlands	combination of dialling tones
Baudot/TDD (45.45 bit/s)	USA, Ireland, Iceland, partly UK	FSK 1400/1800 Hz
Bell (300 bit/s)	USA	full duplex

both parties are mixed on one screen. This made it necessary to use special codes like "*" or "GA" (for go ahead) to indicate the end of a message string and requesting the partner to reply (6,72).

Modern text telephone standards, however, support full duplex dialogues where sent and received texts are presented in different screen windows. Spontaneous replies are possible even while receiving text from the conversation partner.

To overcome the incompatibility of the different national text telephone standards and to offer all the features possible with modern telecommunication protocols (full duplex, voice over data), a new worldwide standard is in preparation. The proposed new standard is called V.18 and will offer the following main advantages: Downward-compatibility with all already existing text telephone standards. The user will not have to care about the standard of the other party's text telephone. A V.18 modem will automatically connect in the highest possible communication protocol. As text telephones are not only beneficial for profoundly deaf persons or for persons completely lacking speech, V.18 will offer the possibility to switch between text and voice communication at any time.

All signals indicating the status of the telephone line and the call progress (dial tone, ringing, engaged, etc.) have to be indicated in a way suitable for the disabled user.

Often the use of the Fax is proposed to replace text telephony. It certainly is true that with the rapid growth of the number of Fax users (even in the private sector), deaf and speech-impaired persons would find many more communication partners addressable in a nonvocal way. However, it must be remembered that the Fax is only a one-way connection and does not support a dialogue (73).

Using the "chat" capabilities of the Internet, therefore, would be an alternative with respect to the true dialogue functionality. The drawback here is, that only logged-in partners can be reached and that there is no possibility of sending an awareness signal to the other party as in standard telephony.

Videophones

In person-to-person conversation, deaf people either use lipreading or sign language, provided the partner has the appropriate skills. By using videophones (picture telephones), the same methods can be applied for telecommunication.

Despite of the already existing camera and display technology, for a long time video telephony could not be realized due to the narrow bandwidth of existing telephone lines. Today, modern image compression algorithms running on powerful microprocessors have drastically changed the situation, as only a fraction of the real image contents has to be transported.

With respect to today's technology in image processing, the use of videophones by disabled persons can be grouped in two classes:

- Videophones offering low frame rates (< 15 frames/s) and modest picture quality (resolution, contrast, gray scale) can be used with existing narrowband telephone lines. This type of videophone is, for example, beneficial for persons with mental disabilities, as seeing the partner augments the verbal communication.
- Videophones used together with broadband networks will offer frame rates of 15 frames/s and more, which is a prerequisite for lipreading and under-

standing sign language. Experiments have shown that using an ISDN line (2 × 64 Kbit/s) and presently available image compression is just not sufficient for this purpose, whereas using twice the capacity worked quite well. So, some future improvement of codec technology could make it possible to cope with ISDN lines for sign language transmission quite soon (74).

Relay Services

Text telephones and videophones will only work if the other party is using the same kind of equipment. Deaf and speech-impaired persons, therefore, have far less telecommunication possibilities as their hearing and speaking peers who use the (audio) telephone. As in industrialized countries telecommunication can be considered a social and occupational necessity, the access to the telephone should be counted as one of the human rights of all citizens.

As long as the public at large is using "POTs" (plain old telephones) and has not yet shifted to multimedia terminals which combine speech, text, and video (which is sure to come sooner or later), a bridge between text telephones and the rest of the world will be necessary. This "bridge" is accomplished by so-called relay services.

The operator of the relay service is the third party to a telecommunication between a text telephone or videophone user and the user of a standard telephone. The deaf person calls the relay service via their text (or videophone) access number and asks the operator to forward the call to the desired hearing subscriber. The operator will now, using a second telephone line, call the hearing customer and, with both parties on-line, he/she will translate between speech and text. If a videophone is used and the operator is capable of sign language, he/she will translate between speech and signing.

If the communication impairment of the disabled party affects hearing alone, the operator usually will only translate in one direction. For the way back, a direct audio connection is established. The same is true for the other direction, if the disabled person is speech-impaired only.

Today, relay services still have to employ operators. At the relay center, computers are used as multimedia terminals to handle the different types of calls and to run programs for improving the typing speed (64,65,75,76).

In the future, the following computer-supported automatic translations seem to be feasible:

- **Speech to text:** For this, improved speaker-independent speech recognizers for continuous speech will be necessary. Presently, only speaker-dependent single-word recognition can be considered to be state-of-the-art (73).
- **Speech to lip images or sign language (gestures):** Here, some special computer animation software to synthesize the image of a speaking or signing person is necessary, in addition to the above-mentioned speech recognizer. Programs for this purpose are already available on the laboratory level (77,78).
- **Speech to Braille or mechanical hand:** Instead of text displays or video screens, deaf–blind persons have to use Braille displays or mechanical hands connected to the output of the speech recognizer.

- **Text to speech:** Speech synthesizer technology is readily available for most languages. Future improvements will concern a wider selection of available voices and the capability to express emotions (73).
- **Sign language (gestures) or finger-spelling to speech:** Laboratory experiments using data gloves for the automatic translation of the finger alphabet already show the feasibility of this approach. By adding position sensors, even basic elements of sign language can be read by the computer (79,80).

Picture Communication

Persons suffering from a language impairment (not to be confused with speech impairment) which is often also addressed as aphasia cannot speak because they lack or have lost the ability to think or express themselves in terms of words and sentences. Therefore, it is obvious that just providing a writing tool would make no difference. In most cases, however, this group of people can recognize and associate images and graphical symbols and can use them for communication.

Disabled children and severely mentally handicapped persons are using smaller or larger sets of symbols (pictures, graphics) where each element stands for a specific message. Let us assume the language-disabled person is pointing to an image showing an apple in order to communicate the message: "I would like to eat an apple now." This example shows two things: First, there has to be some agreement between the disabled person and the other party about the message which the specific symbol represents. Second, only such messages can be delivered for which a symbol has been provided.

Electronic devices with text or speech output can be used as programmable links between symbols and associated messages. The pictures will be placed on single switches, on the overlay of a concept keyboard (touch panel, membrane keyboard), or on a touch screen. By addressing the icon (closing a switch, touching the concept keyboard, or pointing with the mouse or cursor), the corresponding message will be issued. Larger vocabularies can be achieved when the icons are displayed on a computer screen, as topic-related sets of pictures can be arranged in hierarchical menus (81).

Language impairment does not necessarily mean that the afflicted person cannot think about complex and abstract things. This is especially true for persons losing their language capability due to a stroke. It would be a severe constraint if these persons would only have access to some predefined symbols and messages. They would like to express anything they want to say. To accommodate their needs, complete languages based on symbols instead of words have been created, of which Bliss is the most popular and widespread. By using more than 1400 different symbols which can be combined to form other expressions, an almost unlimited communication is possible.

These symbolic languages (like Bliss) are languages in the true sense of the word. To "speak" and to understand them requires learning. Here, computers can do a lot for the nondisabled communication partner by translating the symbols into spoken language. The entire set of Bliss symbols is printed on the overlay of a touch tablet or displayed on a computer screen (in portions which can be scrolled or accessed in pages). The language-disabled person will compose a message by selecting and combining several icons. Sentence by sentence, the computer will parse the input string, translate it into the correct syntax of the corresponding spoken message, and output it via a speech synthesizer (11). Thus, even persons who never have learned Bliss can understand messages composed by language-impaired people.

Calling and Alarm Systems

For many good reasons, the trend is to favor the independent living of disabled and elderly persons and to avoid or at least postpone institutional care as long as possible. Independent living at home, alone or together with the family, calls for assistive devices and for systems to summon human assistance whenever help is needed.

The classical alarm system developed especially for elderly persons is just a hands-free telephone with a built in automatic dialer which will call a service provider whenever an alarm is triggered. Modern devices make use of computer technology in the alarm telephone as well as at the service center.

Stationary Alarm Systems

A state-of-the-art alarm system linked stationary to the telephone line will offer the following features:

- Triggering the alarm

  Pressing a button on a wrist-worn remote controller
  External signals (burglar or fire alarm)
  Dead-man's device (signal triggered automatically if the person in question is not showing some activity within a predefined time span)
  Medical sensors

- The number to be called will be dependent on the type of alarm, the hour, and the day of the week (e.g., automatically calling a relative at the office, at home, or via the mobile phone).
- Calling a sequence of predefined numbers and replaying a prestored spoken alarm message until the call is answered and confirmed by entering a defined PIN code via the touch tone keys. The telephone will then switch to the hands-free mode and establish a voice connection.
- When a computer-equipped service center is called, the unit will transmit an identification number, automatically causing all relevant data to appear on the operator's screen (name, address, medical data, map showing the location, etc.).
- The alarm telephone can be equipped with a link to the door opener. By entering a code, the alarm center can remotely open the door when the helpers arrive.
- Self-test and power-fail provisions to increase the reliability of the system.

Mobile Alarm Systems

Presently, only stationary alarm systems are available. The increasing mobility of disabled and elderly persons does not lower their demand for safety and security. Modified cellular (mobile) phones certainly could be used as alarm phones for outdoor applications. However, it must be guaranteed that the rescuers are guided to the right place even if the user does not know his/her position or is even unable to communicate at all. Therefore, satellite navigation [like GPS (Global Positioning System) and GIS (Geographical Information Systems)] will play an essential role in the development of future mobile alarm telephones.

Alerting Systems

In contrast to the previously described alarm systems, by which the user is able to call for help, alerting systems work into the opposite direction: The user is warned about a danger. As public alarm signals (fire, disaster) usually are given by ringing a bell, blowing a horn, or sounding a siren, hard-of-hearing or deaf persons are running the risk of not being informed in time. Other acoustic signals are important in daily life: the ringing of the phone or the doorbell, the whistling of the water kettle, or the signal of the kitchen timer.

Domestic Applications

Some of these problems could be solved without computers or high tech by just establishing a suitable link that will transfer the usually acoustic event into an optical (blinking lamps/flashlights) or vibrotactile message. Examples are as follows: ringing of the doorbell causes the room light to go on and off; the crying of the baby triggers a flashlight in the kitchen; the alarm clock activates a vibrator beneath the pillow. By using carrier frequency (via power lines), infrared, or radio transmission, additional wiring in the house can be avoided.

There are also portable systems (like pagers) available which can easily be carried around in the house or in the garden without losing contact to the most important signals.

Recently, a different approach using signal processing and neural networks has reached the laboratory stage. Instead of wiring the signaling unit to all sources from which signals can come, the central unit receives the sounds in question via a microphone. The patterns of the different sounds are stored in the device in a training phase. Using a flashlight or a wireless (vibrotactile) pager, the deaf user is informed about the occurrence of the different sounds in his/her house (82).

Public Applications

For relaying a civil alarm signal to a deaf user, the following information channels can be used:

- A dedicated radio frequency
- A subcarrier or RDS code of the local FM station (83)
- The short message service (SMS) of the GSM cellular phone

Prototypes of alerting systems (e.g., integrated into a wristwatch with a vibrotactile ringer) were developed by different projects. Which technology will be preferred certainly is a question of future standardization, as only a system with a large-area coverage makes sense for the deaf and hearing-impaired users.

Manipulators and Robots

As this article deals primarily with computer (and microprocessor) applications, it could be argued that robots and manipulators should not be included here. However, robots in the field of rehabilitation cannot be considered as mere mechanical devices. To become a useful, reliable, and safe partner of a human being, they need complex control and a lot of sensors. Presently, the use of robots in rehabilitation is rather rare. The number of ongoing research, development, and field studies indicates that a boom is expected in the near future (84).

Without going into the details of robot construction, this section will give an overview of the different areas of application.

Fixed Manipulators for Handling Objects in the Environment

Severely motor-impaired persons today can get much help by using computers, remote control, and telecommunication (see the subsection Remote Control). Writing documents, controlling electrical appliances, or making telephone calls are tasks which can be performed without any human assistance. However, when it comes to changing a diskette, inserting a backup tape, or placing a book on the automatic page turner, the standard environmental control system (ECS) cannot help.

By implementing a numeric controlled manipulator into the concept of the ECS, tasks like the above-mentioned ones can be accomplished. Usually, the environment will be adapted to the functionality of the manipulator. All objects to be handled are stored in dedicated magazines and slots to which the gripper easily has access without positioning problems. Most projects in this field are using Cartesian ($x/y/z$) manipulators (85–87).

Fixed Robots for Personal Care and Assistance

Robots of this type are directly serving the disabled person (e.g., by fetching a drinking glass or a beverage bottle and bringing it to the mouth of the user). By using appropriate sensors, not only the exact target position in front of the user has to be determined but also any risk of collision which inevitably would injure the immobile user must be ruled out reliably.

Mobile Robots for Handling Objects

Instead of stationary mounting or running on rails, manipulators can be placed on top of some kind of trolley or movable platform, forming a remote-controlled vehicle with a versatile gripper. The unit can move freely around the disabled person's environment and thus perform most of the pick, transport, and place operations a human assistant would do.

So much for theory. The reality is not as simple as could be assumed at the first glance. A mobile robot has more than half a dozen axles for movement (for the trolley plus the manipulator and the gripper). As a matter of fact, a person in need of such a device will have no or not much dexterity to handle complex controls. The human–machine interface, therefore, will be just a few switches or voice input. This makes controlling the robot a tricky and slow task, especially if there is no direct line of sight between the user and the gripper and the disabled person will have to watch a TV monitor to guide the manipulator.

By adding video and ultrasound sensors plus sophisticated image processing systems, the manipulator will be able to precisely home in on its targets even if the remote control delivers only coarse coordinates. Presently, solutions along these lines are rather expensive and are still the object of intensive research (87–91).

Wheelchair-Mounted Robotic Arms

If the user is able to handle a (powered) wheelchair, the task will be not as difficult as described above. Here, the manipulator can be attached directly to the wheelchair and the user will always be in a suitable position to monitor the movements of the manipulator and gripper from a close distance. Wheelchair-mounted robotic arms are mainly used for picking up objects from the floor or getting things down from a shelf (92).

Mobile Robots for Guidance

Investigations are proceeding to find out if mobile robots could be beneficial for guiding blind persons in unfamiliar environments. Apart from reliable navigation and obstacle-detection subsystems, problems like overcoming steps and stairs have to be solved. Despite some experimental designs, only time can tell if such robots in future will be able to replace a well-trained guide dog at reasonable costs (93).

Mobile Robots for Personal Transport

A mobile robot can also be used as a means of transportation for the disabled person. In other words, this would be nothing else than an intelligent wheelchair which is able to perform certain driving and navigation tasks in an autonomous way. Idealistically, the user would only have to tell the system the desired target position and the wheelchair would automatically move to the new location. More realistic approaches are using "shared control," which means that the wheelchair will assist its user to follow a corridor along a straight line, to pass through a narrow doorway without hitting the door posts, or avoiding a collision with an obstacle which suddenly appears. Image analysis, processing, and understanding are the key technologies to be used here (94–96).

Prosthetics

From the literature it can be seen that there are no clear borderlines between robotic arms and modern prostheses which can also be considered body-mounted robots (97).

Speech Recognition

Several aspects and applications of speech recognition have already been mentioned in earlier sections. Here, a short synopsis of the most important terms are given.

Speaker-Dependent/Independent Speech Recognition

The general goal of developers of speech recognition equipment is the creation of a completely speaker-independent recognition system. Whoever talked to such a system would be understood. This approach is necessary for applications like automatic public information and translation systems (see also the subsection Alternative Telecommunication). No user-specific voice training would be necessary. Systems fulfilling this condition are still rare and have rather restricted vocabularies.

For assisting disabled users, however, speaker dependency should not be considered a drawback but an advantage. On the one hand, it is important that the system is reacting only to "his masters voice," ignoring most of other sounds (voices from other persons in the room or from a radio or TV). On the other hand, a disabled person's voice for many reasons can be out of the range of what the speech system developers consider to be the average. So specific training can overcome a lot of problems and possible interferences.

At this point, it has to be mentioned that motor disabilities can influence the user's speaking in a way that the voice is dependent on the momentary general condition of the person. The voice in the morning can be different from that in the evening. Stress or fatigue can leave traces in the pronunciation and tone. Systems which are able either to learn and store the entire possible spectrum of the user's voice or to adaptively follow occurring changes are the answer to these problems.

Continuous Speech/Isolated Word Speech Recognizers

For a human listener, it seems quite simple to locate the boundaries of single words when listening to another person. Precise analysis of spoken sentences, however, reveals that in many cases there are no significant boundaries at all. The end of the first word can be merged with the beginning of the next one. For a technical system, it is not a trivial task to separate the words in natural speech. Almost all presently commercial available speech recognizers, therefore, require some discipline from the speaker with respect to clearly separating one word from the next one.

Small Vocabulary/Large Vocabulary Speech Recognizers

With respect to the size of the vocabulary, two classes of speech recognizers have been developed for commercial products. Devices with small vocabularies have been built for applications like telephones with speech-controlled dialing. It is evident that some 20 to 50 commands are sufficient to control all necessary functions. Large vocabularies (30,000 words and more), however, are imperative for dictation systems (text entry into the computer for editing purposes).

Speech recognition applications useful for disabled persons are presented in Table 4.

Gesture Recognition

The application of gesture recognition for translating from finger-spelling and sign language was already discussed. See also Refs. 79 and 80.

Another future application of this technology will be to provide an additional input device for a communication aid or a computer for persons with speech and

TABLE 4   Applications for Speech Recognition Systems

Application	speaker dependent/independent	recognition isolated/continuous	vocabulary small/large
Voice dictation	dependent	single	large
Speech-to-text/gestures	independent	continuous	large
Remote control	dependent	single	small
Speech re-synthesis	dependent	continuous	large

motor impairments (neurophysical impairment, athetoid cerebral palsy). This group has significant problems with hitting a switch or operating a pointer, due to their spastic movements. Nevertheless, it could be proven that they are able to express themselves using natural arm gestures. The sensors and the recognition system must be able to differentiate between a voluntary gesture and an involuntary spasm-induced movement. For this reason, not only position sensors but also accelerometers are used. The subsequent recognition process is similar to speech recognition (98–101).

Optical Character Recognition

When looking at the machine-readable line on a check or on a credit card, a few people will be aware that in the beginning the development of optical character recognition was driven by the desire to create a system which could read to blind persons without using a human interpreter.

Today, optical character recognition (OCR) is a well-established commercial discipline. The applications range from automatic processing of financial transactions to reading license plates for road pricing, from address reading for automatic mail sorting to the recognition of handwriting in personal digital assistants (pen computers).

The typical processing steps necessary for converting a printed document into a text file are as follows:

- **Scanning:** generating an image file of the printed document
- **Segmentation:** separating information from the background (isolating columns, paragraphs, lines, and finally, single characters)
- **Feature Extraction:** extracting the significant information from the image of a character
- **Classification:** comparing the features of the character to be recognized with the features of known characters or with a set of programmed rules; assigning the best match to the result

Today, two classes of OCR systems (programs) with respect to the necessity of a training phase are available.

Systems Which Require Training

When starting on a new document, the system will not be able to recognize any of the characters but will display an image of the character in question on the screen. It is the job of the user to recognize this character and to assign it to a code by hitting the corresponding key on the keyboard. This procedure will be repeated until all characters of the used font are entered at least once. If the print quality of the document is poor, it will be necessary to enter more than one representative of each character.

Once trained, such systems will (fair print quality provided) recognize the characters of a font with an accuracy of much more than 99%. Advanced systems can handle more than one font in parallel and even mark the changes from one font to another or from plain print to bold or italics. This is important for reading tasks where not only the text but also text attributes have to be taken into consideration.

As the system has to be trained by the user, even special fonts (like the phonetic alphabet) or special characters (like in scientific literature) can be handled.

Systems Which Do Not Need Training

There are also systems available which are already factory pretrained to the most common fonts and print styles. Usually, no user interaction will be necessary after starting the reading process. If the document to be read matches the specifications the system expects, the result will be satisfying. If more or less exotic fonts or print styles occur or when special symbols are used, the system will fail.

Both approaches have benefits for blind users. For the direct and personal uses, only systems which require no training are acceptable. (This, at least, is true as long as there is no viable solution to interactively present tactile graphics to the blind user so that he/she could run an OCR training phase).

The OCR systems, however, are not only used by blind persons themselves but also by institutions which are producing Braille literature. Here, systems with training can be the better choice because of their flexibility and accuracy.

It must not be forgotten that extracting the text contents of a document is only part of the entire reading process. A document reading system to be used by blind persons must be able to perform at least basic document analysis which comprises the following:

- Automatic determination of the orientation of the text (portrait, landscape, upside-down)
- Fast skipping of blank areas
- Reading columns and headlines which run across more than one column
- Skipping (and indicating) illustrations without getting confused and without omitting text content

Color Recognition

"He is talking like a blind person about color" is a German idiom used when someone is criticized about talking too much about things without deeper knowledge. Since the development of electronic color recognition devices for blind (or color blind) persons, this saying is no longer true. For many reasons, it can be important for blind people to know the color of an object: Identically shaped food packs often significantly differ in color (e.g., milk versus orange juice); blind weavers or carpet makers have to know the color of the wool they are working with; blind professional gardeners want to distinguish flowers by their color (a reality in the tulip fields of the Netherlands).

The hand-held, battery-operated color probe consists of the following:

- A light source
- A three-color sensor for extracting the red, green, and blue color components of the object in question
- A microprocessor which assigns the three-dimensional feature vectors to the names of the different colors
- A speech output device (prerecorded speech) to announce the color to the blind user

About 30–50 different colors and shades can be distinguished by name. For more precise measurements, the percent rating for the three color components plus the brightness can be given as numerical values. Even if it is not easy to imagine a color by four figures, this output mode is essential for comparing the colors of two objects to prove whether two objects (e.g., a pair of stockings) have the identical color (102,103).

Image Processing

Within the wide field of image processing, three subdisciplines are relevant for assisting blind and visually impaired persons:

- Image enhancement
- Image analysis (scene analysis) and image understanding
- Image coding

The applications of image processing aim at restoring impaired vision or creating vision substitution systems where visual information is transformed in a way to be perceived by auditory or tactile means.

Image Enhancement

The first steps toward image enhancement for persons with low vision can be seen in the advent of more or less complex document-reading aids using CCTV (closed circuit television). The document to be read is placed beneath the lens of a television camera which is connected to a CRT, LCD, or fluorescent display. The main purpose is to achieve magnification levels (4–40 times) which cannot be reached by optical means. In addition, such devices offer brightness and contrast enhancement, image inversion (displaying white print on black background), or color transformation (the user can assign any color to print and background which will yield the optimum contrast for his/her personal situation).

Stationary and portable image enhancement devices for document reading can be considered as state-of-the-art. Applying vision enhancement methods for orientation and mobility, however, is a rather new field.

There are several eye diseases which do not lead to such a degree of blindness that the visual sense becomes worthless for orientation and activities of daily living. Let us consider night blindness caused by a damage to the retina's rods, which are responsible for the perception at low light levels. As the cones (working at high illumination levels) are not affected, the night-blind person will have almost unimpeded visual perception under daylight (photopic) conditions but turn blind at dusk (scotopic conditions).

By using miniature television cameras linked to head-mounted displays, two projects currently tackle night blindness and other visual impairments where optical devices cannot solve the problem: In the United States, the helmetlike LVES (Low Vision Enhancement System – pronounced "elvis") has already reached production stage (104,105). The European POVES (Portable Optoelectronic Vision Enhancement System) featuring a smaller, goggle-shaped head-mounted unit is presently (1997) available as a prototype (106–108). Now or in future, these devices will provide the following:

- Increase the brightness
- Enhance the contrast
- Recalculate and adapt the image contrast to specific user needs
- Modify the viewing angle (zooming, wide angle, fish-eye)
- Emphasize lines and edges
- Remap the entire image to bypass blind spots on the retina (scotomae)

Image Analysis and Image Understanding

Vision enhancement systems improve the image but leave all tasks concerning the interpretation of the image to the user. Image analysis and understanding goes one step further and is able to deliver a description of the scene. Due to the complexity of real-world scenes and the hard-to-predict effects of shadows, image understanding to assist blind persons is still on the laboratory level. Even if all image analysis problems could be solved, the question of how to communicate all this information to the blind user will remain (109,110).

However, it can be expected that some less spectacular but rather useful subsets of the total solution, like an optical obstacle detector, will emerge.

Image Coding

Image coding can be considered a mixture of the above-mentioned scenarios. No interpretation of the scene will be accomplished by the technical system, leaving the recognition task completely to the user. However, the system will transform visual information to auditory (or tactile) stimuli which, by training, can be understood by the blind user.

Until now, all experiments which tried to transform a real-world scene into a real-time tactile representation failed due to the insufficient performance of the tactile sense. Maybe, better image preprocessing (compression, feature extraction) and improved tactile stimulators will offer new chances in the future.

Using the auditory sense looks more promising today. The two-dimensional image delivered by a camera can be transformed into a stereophonic sound pattern. Experiments have shown that at least simple images (like lines, characters, symbols) can be interpreted by listening to a sound pattern (111).

However, it is questionable if any of the above-mentioned vision substitution methods will be ready for practical use before optoelectronic implants (artificial retina, direct stimulation of the visual nerve or the visual cortex) will be available.

Navigational Aids

Presently, geographical information systems (GIS) and navigation devices are booming. Wayfinders for cars, digitized maps, computer-assisted route planning, and fleet management are just some examples where orientation tasks are tackled by using information technology. The general availability of the GPS (global positioning system), a high-precision satellite navigation system, created the basis for numerous compact and efficient location devices.

In principle, the accuracy of GPS is well below one meter. Because the entire system was launched for military purposes, the satellite positioning signals are artificially overlaid by a random code so that all general users will achieve much less accuracy, say 20–100 meters (Selective Availability Program). This artificial inaccuracy can be removed to a large extent if the positioning signal can be real-time compared with the signal received at a known position. By calculating the difference between the coordinates resulting from the GPS signal and the real position, the momentary deviation can be determined. If this difference is applied to a GPS signal received in the same area where the reference station is located, the error can be reduced. For this purpose, in some areas the momentary GPS deviation is available on FM subcarriers, via the RDS (Radio Data System) or by using a cellular phone. In other words, for precision positioning, there must be a link not only to the satellite signals [for a three-dimensional position (i.e., longitude, latitude, and altitude), the GPS receiver must have simultaneous contact to at least four satellites] but also to a terrestrial reference station.

Computer-assisted wayfinding may be considered as a sequence of three tasks:

- **Route planning** (prejourney planning): Localizing the coordinates of the destination, finding all possible routes between present position and target position, and determining the optimum path according to defined criteria (speed, accessibility, available means of transport, etc.). This is the domain of PC-based GIS, digitized maps, electronic time tables, and databases.
- **Orientation:** This is the perception and understanding of the spatial relations between the traveler and the three-dimensional environment. It is finding the answer to the questions "Where am I?" and "What are the essential factors of the environment surrounding me?" To some extent, not only the spatial dimensions but also the time will play a role, whenever schedules have to be taken into account. Here, information and positioning systems enter the scene, calculating the coordinates, and delivering a description of the surroundings.
- **Navigation:** This task covers finding the right way and keeping track in order to reach the destination (or an in-between stop for reorientation and resuming navigation). For this purpose, electronic compasses, accelerometers, guidance systems, and so forth can be applied.

The development of navigation and orientation devices for disabled persons started on a much lower level. These first devices were mainly designed to guide blind and visually impaired persons in complex environments. By gradually using more and more sophisticated technology, language, cognition, and mentally handicapped persons are also benefitting from navigation aids. The following subsections present some examples of guidance systems for disabled persons, starting with the simplest devices and ending at the most sophisticated ones.

Acoustic Beacons

To accommodate blind or visually impaired pedestrians, a target to be approached (or an obstacle to be avoided) is marked by a simple, well-perceived sound source. As a permanent sound in many cases will annoy persons in the neighborhood, remote-controlled sound signals were designed, which can be activated on demand by using a radio-frequency transmitter (garage door opener) (112).

The sound signal can be a simple tone, just enough to indicate the walking direction or a speaker system which can, in addition to the navigation purpose, also deliver certain helpful information about the environment (113).

Infrared Beacons

Instead of directly using acoustic signals for orientation and information, infrared transmission technology can be applied to avoid any interference with persons not to be addressed by the system. In this case, the user will have to carry some kind of receiver which will transform the infrared signal into an audible message.

In order to find the right direction, the user will scan the environment with a hand-held infrared receiver and walk toward the direction from which he/she is receiving the strongest signal (114). Another possible approach is to convert the direction from where the infrared signal is received into stereophonic audio. Thus, a spatial sound source is mimicked, which the user easily can approach (103,115).

Complex Mobility and Orientation Systems

In Europe (116,117) as well as in the United States (118), rather complex navigation systems for blind and visually impaired pedestrians are under development, featuring the following:

- Prejourney planning by using digital maps which can be accessed by Braille or synthetic speech
- In-journey guidance by using the GPS

Interactive Mobility Assistance

By combining a GPS receiver, a cellular phone, a still-video camera, and a PDA (personal digital assistant), project ISAAC tries to create a universal mobility tool especially for cognition- and mentally impaired persons. The main difference among the systems mentioned above is that by using the cellular phone a human assistant at a service center can be involved in the orientation and information process. In a situation of disorientation, the user will contact the service center. The GPS will relay the coordinates of the user and by the still-video camera, images from the environment can be sent to the service center. Several other useful off-line functions are implemented in the PDA which acts as the controller for the entire device (119).

REFERENCES

1. J. R. Berliss, P. A. Borden, K. Ford, and G. C. Vanderheiden (eds.), *Trace Resource-Book — Assistive Technologies for Communication, Control & Computer Access*, Trace Research and Development Center, University of Wisconsin-Madison, 1991/92.
2. World Health Organization (WHO), Division of Mental Health and Prevention of Substance Abuse, *The International Classification of Impairments, Disabilities and Handicaps*, WHO, Geneva, 1980; *http://www.who.ch/whosis/icidh/icidh.html*.
3. International Organization for Standardization, *ISO 9999/Technical aids for disabled persons* — Classification. TC 173/SC 2 (1992).
4. S. Carruthers, A. Humphreys, and J. Sandhu, "The Market for R.T. in Europe: A Demographic Study of Need," in *Rehabilitation Technology — Strategies for the European Union, Proceedings of the 1st TIDE Congress*, edited by E. Ballabio et al., IOS Press, Brussels, 1993, pp. 158-163.
5. K. G. Olesen, "COST 219 Survey on Texttelephones and Relay Services in Europe," COST 219/Jytland Telephone, Ref. No. COST-075-89.

6. G. Hellström and K. Currie, "Text Telephony and Relay Services," in *Telecommunications for ALL*, edited by P. Roe, Publication of COST 219, 1995.

7. J. L. Arnott, J. M. Hannan, and R. J. Woodburn, "Linguistic Prediction for Disabled Users of Computer-Mediated Communication," in *Proceedings of the ECART 2 Conference*, Kommentus Förlag, Stockholm, 1993, p. 11.1.

8. H. Kamphuis, W. Beattie, J. L. Arnott et al., "A Comparison of English and Dutch Pals: Predictive Adaptive Lexica in Two Languages," in *Proceedings of the ECART 2 Conference*, Kommentus Förlag, Stockholm, 1993, p. 1.1.

9. J. Bertenstam and S. Hunnicutt, "Adding Morphology to a Word Predictor," in *The European Context for Assistive Technology, Proceedings of the 2nd TIDE Congress*, edited by I. P. Porrero and R. Puig de la Bellacasa, IOS Press, Paris, 1995, pp. 312–315.

10. P. Boissiere and D. Dours, "VITIPI — Versatile Interpretation of Text Input by Persons with Impairments," in *Interdisciplinary Aspects on Computers Helping People with Special Needs, Proceedings of the 5th ICCHP*, edited by J. Klaus et al., Oldenbourg, Linz, 1996, pp. 165–172.

11. J. H. Magnusson, "Application of the IsBliss Symbolic Processing Program," in *Computers for Handicapped Persons, Proceedings of the 3rd ICCHP*, edited by W. L. Zagler, Oldenbourg, Vienna, 1992, pp. 317–328.

12. International Organization for Standardization, *Draft International Standard ISO/DIS 11548/Communication aids for blind persons — 8-dot-Braille graphic characters — Identifiers, names and assignation to 8-bit codetables.* TC 173/SC 4 (1995).

13. M. Novak, G. C. Vanderheiden, J. Hinkens, and J. M. Schauer, "Development of Extensions for Standard Computers and Operating Systems to Allow Access by Users with Motor Impairments," *Rehabil. R&D Prog. Rep., 32*, 145–146 (June 1995).

14. P. L. Emiliani, "Graphical User Interfaces for Blind People," in *Proceedings of the ECART 2 Conference*, Kommentus Förlag, Stockholm, 1993, p. 2.1.

15. G. Weber, D. Kochanek, C. Stephanidis, and G. Homatas, "Access by Blind People to Interaction Objects in MS-Windows," in *Proceedings of the ECART 2 Conference*, Kommentus Förlag, Stockholm, 1993, p. 2.2.

16. L. H. D. Poll and R. P. Waterham, "Graphical User Interfaces and Visually Disabled Users," *IEEE Trans. Rehabil. Eng., RE-3*(1), 65–69 (1995).

17. U. Zeun, "Large Print Desktop-Publishing by PC for the Partially Sighted," in *Computers for Handicapped Persons, Proceedings of the 4th ICCHP*, edited by W. L. Zagler et al., Springer-Verlag , Vienna, 1994, pp. 507–517.

18. B. Stöger and K. Miesenberger, "The Conventional Braille Display — State of the Art and Future Perspectives," in *Computers for Handicapped Persons, Proceedings of the 4th ICCHP*, edited by W. L. Zagler et al., Springer-Verlag, Vienna, 1994, pp. 447–454.

19. R. Kowalik and I. Postawka, "The Concept of a Full Screen Tactile Display (FSTD) Driven by Electrochemical Reactions," in *Computers for Handicapped Persons, Proceedings of the 4th ICCHP*, edited by W. L. Zagler et al., Springer-Verlag, Vienna, 1994, pp. 455–460.

20. J. Fricke and H. Bähring, "A Graphic Input/Output Tablet for Blind Computer Users," in *Computers for Handicapped Persons, Proceedings of the 3rd ICCHP*, edited by W. L. Zagler, Oldenbourg, Vienna, 1992, pp. 172–179.

21. J. Fricke and H. Bähring, "Displaying Laterally Moving Tactile Information," in *Computers for Handicapped Persons, Proceedings of the 4th ICCHP*, edited by W. L. Zagler et al., Springer-Verlag, Vienna, 1994, pp. 461–468.

22. B. Schulz, "A New Architecture Conception for a Two Dimensional Tactile Display," in *Computers for Handicapped Persons, Proceedings of the 4th ICCHP*, edited by W. L. Zagler et al., Springer-Verlag, Vienna, 1994, pp. 469–470.

23. A. Parreño and P. J. Magallón, "Teresa '80: An 80 Character Single Cell Braille Line," in *Computers for Handicapped Persons, Proceedings of the 3rd ICCHP*, edited by W. L. Zagler, Oldenbourg, Vienna, 1992, pp. 403–408.

24. D. Gilden and S. Orlosky, "Braille Computer Screens: A New Perspective," in *Computers for Handicapped Persons, Proceedings of the 2nd ICCHP*, edited by A Min Tjoa et al., Oldenbourg, Zurich, 1990, pp. 101–111.

25. B. Schulz and R. H. Wolf, "Design and Possible Applications of a Dynamic Graphic Tactile Display," in *Interdisciplinary Aspects on Computers Helping People with Special Needs, Proceedings of the 5th ICCHP*, edited by J. Klaus et al., Oldenbourg, Linz, 1996, pp. 741–747.

26. W. Schweikhardt, "Interactive Exploring of Printed Documents by Blind People," in *Interdisciplinary Aspects on Computers Helping People with Special Needs, Proceedings of the 5th ICCHP*, edited by J. Klaus et al., Oldenbourg, Linz, 1996, pp. 451–458.

27. P. Nater, "Dotgraph – A Drawing Program for a Conventional Braille Printer," in *Computers for Handicapped Persons, Proceedings of the 3rd ICCHP*, edited by W. L. Zagler, Oldenbourg, Vienna, 1992, pp. 373–381.

28. F. P. Seiler, J. Haider, P. Mayer, and W. L. Zagler, "Fortec's Efforts to Support Mainstream Education through Research and Technology Development," in *Computers for Handicapped Persons, Proceedings of the 4th ICCHP*, edited by W. L. Zagler et al., Springer-Verlag, Vienna, 1994, pp. 479–486.

29. A. Arató and T. Vaspöri, "An Intelligent Screen Reader Integrated with Synthetic Speech for the Blind," in *Computers for Handicapped Persons, Proceedings of the 3rd ICCHP*, edited by W. L. Zagler, Oldenbourg, Vienna, 1992, pp. 8–13.

30. P. Blenkhorn, "Requirements for Screen Access Software Using Synthetic Speech," in *Computers for Handicapped Persons, Proceedings of the 3rd ICCHP*, edited by W. L. Zagler, Oldenbourg, Vienna, 1992, pp. 31–37.

31. F. P. Seiler and W. Oberleitner, "WineTU, German Language Grade 2 to ASCII Braille Translator," *J. Microcomputer Applic., 13*, 185–191 (1990).

32. P. Blenkhorn, "A System for Converting Braille into Print," *IEEE Trans. Rehabil. Eng., RE-3*(2), 215–221 (1995).

33. J. Freeman and T. Wesley, "The Translation of British Mathematical Braille into Inkprint," in *Proceedings of the ECART 2 Conference*, Kommentus Förlag, Stockholm, 1993, p. 17.1.

34. M. Batusic, F. Burger, K. Miesenberger, and B. Stöger, "Access to Mathematics for the Blind – Defining HrTeX Standard," in *Interdisciplinary Aspects on Computers Helping People with Special Needs, Proceedings of the 5th ICCHP*, edited by J. Klaus et al., Oldenbourg, Linz, 1996, pp. 609–616.

35. R. D. Stevens, P. C. Wright, A. D. N. Edwards, and S. A. Brewster, "An Audio Glance at Syntactic Structure Based on Spoken Form," in *Interdisciplinary Aspects on Computers Helping People with Special Needs, Proceedings of the 5th ICCHP*, edited by J. Klaus et al., Oldenbourg, Linz, 1996, pp. 627–635.

36. N. Baptiste and M. Truquet, "A Complete Solution to Help a Blind Musician to Access Musical Data," in *Proceedings of the ECART 2 Conference*, Kommentus Förlag, Stockholm, 1993, p. 17.2.

37. G. Firsching, R. Lindner, A. Michienzi, and E. Schmid, "Systems for Input, Processing and Output of Music and Music Notation for Visually Impaired People," in *Interdisciplinary Aspects on Computers Helping People with Special Needs, Proceedings of the 5th ICCHP*, edited by J. Klaus et al., Oldenbourg, Linz, 1996, pp. 723–729.

38. N. Ayres and T. Wesley, "Automated Braille Production from ODA Documents," in *Proceedings of the ECART 2 Conference*, Kommentus Förlag, Stockholm, 1993, p. 27.2.

39. D. Forer, "Using SGML to Create Accessible Information," *Interdisciplinary Aspects on Computers Helping People with Special Needs, Proceedings of the 5th ICCHP*, edited by J. Klaus et al., Oldenbourg, Linz, 1996, pp. 219–228.

40. T. Kahlisch, "Improving Access to Hypertext Based Study Material for the Blind," in *Interdisciplinary Aspects on Computers Helping People with Special Needs, Proceedings of the 5th ICCHP*, edited by J. Klaus et al., Oldenbourg, Linz, 1996, pp. 229–236.

41. L. Colombini and M. Somalvico, "Bliss for Disabled People and Able Ones," in *Computers for Handicapped Persons, Proceedings of the 2nd ICCHP*, edited by A. Min Tjoa et al., Oldenbourg, Zürich, 1990, pp. 43–49.

42. S. Besio and L. Ferlino, "Blissymbolics Software Worldwide: From Prototypes towards Future Optimized Products," in *Proceedings of the ECART 2 Conference*, Kommentus Förlag, Stockholm, 1993, p. 34.2.

43. D. L. Jaffe, "Evolution of Mechanical Fingerspelling Hands for People who are Deaf-Blind," *J. Rehabil. Res. Dev., 31*(3), 236–244 (1994).

44. A. S. Khalsa, "IntelliKeys: The Smart Keyboard," in *Computers for Handicapped Persons, Proceedings of the 3rd ICCHP*, edited by W. L. Zagler, Oldenbourg, Vienna, 1992, pp. 263–272.

45. A. Brandt, "Control of Computers for People with Physical Disabilities," in *Computers for Handicapped Persons, Proceedings of the 3rd ICCHP*, edited by W. L. Zagler, Oldenbourg, Vienna, 1992, pp. 71–76.

46. W. Kerstner, G. Pigel, and M. Tscheligi, "The FeelMouse: Making Computer Screens Feelable," in *Computers for Handicapped Persons, Proceedings of the 4th ICCHP*, edited by W. L. Zagler et al., Springer-Verlag, Vienna, 1994, pp. 106–113.

47. A. D. Cherry, M. S. Hawley, M. Freeman, and P. A. Cudd, "Human–Computer Interfacing for the Severely Physically Disabled," in *Computers for Handicapped Persons, Proceedings of the 4th ICCHP*, edited by J. Klaus et al., Springer-Verlag, Vienna, 1994, pp. 177–184.

48. V. Lauruska, "Computerized Control and Communication System for Handicapped," in *Interdisciplinary Aspects on Computers Helping People with Special Needs, Proceedings of the 5th ICCHP*, edited by W. L. Zagler et al., Oldenbourg, Linz, 1996, pp. 517–519.

49. C. Clayton, R. G. S. Platts, M. Steinberg, and A. M. Trudgeon, "Palatal Tongue Controller," in *Computers for Handicapped Persons, Proceedings of the 2nd ICCHP*, edited by A. Min Tjoa et al., Oldenbourg, Zürich, 1990, pp. 39–42.

50. W. Schmitt and W. Zang, "The New Wireless LinguControl," in *Computers for Handicapped Persons, Proceedings of the 4th ICCHP*, edited by W. L. Zagler et al., Springer-Verlag, Vienna, 1994, pp. 101–105.

51. D. G. Evans, S. Pettitt, and P. Blenkhorn, "A Head Operated Joystick," in *Interdisciplinary Aspects on Computers Helping People with Special Needs, Proceedings of the 5th ICCHP*, edited by J. Klaus et al., Oldenbourg, Linz, 1996, p. 85–91.

52. T. Söderlund, "Trial with Eye Pointing User Interface for Computer Access," *Proceedings of the ECART 2 Conference*, Kommentus Förlag, Stockholm, 1993, p. PI.

53. E. Unger, M. Bijak, E. Mayr et al., EOG-Controller for Rehabilitation Technology," in *Interdisciplinary Aspects on Computers Helping People with Special Needs, Proceedings of the 5th ICCHP*, edited by J. Klaus et al., Oldenbourg, Linz, 1996, pp. 401–408.

54. J. Gips, P. DiMattia, F. X. Curran, and P. Olivieri, "Using Eagle Eyes – An Electrodes Based Device for Controlling the Computer with your Eyes – To Help People with Special Needs," in *Interdisciplinary Aspects on Computers Helping People with Special Needs, Proceedings of the 5th ICCHP*, edited by J. Klaus et al., Oldenbourg, Linz, 1996, pp. 77–83.

55. M. Hashimoto, Y. Yonezawa, and K. Itoh, "New Mouse Function Using Teeth-Chattering and Potential around Eyes for the Physically Challenged," in *Interdisciplinary Aspects on Computers Helping People with Special Needs, Proceedings of the 5th ICCHP*, edited by J. Klaus et al., Oldenbourg, Linz, 1996, pp. 93–98.

56. G. Pfurtscheller, J. Kalcher, and D. Flotzinger, "A New Communication Device for Handicapped Persons: The Brain–Computer Interface," in *Rehabilitation Technology—Strategies for the European Union, Proceedings of the 1st TIDE Congress*, edited by E. Ballabio et al., IOS Press, Brussels, 1993, pp. 123–127.

57. J. Kalcher, D. Flotzinger, S. Gölly, Ch. Neuper, and G. Pfurtscheller, "Graz Brain-Computer Interface (BCI) II," in *Computers for Handicapped Persons, Proceedings of the 4th ICCHP*, edited by W. L. Zagler et al., Springer-Verlag, Vienna, 1994, pp. 170–176.

58. N. Hormann, J. Kalcher, C. Neuper et al., "Graz Brain–Computer Interface (BCI)—A Pilot Study on Patients with Motor Deficits," in *Interdisciplinary Aspects on Computers Helping People with Special Needs, Proceedings of the 5th ICCHP*, edited by J. Klaus et al., Oldenbourg, Linz, 1996, pp. 155–160.

59. J. Kalcher, C. Neuper, G. Raich, and G. Pfurtscheller, "Graz Brain-Computer Interface (BCI)—Hardware and Software Components," in *Interdisciplinary Aspects on Computers Helping People with Special Needs, Proceedings of the 5th ICCHP*, edited by J. Klaus et al., Oldenbourg, Linz, 1996, pp. 161–164.

60. C. Flachberger, P. Panek, and W. L. Zagler, "Compose Autonomy!—An Adaptable User Interface for Assistive Technology Systems," in *The European Context for Assistive Technology, Proceedings of the 2nd TIDE Congress*, edited by I. P. Porrero and R. Puig de la Bellacasa, IOS Press, Paris, 1995, pp. 413–416.

61. P. Panek, C. Flachberger, and W. L. Zagler, "The Integration of Technical Assistance into the Rehabilitation Process: A Field Study," in *Interdisciplinary Aspects on Computers Helping People with Special Needs, Proceedings of the 5th ICCHP*, edited by J. Klaus et al., Oldenbourg, Linz, 1996, pp. 529–537.

62. C. Bühler, "Uniform User Interface for Communication and Control," in *Proceedings of the ECART 2 Conference*, Kommentus Förlag, Stockholm, 1993, p. 22.3.

63. W. W. Maltzahn, M. Daphtary, and R. L. Roa, "Usage Patterns of Environmental Control Units by Severely Disabled Individuals in Their Homes," *IEEE Trans. Rehabil. Eng.*, RE-3(2), 222–227 (1995).

64. J. E. Oakey, "Real-Time Voice to Text with Stenographers," in *Computers for Handicapped Persons, Proceedings of the 3rd ICCHP*, edited by W. L. Zagler, Oldenbourg, Vienna, 1992, pp. 403–408.

65. J. E. Oakey, "Further Advances in Real-Time Voice to Text with Steno Interpreters," in *Computers for Handicapped Persons, Proceedings of the 4th ICCHP*, edited by W. L. Zagler et al., Springer-Verlag, Vienna, 1994, pp. 46–50.

66. E. Abadjieva, I. R. Murray, and J. L. Arnott, "An Enhanced Development System for Emotional Speech Synthesis for Use in Vocal Prostheses," in *Proceedings of the ECART 2 Conference*, Kommentus Förlag, Stockholm, 1993, p. 1.2.

67. P. A. Cudd, S. Hunnicutt, J. Arthur et al., "Voices, Attitudes and Emotions in Speech Synthesis," in *The European Context for Assistive Technology, Proceedings of the 2nd TIDE Congress*, edited by I. P. Porrero and R. Puig de la Bellacasa, IOS Press, Paris, 1995, pp. 344–347.

68. F. Guenthner, K. Krüger-Thielmann, R. Pasero, and P. Sabatier, "Communication Aids for Handicapped Persons," in *Proceedings of the ECART 2 Conference*, Kommentus Förlag, Stockholm, 1993, p. 1.4.

69. A. D. N. Edwards and A. Blore, "Speech Input for Persons with Speech Impairments," in *Computers for Handicapped Persons, Proceedings of the 3rd ICCHP*, edited by W. L. Zagler, Oldenbourg, Vienna, 1992, pp. 120–126.

70. E. Rosengren, P. Raghavendra, and S. Hunnicutt, "How Does Automatic Speech Recognition Handle Severely Dysarthric Speech?" in *The European Context for Assistive Technology, Proceedings of the 2nd TIDE Congress*, edited by I. P. Porrero and R. Puig de la Bellacasa, IOS Press, Paris, 1995, pp. 336–339.

71. D. Bauer, "SICONA – Signal Conditioning Communication Aids for the Hearing Impaired," in *TIDE bridge phase synopses*, European Commission, DG XIII, 1994.

72. H. Karlsson and M. Jevelind, "Text-Telephone (TDD) for MacIntosh and MS-Windows," in *Proceedings of the ECART 2 Conference*, Kommentus Förlag, Stockholm, 1993, p. 6.2.

73. S. Price, "Telephone Access to Deaf People," in *The European Context for Assistive Technology, Proceedings of the 2nd TIDE Congress*, edited by I. P. Porrero and R. Puig de la Bellacasa, IOS Press, Paris, 1995, pp. 428–431.

74. J.-I. Lindström and L. M. Pereira, "Videotelephony," in *Telecommunications for ALL*, edited by P. Roe, Publication of COST 219, 1995.

75. O. Dopping, "Improved Telecommunication Between Deaf Text Telephone Users and Hearing Persons," in *Proceedings of the ECART 2 Conference*, Kommentus Förlag, Stockholm, 1993, p. 6.3.

76. N. Wikman, "Evaluation of Transcribing to Hard of Hearing People and People with Acquired Deafness," in *Proceedings of the ECART 2 Conference*, Kommentus Förlag, Stockholm, 1993, p. 4.3.

77. H.-H. Bothe and F. Rieger, "Computer-Animation for Teaching Lipreading," in *Proceedings of the ECART 2 Conference*, Kommentus Förlag, Stockholm, 1993, p. 4.4.

78. H.-H. Bothe and E. A. Wieden, "Artificial Visual Speech Synchronized with a Speech Synthesis System," in *Computers for Handicapped Persons, Proceedings of the 4th ICCHP*, edited by W. L. Zagler et al., Springer-Verlag, Vienna, 1994, pp. 32–37.

79. G. N. Newby, "Gesture Recognition Using Statistical Similarity," in *Proceedings of the 1993 Virtual Reality and Persons with Disabilities Conference*, 1993.

80. M. B. Waldron and S. Kim, "Isolated ASL Sign Recognition System for Deaf Persons," *IEEE Trans. Rehabil. Eng.*, RE-3(4), 354–359 (1995).

81. M. Lundälv, "COMSPEC – A Modular and Open Software Platform for AAC Aids on the Drawing Board," in *The European Context for Assistive Technology, Proceedings of the 2nd TIDE Congress*, edited by I. P. Porrero and R. Puig de la Bellacasa, IOS Press, Paris, 1995, pp. 41–44.

82. R. I. Damper and M. D. Evans, "A Multifunction Domestic Alert System for the Deaf-Blind," *IEEE Trans. Rehabil. Eng.*, RE-3(2), 222–227 (1995).

83. T. Israelsson and A. Hjälm, "Research and Development Project: Warning and Disability," in *Proceedings of the ECART 2 Conference*, Kommentus Förlag, Stockholm, 1993, p. PII.

84. J. L. Dallaway, R. D. Jackson, and P. H. A. Timmers, "Rehabilitation Robotics in Europe," *IEEE Trans. Rehabil. Eng.*, RE-3(1), 33–45 (1995).

85. H. Eftring and G. Bolmsjö, "RAID – A Robotic Workstation for the Disabled," in *Proceedings of the ECART 2 Conference*, Kommentus Förlag, Stockholm, 1993, p. 24.3.

86. L. Holmberg, "The Installation of a Robotized Workstation at Samhall-HADAR," in *Proceedings of the ECART 2 Conference*, Kommentus Förlag, Stockholm, 1993, p. 29.2.

87. G. Bolmsjö, H. Neveryd, and H. Eftring, "Robotics in Rehabilitation," *IEEE Trans. Rehabil. Eng.*, RE-3(1) 77–83 (1995).

88. H. Neveryd and G. Bolmsjö, "WALKY, an Ultrasonic Navigating Mobile Robot for the Disabled," in *The European Context for Assistive Technology, Proceedings of the 2nd TIDE Congress*, edited by I. P. Porrero and R. Puig de la Bellacasa, IOS Press, Paris, 1995, pp. 366–370.

89. H. Neveryd and G. Bolmsjö, "Mobile Robot System for the Disabled," in *Proceedings of the ECART 2 Conference*, Kommentus Förlag, Stockholm, 1993, p. 24.1.

90. T. Komeda, T. Uchida, H. Matsuoka et al., "Mobile Robot System to aid the Daily Life of Bedridden Persons in the Private House," in *Proceedings of the ECART 2 Conference*, Kommentus Förlag, Stockholm, 1993, p. 24.4.

91. M. Fujii, T. Komeda, T. Uchida et al., "Development of the Mobile Robot System to Aid the Daily Life of Bedridden Persons (Interface Between Human and Robot)," in *Interdisciplinary Aspects on Computers Helping People with Special Needs, Proceedings of the 5th ICCHP*, edited by J. Klaus et al., Oldenbourg, Linz, 1996, pp. 107–111.

92. T. Øderud, J. E. Bastiansen, and S. Tyvand, "Experiences with the MANUS Wheelchair Mounted Manipulator," in *Proceedings of the ECART 2 Conference*, Kommentus Förlag, Stockholm, 1993, p. 29.1.

93. G. Lacey and K. M. Dawson-Howe, "Autonomous Guide for the Blind," in *The European Context for Assistive Technology, Proceedings of the 2nd TIDE Congress*, edited by I. P. Porrero and R. Puig de la Bellacasa, IOS Press, Paris, 1995, pp. 294–297.

94. S. P. Levine, D. A. Bell, and Y. Koren, "NavChair: An Example of a Shared-Control System for Assistive Technology," in *Computers for Handicapped Persons, Proceedings of the 4th ICCHP*, edited by W. L. Zagler et al., Springer-Verlag, Vienna, 1994, pp. 136–143.

95. G. Bourhis and P. Pino, "Mobile Robotics and Mobility Assistance for People with Motor Impairments: Rational Justification for the VAHM Project," *IEEE Trans. Rehabil. Eng.*, RE-4(1), 7–12 (1996).

96. N. Katevas, S. Tzafestas, J. M. Bishop et al., "SENARIO – The Autonomous Mobile Robotics Technology for the Locomotion Handicap: Operational & Technical Issues," in *The European Context for Assistive Technology, Proceedings of the 2nd TIDE Congress*, edited by I. P. Porrero and R. Puig de la Bellacasa, IOS Press, Paris, 1995, pp. 371–374.

97. P. J. Kyberd, O. E. Holland, P. H. Chappell et al., "MARCUS: A Two Degree of Freedom Hand Prostheses with Hierarchical Grip Control," *IEEE Trans. Rehabil. Eng.*, RE-3(1), 70–76 (1995).

98. D. M. Roy, W. Harwin, and R. Fawcus, "The Enhancement of Computer Access for People with Cerebral Palsy Through the Computer Recognition of Imprecise Gestures," in *Proceedings of the ECART 2 Conference*, Kommentus Förlag, Stockholm, 1993, p. 71.

99. D. M. Roy, M. Panayi, R. Foulds et al., "The Enhancement of Interaction for People with Severe Speech and Physical Impairment Through the Computer Recognition of Gesture and Manipulation," *Presence: Teleoperators Virtual Environ.*, 3(3), 227–235 (1994).

100. M. E. Harrington, R. W. Daniel, and P. J. Kyberd, "Gesture Recognition of Arm Movements Using Accelerometers," in *The European Context for Assistive Technology, Proceedings of the 2nd TIDE Congress*, edited by I. P. Porrero and R. Puig de la Bellacasa, IOS Press, Paris, 1995, pp. 432–435.

101. H. Brinkmann and F. M. Boland, "A Gesture Input Interface (G.I.I.) Implemented Using Neural Networks," in *The European Context for Assistive Technology, Proceedings of the 2nd TIDE Congress*, edited by I. P. Porrero and R. Puig de la Bellacasa, IOS Press, Paris, 1995, pp. 436–439.

102. F. Furuno, "Colour Discriminating Apparatus for the Blind," in *Computers for Handicapped Persons, Proceedings of the 1st ICCHP*, edited by A Min Tjoa et al., Oldenbourg, Vienna, 1989, pp. 134–143.

103. W. L. Zagler, P. Mayer, N. Winkler, and M. Busboom, "Microprocessor Devices to Lower the Barriers for the Blind and Visually Impaired," in *Computers for Handicapped Persons, Proceedings of the 2nd ICCHP*, edited by A Min Tjoa et al., Oldenbourg, Zürich, 1990, pp. 301–312.

104. R. W. Massof, "High-Tech Help for Low Vision," *NASA Tech Briefs, 17*(2), 20–22 (1993).

105. R. W. Massof, F. H. Baker, G. Dagnelie et al., "The Low Vision Enhancement System: Early Results," in *Proceedings of Vision '96 — International Conference on Low Vision*, 1996.

106. W. L. Zagler, R. Grünfelder, P. Mayer et al., "The Development of POVES — A Portable Optoelectronic Vision Enhancement System," in *The European Context for Assistive Technology, Proceedings of the 2nd TIDE Congress*, edited by I. P. Porrero and R. Puig de la Bellacasa, IOS Press, Paris, 1995, pp. 352–355.

107. P. Mayer and G. Edelmayer, "Electronic Vision Enhancement System," in *Interdisciplinary Aspects on Computers Helping People with Special Needs, Proceedings of the 5th ICCHP*, edited by J. Klaus et al., Oldenbourg, Linz, 1996, pp. 661–669.

108. P. Mayer and G. Edelmayer, "Development and Tests of a Prototype for the Enhancement of Night Vision in the POVES Project — EC TIDE Project 2111," in *Proceedings of Vision '96 — International Conference on Low Vision*, 1996.

109. M. Adjouadi, J. Riley, and F. Candocia, "An Augmented Computer Vision Approach for Enhanced Image Understanding," *J. Rehabil. Res. Dev., 32*(3), 264–279.

110. M. Midon, M. Adjouadi, N. Fernandez et al., "Computer Applications and Information Access for the Visually Impaired," in *Interdisciplinary Aspects on Computers Helping People with Special Needs, Proceedings of the 5th ICCHP*, edited by J. Klaus et al., Oldenbourg, Linz, 1996, pp. 149–154.

111. C. Veraart, C. Capelle, M. C. Ahumada, and C. Trullemans, "Rehabilitation of Blindness Using Sensory Substitution of Vision by Audition," in *Proceedings of the ECART 2 Conference*, Kommentus Förlag, Stockholm, 1993, p. 2.3.

112. D. G. Evans, P. Blenkhorn, and S. Pettitt, "Benevolent Sirens: Personal Sound Marking Systems for Orientation," in *Interdisciplinary Aspects on Computers Helping People with Special Needs, Proceedings of the 5th ICCHP*, edited by J. Klaus et al., Oldenbourg, Linz, 1996, pp. 645–651.

113. G. Whitney, "The Remote Activator (REACT) System," in *Proceedings of the ECART 1 Conference*, 1990, p. 28.2.

114. W. Gerrey, *Remote Information Accessibility by Infrared Signage*, Smith-Kettlewell Eye Research Institute, San Francisco, 1991.

115. P. Mayer, M. Busboom, A. Flamm, and W. L. Zagler, "IRIS — A Multilingual Infrared Orientation and Information System for the Visually Impaired," in *Computers for Handicapped Persons, Proceedings of the 3rd ICCHP*, edited by W. L. Zagler, Oldenbourg, Vienna, 1992, pp. 344–352.

116. T. Strothotte, H. Petrie, V. Johnsson, and L. Reichert, "MoBIC: User Needs and Preliminary Design for a Mobility Aid for Blind and Elderly Travellers," in *The European Context for Assistive Technology, Proceedings of the 2nd TIDE Congress*, edited by I. P. Porrero and R. Puig de la Bellacasa, IOS Press, Paris, 1995, pp. 348–351.

117. V. Johnson and H. Petrie, "Evaluation Methodologies for Navigational Aids for Blind People," in *Interdisciplinary Aspects on Computers Helping People with Special Needs, Proceedings of the 5th ICCHP*, edited by J. Klaus et al., Oldenbourg, Linz, 1996, pp. 653–659.

118. Arkenstone Inc., "Atlas Speaks" and "Strider," see *http://www.arkenstone.org*

119. B. Jönsson and A. Svensk, "ISAAC — A Personal Digital Assistant for the Differently Abled," in *The European Context for Assistive Technology, Proceedings of the 2nd TIDE Congress*, edited by I. P. Porrero and R. Puig de la Bellacasa, IOS Press, Paris, 1995, pp. 356–361.

WOLFGANG L. ZAGLER

DEFECT PREVENTION

INTRODUCTION

When we perform work of any kind, we produce outputs. Because our work processes are not perfect, we also produce defects. Broadly speaking, a defect is an imperfection or flaw in our work output. The usual response when defects appear in work outputs is to include activities in the process to detect and fix them. However, there is an increasing emphasis within the computer industry on preventing defects rather than just detecting and fixing them. The motivation to prevent defects is threefold:

- Prevention is more cost-effective than detection: During development and manufacturing, it is more cost-effective to prevent defects than to expend extra effort both to find the defects through inspection and testing and then to fix them once they are found.
- Low product defect levels have benefits to customers and thus economic benefits to vendors: A product with fewer injected defects can usually be delivered to the customer more quickly. Such products do not need to be repaired as often once they are shipped. Thus, customers are more satisfied with products with fewer defects. These factors translate into increased revenues and lower service costs to the vendor.
- Low defect levels cannot be achieved with detection alone: Our processes for defect detection are not completely effective. For software development, defect detection is accomplished by design and code inspections and various levels of test. Software inspections may be only 60% effective in discovering defects, whereas software tests may be only 50% effective. Therefore, residual defects will remain in the work product even after it has been shipped to customers. Many applications, for example, safety critical applications, require a level of quality that cannot be achieved simply through inspections and product testing.

The discussion in this article focuses on defect prevention with an emphasis on its application in software development. However, the principles described here apply to all processes, including hardware development, manufacturing, and administrative tasks. Indeed, certain facets of defect prevention discussed here, such as statistical process control, have traditionally been applied primarily to manufacturing processes.

This article first presents some of the general principles governing defect prevention and the typical elements found in the various defect prevention methods, followed by a more detailed description of specific approaches to causal analysis and preventive actions, a description of less formal prevention methods, and a summary of full defect prevention processes. Finally, specific defect prevention practices and results reported in the literature are presented.

GENERAL PRINCIPLES

Defects are *caused* by flaws in our processes, tools, and methods. For example, an improperly aligned machine tool will produce defective parts; a software developer who overlooks certain details will produce defective software. Defects may be *prevented* by eliminating their causes, that is, through adjusting and improving the processes, tools, and methods where the defects occurred. For example, a procedure that checks machine tool alignment prior to use will prevent defective parts; a checklist used by the software developer as a reminder will prevent software defects.

Defect prevention may, thus, be defined as preventing defects before they have a chance to occur, through improvements to our processes, tools, and methods. We can identify such improvements in a number of ways:

1. Through our general knowledge of the state of the art. We may be aware of certain improved methods that reduce defects, for example, the Cleanroom methodology for software development or Computer-Aided Design (CAD) tools for hardware design.
2. Through benchmarking activities. When we study how other organizations perform similar processes and tasks, we may identify improvements to our processes that will prevent defects, for example, a better way to control software configurations, an improved solder bath process, or a better way to validate customer requirements.
3. Through process reengineering activities. When we analyze how our current processes work, we may uncover inefficiencies and problem areas that can be corrected and improved. For example, an analysis of the requirements collection process may disclose missing verification steps and problems with communication of requirements changes, both of which can be addressed through processing restructuring.
4. Through causal analysis. If we look at the specific defects that have occurred in our processes and understand their causes, we can propose process improvements to eliminate those causes in the future and, thus, prevent the defects. For example, we may identify a failure in communication as the cause of one or more defects and propose improved communications procedures to prevent similar defects in the future.

Each of these sources of process improvement has limitations. Whereas the use of state-of-the-art improvements and benchmarking can result in quality and productivity improvements to the process, these approaches may not address the majority of defects that are actually occurring. Thus, these improvements may be less effective overall than those derived, for example, from causal analysis. Process reengineering takes considerable time and effort and can only be done reasonably at 2–4 year intervals on the same process. Thus, process reengineering cannot be relied on to address defects as they occur in the process.

Causal analysis occurs after the fact, when defects have already occurred and, therefore, is always a reactive method. However, of the four sources of process improvement, causal analysis is the most systematic approach to address the defects that actually occur within a process. The defects that have already occurred are indications of process weakness or process failure, which are clear opportunities for improvement.

Although the first three approaches should not be overlooked by organizations seeking to improve their processes, this article will concentrate on defect prevention approaches that are based on causal analysis. Thus, a more restrictive definition of *defect prevention* is:

> The systematic improvement of processes, tools, and methods to prevent the recurrence of defects, through the analysis of defects that have occurred in the process.

Defect prevention becomes *systematic* when it involves ongoing activities that are part of the process, that is, part of the everyday work. Defect prevention involves *analysis* in one of a number of possible forms, including causal analysis of individual defects or problems, analysis of defect classification data, or analysis of statistical data of process performance. Defect prevention results in *process improvement* when the results of analysis are actions that alter the organization's processes, tools, or methods so that defects do not recur.

There are a number of principles or premises on which defect prevention is based. These principles have proven to be valid in all processes where prevention activities have been applied:

1. Defects are recurrent. Almost all defects occur repeatedly within a process, regardless of the people who are working within the process.
2. The causes of defects can be known and eliminated or mitigated. The causes of software development defects, for example, fall into one of several broad categories: oversight errors, education problems, communications failures, transcription errors, and process failures. The causes of manufacturing defects may be classified by the 5M's: men, methods, machines, materials, and measurements.
3. If the causes are eliminated, the defects will not recur. When we eliminate or mitigate the causes, the defects will no longer occur or will occur less frequently.
4. Defect causes can be eliminated through process changes. Changing the way we work will eliminate the causes of defects. Such changes can address all types of causes. Some process improvements may be more effective than others in eliminating causes. For example, a tool may automatically eliminate a cause, whereas a checklist may be less effective. Similarly, some improvements will be more costly than others.
5. Defects will recur unless we change the process. A corollary of the previous two principles is that defects will continue to occur unless we change something to stop them. The change must be made in the way we perform the work, that is, in the process.

TYPICAL ELEMENTS OF DEFECT PREVENTION

A number of different methods for defect prevention have been developed. Their features vary depending on the nature of the work being done, the process, and the data collected. For example, a manufacturing process producing machined parts involves repetitive tasks performed on a machine, whereas a software development process has much less repetition of tasks in a given time period and the work is performed in a variety of settings, such as at a blackboard or computer terminal.

To achieve defect prevention, the machine operator in the manufacturing process can strive for statistical control of the process and take preventive action when the process indicates an out-of-control condition. To achieve prevention, the software developer can use techniques like design templates and checklists to reduce defects as the work is performed and recommend preventive process improvements when defects are discovered and analyzed.

Despite such wide process differences, defect prevention methods share a number of typical elements described below. Although no defect prevention method embodies all of these elements, they are common to many of the methods.

Identify, Record, Classify, and Verify Defects

The first requirement of defect prevention is to identify and capture the process's defects. For some processes, capturing the defects is a natural outcome of the process (e.g., recording and tracking defects during the software test to ensure that all defects are fixed), whereas other processes must introduce defect recording in order to perform subsequent preventive activities (e.g., recording defects in a clerical process).

What is a defect? This depends on the work done. Most processes need an operational definition of what a defect is for that process. Some examples of operational definitions follow:

- For a software product, there are major and minor defects. A major defect is one which, if left uncorrected, would be identified by a customer as needing correction. Thus, in broad terms, a major defect is a failure to meet customer expectations. Minor defects are all other defects in the software product.

- A customer callback process typically involves a technical person who discusses a problem with the customer, investigates the problem, and then calls the customer back with a response. The problem is assigned a level of severity to indicate the degree of impact on the customer. Each severity level has a prescribed response time (e.g., respond within 1 hour for severity 1 problems). If the time to respond back to the customer exceeds this prescribed response time, the late response may be considered a defect.

- In manufacturing parts and subassemblies, the part must meet certain specifications and tolerances. If the part or subassembly fails to meet that specification, it is a defect.

- For repetitive procedures (e.g., in manufacturing), the work product may be measured along certain criteria or dimensions (e.g., the width of the hole in a drilling operation, the thickness of solder joints in a soldering operation). The variability of the work product may then be plotted to determine the process's normal variation and its statistical "control limits." Various indications of out-of-control conditions, such as measurements that lie outside the control limits, are defects.

- Problems which occur within a process which are not part of the usual process measurements may be considered defects. Such problems may not even result in defects in a work product (e.g., a process problem that wasted time). One operational definition of this sort of defect was devised by the IBM Mid-Hudson Valley Development Laboratory in Poughkeepsie, NY (2):

A defect is anything that impacts or interferes with maintaining or improving quality or productivity.

Such a problems may not involve product defects but nonetheless are defects in this broader sense. They might include machine downtime, tool failures, usability problems, communications failures, excessive scrap, increases in warranty costs, and customer dissatisfaction or complaints.

The steps in handling defects for defect prevention include the following:

(a) *Collect and record data from the process.* Defect data may be obtained from a number of different sources, for example, from process output measurements, from detection activities such as inspections and testing, from interactions with customers (complaints or comments on the product), from occurrences of rework, from occurrences of scrap, from schedule slippages, and so forth.

(b) *Verify that there is a defect.* Once data indicate a potential defect, the defect may need to be verified against the operational definition; for example, Is there a deviation from the norm? Does the process exhibit out-of-control signals? Do the data indicate that a defect has occurred? In some processes, we need to distinguish the defect, that is, what is actually wrong in the work product, from a symptom of the defect (i.e., an outward manifestation of the defect). For example, the outward manifestation of a defect in a software product may be an incorrectly computed result. The actual defect would be something wrong in the code, for example, an uninitialized variable or an incorrect algorithm.

(c) *Classify the defect.* When the defect is captured and again when it is corrected, it may need to be classified for later analysis according to criteria such as defect trigger, defect type, or other dimensions. Only certain methods of defect prevention rely on defect classification.

Select Defects for Analysis

Most processes cannot include all occurrences of defects for analysis. One hundred percent analysis may be too costly and, because of duplication of defects, additional analysis may yield diminished returns. Focusing the analysis on the most commonly occurring defects, on the other hand, can help develop preventive actions that will address the most defects in the most effective manner.

If we cannot analyze all of the defects, how do we select which defects to analyze? This depends on the process, the kind of defect data, and the method of defect prevention. Some strategies are as follows:

• Pareto analysis. Select the most commonly occurring types of defects for analysis first. This method implies that the defects have been classified according to some criteria, such as defect type. The most commonly occurring defects are those most worthwhile preventing.

- Attribute focusing. The Orthogonal Defect Classification methodology (25,26) uses a number of different classifications for each defect. An analysis method called *attribute focusing* (27,28) is then used to compute the degree of "interestingness" of different sets of defects. The most "interesting" defect sets are those selected for consideration by the development team.
- Selection by severity. Select those defects that have the greatest impact or severity. This method assumes that the defects have been classified by severity. For some processes, the most severe defects are the most worthwhile to prevent.
- Random selection. If the defects have not been classified in any way, a random selection method can be used, for example, selecting every fifth defect. If a large enough sample of defects is selected, the high-frequency defects will be represented in the sample. This method of selection has been successfully applied to software defects. One variation is a random sample which ensures that defects from each member of the software development team are included for analysis.

Perform Preliminary Cause Investigation

For some processes, the cause of most defects is evident. In software development, for example, the defects are introduced by developers who can very frequently identify the cause or causes of the error. When other team members are included in the identification of the causes, almost all defects can be successfully analyzed for cause.

But for many types of defects, the cause may not be obvious. In manufacturing operations, for example, common sources of defects such as changes in the operating conditions, manufacturing equipment, input components, supplier procedures, and so on are not evident. Such cases may need a preliminary investigation of the defect's causes to enable further analysis and preventive suggestions. Such preliminary investigation can include listing the possible causes (e.g., using a cause and effect or fish-bone diagram), narrowing down the possibilities through investigation and then deciding on the *root cause*, or actual cause, for the defect.

Perform Causal Analysis of the Selected Defects, Verify the Causes

Causal analysis of a defect involves understanding the defect and identifying and verifying its causes in order to suggest actions that will prevent the defect in the future. Usually the people involved in causal analysis are the people directly involved in the process that produced the defect, because they are the most knowledgeable about the process. If preliminary cause investigation has been performed, the causal analysis may only involve verification that the actual or root causes have been identified. Otherwise, a detailed discussion may be involved to reach consensus on the causes, and further investigation and confirmation of the causes may be needed.

A defect's causes may involve a chain of causes (where a cause was itself caused by an earlier cause, and so on) or they may involve a direct cause plus contributing or secondary causes. With a chain of causes, the later causes can themselves be viewed as defects in their own right. An example of a chain of causes with contributing causes would be as follows:

- A defect in software code was caused by defects in the earlier design of the software.
- The design defects were caused by miscommunication of changes to the design of another component, which was being developed by another organization at another location.
- The miscommunication of changes was caused by poor communications procedures between the organizations at the different locations.
- The poor communications procedures were caused by a failure to recognize the need for rigorous procedures between the two organizations.
- The failure to recognize the need for procedures was due to lack of experience of the management and senior technical people with developing a product between two organizations at different locations.
- A contributing cause was the development team's general lack of knowledge of the other component's function.
- A contributing cause was time constraints imposed on the project due to the need to introduce the software product in the market quickly.

The entire set of causes is relevant for prevention because each cause contributed to the overall process failure that resulted in the defect. Moreover, some causes are easier to prevent than others, so they should all be considered in developing the most effective preventive actions.

Propose Preventive Actions

Once a defect's causes have been uncovered, it is usually easy to propose preventive actions, that is, actions that will improve the process to prevent similar defects from recurring. The process improvement can address any aspect of the process (e.g., the sequence of the process, its methods, tools, techniques). Some potential preventive actions for the previous example of a chain of causes might be as follows:

- Establish procedures for communicating changes between the two organizations. For example, conduct biweekly project status meetings between the technical team leaders of both organizations to review technical changes.
- Appoint a liaison or contact point in each organization who can field questions from the other organization and direct them to the proper person.
- Change the process to include education sessions for developers in both organizations on the details of the other organization's product function.
- Change the project management guidelines to include recommendations for managing projects that span separate organizations.

In suggesting preventive actions, the team should consider all aspects of the defect, its causes, and the process that enabled the defect to occur. The most obvious aspect for preventive actions to address is to eliminate the actual causes of the defect. However, the team may also want to probe deeper and improve any detection methods, such as inspections and tests, that failed to uncover the defect earlier than it was actually found. The team may want to consider whether there are any other occurrences of similar defects in the product that should be found and removed.

Thus, there are five possible focuses for improvement actions:

1. *Actions to eliminate first-order causes and prevent future occurrences of the defect.* First-order causes are the primary causes of the defect, that is, those causes that directly brought about the defect. For example, a software defect might be that parameters were coded incorrectly in software under development when the software accessed another software component. A first-order cause might be the lack of knowledge about the component which was accessed. A preventive action might be to make available a description of that software component. A broader action would be to make available the descriptions of all components which developers might access.

2. *Actions to eliminate second-order and contributing causes.* Second-order causes are those that occur in a chain of causes, that bring about the first-order causes. For example, a second-order cause for the lack of knowledge about the component might be that documentation of a software component's function is not saved when the components are developed or modified. The preventive action would be to change the development process to save the documentation so that it will be available whenever developers need it.

   Contributing causes are those causes that aided the defect to occur but did not directly cause it. A contributing cause for the lack of knowledge of a component might have been the lack of time to do a thorough investigation of all items. A preventive action for this cause might be to change the planning process to include consideration of the complexity of the items under development when allocating time for this development activity in the future.

3. *Actions to improve detection methods if they failed to detect the defect.* When defects occur, they are detected at some point, either during the process itself or after the work product is shipped to the customer. If the defect was not uncovered by any of the detection steps of the process (e.g., inspection or testing), then we may consider the failure to detect the defect as a defect itself, in the detection process. Thus, one type of preventive action would be to improve the detection process so that similar defects will be detected in the future.

   For example, the defect caused by lack of knowledge of a software component might not have been caught in the code inspection. A preventive action would then be to add an item to the code inspection checklist to check the parameters to all accessed software components.

4. *Actions to remove similar occurrences of the defect that may also have occurred.* If a particular type of defect has occurred, it is likely that other occurrences of that defect or similar defects have also occurred but have not yet been detected. Such similar defects may have related causes, particularly if the same process is being followed. Therefore, it can be worthwhile to look for additional occurrences of the defect.

   In the example of the defect where parameters were coded incorrectly in the software, it may be worthwhile checking all instances of parameters where that software component is accessed.

5. *Actions for general process improvement, not directly motivated by the defect or problem.* In the discussion of defects, causes, and preventive actions, team members may have ideas that will lead to general process improvements but which are not directly related to any defect or cause under discussion. For example, a member may notice a trend in the defects and suggest a general action to address it, or may just have a good idea. Such process improvement suggestions are valuable and should not be lost. Moreover, the defect prevention procedures may actually encourage discussions which lead to such suggestions, as discussed in the next defect prevention element.

Perform Causal Analysis on Trends and General Process Problems

One difficulty with defect causal analysis is that it can focus too narrowly on specific problems, with the result that broader process problems are not addressed. As a result, some defect prevention methods include a focus on broader problems in the process. Such general process problems may not result in work product defects. For example, there may be inefficiencies in the process that should be eliminated, even though they do not result in defects. Also, there may be problems that occur which do not fall within the scope of the organization's definition of a defect. In both of these cases, the broader definition of a defect—anything that impacts or interferes with maintaining or improving quality or productivity—may be applied.

IBM's Defect Prevention Process (DPP) (1) is an example of a method that includes general problem analysis. In its causal analysis meeting, the first 1.5 hours are devoted to individual defect causal analysis, that is, taking a defect, identifying its causes, and proposing preventive actions. The last half-hour of the causal analysis meeting is then devoted to considering three items:

1. *Are there any trends or commonalities in the defects, causes, and suggested actions?* If a trend is identified, additional suggestions are made to address the overall problem which is implied by the trend. For example, if a large number of the defects analyzed involved new hires and others new to the organization, further general suggestions would be made as to how to bring new people in the organization up to speed.

2. *What went wrong during the last few months?* What general problems did the team encounter, regardless of whether it caused defects? For example, there may be problems that wasted time or caused rework. These problem areas are analyzed and further suggestions are made to prevent them in the future.

3. *What went right during the last few months?* If the team has experienced things that went well during the last development step, for example, or the last few months, the team may consider these things more thoroughly. For example, the team may have adopted an improved procedure for doing their work, or improved the way they communicate key information, or enhanced a tool that they use. The team may have found a way to save time, improve accuracy, or improve morale. If these improved procedures, tools, or methods are not generally used in the rest of the organiza-

tion, then the suggestion may be proposed to adopt the process improvement and deploy it to the rest of the organization.

Track the Preventive Actions

Many defect prevention methods generate several suggestions for actions, usually one to three per defect. If a large number of defects is analyzed, the number of actions to keep track of soon grows unmanageable without a mechanism of some sort to track them. Frequently, the tracking is done with a computerized action file or database.

The action database typically includes a means of recording actions and their related defects. It would support tracking the actions from the time they are suggested until they are implemented, to ensure that the actions are implemented in a timely manner and are implemented correctly. The database may allow actions to be assigned to individuals or teams. The details of the implementation can be recorded as well as its current status. Among the data that may be kept for each action are its priority, target date, estimated cost, and estimated effectiveness.

The action database may be used to produce periodic management reports on the status of the process as a whole; for example, how many prevention-related activities have occurred in the last time period (e.g., how many causal analysis sessions were held, how many actions have been implemented, how much time has been spent on these activities).

Implement the Preventive Actions for Process Improvement

Once actions have been proposed, they need to be implemented. For some prevention methods, there is no special mechanism for action implementation. It is assumed that once a preventive action has been proposed, it will be implemented by the appropriate people in the organization. In some instances, it is the individual or team that proposes the action who is expected to implement it. This approach may be problematic if those charged with implementation do not have adequate resources or time, or the necessary skills and authority to change the process.

Other prevention methods (e.g., DPP) call for people to be identified in the organization as the action implementers or action team. Some portion of the action team's time is set aside for implementation work. People are selected who have skills in the right areas (e.g., education, process, tools) and the team is given the authority to change what is necessary in the area's processes and practices to prevent the recurrence of defects.

Provide Feedback to the People in the Process

As the organization's processes are changed, those changes need to be communicated to the workers. Such communication may be thought of as part of the action implementation. For example, if machine operating procedures are changed, the operators will need training in the revised procedures and the revisions need to be reflected in the machine procedures manual.

Such communication can also be less formal, for example, in the form of bulletin board notices or articles in the organization's newsletter. The form of communication will depend on the nature of the process change.

With some prevention methods the process changes may be so numerous and require notification to so many people that a better approach is to schedule periodic process feedback sessions. Not only do the workers learn of the changes that have occurred to the process but they also review the overall process that is to be followed, thereby reinforcing their overall process awareness.

Some processes involve stages or steps of work. Over time, the workers follow a number of different process steps. For example, in software development, the developers perform several design steps, then a coding step, then several testing steps. In these cases, each process step can have a feedback session (sometimes called a process step "kickoff") at the beginning of the step. These sessions prepare the workers for the next step of the process. The process for the step is reviewed in its entirety, as well as the process changes that have occurred recently. The process step kickoff or review session can be very effective in preventing defects.

Check the Effectiveness of Implemented Actions

Once preventive actions have been implemented and deployed within the organization, the defects that were addressed should cease. However, this does not always happen. The actions may not be completely effective in preventing the defect and the deployment of the actions may not be perfect. Thus, it is important to check the result of the implemented actions and take further action if the defects still occur. This step is reflected in the last two parts of the Shewhart cycle of Plan-Do-Check-Act: check the results of the actions and make the necessary adjustments to ensure that the defects are completely eliminated.

In some processes, it is possible to monitor the results of preventive actions through ongoing process measurements. Manufacturing processes, for example, may employ control charts or defect classification. These process measurements can be checked to see whether the defects that were addressed have been reduced or eliminated. If not, further causal analysis may be performed and further actions may be taken.

Other processes such as software development are not as repetitive and tend to have a large number of different defects so that the recurrence of a specific defect may be difficult to detect and the absence of the defect in the process may be impossible to prove in any practical sense. In these cases, we must rely simply on ongoing causal analysis. If the defect that should have been prevented recurs, further actions will be proposed and implemented. Very stubborn, chronic types of defects will be recognized as such and extra effort in preventing them is usually warranted.

Check the Effectiveness of the Prevention Method

In addition to checking the effectiveness of individual actions, the overall effectiveness of the prevention method may be checked. This kind of checking may take one of three forms:

- Monitor the overall defect levels of the process. If a number of preventive actions have been implemented, the overall defect levels should drop, reflecting the cumulative contributions of each of the actions. As more and more actions are implemented, the defect levels should continue to drop.

- Monitor the activity of the prevention method itself. Various aspects of the prevention method itself can be monitored by management to ensure that the prevention activities are occurring and that the overall prevention method is functioning smoothly. The aspects to monitor could include, for example, the number of causal analysis sessions conducted per quarter, the number of actions implemented, the cost of the implemented actions, the number of open actions awaiting implementation (i.e., the action backlog), and so on.
- Monitor the level of deployment of the prevention method in the organization. When a prevention method is introduced, it may take time for the method to be fully deployed in all areas of the organization. The method's degree of deployment may be measured by a "maturity model" which rates an area in terms of different aspects of deployment. Such aspects might include, for example, the proportion of the workers who have been trained in the method, the level of activity of defect recording and causal analysis, the assignment and level of activity of the action implementers, and the installation and operational status of the action tracking tool.

METHODS OF CAUSAL ANALYSIS

The basic idea of causal analysis is to understand the nature of the defect and its underlying causes so that preventive actions can be proposed. However, different processes have different ways to identify the defects and determine their causes. The approach may be to analyze the defects individually, or consider defects grouped according to a classification scheme, or analyze causes for any abnormal variation in the process output.

Individual Defect Causal Analysis

The simplest approach to causal analysis is to take individual defects and analyze them for their causes. The advantage of individual defect causal analysis is that specific defect causes are pinpointed and specific preventive actions can be identified. This specificity is not as likely to be achieved with defect classification methods where a number of defects are grouped together according to the classification but which may have different specific causes. Thus, the actions resulting from the classification may miss these specific causes and be less effective.

In comparison to defect classification, the cost of analyzing individual defects may appear relatively high. For example, a team may take 6–8 minutes on average to analyze a software defect. However, with individual defect analysis, not every defect need be analyzed and a representative sample may be used instead. If representative samples of defects are analyzed, the resulting process improvement actions will be sufficient to reduce overall defect levels.

Individual defect causal analysis is specified in several defect prevention processes, including IBM's Defect Prevention Process (1), Kane's problem analysis system (29), and the Space Shuttle Onboard Software defect prevention process (12).

As an example of individual defect causal analysis, a portion of a causal analysis session is given in Table 1. The causal analysis technique used in this

TABLE 1   Example of Individual Defect Causal Analysis (Using the DPP Method)

Defect No.	Defect abstract	Cause category	Cause abstract	Step created	Suggested preventive actions
1	Referenced the wrong Response Unit control block	Education	Did not understand the router/sender build interface	Code	Create a user's guide for the router/sender interface. Include in all subsequent design documents descriptions of the subcomponent functions used and how to interface to them.
2	Wrong keyword was used on the YY-CALL macro	Education	Did not know how to look up the parameters for a macro	Code	Create a New Hire's Guide to resources in the product area Clean up the macro description text so it is clearer Create a code reuse library for reusable parts
3	Incorrect use of the XXXABORT function	Communications failure	Design document was not easily understood	Code	Improve the documentation of the utility functions of the product
4	Logic in the code was incorrect	Communications failure	Team leader did not give enough information to the developer	Code	Team leaders need more time to work with new hires
5	Condition check in the code was invalid	Transcription	Implemented the module in phases	Code	Recommend to developers to write an implementation plan for modules that are developed in phases
6	XXXXZZ was declared on an invalid boundary	Transcription	Simple mistake	Code	Add control block boundary problems to the Code Common Error List Create a technical write-up on control block boundaries
7	XXXXYY control block field was moved that couldn't move (boundary problem)	Communications failure	There ws no documentation for that requirement in the control block commentary	Code	(Handled by previous actions)
3	XXX call parameter was specified incorrectly	Education	Did not read the module interface documentation carefully enough	Code	Add this error to the Code Common Error List

example is the one used in IBM's Defect Prevention Process. The results of causal analysis of several software defects from a coding process step are presented, with the resulting suggested preventive actions.

Individual defect analysis is not appropriate for certain processes, such as manufacturing, where individual results of a repetitive work process may or may not indicate even the presence of a defect. In such cases, statistical process control methods are more suited to identifying and analyzing defects from the process.

General Defect Classification Methods

A second form of causal analysis is defect classification which involves assigning defects to one or more classes, selecting a group of defects by class, and performing causal analysis on the group. Preventive actions may be suggested that deal with the entire group of defects, thus providing coverage of a number of defects for a relatively small analysis effort. The effort to classify all of the defects, of course, must also be considered in comparing this method with individual defect causal analysis.

The advantage of defect classification is its ability to provide a view of the overall process and, thus, to identify broad areas of prevention. This broadness is also a disadvantage because specific preventive actions may be overlooked.

Among the defect classification methods used for defect prevention are IBM's Orthogonal Defect Classification method (described in the next section), defect analysis via classification (21), and cause–effect analysis (22,23).

Grady (21) describes a defect classification structure for analyzing defect causes that includes defect origin, defect type, and mode (missing, wrong, unclear, etc.). In order to focus attention on causes of defects that cost the most to fix, the defect classes can be weighted by the cost to fix the defect if it is not found until testing. If the objective is to help reduce the backlog of defects needing to be fixed, an alternative focus can consider the defect groups that are most quickly resolved. From the data thus analyzed, recommendations are made to change the process and are accompanied by a cost/benefit analysis of the change.

The cause–effect analysis (23) categorizes defects according to program faults (the basic type of defect), human errors (a level of cause), and process flaws (a further level of cause). From the intersection of defect types and causes, common error mechanisms can be identified and general recommendations can be made about process improvements to prevent the error mechanisms. For example, module interface faults are caused by misunderstandings of the interface specifications (human error) which are caused by lack of methods to specify the interfaces (process flaw). This error mechanism can be prevented by adopting structured analysis/ structured design methods.

Collofello and Gosalia (24) report the use of a defect classification scheme using defect causal categories such as system knowledge or experience, communication, software impacts (failure to consider all impacts), human error, and so on. A fault category (defect type) is also used. The most frequently occurring defect causes are examined and process improvements are suggested and implemented.

Orthogonal Defect Classification Analysis

Orthogonal Defect Classification (ODC) is a method of software defect classification developed at IBM to provide detailed analysis for process improvement (25–28). ODC uses a set of orthogonal classes, that is, classifications that identify defects according to nonoverlapping (orthogonal) dimensions, that are consistent across development phases, and that are uniform across different development projects. The orthogonal classes that are used are as follows:

- Defect type: Identifies what was corrected to fix the defect. Examples of defect type are function, interface, assignment, checking, data structure, document, and so on. The defect type is also qualified by *missing* (or) *incorrect*, that is, whether something new, that was missing, had to be added to fix the defect, or something existing, that was incorrect, had to be changed to fix the defect.
- Defect trigger: Identifies what caused the defect to surface. Examples of defect trigger are operational semantics, language dependencies, concurrency, side effects, backward compatibility, and so on.
- Defect source: Identifies in what part of the system the defect occurred, for example, in new function that was being added, in a part that was being rewritten, in scaffolding code, and so on.
- Defect impact: Identifies aspects of the customer's use of the software that would be affected by the defect, for example, capability or function, usability, performance, and so on.

Defects are classified at two points in the inspection or test process. At the time the defect is reported, its defect trigger and impact are recorded, and at the time it is fixed, its source and type are recorded. When the development phase is complete (or when it is complete for some portion of the project), the defects are analyzed using a machine-assisted technique called *attribute focusing*. Attribute focusing groups the classified defects by their degree of "interestingness" for human analysis and displays them as charts in decreasing order of interestingness.

A feedback meeting is conducted by a domain specialist (for example, a person familiar with the development process) with the development team, to identify the cause of the interestingness, for example, why a disproportionate number of a certain type of defect occurred. Two sets of questions are asked to attempt to understand the interestingness:

- Understand the cause of interestingness: Defect class Q occurs frequently with R but infrequently with W: Why? What event could have led to such occurrence?
- Understand the implication of interestingness: Defect class Q occurs frequently with R but infrequently with W: Is this desirable? What will happen if no action is taken?

Not all interesting attribute combinations can be assigned a cause. However, when a cause can be assigned and verified by the team, changes to the development process may be indicated which will correct the process problem and prevent similar problems in the future. Analyses of defects from subsequent development phases can be used to verify that the corrective actions have been effective in overcoming the problem.

For example, the defects from a design inspection had a disproportionate percentage that were classified as "missing function." Further investigation revealed that these defects dealt with error recovery. The cause was that the design did not adequately focus on error recovery. The corrective action was to review the design to ensure that, after correcting the defects found in the inspection, all error recovery functions had been included. The preventive action was to modify both the design process guidelines and the design inspection guidelines to ensure that error recovery function is considered during the design phase.

Statistical Process Control Methods

Statistical process control (SPC) is a collection of statistical techniques and practices that is well described in the literature, for example, Refs. 29–33, and is widely practiced in industry. Repetitive processes, such as manufacturing operations, where the work product is intended to be identical, may be measured and controlled by relatively simple statistical techniques. Measures of the work product along relevant dimensions are taken and plotted. The variation of the measurements gives an indication both of the process's capability (how much "normal" variation occurs in the process) and whether the process is in control (whether the observed variations remain within the normal limits).

In SPC, variation in the process is categorized according to either special or assignable causes (those that result in variation outside the process's normal limits) and common causes (those that contribute to the normal variation of the process). Eliminating special causes addresses conditions that cause the process to be "out of control." Eliminating common causes addresses the overall capability of the process, reducing the variability that is an inherent property of the process.

Whether specific work product measurements may be considered a defect depends on the specification for the part, not on the variability of the process producing the part. The objective of applying SPC to a process is to produce parts that are within the required specifications. Thus, the first objective is to eliminate special causes to bring the process under statistical control. Then it may still be necessary to eliminate common causes, through process improvements, to further reduce the variability to be within product specifications. Subsequently, the process is monitored with further measurements to ensure that unforeseen special causes are not introduced, resulting in out-of-control conditions.

SPC is thus a form of causal analysis involving two steps: (a) monitoring process measurements to determine both special and common process variation and (b) identifying and eliminating the causes of the variability. The most common statistical technique used to determine variability is the control chart which plots process measurements over time, showing the mean and upper and lower control limits. Out-of-control conditions may then be identified through a number of heuristics:

- Points outside the upper or lower control limits
- Run of two of three points near the upper or lower control limits
- Run of eight or more consecutive points above or below the centerline
- Run of six or more points ever-increasing or ever-decreasing
- Points not conforming to a normal distribution around the centerline

The most common method of identifying the causes of variation is the cause and effect (C&E) or fish-bone diagram. The C&E diagram lists the potential causes for the variation, starting with broad categories of causes (commonly they are men, methods, machines, materials, measurements, and environment). Then more specific causes are added as offshoots or twigs from these primary branches. Then further, more specific causes are added as smaller offshoots to these twigs, and so on. Kane (29) describes several different forms of the C&E diagram.

Once the set of possible causes has been identified, the most likely causes are prioritized and selected for further investigation. The process of investigation may involve direct checking for the presence of the cause, modifying the process under controlled conditions to see if the cause is present, collecting additional data from the process, and so on. The use of design of experiments methods, for example, see Ref. 30, is frequently useful in this process to minimize the number of samples that need to be taken. The result of the investigation is identification of the *root causes* of the variation, that is, those potential causes that can, in fact, cause the problem and are present in the process. One simple test to validate a root cause is to demonstrate that the problem occurs when the cause is present and is eliminated when the cause is absent.

Once the root causes have been identified, process modifications are implemented to eliminate the causes.

APPROACHES TO PREVENTIVE ACTIONS

There are a number of different approaches to preventive actions, depending on the focus of the improvement. The focus may be on the process itself with an emphasis on making it impossible for the mistake to be made again, on the detection methods that failed to catch the primary defect earlier in the process, or on duplicate defects similar to the one under consideration, that the process may have allowed to occur which should also be found and corrected.

Poka-Yoke (Mistake Proofing) and Automatic Elimination of Causes

Shigeo Shingo (44) introduced the *poka-yoke* or mistake proofing method. Poka-yoke (pronounced "poka yokay") seeks to develop preventive actions whereby a specific error can no longer be made. Such devices are usually simple and inexpensive but make it impossible for a particular error to recur. For example, an electronic device required the application of insulation tape in 10 places. However, sometimes not all 10 strips of tape were applied. To prevent this error, the strips were precut and arranged on a rod in groups of 10 so that the worker could tell if all strips had been used. Thereafter, there were no missing insulation strips.

Poka-yoke is most readily applied to highly repetitive manual operations. Poka-yoke devices frequently employ limit switches, photoelectric switches, and similar simple sensors. When poka-yoke is practiced effectively, assembly machines can have a dozen or more different devices each. Shingo notes that a poka-yoke system has two functions: It performs 100% inspection automatically, and if an abnormality occurs, it provides immediate feedback which then prompts action.

A similar concept is used in other defect prevention methods, for example, the idea of *defect extinction* in IBM's Defect Prevention Process (1). Here, the use of software tools is proposed to automatically eliminate errors in software development. One type of tool is the "module checker" which scans the source code for typical errors whenever a source module is changed and recompiled. A similar scan

can also be run on a set of source modules to uncover and remove existing defects. A module checker tool of this sort, called FUNCTOR, is used by Fujitsu (18) to eliminate simple coding bugs.

Improving Defect Detection Methods

Work processes usually involve defect detection or verification methods such as testing or inspections, whose purpose is to uncover any defects that have been injected during the primary process. The failure to detect a defect may be viewed as a defect in the detection process (provided the defect *should have been detected* by that verification step or method).

Such defect "escapes" (defects that escaped a detection step) may be analyzed and improvements in the detection step proposed. This causal analysis is best done by the people involved in the detection process, that is, the testers or inspectors. The actions will be to improve the methods of detection to make them more effective. Such actions will be in addition to actions that may be proposed to prevent the original defect from recurring.

The Space Shuttle Onboard Software defect prevention process (12) routinely includes consideration of improvements to any verification steps that allowed the defect to go undetected through the process.

Finding and Removing Duplicate Defects

The presence of a defect is evidence that other similar defects may also exist. The uncovered defect indicates a flaw in the work process which may have allowed similar defects to occur. Some or all of these defects may not have been detected yet. Therefore, it may be worthwhile to make a special effort to find any similar defects and remove them.

In a strict sense, such supplemental detection activities are not prevention because the defects have already occurred. However, in some applications, particularly in safety critical systems, this extra focus can be an integral part of the defect prevention activities. Such supplemental detection efforts are well cost justified for such systems, although they may not be cost justified in other applications.

The Space Shuttle Onboard Software defect prevention process (12) includes this focus. An example of such an effort in their process involved an error in the use of global data elements in the multiple-pass operation of the software (15, pp. 886–887). The software failed to reinitialize certain variables on subsequent passes, causing a critical failure. The software was analyzed in detail to uncover any other situations where a global variable might not be reinitialized correctly. The developers uncovered an additional 17 defects, of which one would have caused a serious failure (loss of certain safety checking during space shuttle ascent).

LESS FORMAL DEFECT PREVENTION METHODS

Two "less formal" defect prevention methods, postmortems and quality control circles, have been in use for many years. They are less formal because they do not prescribe a full process that is integrated with the process of work. Nevertheless, they have been applied successfully in many companies.

Postmortems

A postmortem is the systematic review and analysis of the results and experiences of a development project. The postmortem is usually conducted just after the project has completed. The report may include the product's quality and other in-process measurements, project statistics, a narrative history, and so on. One purpose of these data is for comparison with other projects. Another major reason for the postmortem is for systematic feedback, including causal analysis, to identify areas for improvement.

The postmortem process used at AT&T (34) includes the following steps:

1. Gather the needed data and observations during the process
2. Identify the key messages, themes, and recommendations from the project
3. Conduct a postmortem meeting of the key technical staff and managers
4. Publish meeting minutes and recommendations
5. Follow up throughout the year to ensure that recommendations have been adopted

Postmortems can be conducted at key points during the development cycle, for example, after planning, after first product ship, and 1 year after product ship. In addition, "mini" postmortems may be held at the end of each development stage (design, development, test) or for a particular component of the product. Such "mini" postmortems tend to be more focused and involve more in-depth analysis.

Quality Control Circles

A quality control circle (QCC) consists of a group of workers, usually from the same area, who meet regularly to discuss quality problems and ways to overcome them. The team may use statistical process control methods or other forms of causal analysis to identify problems and their causes. The QCC then proposes improvements to management and implements the improvements when they are approved.

To support a QCC program, there is usually a training program for QCC facilitators, QCC leaders, and members. The training includes basic techniques such as brainstorming, cause and effect (fish-bone) diagrams, Pareto diagrams, control charts, and problem-solving techniques.

FULL DEFECT PREVENTION PROCESSES

Three full defect prevention processes are described in the literature. Each integrates most of the elements of defect prevention described earlier.

Space Shuttle Onboard Software Defect Prevention Process

The Space Shuttle Onboard Software defect prevention process (12–14) was developed at IBM Houston to address the need for extremely high levels of quality in the space shuttle onboard software, a highly visible, safety critical software system. This rigorous process includes the following elements:

1. Identify defects through inspections, testing, and field usage; fix the defects

2. Identify the root cause of each defect through causal analysis and implement process changes to eliminate the cause and prevent the recurrence of the error
3. Fix other faults in the inspection and testing processes that allowed the defect to go undetected through the process (i.e., an "escape")
4. Look for similar, as-yet-undetected defects and fix them

Special teams consisting of members from all phases of the development process (requirements, design, code, verification) are responsible for the investigation of every defect, to determine how it escaped detection and to find any similar defects. In addition, a periodic analysis of error trends is conducted. From these analyses, further process improvements are proposed and implemented.

Kane's Defect Prevention System

Victor Kane (29) describes a comprehensive Defect Prevention System (DPS) including a 10-step problem analysis system for causal analysis and prevention. These systems are most applicable to a manufacturing type of process. Participation by both managers and employees is critical to the success of implementing a DPS. Kane recommends an overall 10-step process to work toward establishing a DPS:

1. Establish open communications among supervisors and employees, encouraging employees to address quality in their work area
2. Change operating systems that are critical to prevention such as preventive maintenance, training, tool control, and gauge control
3. Initiate customer feedback systems to ensure feedback on product performance and customer problems
4. Develop key quality and productivity indicators to ensure that the process can be monitored and the effect of changes evaluated
5. Utilize problem-solving teams to address the top problems identified by the key indicators; use the problem analysis system to understand the causes and eliminate them
6. Define process relationships to identify process parameters that may be contributing to variability in process output
7. Develop and implement process control plans to sample and monitor process outputs and evaluate process capability
8. Develop an incoming material defect prevention system to ensure that suppliers use similar prevention and problem-solving methods
9. Emphasize management evaluation of systems so that management becomes involved in the improvement and problem-solving process
10. Develop a continuous improvement mindset as opposed to focusing on short-term performance targets

The two key preventive aspects of the DPS are the statistical tools which are used to identify processes that are unstable or are out of statistical control (Steps 6 and 7) and the problem analysis system (Step 5). The latter involves 10 steps in identifying process problems, understanding their causes, and implementing solutions that will prevent the problems from recurring:

1. Form a team of 5–10 members with the appropriate process knowledge and work experience

2. Define the problem in terms of who, what, where, when, why, how, and how much
3. Implement interim containment actions so that the problem does not cause further disruption until it has been solved
4. Identify potential causes via cause and effect diagrams, time line analysis (what changed in the process, when), comparison analyses, and so on
5. Analyze potential causes to test whether they may cause the problem
6. Validate root causes (i.e., those causes that can cause the problem and are present)
7. Identify alternative solutions that will address the root causes
8. Verify and implement permanent corrective actions
9. Implement ongoing controls to ensure that the problem will not recur
10. Change the system that did not prevent the problem: identify the management or operating system that should have prevented the problem and make changes to the system to prevent recurrence of similar problems

There are two levels of prevention addressed by the problem analysis system: first order causes of the defect are eliminated by Steps 6-9, and second order and contributing causes are addressed by Step 10.

IBM's Defect Prevention Process

The Defect Prevention Process (DPP) (1-6) was first developed in connection with software development but has since been successfully applied to hardware development, manufacturing, and administrative processes. DPP includes five major elements (see Fig. 1):

- Causal analysis of defects: This usually involves defect selection from the set of defects that have occurred in the work process (e.g., a development step). The selected defects are handled in a causal analysis meeting involving the team members who participated in the process where the defects occurred. The result of causal analysis is a set of suggested actions for process improvement. The details of conducting a causal analysis meeting are described in Ref. 6.
- Action database: The suggested actions are recorded in a database for tracking as they are being implemented
- Action team: An action team consisting of experts in the organization's process, tools, and methods screens, prioritizes, and implements the suggested actions. Some of the actions will involve changes to the product, the introduction of new or improved tools and technical education. The overall effect of the implemented actions is continuous improvement of the organization's processes.
- Repositories of process and product information: Many suggestions result in changes to the process or the accumulation of product information. Such actions may involve, for example, clarifications to the process, checklists, guidelines, common error lists, document templates, and technical product information. These data are stored in on-line repositories for convenient access by the workers.
- Periodic feedback to the workers: Because it is important to communicate

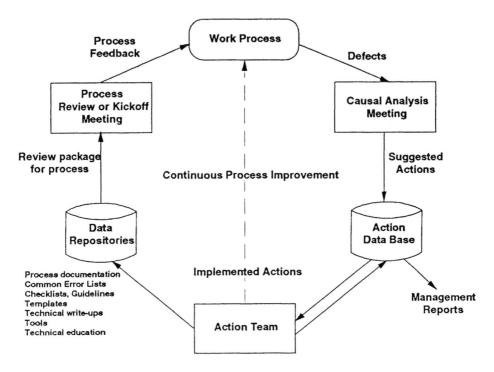

FIGURE 1   IBM's Defect Prevention Process.

the changes that are made to the process and also to review the process periodically, regular process review, or kickoff meetings are conducted at the team level to review the process, with special emphasis on the changes which have been implemented since the last review.

SURVEY OF DEFECT PREVENTION PRACTICES AND RESULTS

This section describes the various approaches to defect prevention that have been reported in the literature. The focus is on their use in the computer industry, in particular in software development. The approaches are grouped by related methods.

Poka-Yoke

The use of poka-yoke or mistake proofing methods in telecommunications hardware manufacturing at AT&T is reported by Cassidy (45), with two examples described that resulted in no further defects. Bandyopadhyay (46) provides a summary of poka-yoke methods and a survey of reported results in the literature.

Postmortems

Postmortems are used routinely in companies but are not often described in the literature. Tiedeman (34) reports on their use in AT&T.

Quality Control Circles

In contrast to postmortems, quality control circles are described frequently in the literature (35–38) with most applications being in manufacturing processes. Companies that have reported use of quality circles in software development include Bell Communications Research (Bellcore) (39, 40), NEC Corporation (41), Digital Equipment Corporation (42), and Nippon Steel Corporation (43).

The use of software quality control (SWQC) groups or circles at NEC (41) is described in connection with their overall "software factory architecture." Hutchings at DEC (42) describes the use of cause and effect analysis by a quality circle to identify improvements to their software inspection process. The circle would then use defect categories from subsequent inspections to determine if the preventive actions had an effect. Ogawa et al. of Nippon Steel (43) report the use of small groups and a "software quality committee" following the Shewhart Plan–Do–Check–Act cycle, with a resulting reduction in defects in their software.

Defect Classification

The use of defect classification is reported by Hewlett-Packard in two forms. Grady (21) reports the use of defect classification to analyze defect causes and develop recommendations for process improvement. He cites an example of introducing inspections to reduce the errors fixed in test. Nakajo and Kume (23) report the application of a cause–effect analysis that categorizes defects according to program faults, human errors, and process flaws. From these data, common error mechanisms can be identified and general recommendations can be made about process improvements. An example is given where the common error mechanisms dealing with module interface errors can be corrected with the use of structured analysis/ structured design methods. The use of these methods in developing six subsystems was compared to the development of six other subsystems without these design methods, with a consequent reduction in overall errors and, in particular, for interface errors.

Collofello and Gosalia (24) report the use of defect classification at AG Communications Systems Corporation employing causal categories which are then used to propose improvements to the process. By implementing improvements in the review process, in training, and in communications, a substantial reduction in software faults was achieved.

Variations of Causal Analysis

Various forms of causal analysis have been reported by different companies. Casey et al. of Bell Communications Research (Bellcore) (17) describe a Defect Analysis model wherein individual defects are analyzed for their root cause and are then grouped together by common or related root cause. From these groups a team makes recommendations for process changes to prevent the group of defects and/or to detect them earlier in the life cycle. The results from four projects showed a potential reduction in field defects from 75% to 90% with a potential savings from the reduction of these defects of two to four times the cost of doing the defect analysis. Specific examples from two of the projects are given. Nakamura et al. of Fujitsu (18) report on the "NAZE NAZE" (Why? Why?) process of causal analysis which identifies the underlying causes of software bugs and proposes improvements to working procedures and designers' capabilities. Among the preventive actions reported are various automated checking tools to prevent common development and test errors.

Boteler of Lockeed (19) reports on the use of causal analysis and preventive actions in a Research and Engineering department with the result that rejection rates dropped from 14% to 1.6% per month over 20 months with a reduction of scrap and rework costs dropping from $3800 to $100 per month.

MacLeod of Hewlett-Packard (20) reports on the use of causal analysis integrated with software inspections. Three to five major defects are selected from the defects reported during the inspection. From the defect causes, areas of process improvement are identified.

Causal Analysis and Defect Prevention Within IBM

Within IBM, causal analysis and defect prevention work developed independently in several different labs. In IBM United Kingdom (16), a formal process of causal analysis was established to identify defect causes and implement preventive actions. The result of these efforts and other quality efforts brought about a decrease in errors from 545 to 150 within 2 years with a consequent cost avoidance of 33 person years in those 2 years.

Orthogonal Defect Classification was developed at IBM Research in the late 1980s and is described in detail in several papers (25-28) with examples taken from many different development projects. The results include process improvements to design and development methods, inspections, and test. In particular, the use of the attribute focusing technique in a number of projects (28) yielded numerous corrective and preventive improvements.

The Space Shuttle Onboard Software organization at IBM Houston (now part of Loral Corporation) implemented a defect prevention process beginning in the early 1980s (12-14) which incorporates causal analysis, prevention of the original defect, improving the verification processes that failed to detect the defect, and detecting other similar defects that may still be present in the software. As a result, the product defect rate dropped from about 3 per thousand lines of source code to about 0.1 over the period of 1983 through 1992.

IBM's Defect Prevention Process

At the IBM Networking Software Laboratory in Research Triangle Park, NC, the Defect Prevention Process (DPP) was developed beginning in 1983 (1-6). DPP includes causal analysis, action implementation, action tracking, and periodic feedback of process improvements. DPP is now practiced in most major IBM software development laboratories and has also found application in hardware engineering, manufacturing, and administrative processes. The results are that software projects typically achieve two to three times reduction in defect rates within 1-2 years while expending 1% to 1.5% of their resources on the process, including the cost of action implementation.

Other companies have also adopted some or most of the Defect Prevention Process, with similar results. Northern Telecom and Bell Northern Research adopted DPP as part of their overall total quality management program (7,8). In a development project for Nippon Telephone and Telegraph (9), near-zero-defect error rates were achieved over several releases of the software, with consequent high customer satisfaction.

Dangerfield et al. (10) and Card (11) report on the use of defect causal analysis (DCA) at Computer Sciences Corporation, which incorporates several of the concepts of DPP. CSC reports a 50% reduction in defects within 2 years with an expenditure of about 1.5% of project resources.

REFERENCES

IBM's Defect Prevention Process

1. R. G. Mays, C. L. Jones, G. J. Holloway, and D. P. Studinski, "Experiences with Defect Prevention," *IBM Syst. J., 29*(1), 4-32 (1990).
2. J. L. Gale, J. R. Tirso, and C. A. Burchfield, "Implementing the Defect Prevention Process in the MVS Interactive Programming Organization," *IBM Syst. J., 29*(1), 33-43 (1990).
3. R. G. Mays, "Applications of Defect Prevention in Software Development," *IEEE J. Selected Areas Commun., 8*(2), 164-168 (1990).
4. C. L. Jones, "A Process-Integrated Approach to Defect Prevention," *IBM Syst. J., 24*(2), 150-167 (1985).
5. R. G. Mays, "Defect Prevention and Total Quality Management," *Total Quality Management for Software*, G. G. Schulmeyer and J. I. McManus (eds.), Van Nostrand Reinhold, New York, 1992, Chap. 15.
6. R. G. Mays, "Practical Aspects of the Defect Prevention Process," in *Software Inspection*, T. Gilb and D. R. Graham, Addison-Wesley, London, 1993, Chap. 17.

Applications of DPP

7. T. J. Bradley, "The Use of Defect Prevention in Achieving Total Quality Management in the Software Life Cycle," *ICC 91. International Conference on Communications Conference Record, 1*, 356-359 (1991).
8. W. M. Pratt, "Experiences in the Application of Customer-Based Metrics in Improving Software Service Quality," *ICC 91. International Conference on Communications Conference Record, 3*, 1459-1462 (1991).
9. Y. Ueyama and C. Ludwig, "Joint Customer Development Process and Its Impact on Software Quality," *ISS 92. XIV International Switching Symposium, 2*, 374-378 (1992).
10. O. Dangerfield, P. Ambardekar, P. Paluzzi, D. Card, and D. Giblin, "Defect Causal Analysis: A Report from the Field," in *Proceedings: Second International Conference on Software Quality*, American Society for Quality Control, Milwaukee, WI, 1992, pp. 109-113.
11. D. N. Card, "Defect-Causal Analysis Drives Down Error Rates," *IEEE Software, 10*(4), 98-99 (1993).

Space Shuttle Onboard Software Defect Prevention Process

12. C. Billings, J. Clifton, B. Kolkhorst, E. Lee, and W. B. Wingert, "Journey to a Mature Software Process," *IBM Syst. J., 33*(1), 46-61 (1994).
13. J. M. Haugh, "Never Make the Same Mistake Twice — Using Configuration Control and Error Analysis to Improve Software Quality," *IEEE Aerospace Electron. Syst. Mag., 7*(1), 12-16 (1992).
14. B. G. Kolkhorst and A. J. Macina, "Developing Error-Free Software," *IEEE Aerospace Electron. Syst. Mag., 3*(11), 25-31 (1988).

15. A. Spector and D. Gifford, "The Space Shuttle Primary Computer System," *Commun. ACM, 27*(9), 874–900 (1984).

Other Causal Analysis

16. A. M. White, "Modern Practical Methods of Producing HIgh Quality Software," *Qual. Assurance, 14*(3), 96–102 (1988).
17. B. K. Casey, E. M. Kaldon, J. L. Sun, and J. M. Watters, "Application of Defect Analysis Techniques to Achieve Continuous Quality and Productivity Improvements," *ICC 91. International Conference on Communications Conference Record, 3*, 1450–1454 (1991).
18. K. Nakamura, M. Sugawara, and M. Toyama, "Defect Prevention Activities and Tools," *ICC 91. International Conference on Communications Conference Record, 1*, 360–363 (1991).
19. J. L. Boteler, "Using Prevention Techniques," *Qual. Prog., 26*(7), 105–107 (1993).
20. J. M. MacLeod, "Implementing and Sustaining a Software Inspection Program in an R&D Environment," *Hewlett-Packard J., 44*(3), 60–63 (1993).

Defect Classification Methods

21. R. B. Grady, "Dissecting Software Failures," *Hewlett-Packard J., 40*(2), 57–63 (1989).
22. T. Nakajo, K. Sasabuchi, and T. Akiyama, "A Structured Approach to Software Defect Analysis," *Hewlett-Packard J., 40*(2), 50–56 (1989).
23. T. Nakajo and H. Kume, "A Case History Analysis of Software Error Cause–Effect Relationships," *IEEE Trans. Software Eng., SE-17*(8), 830–838 (1991).
24. J. S. Collofello and B. P. Gosalia, "An Application of Causal Analysis to the Software Modification Process," *Software — Practice Experience, 23*(10), 1095–1105 (1993).

Orthogonal Defect Classification

25. R. Chillarege, I. Bhandari, J. K. Chaar, M. J. Halliday, D. S. Moebus, B. K. Ray, and M. Wong, "Orthogonal Defect Classification — A Concept for In-Process Measurements," *IEEE Trans. Software Eng., 18*(11), 943–956 (1992).
26. J. Chaar, M. Halliday, I. Bhandari, and R. Chillarege, "In-Process Evaluation for Software Inspection and Test," *IEEE Trans. Software Eng., 19*(11), 1055–1070 (1993).
27. I. Bhandari, M. Halliday, E. Tarver, D. Brown, J. Chaar, and R. Chillarege, "A Case Study of Software Process Improvement During Development," *IEEE Trans. Software Eng., 19*(12), 1157–1170 (1993).
28. I. Bhandari, M. J. Halliday, J. Chaar, R. Chillarege, K. Jones, J. S. Atkinson, C. Lepori-Costello, P. Y. Jasper, E. D. Tarver, C. C. Lewis, and M. Yonezawa, "In-Process Improvement Through Defect Data Interpretation," *IBM Syst. J., 33*(1), 182–214 (1994).

Statistical Process Control

29. V. E. Kane, *Defect Prevention: Use of Simple Statistical Tools*, Marcel Dekker, Inc., New York (1989).
30. E. R. Ott and E. G. Schilling, *Process Quality Control*, 2nd ed., McGraw-Hill, New York, 1990.
31. G. B. Wetherill and D. W. Brown, *Statistical Process Control*, Chapman & Hall, London, 1991.
32. K. Ishikawa, *Guide to Quality Control*, Asian Productivity Organization, Tokyo, 1976.
33. A. V. Feigenbaum, *Total Quality Control*, McGraw-Hill, New York, 1983.

Postmortems

34. M. J. Tiedeman, "Post-mortems – Methodology and Experiences," *IEEE J. Selected Areas Commun.*, 8(2), 176–180 (1990).

Quality Control Circles

35. K. Ishikawa, *What is Total Quality Control? The Japanese Way*, D. J. Lu (transl.), Prentice-Hall, Englewood Cliffs, NJ, 1985.
36. J. M. Juran and F. M. Gryna, Jr., *Quality Planning and Analysis*, McGraw-Hill, New York, 1980.
37. S. Watanabe, "The Japanese Quality Control Circle: Why It Works," *Int. Labour Rev.*, 130(1), 57–79 (1991).
38. I. Nonaka, "The History of the Quality Circle," *Qual. Prog.*, 26(9), 81–83 (1993).

Quality Control Circle Applications

39. B. K. Lee, "Implementing a Quality Circle Programme for Computer Professionals," *Computer Syst. Sci. Eng.*, 1(1), 65–67 (1985).
40. P. H. Ephrath, "Quality Software: A Never Ending Cycle," *Proceedings of the IEEE International Conference on Systems, Man and Cybernetics*, IEEE Service Center, Piscataway, NJ, 1990, pp. 882–883.
41. K. Fujino, "Concept of Software Factory Engineering," *NEC Res. Develop.*, No. 94, 103–119 (1989).
42. T. Hutchings, "Formal Inspections and Continuous Improvement," *Electro/92 Conference, 5*, 22–28 (1992).
43. Y. Ogawa, T. Yamazaki, and E. Teratsuji, "Software Quality Improvement Activities at Nippon Steel Corporation," *Proceedings of the Third IFAC/IFIP Workshop, Indiana, USA*, Pergamon Press, New York, 1989, pp. 21–25.

Poka-Yoke

44. S. Shingo, *Zero Quality Control: Source Inspection and the Poka-yoke System*, A. P. Dillon (transl.), Productivity Press, Stamford, CT, 1986.
45. M. P. Cassidy, "Employee Empowered Quality Improvement," in *Eleventh IEEE/CHMT International Electronics Manufacturing Technology Symposium*, September 1991, pp. 39–43.
46. J. K. Bandyopadhyay, "Poka Yokay Systems to Ensure Zero Defect Quality Manufacturing," *Int. J. Manag.*, 10(1), 29–33 (1993).

ROBERT G. MAYS

ENVIRONMENTAL VISUALIZATION: SCIENTIFIC VISUALIZATION IN ENVIRONMENTAL RESEARCH

INTRODUCTION

What Is Environmental Visualization?

Environmental visualization is part of scientific visualization or information visualization. It uses traditional visualization techniques and applies them to environmental research. The complexity of environmental data often requires understanding not only the visualization techniques but also a variety of science and engineering. The environmental samples and modeling output are often huge and their visualization needs the collaboration between visualization specialists and scientists. Often, the specialists have the scientific background to understand the datasets.

The technical basis of scientific visualization is computer visualization. Computer visualization is a form of communication that transcends application and technological boundaries. It is a tool for discovery and understanding. It is also a tool for communication and teaching (1). Computer visualization, in its simplest sense, is the process of making the invisible visible.

Computer visualization is different from traditional computer graphics. Although computer graphics plays an important role in computer visualization, other computer technologies such as multimedia production and Internet technology have also contributed to make scientific visualization and virtual reality results meaningful. The difference between visualization graphics and presentation graphics is that the latter is primarily concerned with the communication of information and results that are already understood.

Scientific visualization is a technology which helps to explore and understand scientific phenomena visually, objectively, qualitatively, and quantitatively. Scientific visualization allows scientists to see the invisible and to think the unthinkable. In scientific visualization, we are seeking to understand the data. For example, we can draw a car and display it in a nice layout. We can generate very beautiful pictures using computer graphics. After we add the scientific information (temperature, exhaust emission, or velocity field around the vehicle), then it becomes a scientific visualization product.

There are different definitions for scientific visualization in different stages of this technology and there are different definitions for different users. For environmental scientists, scientific visualization is a technology to help them to display a large multidimensional dataset, to animate the dataset, to explore the information graphically — as a means of gaining insights into the data, to convey the findings of the dataset effectively, and to support environmental decision making. For numerical modelers, scientific visualization is a graphical process analogous to numerical analysis. Scientific visualization is the key to our understanding these modeling results and leads us to the discovery of unknown aspects of the environmental phenomena. It provides us with tools and techniques that seek to promote new dimensions of insight into problems solving using current technology.

The goals of scientific visualization are to promote a deeper level of understanding of the data under investigation and to foster new insight into the underlying processes, relying on the human's powerful ability to visualize. To achieve these goals, scientific visualization utilizes aspects in the areas of computer graphics: user-interface methodology, image processing, system design, and signal processing. These formerly independent fields are brought together by the use of the analogous techniques in the different areas. Scientific visualization is an additional tool for scientific research and investigation.

History of Scientific Visualization

Scientific visualization originated from the practice of using computer graphics to support better understanding of general science. In October 1986, the Division of Advanced Computing of the National Science Foundation sponsored a meeting: Panel on Graphics, Image Processing and Workstations. Several supercomputing centers had been requesting funds to provide graphics hardware and software to scientific users, because the existing tools were not adequate to meet their needs. The Panel maintained that visualization in scientific computing is a major emerging computer-based technology needing significantly enhanced federal support. Then The Workshop on Visualization in Scientific Computing was held February 1987; it brought together researchers from academia, industry, and government research labs. The ViSC report (2) presents the findings and recommendations of the panel for a new initiative in visualization in scientific computing. The report focused on the perceived need to develop revolutionary approaches to render the tides of computer-based data comprehensible in some easy-to-grasp form. The goal of visualization is to leverage existing scientific methods by providing new scientific insight through visual methods. After the report, this process was termed scientific visualization.

Scientific visualization is a growing and changing field and has emerged as a technology in 10 years. Just several years ago, large scientific research centers responded by establishing and/or expanding groups devoted to the development of visualization methodologies and tools for an integrated understanding of very large datasets. The large dataset gives rise to problems of scale and of finding relationships between different parts of the data. By displaying multidimensional data in an easily understandable form on a two-dimensional (2D) screen, it enables insights into three-dimensional (3D) and higher-dimensional data and datasets that were not formerly possible.

Scientific visualization systems are combinations of hardware and software systems and techniques. A scientific visualization system includes hardware rendering engine, graphics kernel, graphical user interface, and visualization modules. These systems usually come with mass storage, high-speed computer network, and other components such as stereo visual glass, multidimensional freedom mouse/ space ball, and immersion gadgets.

Information visualization emerged as the result of expansion of visualization. Analog to scientific visualization, which is a relatively mature technology, information visualization uses state-of-the-art computer hardware and software to achieve a new understanding of the information data. The Internet and quickly proliferating Intranets have fueled the growth of information visualization applications.

SCIENTIFIC VISUALIZATION IN ENVIRONMENTAL RESEARCH

Environmental Visualization Is a Field

As defined by Zannetti (3), environmental modeling is a process in which environmental scientists study the environmental problems quantitatively by solving a set of mathematical equations, and then, simulate and forecast the environmental impact of such problems. Today, complex environmental models, especially when linked with 3D visualization techniques, have become a new branch of science, not just a solution method to assist scientific researchers.

Scientific visualization allows environmental researchers to plot complex masses of raw data in several dimensions over time to compare the images produced to theoretical models or simulations. By comparing field data to theoretical formulations, researchers may gain insights that confirm or refine their hypotheses – or they might discover anomalies that lead them in new directions (4). For example, environmental modelers often deal with a huge geographical-based dataset, scientific visualization allows the modelers to manage the dataset and modeling results, as well as do quality assurance to these data and results.

Scientific visualization highlights applications and application areas because it is concerned about providing leverage in these areas to enable the user to achieve more with the computing tools now available. In a number of instances, the tools and techniques of visualization have been used to analyze and display large volumes of, often time-varying, multidimensional data in such a way as to allow the user to extract significant features and results quickly and easily. Such tools benefit from the availability of modern workstations and personal computers with good performance, large amounts of memory and disk space, and with powerful graphics facilities – both in terms of range of colors available and also speed of display. This close coupling of graphics and raw computational performance is a powerful combination for those areas where visual insight is an important part of the problem-solving capability. Visualization is the interactive language uniting the scientific world.

Visualization in Environmental Research

There are many problems an environmental scientist faces, and scientific visualization has helped solve some of these problems since it emerged as a field 10 years ago. We need scientific visualization for the three reasons (5):

> **First,** most of the environmental impact is invisible, unless severe damage appears. For example, we usually cannot see the concentration of the pollutants (except in Los Angeles) quantitatively, yet everyone may "feel" if the concentration is too high. It is difficult to see things that are not visible. Scientific visualization can help the public see the invisible by matching visible colors with numbers.
>
> **Second,** environmental problems are very complex. Most of the environmental simulations or forecasts are associated with huge datasets. Scientific visualization plays an important role in the interpolation of these large multidi-

mensional datasets and cooperate with other information at different time/
space scales. A *Wall Street Journal* article reported that only a very small
portion (estimated at 5%) of NASA's satellite data had been analyzed.
There were just too many numbers to deal with that data effectively. The
article claimed that if more of the numbers had been converted to pictures,
the hole could have been detected in the ozone layer 10 years earlier (6).

Third, many environmental problems are GIS (geographical information system) based, and results make much more sense when displayed against the
corresponding geographic features. GIS provides a powerful tool for terrain
analysis: spatially distributed models are used within the context of a complex terrain and heterogeneous landscape environments represent a key link
between environmental models and GIS technology (7). The visualization of
GIS-related datasets has become one of the important aspects of scientific
visualization.

Scientific visualization makes it easier to integrate environmental models, to
disaggregate them to greater levels of spatial detail, and to reaggregate results over
politically relevant areas. The visualization of the modeling data can be used to
make striking products that carry far more weight than tables of numbers, and
the interactive nature of much of the current visualization software allows the
decision-maker to work with complex models in a comfortable, reassuring environment that does not demand a great depth of scientific understanding. Thus, environmental visualization is the essential bridge between the science and policy that will
make science more relevant and policy development more scientifically honest.

VISUALIZATION METHODOLOGY

It is impossible to cover every visualization technique of general interest—there are
simply too many. As a result, we include only traditional visualization techniques
such as line graphs, vector fields, and volume visualization. Nielson et al. (8) presents a wide variety of current applications of scientific visualization and also an
excellent bibliography of scientific papers. Frenkel (9) provides a general introduction to basic visualization techniques. Thalmann (10) cites a number of papers in the
areas of scientific visualization and graphical simulation. For detailed descriptions
including some software description, the reader may also refer to the works of
Rosenblum (11), Pickover and Tewsbury (12), and Zhang (5).

We divide the techniques into two categories: basic techniques and advanced
techniques. The so-called basic techniques are the popular methods widely used in
the environmental community in visualizing the environmental dataset; they are
considered essential. The advanced techniques may be used only occasionally by
scientists.

Basic Techniques

Zooming, Rotating and Panning

Zooming provides the ability to zoom in/out of the image, which allows the users
to look at a smaller part or a larger part of the display; rotating allows the user to
turn the object in the display to different angles, and panning moves the image in
horizontal and vertical directions.

Annotation

This provides the ability to annotate the graphical results with labels, scales, and titles. It is essential that good visualizations contain sufficient annotations for a viewer to derive appropriate information from the imagery. A colored height field or streamlines set with no supporting labeling can make perfectly beautiful, but meaningless, computer graphics. Some softwares provide more advanced annotations, like "clocks" and "meters."

Color Legend Editing

This is the capability of editing the color legend which represents the scalar value of the field, including its range (minimum, maximum) and style of the color arrangements.

Scatterplot

This category includes major areas of visualization of multivariate data, where each element of the data is considered a point in a multidimensional space. This kind of data can be visualized by projecting the data from the multidimensional space to the 2D viewing surface. The one-dimensional (1D) scatterpoint is the simplest case, where values may be marked as points on a single axis. For the 3D case, it is possible to project the points to a 2D plane and take some attribute of the marker glyph used to indicate the third component. Other techniques for higher-dimensional datasets are reviewed by Brodlie et al. (13). Figure 1 provides example of displaying point source data over Thailand.

Histogram

The basic idea of a histogram is to regroup a set of data into different subsets (acts like a form of filter on your dataset) and to indicate the number of data in each subset. The output can be plotted using bars on the histogram. The height of each histogram bar is proportional to the number of samples of original data that occur in the range covered by that bar. This technique is often used with scattered datasets. Take the example of 2D scatterplot of the intake of pollutants for individuals of different ages. The corresponding histogram can show the average intake of pollutants per day for each age group.

Bar Chart (Balls and Sticks for 1D Unstructured Data)

Given values of items in a set, a bar chart presents these values by the length of bars drawn horizontally or vertically. Often, we can add sophisticated rendering effects, with shadow effects on bars, for example. Pie charts also belong to this category. An example would be the CO concentration level in North Carolina for each year between 1970 and 1995.

Line Graph (Including Time Series)

This is one of the elementary but widely used basic visualization techniques. Given a set of data points, a line is drawn through the data points to visualize the underlying function. The traditional method can be either linear, or of higher order with cubic splines. Several graphs are often displayed on the same plot using different rendering techniques or colors to distinguish the graphs. The line styles and data-point

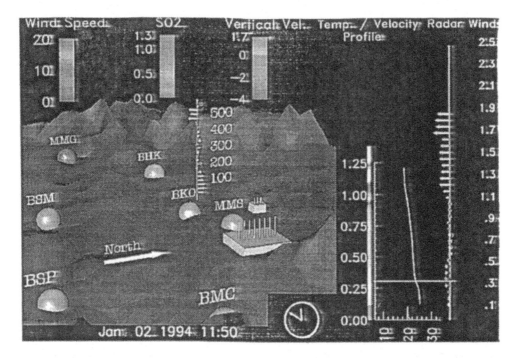

FIGURE 1   Point source data over Thailand, by Mark Bolstad, EPA Scientific Visualization Center. Software: IBM Data Explorer.

styles can also be controlled. An example would be to plot a ground-level concentration along the wind direction through the point source. Care is needed here in choosing the interpolation techniques.

Surface View (2D Surface)

A traditional alternative to contouring is to display a mesh of lines parallel to the x and y axes and lying on the underlying surface, the mesh being projected on to a 2D plane. The surface is then projected onto the display screen. Hidden lines may or may not be removed. The largest values in the field are represented by the highest peaks on the mesh, and the smallest values are represented by the lowest valleys. Alternatively, the surface can also be rendered as a solidly shaded object. As with mesh surfaces, the values in the scalar field are mapped to the heights of the surface. The surface is then shaded directly, using a standard lighting model, with the mesh optionally overlaid.

Contour Graph

Line-Based Contouring: Two-dimensional line contours represent 2D scalar fields by drawing curves representing constant-function (z) values. With most visualization software, the contour lines can be labeled with the values they represent, and attributes of the lines, such as color, thickness, and pattern, can be set. Some contouring packages allow interpolations to be applied to the contour lines or to the scalar data before it contoured. Some advantages of line contour plots in visualizing

2D scalar fields include that it is well suited to monochrome and gray-scale reproduction.

Discrete Shaded Contouring: From a set of values at points on the 2D plane, areas between two isolines are indicated by a particular style of shading. Thus, areas of constant color represent a constant range of values in the scalar field. Often, a legend is drawn next the contour plot to show what range of values each color represents. With most packages, line contours can be plotted over the shaded contours. Some advantages of shaded contour plots in visualizing 2D scalar fields are its easy detection of areas of rapid change and areas of constant value and its easy detection of minimum and maximum values.

2D Halftone Images: Two-dimensional halftone images are gray-scale images which are generated by imaging blacks dots of varying sizes on a white surface. As the dots are very tiny, the eye perceives a continuous-tone image. This is more or less the printing definition, but in computer graphics, the term halftone is used to describe a number of techniques which basically achieve the same effect as varying dots. Halftone images can be used to visualize 2D scalar fields by mapping the values in the field to gray levels in the halftone image. For the smallest value in the field is mapped to white, the largest value is mapped to black, and the values in between map linearly to the gray scale from white to black. Currently, most PostScript printers support the image PostScript operator which simply takes an array of 1-, 2-, 4-, or 8-bit values and creates the halftone image in hardware.

Colored Tile: The domain is divided into a grid of cells (typically corresponding to pixels on display), and the color of each cell represents the corresponding value of the function. This technique is often used where there is a dense grid of data (e.g., data from satellites or scanners); therefore, interpolation is rarely an issue.

Colored Mesh Contour: The color at each pixel on display can be interpolated from available data to provide a smooth contour plot or a colored mesh plot. The interpolation technique depends on the arrangement of the data points. Figure 2 is a great example of the colored tile contour describing the concentration level for different species from the Urban Airshed Model (UAM).

Isosurfaces

They display surfaces of constant value within a volume. The general approach is to apply a surface detector to the sample array and then fit geometric primitives to detect surfaces. Surfaces are then rendered by an appropriate technique.

Arrow Plots

For vector fields, it is typical to display vector data by the use of arrows. In the simplest case, a 2D vector in the plane can be visualized by 2D arrows. We may also superimpose the vector on a field rendered using shades, hue, and lightness. The difference between a 3D and a 2D vector is that the arrows can point out of or into the display surface. This is a useful method for visualizing 3D flow in a planar cross section of a volume. Scalars may also be mapped onto the vector using a different color to provide extra scale information or representation of a totally separate variable. The choice of vector type and arrowhead can affect the perceptibility of

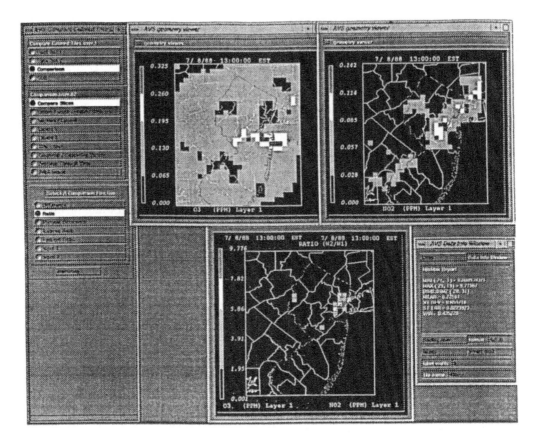

FIGURE 2   Modeled concentration level for different pollutants produced by Todd Plessel, U.S. EPA Scientific Visualization Center. Software: AVS.

the direction of the vector. Figure 3 shows the 3D vectors are displayed using isosurfaces and overlaying a satellite image.

Advanced Techniques

Bounded-Region Plot (Contour)

There are several applications where the entity to be displayed is defined over a set of regions. For example, the density of the population for different cities on a map. This type of display is known as a bounded-region plot. The value associated with the region is coded by means of contour and shading. Figure 4 displays human exposure in the Denver, CO area overlaid with the geographical information in that area.

Height Field Plot (or Height Map)

This is a visualization technique used to visualize data collected on a 2D grid. Conceptually, a height map is drawn by elevating the 2D grid into the third dimen-

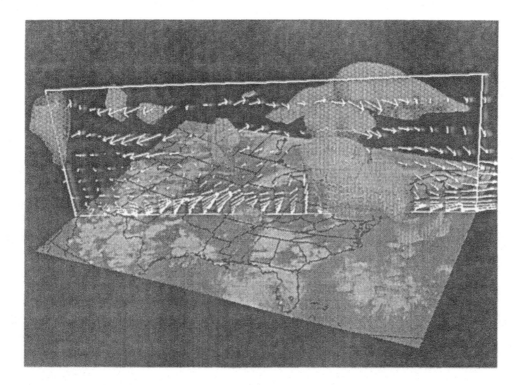

FIGURE 3   Three-dimensional vectors displayed with isosurfaces are overlaying a satellite image; software: Vis5D.

sion (*Z* direction, for example) with our original grid lying in the *X-Y* plane. The height or *Z*-value given to each vertex of the original grid is proportional to the specified scalar data value at that vertex. This is also called an elevated contour plot. The result usually looks like a map of the surface of the earth with hills and valleys. A height field plot also enables two scalar fields over a 2D domain to be displayed. An example, presenting topographic data with concentration levels which are represented by using a shaded contour on the surface is presented in Figure 5.

Volume Rendering

Color and partial opacity are assigned to each possible voxel value via classification tables (usually accessed with transfer functions). The color is usually based on the value of the voxel (or given independently for the voxel) and the gradient at the voxel; the opacity is based on how close the voxel value is to a given threshold(s) and what the gradient at the voxel is. The results of volumetric rendering can often give the impression of a cube of multicolored glass with opaque objects contained within it. This type is volumetric rendering is useful for revealing the internal structures, details, and relationships of 3D scalar fields.

Streamlines, Streaklines, and Particle Tracks (2D and 3D)

An alternative representation for vectors is to show streamlines of particle tracks (streaklines). Streamlines produce a set of lines that show the flight path of each

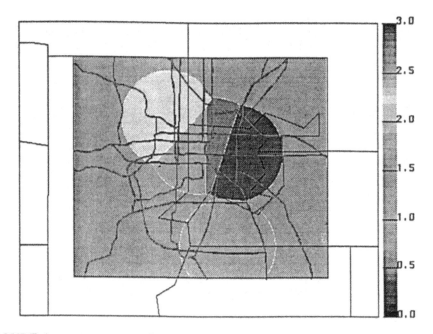

FIGURE 4   Human exposure in Denver, CO overlaid with the geographical information; software: AVS 5. [From *A VS Network News*, Imagery Gallery Edition, *3*(2) (1994).]

"ball and streamer." These are static polylines which indicate the direction of the flow in CFD, present the vortices in the field. Color may also be added to indicate the velocity of the particle at each point in the streamline. Some of the software (e.g., IBM Data Explorer) also allows one to visualize the streamlines' associated "twist" using the ribbon, curl, and flag parameters of streamline to force computation of the vorticity field.

A streakline is used to study a dynamic or unsteady vector field. The streakline is drawn by tracing the styroform balls and streamers which fly through the vector field. The direction and speed of the balls and streamers are updated as their flight is affected by the changing field; that is, at each moment, we provide new data for vector direction and intensity at each sample point. This technique is also called "particle advection" or "particle tracing." Figure 6 is an example of flow and dispersion inside street canyons using streamlines.

Vector Field Topology Plots

The critical points of the field are identified by analysis of the Jacobian matrix of the vector with respect to the position; saddle points, attracting nodes, repelling nodes, and so forth are selected. Streamlines are drawn from each appropriate critical point. The result is typically a very simple and uncrowded plot, but one from which an observer can infer the entire vector field. The length of the vector is usually proportional to the magnitude of the vector. The direction of the vector will be the direction of that point.

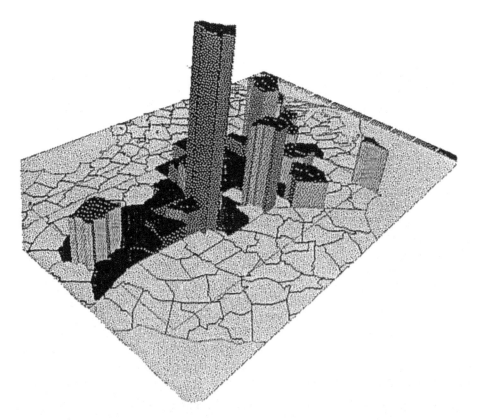

FIGURE 5   Concentration level in different counties in North Carolina. The height represents the concentration level and the color of the cylinder displays the second scalar. Produced by Jeff Wang, MCNC; software: AVS 5. [From *A VS Network News*, Imagery Gallery Edition, *3*(2) (1994).]

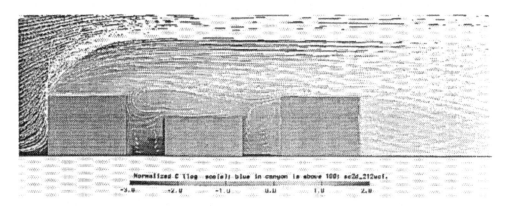

FIGURE 6   Flow and dispersion inside street canyons; streamlines overlaid with concentration field; software: AVS.

Animation

There are two basic types of animation: showing a series of steps one after another and causing an object to move or rotate or change scale in order to study it from different points of view.

Visualization Functionality

Other than the visualization techniques we discussed, some of the functionalities of the software are also very important for the end users. For example, the support of audio/video production including the capability to produce JPEG or MPEG output files. The interactivity, flexibility, and user-friendliness of the visualization systems are among the first things to check. Graphical user interface (GUI) is quite standard among visualization software. Another important functionality is called X-support (i.e., support of X11 protocol), which allows an X-server to be used. This allows the software to be distributed across a number of different platform types via the X-server. We will discuss these further in the next section.

To enhance the quality of the data, we may need to polish them using image processing techniques. We may also use other techniques, such as controlled light to objects, and mirrored and shadowed walls, to make the visualization results better looking. The readers may obtain more details in Ref. 13.

CURRENT STATUS OF USING SCIENTIFIC VISUALIZATION IN ENVIRONMENTAL RESEARCH

Scientific visualization has been able to display and analyze a large environmental dataset on all kinds of computer platforms—from supercomputers, to high-end UNIX graphic workstations, to PC and Macintosh. Advanced computer graphics technology, such as virtual buffer, volume rendering, and optimal geometric approximation, has been widely implemented on all computer platforms. There are hundreds of visualization packages available commercially or free to the environmental scientists. With the low-cost systems beginning to provide sufficient CPU memory, coupled with floating-point computing speed which placed them within an order of magnitude of contemporary "supercomputers," the slope of performance increase of workstations has been quite steep in the last several years (14).

Graphical user interface (GUI) and object-oriented user interface (OOUI) are widely implemented in many software packages. This makes software tools for visualization more user friendly and accessible to a wide variety of application areas, thus increasing their potential and usability. An interactive graphics environment has been introduced to the environmental community. Such exotic technology as virtual reality, immerse vision hamlet, vision dome, and DOOM are just beginning to be available for environmental modeling. Visual interface, the interface that uses graphics itself as a navigator (different from the GUI), has been introduced into the environmental science community to allow a better understanding of the environmental models.

The vast computer network available to environmental researchers permits them to share data and resources from the earlier stage of network development. Now, a high-speed network environment has been developed to allow data to be shared among various workstations. Therefore, scientific visualization in the environmental science field is no longer discrete and stand-alone. Parallel visualization is also emerging. Today, most of the scientific visualization work is accomplished on workstations and minicomputers, which are more cost-effective visualization tools than supercomputers. Although we have not reached the stage where every scientist or engineer owns a personal workstation, many of us do have the opportunity to access the visualization software on a wide variety of platforms.

Scientific visualization has been used more and more for supporting environmental decision making and helping environmental researchers to communicate ideas and play "what-if" game in reasonable time frame. The advanced technologies in visualization are beginning to be integrated into U.S. EPA planning and decision making with respect to any computational modeling used to derive federal policy governing environmental issues. With the help of either commercial or public-domain runtime application builders, it is no longer crucial for an environmental modeler to understand how to program computer graphics required for visualization to visualize their data.

The visualization technology has evolved from the 2D linear stage to the 3D time-series stage and is now entering to the four-dimensional (space and time) multimedia stage. Multimedia applications have become a major part of environmental scientific visualization. Audio and video capabilities have been integrated into many visualization softwares and have helped environmental researchers understand and present their modeling results.

Ecosystem visualization has emerged as a new area of environmental scientific visualization. The ecosystem visualization projects visualize modeling results, observations (e.g., satellite image, measurements, point sources, etc.), GIS data, and socioeconomic effect together to demonstrate the ecosystem activity and find the relationship among them.

The pure scientific visualization in environmental research has evolved from focusing on pure spatial data analysis to information visualization, which transforms both spatial and abstract data into visual forms.

However, there are many problems remaining in the environmental scientific visualization field. Most of the environmental researchers are doing visualization-related work on workstations. None of the visualization systems can provide all the functionally the scientists and modelers want. Also, there is a wide range of platforms being used by the scientists. Some of these platforms may not run the software. A significant percentage of people are using personal computers (PC or Macintosh) to do scientific visualization. Although we see more vendors beginning to support the personal computer environmental due to the popularity of the desktop environment, many of the sophisticated visualization software still do not support Windows or the Macintosh operating system (15). It is encouraging to see some vendors are aggressively pursuing the support of collaborative and interactive visualization via the Internet using emerging technologies like Java. Some vendors are even developing the whole visualization system using JAVA: VisAD (16) is one of the examples, whose next release will be written in Java. It is still very expensive to publish colored graphs. As a result, most of the scientific journals are not encouraging the use of color in their publications. Generating high-quality black-and-white images that summarize results for publication is still a priority for scientists. With the popularity of the electronic publishing like the CD-ROM and Web pages, we can see the days when the publication of the visualization results will not be a problem at all.

There are recent attempts through the research and development initiatives on developing a user-friendly scientific modeling framework (e.g., CAMRAQ CMS project and U.S. EPA HPCC Models-3 project). These initiatives focus on establishing the desktop visualization system, integrating GIS and remote sensing data with environmental modeling, utilizing Internet technology, and better visual interfacing for environmental management and decision making.

CONCLUSIONS—THE FUTURE OF ENVIRONMENTAL VISUALIZATION

The future of scientific visualization will depend less on the development of visualization software, and more on design, communication, and presentation. Most of the scientific visualization software already support the basic elements of scientific visualization (i.e., basic 2D and 3D graphics and animation). The developers will concentrate on better design and a more comprehensive presentation. The materials developed in a scientific visualization project are good not only for scientific research but also for education.

The advance of computer hardware has changed the fate of scientific visualization. The number of polygons rendered per second increases from a few hundred 10 years ago to tens of millions today. The main memory of the graphics workstation increase from 32 megabytes to 256 megabytes. Many restrictions have disappeared. Several years ago, the Z buffer was a lucrative technology that was claimed would never be popular because of the memory constraint; now the Z buffer is a very standard technology on graphics workstations. Ray tracing is another technology which was almost claimed not useful years ago because it was very expensive, considering the computer speed. Now, we can see ray tracing is widely used. The speed of graphics workstation makes real-time, instantaneous scientific visualization possible.

In the next few years, environmental visualization will offer more to the environmental community:

1. Large, complex scientific visualization projects targeting at integration of information. In these projects, the earth's ecosystem as a whole will be visualized via the state-of-the-art visualization hardware and software.
2. High-speed network will emerge as a crucial element of the visualization environment. With a gigabit-per-second speed network, we can visualize data as well as information.
3. Collaborative visualization projects fueled by the high-speed network will become more popular. Analog to the memory situations in the late 1980s, as soon as the bandwidth problem is resolved, most of the scientific visualization projects will be collaborative in nature.
4. Real-time, instantaneous visualization and analysis will emerge as the next technology frontier in environmental visualization. Many data will be collected, visualized, and compared with the modeling or measuring results instantaneously, then archived to the mass storage.
5. Large-scale, multidiscipline data integration will occur as a result of more interagency collaboration. These integration includes, but is not limited to, GIS–environmental modeling result integration; ecosystem activity and economic, social, and demographical movement integration; and global environmental impact (at the planetary system level) visualization.

6. Virtual reality used to be an entertainment prototype. It will play an important role in the future environmental visualization project, because many projects will aim to add educational value to the environmental modeling results. An immersed virtual environment also helps the environmental researchers to see things from the inside and do analysis in a more controllable way.

7. Multimedia visualization, a fifth-dimensional approach, will also prevail in environmental scientific visualization projects.

8. Desktop visualization becomes popular due to advances in the hardware of personal computers. More environmental scientists will be using scientific visualization in the environment familiar to them. The recent development of Internet technology, such as Web-based browsers, the JAVA programming language, and the network PC, also introduce opportunity for the scientist to use visualization software online, on demand, and on budget.

In the following decades, new projects for environmental visualization will arrive in the environmental community. Here are a few examples: visualization of ecosystem activities, airshed, watershed, and cross-media environmental models will be integrated and visualized; the economic effect on an environmental project and the economic effect of a solution; visualization of an environmental database and data structure; in contrast to the traditional 2D GUI, a multidimensional visual interface will emerge, the graphics-based visual interface for environmental models; an experimental collaborative visualization prototype will become an important part of environmental visualization.

ACKNOWLEDGMENTS

This manuscript could not be finished without the constructive suggestions and comments from Dr. Jeff Wang. Several Graphs in the manual are produced at the U.S. Environmental Protection Agency Scientific Visualization Center.

REFERENCES

1. T. A. DeFanti, M. D. Brown, and B. H. McCormick, "Visualization: Expanding Scientific and Engineering Research Opportunities," *22*(8), 12–25 (1989).

2. B. H. McCormick, T. A. DeFanti, and M. D. Brown, "Visualization in Scientific Computing," *Computer Graphics, 21*(6) (1987).

3. P. Zannetti, *Environmental Modeling I*, P. Zannetti (ed.), Computational Mechanics Publications/Elsevier Applied Science, London, 1993.

4. R. Cassidy, "Scientific Visualization: A New Computer Research Tool," *Res. Devel.*, *32*(4), 50–60 (1990).

5. Y. Q. Zhang, "Scientific Visualization in Environmental Research," in *Environmental Modeling III*, P. Zannetti (ed.), Computational Mechanics Publications/Elsevier Applied Science, London, in press.

6. C. Machover, *Proceedings at the Third International Environmental Visualization Exposition* (1995).

7. L. T. Steyert, "A Perspective of the State of Environmental Simulation Modeling," in *Environmental Modeling with GIS*, M. Goodchild, B. O. Parks, and L. T. Steyaert (eds.), Oxford University Press, Oxford, 1993.

8. G. M. Nielson, B. Shriver, and L. Rosenblum, *Visualization in Scientific Computing*, IEEE Press, New York, 1990.

9. K. A. Frenkel, "The Art and Science of Visualizing Data," *Commun. ACM*, *31*(2), 110–121 (1988).

10. D. Thalmann, *Scientific Visualization and Graphics Simulation*, John Wiley and Sons, New York, 1990.

11. L. Rosenblum, *Scientific Visualization: Advances and Challenges*, Academic Press, London, 1994.

12. C. A. Pickover and S. K. Tewsbury, *Frontiers of Scientific Visualization*, John Wiley and Sons, New York, 1994.

13. K. W. Brodlie, L. A. Carpenter, R. A. Earnshaw, J. R. Gallop, R. J. Hubbold, A. M. Mumford, C. D. Osland, and P. Quarendon, *Scientific Visualization: Techniques and Applications*, Springer-Verlag, New York, 1992.

14. N. Lincoln, "The Future of Environmental Modeling," in *Environmental Modeling I*, P. Zannetti (ed.), Computational Mechanics Publications/Elsevier Applied Science, London, 1993, pp. 513–532.

15. T. Plessel, "Implementation Plan for Models-3 Visualization Development," Report for U.S. EPA HPCC Task (1995).

16. B. Hibbard, "VisAD," http://www.ssec.wisc.edu/~billh/visad.html

YANCHING Q. ZHANG

FORMAL SOFTWARE DEVELOPMENT METHODS: AN ENGINEERING PERSPECTIVE

INTRODUCTION

In the past four decades, computers and computer software have become an important factor in our society. Many devices used in our daily lives depend for their functioning on software, and technological advances could be made through the use of software. Software technology has also become crucial to business success. Organizations depend on software for their profitability and their long-term competitive survival. At the same time, the computer field itself is rapidly changing. We have seen exponential growth over the past four decades. These changes and growth have not only changed the world we live in, but have also raised our expectations, leading to increasingly ambitious systems.

The recognition that systematically producing large-scale software systems is an engineering discipline took place at a NATO conference held in Garmisch (Germany) in 1968 (1). Initial experience in building large software systems showed that existing methods for software development were inadequate. On this occasion, the term 'Software Engineering' was first introduced, thus stressing the consensus that an approach to producing software was needed which uses engineering principles in the process of development, made up of both technical and nontechnical aspects. Software Engineering and traditional engineering disciplines share the pragmatic approach to the development and maintenance of technological artifacts. Software Engineering is not just about producing software, it also means producing software in a cost-effective way. Given unlimited resources, most software problems can probably be solved, but the challenge for the software engineer is to produce high-quality software with a finite amount of resources and on a predicted schedule.

The problems involved with the systematic production of large-scale software are numerous and hard to tackle. Many improvements have been proposed over the years, some of which have proved their value, whereas others have been silently discarded. One technique that is steadily growing in importance is the application of methods with a sound basis in mathematics, so-called *formal methods*. The link with mathematics means that formal methods have valuable properties which make the development of verified software systems possible. The global aim of this article is to increase the understanding of the role and limitations of formal methods in software development — in particular, their relationship to other (nonformal) methods, techniques, and models for software development.

Introductions to formal specifications and formal methods can be found in Refs. 2–4. See Ref. 5 for a comprehensive overview of the state of the art in formal methods. A good entry point to formal methods is the WWW virtual library formal methods page located at *http://www.comlab.ox.ac.uk/archive/formal-methods. html.*

Formal Methods

Formal methods can be described in different ways. De Roever defines formal methods as "that branch of research in the foundation of computer science which deals with modeling and reasoning about (properties of) sequential and distributed systems" (6). De Roever emphasizes in his definition the possibilities for reasoning about systems, but does not elaborate on any methodological aspects. Landwehr et al. describe a formal method as having "an effective procedure for determining whether [. . . the method has . . .] been correctly applied" (7). In this definition, emphasis is placed on checking the application of a method. No mention is made, however, of whether the effective procedure should be based on mathematics or not. Wing describes formal methods as "mathematically based techniques for describing system properties. Such formal methods provide frameworks within which people can specify, develop and verify systems in a systematic, rather than ad hoc manner" (8). According to this definition, formal methods essentially are formal systems; they provide frameworks to inspect the satisfiability of specifications, to prove the correctness of an implementation of a system, and to prove properties of systems without the need to have an executable representation of the system. In Ref. 9, Bjørner describes the notion of *method* as "a procedure with selection criteria for choosing among and using a number of techniques and tools in order to efficiently achieve the construction of a certain efficient artifact." The guidelines and principles together provide a design philosophy according to which specifications can be developed into implementations. Such a design philosophy will normally include principles which are also found in nonformal methods, like decomposition, refinement, and so forth.

Clarke and Wing capture the essential elements of formal methods, by describing them as "mathematically-based languages, techniques and tools for specifying and verifying [. . .] systems" (5). Thus, a formal method comprises one or more formal languages, techniques that use the mathematical basis, and tools that automate part of these techniques. Furthermore, formal methods are methods for the *specification* and *verified development* of software systems. Using a formal notation forces the specifier to model requirements and designs in a concise manner, leaving no room for ambiguities. It prevents inconsistent designs and enforces implicit assumptions to be made explicit. Errors, ambiguities, and incompletenesses are thus being detected at an early phase in the development process. The second key aspect of formal methods is related to the correctness of design steps in the development of a system. The mathematical basis of formal notations facilitates the application of formal verification. Specifications and design steps can be mathematically proved to have certain desired properties. Such a claim is much stronger than the level of assurance that results from the application of informal analysis techniques.

Furthermore, a formal notation provides a framework for organizing the mental process of design that can be taught and transferred. Systematic approaches are much easier to teach than those that rely on common sense without much explicit guidance. Mathematics provides a set of general concepts that can be used as building blocks in solving many different kinds of problems. Recognizing that a particular problem in software development is a special case of a familiar general structure can help to impose order and simplicity on a maze of details. This is important because conceptual complexity imposes the ultimate limits on the software systems that can be built.

Formal methods potentially enable the development of complex software (and hardware) systems at a higher level of correctness than can be reached with conventional, informal methods, without increasing the costs of software development (4,10). However, formal methods do not represent a solution for the complete development of software systems; instead, their usage is focused on particular types of system or components (e.g., safety critical systems), or particular aspects of systems. Thus, to be of practical use, formal methods have to be embedded in software development processes along with other techniques.

Formal Methods in Software Development

The recognition of the importance of formal methods is also growing outside academic circles. In the United Kingdom, for example, the use of formal methods has become obligatory for the development of safety-critical systems for the MoD (Ministry of Defence). The requirements for the development of such systems are defined in interim defence standards 00-55 (11) and 00-56 (12). Projects in which formal methods are used have been carried out or are being carried out in industry by a few companies. Some cases of great efforts in applying formal methods in industry are known. Examples are the formal specification in Z of IBM's transaction processing system CICS (13,14) and the development of a distributed fault-tolerant information-display system using VDM and CCS (15). The effective transfer of a new technology—like formal methods—into industry is a complex affair which must be handled with care. New technologies are not only required to be effective but also have to solve a perceived problem and have to be acceptable to their intended users.

Larsen (16) reports on an experiment in industry that intends to assess the effectiveness of the use of formal methods in the development of a safety-critical system. This was done by letting two groups, one using formal methods (VDM) and the other using conventional methods, develop the same application. Results confirmed those from other studies (e.g., Ref. 15) that formal methods increase the costs in the early stages of development, whereas in later stages, formal methods result in considerable cost reductions. The use of formal methods in commercial situations has been limited (17). Coleman reflects on his experience with the introduction of formal methods in industrial organizations in Ref. 18. Craigen et al. (19) provide a survey on the use and problems of formal methods in 12 applications; a summary of their findings can be found in Ref. 20. A more extensive survey is presented in Ref. 21, comprising both a literature survey as well as an analysis of questionnaires returned by 126 organizations, mainly in the United Kingdom. Hall (22) and Bowen (23) present overviews of several problems—or to be more precise, what *appear* to be problems—with the wider industrial acceptance of formal methods.

Although theoretic issues with respect to formal methods as such are being further developed at a steady pace, questions remain on the stage in the software development process during which formal methods should be applied, and on the benefits of applying formal methods for the total development process. An insufficient understanding of the relationship between the software process and formal methods hinders the actual application of formal methods for the development of "real" systems to a large extent, as argued in Refs. 5, 17, 18, and 24. It is, therefore, necessary to investigate how formal methods fit in the "software life cycle" and to analyze how formal methods can be used together with techniques and methods that are currently used in industry. Fraser et al. give a comprehensive overview of current strategies in embedding formal specification in the software production process (17).

This article highlights, in particular, formal methods for the development of complex computer systems. In the following section, first the essence of formal methods is clarified. We explain what a formal method consists of, give working definitions of the terms *formal specification* and *formal method*. We give different criteria for classification of formal methods. In the section Formal Methods: Examples, we give a summary of four widely used formal methods, VDM, Z, LARCH, and LOTOS. The section Formal Methods in Complex Computer Systems links formal methods to the engineering of complex computer systems. Here, two innovative approaches are introduced: H-ASTRAL and MTCCS. These two approaches offer constructions to specify both complex data and control structures, combined with facilities to model concurrency, real-time behavior, and continuous variables. The last section sums up our presentation and briefly looks into the future.

FORMAL METHODS

Software Specifications

Formal specifications form a class of specifications that satisfies the requirement of precise and unambiguous descriptions. Preciseness by formal specifications is achieved through the use of a mathematically defined notation for the representation of a specification, and the absence of ambiguity is achieved through the fact that the meaning of a formal specification is defined in terms of an underlying mathematical model; that is, the interpretation of such a specification is unambiguous with respect to the underlying mathematical model. The interpretation of a specification in terms of the underlying model is what is referred to as *its semantics*. This observation introduces two domains: a *specification domain* and a *semantic domain* (see Fig. 1).

Formal specification notations provide facilities to express abstraction. As such, the concept of abstraction is not fundamental for formal specifications, but, in practice, the use of abstraction techniques turns out to be almost always possible. This usage allows the specifier to express requirements or designs at a suitable level of abstraction. Hereby, a transformational model is introduced, well known in software development; systems are initially modeled by high-level abstract descriptions and are iteratively refined through a number of transformation steps to finally arrive at an implementation.

The following definition of a formal specification language can be given.

Definition 1. A *formal specification language* is a specification language with a well-defined syntax and semantics, both defined on a mathematical basis. □

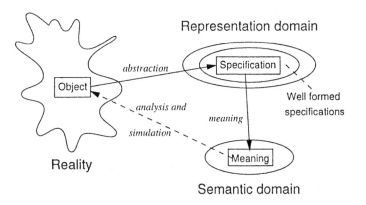

FIGURE 1   The specification domains.

The syntax of a formal specification language is usually defined by a context-free grammar. The symbols of the language can either be textual or graphical, but, usually, they are textual. The semantics usually consists of static semantics and a dynamic semantics. The static semantics defines which sentences from the language generated by the grammar are well formed. The dynamic semantics defines a mathematic interpretation of a well-formed specification in terms of an underlying semantic model.

Formal Methods

The word "method" in formal method implies that a formal method includes *techniques* to apply its mathematical basis, and guidelines to do so sytematically, along with a set of general principles. With respect to the transformational model for software development, this means that the formal method should address one or more elementary transformation steps of the total transformation process. The rigor with which this is done may differ, but in order to reason about the correctness of a single elementary transformation step, it is necessary that at least the relationship that exists between two consecutive specifications is defined; usually this relationship is called a "refinement" relationship. It is not necessary that a formal method use a single specification language in which specifications are expressed; in fact, several specification languages may be used for specifications at different stages of development.

We can now define a formal method as follows.

Definition 2. A *formal method* is a (collection of) formal specification language(s), and defines mathematically the relationships that exist between formal source and target specifications in one or more elementary transformation steps. □

A formal method should include techniques and tools that support the establishment and/or verification of the formal relations.

Classifying Formal Methods

To be able to classify formal methods, it is necessary to have a classification of formal methods. Formal methods are usually arranged in what in this article is called the *semantic foundation-based* classification.

Semantic Foundation-Based Classification

The most commonly accepted classification of formal methods is based on the semantic foundation of the formal specification languages that they use. The two main semantic approaches that can be distinguished are the *model-oriented approach* and the *property-oriented approach*; each has served as a basis for a broad class of formal methods. Also, methods exist that combine the two approaches. A comparison of the two approaches can be found in Ref. 25.

Model-Oriented Formal Methods: In a model-oriented approach, the specification language provides constructs which enable the user to specify a *model* of the system's behavior in terms of a mathematical model using abstract data structures such as sets, sequences, cartesian products, maps, and functions. The intended behavior of the system can be understood by inferring behavior from the model. The main advantage of this approach is that such models are natural for humans to understand.

Model-oriented formal methods can be further categorized as *process algebra methods* [e.g., CCS (26–28), CSP (29), ACSR (30)], *state machine methods* [e.g., ASLAN and ASTRAL (31,32), Timed and Hybrid Automata (33,34), PAISLey (35,36), Petri nets (37), and Statecharts (38–40)], or set theoretic methods [e.g., RAISE (41,42), VDM (43), Z (44), and the B-method (45)].

Property-Oriented Formal Methods: Property-oriented formal methods use formal specification languages which enable the expression of the necessary minimal constraints of the system's behavior, without prescribing an internal structure or a model of the system. This means that no specific architecture of the system is implied by the formal specification (no bias toward a particular implementation), giving the designer some freedom in the further development of the system. A disadvantage of property-oriented formal methods is that they seem to be difficult to understand for many humans.

Property-oriented formal methods fall into two subcategories: *axiomatic methods* and *algebraic methods*. Axiomatic methods are based on first-order predicate logic, which is used to state preconditions and postconditions of operations over abstract data types. Examples of such methods are Larch (46), ANNA (47,48), and EHDM (49).

Algebraic methods are based on multisorted algebras, where properties of the behavior of the specified system are related to equations over the entities of the algebra. Methods in this group based on equational logic are, for example, Clear (50,51), ASF (52), and ACT ONE (53). Property-oriented methods based on temporal logic include Temporal Logic (54), TLA (55), and ProCos (56). Property-oriented methods based on higher-order logic include EVES (10,57), HOL (58), and OBJ3 (59). A well-known hybrid method is LOTOS (60,61), which is based on a combination of different semantic concepts: It combines a process algebra approach with an equational logic approach. The latter is used to define the data aspects of systems.

Application-Based Classification

Another classification of formal methods can be made by examining the application domain; languages are usually focused on certain types of systems. One category consists of methods focused on the modeling of *sequential* systems. Formalisms associated with these methods often employ powerful structures like sets, maps, relations, and functions to model data and operations on data. Examples are set-theoretic methods like VDM, Z, and Larch.

When modeling parallel and distributed systems, other formalisms are needed. Most formalisms for *concurrent* systems are focused on modeling processes *and* their interactions. They usually do not model data or only model data through primitive structures flike integers. Formalisms that fall into this category are process algebras, state machine formalisms, Petri nets, statecharts, and algebraic formalisms. Some approaches combine the modeling of concurrency with the modeling of more complex data structures, like LOTOS and MTCCS.

If quantitative time plays a role in modeling systems, *real-time* formalisms are needed. These formalisms allow the modeling of events in time; not only is their ordering of importance but also their distance in time. Examples are timed and hybrid automata, ET-LOTOS (62), ACSR, ASTRAL, and MTCCS.

One type of systems for which formal methods are of great importance are complex, embedded systems. Embedded software systems are software systems incorporated in physical devices like flight control systems or televisions. To model these systems accurately, it is often necessary also to model their environment, which is usually of a continuous nature. Therefore, *hybrid system* specification languages are needed, which are capable of modeling — besides the discrete software component — the continuous physical environment. Examples are hybrid automata and Hybrid ASTRAL.

Verification Approaches

Two fundamental techniques to verification of software systems can be discerned:

Deductive verification (theorem proving): Proving correctness statements by formal reasoning in some logic (deduction), applying axioms and interference rules provided by that logic. Typically, one proves the correctness of a formula $f \Rightarrow g$, where f is a formula representing a model and g is a formula representing a more abstract model or a property. Examples are HOL (58), NQTHM (63), PVS (64), and Z-EVES (65).

Algorithmic verification (model checking): Proving correctness statements by algorithmically evaluating the state space of the system under consideration. The problem to be solved is how to make the state-space evaluation sufficiently efficient to allow interesting properties to be proved. Model-checking approaches usually combine a model-oriented approach with a property-oriented approach. Abstract properties are described in some form of temporal logic, whereas more concrete systems are specified in some operational language. To make verification possible, the semantics of the two formalisms have to relate to the same underlying model. Important representatives are SMV (66), SPIN (67), and model checking for timed/hybrid automata (68,69). See Ref. 5 for a comprehensive overview.

When comparing the two techniques, each has particular advantages over the other. In some cases, theorem proving allows verification of quite complex models. A great disadvantage, however, is that this kind of verification involves a great deal of human interaction. Although it is often possible (and necessary) to automatically check a (handwritten) proof, the actual generation of such a proof is usually too complex to be automated. Furthermore, the user involvement is often of a very complex and time-consuming nature and requires extensive specific knowledge of the user. Model checking, on the other hand, can often be fully automated, allowing fast and user-independent verification. The disadvantage here is that the complexity of the verification problems that can be handled is limited due to the explosion in the size of the state space.

A promising approach is the combination of model-checking and theorem-proving techniques, as these techniques are, to a great extent, complementary to another. One approach is to use a model-checker as an automatic decision procedure within a theorem-prover (70), whereas other approaches use theorem-provers as the supporting tool in the application of model-checking techniques (e.g., for the formalization of abstractions needed to make model checking feasible) (71). When considering the complexity of software systems that are built nowadays, it seems that truly useful verification tools should fully integrate both verification approaches. The model-checking aspect is needed to cope with the complex interactions and control structures, whereas theorem proving is indispensable in dealing with complex data structures.

FORMAL METHODS: EXAMPLES

This chapter gives an introduction into four much used formal methods: VDM, Z, Larch, and LOTOS. These methods are currently the most general methods that are adopted by the software industry. The section is not meant as a comprehensive overview but intends to introduce the reader to some concrete examples of representative formal methods.

The Vienna Development Method

The Vienna Development Method (VDM) is a formal specification method based on the model-oriented paradigm. Its semantics are based on the denotational semantics approach and a three-valued logic, called the Logic of Partial Functions [LPF (43)]. In this section, we will give a summary of its characteristics.

History

"VDM" is a generic term because several VDM "dialects" exist. The development of VDM started in 1970, when a group formed by Heinz Zemanek worked on formal language definition and compiler design in the IBM laboratory in Vienna. They built on ideas of Elgot, Landin, and McCarthy to create an operational semantics approach capable of defining the whole of PL/I, including the parallel features of the language. For this purpose, they used a meta-language which was called *Vienna Definition Language* (VDL). The approach taken was successful, but it also showed that operational semantics could complicate formal reasoning in an unnecessary way. A new approach was taken, called *denotational semantics*, in late 1972. A PL/ I compiler was designed uisng a meta-language called Meta-IV. Due to external reasons, the compiler was never finished, but the formal definition of PL/I in a denotational style is generally seen as the birth of VDM.

The diversion of the IBM group to handle more practical problems led to its dissolution. From then on, further development mainly took place at two locations: in Lyngby, Denmark (Prof. Dines Bjørner) and in Manchester, United Kingdom (Prof. Cliff B. Jones). The Danish VDM research has concentrated on systems software specifications, which has led *inter alia* to a complete formal definition of the Ada language, whereas the English research has mainly concentrated on algorithm and data structure refinement. VDM's proof obligations are one of the major results of the latter research. Thus, the main reason for the existence of different VDM dialects is the different areas of application for which VDM can be used. Unfortunately, such a diversion does not stimulate industrial acceptance of VDM. Therefore, in 1986, work started on the establishment of a standard version of VDM'S formal specification language: VDM-SL.

The standardization effort was initiated by the British Standards Institution (BSI), establishing a Panel (BSI IST/5/-/50 until 1990; since then, BSI IST/5/-/19) whose membership was also open to members from foreign organizations. In 1990, the need for a VDM-SL standard was also recognized by ISO/IEC JTC1* by accepting a new work item. A Working Group (WG19) was formed by SC22. Two of the authors of this article were active members of SC22/WG19, relevant publications are Refs. 72–74. In 1993, the draft standard for VDM-SL was completed (75).

The Language

VDM is a model-oriented formal method based on denotational semantics, intended to support stepwise refinement of abstract models into concrete implementations. The method includes a formal specification language, VDM-SL, which supports various forms of abstraction.

Representational abstraction is supported through data-modeling facilities. These facilities are based on six mathematical data-structuring mechanisms: sets, sequences, maps, composite types, cartesian products, and unions. At a lower level, the language provides various numeric types, booleans, tokens, and enumeration types. By using the data-structuring mechanism and the basic data types, compound data types can be formed; in VDM, they are denoted by the term *domains*. Domains form in general infinite classes of objects with a specific mathematical structure. Subtyping is supported by attaching invariants to domain definitions.

A VDM specification typically consists of a state description (possibly augmented with invariant and initialization predicates), a collection of type definitions (possibly augmented with invariants), a collection of constant definitions, a collection of operations, and a collection of functions.

Operational abstraction is supported by both functional abstraction and relational abstraction, the first by means of (fully referentially transparent) function

---

*Joint Technical Committee 1 of the International Standards Organization and the International Electrotechnical Commission.

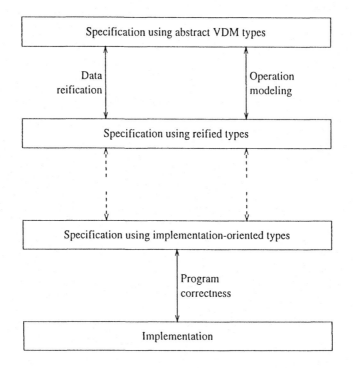

FIGURE 2   VDM development paradigm.

specification and the second by operation specification. Both functions and operations may be specified *implicitly* using *preconditions* and *postconditions*, or *explicitly* using *applicative* constructs (expressions) to specify functions and *imperative* constructs (statements) to specify operations. Operations have direct access to a collection of global objects: the *state* of the specification. The state is specified as a composite type consisting of labeled components.

Methodological Aspects

The VDM development paradigm (Fig. 2) matches the transformational model for software development. An initial VDM specification should be as abstract as possible. Two techniques are available for the development of an initial specification: *data reification*, which addresses lowering the level of abstraction of data types, and *operation modeling*, which addresses the development of VDM functions and operations.

Data reification involves the transition from abstract to concrete data types and the justification of the transition. Choosing a more concrete data model implies a redefinition of all operations and functions on the original model in terms of the new model, a process called *operation modeling*. Central to data reification is the notion of adequacy, expressed through two functions on the abstract and concrete domains: the *abstraction* function and the *retrieve* function. The abstraction function maps abstract values upon concrete values; the retrieve function does the opposite, mapping concrete values onto abstract ones.

The introduction of representation details in the specification forces operations and functions to become more algorithmic (and hence more concrete). The final step within the development is the transition of a low-level specification into the programming language of choice. This process is supported by the operation decomposition rules for VDM-SL constructs. These rules render the possibility of a constructive mapping of VDM-SL constructs into programming language constructs.

Several tools are available for VDM. One of them is the IFAD VDM-SL toolbox (76), which offers syntax and static semantics checking, test facilities, and C + + code generation. This toolbox is much used in industry and follows a pragmatic approach to formal methods. For truly formal development in VDM, the mural system (77) is available which supports formal reasoning about VDM specifications.

For an extensive overview of the use of VDM and its formal specification language VDM-SL we refer to textbooks such as Refs. 43 and 78–81.

Variants

A number of extensions of VDM were defined and several other formal specification languages were inspired by VDM. VDM + + (82) is an object-oriented extension of VDM. It allows the modeling of both concurrency aspects as well as real-time aspects of systems. VVSL (83) is a language that facilitates the construction of structured VDM-SL specifications. It extends VDM-SL through the introduction of modularization constructs and constructs for dealing with processes acting on a shared state.

The RAISE specification language (RSL) (41), the specification language of the RAISE method (84) was derived from VDM-SL. Added were facilities to express modularity, concurrency, and alternative specification styles. It is a broad-spectrum language; for example, data can not only be expressed in a model-oriented style but also in an algebraic property-oriented style. Furthermore, concurrency can be expressed in process-algebraic style (based on CSP).

Z

Z is a formal specification notation based on set theory and first-order predicate logic. Its semantics are based on two-valued logic (VDM, for instance, is based on three-valued logics) and set theory.

History

Z has been developed at the Programming Research Group at the Oxford University Computing Laboratory and elsewhere since the late 1970s. Currently, Z is subject to international ISO standardization.

The Z Methodology

In Z, a specification is split into schemas. A Z schema is a mixed graphical and textual representation. Each schema can be linked with a commentary which informally explains the significance of the formal mathematics used in the schema. In Z, schemas describe both static and dynamic aspects of a system. The static aspects consists of the states a system can occupy and the invariant relationships that are maintained as the system moves from state to state. The dynamic aspects include the possible operations, the relationship between their inputs and outputs, and the changes of state that may occur.

Each schema consists of two parts and a line separating them. The part above the central dividing line is called the declaration part; the part below is called the predicate part. In the declaration part, all variables of the schema are declared. If a variable is not declared in the declaration part of a schema, the predicate part of the same schema may not refer to that variable. The predicate part of a schema gives the relationship between the values of the variables, declared in the declaration part. It is possible to specify operations, which can only be performed if a certain condition is met. These operations are specified with a schema in which that condition is stated as a precondition right below the central dividing line. If the precondition is satisfied, the following lines state the result of the operation. Figure 3 presents the *square root* schema as an example. This schema has two variables, in? and out!, and a precondition for narrowing the set of acceptable input values. The final line of the schema gives the relationship between the variables.

To specify greater systems, several simple schemas can be combined into a single greater schema. This combining or composing can be done by taking the conjunction or disjunction of the smaller schemas. Another way to specify greater systems is to abstract from unimportant details in the beginning and focus on the big picture. Later, the resulting abstract, high-level schemas can be refined into more concrete schmeas by data refinement and the addition of details.

Tools

There are a number of tools, both commercial and noncommercial, available to support the Z notation. Most of these tools provide assistance in formatting, editing, or typechecking Z specifications. Furthermore, there are some analysis tools available, such as Z-EVES, Nitpick, Zola, and ProofPower. These analysis tools help in analyzing Z specifications and proving simple conjectures. References to these tools can be found on the WWW Virtual Library: The Z notation is located at *http://www.comlab.ox.ac.uk/archive/z.html.*

Variants

Several object-oriented extensions to or versions of Z have been developed over the years; among them, ZERO, MooZ, Object-Z, OOZE, Z++, and ZEST. Stepney (85) is a collection of papers and presents object-oriented approaches of Z (including those mentioned above), together with a specification of the same two examples in each approach.

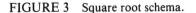

in?, out! $\in \mathbb{R}$

in? ≥ 0

out! $= \sqrt{in?}$

FIGURE 3   Square root schema.

Z++ originated in 1989 within the European ESPRIT project "REDO." Z++ extends the Z specification notation with a class construct and mechanisms for specifying concurrency and real-time behavior via real-time logic (RTL). It has a semantics defined via logical theories in a hybrid form of RTL and temporal logic and an associated development method utilizing OMT (86).

LARCH

Larch is geared toward specifying program modules (as if defining abstract data types) to be implemented in particular programming languages. Predicate-oriented *interface languages* are used to describe the intended behavior of procedures and abstractions are formulated in the *Shared Language*.

History

The Larch Project at MIT's Laboratory for Computer Science and DEC's Systems Research Center is the continuation of collaborative research into the uses of formal specification that started with the work reported in Ref. 87. In 1975, the Ph.D. thesis of Guttag showed that all computable functions over an abstract data type could be defined algebraically using equations of a simple form. It also considered the question of adequacy of such a specification. The essence of the two-tiered style of specfication of Larch evolved in 1980. A description of an early version of the Larch Shared Language was published in 1983, and by 1985, a reasonable comprehensive description of Larch, "Larch in Five Easy Pieces" (88), was published. Early in 1990, tools supporting Larch were becoming available and they were used to check and reason about specifications. A book about Larch, *Larch: Languages and Tools for Formal Specification* (46) appeared in 1993.

The Larch Project

The project is developing both a family of specification languages and a set of tools to support their use, including language-sensitive editors and semantic checkers based on a powerful theorem-prover.

The Larch Project is based on a two-tiered approach to specification. Each Larch specification has components written in two languages, a Larch interface language and the Larch Shared Language (LSL). A Larch interface language is designed for each specific programming language and used to specify program components. Each interface specification should provide the information needed to write programs that use the specified component.

Interface languages are used to specify the interfaces between program components. Subtle differences arise from the various parameter-passing and storage-allocation mechanisms used by different languages.

Interface specifications rely on definitions from auxiliary specifications, written in LSL, to provide semantics for the primitive terms they use. Specifiers are not limited to a fixed set of notations but use LSL to define specialized vocabularies suitable for particular interface specifications or classes of specifications.

Larch Shared Language is used to define terms used in interface specifications and generates theories independent of any programming language. It uses equations to define relations among operators, giving meaning to the notion of equality between terms that appear in interface specifications.

The Larch Project is influenced by the following four considerations:

- Scale: In order to write large specifications, it is important that the Larch languages are readable and that the incremental construction of such specifications is possible. Furthermore, it is essential that large specifications can be composed from small ones, that can be understood separately.
- Tools: The writing of specifications is an error-prone process. Therefore, it is important to do a substantial amount of checking on the specifications themselves. An important aspect of this approach is the use of a powerful theorem-prover for semantic checking to supplement the syntactic checking.
- Language dependencies: The environment in which a program component is embedded is likely to depend on the semantic primitives of the programming language. Any attempt to disguise this dependence will make specifications more obscure. On the other hand, many of the important abstractions in most specifications can be defined independently of any programming language.
- Reusability: A repository of reusable specification components that have evolved to handle the common cases well is needed to stop inventing the wheel time and time again.

The basic unit of specification of the LSL is the trait. A trait introduces operators and specifies their properties. Sometimes, the collection of operators corresponds to an abstract data type. Frequently, however, it is useful to define properties that do not fully characterize a type. Figure 4 presents the associative trait as an example. In this figure, the infix symbol #∘# is used to denote a generic binary operator and T denotes a generic type.

A specification of an abstract data type in a Larch Interface Language consists of three parts: (i) a header giving the type name and the names of the externally visible routines, (ii) an associated trait and a mapping from the types in the data abstraction to sorts in the trait, and (iii) interface specifications for each routine (procedure or function) of the type. A specification of a routine has three parts: (i) a header giving the name of the routine, and the names and types of its formals (parameters and returned values), (ii) an associated trait providing the theory of the operators that appear in the body, and (iii) a body stating requirements on the routine's parameters and specifying the effects the routine must have when those requirements are met.

Associative: trait

$$introduces \ \#\circ\#: T, T \rightarrow T$$

$$asserts \ for \ all \ [\ x,y,z: T]$$

$$(x \circ y) \circ z = x \circ (y \circ z)$$

FIGURE 4   The Larch associative trait.

Tools

The first tools supporting Larch started to become available in the spring of 1990. These tools were used to check and reason about specifications. Currently, the Larch toolset consists of the following three tools: the Larch Prover, the LSL checker, and LCLint checker.

The Larch Prover, LP, is an interactive theorem-proving system for multi-sorted first-order logic. It is used to reason about circuit design, concurrent algorithms, hardware, and software. LP is intended to assist users in finding and correcting flaws in conjectures (the predominant activity in the early stages of the design process).

The LSL checker checks for syntax and type errors in LSL specifications. It can also be used to generate two input files for the Larch Prover. The first file contains an LP axiomatization for an LSL specification. The second contains the proof obligations associated with logical claims made by specifiers about the logical properties of their specifications.

LCLint is a tool for statically checking C programs. When annotations are added to programs, LCLint can perform stronger checks, which may reveal a number of problems, such as memory management errors and dangerous data sharing or unexpected aliasing.

LOTOS

LOTOS is a formal specification language that combines a model-oriented semantics with a property-oriented semantics. Processes and their interactions are defined in a process-algebraic manner, and data aspects are defined through abstract-data-type specifications using equational logic. This section briefly discusses the LOTOS specification language.

History

LOTOS was developed within the International Organization for Standardization (ISO) from 1981 until 1986. Its development was triggered by the need for a Formal Description Technique (FDT) for the exact specification of protocols and services of the Open Systems Interconnection (OSI) architecture. The language however, is sufficiently general to be useful for the description of distributed and concurrent systems. In 1987, the language was complete; in 1989, it became an International Standard (61).

The Language

LOTOS is founded on a merging of two different modeling formalisms – one for the control part and one for the data part. The control part is defined by a process-algebraic formalism that is mostly based on CCS (28) and has some features of CSP (29). The data part is based on ACT ONE (53), an abstract-data-type formalism based on equational specification.

The (control) state of a process is represented by a behavior expression. A behavior expression describes which actions can be performed next. By performing an action, a behavior expression is transformed into a new behavior expression defining the subsequent behavior. An action is either an internal action or an action that needs synchronization with another process or the (non-LOTOS) environment.

For example, a behavior expression (a; B) represents a process that can perform an action a and subsequently evolve into the behavior expression B. Besides the action prefix operator, other operators are defined that express for example choices, interrupts, and the parallel composition of processes. Consider, for example, the behavior expression a; A [] b; B, which models a process that can either synchronize on event a and then become A, or synchronize on b and then become B. The actual choice is determined by the behavior of the environment of the process. The communication model of LOTOS is derived from that of CSP and is based on multiway synchronization. Interactions are instantaneous events, in which two or more processes synchronize. Interaction points are specified by means of gates.

Parallelism is expressed by parallel composition operators though which one explicitly defines at which gates the component processes have to synchronize. For example, $a!3$; A $|[a]|$ $a?x$; $B(x)$ defines two processes synchronizing through gate a. After synchronizing, the system evolves to A $|[a]|$ $B(3)$ in which x is bound to 3 in B.

Basic LOTOS (i.e., LOTOS without data modeling facilities) is completely defined by this operational semantics. Full LOTOS extends basic LOTOS through the introduction of data types and values which can be used in interactions. The data component of LOTOS is defined by an abstract-data-type specification language (ACT ONE), in which data elements are specified by only defining its essential properties, without assuming any concrete representation.

Methodological Aspects

The fact that LOTOS is a broad-spectrum specification language allows for different *specification styles*. For example, the constraint-oriented style defines a system as a combination of different constraints, each of which is concerned with a different aspect of the system. These constraints are integrated using a parallel composition operator. The resource-oriented style, on the other hand, decomposes a system according functional units that reflect design decisions. The constraint-oriented style is very useful for defining requirements of systems, whereas the resource-oriented style is typically used in the implementation of a design.

LOTOS can thus be used in many stages of the software design process. Numerous tools and techniques have been developed for the support of the design phases. Tools exist of verification, simulation, prototyping, formal transformation code generation, syntax and static semantics checking, test generation, and more. The European ESPRIT II "lotosphere" project was aimed at arriving at a design methodology based on LOTOS. The result was the Lotosphere Design Methodology together with an integrated tool environment (89).

In the past years, work has been done on extending LOTOS with capabilities to describe real-time behavior (62). Currently, work is in progress within ISO/IEC to construct an enhanced LOTOS version in which, among other things, the modeling of time is introduced and the data model is revised (90).

More elaborate information on LOTOS can be found in Refs. 61 and 91.

FORMAL METHODS IN COMPLEX COMPUTER SYSTEMS

One important application area of formal method is the development of complex software systems. These systems are typically concurrent and distributed and often have real-time properties. An important class of complex software systems is that of *embedded systems*: software systems incorporated in a physical environment with which they interact. These *reactive* systems require modeling notations that are different from traditional sequential ones. All those systems introduce an additional source of complexity; to reliably analyze these systems, one often also has to model its environment. Furthermore, for certain type of systems (like process control systems), this environment is of a *continuous nature*, resulting in systems that are built from both discrete and continuous components. Such systems are called *hybrid systems*. Modeling notations for hybrid systems require constructions that can deal with discrete as well as continuous aspects.

Many of these systems are also *safety-critical* systems, meaning that failures of these systems could lead to human loss or huge economic or environmental costs. In the development of these systems, a high degree of correctness needs to be guaranteed. Together with the earlier described complex nature of these systems which introduces many sources of potential errors, this poses a challenge to this particular area of software engineering. Formal methods are therefore well suited for the development of these systems. Specification and verification technologies are needed that can effectively deal with the above-mentioned aspect of these systems.

First, we give a short introduction to hybrid systems. The remainder of the section is devoted to two formal methods *under development* that are aimed at the description of complex safety-critical software systems. First, we will discuss ASTRAL, a formal specification language aimed at describing real-time systems, and Hybrid ASTRAL, an extension that allows the modeling of hybrid systems. The second method, MTCCS, is focused at building system models in which not only process structure and timing is relevant but also complex data structures need to be modeled in an effective way.

Hybrid Systems

Hybrid systems are systems, which combine discrete and continuous components. The discrete components are used to describe the behavior of the software, and the continuous components are used to model the behavior of the environment. Depending on the method used to model the environment, hybrid system specification notations can be divided into two subclasses: timed automata and hybrid automata.

The basic building block of hybrid system specifications is the finite state machine. A finite state machine consists of vertices, edges, and real-numbered variables. The vertices, also called locations, represent the control state of the system and are connected to each other by edges, also called transitions. These transitions consist of a guard and a set of events. The guard is a predicate on the variables of the system, and when it is enabled, the corresponding transition may execute. The set of events consists of assignments to the variables, which are performed when the associated transition is performed. The behavior of a finite state machine can be characterized by a (possible infinite) sequence of visited locations and executed transitions.

Timed automata extend this basic model by adding a special kind of variable, so-called clocks. Clocks change their values continuously with a rate equal to one and can only be reset to zero by transitons. This addition of clocks to finite state machines changes the way in which the behavior of the system is described. It is, for instance, possible to spend a certain amount in a location, before executing a transition. The time spent in a location can be restricted by the addition of a location invariant. This location invariant is a predicate over the clocks of the system and has to be satisfied when the system is in this particular location. The behavior of a timed automata can be characterized by a sequence of visited locations, time spent in those locations, and executed transitions. More about timed automata can be found in Ref. 33.

Hybrid automata can be subdivided into linear and nonlinear hybrid automata. Linear hybrid automata extend timed automata by allowing clocks to run at a constant rate. This results in piecewise linear relation between time and the value of a continuous variable. This linearity has several advantages, which can be exploited in the verification of the automata. Nonlinear hybrid automata extend linear hybrid automata by allowing nonconstant rates. Hybrid systems also have a connection to the description of dynamic behavior by differential equations in control theory. In Ref. 34, Henzinger presents an overview of the current state of hybrid automata.

Example

Figure 5 presents the hybrid automata of a water-level controller. In this hybrid automata, the variable x represents the height of the water level and x' is the derivative of x. Initially, the water level equals MIN and rises until it reaches MAX. When the water level equals MAX, it cannot rise without violating the location invariant and it has to take the transition to the right location, where the water level will decrease.

ASTRAL and Hybrid ASTRAL

History

The formal specification language ASTRAL (32,92) has been developed by Ghezzi and Kemmerer at the Politecnico di Milano and the University of California at Santa Barbara. It is based on ASLAN (93) and RT-ASLAN (31) and was given formal semantics by a translation into TRIO (94,95), a logic language developed for the specification of real-time systems.

ASTRAL Specification Language

An ASTRAL specification consists of a **global** specification and a collection of **process type** specifications. In the global specification, (new) types may be intro-

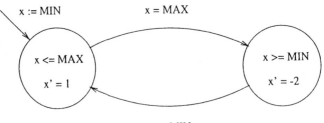

FIGURE 5   Water-level controller.

duced and global constants may be declared. A process type may have multiple process instances, the number of which is specified in the global specification. It is assumed that each process instance executes on its own dedicated processor and has enough memory to complete its task (maximal parallelism).

The process-type specification consists of a **state** specification and the specification of a set of **transitions**, which may transform that state. The state of a process-type specification consists of a **variable** clause, in which variables of that process type may be declared, and a **constant** clause, in which constants of that process type may be declared. Furthermore, these variables and constants may be exported to other processes by including them in the **export** clause. These other processes may import exported variables and constants by including them in their **import** clause. This is the only means of communication between ASTRAL processes. The initial state of a process is described in its **initial** clause.

A transition consists of an **entry** clause and an **exit** clause and has a certain **duration**. The **entry** clause may refer to variables and constants, declared in the variable and constant clauses of its process type and to the variables and constants, which are included in the import clause of its process type. It describes in which part of the state space its corresponding transition is enabled. If a transition is enabled and no other transition of the same process is executing, it has to start executing immediately (maximal progress).

The result of a transition is described by its **exit** clause. The exit clause may refer to variables and constants, declared in the variable and constant clauses of its process type and to variables and constants, which are included in the import clause of its process type. However, it can only change the values of the local variables; but in order to describe that change, it may use the values that imported variables had at the start of the transition. During the execution of a transition the values of the local variables remain the same, but their value may change at the completion of a transition, depending on that transition. So, when a process inquires about the value of variables of another process during the execution of a transition, it gets the values which those variables had at the start of the execution of that transition. At the end of a transition, the corresponding process broadcasts the values of its exported variables to all interested processes. It is assumed that this communication is performed instantly (instantaneous broadcast mechanism).

The **duration** of a transition is indicated by a constant number. This constant must have been declared in the constant clause of the corresponding process type or included in the import clause of that process type. Note that durations may not be equal to zero, as this would lead to an inconsistent space state (e.g., one variable could have multiple values at the same time).

One of the advantages of ASTRAL over other specification languages is the possibility to explicitly state properties of an ASTRAL specification in the same specification. Such properties can be divided into global properties, which involve variables of multiple process types, and local properties, which only involve variables of a single process type. The global properties are stated in the global part of the specification, and the local properties are stated in their corresponding process type. More specific, ASTRAL has the following kinds of properties:

- **Invariants**, which have to hold in every reachable state
- **Constraints**, which restrict the possible state changes
- **Schedules**, which express temporal relations between transitions

Constraints and invariants always have to be proved correct. A number of proof rules to prove invariants and constraints of ASTRAL specifications are presented in Ref. 96. The duration of transitions influences the behavior of a specification. However, time may also be referred to in entry and exit clauses of transitions and in local and global properties of specifications. The current time is available in ASTRAL by the special variable **now**, which represents an external global clock. Furthermore, ASTRAL provides the specification functions **Start** and **End**, which can be used to refer to the starts and endings of transitions, which occurs frequently in the schedule clauses. The specification function **past** can be used to refer to the values of variables in the past. For instance, **past**(*var*, *t*) refers to the value of variable *var* at time instant *t*, only if *t* is smaller than or equal to the current time.

Hybrid ASTRAL

Hybrid ASTRAL (H-ASTRAL) is an extension of the formal specification language ASTRAL. It extends ASTRAL with variables which may change continuously instead of at discrete points in time like the variables of ASTRAL. The value of these continuous variables can be given as a function of time. As the time model used in ASTRAL is dense, within a finite time interval these continuous variables may have an infinite number of different valuations. Discrete variables, variables of ASTRAL, always have a finite number of different values during a finite time interval.

This extension to ASTRAL was defined in order to model a particular kind of control system specification, the so-called block diagrams, from the domain of control engineering. These block diagrams can be interpreted as differential equations about relevant behavior of the environment. In a joint project between the control engineering lab and the software engineering lab, we tried to close the gap between control engineering and software engineering in the development of real-time control systems. This has resulted in an integrated development method (97). H-ASTRAL has been chosen as the formal specification language of this development method.

In H-ASTRAL, a new kind of process type is added. This new kind of process type has a **relation** clause, in which the behavior of continuous variables is described. Furthermore, transitions are absent. As there are no transitions, there is no need for the constraint, invariant, and schedule clauses. As the behavior of the continuous variables is influenced by the values of imported variables from other, discrete processes, local invariants which refer only to local variables and constants cannot be formulated. Furthermore, the absence of transitions eliminates the constraint clause, as continuous variables do not change at discrete points in time, which is essential to constraints. Instead, continuous variables may change at any point in time and properties concerning their value are stated in the global specification. As schedules express temporal relations between the executions of transitions, they are also not needed in continuous process types. The initial value of the continuous variables can be stated in an initial clause, but they must comply with the initial value of **now** and with the initial clauses of the process types of the imported discrete variables.

It is assumed that every variable declared in a continuous process type is a continuous variable. The value of these continuous variables is expressed by a function and depends on the time and possibly on imported discrete variables and constants. Assertions about the value of continuous variables can be placed in the invariant clause of the global specification. The new process type still has the import, export, constant, and variable clauses. The **import** clause is used to import the discrete controller variables, which influence the behavior of the continuous variables. The **export** clause exports the continuous variables to other processes, which may start transitions depending on the value of continuous variables. The **constant** clause declares constants, which are needed to describe the behavior of the continuous variables of the process type and the **variable** clause lists the continuous variables of the process type.

Example

Consider a water-level control system, which consists of a controller and a water tank. The controller is required to regulate the water level in the tank such that it is always within some minimum and maximum level.

Only two different control actions are possible: either (i) the inflow of water is disabled while the outflow of water is enabled, or (ii) the outflow of water is disabled while the inflow of water is enabled.

In the specification of this problem, the following assumptions have been made:

- The availability of a precise mathematical model of the water level (when either rising or falling)
- The existence of sensory device, capable of continuously monitoring the current water level

The resulting specification in Hybrid ASTRAL is shown below. In this specification, r represents the rate of water inflow, h represents the current height of the water level, h_0 represents the height of the water level when the last transition was completed, which is represented by the variable *last_change*. Note that primed variables in the exit clauses of transitions refer to the values of those variables at the start of the corresponding transition.

```
GLOBAL SPECIFICATION Water_Level_Control_System
CONSTANT
    MIN = 2;
    MAX = 10;
TYPE
    Control_Val = { -1, 1};
IMPORT h;
EXPORT MIN, MAX, Control_Val;
PROCESSES
    tank      : Water_Tank;
    wlcontrol: Controller;
INVARIANT
    1 ≤ h ∧ h ≤ 12
END GLOBAL SPECIFICATION

PROCESS Controller
IMPORT Control_Val, MIN, MAX, h;
EXPORT r;
```

```
CONSTANT
    T__o,T__i;
VARIABLES
    r              : Control__Val;
    h__0           : Real;
    last__change: Real;
INITIAL
    r = 1 ∧ last__change = 0 ∧ h__0 = MIN
TRANSITION Outlet      T__o
ENTRY
    h ≥ MAX ∧ r = 1
EXIT
    r = −1 ∧ h__0 = h′ + T__o
    ∧ last__change = now′ + T__o
TRANSITION Inlet       T__i
ENTRY
    h ≤ MIN ∧ r = −1
EXIT
    r = 1 ∧ h__0 = h′ − T__i
    ∧ last__change = now′ + T__o
END Controller;

PROCESS Water__Tank
IMPORT r,h__0,last__change;
EXPORT h;
VARIABLES
    h            : Real;
INITIAL
    h = MIN
RELATION
    h = h__0 + r * (now − last__change)
END Water__Tank;
```

MTCCS

When modeling complex computer systems, formalisms are needed that allow the expression of (i) concurrency, (ii) real-time aspects of a system, and (iii) data aspects of a system. MTCCS (Model-oriented Timed Calculus of Communicating Systems) (98,99) is a formal specification language aimed at defining real-time concurrent systems with a nontrivial data component. MTCCS is the result of the merging of a process definition formalism and a data description formalism in a similar fashion, as is done in LOTOS. The process part is based on Timed CCS (100), a timed version of the process algebra notation CCS (26). Timed CCS does not allow the description of data elements. It is therefore combined with VDM-SL, the specification language of VDM, to allow manipulation of data components. The reason to choose two different models for process/control and data is that the two aspects are, in itself, fundamentally different and require different approaches to their description. MTCCS is based on earlier work on a language called MOSCA (101, 102).

An MTCCS specification describes four aspects of systems of communicating processes: their data-containment, their functional behavior, their process structure and their behavior in time. Associated with these aspects are the following MTCCS constructions: data type and state definitions, functions and operations on data, agent definitions, and timed actions. The former two are taken from VDM-SL; the process and time aspects are based on Timed CCS.

At the top level, an MTCCS specification consists of one or more (global) agent definitions, and an initial behavior expression. Global agents can only be instantiated in the initial behaviour expression. The initial behavior expression can thus be seen as defining the main process structure. A global agent has a state and a number of local agents, sharing the state of the global agent. They can only be instantiated from within the global agent in which they are defined.

As in value passing CCS, processes communicate through channels; for example, $\bar{a}(3).A \,|\, a(x).B$ represents two processes communicating over a channel a. As a result of this communication, x is bound to 3 in B.

The time model of Timed CCS is a simple but effective way to model timed behavior. Time is assumed to flow continuously and the passing of time is modeled by *Idle* actions. For example, the behavior expression *Idle*(10).B models a process that idles for 10 time units and subsequently behaves according to expression B. Furthermore, the passing of time can be measured; in $a(x) \star d.B$ the amount of time between enabling and executing $a(x)$ is recorded in d. The fact that MTCCS also incorporates data, increases the power of our time modeling constructs. It allows, for example, the expression of intervals in delays, and dealing with elapsed time values as normal data values.

The semantics of MTCCS integrate two different semantic models; the process part is given a process-algebraic semantics in the spirit of CCS, and the data part is given a denotational semantics. The latter is embodied by (a subset of) VDM-SL.

To express properties of MTCCS specifications we use a variant of TCTL (timed computation tree logic) (103), which allows the expression of many interesting real-time properties. Our method for verifying the correctness of property specifications with respect to system specifications is based on model checking, which allows the verification of temporal logic properties in a highly automatic manner. To apply model checking, MTCCS specifications are transformed into a timed-automaton-based representation called XTGraphs (99). This two-phased approach to verification of process-algebra specifications has been applied before [e.g., to ET-LOTOS (104)] but not to formalisms that incorporate the formal definition of data components. The resulting XTGraph models are used as input for the subsequent symbolic model-checking step. A secondary benefit of our transformation is that the resulting XTGraphs can be used as the basis for other analysis techniques like simulation, or for the implementation of specifications.

Model-checking techniques are generally not well suited for dealing with complex data structures. Therefore, when applying model checking to languages like MTCCS, *abstraction techniques* are needed. These abstraction techniques transform system models into simpler ones while preserving the possibilities of checking the properties of interest. We are therefore working on combining model checking with the application of abstraction techniques to VDM-SL structures. A disadvantage of the usage of abstractions is that it destroys the automatic character of the verification procedure. Human interaction is needed to create useful abstraction and to prove them correct. To support the latter activity we are studying, the possibilities of integration with a theorem-proving tool.

Below, a small example specification of the water-level control system introduced in the subsection ASTRAL and Hybrid ASTRAL is given.

specification *Waterlevel__controller*
const INFLOW = 1
    OUTFLOW = 2
    HIGHLEVEL = 10
    LOWLEVEL = 5
    PUMPREACTTIME = 1
    CONTRREACTTIME = 0
    POLLDELAY = 1

agent *Tank*
ports $\overline{sense}$: $\mathbb{R}$
    stop, go
local *PumpOn* $\langle \mathbb{R} \rangle$, *PumpOff* $\langle \mathbb{R} \rangle$
    PumpOn $\langle level \rangle \triangleq$
        $\overline{sense}$ ★ d (*level* + INFLOW * d) $\odot$ *PumpOn* $\langle level + \text{INFLOW} * d \rangle$
        $\oplus$
        stop ★ $d \odot$ idle(PUMPREACTTIME) $\odot$ *PumpOff* $\langle level + \text{INFLOW} * (d +$
PUMPREACTTIME)$\rangle$
    PumpOff $\langle level \rangle \triangleq$
        $\overline{sense}$ ★ d (*level* − OUTFLOW * d) $\odot$ *PumpOff* $\langle level - \text{OUTFLOW} * d \rangle$
        $\oplus$
        go ★ $d \odot$ idle(PUMPREACTTIME) $\odot$ *PumpOn* $\langle level - \text{OUTFLOW} * (d +$
PUMPREACTTIME)$\rangle$
    Tank $\triangleq$ *PumpOn* $\langle 0 \rangle$

agent *Controller*
ports *sense* : $\mathbb{R}$
    $\overline{stop}, \overline{go}$
local C_1, C_2
    $C_1 \triangleq$
    idle (POLLDELAY) $\odot$ *sense(l)* $\odot$
        if $l \geq$ HIGHLEVEL then idle(CONTRREACTTIME) $\odot$ $\overline{stop}$ $\odot$ C_2 else C_1
    $C_2 \triangleq$
    idle (POLLDELAY) $\odot$ *sense(l)* $\odot$
        if $l \leq$ LOWLEVEL then idle(CONTRREACTTIME) $\odot$ $\overline{go}$ $\odot$ C_1 else C_2
Controller $\triangleq$ C_1

Specification $\triangleq$ (*Tank* | *Controller*)

The specification defines two processes, a *Tank* and a *Controller*. The tank can either be in a state in which the pump is on (*PumpOn*), or in a state in which the pump is turned off (*PumpOff*). The states are parameterized with the current value of the water level. If the pump is on, two things can happen [modeled by the "$\oplus$" (choice), it can be asked for the current water level (the *sense* action), or it can be triggered to turn off the pump (the *stop* action]. The ★d construct causes the variable *d* to be bound to the amount of time elapsed between enabling and execution of the action *sense*. The value of *d* can be used to compute the new value of the water level that is output in the communication over the sense port. If a *stop* synchronization takes place, it evolves to *PumpOff* after a delay modeling the reaction time of the pump. Notice that *stop* and *go* are pure synchronizations, whereas *sense* models the communication of a value. *PumpOff* is analogous; instead of synchronizing on *stop*, it synchronizes on *go*, causing the pump to be turned on again.

The *Controller* polls the tank through the *sense* port. If the water level reaches the lower bound, it issues a *go* command to the tank. Alternatively, if the water level reaches the upper limit, a *stop* command is issued.

CONCLUSIONS

The Application of Formal Methods in the Software Process

It is possible to use formal methods in the software process for a variety of activities, starting during preliminary design through detailed design and coding and testing. During these phases, formal methods provide distinct benefits over their nonformal counterparts:

- They include formal notations which can be unambiguously interpreted and which – for a large class of these formal notations – provide extensive means to express (representational and procedural) abstraction. These notations can be used to verify formally characteristics of the design. Besides this, they are used as "thinking tools" that have been shown to be important aids during design;
- They provide the means to formally verify the correctness of the design steps made. Although it is clear that formal verification cannot be done when using nonformal methods, due to technical reasons it is currently not always feasible to completely prove the correctness of all design steps. The application area should be considered when deciding whether to prove the correctness of *all* design steps (completely formal), *some* of the design steps (rigorously formal), or *none* of the design steps (nonformal) made.

Improvements of Formal Methods

Until now, formal methods have been based on one strong concept, *mathematics*, using very simple paradigms for the development of software. They do not (completely) address the issues which are important for the development of large software systems. It has been shown that the application of formal methods in an established software process model is indeed possible and beneficial, but problems occur with the integration of these methods.

The first area in which improvements can be made is in the construction of the initial source specification in the Preliminary Design. None of the known formal methods provide support, either by providing guidelines for the actual construction or by providing requirements that an initial source specification should fulfill *how* such an initial source specification can be constructed (see, e.g., Ref. 105). To improve this, formal methods should be extended (for example, with ideas from another already existing design method) to make a structured composition of an initial system model possible.

A second area for improvement is the connection with the coding phase of the software process. The step to go from a formal specification to source code may sometimes seem trivial, but this is certainly not true for large programs. This problem can be approached in two ways:

1. Defining an executable subset of the formal specification language, which can be used as a programming language. To make it possible to use this subset for large programs, it would then become even more necessary to extend this language with a proper structuring mechanism and, most likely, other constructs present in modern programming languages as well.
2. Defining a formal relationship between the specification language and the programming language used. The existence of a formal relationship makes it possible to prove that the transformation from a low-level specification into a program expressed in that programming language is correct.

The importance of tool support for the development of software has increased during the last three decades and will also be essential for the effective use of formal methods in industry. There are several computer-based tools that support working with formal methods. These tools, however, are suited for the support of the *specification* and *verification* activities only. However, by their nature, formal methods seem to be very well suited to be supported by computer-based tools for the development activities performed during the software process.

REFERENCES

1. P. Naur and B. Randell (eds.), *Software Engineering — Report on a Conference Sponsored by the NATO Science Committee* January 1969.
2. N. G. Leveson (ed.), *IEEE Trans. Software Eng., SE-16*, (9) (1990).
3. S. L. Gerhart (ed.), *IEEE Software, 7*(5) (1990).
4. H. Saiedian, "An Invitation to Formal Methods," *IEEE Computer, 29*(4), 16–30 (1996).
5. E. M. Clarke and J. M. Wing, "Formal Methods: State of the Art and Future Directions," Technical Report CMU-CS-96-178, Carnegie Mellon University, School of Computer Science, 1996; *ACM Comput. Surv.* (in press).
6. W.-P. de Roever, "Foundations of Computer Science: Leaving the Ivory Tower," *Bull. Eur. Assoc. Theoret. Computer Sci., 44*, 455–492 (1991).
7. C. Landwehr, J. McLean, and C. Heitmeyer, "Defining Formalism," *Commun. ACM, 34*(10), 15–16 (1991).
8. J. M. Wing, "A Specifier's Introduction to Formal Methods," *IEEE Computer, 23*(9), 8–22 (1990).
9. D. Bjørner, "Towards a Meaning of 'M' in VDM," in *TAPSOFT'89; Proceedings of the International Joint Conference on Theory and Practice of Software Development,* edited by G. Goos and J. Hartmanis, Springer-Verlag, New York, 1989, pp. 1–35.
10. D. Craigen et al., "EVES: An Overview," Technical Report CP-91-5402-43, Odyssey Research Associates, Ottawa, Ontario, Canada (1991).
11. *Interim Defence Standard 00-55*, UK Ministry of Defence (May 1989).
12. *Interim Defence Standard 00-56*, UK Ministry of Defence (May 1989).

13. I. J. Hayes, "Applying Formal Specification to Software Development in Industry," *IEEE Trans. Software Eng., SE-11*(2), 169–178 (1985).

14. I. Houston and S. King, "CICS Project Report; Experiences and Results from the Use of Z in IBM," in *VDM'91; Formal Software Development Methods*, Springer-Verlag, New York, 1991, pp. 588–596.

15. A. Hall, "Using Formal Methods to Develop an ATC Information System," *IEEE Software, 12*(6), 66–76 (1996).

16. P. G. Larsen, J. Fitzgerald, and T. Brookes, "Applying Formal Specification in Industry," *IEEE Software, 13*(3), 48–56 (1996).

17. M. D. Fraser, K. Kumar, and V. K. Vaishnavi, "Strategies for Incorporating Formal Specifications in Software Development," *Commun. ACM, 37*(10), 74–86 (1994).

18. D. Coleman, "The Technology Transfer of Formal Methods: What's Going Wrong?" in *Proceedings of the Workshop on Industrial Use of Formal Methods*, March 1990.

19. D. Craigen, S. Gerhart, and T. Ralston, "An International Survey of Industrial Applications of Formal Methods. Volume 1: Purpose, Approach, Analysis, and Conclusions. Volume 2: Case Studies," Report NISTGCR 93/626, US Department of Commerce, National Institute of Standards, Computer Systems Laboratory, Gaithersburg, MD (March 1993).

20. D. Craigen, S. Gerhart, and T. Ralston, "Formal Methods Reality Check: Industrial Usage," *IEEE Trans. Software Eng., 21*(2), 90–98 (1995).

21. S. Austin and G. I. Parkin, "Formal Methods: A Survey," Technical Report, Division of Information Technology and Computing, National Physical Laboratory, Teddington, Middlesex, U.K. (March 1993).

22. A. Hall, "Seven Myths of Formal Methods," *IEEE Software, 7*(5), 11–19 (1990).

23. J. P. Bowen and M. G. Hinchey, "Seven More Myths of Formal Methods," *IEEE Software, 12*(4), 34–41 (1994).

24. W. G. Wood, "Application of Formal Methods to System and Software Specification," *ACM Software Eng. Notes, 15*(4), 144–146 (1990) (Proceedings of the ACM Workshop on Formal Methods and Software Development, 1989).

25. D. A. Duce and E. V. C. Fielding, "Formal Specification – A Comparison of Two Techniques," *Computer J., 30*(4), 316–327 (1987).

26. R. Milner, *A Calculus of Communicating Systems*, Springer-Verlag, New York, 1980.

27. D. Walker, "Introduction to a Calculus of Communicating Systems," Technical Report, Laboratory for Foundations of Computer Science, Department of Computer Science, University of Edinburgh (February 1987).

28. R. Milner, *Communication and Concurrency*, Prentice-Hall International, Englewood Cliffs, NJ, 1989.

29. C. A. R. Hoare, *Communicating Sequential Processes*, Prentice-Hall International, Englewood Cliffs, NJ, 1985.

30. I. Lee, H. Ben-Abdallah, and J.-Y. Choi, *A Process Algebraic Method for the Specification and Analysis of Real-time Systems*, John Wiley and Sons, New York, 1996, Chap. 7.

31. B. Auernheimer and R. A. Kemmerer, "RT-ASLAN: A Specification Language for Real-time Systems," *IEEE Trans. Software Eng., SE-12*(9), 879–889 (1986).

32. A. Coen-Porisini, C. Ghezzi, and R. A. Kemmerer, "Specification of Realtime Systems Using ASTRAL," Technical Report TRCS 96-30, University of California, Santa Barbara (July 1996).

33. R. Alur and D. Dill, "The Theory of Timed Automata," in *Proceedings REX Workshop on Real-Time: Theory and Practice*, Springer-Verlag, New York, 1991, pp. 45–73.

34. T. A. Henzinger, "The Theory of Hybrid Automata," in *Proceedings of the 11th*

IEEE Symposium on Logic in Computer Science, IEEE Computer Society Press, Los Alamitos, CA, 1996, pp. 278–292.

35. P. Zave and R. T. Yeh, "Executable Requirements for Embedded Systems," in *Proceedings of the 5th International Conference on Software Engineering*, IEEE Computer Society Press, Los Alamitos, CA, 1981, pp. 295–304.

36. P. Zave, "An Operational Approach to Requirements Specification for Embedded Systems," *IEEE Trans. Software Eng., SE-8*(3), 250–269 (1982).

37. J. L. Peterson, "Petri Nets," *ACM Comput. Surv., 9*(3), 223–252 (1977).

38. D. Harel, "Statecharts: A Visual Approach to Complex Systems," Technical Report CS84-05, The Weizmann Institute of Science, Rehovot, Israel (February 1984).

39. D. Harel, A. Pnueli, J. P. Schmidt, and R. Sherman, "On the Formal Semantics of Statecharts," in *Proceedings of the 2nd IEEE Symposium on Logic in Computer Science*, 1987, pp. 54–64.

40. D. Harel, "Biting the Silver Bullet: Towards a Brighter Future for System Development," *IEEE Computer, 25*(1), 8 (1992).

41. The RAISE Language Group, *The RAISE Specification Language*, Prentice-Hall International, Englewood Cliffs, NJ, 1992.

42. C. George and S. Prehn, *The RAISE Justification Handbook*, Prentice-Hall International, Englewood Cliffs, NJ, 1992.

43. C. B. Jones, *Systematic Software Development using VDM*, 2nd ed., Prentice-Hall International, Englewood Cliffs, NJ, 1990.

44. M. Spivey, *Understanding Z — A Specification Language and its Formal Semantics*, Cambridge University Press, Cambridge, 1988.

45. J.-R. Abrial, *The B-Book: Assigning Programs to Meanings*, Cambridge University Press, Cambridge, 1996.

46. J. V. Guttag and J. J. Horning (eds.), *Larch: Languages and Tools for Formal Specification*, Springer-Verlag, New York, 1993, with Stephen J. Garland, Kevin D. Jones, Andrés Modet, and Jeannette M. Wing.

47. D. C. Luckham and F. W. von Henke, "An Overview of ANNA, a Specification Language for Ada," *IEEE Software, 2*(2), 9–22 (1985).

48. D. C. Luckham, *Programming with Specifications: An Introduction to ANNA — A Specification Language for ADA*, Springer-Verlag, New York, 1990.

49. J. Rushby, F. von Henke, and S. Owre, "An Introduction to Formal Specification and Verification Using EHDM," Technical Report SRI-CSL-91-2, Computer Science Laboratory, SRI International (1991).

50. R. M. Burstall and J. A. Goguen, *The Semantics of Clear, a Specification Language*, Springer-Verlag, New York, 1980.

51. R. M. Burstall and J. A. Goguen, "An Informal Introduction to Specifications using Clear," in *The Correctness Problem in Computer Science*, edited by R. S. Boyer and J. S. Moore, Academic Press, London, 1981, pp. 185–213.

52. J. A. Bergstra, J. Heering, and P. Klint, "ASF — An Algebraic Specification Formalism," Technical Report CS-R8705, Centre for Mathematics and Computer Science (CWI), Amsterdam (January 1987).

53. H. Ehrig, W. Fey, and H. Hansen, "ACT ONE: An Algebraic Specification Language with Two Levels of Semantics," Technical Report, Institut für Software und Theoretische Informatik, Technische Universität Berlin (1983).

54. A. Pnueli, "Applications of Temporal Logic to the Specification and Verification of Reactive Systems," in *Current Trends in Concurrency*, edited by J. W. de Bakker, W. P. de Roever, and G. Rozenberg, Springer-Verlag, New York, 1986, pp. 510–585.

55. L. Lamport, "The Temporal Logic of Actions," *ACM Trans. Program. Lang. Syst., 16*(3), 872–923 (1995).

56. D. Bjørner, "Draft Final Report ProCos," Report ID/DTH DB 13/1, Department of

Computer Science, Technical University of Denmark (October 1991); ESPRIT BRA 4104.

57. M. Saaltink and D. Craigen, "Simple Type Theory in EVES," in *Proceedings of the 4th Banff Higher Order Workshop*, Springer-Verlag, New York, 1991.

58. M. J. C. Gordon, "HOL: A Proof Generating System for Higher-Order Logic," in *VLSI Specification, Verification and Synthesis*, edited by G. Birtwistle and P. A. Subrahmanyam, Kluwer Academic Publishers, Boston, 1988.

59. J. A. Goguen and T. Winkler, "Introducing OBJ3," Technical Report SRI-CSL-88-9, Computer Science Laboratory, SRI International (August 1988).

60. T. Bolognesi and E. Brinksma, "Introduction to the ISO Specification Language LOTOS," *Computer Networks ISDN Syst., 14*, 25–59 (1987).

61. ISO8807, *Information Processing Systems – Open Systems Interconnection – LOTOS: A Formal Description Technique Based on the Temporal Ordering of Observational Behaviour*, 1989.

62. L. Léonard and G. Leduc, "An Enhanced Version of Timed LOTOS and its Application to a Case Study," in *Proceedings of the 6th International Conference on Formal Description Techniques*, North-Holland, Amsterdam, 1994, pp. 483–498.

63. R. S. Boyer and J. S. Moore, *A Computational Logic Handbook*, Academic Press, New York, 1988.

64. N. Shankar, S. Owre, and J. M. Rushby, "The PVS Proof Checker: A Reference Manual (Beta Release)," Computer Science Laboratory, SRI International (March 1993).

65. I. Meisels and M. Saaltink, "The Z/EVES Reference Manual," Technical Report TR-96-5493-03a, ORA Canada, Ottawa, Ontario (April 1996).

66. K. L. McMillan, *Symbolic Model Checking*. Kluwer Academic Publishers, Boston, 1993.

67. G. J. Holzmann and D. Peled, "An Improvement in Formal Verification," in *Proceedings of the 7th International Conference on Formal Description Techniques*, Chapman & Hall, New York, 1995, pp. 197–209.

68. K. G. Larsen, P. Petterson, and W. Yi, "Model Checking for Real-Time Systems," in *Proceedings of Fundamentals of Computation Theory*, Springer-Verlag, New York, 1995, pp. 62–88.

69. R. Alur, C. Courcoubetis, N. Halbwachs, T. A. Henzinger, P.-H. Ho, X. Nicollin, A. Olivero, J. Sifakis, and S. Yovine, "The Algorithmic Analysis of Hybrid Systems," *Theoret. Computer Sci., 138*, 3–34 (1995).

70. S. Rajan, N. Shankar, and M. K. Srivas, "An Integration of Model Checking with Automated Proof Checking," in *Proceedings 7th International Conference on Computer Aided Verification, CAV'95*, Springer-Verlag, New York, 1995, pp. 84–97.

71. J. Dingel and T. Filkorn, "Model Checking for Infinite State Systems Using Data Abstraction, Assumption-Commitment Style Reasoning and Theorem Proving," in *Proceedings 7th International Conference on Computer Aided Verification, CAV'95*, Springer-Verlag, New York, 1995, pp. 54–69.

72. N. Plat and P. Gorm Larsen, "An Overview of the ISO/VDM-SL Standard," *ACM SIGPLAN Notices, 27*(8), 76–82 (1992).

73. N. Plat and H. Toetenel, "A Formal Transformation from the BSI/VDM-SL Concrete Syntax to the Core Abstract Syntax," Technical Report 92-07, Faculty of Technical Mathematics and Informatics, Delft University of Technology (March 1992).

74. P. G. Larsen and N. Plat, "Standards for Non-Executable Specification Languages," *Computer J., 35*(6), 567–573 (1992).

75. ISO/IEC JTC1/SC22/WG 19, *VDM-SL, First Committee Draft Standard: CD 13817-1*, 1993.

76. R. Elmstrøm, P. G. Larsen, and P. B. Lassen, "The IFAD VDM-SL Toolbox: A

practical Approach to Formal Specifications," *ACM Sigplan Notices, 29*(9), 77–80 (1994).

77. C. B. Jones, K. D. Jones, P. A. Lindsay, and R. Moore, *MuRAL: A Formal Development Support System*, Springer-Verlag, New York, 1991.

78. D. Bjørner and C. B. Jones, *Formal Specification & Software Development*, Prentice-Hall International, Englewood Cliffs, NJ, 1982.

79. C. B. Jones and R. Shaw (eds.), *Case Studies in VDM*, Prentice-Hall International, Englewood Cliffs, NJ, 1990.

80. D. Andrews and D. Ince, *Practical Formal Methods with VDM*, McGraw-Hill, New York, 1991.

81. J. Dawes, *The VDM-SL Reference Guide*, Pitman, London, 1991.

82. E. Dürr and J. van Katwijk, "VDM + + – A Formal Specification Language for Object-oriented Designs," in *Proceedings of CompEuro'92*, IEEE Computer Society Press, Los Alamitos, CA, 1992, pp. 214–219.

83. C. A. Middleburg, *Logic and Specification – Extending VDM-SL for Advanced Formal Specification*, Chapman & Hall, New York, 1993.

84. The RAISE Method Group, *The RAISE Development Method*. Prentice-Hall International, Englewood Cliffs, NJ, 1995.

85. S. Stepney, R. Barden, and D. Cooper (eds.), *Object Orientation in Z. Workshops in Computing*, Springer-Verlag, New York, 1992.

86. J. Rumbaugh, M. Blaha, W. Premerlani, F. Eddy, and W. Lorensen, *Object-Oriented Modelling and Design*, Prentice-Hall, Englewood Cliffs, NJ, 1991.

87. J. V. Guttag, "The Specification and Application to Programming of Abstract Data Types," Ph.D. thesis, University of Toronto, Department of Computer Science (1975).

88. J. V. Guttag, J. J. Horning, and J. M. Wing, "Larch in Five Easy Pieces," Report 5, DEC Systems Research Center (July 1985).

89. T. Bolognesi, J. van de Langemaat, and C. Vissers, *LOTOSphere: Software Development with LOTOS*, Kluwer Academic Publishers, Boston, 1995.

90. *ISO/IEC JTC1/SC21/WG7*, Enhancements to LOTOS, 1997.

91. P. H. J. van Eijk, C. A. Vissers, and M. Diaz, *The Formal Description Technique LOTOS*, North-Holland, Amsterdam, 1989.

92. C. Ghezzi and R. A. Kemmerer, "ASTRAL: An Assertion Language for Specifying Realtime Systems," in *Proceedings of the Third European Software Engineering Conference*, October 1991, pp. 122–146.

93. B. Auernheimer and R. A. Kemmerer, "ASLAN User's Manual," Technical Report TRCS 84-10, University of California, Santa Barbara (March 1985).

94. C. Ghezzi, D. Mandrioli, and A. Morzenti, "TRIO: A Logic Language for Executable Specifications of Real-Time Systems," *J. Syst. Software, 12*, 107–123 (June 1990).

95. C. Ghezzi and R. A. Kemmerer, "Executing Formal Specifications: The ASTRAL to TRIO Translation Approach," in *TAV'91, Symposium on Testing, Analysis, and Verification*, October 1991.

96. A. Coen-Porisini, R. A. Kemmerer, and D. Mandrioli, "Formal Verification of Realtime Systems in ASTRAL," Technical Report TRCS 92-22, University of California, Santa Barbara (September 1992).

97. K. Brink, L. Bun, J. van Katwijk, and W. J. Toetenel, "Closed World Specification of Embedded Real-Time Controller," in *Proceedings 8th Euromicro Workshop on Real-Time Systems*, IEEE Press, New York, 1996.

98. J. van Katwijk, R. F. Lutje Spelberg, S. Stuurman, and W. J. Toetenel, "Modeling and Analysis of Complex Computer Systems; the MTCCS Approach," in *Proceedings of the Second IEEE International Conference on Engineering of Complex Computer Systems*, IEEE Computer Society Press, Los Alamitos, CA, 1996, pp. 423–430.

99. L. Spelberg, R. J. Toetenel, and W. J. Toetenel, "Transformation of MTCCS into an

Extension of Timed Automata," in *Proceedings of the Northern Formal Methods Workshop*, Springer-Verlag, New York, 1996.

100. W. Yi, "CCS + Time = An Interleaving Model for Real-Time Systems," in *Proceedings of the 18th International Colloquium on Automata, Languages and Programming*, Springer-Verlag, New York, 1991, pp. 217–228.

101. W. J. Toetenel, "VDM + CCS + TIME = MOSCA," in *Proceedings of the IFIP/IFAC Workshop on Real-time Programming*, 1992.

102. W. J. Toetenel, "Loose Real-Time Communicating Agents," in *Proceedings of the 1st Workshop on Semantics of Specification Languages*, Springer-Verlag, New York, 1993, pp. 135–151.

103. R. Alur, C. Courcoubetis, and D. Dill, "Model-Checking in Dense Real-Time," *Inform. Comput., 104*, 2–34 (1993).

104. C. Daws, A. Olivero, and S. Yovine, "Verifying ET-LOTOS Programs with KRONOS," in *Proceedings of the 7th International Conference on Formal Description Techniques*, Chapman & Hall, New York, 1995, pp. 227–242.

105. B. Dandanell, J. Gørtz, J. Storbank Pedersen, and E. Zierau, "Experiences from Applications of RAISE," in *FME'93; Industrial-Strength Formal Methods*, Springer-Verlag, New York, 1993, pp. 52–63.

LEON BUN

JAN VAN KATWIJK

RONALD LUTJE SPELBERG

HANS TOETENEL

NICO PLAT

FUNCTIONAL PROGRAMMING

The very earliest of programming languages were designed with one simple goal in mind: to provide a vehicle through which one could control the behavior of electronic digital computers. Not surprisingly, these early languages reflected fairly well the structure of the underlying machines. Although at first blush this seems eminently reasonable, this viewpoint quickly changed, for two very good reasons. First, it became obvious that what was easy for a machine to reason about was not necessarily easy for a human to reason about. Second, as the number of different kinds of machines increased, the need arose for a common language with which to program all of them.

Thus, from primitive assembly languages (which were at least a step up from raw machine code), there grew a plethora of high-level programming languages, beginning with Fortran in the 1950s. The development of these languages grew so rapidly that by the 1980s they were best characterized by grouping them into "families" that reflected a common computation model or programming "style." Debates over which language or family of languages is best will undoubtedly persist for as long as computers need programmers.

The most popular languages such as Fortran, C, Pascal, and Ada fall into the family of *imperative* languages, as computation is based primarily on the notion of a *command*. Languages such as C++, Eiffel, and Java are called *object-oriented* languages because they are based on the concept of *objects* and communication among them. Finally, of interest in this section is the family of *functional* languages, which compute entirely through the application of *functions* or, more generally, through the *evaluation of expressions*. Languages such as LISP, Scheme, and APL fall generally into this family, but today the most popular functional languages are ML (1) and Haskell (2). All of the examples given here are based on Haskell.

Among the claims made by functional programming advocates are that programs can be written quicker, are more concise, are "higher level" (resembling more closely traditional mathematical notation), are more amendable to formal reasoning and analysis, and can be executed more easily on parallel computers. Some of these issues are addressed in the following paragraphs; to learn more, see Refs.3–5.

IMPERATIVE VERSUS FUNCTIONAL LANGUAGES

Imperative languages are characterized as having an *implicit state* that is modified (i.e., side-effected) by *commands*. As a result, such languages generally have a notion of *sequencing* (of the commands) to permit precise and deterministic control over the state. As an example, the *assignment statement* is a very common command whose effect is to alter the implicit state so as to yield a different binding for a particular variable. The begin . . . end construct is the prototypical sequencer of commands, as are the well-known *goto statement* (unconditional transfer of control), *conditional statement* (qualified transfer of control), and *while loop* (an iteration command). With these simple constructs, we can then, for example, compute the factorial of the number x by

```
n : = x;
a : = 1;
while n > 0 do
begin a : = a*n;
      n : = n - 1
end;
   . . .
```

After execution of this program, the value bound to the variable a will be the desired result.

In contrast, functional languages are characterized as having *no* implicit state; instead, the emphasis is placed entirely on programming with *functions* or, more generally, *expressions*. State-oriented computations are accomplished by carrying the state around explicitly rather than implicitly, and looping is accomplished via *recursion* rather than by sequencing. For example, here is a Haskell program that simulates as closely as possible the factorial computation given above:

```
let fac a n = if n > 0
              then fac (a*n) (n - 1)
              else a
in fac 1 x
```

in which the definition of the function fac is introduced using a let expression, and then used "in" the result fac 1 x. The formal parameters a and n are examples of "carrying the state around explicitly," and the recursive structure mimics the while loop given in the previous example. Note that the conditional in this program is an *expression* rather than *command*; that is, it denotes a *value* (conditional on the value of the predicate) rather than denoting a sequencer of commands. Indeed, the *value of the program* is the desired factorial, rather than it being found in an implicit state.

Functional programming is often described as expressing *what* is being computed rather than *how*, although this is really a matter of degree. For example, the above program may say less about how factorial is computed than the imperative program given earlier, but it is perhaps not as abstract as this Haskell program:

```
let fac 0 = 1
    fac n = n * fac (n - 1)
in fac x
```

which happens to look a lot like the mathematical definition of factorial:

$$fac\ n = \begin{cases} 1 & \text{if } n = 0 \\ n * fac(n - 1) & \text{if } n > 0. \end{cases}$$

This "mathematical flavor" is a distinguishing feature of modern functional languages and lends weight to the argument that they are easier to reason about, because conventional mathematics can be employed. As can be seen in the above examples, modern functional languages have an "equational" look, in which functions are defined using mutually recursive equations and pattern matching.

As most programming languages have expressions of some sort (e.g., you can write the arithmetic expression x + y in almost any programming language), it is tempting to take our definitions of language families quite literally and describe functional languages via derivation from a convention programming language: Simply drop the assignment statement and any other side-effecting commands, and there you have it! Unfortunately, the result of such a derivation is almost always far less then satisfactory, as the purely functional subset of most imperative languages is hopelessly weak.

Rather than saying, then, what functional languages *do not* have, it is better to characterize them by the features they *do* have. For modern functional languages, those features include higher-order functions, lazy evaluation, pattern matching, and various kinds of data abstraction. Indeed, this discussion suggests that what is important is the functional programming *style*, in which the above features are manifest and in which side effects are strongly discouraged but not necessarily eliminated. This is the viewpoint taken by the ML community.

On the other hand, there is a compelling "purist" viewpoint which argues that purely functional languages are not only sufficient for general computing needs but also better because of their purity. To those most familiar with conventional programming languages, such a purist viewpoint seems untenable. How, for example, can one perform input/output without some kind of a command? We will see that, indeed, there is a purely functional way to achieve this which does not compromise expressiveness or performance.

REFERENTIAL TRANSPARENCY AND EQUATIONAL REASONING

The emphasis on a pure declarative style of programming is perhaps the hallmark of the functional programming paradigm. The term *referentially transparent* is often used to describe this style of programming, in which "equals can be replaced by equals." For example, consider the Haskell expression:

```
let x = f a
in . . . x + x . . .
```

The function application (f a) may be substituted for any free occurrence of x in the scope created by the let expression, such as in the subexpression x + x; this is called *equational reasoning*. This cannot generally be done using an imperative language, because one must first be sure that no assignment to x is made in any of the statements intervening between the initial definition of x and one of its subsequent uses. In general, this can be quite a tricky task, for example, in the case where a procedure is called with x as an argument, which may require finding and inspecting the definition of that procedure, which in turn might require inspecting other procedures, and so on. In a language such as Haskell, the definition of x can *always* be substituted immediately for any of its occurrences, with no further considerations required.

Although the notion of referential transparency may seem like a simple idea, the clean equational reasoning that it allows is very powerful, not only for reasoning formally about programs but also informally in writing and debugging programs. A program in which side effects are minimized, but not eliminated, may still benefit from equational reason, although naturally more care must be taken when applying such reasoning. The degree of care, however, may be much higher than one might think at first: Most languages that allow "minor" forms of side effects do not minimize their locality lexically—thus, any call to any function in any module might conceivably introduce a side effect, in turn invalidating many applications of equational reasoning.

HIGHER-ORDER FUNCTIONS

If functions are treated as "first-class values" in a language—allowing them to be stored in data structures, passed as arguments, and returned as results—they are referred to as *higher-order functions*. Philosophically speaking, functions are values just like any others, so why not give them the same first-class status? But there are also compelling pragmatic reasons. Simply stated, functions facilitate *abstraction* over computational strategies, which, in turn, enhances modularity and conciseness.

As an example of a higher-order function, consider

twice f x = f (f x)

which takes its first argument, a function f, and "applies it twice" to its second argument, x. The syntax used here is important: twice as written is *curried*, meaning that when applied to one argument, it returns a function which then takes one more argument, the second argument above. For example, the function add2:

add2 = twice succ
            where succ x = x + 1

is a function that will add 2 to its argument. To see this, we just use equational reasoning, as follows:

twice succ x
 = succ (succ x)
 = succ (x + 1)
 = (x + 1) + 1
 = x + 2

In modern functional languages, functions can be created in several ways. One way is to name them using equations, as above, but another way is to create them directly as *lambda abstractions*, thus rendering them nameless, as in the Haskell expression

 \x → x + 1

which is the same as the successor function succ defined above. add2 can then be defined more succinctly as add2 = twice (\x → x + 1)

From a pragmatic viewpoint, we can understand the usefulness of higher-order functions through an appreciation of abstraction in general. A function is an abstraction of values over some common behavior. Limiting the values over which the abstraction occurs to nonfunctions seems unreasonable; lifting that restriction results in higher-order functions.

Higher-order functions increase modularity by serving as a mechanism for "gluing" program fragments together (6). That gluing property comes not just from the ability to *compose* functions but also the ability to *abstract* over functional behaviors as described above.

To give an example of this, let us first introduce the paradigmatic data structure in functional languages: the ordered *list*. The empty list in Haskell is denoted [ ], and the list whose first element is x and remaining elements comprise the list xs, is given by x : xs. (Note the naming convention used here; xs is the plural of x, and should be read that way.) Finally, the list [1,2,3] is shorthand for 1 : (2 : (3 : [ ])).

Continuing, suppose in the course of program construction we define a function to add together the elements of a list:

sum [ ]   = 0
sum (x : xs) = x + sum xs

For example, sum [1,2,3] returns 6. Then suppose we later define a function to multiply the elements of a list:

prod [ ]   = 1
prod (x : xs) = x * prod xs

But now we note a repeating computational pattern, and anticipate that we might see it again, so we ask ourselves if we can possibly abstract the common behavior. In fact, this is easy to do: we note that + / * and 0 / 1 are the variable elements in the behavior, and thus we *parameterize* them; that is, we make them formal parameters, say & and init. Calling the new function fold, the equivalent of sum/prod will be fold f init, and thus arrive at

fold (&) init [ ]   = init
fold (&) init (x : xs) = x & (fold (&) init) xs

[An infix operator may be passed as an argument by surrounding it in parentheses; thus, (&) is equivalent to \x y → x&y.]

From this, we can now derive new definitions for sum and prod:

sum = fold (+) 0
prod = fold (*) 1

It is easy to verify that the new definitions are equivalent to the old, using simple equational reasoning. It is also important to note that in arriving at the main abstraction, we did nothing out of the ordinary—we are just applying classical data abstraction principles in as an unrestricted a way as possible, and that means allowing functions to be "first-class citizens."

Of course now that the fold abstraction has been made, many other useful functions can be defined, even something as seemingly unrelated as (+ +), a function that concatenates two lists together:

xs + + ys = fold (:) ys xs

For example, [1,2,3] + + [4,5,6] returns [1,2,3,4,5,6].

Another useful operation on lists is one that applies a function to every element, yielding a new list. This is called map:

map f [ ]   = [ ]
map f (x : xs) = f x : map f xs

For example, using add2 defined earlier, map add2 [1,2,3] returns [3,4,5].

LAZY EVALUATION

Most programming languages evaluate arguments to functions or procedures *before* the actual call is made. For example, given a function definition such as

f x = 42

then the call f (5 ∗ 3) will evaluate the expression (5 ∗ 3) before the call is made. This is unfortunate, in that the function did not actually need the argument, as it simply returns the value 42.

In contrast, some functional languages only evaluate arguments at the point that the value is needed and, furthermore, ensure that the evaluation happens at most once. This is called *lazy evaluation* and is the evaluation mechanism used in Haskell.

Lazy evaluation has two advantages over conventional evaluation. First, *it frees a programmer from concerns about evaluation order*. The fact is, programmers are generally concerned about the efficiency of their programs; thus, they prefer not computing things needlessly. As a simple example, suppose we *may* need to know the greatest common divisor of b and c in some computation involving x. In Haskell, we might write

let a = gcd b c
in f a x

without worrying about a being evaluated needlessly: If in the computation of f a x the value of a is needed, it will be computed, otherwise not. If this were written in a language not supporting lazy evaluation, the greatest common denominator (gcd) of b and c would *always* be computed. To get around this, we might try modifying f so that it took both b and c as arguments rather than just a, and computed the gcd internally. But this is a severe violation of modularity, which arose solely out of the programmer's concern about evaluation order. Lazy evaluation eliminates that concern and preserves modularity.

The second argument for lazy evaluation is perhaps the one more often heard: *the ability to compute with unbounded ("infinite") data structures*. The idea is that a programmer should be able to describe a specific data structure without worrying about how it gets evaluated. Thus, for example, one could describe the sequence of natural numbers by the following simple program:

```
numsfrom n  = n : numsfrom (n + 1)
nats        = numsfrom 0
```

By unwinding these definitions using equational reasoning as defined earlier:

```
nats
= numsfrom 0
= 0 : numsfrom 1
= 0 : 1 : numsfrom 2
= 0 : 1 : 2 : numsfrom 3
= 0 : 1 : 2 : 3 : numsfrom 4
. . .
```

It is easy to see that nats is the list 0, 1, 2, 3, ... This is an example of an "infinite list" or stream, and in a language that did not support lazy evaluation would cause the program to diverge. With lazy evaluation, the list is only evaluated as it is needed, or "consumed," by some other computation.

For example, we could define a function that filters out only those elements satisfying a property p:

```
filter p (x : xs) = if (p x) then (x : rest) else rest
                  where rest = filter p xs
```

in which case "filter p nats" could be written knowing that the degree of the list's computation will be determined by its context (i.e., the consumer of the result). Thus, filter has no operational control within it and can be combined with other functions in a modular way. In particular, suppose head is defined by

```
head (x : xs) = x
```

Then head (filter (\ x → x > 10) nats would return the first natural number greater than 10, which is, of course, 11. Exactly 12 elements of the infinite list nats would be computed to generate this result.

TYPES AND POLYMORPHISM

Many programming languages have a notion of *type*, and modern function languages have particularly rich type systems. Just as expressions denote values, *type expressions* denote *types*. Examples of type expressions include the atomic types Int (fixed-precision integers), Char (ASCII characters), Int → Int (functions mapping Int to Int), as well as the structured types such as [Int] (homogeneous lists of integers) and (Char,Int) (character/integer pairs). Types in a sense *describe* values, and the association of a value with its type is called a *typing*. For example,

```
    5 : : Int
  'a' : : Char
 succ : : Int → Int
[1,2,3]: : [Int]
('b',4) : : (Char,Int)
```

are all typings, where the : : can be read "has type."

Most functional languages also have *polymorphic* types — types that are universally guantified in some way over *all* types. Polymorphic type expressions essentially describe *families* of types. For example, (∀a)[a] is the family of types consisting of, for every type a, the type of lists of a. Lists of integers (e.g., [1,2,3]) lists of characters (['a','b','c']), even lists of lists of integers, and so forth, are all members of this family. (Note, however, that [2,'b'] is *not* a valid example, as there is no single type that contains both 2 and 'b'.)

We can also define *polymorphic functions*. For example, consider the problem of counting the number of elements in a list:

```
length         : : [a] → Int
length [ ]     = 0
length (x : xs) = 1 + length xs
```

This definition is almost self-explanatory. It can be read as, "The length of the empty list is 0, and the length of a list whose first element is x and remainder is xs is 1 plus the length of xs." Being polymorphic, length can be applied to a list containing elements of any type.

For example,

```
length [1,2,3]     = 3
length ['a','b','c'] = 3
length [[ ],[ ],[ ]]  = 3
```

USER-DEFINED DATA TYPES

We have seen examples of integers, lists, tuples, and a few other data types, but it is often the case that a programmer wishes to define his or her own data type. Most modern functional languages provide powerful mechanisms to support this kind of abstraction. For example, a data type of colors could be defined as

```
data color = Red | Green | Blue | Indigo | Violet
```

Functions can then be defined on this data type by matching against the arguments, just as we did for integers and lists:

```
isRed Red = True
isRed  c  = False
```

Of course, much richer data types can also be defined. The following is a data type of *trees* that is both polymorphic and recursive:

```
data Tree a = Leaf a
            | Branch (Tree a) (Tree a)
```

This can be read: "for all types a, a tree of type Tree a is either a leaf with a value of type a, or a branch whose two subtrees are each of type Tree a."

With this example, we have defined a type sufficiently rich to allow defining some interesting (recursive) functions that use it. For example, suppose we wish to define a function fringe that returns a list of all the elements in the leaves of a tree from left to right. A suitable definition is

```
fringe                      : : Tree a → [a]
fringe (Leaf x)             = [x]
fringe (Branch left right)  = fringe left + +  fringe right
```

PURELY FUNCTIONAL INPUT/OUTPUT

Earlier, we mentioned that it was possible to perform input/output (I/O) operations in a purely functional language, even though there is no primitive notion of a "command." This is achieved by defining a special kind of value that is interpreted by the operating system as if it were a command. In Haskell, this special type is called a *monad*.

The I/O monad used by Haskell mediates between the "values" natural to a functional language and the "actions" which characterize I/O operations and imperative programming in general. The order of evaluation of expressions in Haskell is constrained only by data dependencies; normally, an implementation has a great deal of freedom in choosing this order. Actions, however, must be ordered in a well-defined manner for program execution—and I/O in particular—to be meaningful. Haskell's I/O monad provides the user with a way to specify this sequential chaining of actions, and an implementation is obliged to preserve this order.

The term "monad" comes from a branch of mathematics known as *category theory*. From a programmer's perspective, however, it is best to think of a monad simply as an abstract data type which has operations to create actions—corresponding to convention I/O operations—and operations (mentioned above) to sequentially compose actions— corresponding to sequencers (such as the semicolon) in imperative languages. The "hidden implementation" of monad can be thought of as the "system state" (i.e., the state of the world).

An I/O operation which returns a value of type a has the type IO a. For example, the getChar primitive has the type IO Char, as its effect is to return one character from the keyboard. When an I/O operation does not return a value, the type IO ( ) is used. I/O operations may also *receive* arguments. For example, putChar, whose effect is to display its character argument on the screen, has type Char → IO ( ).

Linear sequencing of I/O operations is achieved using two functions. The ≫ function corresponds to simple sequential execution:

```
(≫) : : IO a → IO b → IO b
```

This performs the first I/O action, ignoring any result produced, and then performs the second action; thus, it is like the semicolon in an imperative language. For example, two calls to putChar can be sequenced as follows:

```
putChar 'a' ≫ putChar 'b'
```

When an I/O action returns a value, it can be transmitted to a subsequent I/O operation using ≫ = :

```
(≫ =) : : IO a → (a → IO b) → IO b
```

For example, to read a character and then print it, we could write

```
getChar ≫ = ( \c → putChar c)
```

The I/O monad also provides a *null* I/O function, return. This function takes a value and creates an action which will return that value when executed, Its type is

return : : a → IO a

It is important to remember that these I/O functions are no different from any other Haskell function. For example, ≫ can be used as an argument to fold to define a function that will print a list of characters:

putStr : : [Char] → IO ( )
putStr s = fold (≫) (return ( )) (map putChar s)

CONCLUSIONS

Functional languages are very high-level languages, indeed resembling traditional mathematics in many ways. They center on the evaluation of functions and do not rely on side-effecting commands as most conventional languages do. The perils of side effects are appreciated by experienced programmers in any language, although most are loathe to give them up completely. It remains the goal of the functional programming community to demonstrate that one can do completely without side effects, without sacrificing efficiency or modularity.

REFERENCES

1. R. Milner, M. Tofte, and R. Harper, *The Definition of Standard ML*, The MIT Press, Cambridge, MA, 1990.
2. P. Hudak, S. Peyton Jones, and P. Wadler (eds.),"Report on the Programming Language Haskell, A Non-strict Purely Functional Language (Version 1.2)," *ACM SIGPLAN Notices, 27*(5), 000–000 (1992).
3. R. Bird and P. Wadler, *Introduction to Functional Programming*, Prentice-Hall, New York 1988.
4. A. J. Field and P. G. Harrison, *Functional Programming*, Addison-Wesley, Workingham, U.K., 1988.
5. P. Hudak, "Conception, Evolution, and Application of Functional Programming Languages," *ACM Comput. Surv., 21*(3), 359–411 (1989).
6. J. Hughes, "Why Functional Programming Matters," Technical Report 16, Programming Methodology Group, Chalmers University of Technology (November 1984).

PAUL HUDAK

IMAGE ANALYSIS AND SYNTHESIS

INTRODUCTION

Since the early phases of Artificial Intelligence, the process of perception has been recognized as a major means to provide an agent (natural or artificial) with information. Perception is initiated by sensors. Among the multitude of sensor types, visual sensors are among the most useful ones for dealing with and extracting information from the physical world. The long-sought quest to imitate human perceptual abilities by building autonomous systems, robots, or even anthropomorphic automata requires a solution of the image analysis problem. Image analysis transforms the sensory signal (a two-dimensional array of numbers) into useful information to achieve a required task.

In order to understand what sort of processing we will need to do, let us look at some of the possible uses for image analysis:

- **Manipulation:** In a factory for automating various production processes, robots are used that will need to perform tasks as grasping an object, inserting, piling, and so on. These tasks need local shape information and feedback ("decrease distance to object", "turn left", "turn right", etc.) for motor control.

- **Navigation:** A very active area of research today is to build autonomous vehicles such as cars that can drive without the assistance of a human driver, and spacecraft and airplanes that can navigate relative to some surface, planetary or on Earth. Such tasks require image analysis for supplying adequate models of the terrain where the vehicle operates, for obstacle avoidance, and calculating one's current position and orientation.

- **Industrial inspection:** Factory automation requires image analysis for all sorts of quality control applications. This ranges from finding defects in a product (wooden boards, circuit boards, leather, glass, metal, food, and so on). Such problems may be approached by using two-dimensional images (e.g., images that have been acquired by just one camera looking at the object) or three-dimensional information. Three-dimensional inspection may be aimed at finding defects on objects that have three-dimensional extent, or of inspecting the three-dimensional parameters of the surface (e.g., does a workpiece comply to the desired specifications).

- **Character recognition:** Character recognition, also called optical character recognition (OCR), aims at the automatic conversion of an image of a character, or of characters in running text, into the corresponding symbolic (ASCII) form. The long history of research in this area, some commercial successes, and the continuing need for implementations to handle less restricted forms of text makes character recognition one of the most important application areas to date in image analysis. The ability of humans to read printed text effortlessly is far from matched by today's machines which makes this an important research topic in artificial intelligence.

- **Range data analysis:** Images obtained by two-dimensional cameras usually acquire luminance information of the object or scene that is imaged. Another type of sensor can be built that stores the distance of each object point imaged from the camera. Information of this kind can be acquired directly using principles of time-of-flight in a laser beam arrangement, or a so-called stereo system, based on multiple two-dimensional images that can be combined to compute range. The purpose of analyzing range data is to extract three-dimensional properties of the object (how far away it is, the curvature of the surface at pertinent points, spatial relations between several objects, and the like). The information analyzed should be sufficient to describe what is being seen and how sensed objects are related to each other in space. When one uses ranging systems, the prevailing task is to obtain the description of a scene in three-dimensional space.

Endeavors to build such systems have sometimes used psychophysical evidence on how the human visual system might work as an ideal and tried to simulate it. Between the areas of computer vision and human visual psychophysics there is a two-way interplay that has been of mutual benefit for both areas. Computer scientists have played a role in the generation of psychophysical models of human vision both in identifying how information about the visual environment is represented in the retinal image and in formulating algorithms that would allow the information to be extracted. On the other hand, in the human visual pathway we have a physical structure that already for a great many years has been able not only to detect and recognize objects but also to perform many other extremely advanced visual functions—and with no apparent effort. In this sense, many of the major problems of robot vision have already been solved. Here, the psychophysicist has aided the computer scientist by experimentally teasing out the methods used by the human visual system to recover environmental information, and then expressing these methods in the form of algorithms.

Definitions

Image analysis in the context of artificial intelligence is the process of using computers to extract useful information about the physical world from images. It uses approaches from *image processing*, which take images as input and computes other images as output. *Pattern recognition* in the context of images uses images as input and *statistical features* as output. The distinction between the two is fuzzy, because sometimes statistical features can also be represented as images. *Computer vision* is closely related to image analysis, stressing the photogrammetric aspects with the goal of deriving information on the *three-dimensional shape* of the objects imaged. *Machine vision* has recently been used mostly in the context of building systems that automate a visual task in manufacturing. In this article, we view *image analysis* as the generic term forming the superset of the terms mentioned above. Other related terms are *machine perception, pattern recognition engineering, industrial automa-*

tion, remote sensing, electronic imaging, motion analysis, and *robotics*, covering various subsets of the problem.

A similar distinction is sometimes made in terms of low-level and higher-level vision. Low-level vision covers topics of binary machine vision, mathematical morphology, neighborhood operators, conditioning operators, labeling operations, texture analysis, region segmentation, and linear feature extraction. Higher-level vision covers illumination, perspective projection, analytical photogrammetry, motion, image matching, model matching, and knowledge-based vision systems.

Image synthesis is the process of artificially creating digital images using computers. The information used to create these images can be *represented explicitly* by storing building blocks like lines, circles, rectangles, and so forth in a computer. This type of synthesis is mostly referred to as *computer graphics* and was the initial application. In an implicit representation, the information is stored in mathematical formulas specifying the synthesis procedure; *fractal image synthesis* is an example. A third type of synthesis is used in the context of *visualization*, where images are computed from one or more types of simple representation. In *scientific* visualization, the goal is to compute images making results of a computation easily understandable for human observers. In *virtual reality*, the computation of images aims to replace cameras and the physical image acquisition process. Other related terms are *computer animation, motion recovery, texture mapping*, and *computer-aided design* (CAD).

Image analysis and synthesis. Modern approaches to image analysis, especially computer vision, have combined methods using synthesis results in the process of analysis. In this interpretation, image analysis procedures compute information (e.g., features). This information is used to synthesize images that would have given rise to those features. The comparison of the original images and the synthesized ones can assist to select an optimal feature set for a specific task. An example is the combined used of CAD data and image analysis techniques, or the computation of navigation data for autonomous robots, where synthesized three-dimensional (3D) models of the environment is used as a basis for recognition of hazards. See details below.

REVIEW OF CONCEPTS AND VOCABULARY

In this section, we summarize some of the major concepts and vocabulary in order to understand image analysis and synthesis for the later sections. The earlier companion articles IMAGE PROCESSING, PATTERN RECOGNITION, COMPUTER VISION should also be consulted for details.

For both biological systems and machines, image analysis begins with a large array of measurements of the amount of light reflected from surfaces in the environment. The goal of image analysis is to recover physical properties of objects in the scene, such as the location of object boundaries and the structure, color, and texture of object surfaces, from the two-dimensional image that is projected onto the eye or camera. The first clues about the physical properties of the scene are provided by the changes of intensity in the image. For example, Figure 1, the boundaries of the cars parked on the parking lot, the reflections on car surfaces and windows, the shadows, the stochastic appearance of leaves all give rise to spatial changes in light

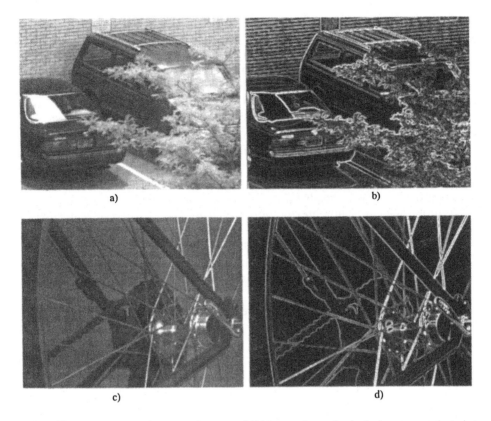

FIGURE 1   An image of a natural scene exhibiting various physical phenomena that give rise to intensity changes. (a) and (c) are original images; (b) and (d) are the images after applying an edge-operator.

intensity captured by the camera. The geometric arrangement, contrast, brightness, and size of these intensity changes contain information about the physical objects in the scene. It should be observed from these examples that the phenomenon "intensity change" is caused by a set of physical phenomena and the detection of intensity changes alone is in no way sufficient to recognize objects.

We have tacitly assumed that the images we are talking about are two-dimensional matrices of bytes, where each byte forms one pixel. In fact, many simple and complex data structures can be combined in a two-dimensional arrangement to form an image. Pixels can be real-valued numbers, integers of arbitrary bit length, real-valued vectors (e.g., a pixel in a color image could be a 3D color vector using one element for each of the red, green, and blue colors). These vector-valued pixels form a *panchromatic* image as opposed to *monochromatic* images that store only information of one spectral channel.

Image Processing

In the strict sense, image processing is the process of computing a new image from an existing image. It is sometimes also defined to encompass all the various operations that can be applied to image data. These include, but are not limited to, image compression, image restoration, image enhancement, preprocessing, quantization, spatial filtering, matching, and recognition techniques. *See* IMAGE PROCESSING.

Image processing can be applied in its own right to generate "better" images from existing ones, or it can be a first step in image analysis. Due to the increased application of digital images in the graphic arts, image processing has become a very large field. Important processing steps are *restoration* and *enhancement*, where radiometric operations are used to convert the original pixel values using a lookup tables. One important applications is histogram equalization, where the histogram of an image is changed by various gray-level transformation functions to enhance the visible contrast. Again, *see* IMAGE PROCESSING.

During image formation with a camera, geometric distortions occur. These may not be critical in some cases, but when the final task of image analysis is to measure objects in the scene in terms of geometric properties (e.g., the length and width of an object), distortions must be corrected. Methods that achieve this comprise *rectification* and *calibration*. This can be achieved by measuring the real-world coordinates of special points in the image. These points (sometimes also called *landmarks* or *control points*) are used to measure distortion parameters and resample the image into a distortion-free one.

Pattern Recognition

Image processing as viewed above is an information-enhancement process. It is primarily geared at making images better suited for interpretation by a human observer. So the information produced by image processing is still an image or set of images. A process is needed to reduce the information contained in the image pixels and produce quantitative or qualitative statements about the image content. A major set of tools to achieve this is pattern recognition. A widely accepted view of pattern recognition uses the following major steps: extraction, identification, classification, and description of patterns. The first step, extraction, finds an intermediate representation of relevant information in the raw image. It may use edge-detection techniques to find edges in images, or group pixels into homogeneous areas that may belong to a single object.

Here, *object* could be a single pixel or a group of pixels (e.g., a chain of pixels linked together, or an area of pixels connected together). The major goal is to find subgroups of pixels that will be described by some sort of attributes. Usually, this set of attributes is called *features*. A particular approach to finding such subgroups are clustering techniques. These techniques seek to group pixels into meaningful subsets based on the attributes of the single pixels. In general, only one attribute is not sufficient to describe an object. This leads to the notion of a feature vector – a collection of attributes that describe the object. Pattern recognition usually deals with numeric features; that is, features that form a vector in the domain of real numbers. However, this needs not be the case. Features can also be of linguistic type, leading to more advanced techniques.

Using the feature vector representation, techniques can be used to construct decision rules that enable one to identify units on the basis of their measurement patterns. One possibility is to build mathematical functions of the feature vectors that assigns a class to each feature vector. Given the class of on object, it is possible for an automatic system, for example, to make a decision and change its course of action. In the following paragraphs, we will elaborate on these techniques and give examples. The reader should also refer to the special article PATTERN RECOGNITION in this Encyclopedia.

There is no general approach to the process of feature extraction. The type of features extracted depends mostly on the task at hand and the kind of images used. As shown in Figure 1, many different phenomena can occur in real-world scenes, and a major task for the designer of image analysis systems is to confine the occurring phenomena to a set as small as possible. If the illumination of the scene can be controlled, useful results can be achieved already with a relatively simple set of features. Many industrial systems, for example, use controlled illumination and simple thresholding techniques to make decisions and provide measurement results.

Pattern recognition provides a very useful tool to at least semiautomate this process, called **feature selection**. Using an image as input, one can compute a large set of feasible features. The types of features could include geometrical features (spectral features, Karhunen–Loeve components, spatial features, FFT features, moment features) and structural features (line segments, curve segments, blobs, corner points, line intersections). None of these features will be useful in general, but using statistical techniques, the contribution of each feature to the given task can be measured.

We will leave this general overview of pattern recognition by noting that it knows two basic paradigms: *statistical pattern recognition* and *structural pattern recognition*. For the underlying mathematics and a description of applications in character recognition, with the special case of contextual character recognition, *see* PATTERN RECOGNITION.

Computer Vision

In the above, we have briefly summarized the key components of image analyses. Image processing and pattern recognition combined yield the (mostly) quantitative result of our desired information reduction process. One possible next step is to combine these results with artificial intelligence techniques and focus on the computer analysis of one or more images, possibly taken in a time sequence, and to try to interpret three-dimensional scenes. Sometimes, this process is termed computer vision, image understanding, or scene analysis. It should be stressed, however, that no clear-cut definition exists, and these terms are used interchangeably with image analysis. In the following, we will outline the basic steps in a computer vision system, defined here as a system that takes two-dimensional image(s) as input and outputs an interpretation of the three-dimensional scene that was imaged.

Note that this process will have two major parts. One part will process the two-dimensional image(s); a second part will derive the *three-dimensional* information. In the first part, the two-dimensional image (e.g., a gray-level image of the scene) will be analyzed much like was discussed above. We will derive property measurements, symbolic images, or labels, find the relational structure of these labels, and possibly achieve segmentation. Using the segments detected, we can match these segments to stored models via model matching and finally achieve recognition. In the literature, sometimes the term *feature* loosely refers to a specific part of an object (e.g., a vertex or a line), but we will adhere to the strict sense, where a feature is a (sometimes statistical) property of an image or segment of an image. For example, the gray value is a feature of a pixel; the mean value of a region is a feature of that image part. For recognition, often features defined for a single entity are combined to form feature vectors. A feature vector is an *N*-tuple of features.

As can easily seen, the process of **segmentation** is very difficult in practice. See, for instance, Figure 3, where reasonable segments are easily recognizable by a human observer, but due to the overlapping areas, segmentation by computer is not as trivial. By segmentation, we mean the detection of connected areas in an image. Such techniques include edge detection, color and texture edge detection, lines, curves, blobs, spots, and corners. Segmentation aims at the computation of "coherent" point subpopulations. To achieve segmentation, the techniques to isolate *connected components* like holes, concavities, borders, arcs, branches, and elongated parts are used. They deal with thinning and the computation of skeletons, shrinking, expanding, opening, closing, and resegmentation of arcs and curves. A particular ingenious methods for detection of such image parts is the *Hough transform*.

In a three-dimensional world, the segmentation is even more complex. For instance, consider, again, Figure 1. Here, the cars are partially occluded by the leaves of the trees in the foreground. Two-dimensional segmentation will fail when we cannot incorporate the knowledge of occlusion in some way. One possibility would be to incorporate three-dimensional information like the distance of the various parts of the image from the camera and combine it with the two-dimensional information of the image. Now, three-dimensional information cannot, at least in general, be inferred from one image alone, although there are instances where this is possible. We will need to include a second view of the scene using a stereo camera system or range system, for example.

Three-dimensional image analysis was strongly influence by the work of Marr (1), who was among the first to define the 3D scene analysis paradigm. He suggested a chain of processing consisting of the following steps:

- 2D features extraction, recovery
- 2½D feature extraction
- Segmentation
- Resegmentation
- 2½D property measurement
- Constraint analysis (3D)

The central aim in **Marr's paradigm** was recovery (i.e., the computation of the full depth map to recover the three-dimensional information). Many approaches to achieve this goal have been studied. The list includes *shape from contour* (or *shape from shape*), *shape from focus, shape from shading, shape from stereo, shape from texture*, and *shape from motion*. This approach was studied so widely that the generic term of *shape from X* was coined. This paradigm is explained in more detail in the special article, COMPUTER VISION in this Encyclopedia.

THE GENERIC IMAGE ANALYSIS PROCESSING CHAIN

In this section, we describe a full-image analysis processing chain. As was discussed above, it includes steps to successively reduce the amount of raw data and increase the amount of information extracted. These steps form *levels of abstraction*, where the type of information changes from pure *numeric* to a *symbolic* one. Image analysis aims to answer questions as: What kind of objects does this image contain? Where are the objects? What are the properties of the objects? The generic building blocks that became useful mostly in the two-dimensional case are preprocessing and feature computation, labeling, segmentation, and statistical classification.

From Features to Objects

Throughout this article (unless otherwise noted), the term *feature* is used in the sense of statistical classification (2) as a *number* or *measurement*. Features are used to *describe* entities like pixels, objects, or a whole image. The *intensity* of a pixel could be such a feature, or the diameter of an object is other one. Features are not to be understood as the entities themselves (as sometimes used in image processing or remote sensing terminology), where edges, lines, or blobs are understood as features.

When several such numbers are needed to describe an entity, they form a set of features, or *feature vector*. When entities are described by sets of features, not all of them may be useful for classification. The process of finding a useful subset of features is termed *feature selection*. When several features are used to compute new features (usually a smaller number of features), the term *feature extraction* is used.

The term *object* in this context designates segments of an image that contain some effect of relevance. Often but not always, an object is a compact, connected set of pixels clearly distinguishable from the regular (background) texture. Examples for objects are edges, lines, or vertices in a drawing. An object can be *represented* by a feature vector, much the same as single pixels, although the type of features will be different. For object recognition, it may sometimes be useful to represent each objects by a number of subobjects.

As shown in Figure 2, the first step in our image analysis chain is **preprocessing and feature computation**. In general, this process assigns to each pixel a feature vector. The type of features computed varies based on the application. This step may result in a data reduction process (e.g., in image thresholding, where the feature assigned is a binary value, and only one such feature is assigned), or it may increase the amount of data (e.g., in edge detection, where the output of several *two-dimensional filters* is assigned to each pixel). Useful features include the output of filters, the output of texture operators, and the output of edge operators.

The results of the feature computation step for each pixel are used to assign labels to each pixel in the **labeling** step. Such a label can be of symbolic nature as used in edge detection, corner detection, or the identification of pixels that participate in forming shape primitives, or it can have a numeric value. A review of

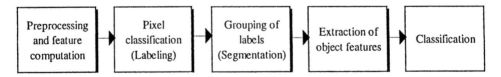

FIGURE 2   A generic processing chain for image analysis.

labeling algorithms can be found in Ref. 3 and 4. The labels assigned to pixels are the input to **segmentation**. Segmentation aims at finding maximal connected sets of pixels whose labels share some property. If the labels are symbolic, segmentation is a grouping process called *connected component analysis*. If the labels are numeric, segmentation can be achieved by a process called *region growing*.

We have now achieved one of the most difficult steps in image analysis. In fact, whenever segmentation results in a clear partitioning of the image into the objects of interest and every object is represented by just one such segment, the proceeding processing is straightforward. In practice, however, segmentation will need improvement. The objects of interest may be spread out over several segments, or on the contrary, one segment may contain several objects. This is where a process called *resegmentation* may be invoked. In this step, all the segments are analyzed as to whether some of them should be joined together or split up into separate segments. A principle, which turned out to help in this step, is the *principle of least commitment*. It suggests trying to segment the image into rather small parts to ensure that no segment contains more than one object. The following resegmentation step then needs to take into account only possibilities for merging, not for splitting.

Having achieved a reasonable segmentation, we can extract separate features for every single object found (**feature extraction** or **computation**). The segments found by grouping or connected component labeling are assigned properties or features. Such properties might include the centroid, area, orientation, spatial moments, and so on. These features are used as input to classification or matching with previously acquired samples. Basically, every segment is described by a feature vector for statistical classification or by a set of symbolic descriptions derived from the distribution of labels within the segment.

The step of extraction of object features results in a separate feature vector for each object. Now, **statistical classification** follows. This step uses the feature vectors computed during extraction and assigns classes to each segment. This is one of the most intensely studied areas in image analysis. It is useful on every level of processing, be it pixels, subobjects, or objects. Recently, the area has found useful additions through the advance of *artificial neural network* (ANN) techniques (see below). A very comprehensive review of the state of the art, with an emphasis on the mutual benefits of both approaches, can be found in Refs. 5 and 6.

Practical Variants

In practice, the generic processing chain described above will need to adapt to the problem at hand. Often, a very effective approach is **hierarchical processing**. The processes of feature computation, labeling, and grouping can be performed not only on pixels but on groups of pixels. Such a technique could use combinations of 4 × 4 pixels on a regular grid yielding 16 feature vectors. These features are combined to form one single label. The aim of this process is to reduce the amount of data to be processed. This technique is frequently used in real-time processing. After labeling, the subsequent processing steps have only a sixteenth of the storage requirements. Another area where this approach is used is in texture segmentation. As texture segmentation cannot be done locally, such a data reduction process is mandatory.

A special method for computing features is based on correlation of the image with a set of filters, whose coefficients are defined by a *Gabor* function, yielding so-called Gabor features. The Gabor function is complex-valued in the image domain. For image representation and compression, the real part of the Gabor function is sufficient, and usually only the real part of the Gabor function has been used for detection of objects. For distortion of invariant multiclass object detection, a number of different Gabor functions are necessary (7). The imaginary part of a Gabor filter has been shown to be a good (tunable) edge detector, whereas the real part is a (tunable) blob detector. Extensions of these ideas combine the advantages of both parts using a fusion concept (8,9). In this approach, optimal filters can be derived by tuning the parameters of a filter to achieve the best trade-off between correct classification and false alarms. Other examples of how Gabor filters can be used for various applications are found in Ref. 10, which is also a good introductory text for the area.

The step of statistical classification was only briefly described above. A prerequisite to make statistical classification work is the knowledge (or computation) of the probability density functions for the features used. In some cases, this can be avoided by applying simple classifiers that use only statistical parameters like the mean and variance of the feature distribution — a procedure that will work when the features follow the assumption of Gaussian distribution function. A very useful set of tools as an alternative to statistical classification would be using **neural networks**. The field of neural networks has arisen from diverse sources ranging from physiology, psychology, and signal processing (1D and 2D) through language processing. A neural network is a set of units, each of which takes a linear combination of values from either an input vector or the output of other units. The linear combination then goes through a nonlinear function, such as a threshold or a sigmoid. Associated with the neural network is a training algorithm, where the pattern feature vectors are analyzed by the network. The network changes its parameters (*weight*) according to the output of this analysis. A widely used technique for this adaptation process is the *back-propagation* algorithm. In the simplest networks, the output from one node is fed into another node in such a way as to propagate information through layers of interconnected nodes. More complex behavior may be modeled by networks in which the final output nodes are connected with earlier nodes, and then the system has the characteristics of a highly nonlinear system with feedback.

It has been argued that neural networks mirror, to a certain extent, the behavior of networks of neurons in the brain. The anthropomorphic name with implicit high-aiming expectations led to a widely discussed controversy. The limitations of the networks that Rosenblatt and Block discussed were explored by Minsky and Papert (11). After the publication of their book, interest in perceptrons and neural networks decreased. Kohonen (12) showed how to use the neural network paradigm for associative memories, followed by further improvements in form of the self-organizing map (SOM) and learning vector quantization (LVQ), both reviewed extensively in Ref. 6.

Program packages. Many extensive software packages exist. A selection is provided in Refs. 6, 13, and 14. Many programs are available on the Internet; one of the largest packages is Khoros.

COMPUTATIONAL TECHNIQUES

In the previous section, we have shown a generic image analysis processing chain. Every single step in this chain can consist of a serious of computational techniques that assist in improving the intermediate results. As an example, we could choose a simple thresholding technique to label an image into just two classes: background and object regions. This will often result in erroneous segmentation. An alternative to the resegmentation step mentioned above would be to work on the labeled image and try to remove those pixels from the object regions that cause the wrong segmentation. From a large set of methods, also termed image operations, we will select morphological processing as a further example of elegant processing that can drastically improve segmentation in some cases.

Image Operations

Mathematical morphology refers to an area of image processing concerned with the analysis of shape. The basic morphological operations consist of dilating, eroding, opening, and closing of an image with a structuring element. For an introduction, see Ref. 15 or the overview in Ref. 3. Morphological processing can be applied to both binary and gray-level images. An illustration is given in Figure 3. Let us assume that our processing steps achieved a binary image consisting only of black and white pixels, where a black pixel is represented by the value zero (0) and a white pixel by the value one (1). This binary image can be "improved" depending on the task by the following steps, or a combination of them.

- Erosion. This function uses the binary image and tests the neighborhood of every pixel. When it finds a white pixel that has a black pixel as neighbor, the white pixel is set to black. The neighborhood function used is

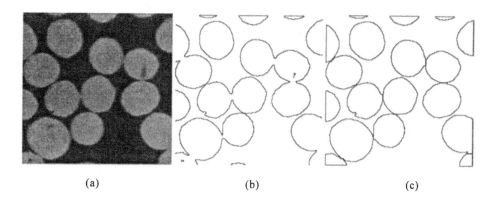

(a)   (b)   (c)

FIGURE 3 An example for morphological image processing. Here, an application of morphology is shown for the purpose of segmentation of blobs in a binary image. (a) The original image; (b) after thresholding the image, binary-connected component labeling is performed and the detected boundaries are plotted; (c) after thresholding, a sequence of binary erosions and dilations are performed, the remainder is the same as in (b). The boundaries of the objects have been improved, and the cells of (a) have been correctly segmented.

typically 8-connected referring to the fact that all 8 neighbors — left, right, top, bottom, and the diagonal neighbors — of the pixel are inspected. A more general view of erosion uses the notion of a structuring element. The structuring element is a small binary template, defining the morphological operation. For the case of eroding with the 8-connected neighborhood function, we used a 3×3 binary template as the structuring element. Erosion results in an image that gives all locations where the structuring element is contained in the original image.

- Dilation. This function is the inverse of erosion. It identifies all background pixels that are 8-connected to a foreground pixel, or, in general terms, it gives all locations where in the neighborhood defined by the structuring element at least one foreground pixel is present.
- Open. This is an erosion followed by a dilation.
- Close. A dilation followed by an erosion.

The following operations on binary images are not strictly morphological, but may use the morphological operation defined above.

- Skeletonize. This function seeks to find the approximate centerline for each connected component in the foreground. It assumes that we have identified, or labeled, the segments in the binary image already. The centerline is found by iteratively removing pixels at the boundary of the component.
- Thinning. After connected component labeling of the binary image, this operation applies to morphological hit-or-miss transform to the foreground until there is no further change. The goal of thinning is to identify a set of pixels that describe the underlying shape of the components. A major problem with thinning are the resulting "hair" that protrude from the objects. Usually, a step called *pruning* is applied after thinning to remove these protrusions.
- Thicken. Thickening proceeds in iterations, where, at every step, small holes on the boundary of the component are removed. After several thickening iterations, the shape of the component will approach an enclosing octagon.
- Watershed separation. This function is very effective, yet time-consuming, in separating touching blobs. Touching blobs are segments that are labeled as one large segment, whereas, in fact, it contains two or more smaller segments. The function applies the so-called watershed algorithm to an intermediate image derived from the foreground components of the segmented image. The intermediate image is formed by inverting the distance transform of the binary image.
- Distance transform. Here, for every pixel in an object, the distance to the nearest background pixel is computed. The resulting image contains this distance as the gray value for every pixel.

We conclude this section with an example for an image, where morphological operations are used to improve the segmentation result. In Figure 3, the improvement was achieved by a series of erosions and dilations; in Figure 4, the watershed algorithm was used to improve segmentation.

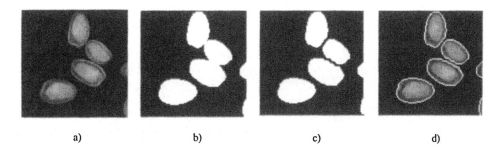

a)   b)   c)   d)

FIGURE 4 An example for the watershed algorithm. Here, the task was to separate the touching objects. (a) The original image; (b) result of thresholding; (c) result of the watershed algorithm; (d) the resulting object boundaries.

TWO-DIMENSIONAL IMAGE ANALYSIS

The preceding sections have described the major processing steps that lead us from the iconic image representation (i.e., the representation in form of pixels) to the representation in form of segments. Let us assume that this segmentation has resulted in an assignment of each pixel to a certain segment, or to the background. We will now proceed with a description of what can be done with each segment, especially how it can be represented in a data structure and how we can derive a classification or recognition. We have already seen a very simple representation in Figures 3 and 4, where the boundaries of the segmented objects are shown as a chain of bright pixels. We will now proceed to more elaborate data structures that are applicable for the classification task.

Two-dimensional shape analysis can use representations that are *imagelike* such as binary images with assigned labels (from connected component analysis) or can consist of more complicated data structures like *graphs, strings, skeletons, lists of edge elements*, and so on. The image analysis part uses two steps. The first step builds up the data structure; the second interprets the computed data structure. Figure 5 illustrates this sequence of processing.

One of the most important and efficient algorithms to transform a feature image into a segmented image is connected component analysis. Also called *blob coloring* or *labeling*, connected component analysis uses features defined on images. (Note as an example that the result of thresholding on a gray-level image is a special kind of feature image. The feature assigned to each pixel has the value 0 or 1.) The algorithm parses through all pixels in an image and assigns a unique number to all pixels that are connected and similar. The definition of connectedness is based on the selection of a neighborhood function. The definition of similarity uses the feature values (or vectors) at each pixel. A simple measure of similarity occurs in binary images, where two pixels are said to be similar if they have the same gray value (0 or 1). Examples for how labels can be connected are 4-connectedness, or 8-connectedness, or more-connection function using also similarity criteria (3,16, 17). An example for a result of connected component labeling is shown in Figure 5.

Depending on the data structure used to represent the image information, different kinds of *properties* can be computed. In the case of imagelike representa-

a) Graylevel image

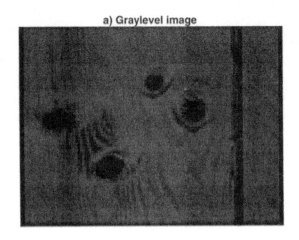

b) Symbolic image

```
                @  @  @  @
                @  @  @  @                                              @
                @  @  @  @
                @  @  @  @                                              @
    @           @  @  @  @           0  e  D
    @     @  @  @  @  @  @           d  +  D
          @  @  @                    8  E  4        d  e
          e                         8  4        0  e  2                 @
        e  e  @      @  @  @               e  d  V  D                   @
    0  +  +  2          @  @                  d  @  E  4
  d  8  E  4  4          @  @  D            8  8        4  E             @
    E  E  E  +  @  +  e  @  @                    E  E          @  @
          @  +  +  +  E  D                  @                8          @
          @  @  +  E  4  e  e  D                                    @  @
          @  @  @  D  0  e  2  D                                    @  @
    @     @  @  @  d  d  +  4  2                                    @  @
          @     @  @  8  E  4                                       @  @
          @        @  E  @                                          @  @
          @  @  @  @        @                                          @
             @  @  @        @                                          @
          @  @  @  @  @                                                @
```

c) Label image

```
                6  6  6  6
                6  6  6  6                                        42
                6  6  6  6
                6  6  6  6                                        43
      44        6  6  6  6        454545
      44     6  6  6  6  6  6     454545
                6  6  6          454545    4647                   48
               49                4545         474747
          505051    525252                 53475447              55
        50505050       5252                47564747
      5050505050    525257                  4747    4758         59
       505050606160625252                      4747              5959
             636060606262               64          65           59
             6363606070606666666                                 5959
             6363636766666666                                    5959
      68     6363636666666669                                    5959
             63    6363666666                                    5959
             63         636663                                   5959
             63636363      63                                    59
               636363    63                                      59
             6363636363                                          59
```

FIGURE 5 Example of the sequence of processing steps in image analysis. From the gray-level image, a symbolic image is derived, followed by the computation of a label image, boundary representation, and feature representation of the objects found in the image. (a) Gray-level image; (b) symbolic image; (c) label image; (d) boundary representation for object with number 47; (e) typical feature representation for object 47 as used for further analysis.

d) Boundary representation for object 47

object# 47 → e2D44E8dd0

e) Feature representation for object 47

object# 47

npix	14.0	i0	22.9	j0	123.7		
y_min	6.0	n_dark	3.0	n_hole	0.0	phi	91.9
l1	32.9	i2	15.7	y_max_min	48.0	elong	0.3
orient	99.9	r1	2.5	r2	1.8	p_count	0.0
c_count	0.0	feat_c	-8.0	feat_d	20.0	feat_e	18.0
feat_y	40.0	feat_cv	-9.0	c_max	16.0	d_max	34.0
e_max	29.0	y_max	87.0	cv_max	17.0	dD_count	21.0
pl_count	0.0	a	15.7	b	-1.1	c	32.9
class_form	3.0	obj_name	0.0	Cc_avg	0.0	y_max_avg	87.0

FIGURE 5   Continued.

tion, algorithms exist to efficiently compute the properties for the regions found in the image: *perimeter, area, centroid, moments* and *center of gravity*. An important set of properties are those that are invariant against rotation and scale. Certain moments can be computed that are invariant. Others are the *Euler number for a region* (the number of connected components minus the number of holes) and the *compactness* (length of the perimeter divided by the area). Many other properties can be computed: the *bounding rectangle of a region, extremal pixel, elongation, symmetric axis*, or *signature analysis*.

In signature analysis, a binary image is analyzed in terms of its projections. Projections can be vertical, horizontal, diagonal, circular, radial, spiral, or general. The analysis computes such projections, segments each projection, and takes property measurements of each projection segment.

The *skeleton* of a region is often computed for the analysis of linelike structures (e.g., line-drawing analysis). It is achieved by the successive applications of a *thinning* operator which reduces a regions to a set of arcs that constitutes a skeleton. A thinning operator is a symbolic image neighborhood operator that deletes, in some symmetric way, all the interior border pixels of a region that do not disconnect the region.

When image regions are described in a symbolic manner, approaches from the area of formal languages can be applied for recognition. An example would be the representation of the contour of an object by symbolic shape primitives (see Fig. 5). The contour is a string of symbols and defines a sentence from formal language. The language is defined by a formal grammar. Recognition is achieved by parsing the string successively with a set of grammars. The grammar which causes the least amount of syntactical errors defines the class assigned. *See* PATTERN RECOGNITION.

Color and Texture

When we observe natural surfaces like textiles, a road surface, stones, wood, or stones, we perceive that their surfaces are homogeneous, in spite of fluctuations in brightness or color. Such a homogeneous visual pattern is called *texture*. All objects have a specific texture and human beings can use textures as cues to recognize many kinds of objects in the world. In our generic image analysis chain, the analysis of texture can be placed in several places. One possibility would be to compute mathematical parameters that describe the texture locally (i.e., around a certain region around each pixel). The parameters computed again form a feature vector. Typically, such feature vectors have high dimensions, due to the great variety in which textures may appear. A second approach would be to achieve a first segmentation based on crude texture measures and to use finer texture measure to split up the segments, or classify them.

Texture is an important characteristic for the analysis of many types of images. Despite its importance and ubiquity in images, a formal approach or precise definition of texture does not exist. The texture discrimination techniques are, for the most part, ad hoc. In the following, we discuss some of the extraction techniques and models that have been used to measure textural properties and to compute three-dimensional shape from texture. The following three issues for analyzing the texture of an image region are of interest (18):

1. Classification: determine to which of a finite number of classes the region belongs
2. Modeling: determine a description or mathematical model of the texture
3. Segmentation: determine the boundaries between differently textured regions

To characterize texture, we must characterize the gray-level primitive properties as well as the spatial relationships among them. This implies a two-level analysis: The first level has to do with specifying the local properties that manifest themselves in gray-level primitives; the second layer has to do with specifying the organization among the gray-level primitives. Methods for texture analysis include *gray-level co-occurrence, generalized co-occurrence, autocorrelation function, digital transform methods, textural energy, textural edginess, vector dispersion, relative extremal density, mathematical morphology, autoregression models, discrete Markov random fields, random mosaic models,* and *structural approaches.* See Refs. 3 and 19. In order to capture the spatial dependence of gray-level values a two-dimensional dependence matrix known as a gray-level co-occurrence matrix is extensively used in texture analysis. Another measure that has been used extensively is the autocorrelation function. These are discussed briefly in this section.

Gray-Level Co-Occurrence Matrix

The gray-level co-occurrence matrix $P(i, j, d)$ is a parameter of a displacement vector $d = (dx, dy)$. Using a particular value of d, we consider all pixels whose distance to each other is d and count how often these pairs have gray-levels i and j. In general, $P(i, j, d)$ is not symmetric because the number of pairs of pixels having gray-levels (i, j) does not necessarily equal the number of pixel pairs having gray-levels (j, i). The elements of $P(i, j, d)$ are normalized by dividing each entry by the total number of pixel pairs. For analysis purposes, the matrices P are not used as such, but we compute new features from them. Examples for such feature are the following:

$$\text{Entropy} \quad = -\Sigma \, \Sigma \, P(i, j, d) \log P(i, j, d),$$
$$\text{Energy} \quad = \Sigma \, \Sigma \, P^2(i, j, d),$$

Contrast $\quad = \Sigma \Sigma (i - j)^2 P(i, j, d),$

Homogeneity $= \Sigma \Sigma \dfrac{P(i,j,d)}{1 + |i - j|}.$

The choice of the displacement d is an important parameter in the definition of the gray-level co-occurrence matrix. Usually, a set of displacements is chosen and the parameters are computed for all of them. Automatic feature selection methods are then applied to select the subset of parameters that achieves the highest classification accuracy in a given task.

Color

With the advent of priceless color sensors, color processing has become a feasible option for increasing the information contents of images. Basically, a color image can be viewed as an image where each pixel has three features—the values of the red, green and blue (RGB) color channels of the camera. This view enables us to apply all methods from multifeature classification. In addition, direct transforms on the color information are widely used. The IHS transform, for instance, converts the RGB information, which contains brightness and color into *intensity, hue,* and *saturation* (IHS) values. The major advantage of using IHS representation rather than the RGB representation is the fact that color variations will usually affect all three colors. Take the simple case, where the color stays the same, only the brightness varies. In this case, all three values of RGB change; yet, in the IHS model, only the intensity value changes. Using the IHS model, a simple threshold or range selection on the hue parameter can be used to select a particular color. With RGB, one would have to select three different ranges simultaneously to select the color.

MATCHING AND STEREO

So far, we have considered the analysis of only one image at a time. Many image analysis tasks require the simultaneous analysis of two or more images. In some applications, the information about an object must be collected over a series of images. For example, when a workpiece on a conveyor belt is to be inspected for its three-dimensional shape, several images must be taken to acquire all possible aspects of the object. Multiview images are a standard requirement when objects are just too large to fit within the view of one camera. An example would be the three-dimensional modeling of the surface of a planet, in order to provide the vital information for the landing and navigation system of a spacecraft. But not only does three-dimensional modeling need several images. The monitoring of land-use, for instance, needs to cover large areas, and several images must be "pasted" together to map an entire scene. In these tasks, the imaged areas overlap. One must find out where the overlap occurs and take proper steps to adapt the various images so they fit together into the mosaic.

In these tasks, image matching is the central task. Image matching refers to the process of determining the pixel-by-pixel, arc-by-arc, or region-by-region correspondence between two images taken of the same scene, but with different sensors, different lighting, or a different viewing angle. Image matching can be used in the spectral/temporal pattern classification of remote sensing or in determining corresponding points for stereo, tracking, change analysis, and motion analysis. In one group of approaches, subimages of one image are translated over a second image. For each translation, the differences between appropriately transformed gray-tone intensities and/or edges are measured.

Image matching can be achieved by *symbolic registration* (or *symbolic matching*) or by *feature point matching*. In symbolic matching, higher-level units are used. For example, the scene can be segmented and a region matching then performed by using segment features, such as area, position, perimeter^2/area, orientation, and so on. In feature point matching, selected points of each image are first determined on the basis of the distinctive image values in a neighborhood or on the basis of intersection between two feature lines. The location of each point can be determined to subpixel precision. After the locations of distinctive points are determined, a correspondence process associates as many selected points of one image as possible with selected points on the second image (Fig. 6). The correspondence is based on similarity of the feature characteristics of the points. See Ref. 20 for a review and comparison of the various techniques.

The techniques of image matching can be the last resort when other methods fail. One possibility would be to store the image of a prototype object for every possible class, match all prototypes to the new image, and select the best-fitting prototype as classification. Such cases are examples of where the generic processing chain of extracting features, segmentation, and classification, is interrupted, because one link in the chain cannot be performed. Take, for example, the task of detecting scratches on a metallic surface, which is corrupted by small particles. Although scratches form connected lines in an image, the small particles make it impossible find continuous objects. This application was the initial task to be solved by the **Hough transform** method. Although first utilized for detecting lines in extremely noisy images, the method is mathematically equivalent too pattern matching.

The Hough transform is a technique to find patterns of a given shape. It is, mathematically, an efficient implementation of template matching (21). It has also been used successfully in the detection of three-dimensional object shapes. The technique uses forms or shapes having free parameters that, when specified precisely, define the arc, shape, or form. For example, a circle is described by the parameters radius and center coordinates – a total of three parameters. Whenever a point in an image is found that could belong to a circle, an estimate is computed of which parameter values could have created this point. For instance, could we apply an edge detection operator to the image containing a circle? All points with high output of this operator could be circle points. Now, from the orientation of the edge, we would have an estimate of where the center of the circle would lie (Fig. 7). A voting scheme is then implemented using a set of accumulators, where each accumulator corresponds to one value set of the parameters.

The so-called free parameters constitute the transform domain or the parameter space of the Hough transform. Depending on the information available to the Hough transform, each neighborhood of the image or object surface being transformed will map to a point or a set of points in the Hough parameter space. The Hough transform discretizes the Hough parameter space into bins and counts, for each bin, how many neighborhoods on the image or object surface have a trans-

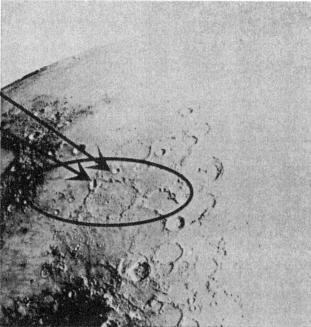

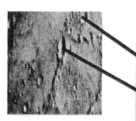

Camera Image
(acquired during
navigation)

Orbital model
(images acquired during orbit)
The ellipse of uncertainty (EU) is the
estimate for the current location of
the spacecraft (100m/pixel)

FIGURE 6   Illustration of image matching as used in the context of spacecraft navigation. A spacecraft uses a camera system to acquire images during its flight. Using a prestored model of the terrain and image matching techniques, the current position of the spacecraft relative to the terrain can be computed. See also Figure 14.

formed point lying in the volume assigned to the bin. The bin with a maximum number of counts corresponds to the sought-after parameter combination.

Another very important instance of matching of images occurs in the task of three-dimensional modeling of objects using several cameras. We will look into the case of stereo, where an object is viewed by at least two cameras, and information about the object in three-dimensional coordinated systems can be obtained. In particular, stereo—from *stereos*, Greek for solid—indicates the involvement of three-dimensional space. Image analysis is has traditionally been restricted to the recovery of a three-dimensional scene from multiple images of the scene. Our focus shall be the recovery of a scene from a pair of images of the scene, each image acquired from a different viewpoint.

By far, the most widely investigated stereo technique employs the variation of

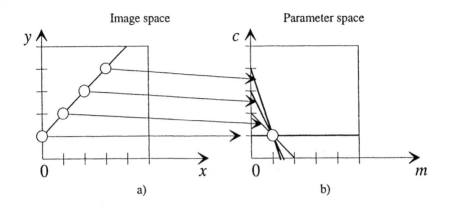

FIGURE 7 An example for the application of the Hough transform to detect a line in an image. (a) The image space $y = f(x)$, or $y = mx + c$. (b) The parameter space (or Hough space) $m = g(c)$, or $c = y - mx$. Every point in (a) gives rise to certain combinations of parameter values m and c in (b).

camera position, called geometric stereo. Whereas the theoretical basis for geometric stereo is straightforward, the implementation of geometric stereo is a nontrivial undertaking. It requires that we establish correspondence between points in one image with points in the other image such that each of two matched points is the image of the same point in space. Refs. 16 and 22.

Triangulation. The principle that underlies geometric stereo is triangulation. As illustrated in Figure 8, under the assumption of perspective projection, each image point is the projection of some point along the ray through the image point and its center of projection. If the corresponding point in the other image is known, then the object point must also lie on the corresponding ray through that point. The object point must lie at the intersection of the two rays and the determination of this intersection is called *triangulation*.

Correspondence. The practical difficulty with geometric stereo is the establishment of *correspondence*. As illustrated in Figure 9, ambiguous correspondence between points in the two images may lead to several different consistent interpretations of the scene. However, such local ambiguities often can be resolved at a global level. The problem of correspondence establishment is further confounded by the fact that some points in each image will have no corresponding points in the other image. There are two reasons for this absence of corresponding points. First, the two cameras will have different fields of view; second, objects in the scene may occlude differently in the two images.

Epipolar constraint. Suppose we have two image planes, each with a different center of projection. Then each of the possibly two images of every object point that lies within a particular plane passing through the two centers of projection is restricted to the intersection of this plane with the image plane. A plane that passes through the two centers of projection is called an *epipolar plane*, and the two straight-line intersections of an epipolar plane with the two image planes are called *conjugate* (or *corresponding*) *epipolar lines*. As is clear from Figure 9, conjugate epipolar lines exhibit the following important property: The conjugate, if any, or a point on one epipolar line is restricted to the corresponding epipolar line in the other image.

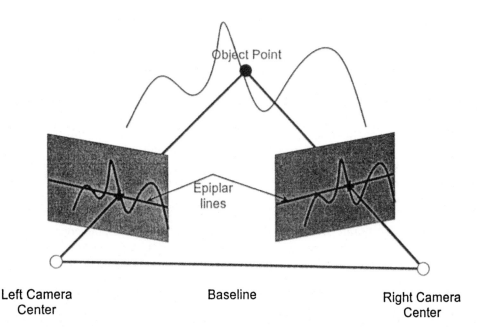

FIGURE 8 Geometric stereo is based on triangulation. Given a single image, the three-dimensional location of any visible object point is restricted to the straight line that passes through the center of projection and the image of the object point.

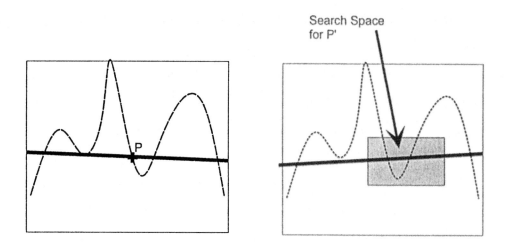

FIGURE 9 The correspondence problem in stereo. When the camera calibration parameters are known, the search space to find the conjugate point P′ to a given point P is the epipolar line. Still, the search is complex due to ambiguity. Several points in the left image may correspond to P.

Calibration for stereo. For geometric stereo, we need geometric models of the cameras. Often, the *intrinsic* parameters of a camera are known a priori, perhaps due to a camera calibration. Then, to specify the geometric model of the camera, we need only to determine the six degrees of freedom associated with the camera's orientation and position. As far as geometric stereo is concerned, it may be sufficient (and possible) to determine only the orientation and position of one camera with respect to the other. Such a determination would allow us to compute the spatial position of the imaged scene points with respect to the camera pair. Typically, stereo calibration is pursued using a known calibration object containing points with known 3D coordinates. Based on the image positions of six or more points, the position and orientation of the camera(s) can be determined in the coordinate system of the object.

In many situations, absolute calibration is not possible and we may have no choice but to calibrate a stereo system by establishing correspondence between individual points in the *two images* such that each point in a pair of matched point is the image of the same object point. Under such circumstances, the distance between the two camera positions cannot be determined. Only the *direction of relative displacement* between the two cameras can be determined. We are then left with just five determinable degrees of freedom: three for the orientation of one camera with respect to the other, and two for the direction of displacement between the two cameras. Longuet-Higgins (23) has shown that barring the case where all the points in the scene lie on a quadric surface that passes through the two viewpoints (24), eight point pairs determine a set of simultaneous linear equations that provide a unique closed-form solution to the five degrees of freedom. Other extensions followed (25-28). However, when the data are noisy, the underutilization of data is a concern. In this case, no closed-form solutions exist. One possible strategy is to use the eight-point approach to determine a tentative solution that serves as a starting point for an iterative numerical solution to the complete set of constraints that are imposed on the solution by the data.

Of the various techniques for shape recovery, geometric stereo, typically, has been the most effective. This relative effectiveness of geometric stereo should come as no surprise. The underlying principle is simple, and depth computations are direct. Note, however, that geometric stereo, at best, provides depth estimates at only those image points that are locally distinguishable along epipolar lines (e.g., edge crossings). The distribution of such points in an image is, in general, sparse and irregular in untextured environments. Hence, several authors have suggested various interpolation schemes to estimate depths at intervening points (e.g., Refs. 29-32. See Refs. 33 and 34 for reviews. All such schemes seek to determine the imaged surface uniquely by restricting the class of admissible solutions severely — for example, to models of thin elastic membranes or plates.

THREE-DIMENSIONAL COMPUTER VISION

Three-Dimensional Representation

In the previous section, we have discussed various techniques to compute three-dimensional information from images of an object. Although techniques exist to derive this information from one image alone, these are restricted to very special constraints of how objects are imaged (illumination and special surface conditions).

The most widely used techniques use multiview stereo and image sequences. Given a representation of the object's points in terms of their location in a three-dimensional coordinate system, the next step is to combine these coordinate measurements into a meaningful model of the object's surface or volume, or some kind of parametric representation so that the surface can be treated as a whole and used for recognition purposes. We will first discuss some current methods to represent surfaces in a mathematical model, followed by a brief discussion on their application to recognition. It should be noted that three-dimensional recognition is one of the most challenging areas of research, and also one of the most immature ones. Note that before we are able to model a surface with mathematical models, we must first segment the surfaces found in a scene into parts, which then are subject to modeling. Methods dealing with breaking up a surface in several parts are described in the article on COMPUTER VISION. They comprise *range sensing* and *range segmentation*, as well as *recovery from shading, texture*, and *contours*. For our discussion here, we assume that a range sensor or a stereo sensor has provided surface information, and segmentation has been achieved.

Object recognition is one of the most important aspects of computer vision. In order to recognize and identify objects, the vision system must have one or more stored models of the objects that may appear in the universe with which it deals. To achieve the goal, it must first represent the entity, or at least represent relevant aspects of it. **Representation** is a key issue in several domains: artificial intelligence, computer-aided design, computer-aided manufacturing, computer graphics, computer vision, and robotics. Representation schemes must have certain desirable attributes: It must be *sufficient*, must have a *wide domain*, it must be *unique*, and it must be *unambiguous, generative, local, additive, stable* and *convenient* (see Ref. 35 for details). In computer vision and computer graphics, a large body of work devoted to shape representation exists. See Ref. 36 for a review. They can be classified into *volumetric* and *surface-based* schemes. We will consider briefly the most influential approaches to shape representation:

- **Parametric Bicubic Patches** (surface based). Parametric bicubic patches are a popular tool for describing surfaces in computer graphics (37). The strategy in this approach is to segment the surface into a set of patches and then to approximate each patch by a parametric bicubic patch such that continuity in position and surface normal across patch boundaries is preserved.
- **Symmetric-Axis Transform** (volumetric). The symmetric-axis transform (SAT), also known as the *Blum transform* or the *medial axis transform* is a widely used shape description technique that was first proposed by Blum in 1967 (38). A description in two dimensions is as follows and its three-dimensional extension is obvious. The SAT uses a circular primitive (circles in two dimensions, balls in three dimensions). Objects are described by the collection of maximal primitives. These are the ones which fit inside the object but cannot be contained in another primitive inside the object. The object is the logical union of all of its maximal primitives. The description is in two parts: the locus of centers, called the symmetric axis, and the radius at each point, called the radius function. An example for a two-dimensional object is given in Figure 10.

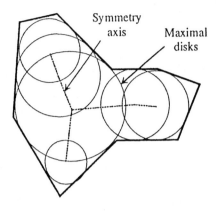

FIGURE 10   The symmetry axis of a simple two-dimensional shape.

- **Generalized Cylinders** (surface based or volumetric). The generalized cylinder (GC) representation, first proposed by Binford in 1971 (39), is perhaps the most popular shape-description method in computer vision today. We can generate any cylinder by sweeping a cross section along a straight line, called the cylinder's *axis*. A *generalized cylinder (GC)* generalized the notion of an ordinary cylinder in two ways: by sweeping the *cross section* along an arbitrary space curve, called the generalized cylinder's *axis* or *spine*, and by allowing the cross section to transform (i.e., scale, rotate, and distort) as it is swept, the transformation rule being called the *sweep rule*.
- **Visual Potential** (nonmetric). The visual potential is a nonmetric description quite unlike the other representations we have discussed. The visual potential of an object is a graph in which each node represents an *aspect* of the object, and each edge represents the possibility of transiting from one aspect to another under motion of the observer (40).

Object Recognition

So far, we have discussed the necessary part to represent an object (two dimensional or three dimensional) and can now proceed with recognition and classification. Recognition is often referred to as a high-level task, stressing the information from additional sources that must flow into this process. Practical applications have shown that recognition cannot be realized without a feedback loop. Feedback means that the system tries to recognize an object (i.e., finds its class among a set of possible classes) and then uses synthesis procedures to generate an artificial simulated representation. This simulated representation is then matched with the representation used in the analysis step, and the differences encountered give rise to change the analysis. The matching between the simulated and the actual representation can be performed on many possible levels: on the feature level, on the level where segments have been found, by comparing the two representations, and even on the level of images. The procedure is performed until convergence criteria are met. The process outlined here can be also thought of as building descriptions of the scene (analysis) and predictions (hypothesis). This paradigm is often also called model-based recognition. (See Fig. 11).

Active Vision

Since the appearance of the first technical results on *active vision* (41,42), researchers are beginning to realize that perception must integrate the observer in the vision process. In an effort to build intelligent visual systems, we must consider the fact that perception is intimately related to the physiology of the perceiver and the tasks that it performs. This viewpoint, known as *purposive, qualitative,* or *animate* vision, is the natural evolution of the principles of *active vision*. An active observer that wants to reconstruct an accurate and complete representation of its extrapersonal space needs an unrealistically large amount of computational power. Complete visual reconstruction is impossible. Purposive vision calls for partial and op-

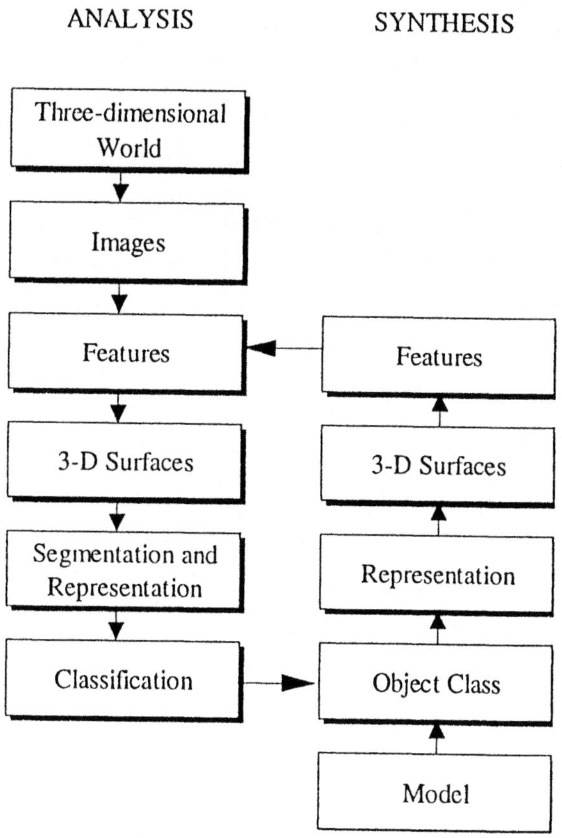

ANALYSIS   SYNTHESIS

FIGURE 11   A model for recognition of three-dimensional object showing the interaction between analysis and synthesis. Many parts of this paradigm are similar to those used in model-based recognition. Notice the iterative (loop) control structure where the analysis results feed into the synthesis chain, which then may change the recognition result.

portunistic visual reconstruction and for the development of new, flexible representations related to action. The current state of research as well as applications can be found in Ref. 43. The thesis that vision is necessarily an active process was first outlined in the context of human vision by Gibson (44).

MOTION

Egomotion and Rigid Objects

Until now, we have restricted ourselves to visual perception by a stationary observer. Let us now explore the recovery of a three-dimensional scene from multiple images of the scene, which were captured by a camera that is in motion with respect to the scene. The continuous stream of images available to an observer who is in motion with respect to the environment provides the observer with information not only about the observer's motion relative to the environment but also about the depths of the observed scene points. Let us consider the case of a forward-moving camera (for instance, the situation seen by a driver of a car on a straight road). Here, points in the scene that are very distant from the observer will not change their positions in the image very much. Also, points that lie along the viewer's direction of translation will have small position changes in all images of the sequence. Other points appear to move radially outward from the observer's point of approach. The amount by which image points change their image positions from one frame to the next is called **motion parallax**. When objects are stationary but viewed by a moving observer, he will have the impression of the objects moving relative to each other. This impression is called apparent relative motion. Apparent motion occurs when the objects lie at different depths along a common line of sight of the observer. Motion parallax was first outlined by Euclid in his treatise *Optics*, circa 300 B.C.

Image capture with camera motion that includes camera translation provides the image data with an extra dimension: the dimension of a varying viewpoint. We have intensity variation over the image plane and over time (i.e., *spatiotemporal variation*). Shape recovery using time-varying imagery is a generalization of geometric stereo. Every scene point lies on all its projection rays; hence, multiple identifiable rays from a scene point determine the spatial position of the point. There is, however, one major difference between three-dimensional recovery through stereo (using a calibrated multicamera system) and that is the unknown motion parameters (or calibration of the camera system). To recover shape from motion requires that the relative motion from one image frame to the next be determined.

When we take two successive image frames, the motion of the camera between these two time instances is described by a **nonlinear equation of six unknowns** (three unknowns for translation, three for rotation). When we assume that point correspondences for these two frames exist, the motion can be recovered up to a scale factor for the translation. Many methods to solve this problem exist (45).

Motion Field

In Figure 12, two frames of an image sequence are shown. The way image points move from one frame to the next have been drawn as vectors. These vectors, which are the projections of the motion of scene points relative to the observer, constitute

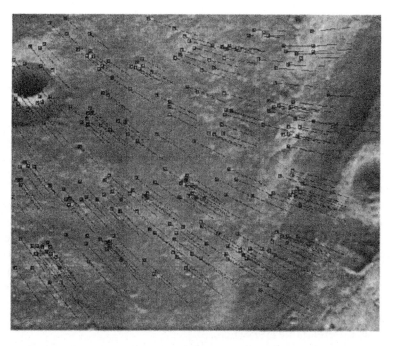

a)

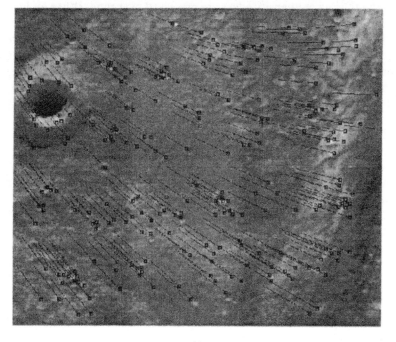

b)

FIGURE 12 The problem of tracking is to find conjugate points in a sequence of image frames. They can either be found by matching or based on the idea of optical flow by using gray-level derivatives. Here, the results of a feature-based tracking algorithm are shown. (Adapted from Ref. 46.)

the observer's so-called *motion field*. The image motion (also called the *optical flow*) that is represented in a motion field may be either the instantaneous image velocities or the interframe displacements of the projections of scene points. In general, it is possible to estimate the motion field over the image plane at only sparsely distributed image locations. This notions of a motion field, as defined here, entails first-order (i.e., straight-line) approximations to the image trajectories of scene points. It is likely that this notion will need to be refined in the not too distant future to include higher-order trajectory information – for instance, to include the curvatures of the image trajectories of scene points.

One set of techniques to estimate the motion field is based on the *spatiotemporal derivatives* of the image data. Recall that *spatio* refers to the two dimensions of a single image, and *temporal* refers to the time axis over which the image evolves. Each technique in this class computes the intensity flow – the image motions of image isobrightness contours; these motions lead to the motion field under the assumption that the image intensities of scene points are strictly preserved over time. Techniques that depend on spatiotemporal differentiation to estimate the motion field assume implicitly that the spatiotemporal variation in the image intensity is continuously differentiable everywhere.

Another class of techniques for motion field estimation is based on *spatiotemporal coherence*. These techniques assume that either one or both of the image intensity and the image-intensity edges are preserved over time. When an image edge evolves under relative motion between the camera and the scene, the edge sweeps out a coherent structure of one higher dimension than itself in spatiotemporal image space: It sweeps out a spatiotemporal surface across which the image intensity undergoes an abrupt change. Analogously, a locally discriminable image point sweeps out a locally discriminable spatiotemporal image curve, and a constant-intensity image region sweeps out a spatiotemporal constant-intensity image volume. Contrary to spatiotemporal derivatives, coherence-based approaches do not require differentiability of the image data.

For the problem of estimating the observer's motion from the motion field, it sometimes suffices to identify the so-called **focus of expansion**. This is a single point in the image sequence where the image points to not move. The focus of expansion of a motion field image arising from a moving camera and a stationary scene is that point on the image where the optic flow is zero and such that the optic flow of the neighboring point are directed away from it. In cases of relative motion toward the camera, there will be exactly one focus of expansion point in such a motion field image. In a motion field image arising from an object in relative motion to the camera, the focus of expansion is that point on the image having all the optic flow vectors arising from the moving object directed away from it.

The Aperture Problem

A special case of optical flow is *edge flow*, where the vectors in the flow image represent the motion of edges. The *aperture problem* for edge flow is the following. In the absence of knowledge of camera motion, when we are looking at a viewpoint-independent edge in an image through an aperture, all we can say about the evolving image position of an indistinguishable point along the edge is that this position continues to lie somewhere along the evolving image of the edge. In the limit, we can locally determine only that component of the image motion of an image-intensity edge that is orthogonal to the edge, and not the component that is tangent to the edge. (See Fig. 13).

Motion Analysis

Motion analysis is determined to find the camera motion parameters from the observed images. It is based on **Euler's theorem** pertaining to rotation about a point: Any arbitrary rotation of a rigid body about a point can be accomplished by a rotation about a unique line through the point. It follows from this theorem that any rigid-body (relative) motion (or velocity) can be decomposed into two three-degree-of-freedom components: translation and rotation about a line through the center of projection. That an arbitrary motion field can be analyzed as the sum of a translational field and a rotational field has been well known for some time. Nakayama and Loomis (47) derived explicit expressions for the component fields under spherical projection. Subsequently, Longuet-Higgins and Prazdny (48) addressed the all-important inverse question: How can we decompose an arbitrary motion field into a pure rotational field and a pure translational field? Such a decomposition is clearly useful: The component fields have a simple structure and are almost trivial to analyze.

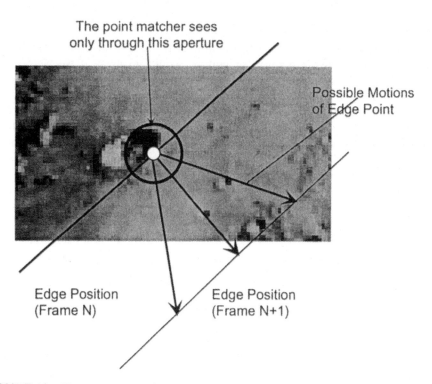

FIGURE 13   The aperture problem appears both in multiview stereo and in motion tracking. See text for explanation.

Nelson and Aloimonos (49) argue that, rather than trying to determine all the motion parameters simultaneously, it is computationally more viable to estimate the relative velocity of the camera by independently computing each of its three rotational velocity components along three mutually orthogonal axes. They show that if we consider motion-field vectors located along a great circle on a spherical projection surface, then the components of these vectors tangent to the great circle will depend on only the following two motions: translation parallel to the plane of the circle, and rotation about an axis orthogonal to the plane of the circle.

As we have discussed above, it is possible to estimate the motion of a camera with respect to a scene when we know the motion field. In addition to estimating the motion parameters, we can compute shape characteristics using the images taken during the movement. The techniques that deal with this problem are called **structure from motion**. Structure from motion refers to the capability of determining a moving object's shape characteristics, and its position and velocity as well from a sequence of two or more images taken of the moving object. Equivalently, if the camera is in motion, structure from motion refers to the capability of determining an object's shape characteristics as well as its position and the camera's velocity from a sequence of two or more images taken of the object by the moving camera. One fundamental kind of structure-from-motion problem is to determine the fixed position of M three-dimensional points from a time sequence of N views, each containing the two-dimensional perspective projection of the M three-dimensional points.

Ambiguity

Note that motion-based image analysis facilitates the recovery of the world only up to a scale factor. This ambiguity, of course, would go away if we were to use multiple (calibrated) cameras to provide stereo. In this connection, see, for instance, Refs. 50 and 51. In addition to removing the indeterminacy of a scale factor, simultaneously acquired stereo images also simplify considerably the recovery of the structure and motion of a scene that exhibits multiple independent motions relative to the camera. Perhaps, then, motion-based image analysis with multiple cameras to provide stereo will turn out to be the primary scene-recovery technique in computer vision, with the other methods filling in the gaps.

IMAGE SYNTHESIS TOPICS

Traditionally, researchers in image processing have become accustomed to a strict distinction between computer vision and computer graphics: Computer vision deals with image analysis, and the field of computer graphics deals with image synthesis. Interestingly, the two fields have evolved rather independently. In the last few years, however, the relation between the two fields has become more intensive. On a superficial level, the two areas assist each other. In computer graphics, *antialiasing techniques* use analysis; in computer vision, the visualization of results use computer graphics. However, the interrelationship between the two fields is much deeper. Because a central theme in both is the relationship between 3D scenes and their 2D views (images), much of the mathematics and physics used in the two fields are

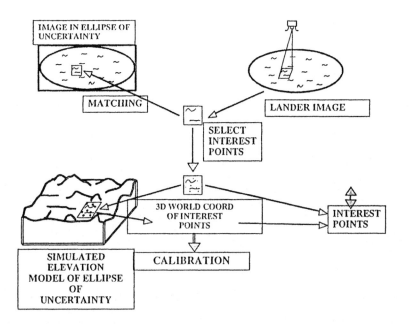

FIGURE 14 Image analysis and synthesis assist each other in a system for spacecraft navigation. After taking a new image (Step 1), it is located in an *ellipse of uncertainty image* (EU). This EU image is a part of the orbiter image, where an initial guess suspects the viewed scene. In Step 2, a combination of interest point selection and matching is used to find the precise location of the new image in the EU image. In Step 3, landmarks are selected and their height information is extracted from the elevation model. This height information acts to define a world-coordinate system and is used with the corresponding image coordinates of the landmarks to compute the calibration parameters. (Adapted from Ref. 46.)

common (52). The basic idea is that a generic model for the class of objects of interest is selected. Then, for a specific object, the parameters of the generic model are estimated via analysis to fit the given object. This customized model is used to generate displays or to do recognition using synthesis. In some cases, the analysis-synthesis cycle is repeated many times to refine the model customization. In the following, we show typical applications and examples of this new area of research.

A generic area, where analysis uses synthesis, is in *CAD-based computer vision*. In this field, typically, a CAD model is used to assist in the recognition of objects. One such approach (53) uses the CAD model to synthesize a view-independent model of objects. This model is generated automatically by a "viewing and reasoning" process. The system inspects the CAD model from a number of different viewpoints, and a statistical inference is applied to identify relatively view-independent relationships among component parts of the object. These relations are stored as a relational model of the object, which is represented in the form of a hypergraph.

Another example is taken from the area of spacecraft navigation (see Fig. 14). In a realistic mission to a planet, a spacecraft performs an orbit phase around the planet to acquire images. Using these images, a digital elevation model is synthesized. This model is used for navigation purposes and during landing, as follows. The images taken by the on-board camera are used in a matching procedure to localize the new scene in the orbiter images. Using the orbiter images, landmarks are automatically selected, for which the elevation information is extracted from the elevation model. These height data are used to estimate the position and orientation parameters of the spacecraft as described in the section on camera calibration.

A further area of interest within the combination of analysis and synthesis is the generation of artificial views of objects using photographs. A variant of this procedure is *texture mapping* and is described in Figure 15. Here, real image data and computer graphics of complex environments like architectural or industrial sites are combined. At least one or more stereo image pairs and additional single images are combined to compute a complete as-built status of the object. In addition to the CAD model of the original design, the CAD model of planned add-ons can be included.

Synthetic Texture Image Generation

A variety of approaches have been developed for the generation of synthetic texture images. A time-series model for texture synthesis has been developed by McCormick and Jayaramamurthy (54) and Tou et al. (55). Yokoyama and Haralick (56) used a structured-growth model to synthesize a more complex image texture. Pratt et al. (57) developed a set of techniques for generating textures with identical means, variances, and autocorrelation functions but different higher-order moments. Gagalowicz (58) gave a technique for generating binary texture fields with prescribed

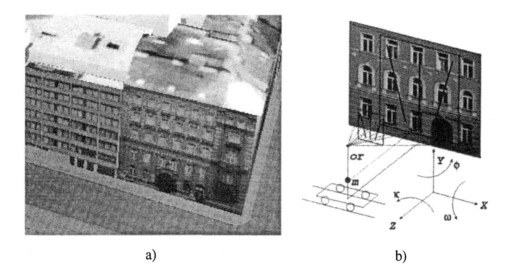

a)   b)

FIGURE 15   A completely synthetic view of a part of Vienna. Real images are transformed into a new geometry-defined CAD model and the viewing parameters selected by the observer. In the case of missing image data, texture mapping fills the gaps.

second-order statistics. Chellappa and Kashyap (59) described a technique for the generation of images having a given Gauss–Markov random field.

Gagalowicz and de Ma (60) described a texture synthesis technique that produced textures as they would appear on perspective projection images of three-dimensional surfaces. Gagalowicz and de Ma (61) described a technique to synthesize artificial textures in parallel form a compressed-data set and retain good visual similarity to natural textures.

CONCLUSION

In this article, the major elements were outlined that defined image analysis as an information-reduction process. We have provided an overview of the most actively studied problem areas, as well as pointed out a starting point for approaching a given image analysis task. It should be noted that although image analysis has seen decades of very active research, no general solution has been found that would have similar functionality as the human visual system. The major milestones could be—however loosely—defined as starting from Robert's thesis (1963), which is often considered to be the first Ph.D. thesis in computer vision and introduced several key ideas including edge detection and model-based matching. David Marr played a major role in connecting computer vision to the traditional areas of biological vision—psychophysics and neurobiology. His main work, *Vision* (1) is often referred to as the groundwork or basis of the Marr paradigm, viewing vision as a reconstruction process. The most solid proof that reconstruction is not necessary for many (or most) tasks came from the work of Dickmanns in Germany, who demonstrated an autonomous car that was able to drive on a highway, computing only very simple visual features. Consequently, active vision was advocated by Bajcsy and Aloimonos to lead away from the "recoverist" school. Current research is expanding on these lines, also combined with considerable efforts not only to show new solutions, but in terms of software engineering efforts that may lay the ground for further fruitful research and build an extensive image understanding environment.

APPENDIX

Journals

The major journals of the field include following IEEE Transactions journals: Pattern Analysis and Machine Intelligence; Systems, Man, and Cybernetics; Neural Networks; Signal Processing; Robotics and Automation; Fuzzy Sets; Geoscience and Remote Sensing; and Image Processing.

Other important journals are *Computer Vision, Graphics, and Image Processing* (now appearing as the two journals *CVGIP: Image Understanding* and *CVGIP: Graphical Models and Image Processing*), the *International Journal of Computer Vision, Image and Vision Computing, Machine Vision and Applications, Optical Engineering, Pattern Recognition, Pattern Recognition Letters*, and *Journal of Mathematical Imaging and Vision*.

Since the publication of the first major books in the field (62,63), the field has grown immensely. International conferences sometimes attract well over 1000 attendees. The list includes the European Conference on Computer Vision (ECCV), the International Conference on Pattern Recognition (ICPR), the International Conference on Computer Vision (ICCV), and the Conference on Computer Vision and Pattern Recognition (CVPR). In addition, many smaller conferences are organized to cover specific subtopics.

Literature

The field of Image Processing is studied under a great variety of subtopics. A widely accepted classification of subtopics is taken from Rosenfeld's annual Survey on Computer Vision (see Table 1). This survey is published annually and gives a bibliography containing important publications published per year. Since the books by Rosenfeld (63) and Duda and Hart (6), many textbooks have appeared (see References). The list includes Refs. 16, 20, 41, 64, and 65. A detailed glossary of computer vision terms appears in Ref. 20. There also exist a number of handbooks (e.g., Refs. 45 and 66).

A selection of relevant books covering the field are given in the Books section of the Bibliography. Review articles about subtopics appear in special issues of the above-mentioned journals. A nonexhaustive list is given in the Bibliography section.

Literature on Electronic Media

Through the last 5 years, together with the growth and expansion of the Internet and the introduction of the World Wide Web (WWW), a galore of resources has become available to the computer vision researcher. Beginning with the first servers on universities, which made available test images, source codes and papers to the user via the file transfer protocol (ftp), so-called mailing lists and *usegroups* soon developed. In the context of this article, the following *usegroups* are of main interest:

comp.ai.vision	computer vision
comp.robotics	robotics (FAQ available)
sci.image.processing	common image processing topics (FAQ available)
comp.soft-sys.khoros	the image processing package Khoros (FAQ available)
comp.dsp	digital signal processing (FAQ available)

Today, the most comfortable way to access the image processing resources on the Internet is through the WWW with the Mosaic software. A suitable starting point for all journeys through the net is the *computer vision home page*. It contains hundreds of pointers to universities and research organizations all over the world, provides access to the FAQs (frequently asked questions), pointers to software, test images, descriptions of algorithms, announcements of conferences, on-line publications, and links to other computer vision pages distributed over the globe.

TABLE I   Classification and Subtopics

1. General references	
2. Related topics	
Not covered systematically	
2.1 Geometry (computational, digital, etc.)	
2.2 Graphics and visualization (see 8.2, 10.3, 12.4 for additional references on image synthesis)	•
2.3 Compression and digitization, scanning, wavelet transforms	
2.4 Processing, enhancement, restoration, image quality	IP
2.5 Optical processing	•
2.6 Neural networks	•
2.7 Artificial intelligence and pattern recognition	•
3. Applications	
3.1 Documents	
3.2 Biomedical	
3.3 Human	
3.4 Industrial	PR
3.5 Robotics	•
3.6 Remote sensing, reconnaissance	IP
4. Architectures	IP
4.1 General	
4.2 Meshes	
4.3 Other systems	
5. Computational techniques	
5.1 Image operations	IP
5.2 Morphological operations	•
5.3 Geometric transformations; calibration	•
5.4 Interpolation	
5.5 Estimation	
6. Feature detection and segmentation; image analysis	
6.1 Feature detection; edges, lines, corners, etc.	
6.2 Segmenttion (including thresholding, feature grouping). See later sections on feature detection and segmentation for shapes (7.1), curves (7.2), color images (8.1–8.2), range data (9.1), and motion fields (12.3).	CV
6.3 Image and scene analysis; general references on control in object recognition systems, and on active vision; see also fusion, learning, and indexing	•
7. Two-dimensional shape; pattern	CV
7.1 Representation, description, decomposion, recognition	CV
7.2 Curves and contours (representation, decomposition)	CV
7.3 Properties (including invariants); see probing	
7.4 Distance and skeletons	
7.5 Formal languages; topolgoy	
7.6 Path planning	
7.x Connected Component Analysis	•
8. Color texture	
8.1 Illumination and reflectance	
8.2 Texture: modeling and synthesis; segmentation	
8.3 Texture: description	

(continued)

TABLE 1   Continued

9. Matching and stereo	
9.1 Matching of strings, arrays, trees, graphs, etc.	CV
9.2 Matching of images, signals, contours, patterns, templates, regions	CV
9.3 Hough transforms	
9.4 Stereo	•
9.5 Stero: extensions, variations, applications	•
9.x Calibration for stereo	
10. Three-dimensional recovery and analysis	
10.1 Range sensing and segmentation	CV
10.2 Recovery from shading, texture, contour	CV
10.3 Display (ray tracing, rendering; 3D images	CV
11. Three-dimensional shape	
11.1 Representations and models	•
11.2 Geometry, aspects	
11.3 Recognition	
11.4 Acquisition and indexing; alignment, matching, and extension; pose estimation	
12. Motion	•
12.1 Flow computation and motion estimation	
12.2 Structure from motion	
12.3 Motion detection and tracking; segmentation	
12.4 Other topics: Motion perception; motion transparency; binocular motion analysis; temporal texture; nonrigid motion; shape deformation and computer animation; motion recovery and event sequence analysis	
13. Items not contained in the above classification, but relevant enough for explicit treatment	
13.1 Pattern classification: statistical	PR
13.2 Pattern classification: syntactic	PR
13.3 Feature selection techniques	PR

The table above is adapted from Rosenfeld's classification. There is indicated which terms have been already covered in the three published contributions to the Encyclopedia. Here IP means "Image Processing," PR "Pattern Recognition," and CV "Computer Vision." The items marked with a bullet (•) are treated in the new contribution "Image Analysis and Synthesis."

BIBLIOGRAPHY

Books

Abidi, M. A., and R. C. Gonzalez, *Data Fusion in Robotics and Machine Intelligence*, Academic Press, New York, 1992.

Anzai, Y., *Pattern Recognition and Machine Learning*, Academic Press, New York, 1992 (translated from the Japanese edition 1989).

Ayache, N., *Artificial Vision for Mobile Robots*, The MIT Press, Cambridge, MA, 1991.

Blake, A., and A. Yuille, *Active Vision*, The MIT Press, Cambridge, MA, 1992.

Carpenter, G. A., and S. Grossberg, *Neural Networks for Vision and Image Processing*, The MIT Press, Cambridge, MA, 1992.

Chen, C. H., L. F. Pau, and P. S. P. Wang, *Handbook of Pattern Recognition & Computer Vision*, World Scientific, Singapore, 1993.

Davies, E. R., *Machine Vision: Theory, Algorithms, Practicalities*, Academic Press, New York, 1990.

De Valois, R. L., and K. K. De Valois, *Spatial Vision*, Oxford University Press, Oxford, 1990.

Dougherty, E. R., *An Introduction to Morphological Image Processing*, SPIE, 1993.

Faugeras, O. D., *Three-Dimensional Computer Vision*, The MIT Press, Cambridge, MA, 1992.

Freeman, J. A., and D. M. Skapura, *Neural Networks, — Algorithms, Applications and Programming Techniques*, Addison-Wesley, Reading, MA, 1992.

Grimson, W. E., *Object Recognition by Computer*, The MIT Press, Cambridge, MA, 1990.

Haralick, R. M., and L. G. Shapiro, *Computer and Robot Vision, Vol. 1 and Vol. 2*, Addison-Wesley, Reading, MA, 1993.

Jaehne, B., *Digital Image Processing*, Springer-Verlag, New York, 1991.

Jain, R., R. Kasturi, and B. G. Schunk, *Machine Vision*, McGraw-Hill, New York, 1995.

Kafri, O., and I. Glatt, *The Physics of Moire Metrology*, John Wiley and Sons, New York, 1990.

Kaplan, H., *Practical Applications of Infrared Thermal Sensing and Imaging Equipment*, SPIE, 1993.

Katsaggelos, A. K., *Digital Image Restoration*, 1991.

Kohonen, T., *Self-Organizing Maps*, Springer-Verlag, 1995.

Lagendijk, R. L., and J. Biemond, *Restoration of Images*, Academic Publishers Group, Doordrecht, 1991.

Lam, D. M.-K., and C. J. Shatz, *Development of the Visual System*, The MIT Press, Cambridge, MA, 1991.

Leavers, V. F., *Shape Detection in Computer Vision Using the Hough Transform*, 1992.

Linggard, R., D. J. Myers, and C. Nightingale, *Neural Networks for Vision, Speech and Natural Language*, Chapman & Hall, New York, 1992.

Masters, T., *Signal and Image Processing with Neural Networks: a C++ source book*, John Wiley and Sons, New York, 1994.

Masters, T., *Advanced Algorithms for Neural Networks: a C++ source book*, John Wiley and Sons, New York, 1995.

Maybank, S., *Theory of Reconstruction from Image Motion*, Springer-Verlag, New York, 1993.

McCafferty, *Human and Machine Vision*, Horwood, New York, 1990.

Michie, D. J., D. J. Spiegelhalter, and C. C. Taylor, *Machine Learning, Neural and Statistical Classification*, Ellis Horwood Limited, Englewood Cliffs, NJ, 1994.

Minsky, M., and S. Papert, *Perceptrons: An Introduction to Computational Geometry*, The MIT Press, Cambridge, MA, 1969.

Mundy, J., and A. Zisserman, *Geometric Invariance in Computer Vision*, The MIT Press, Cambridge, MA, 1992.

Murray, D. W., B. F. Buxton, *Experiments in the Machine Interpretation of Visual Motion*, The MIT Press, Cambridge, MA, 1990.

Myler, H. R., and A. R. Weeks, *Computer Imaging Recipes in C*, Prentice-Hall, Englewood Cliffs, NJ, 1993.

Nadler, M., and E. P. Smith, *Pattern Recognition Engineering*, John Wiley and Sons, New York, 1993.

Nalwa, V. S., *A Guided Tour of Computer Vision*, Addison-Wesley, Reading, MA, 1993.

Pomerleau, D. A., *Neural Network Perception for Mobile Robot Guidance*, Kluwer Academic Publishers, Boston, 1993.

Pratt, W. K., *Digital Image Processing*, 2nd ed., John Wiley and Sons, New York, 1991.

Shapiro, S. C., *Encyclopedia of Artificial Intelligence*, John Wiley and Sons, New York, 1992.

Sonka, M., V. Hlavac, and R. Boyle, *Image Processing, Analysis and Machine Vision*, Chapman & Hall, New York, 1993.

Suen, C. Y., and P. S. P. Wang, *Thinning Methodologies for Pattern Recognition*, World Scientific, Singapore, 1994.

Thorpe, C. E., *Vision and Navigation – The Carnegie Mellon NAVLAB*, Kluwer Academic Publishers, Boston, 1990.

Tomita, F., and S. Tsuji, *Computer Analysis of Visual Textures*, Kluwer Academic Publishers, Boston, 1990.

Watt, R. J., *Understanding Vision*, Academic Press, London, 1991.

Wechsler, H., *Neural Networks for Perception, Volume 1, Human and Machine Perception*, Academic Press, New York, 1992.

Wechsler, H., *Neural Networks for Perception, Volume 2, Computation. Learning, and Architectures*, Academic Press, New York, 1992.

Weng, J., R. J. Huang, and N. Ahuja, *Motion and Structure from Image Sequences*, Springer-Verlag, New York, 1992.

Zeki, S., *A Vision of the Brain*, Blackwell Scientific Publications, Oxford, 1993.

Zhang, Z., and O. Faugeras, *3D Dynamic Scene Analysis, A Stereo Based Approach*, 1992.

Zhou, Y.-T., and R. Chellappa, *Artificial Neural Networks for Computer Vision*, Springer-Verlag, New York, 1992.

Review Articles

Special Issue on Computer Vision, *Proceedings of the IEEE*, 1988.

Aggarwal, J. K., and N. Nandhakumar, "On the Computation of Motion from Sequences of Images – A Review," *Proc. IEEE*, 917–935 (August 1988).

Arman, F., and J. K. Aggarwal, "Model-Based Object Recognition in Dense-Range Images – A Review," *ACM – Comput. Surv.*, 25(1), 5–44 (1993).

Besl, P. J., "Active Optical Range Imaging Sensors," *Machine Vision Applications,* 1(2), 127–152 (1988).

Cox, I. J., "A Review of Statistical Data Association Techniques for Motion Correspondence," *Int. J. Computer Vision,* 10(1), 53–66 (1993).

Dhond, U. R., and J. K. Aggarwal, "Structure from Stereo – A Review," *IEEE Trans. Syst. Man Cybern.*, SMC-19(6), 1489–1489 (1989).

Elliman, D. G., and I. T. Lancaster, "A Review of Segmentation and Contextual Analysis Techniques for Text Recognition," *Pattern Recognition,* 23(3-4), 337–346 (1990).

Feldman, Fanty, Goddard, and Lynne, "Computing with Structured Connectionist Networks," *ACM Commun.* (February 1988).

Fu, K. S., "Learning Control Systems, – Review and Outlook," *IEEE Trans. Pattern Anal. Mach. Intell.*, PAMI-8(3), (1986).

Govindan, V. K., and A. P. Shivaprasad, "Character Recognition – A Review," *Pattern Recognition,* 23(7), 671–671 (1990).

Grant, W. B., "Differential Absorption and Raman Lidar for Water Vapor Profile Measurements: A Review," *Opt. Eng.*, 30(1), 30–48 (1991).

Huang, T. S., and A. N. Netravali, "Motion Structure from Feature Correspondences: A Review," *Proc. IEEE*, 82(2), 251–268 (1994).

Hush, D. R., and B. G. Horne, "Progress is Supervised Neural Networks," *Signal Process. Mag.*, 10(1), 8–39 (1993).

Knight, K., "Connectionist Ideas and Algorithms," *ACM Commun.*, 58–74 (November 1990).

Lau, C., and B. Widrow, "Neural Networks Special Issue I," *Proc. IEEE*, 78(9) (September 1990).

Lau, C., and B. Widrow, "Neural Networks Special Issue II," *Proc. IEEE*, 78(10) (October 1990).

Lippmann, R. P., "Pattern Classification Using Neural Networks," *IEEE Commun. Mag.,* *27*(11), 47–64 (1989).

Maren, A. J., "Neural Networks for Enhanced Human–Computer Interactions," *IEEE Control Syst. Mag., 11*(5), 34–36 (1991).

Marshall, S., "Review of Shape Coding Techniques," *Image Vision Comput., 7*(4), 281–281 (1989).

Meer, P., D. Mintz, D. Y. Kim, and A. Rosenfeld, "Robust Regression Methods for Computer Vision: A Review," *Int. J. Computer Vision, 6*(1), 59–70 (1991).

Meng, M., and A. C. Kak, "Mobile Robot Navigation Using Neural Networks and Nonmetrical Environment Models," *IEEE Control Syst. Mag., 13*(5), 30–39 (1993).

Pal, N. R., and S. K. Pal, "A Review on Image Segmentation Techniques," *Pattern Recognition, 26*(9), 1277–1294 (1993).

Reed, T. R., and J. M. HansduBuf, "A Review of Recent Texture Segmentation and Feature Extraction Techniques," *CVGIP: Image Understanding, 57*(3), 359–372 (1993).

Sarkar, S., and K. L. Boyer, "Perceptual Organization in Computer Vision: A Review and a Proposal for a Classificatory Structure," *IEEE Trans. Syst. Man & Cybern., SMC-23*(1), 382–399 (1993).

Sirkis, J. S., Y.-M. Chen, H. Singh, and A. Y.-H. Cheng, "Computerized Optical Fringe Pattern Analysis in Photomechanics: A Review," *Opti. Eng., 31*(2), 304–314 (1992).

Theordoracatos, V. E., and D. E. Calkins, "A 3-D Vision System Model for Automatic Object Surface Sensing," *Int. J. Computer Vision, 11*(1), 75–99 (1992).

REFERENCES

1. D. Marr, *Vision*, Freeman, San Francisco, 1982.
2. R. O. Duda and P. E. Hart, *Pattern Classification and Scene Analysis*, John Wiley and Sons, 1973.
3. R. M. Haralick and L. G. Shapiro, *Computer and Robot Vision*, Addison-Wesley, Reading, MA, 1992.
4. R. Jain, R. Kasturi, and B. G. Schunk, *Machine Vision*, McGraw-Hill, New York, 1995.
5. D. J. Michie, D. J. Spiegelhalter, and C. C. Taylor, *Machine Learning, Neural and Statistical Classification*, Ellis Horwood Limited, Englewood Cliffs, NJ, 1994.
6. T. Kohonen, *Self-Organizing Maps*, Springer-Verlag, New York, 1995.
7. D. P. Casasent, J. S. Smokelin, and A. Ye, "Wavelet and Gabor Transforms for Detection," *Opti. Eng., 31*(9), 1893–1898 (1992).
8. D. P. Casasent and J.-S. Smolkelin, "Real, Imaginary, and Clutter Gabor Filter Fusion for Detection with Reduced False Alarms," *Opti. eng., 33*(7), 2255–2263 (1994).
9. D. Weber and D. P. Casasent, "Fusion and Optimized Gabor Filter Design for Object Detection," *Proc. SPIE, 2588* (1995).
10. Y.-T. Zhou and R. Chellappa, *Artificial Neural Networks for Computer Vision*, Springer-Verlag, New York, 1992.
11. M. Minsky and S. Papert, *Perceptrons: An Introduction to Computational Geometry*, The MIT Press, Cambridge, MA, 1969.
12. T. Kohonen, *Self-Organization and Associative Memory*, Springer-Verlag, New York, 1988.
13. T. Masters, *Signal and Image Processing with Neural Networks: a C++ source book*, John Wiley and Sons, New York, 1994.
14. T. Masters, *Advanced Algorithms for Neural Networks: a C++ source book*, John Wiley and Sons, New York, 1995.
15. E. R. Dougherty, *An Introduction to Morphological Image Processing*, SPIE, 1993.
16. D. H. Ballard and C. M. Brown, *Computer Vision*, Prentice-Hall, Englewood Cliffs, NJ, 1982.

17. W. Pölzleitner and G. Schwingshakl, "Real-Time Surface Grading of Profiled Boards," *Ind. Metrol., 2*(3&4), 283–298 (1992).

18. R. W. Ehrich and J. P. Foith, "A View of Texture Topology and Texture Description," *Computer Graphics Image Proc., 8*, 174–202 (1978).

19. F. Tomita and S. Tsuji, *Computer Analysis of Visual Textures*, Kluwer Academic Publishers, Boston, 1990.

20. R. M. Haralick and L. G. Shapiro, *Computer and Robot Vision*, Addison-Wesley, Reading, MA 1993.

21. J. Princen, J. Illingworth, and J. Kittler, "Templates and the Hough Transform," in *Active Perception and Robot Vision*, edited by A. K. Sood and H. Wechsler, Springer-Verlag, New York, 1992, pp. 615–634.

22. O. D. Faugeras, "A Few Steps Towards Artificial 3-D Vision," in *Robotics Science*, edited by M. Brady, The MIT Press, Cambridge, MA, 1989, pp. 39–137.

23. H. C. Longuet-Higgins, "A Computer Algorithm for Reconstructing a Scene from Two Projections," *Nature, 293*, 133–135 (1981).

24. H. C. Longuet-Higgins, "The Reconstruction of a Scene from Two Projections – Configurations That Defeat the 8-Point Algorithm," in *Proceedings of the First Conference on Artificial Intelligence Applications*, (1984), pp. 395–397.

25. O. D. Faugeras, F. Lustman, and G. Toscani, "Motion and Structure from Motion from Point and Line Matches," in *Proceedings of the First International Conference on Computer Vision*, 1987, pp. 25–34.

26. R. Y. Tsai and T. S. Huang, "Uniqueness and Estimation of Three-Dimensional Motion Parameters of Rigid Objects with Curved Surfaces," *IEEE Trans. Pattern Anal. Mach. Intell., PAMI-6*(1), 13–27 (1984).

27. J. Weng, T. S. Huang, and N. Ahuja, "Motion and Structure from Two Perspective Views: Algorithms, Error Analysis, and Error Estimation," *IEEE Trans. Pattern Anal. Mach. Intell., PAMI-11*(5), 451–476 (1989).

28. X. Zhuang, "A Simplification to Linear Two-View Motion Algorithms," *Computer Vision, Graphics, Image Proc., 46*, 175–178 (1989).

29. D. Terzopoulos, "Multilevel Computational Processes for Visual Surface Reconstruction," *Computer Vision, Graphics, Image Proc., 24*, 52–96 (1983).

30. W. E. L. Grimson, "On the Reconstruction of Visible Surfaces," in *Image Understanding 1984*, edited by S. Ullman and W. Richards, Ablex Publishing, Norwood, NJ, 1984, pp. 195–223.

31. A. Blake and A. Zisserman, *Visual Reconstruction*, The MIT Press, Cambridge, MA, 1987.

32. R. Szeliski, "Bayesian Modeling of Uncertainty in Low-Level Vision," *Int. J. Computer Vision, 5*, 271–301 (1990).

33. R. Szeliski, "Fast Surface Interpolation Using Hierarchical Basis Functions," *IEEE Trans. Pattern Anal. Mach. Intell., PAMI-12*(6), 513–528 (1990).

34. G. Wolberg, *Digital Image Warping*, IEEE Computer Society Press, Los Alamitos, CA, 1990.

35. V. S. Nalwa, *A Guided Tour of Computer Vision*, Addison-Wesley, Reading, MA, 1993.

36. R. T. Chin and C. R. Dyer, "Model-Based Recognition in Robot Vision," *Comput. Surv., 18*(1), 67–108 (1986).

37. J. D. Foley and A. van Dam, *Fundamentals of Interactive Computer Graphics*, Addison-Wesley, Reading, MA, 1982.

38. H. Blum, "A Transformation for Extracting New Descriptors of Shape," in *Models for the Perception of Speech and Visual Form*, edited by W. Wathen-Dunn. The MIT Press, Cambridge, MA, 1967, pp. 362–380.

39. T. O. Binford, "Visual Perception by Computer," in *IEEE Conference on Decision and Control*, 1971.

40. J. J. Koenderink and A. J. van Doorn, "The Internal Representation of Solid Shape with Respect to Vision," *Biol. Cybern., 32*, 211–216 (1979).

41. J. Aloimonos, I. Weiss, and A. Bandyopadhyaym, "Active Vision," *Int. J. Computer Vision, 1*, 171–187 (1988).

42. R. Bajcsy, "Active Perception," *IEEE Proc., 76*(8), 996–1005 (1988).

43. J. Aloimonos, *Active Perception*, Lawrence Erlbaum, Hillsdale, NJ, 1993.

44. J. J. Gibson, *The Ecological Approach to Visual Perception*, Houghton Mifflin, Boston, MA, 1979.

45. T. Y. Young and K. S. Fu, *Handbook of Pattern Recognition and Image Processing*, Academic Press, New York, 1986.

46. G. Paar and W. Pölzleitner, "Autonomous Spacecraft Navigation Using Computer Vision — A Case Study for the Moon," *Proc. SPIE, 2591* (1995).

47. K. Nakayama and J. M. Loomis, "Optical Velocity Patterns, Velocity Sensitive Neurons, and Space Perception: A Hypothesis," *Perception, 3*, 63–80 (1974).

48. H. C. Longuet-Higgins and K. Prazdny, "The Interpretation of a Moving Retinal Image," *Proc. Roy. Soc. London, 208*, 385–397 (1980).

49. R. C. Nelson and J. Aloimonos, "Finding Motion Parameters from Spherical Motion Fields," *Biol. Cybern., 58*, 261–273 (1988).

50. A. M. Waxman and J. H. Duncan, "Binocular Image Flows: Steps Toward Stereo-Motion Fusion," *IEEE Trans. Pattern Anal. Mach. Intell., PAMI-8*(6), 715–729 (1986).

51. P. Balasubramanyam and M. A. Snyder, "The P-Field: A Computational Model for Binocular Motion Processing," in *Proceedings of the IEEE Computer Society Conference on Computer Vision and Pattern Recognition, CVPR '91*, 1991, pp. 115–120.

52. Special issue on image analysis by synthesis, *IEEE Trans. Pattern Anal. Mach. Intell., PAMI-15*(6), 531–651 (1993).

53. S. Zhang, G. D. Sullivan, and K. D. Baker, "The Automatic Construction of a View-Independent Relational Model for 3-D Object Recognition," *IEEE Trans. Pattern Anal. Mach. Intell., PAMI-15*(6), 531–544 (1993).

54. B. H. McCormick and S. N. Jayaramamurthy, "Time Series Model for Texture Synthesis," *Int. J. Computer Inform. Sci., 3* 329–343 (1974).

55. J. T. Tou, D. B. Kao, and Y. S. Chang, "Pictorial Texture Analysis and Synthesis," in *Proceedings of the Third International Joint Conference on Pattern Recognition*, 1976, p. 590.

56. R. Yokoyama and R. M. Haralick, "Texture Synthesis Using a Growth Model," *Computer Graphics Image Proc., 8*, 369–381 (1978).

57. W. K. Pratt, O. D. Faugeras, and A. Gagalowicz, "Visual Discrimination of Stochastic Texture Fields," *IEEE Trans. Syst. Man Cybern., 8* 796–804 (1978).

58. A. Gagalowicz, "A New Method for Texture Fields Synthesis: Some Applications to the Study of Human Vision," *IEEE Trans. Pattern Anal. Intell., PAMI-3*, 520–533 (1981).

59. R. Chellappa and R. L. Kashyap, "Synthetic Generation and Estimation in Random Field Models of Images," in *Proceedings of the 1981 Pattern Recognition Conference and Image Processing Conference*, 1981, pp. 577–582.

60. A. Gagalowicz and S. de Ma, "Synthesis of Natural Textures on 3-D Surfaces," in *Seventh International Conference on Pattern Recognition*, 1984, pp. 1209–1212.

61. A. Gagalowicz and S. de Ma, "Sequential Synthesis of Natural Textures," *Computer Vision, Graphics, Image Process.* (1985).

62. R. O. Duda P. E. Hart, *Pattern Classification and Scene Analysis*, John Wiley and Sons, New York, 1973.

63. A. Rosenfeld and A. C. Kak, *Digital Picture Processing*, Academic Press, New York, 1982.

64. V. S. Nalwa, *A Guided Tour of Computer Vision*, Addison-Wiley, Reading, MA, 1993.

65. H. Wechsler, *Computational Vision*, Academic Press, New York, 1990.

66. C. H. Chen, L. F. Pau, and P. S. P. Wang, *Handbook of Pattern Recognition & Computer Vision*, World Scientific, Singapore, 1993.

WOLFGANG PÖLZLEITNER

INTERACTIVE INDUCTIVE MACHINE LEARNING AND THE CONDITIONAL PROBABILISTIC LEARNING ALGORITHM

All green birds that I see are parrots.
All birds I see that are not green are not parrots.
Therefore, if I see a green bird in the future, by induction, I will conclude that it is a parrot.

INTRODUCTION

The study of machine learning is concerned with taking data in raw, uninterpreted form, extracting the knowledge inherent in that data, and presenting it in a form that can be applied by a machine, and, preferably, a human. For humans, this extraction is a natural process. We observe and interact with our environment, receiving data and stimuli that we process using some inference process, and arrange in an internal structure for later use in further learning or reasoning. These processes are not well understood; thus, in our models, we can only approximate them. This article will introduce a subfield of machine learning, interactive inductive learning, and will discuss one particular learning model to demonstrate some basic concepts.

Since the mid-1950s (1), much work has been done in machine learning and is thoroughly reviewed in Refs. 2-8. Basic introductions to machine learning may be found in Refs. 9-12. Inductive machine learning from examples is a specialized form of machine learning in which we attempt to learn, from a set of input examples, an intuitive notion of a "concept" (e.g., specific diseases or desirable cars). Our inputs are limited to a set of examples, or observations, and counterexamples of the target concept, and our output is a general concept description or function containing the descriptive "knowledge" inherent in the examples. The output function is then useful for classifying new, previously unseen objects. The output function often takes the form of a decision tree, or set of decision rules (also known as classification trees and rules). For example, given a certain set of symptoms exhibited by a sickly soybean plant, classification rules allow us to determine the disease afflicting the unfortunate plant. An inductive learning system attempts, in a domain-independent way, to create a general, human-understandable, concept description of minimal length and complexity. General descriptions allow the classification of future observations. Human-understandable descriptions of minimal length and complexity allow more efficient representation, storage, and application.

Learning from examples was studied as early as 1959, with Samuel's seminal inductive learning Checkers program (13). Michalski et al. developed a successful sequence of systems, including AQVAL/1, AQ11, and AQ15 (14–17). These systems effectively demonstrated that they could inductively determine diagnosis rules for soybean diseases. The work of Quinlan, best represented by the ID3 and C4.5

systems (18–23), is directed toward the inductive construction of decision trees. Two other well-known applications of inductive learning are Teiresias, a learning component of the expert system MYCIN of Davis and Lenat (24), and Buchanan and Feigenbaum's Meta-DENDRAL (25). Another approach to inductive learning may be referred to as *approximate classification*. This includes the works of Pawlak, Ras, Wong, Ziarko, and others (26–30) and is based on the theory of rough sets, as introduced by Pawlak (30). The *conditional probabilistic learning algorithm* (CPLA) system presented below falls into this class. Practical uses for inductive learning systems include generating production rules for expert systems, and decision support systems (35,41). More extensive histories and surveys of the inductive learning field may also be found (7,9,11,33,34).

Inductive learning from examples is very closely related to the process of knowledge acquisition (35–41). In the construction of expert systems, the transfer of expertise from the expert to the expert system is often complicated and arduous, as the expert may find it difficult to express his or her knowledge completely, succinctly, and consistently. Knowledge acquisition systems typically interact with an expert using some combination of (1) posing system-generated questions (42), (2) incrementally learning from examples presented by the expert as he or she watches the rule base evolve (43–46), and (3) generating examples to be classified by the expert (47). Knowledge acquisition techniques generally function with significant domain knowledge—that is, built-in information about the domain being studied. Clearly, knowledge acquisition systems are interactive to various degrees. As such, they are closely related to interactive (semiautomated) inductive learning (48–50).

Interactive inductive learning systems use inductive inference, use little or no domain knowledge, and interact with a user who is not necessarily an expert. Such systems take advantage of user interaction to refine or guide the rule generation process. Such possible interactions are as follows:

Pruning parameters: A user can adjust a system's decision tree output by adjusting the acceptable error parameters used in the pruning process (51).

Selecting relevant attributes: The user can guide the system's choice of attributes used in the rule-generation process. For example, in Ref. 52, the user must guide the choice of attributes with which to partition the data.

Classifying examples: The system may require feedback on classification or treatment of examples it finds or generates (53).

Manipulating data/values: The user can adjust the partitioning of continuous values into intervals, as in Ref. 53, or equivalences between values, as in CPLA.

Guiding and/or correcting generalizations: This general description covers interaction in which the system turns to the user to choose valid actions from a selection generated during the learning process (see, e.g., Ref. 42).

To summarize and conclude, we can distinguish knowledge acquisition systems from interactive inductive learning systems in the following four ways:

1. Knowledge acquisition techniques are designed specifically to elicit knowledge from an *expert*. Interactive inductive learning systems derive their information from the *data*. The system's user provides only guidance, because he or she does not always know the correct feedback to give the system.

2. Knowledge acquisition systems use a variety of techniques to create their knowledge base, whereas interactive inductive learning is, by definition, restricted to inductive inference.
3. Interactive inductive learning systems have a much wider selection of interaction methods.
4. Interactive inductive learning systems use little or no domain knowledge to perform learning. Knowledge acquisition techniques frequently require a large amount of domain knowledge in order to be able to ask meaningful questions during the elicitation process.

Note, finally, that a successful interactive inductive learning system may even be able to help the user discover new relationships among the data, as CPLA does. For example, system output may indicate that certain attributes are necessary to the knowledge system (superfluous) or that distinctions among attribute values are unnecessary.

CPLA is an interactive inductive learning system that learns from examples and expresses its learning as a set of decision rules. Its interaction takes the form of parameters, called *conditions* — equivalences on attribute values — which are selected and adjusted by the user to tune the rules, as well as analyze the data.

ISSUES IN INDUCTIVE LEARNING

Simply described, inductive learning is the extrapolation of general classification rules from a finite set of example descriptions (the *training sample*). Each example consists of an object or object description, and its classification into a *concept*. It is important to note that inductive learning is nonlogical; that is, it is not *truth-preserving*. For example, the correct classification rule classifying an object o_1 as a positive example does not logically imply that any object o_2 *with an identical description* will also be a positive concept example. It follows, therefore, that it is impossible to create a decision system that guarantees 100% prediction of unseen examples unless the system used the entire universe as a training sample. In order to make the statement that all objects identical to o_1 must be classified as positive examples, we make a very strong assumption about the state of the universe:

The state of the universe is reflected in the state of the training sample.

Obviously, this assumption should be valid if the sample is randomly selected, but that cannot always be guaranteed. We conclude from the above assumption that the distribution of objects in the sample is identical to the distribution of objects in the universe, and, therefore, any conclusions (decision rules) derived from the sample will hold for the universe of objects in general. A second, equally important assumption must be made for induction to succeed:

There is a pattern to the universe that permits a description of a set of sample data to be produced that is shorter in length than actual data. (54)

That is to say, we can find a pattern to describe our sample set that is more efficient than simply listing the elements of the set. Thus, in our introductory example, the pattern is that all parrots are green; therefore, we need not describe our parrot sightings by listing the height, weight, age, and so forth for each bird observation.

In the study of inductive learning, many issues must be addressed. Michalski (34), and Carbonell (7), discuss the following items in detail:

Representation and description language: Knowledge representation is an issue in its own right (8,55,56). We are concerned both with the input language — used to specify the training information — and the output language — used to specify the knowledge accumulated by the system. The input language generally takes the form of a table of objects and attributes, defining attribute-value pairs [e.g., (color, blue) and (height, tall)]. This representation is discussed in more detail below.

The possibilities for an output language are much more varied and include decision trees, decision rules (also known as production rules), decision algorithms, and frames. The first two of these are the most common for inductive systems that learn from examples, and it is possible to convert from one format to the other (57). The ID3/C4 family of algorithms mentioned earlier generates decision trees (other such systems are described in Ref. 58), whereas the AQ series of algorithms and the approximate classification algorithms produce decision rules.

Types of descriptions sought: A system may generate either discriminant or characteristic descriptions. *Discriminant* descriptions are chosen in such a way as to distinguish between positive examples of a concept and negative examples. *Characteristic* descriptions simply characterize positive examples of the concept using common properties of those examples.

Transformation rules: These describe the transformations applied to the input data in order to produce the output. Some basic transformations include *generalization* of rules, *specialization* of rules, and *composition* of rules.

Control strategy: A *top-down* strategy hypothesizes a solution and transforms it to satisfy some stopping criteria, whereas a *bottom-up* strategy generalizes on the input data until a solution is found to cover all inputs.

Source of instances: A system may learn from examples, presented by a teacher and expert, or it may learn by observation, generating training instances and relying on some external oracle to perform classification.

Completeness and consistency: *Completeness* demands that every positive training example must satisfy the description of the concept, whereas *consistency* demands that if an example satisfies the concept description, it cannot be a negative example.

Single- versus multiple-concept learning: Some systems learn one concept from positive and negative examples of that concept, whereas other systems may learn a set of concepts from a collection of examples, each of which is denoted as a positive example of some concept. Note that a single-concept learning is a special case of multiple-concept learning, in which there are only two concepts to learn: the concept itself and its negation.

Noise and instance classification: It is not possible to assume ideal training data in which every example is correctly classified as a positive or negative example of the concept being learned by the system. Statistical and probabilistic techniques are often adopted to deal with noisy data (59). Some systems, such as C4, generate a tree to accommodate all information, and then remove sections of the tree according to the amount of acceptable error

(60). This is known as *pruning* (51,61). Other systems generate probabilistic decision rules, allowing noise to express itself as the *certainty* of a rule. Approximate classification methods, based on rough set theory, have shown themselves to handle this problem well (26,28,30,59,62,63).

Incremental versus one-shot (one-step) learning: One-shot inductive learning methods begin with a set of training examples, and — in one step — generate all output. More recently, the emphasis is on incremental methods that learn gradually, as each new training example is presented to the system (17,64).

Other issues of note in inductive learning include the treatment of missing values (65,66), the calculation of error rates (67), and the overfitting of the concept description to the data (67). In the computational learning approach of Valiant, the focus is on discovering what kind of Boolean functions are learnable and what amount of training examples are required to learn each type of function (68–70). Other more theoretical issues are addressed by Angluin, Smith, Pitt, and others (71–74).

Each choice made from the above issues in the design of a learning system affects its *bias* (75); that is, every system has a bias toward particular outputs, so that some outputs are more likely than others, given that they may be equally correct. For example, a system may be biased toward a smaller set of decision rules or toward short decision trees, with many branches at each decision node.

The CPLA system takes as input a table of attribute-value pairs presented by an expert and, using rough set methodology, generates probabilistic decision rules in one shot. It learns multiple concepts and generates discriminant, complete, and consistent rules using generalization techniques in a bottom-up fashion.

BASIC REPRESENTATIONAL MODEL

We assume that in the process of perception we distinguish entities (*objects*) and their properties. Properties of objects are perceived through assignment of some characteristics (*attributes*) and their values. In this way, we establish a universe of discourse. We use the term *universe of discourse* to refer to that set of elements and information items that our representation method allows us to discuss. Within this universe, we will define a knowledge system. Elements of the universe are referred to as objects. Objects in the universe may be *seen* or *unseen*. Seen objects are those objects of which we have knowledge; that is, those objects which comprise our data. This nonempty set of objects is commonly referred to as the *sample*, and we will denote it by *OBJ*. Elements of *OBJ* may be books, people, and so forth. Unseen objects are simply objects that are describable in our system but for which we have no information (i.e., they are not present in the sample). We partition the sample into two parts: the *training sample* — from which decision rules are inductively derived — and the *test sample* — which is used to test the predictive accuracy of the generated rules. Knowledge about objects is expressed through assignment of some characteristic features to the objects (e.g., humans can be characterized by gender and age, books by title and author's name). These features are represented by attributes and values of attributes. Thus, the components of the system are nonempty set AT of attributes, and for each $a \in AT$, a set VAL_a of values of attribute a.

An information function f: $OBJ \times AT \rightarrow VAL$ assigns attribute values to objects, yielding the description of each object, and may be expressed as a table. A *concept* refers to some subset of the universe (to which we have attached some meaning). The intersection of OBJ and the concept comprises the set of positive examples of that concept. In a single-concept situation, there are two possible decision classes: positive and negative. An expert must assign each example object in OBJ to the correct decision class, denoted by the expert attribute $E \in AT$. This expresses the concepts we want the system to learn; so, in the one-concept case, $VAL_E = \{+, -\}$. Figure 1 shows an example of a multiconcept case, with four decision classes.

CONDITIONAL PROBABILISTIC LEARNING ALGORITHM

Presented here is the model for a system automating the process of inductive learning from a database of examples.* It uses results from Pawlak's rough set theory (30), probabilistic approximation (26), and conditional indiscernibility (76). The resulting system produces approximate classification rules from a database of attri-

Let:

$$
\begin{aligned}
OBJ &= \{car_1, car_2, car_3, car_4, car_5\}, \\
AT &= \{Transmission, Color, Cylinders, Speed\}, \\
E &= \{Rating\}, \\
VAL_{Transmission} &= \{standard, automatic\}, \\
VAL_{Color} &= \{blue, red, green\}, \\
VAL_{Cylinders} &= \{4, 6, 8\}, \\
VAL_{Speed} &= \{fast, med, slow\}, \\
VAL_{Rating} &= \{excellent, good, fair, poor\}.
\end{aligned}
$$

The function, f, is described by the table below.

OBJ	Transmission	Color	Cylinders	Speed	Rating
car_1	standard	blue	4	fast	excellent
car_2	standard	blue	4	med	good
car_3	standard	green	4	med	good
car_4	standard	red	6	slow	fair
car_5	automatic	red	8	slow	poor

FIGURE 1   A multiple-concept case. The right-hand column shows the expert's rating of each car. Each rating value is a label for a concept that we want the system to learn.

---

*An expanded version of this section appeared as a full paper (29).

bute-value pairs. These rules together form probabilistic descriptions of the concepts described by the examples.

The model allows for semantic knowledge to be deduced from the database in ways not previously explored by other systems. The model is distinctive in that it includes the *conditions* feature that allows user control over sets of attribute values and, thus, allows a greater flexibility of analysis. More specifically, conditions specify equivalences on sets of attribute values, with the result that some objects may become indistinguishable. This is essentially the opposite of the discretization process, in which continuous values are separated into intervals, each a discrete value.

Moreover, the model is distinctive in that it defines a feedback relationship between the user and the learning program, unlike other inductive learning systems, which simply input data and output a decision tree. This interactiveness allows for rule (tree) compaction and generalization.

Finally, this model is also distinctive in that it yields a family of production rules using easily comprehended descriptions formed of attribute-value pairs. Compared to the decision trees used by many other inductive learning systems (e.g., Ref. 23), this format is more easily understood and manipulated by humans.

The model defines an interactive inductive learning system, CPLA, which is based on the model of Wong and Ziarko's INFER (26). CPLA is an inductive learning system that uses the probabilistic information inherent in a database and generates a family of probabilistic decision rules based on a minimized set of object attributes. We generalize further on Wong and Ziarko's model by adding *conditions* to the system, as introduced in Refs. 76 and 77. Conditions are a form of user input that makes the system interactive and that can reduce the size of the rule family. Also, the decision rules are input to the *condition suggestion algorithm* (CSA), which generates suggested conditions. Conditions applied to decision rules generalize them, possibly resulting in a smaller and more concisely described family of rules. The entire model is shown in Figure 2.

The diagram in Figure 2 shows how the three elements of the system, CPLA, CSA, and the user, form an *interactive* cycle in which the user moderates the

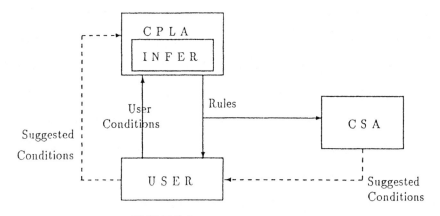

FIGURE 2   The interactive cycle.

feedback from CSA. The cycle begins by taking any (possibly empty) set of user-supplied conditions and running CPLA on the examples database with those conditions. CPLA, by definition, will remove the statistical functional dependencies among attributes, so that a minimal number of attributes are used in the decision rules. It will then output a family of decision rules that will then be passed to CSA, from which suggested conditions will be generated. The user can examine the suggested conditions and select a subset of them to feed back into CPLA for another pass, beginning the cycle again. The suggested conditions may affect the rule family in two ways (in addition to reducing the number of rules generated). They may introduce superfluous attributes that CPLA will remove, and they may change decision-rule certainties. The cycle continues until the *user* is satisfied with the final generation of decision rules.

Wong and Wong (27) presented an inductive learning algorithm, ILS, and showed it to be an improvement over the earlier systems of Michalski (AQ11; Ref. 16) and Quinlan (ID3; Ref. 19), because it allowed for shorter descriptions (and thus shorter decision trees) based on a smaller set of attributes. Furthermore, the output was in the more comprehensible *production rule* format. ILS improved on the above-mentioned methods by using rough set theory, as did INFER, which also took advantage of the probabilistic information inherent in databases to generate probabilistic decision rules.

The probabilistic approach allows us to retrieve some of the information discarded by the deterministic approach by attaching a degree of certainty to probabilistic rules that would have not existed in the earlier deterministic case (see also Refs. 26, 27, 78, and 79).

In later work, Quinlan (21,23) introduced C4 as a method to deal with such probabilistic rules (i.e., rules that Quinlan refers to as having a "central estimate" less than 1). C4 deals with these cases by generating a decision tree and then pruning subtrees when it would not increase the error rating of the subtree root beyond a certain degree. In contrast, the rough set-based methods on which we base our work output the entire family of generated rules, with corresponding certainties, and the user decides which to retain and which to discard. Furthermore, by outputting all rules, we allow the user to see all information compiled by the learning system before deciding which to discard, whereas in the C4 approach, pruning removes information that is then forever lost to the user (without regenerating the entire decision tree). Such manipulation is more practical with decision-rule output as opposed to decision tree output.

Finally, it may be said that the objective of learning systems is to learn *concept descriptions*, in which case a set of descriptive terms seems intuitively more useful as a description, as compared with a decision tree, which acts solely as a classifier. For more discussion on the merits of decision trees versus description rules, see Ref. 57.

The model presented here expands on ILS and INFER by generalizing and adding *conditions* to the system. Conditions introduce into the model a new form of generalization and a mechanism for user feedback, allowing for a more powerful analysis of the dataset.

The knowledge system to be used is specified in the following way. Let $K = (OBJ, AT, E, VAL, f)$, where OBJ is a finite, nonempty set, whose elements are called *objects*, AT is a finite, nonempty set, whose elements are called *attributes,*

$E \in AT$ is the *expert (decision) attributes*, $VAL = \cup_{a \in AT} VAL_a$, where for each $a \in AT$, VAL_a is a finite set with at least two elements and the elements of VAL_a are called *values of attribute a*. The total function f is called the *information function* from the set $OBJ \times AT$ into a set VAL such that $(\forall o \in OBJ)\ (\forall a \in AT)\ (f(o, a) \in VAL_a)$. Every object in OBJ has associated with it a set of values corresponding to the attributes AT and the expert attribute E. The function f maps the attribute of an object to its corresponding value.

Learning

In general, information about objects obtained from such a knowledge representation system is not sufficient to characterize objects uniquely; that is, we are not able to distinguish all the objects by means of the admitted attributes and their values. For example, if we only have the attributes {*Transmission, Color, Cylinders*} to characterize the objects in the example above, then we cannot distinguish between car_1 and car_2. This means that objects are recognized up to an *indiscernibility relation* determined by elementary information items. *Any two objects are indiscernible whenever they assume the same values for all the attributes under consideration.*

The indiscernibility relation is what allows learning systems to generalize. It allows for the possibility of recognizing just the important features of objects. Given an indiscernibility relation, we can use it to define equivalence classes — sets of objects indiscernible based on the given attribute set.

Next, we form concepts; that is, we aggregate some objects into sets. Information about a concept is composed from information about objects that are instances of that concept. As objects are not necessarily distinguishable, information characterizing a concept may be ambiguous to some extent. In this case, we want to have at least some approximation of our information and we express it in terms of an indiscernibility relation, which leads to the definition and theory of *rough sets* that was used to introduce the concept of approximate classification (30,32,80).

Learning is defined in the system as generating descriptions for rules for classifying objects into concepts. A deterministic learning system generates rules only when all objects satisfying a description are members of a concept. A probabilistic system such as CPLA generates a rule and assigns a certainty to it, depending on the probability that an object satisfying a certain description is a member of the corresponding concept.

Conditions

Suppose there is a user who is trying to decide what car to buy (and thus rating every car considered in terms of desirability). In such a case, a user may not care if the car has six or eight cylinders, while still being concerned with the difference between four and six cylinders. Thus, he or she would consider the values six and eight as equivalent.

Conditions are formally defined as a family of equivalence relations $\{cond_a\}_{a \in AT}$ defined in the set VAL_a; that is, for each $a \in AT$, $cond_a \subseteq VAL_a \times VAL_a$, and $cond_a$ is an equivalence relation. By $cond_a(v)$ we mean $\{v' : (v, v') \in cond_a\}$.

(*Notational remark*: Only pairs that define the conditions explicitly are listed;

pairs that assure the reflexive, symmetric, and transitive properties will not be listed.)

Example 1
Let us consider the system from Figure 1. To define the condition mentioned above, we let

$$cond_{Cylinders} = \{(6, 8)\}.$$

Note that implicitly specified are the conditions

$$cond_{Cylinders} = \{(6, 6), (8, 8)\} \cup \{(8, 6)\}.$$

The first set contains pairs that assure the reflexive property; the second set contains the remaining pair for the symmetric property; the transitive property is fulfilled vacuously here.

Relations

As stated earlier, the indiscernibility relation is a key element in most approximate classification systems related to our inductive learning system. It is what allows a system to generalize from examples. What distinguishes our approach from others is that we provide control over which objects are to be indiscernible.

Usually (see Refs. 27, 78, 79, and 81) indiscernibility is defined in the following way. Let $A \subseteq AT$. We say that objects o_1 and o_2 are indiscernible with respect to the subset A of attributes if the following condition is satisfied:

$$o_1 \approx_A o_2 \quad \text{iff } (\forall a \in A)(f(o_1, a) = f(o_2, a)).$$

Example 2
When $A = \{Transmission, Color\}$, then car_1 and car_2 are indiscernible with respect to the attributes *transmission* and *color*; that is $car_a \approx_A car_2$.

We generalize here the notion of indiscernibility by adding to it the notion of conditions, and define, for any $A \subseteq AT$, and any family of conditions $\{cond_a\}_{a \in A}$, a family of binary relations $R(A)$ on OBJ as follows:

$$o_1 R(A) o_2 \quad \text{iff } (\forall a \in A)((f(o_1, a), f(o_2, a)) \in cond_a).$$

Call the *identity conditions* the set of conditions $cond_a = \{(v, v) : v \in VAL_a\}$.

(*Notational remark*: Given $A \subseteq AT$, if we define *only* $cond_a$ for a certain attribute $a \in A$, then we mean that $cond_b$ for all $b \neq a$, $b \in A$, are identity conditions.)

Example 3
Let $A = AT$ in the system from Figure 1. The conditions $cond_{Speed} = \{(fast, med)\}$ defines a relation, $R(A)$, such that

$$car_1 R(A) \ car_2,$$

and the plain indiscernibility relation $\approx_A$ does not hold for car_1 and car_2.

Because $R(A)$ is an equivalence relation, it induces a partition on the set of objects, denoted $R(A)^* = \{A_1, A_2 \ldots, A_n\}$.

Example 4

In the system of Figure 1, if $A = \{Transmission, Color, Speed\}$, $cond_{Speed} = \{med, fast\}$, and $cond_{Transmission} = \{standard, automatic\}$, then we assume $cond_{Color}$ is the identity conditions $\{(v, v) : v \in VAL\}$. These conditions define a relation $R(A)$ such that $R(A)^* = \{A_1, A_2\}$, where $A_1 = \{car_1, car_2\}$ and $A_2 = \{car_3, car_4\}$.

Call a knowledge representation system K together with a family of conditions and a family of relations $\{R(A)\}_{A \subseteq AT}$ defined above, a *conditional knowledge representation system CK*; that is,

$$CK = (K, \{cond_a\}_{a \in A}, \{R(A)\}_{A \subseteq AT}).$$

We now use this knowledge representation system to describe — or "learn" — concepts defined by an expert. The concepts are defined to the system via the *expert classification*, represented by the values of the expert attribute. An expert classifies each object into a concept by assigning an appropriate value to its expert attribute. In our example, the expert is teaching the concepts *excellent car, good car, fair car,* and *poor car* by classifying the cars into the appropriate concept, according to his or her expert opinion.

Probability

The next step is to generalize to a probabilistic model, as in Refs. 26, 27, 78, and 79. The resulting system is a *conditional probabilistic knowledge representation system CPK*

$$CPK = K + conditions + probability.$$

Probability is incorporated into the system by extending the models of the above works. Let A be any subset of AT. Let $R(A)^* = \{A_1, A_2, \ldots, A_n\}$ denote the partition induced by $R(A)$ on OBJ, where A_i is an equivalence class of $R(A)$. Let $R(E)^* = \{E_1, E_2, \ldots, E_m\}$ (where E is the set of expert attributes) denote the partition induced by $R(E)$ on OBJ, so that each element of $R(E)^*$ corresponds to one of the expert-defined concepts. Given a relation $R(A)$ and the partitions $R(A)^* = \{A_1, \ldots, A_n\}$ and $R(E)^* = \{E_1, \ldots, E_m\}$, we let P denote the *conditional probability* $P(E_j|A_i) = P(E_i \cap A_i)/P(A_i)$ where $P(E_j|A_i)$ denotes the probability of occurrence of event E_j conditioned on event A_i.

Deterministic models discard probabilistic information. If the relationship between a class A_i and an expert class E_j is not deterministic, no rule is created between the two. This probabilistic system generates such a rule and attaches a probability to it, thus retaining useful information that otherwise would have been discarded.

We use the probabilistic model because of its ability to capture and make use of the statistical information available in the boundary — the region in OBJ in which we cannot tell whether an object belongs to a concept or not. The probabilistic model has been proven (62,78) to be superior to the deterministic model. It also has benefits as a useful tool for dealing with some more difficult problems in machine learning such as generation of decision rules from inconsistent training examples (82,83).

Superfluous Attributes

In a knowledge representation system, it is possible that some attributes of AT are redundant; that is, they do not provide any additional information about the objects in OBJ. These attributes will be defined as conditionally statistically superfluous.

Wong and Ziarko discussed statistical functional dependency in Ref. 26. Functional dependency in our conditional probabilistic model becomes *statistical conditional functional dependency*. It is referred to here simply as *statistical dependency*.

Several techniques have been suggested to remove the superfluous attributes from a knowledge representation system. We will adopt the probabilistic method described by Wong and Ziarko and extend it to our conditional model and incorporate it into our algorithm, using the definition of conditionally superfluous attributes given below. The result will be that our conditional decision rules will contain no superfluous attributes and, therefore, there will be fewer rules (79).

Given relations $R(A)$, $R(B)$, with $R(A)^* = \{A_1, \ldots, A_n\}$, and $R(B)^* = \{B_1, \ldots, B_m\}$, where A and B are arbitrary set of attributes, define the normalized *entropy function* $H(R(B)^* | R(A^*))$, which provides a plausible measure of statistical dependency, as follows (78):

$$H(R(B)^* | R(A)^*) = \sum_{i=1}^{n} \frac{P(A_i) H(R(B)^* | A_i)}{\log m},$$

where

$$H(R(B)^* | A_i) = -\sum_{j=1}^{m} P(B_j | A_i) \log P(B_j | A_i).$$

We say that B is *conditionally functionally dependent* on A if and only if

$$H(R(B)^* | R(A^*)) = 0.$$

An attribute a is said to be *conditionally statistically superfluous with respect to B* if

$$H(R(B)^* | R(A) - \{a\})^*) = H(R(B)^* | R(A)^*).$$

As mentioned earlier, when we add to a knowledge representation system conditions and conditional probabilities, the result is a conditional probabilistic knowledge representation system CPK. We can now more formally define CPK:

$$CPK = (K, A_p),$$

where K is the deterministic knowledge representation system and A_p is the conditional probabilistic approximation space

$$A_p = (\{(VAL, \{cond_a\}_{a \in A}, R(A))\}_{A \subseteq AT}, P),$$

respectively.

Descriptions

The expert partition represents an expert's classification of objects into concepts. Decision rules describe the relationship between the partition based on the attributes $A \subseteq AT$ and the partition based on the expert's classification E. Such a definition maps the description of an element of the first partition to a description of an element of the second partition. A description as defined in these works is of the form

$$des(A_i) = \bigwedge_{a \in A} (a, v)$$

where (a, v) are pairs such that $f(o, a) = v$ for $o \in A_i$, and $\wedge$ indicates logical conjunction ("and").

Example 5

Let K be the system from Figure 1, $A \subseteq AT$, $A = \{color, speed\}$, and a simple equivalence relation $\approx_A$ induces a partition such that $OBJ = A_1 \cup A_2 \cup A_3 \cup A_4$, such that the class A_1 is the set of cars $\{car_1\}$ and all members of A_1 are *blue* and *fast*, and A_2 is the set of cars that are *blue* and *medium* speed; that is, $\{car_2\}$. The descriptions of A_1 and A_2 are

$$des(A_1) = (color, blue) \wedge (speed, fast),$$
$$des(A_2) = (color, blue) \wedge (speed, med).$$

In this model, a partition depends not only on the set of attributes $A \subseteq AT$ but also on the set of conditions defined for those attributes. Thus, the partition by $R(A)$ in *conditioned* decision rules is a function of the family of conditions applied to the system.

Given a set $A \subseteq AT$ and a family of conditions $\{cond_a\}_{a \in A}$, define the *conditioned description* (from now on referred to simply as the *description*) of any equivalence class $A_i \in R(A)*$

$$\bigwedge (a, cond_a(f(o, a))).$$

We will use $des(A_i)$ as a shorthand notation for the description. When it is not obvious from the context, we will use $des_A(A_i)$ to indicate the attributes from which the description is formed.

[*Notational remark*: Note that in a description, if the only condition on the value of an attribute is that it is equivalent to itself, then in the description we write the pair (*attribute, value*) rather than (*attribute*, {value}).]

Example 6

Let us again consider the system K from Example 5. Assume that the user does not care about the difference between *medium* and *fast* as the speed of a car. This is expressed in our system as the condition $cond_{speed} = \{(fast, med)\}$ [equivalently, $cond_{color}(fast) = \{fast, med\}$]. Now consider a set of attributes $A = \{color, speed\}$ with the condition described. This defines a relation $R(A)$ such that a new partition of OBJ is created. In this partition the first set, A_i is $A_1 = \{car_1, car_2\}$ and

$$des(A_1) = (color, blue) \wedge (speed, \{fast, med\}).$$

Conditioned Decision Rules

Conditioned rules take the form of a mapping from the description of an equivalence class of $R(A)*$ to the description of an equivalence class of $R(E)*$.

We define as in Ref. 78, the family of decision rules $\{r_{i,j}\}$ for the system CPK as

1. $des(A_i) \overset{\triangle}{=} des(E_j)$ if $P(E_j | A_i) > 0.5$
2. $des(A_i) \overset{\triangle}{=} NOTdes(E_j)$ if $P(E_j | A_i) < 0.5$
3. $des(A_i) \overset{\triangle}{=} unknown(E_j)$ if $P(E_j | A_i) = 0.5$

where the *certainty* of a rule is defined as

$$c = \max(P(E_j | A_i), 1 - P(E_j | A_i)).$$

Example 7

Let K be the system of Figure 1 and assume that we have no conditions (besides, obviously, the identity conditions), and the set of attributes $A = (Transmission, Color, Cylinders, Speed)$, then the partition induced is $A_1 = \{car_1\}$, $A_2 = \{car_2\}$, $A_3 = \{car_3\}$, $A_4 = \{car_4\}$, $A_5 = \{car_5\}$. The partition $R(E)^*$ is $E_1 = \{car_1\}$, $E_2 = \{car_2, car_3\}$, $E_3 = \{car_4\}$, and $E_4 = \{car_5\}$. An example of a rule is

> $r_{1,1}$: $(Transmission, standard)$
> $\wedge$ $(Color, blue)$
> $\wedge$ $(Cylinders, 4)$
> $\wedge$ $(Speed, fast) \overset{1.0}{\Rightarrow} (Rating, excellent)$.

Given the same set of attributes and the conditions $cond_{Color} = \{(blue, green)\}$ ($\{cond_a\}_{a \neq Color}$ is the identity conditions), the partition $R(A)^*$ becomes $A_1 = \{car_1\}$, $A_2 = \{car_2, car_3\}$, $A_3 = \{car_4\}$, and $A_4 = \{car_5\}$. $R(E)^*$ does not change. An example of a rule is

> $r_{2,2}$: $(Transmission, standard)$
> $\wedge$ $(Color, \{blue, green\})$
> $\wedge$ $(Cylinders, 4)$
> $\wedge$ $(Speed, med) \overset{1.0}{\Rightarrow} (Rating, good)$.

It is obvious that conditions may decrease the number of classes in a partition, because they may reduce the number of distinguishable objects in *OBJ*. Rules are a function of the partition of the database; therefore, we can see that conditions will reduce the number of rules by decreasing the number of partitions of the database.

Given a conditional probabilistic knowledge representation system, we will now define the system CPLA, which generates a family of probabilistic rules based on a minimal set of attributes, taking into account the conditions defined by the system, if any. Each rule has associated with it a certainty, describing the probability that an object conforming to the description of the rule's domain will belong to the expert class that the rule specifies.

THE ALGORITHM

CPLA traces its roots to Refs. 26, 78, and 79. From Ref. 79, it inherits the procedural structure of the algorithm. As an extension of Wong and Ziarko's INFER algorithm (26), it maintains the property that the output will have no superfluous attributes. It takes the most from Pawlak et al.'s 1988 article (78) as it utilizes the entropy function suggested in their article to calculate attribute dependencies and it uses the probabilistic rules proposed in their article (as discussed above). The algorithm is

- *Input* a conditional probabilistic knowledge representation system (K, A_p) where $K = (OBJ, AT, E, VAL, f)$ and A_p is the conditional probabilistic approximation space.
- Let $OBJ' = OBJ, A = \emptyset, B = AT$.
- Repeat until $OBJ' = \emptyset$ or $B = \emptyset$.
  Loop: Find $a \in B$ such that $H(R(E)^* | R(A \cup \{a\})^*)$ is *minimum* for OBJ'.
  If $A \cup \{a\}$ is statistically dependent on A, then let $B \leftarrow B - \{a\}$, goto *Loop*.
  Let $A \leftarrow A \cup \{a\}$.
  For each $E_j \in R(E)^*$ from OBJ'
    For each A_i such that $P(E_j | A_i) = 1.0$
      Output $des(A_i) \stackrel{1.0}{\Rightarrow} des(E_j)$
      Let $OBJ' \leftarrow OBJ' - A_i$
- If $OBJ' \neq \emptyset$
    For each $E_j \in R(E)^*$
    For each A_i such that $A_i \cap E_j \neq \emptyset$
    Calculate $p_{i,j} = P(E_j | A_i)$.
    Calculate $c = max(p_{i,j}, 1 - p_{i,j})$.
    If $p_{i,j} > 1 - p_{i,j}$
    $\rightarrow$ Output $des(A_i) \stackrel{c}{\Rightarrow} des(E_j)$
    If $p_{i,j} < 1 - p_{i,j}$
    $\rightarrow$ Output $des(A_i) \stackrel{c}{\Rightarrow} NOTdes(E_j)$
    If $p_{i,j} = 1 - p_{i,j}$
    $\rightarrow$ Output $des(A_i) \stackrel{0.5}{\Rightarrow} unknown(E_j)$
- End.

Given a knowledge representation system *CPK* and two equivalence relations $R(A)$ and $R(E)$, defining partitions $R(A)^* = \{A_1, A_2, \ldots, A_n\}$ and $R(E)^* = \{E_1, E_2 \ldots, E_m\}$, respectively, a rule is generated for every pair A_i, E_j such that $P(E_j | A_i) \neq 0$. Therefore, to reduce the number of rules, we must apply conditions to decrease the number of partitions of the data set, so that we will have a smaller number of rules retaining approximately the same amount of knowledge.

Often, a system may contain attributes whose values are irrelevant in determining the expert classification of the objects. These attributes are not conditionally statistically superfluous, but the information they supply has no effect on the expert's global decision. The problem is one of determining which attributes contribute nothing to the expert's classification. There are two possible indicators: (1) two widely separated values (assuming ordered values) of an attribute can be unified through conditions without decreasing the accuracy of the system, and (2) *all* values of an attribute may be unified without loss of accuracy. These indicators can lead us to conclude that the attribute to which these values belong must not be significant to the expert's classification, as differences in the attribute's values do not play a part in the final classification.

This kind of syntactic information is extracted by the CSA.

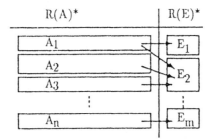

FIGURE 3   Graphical representation of decision rules.

CONDITION SUGGESTION

The main idea behind the condition suggestion is the collapsing of *similar* rules into one rule, or, equivalently, the generalization from a set of specific rules to a more general rule. This is accomplished by the suggestion of conditions that will effectively merge several equivalence classes of a partition into one class. This can best be seen in Figure 3, in which classes are represented as boxes, and rules are represented as arrows from classes in $R(A)^*$ to classes in $R(E)^*$.

Two rules that map classes in $R(A)^*$ to the same class in $R(E)^*$ with the same certainty are considered similar (e.g., A_2 and A_3 in Figure 3). We would like to generate conditions to merge A_2 and A_3, so that the new partition is as shown in Figure 4.

To proceed with the definition of similarity, we introduced a further notational shorthand:

$$DES_1(E_j) = des(E_j)$$
$$DES_2(E_j) = NOTdes(E_j)$$
$$DES_3(E_j) = unknown(E_j)$$

so all rules may now be denoted by

$$des(A_i) \stackrel{c}{\Rightarrow} DES_k(E_j)$$

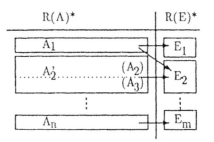

FIGURE 4   Merging equivalence classes.

Similarity

The principle upon which the CSA is based is the idea of *rule similarity*.

Example 8

Given two rules

$$(Color, \; blue) \wedge (Speed, \; med) \stackrel{1.0}{\Rightarrow} (Rating, \; good)$$

$$(Color, \; green) \wedge (Speed, \; med) \stackrel{1.0}{\Rightarrow} (Rating, \; good)$$

the rules are *similar*, as they both map the description of some equivalence class to the same concept with the same certainty.

Specifically, given a conditional probabilistic knowledge representation system *CPK* and a set of attributes $A \subseteq AT$, let $r_{i,j}$ and $r_{p,q}$ be any two rules from the family of rules $\{r_{i,j}\}$:

$$r_{i,j} : des \; (A_i) \stackrel{c_1}{\Rightarrow} DES_k(E_j)$$

$$r_{p,q} : des(A_p) \stackrel{c_2}{\Rightarrow} DES_r(E_q)$$

[where $A_i, \; A_p \in R(A)^*, \; E_j, \; E_q \in R(E)^*, \; 1 \leq k, r \leq 3$]. We define a similarity relation, **sim**, as follows

$$r_{i,j} \; \textbf{sim} \; r_{p,q} \quad \text{iff } c_1 = c_2, j = q, k = r.$$

By definition, **sim** is an equivalence relation. Note that although the value of k (r) is determined by c_1 and j (c_1 and q), we specify the condition $k = r$ to form a more general definition.

Given a rule $r_{i,j} : des(A_i) \stackrel{c}{\Rightarrow} DES_k(E_j)$, we will call the equivalence class $[r_{i,j}]$ a set of similarly acting rules for $r_{i,j}$.

$$SIM(r_{i,j}) = [r_{i,j}].$$

By definition,

$$SIM(r_{i,j}) = \{r_{p,j} : r_{p,j} : des(A_p) \stackrel{c}{\Rightarrow} DES_k(E_j) \text{ for some } p\}.$$

Define the *domain* of some rule, $des(A_i) \stackrel{c}{\Rightarrow} des(E_j)$, as the set of objects whose descriptions match the description of the set $A_i \in R(A)^*$; that is,

$$domain(des(A_i) \stackrel{c}{\Rightarrow} DES_k(E_j)) = \{o : des_A(\{o\}) = des(A_i)\},$$

where $o \in OBJ$. The domain of the above rule is simply the set A_i. Define the *domain of a set of rules* as the union of the domains of the rules in the set.

Define, for each $r_{i,j}$, the domain of a set of similarity acting rules

$$DSIM(r_{i,j}) = \bigcup_{A_p \in R(A)^*} \{A_p : des(A_p) \stackrel{c}{\Rightarrow} DES_k(E_j)\},$$

where c and k are defined by the rule $r_{i,j}$.

Thus, the domain of the two rules mentioned above would be all the cars from the database whose description matches (*Color, blue*) $\wedge$ (*Speed, med*) or (*Color, green*) $\wedge$ (*Speed, med*).

For each $SIM(r_{i,j}) = [r_{i,j}]$ we would like to introduce a new rule

$$des(DSIM(r_{i,j})) \overset{c}{\Rightarrow} DES_k(E_j).$$

This new rule performs the same function as the set of rules $SIM(r_{i,j})$.

In other words, we have taken one set of rules, SIM and created a *generalized* rule to replace it, which covers the same domain of input objects.

Given a set $SIM(r_{i,j})$ of equivalent rules on A, rules are merged by applying conditions that will attempt to collapse all elements of each $DSIM(r_{i,j})$ into one equivalence class. The conditions required are, for all $a \in AT$,

$$cond_a = \{(v, v') : (\forall o \in A_i) (\exists A_j \subseteq DSIM(r_{i,j}))$$
$$(\exists o' \in A_j) (v = f(o, a) \wedge v' = f(o', a))\}.$$

At this point, we must specify what is meant exactly by $des(DSIM(r_{i,j}))$. The precise description of such a set of objects would be

$$\bigvee_{o \in DSIM(r_{i,k})} \left(\bigwedge_{a \in A} (a, cond_a(f(o, a))) \right),$$

but this is equivalent to the original set of rules. Instead, we would like to generate just one conjunctive description of $DSIM(r_{i,k})$. Practically, however, such extensive conditions would quite possibly have the effect of merging domains of dissimilar rules. We are, therefore, obliged to use as few conditions as possible to avoid increasing the total entropy of the system. Our compromise, therefore, is to merge only classes that are described by equal sets of attributes (the same set of attributes). This is reflected in the CSA algorithm below.

Example 9

Given the two rules presented in the previous example

$$(Color, blue) \wedge (Speed, med) \overset{1.0}{\Rightarrow} (Rating, good)$$
$$(Color, green) \wedge (Speed, med) \overset{1.0}{\Rightarrow} (Rating, good)$$

to merge the two classes described by the descriptions, the suggested conditions would be $cond_{Color} = \{(blue, green)\}$.

The Condition Suggestion Algorithm

This algorithm form of a set of suggested conditions to merge similar rules whose domains are described by the same attributes.

- Input a family of rules, $\{r_{i,j}\}$.
- Generate the suggested new conditions, $COND'$:
  let $COND' = \emptyset$
  for each rule, $r_{i,j} : des_A(A_i) \overset{c}{\Rightarrow} DES_k(E_j) \in \{r_{i,j}\}$

  Search $\{r_{i,j}\}$ for all similar rules $r'_{i,j} : des_{A'}(A_l) \overset{c'}{\Rightarrow} DES_k(E_j), A = A'$.
  Let $D = \{A_l\}$, the set of domains of those rules.
  Update $COND'$ with the conditions:
  $cond_a = \{(v, v') : (\forall o \in D) (\exists o' \in D) (v = f(o, a) \wedge v' = f(o', a))\}.$
  output $COND'$.
- End.

Conclusion

This section has proposed a model of probabilistic inductive learning built on the ILS model of Wong and Wong (27), and the INFER model of Wong and Ziarko (26). The model—CPLA—incorporates the concept of *conditions* and allows for direct user interaction with the data. CSA extracts syntactic knowledge from the knowledge representation system and allows the user to convert it to semantic knowledge. The syntactic knowledge is presented as suggested conditions that can reduce the size of the rule family generated by the learning system. These parts have been put together as a three-element system or cycle: CPLA–CSA–user. The user plays an integral part in the cycle by supplying conditions as well as selecting from the suggested conditions to adjust the data so as to maximize the information content of the rules while minimizing the uncertainty of the system. The result is a smaller, more efficient system.

AN EXPERIMENT

CPLA was applied as a learning system to real data.* The results discussed are based on data from a survey of voters in the 1988 U.S. presidential election.† The conditions feature of CPLA was able to yield a roughly 47% decrease in the number of rules, and up to 88% predictive accuracy.

Our analysis was concerned with the following:

1. The semantic analysis of rules and conditions. What information about the election itself could we extract from the rules and suggested conditions?
2. The effect of conditions on the number of rules. How did conditions affect the number of rules output by CPLA?
3. The predictive accuracy of the rules. How did the conditions affect the ability of the rules to classify previously unseen examples?

Item 1 consists of an analysis of CPLA results. This is a nonstandard analysis, as we are discussing the semantic content of the rules themselves. Items 2 and 3 are more traditional analyses of performance issues.

The Data

In the database of election survey responses, example objects were the responses of an individual to a set of questions. Each question is considered an attribute, and each answer a value. The attributes AT and their corresponding values VAL_a ($a \in AT$) are listed in Table 1. The expert attribute was the survey respondent's vote, in this case, a vote for presidential candidates George Bush or Michael Dukakis.

The database consists of 444 records. In order to discuss both rule generation and predictive accuracy, we randomly split the database into two parts. Two-thirds

---

*This section is a summary of results presented in Ref. 84.

†Data acquired courtesy of C. Taber and M. Lodge, Department of Political Science, State University of New York at Stony Brook.

TABLE 1   Database Attributes and Values

	AT	VAL_a
a_1	Party Identification	$\{1, \ldots, 7\}$
a_2	Ideological Distance from Dukakis	$\{0, \ldots, 7\}$
a_3	Ideological Distance from Bush	$\{0, \ldots, 7\}$
a_4	Bush Issue-distance: Government Services	$\{0, \ldots, 7\}$
a_5	Bush Issue-distance: Defense Spending	$\{0, \ldots, 7\}$
a_6	Bush Issue-distance: Health Insurance	$\{0, \ldots, 7\}$
a_7	Bush Issue-distance: Standard of Living	$\{0, \ldots, 7\}$
a_8	Dukakis Issue-distance: Government Services	$\{0, \ldots, 7\}$
a_9	Dukakis Issue-distance: Defense Spending	$\{0, \ldots, 7\}$
a_{10}	Dukakis Issue-distance: Health Insurance	$\{0, \ldots, 7\}$
a_{11}	Dukakis Issue-distance: Standard of Living	$\{0, \ldots, 7\}$
a_{12}	Race	$\{-1, 0, 1\}$
a_{13}	Sex	$\{0, 1\}$
a_{14}	Age	$\{18, \ldots, 100\}$
a_{15}	Education	$\{1, \ldots, 7\}$
a_{16}	Type of Community raised in	$\{1, \ldots, 7\}$
a_{17}	Rate Intelligence: Bush	$\{1, \ldots, 7\}$
a_{18}	Rate Intelligence: Dukakis	$\{1, \ldots, 7\}$
a_{19}	Rate Compassion: Bush	$\{1, \ldots, 7\}$
a_{20}	Rate Compassion: Dukakis	$\{1, \ldots, 7\}$
a_{21}	Rate Morals: Bush	$\{1, \ldots, 7\}$
a_{22}	Rate Morals: Dukakis	$\{1, \ldots, 7\}$
a_{23}	Rate as Inspiring: Bush	$\{1, \ldots, 7\}$
a_{24}	Rate as Inspiring: Dukakis	$\{1, \ldots, 7\}$
a_{25}	Rate as Leader: Bush	$\{1, \ldots, 7\}$
a_{26}	Rate as Leader: Dukakis	$\{1, \ldots, 7\}$
a_{27}	Rate as Decent: Bush	$\{1, \ldots, 7\}$
a_{28}	Rate as Decent: Dukakis	$\{1, \ldots, 7\}$
a_{29}	Rate as Caring: Bush	$\{1, \ldots, 7\}$
a_{30}	Rate as Caring: Dukakis	$\{1, \ldots, 7\}$

Objects Respondent	Attributes				Expert attribute Vote
	Party id.	Ideological dist. duk.	$\cdots$	Caring Dukakis	
1	Independent	2	$\cdots$	7	Dukakis
2	Liberal	1	$\cdots$	5	Dukakis
.	.	.	.	.	.
.	.	.	.	.	.
.	.	.	.	.	.
444	Conservative	6	$\cdots$	3	Bush

of the data are designated as "training data" and used by CPLA to inductively generate rules. The remaining third were designated as "test data" and were used to measure predictive accuracy, as described below. A small portion of the database is given below.

Application Process

In the application of CPLA to the data there were three phases:

Phase A: Application to the training data with all 30 attributes and no initial conditions; i.e., $\{cond_a\}_{a \in AT} = \emptyset$.

Phase B: Application to the training data with all 30 attributes and with the condition that ages (a_{14}) are grouped into intervals of 10. This was done to compensate for the fact that the age attribute yields a very fine partition and thus very specific rules.

Phase C: Application to the training data using only four attributes selected as nonsuperfluous in phase A. Three sets of four attributes chosen are as follows:

1. Party identification (a_1), age (a_{14}), health insurance: Dukakis (a_{10}); ideology: Dukakis (a_2).
2. Party identification (a_1); ideology: Bush (a_3); age (a_{14}), education (a_{15}).
3. Party identification (a_1); age (a_{14}); government services: Bush (a_4); ideology: Dukakis (a_2).

$\{cond_a\}_{a \in AT}$ = ages grouped into groups of 10 and selected conditions suggested by CSA.

Semantic Analysis

From our analysis, we conclude that CPLA/CSA has done a fair job of generating a set of useful rules describing the concepts "voter for Bush" and "voter for Dukakis." We are also able to draw other conclusions, both about voting patterns and about the relevant survey questions. It is interesting to note that all these conclusions seem reasonable and have been made by computer scientists. We must now compare our conclusions to an analysis via standard techniques by political scientists. Such a comparison will be the subject of a future article.

By examining features such as choice of attributes, order of attribute selection, and effects of conditions on performance, we have been able to make the following observations:

- Party identification (a_1), in every trial, is always the first chosen by CPLA. This leads to our conclusion that party affiliation is the most important deciding attribute.
- Almost all attribute value ranges were between 0 and 7, but when conditions eliminating distinctions between 0, 1, 2 and 5, 6, 7 were imposed, the performance of the system did not decrease. A logical conclusion is that such distinctions are unnecessary.
- The attributes party identification, age, and issues $(a_1, a_{14}, a_4-a_{11})$ were chosen to create the rules, whereas personal feelings $(a_{17}-a_{30})$ were dis-

carded as superfluous, indicating perhaps that personal feelings were not reliable predictors of voting patterns.

- The most frequently chosen nonsuperfluous attributes related to Dukakis. We might conclude, therefore, that voters were reacting to Dukakis rather than voting for Bush.

- From the rules, we note that personal feelings about issues (a_4–a_{11}) were often at odds with party affiliation and that voters often voted according to their party affiliation, despite their personal feelings about issues. This also shows the importance of party affiliation.

- The attribute *ideological distance from Dukakis* indicated that (1) respondents far from Dukakis in ideology (value of $a_2 \geq 5$) usually voted for Bush and (2) respondents close to Dukakis in ideology (value of $a_2 \leq 3$) voted for both candidates. We might conclude from this that ideology was not strong enough a factor to make Dukakis sympathizers vote for Dukakis, implying that perhaps there were more important factors involved for those voters.

- The age attribute (a_{14}) is important to the rule family even when grouped by conditions into tens. However, there we saw no obvious trend connecting age to voting patterns.

Performance Issues

Initial results show a significant decrease in the number of rules (see Table 2). The initial family of rules generated was entirely deterministic. After adding conditions, the resulting rules were still all entirely deterministic, indicating a good choice of conditions. Furthermore, in all cases, approximately 85% of attributes were discarded as superfluous. Although, in most trials, the attributes chosen were not exactly the same, they were similar enough to indicate a trend.

Predictive Accuracy

Because the ultimate goal of inductive learning is to use the knowledge acquired to recognize (classify) previously unseen objects, we are interested in measuring this ability. Predictive accuracy is the standard measurement tool. It is a measure of the "usefulness" of the rule family. Therefore, after CPLA generated a family of rules, we tested these rules on the test data to see how well they would predict the expert classification of each test object.

Because we have begun with a well-defined formal model, we can define formally the standard notions used above: *classification* and *prediction*.

TABLE 2   Rule Reduction Results

Phase	Attributes in training set	Nonsuperfluous attributes found	Conditions used	Rules	Improvement (rule reduction %)
A	30	4	None	168	–
B	30	5	By user	89	–47
C	4	4	By CSA and user	89	–41

An object o *satisfies* a_i *in a rule* $r : des_A(A_j) \to des(E_k)$ if, for a pair (a_i, $conda_i(v_i)$) in $des_A(A_j)$, $f(o, a_i) \in cond_a(v_i)$.

Object o and rule $r : des_A(A_j) \Rightarrow des(E_k)$, are an *exact match* if o satisfies all $a_i \in A$.

A rule $r : des_A(A_j) \Rightarrow des(E_k)$, *classifies* an object o into expert class $des(E_k)$ if r is an exact match.

Given a rule $r : des_A(A_j) \Rightarrow des(E_k)$, classifying o, $des(E_k)$ is called the rule's *prediction*.

A rule classifies an object o *correctly* if its prediction for o, $des(E_x)$, is equal to $f(o, E)$, where E is the expert attribute. Otherwise, the classification is *incorrect*.

Predictive accuracy of a family of rules is defined, for a test database, as the percentage of test objects correctly classified by the rules.

If there is no rule that matches an object exactly, then there is no prediction for that object, and the object is *unclassified*.

We have dealt with the problem of unclassified objects by creating a *guessing* heuristic. When we use this heuristic, no test object is ever left unclassified.

For every unclassified object o, we determine $pred(o, r)$ for each rule r

$$pred(o, r) = \frac{\text{Number of attributes satisfied by } o \text{ in rule } r}{\text{Number of attributes in description of rule } r}.$$

We "guess" that objects o satisfies rule r if $m = \max_r pred(o,r)$. This heuristic yields the "closest" match of an object and description, when no exact match is available. Results show this is to be a useful technique.

Performance Conclusions

Overall, for this dataset, *conditions* proved themselves to be useful for system optimization. First, they decreased the number of rules without introducing any probabilistic factors into the rule family. Second, they increased the predictive power of the rule family. Table 3 shows the predictive accuracy of the rules without guessing ("exact match") and with guessing. The improvement described shows the increase in predictive accuracy of testing phases B and C as compared to A, both with and without the guessing heuristic.

TABLE 3   Predictive Accuracy

Phase	Predictive accuracy		Percentage improvement	
	Exact match	With guessing	Exact match	With guessing
A	55	77	–	–
B	77	84	41	9
C	84	88	52	14

Phase A: This case obviously yields the poorest results, as there has been no attempt at generalization. CSA suggest (among others) conditions that, in general, make "highly valued" scales, such as the range 1–7, into "fewer-valued" scales, such as {1,2,3}, {4}, and {5,6,7}.

Phase B: In this case, we have partitioned VAL_{age} into groups of 10, to make that attribute yield a coarser partition, and thus more general rules. Immediately, more general, and therefore fewer, rules are generated. By making the rule family more general, we have increased the number of possible objects that might satisfy a rule's description, and thus the number of correctly classified objects obviously increases also, but not as much.

Phase C: In this case, with the CSA-suggested conditions, we have still decreased the number of rules from phase A, although not as much, but we have significantly increased the predictive accuracy of the rule. Thus, with the "guessing" heuristic in place, we achieve a respectable 88% accuracy for this database.

Thus, we see that conditions have yielded a significant improvement. Conditions alone (no guessing) took the predictive accuracy from 55% to 84%. Furthermore, it is interesting to note that as conditions were added to the system, they seemed to "replace" the guessing algorithm. Whereas in phase A, guessing improves accuracy by 20 percentage points, in phase C, guessing only yields a 4-point improvement. This phenomenon can be explained by noting that both conditions and guessing are a form of generalization. In the first case, generalization is by making classes of attributes equivalent, whereas in the second case generalization is by dropping a clause (somewhat arbitrarily) from the description. Together, these techniques have improved predictive accuracy from 55% (exact match, no guessing) to 88% (conditions + guessing), a 60% improvement.

In this study, we have also noted that CSA conditions may blur distinctions too much. In an attempt to merge many rules, CSA may suggest many conditions. Application of too many conditions leads to overgeneralization. Furthermore, rules need to be assigned some sort of *strength*, indicating how much evidence supports them. "Weakly" supported rules can confuse conclusions. Nevertheless, conditions are still necessary to make sense of such data. In the study, conditions helped indicate the usefulness of various gradations in possible attribute values.

Conclusion

The system presented here has been shown to be effective in the inductive learning task, as well as the task of semantically analyzing the training database. CPLA incorporates the concept of *conditions* and allows for direct user interaction with the data. CSA extracts syntactic knowledge from the knowledge representation system and allows the user to translate it to semantic knowledge. This syntactic knowledge is presented as suggested conditions that generalize attribute values, and thus generalize decision rules.

CPLA, CSA, and the user form a three-element cyclic system. The user plays an integral part in the cycle by supplying conditions, as well as selecting from the suggested conditions, to adjust the data so as to maximize the information content of the rules while minimizing the uncertainty of the system. The application of CPLA/CSA to survey data from the 1988 U.S. election demonstrated the learning system can not only result in a smaller, more efficient set of decision rules to describe a concept but can also allow a nondomain expert to extract useful semantic meaning from the data.

REFERENCES*

1. F. Rosenblatt, "The Perceptron: A Probabilistic Model for Information Storage and Organization in the Brain," *Psych. Rev., 65*, 386–407 (1958).
2. B. Chandrasekaran and M. C. Yovits, "Artificial intelligence," in *Encyclopedia of Computer Science and Technology*, Marcel Dekker, New York, 1975, Vol. 2.
3. J. G. Carbonell, R. S. Michalski, and T. M. Mitchell, "An Overview of Machine Learning," in *Machine Learning: An Artificial Intelligence Approach*, R. S. Michalski, J. G. Carbonell, and T. M. Mitchell (eds.), Tioga Pub. Co., Palo Alto, CA, 1983.
4. T. M. Mitchell, J. G. Carbonell, and R. S. Michalski (eds.), *Machine Learning: A Guide to Current Research*, Kluwer Academic, Boston, 1986.
5. J. W. Shavlik and T. D. Dietterich (eds.), *Readings in Machine Learning*, Morgan Kaufmann, San Mateo, CA, 1990.
6. D. Partridge, "Artificial Intelligence," in *Encyclopedia of Computer Science and Technology*, Marcel Dekker, New York, 1990, Vol. 22.
7. J. G. Carbonell, "Introduction: Paradigms for Machine Learning," in *Machine Learning: Paradigms and Methods*, J. G. Carbonell (ed.), MIT/Elsevier, Cambridge, MA, 1990, pp. 1–9.
8. Z. W. Ras and M. Zemankova, "Intelligent Systems," in *Encyclopedia of Computer Science and Technology*, Marcel Dekker, New York, 1990, Vol. 22.
9. F. Bergadano, *Machine Learning: An Integrated Framework and Its Applications*, E. Horwood, New York, 1991.
10. J. G. Carbonell (ed.), *Machine Learning: Paradigms and Methods*, MIT/Elsevier, Cambridge, MA, 1990.
11. R. Forsyth (ed.), *Machine Learning: Principles and Techniques*, Chapman & Hall, New York, 1989.
12. Y. Kodratoff, *Introduction to Machine Learning*, Pitman Pub. Co., London, 1988.
13. A. L. Samuel, "Some Studies in Machine Learning Using the Game of Checkers," in *Computers and Thought*, E. A. Feigenbaum and J. Feldman (eds.), McGraw-Hill, New York, 1963, pp. 71–105.
14. R. S. Michalski, "On the Quasi-Minimal Solution of the General Covering Problem," in *Proc. Fifth International Symposium on Information Processing (FCIP69)*, 1969, pp. 125–128.
15. R. S. Michalski, "AQVAL/1 – Computer Implementation of a Variable Valued Logic System and Examples of Its Application to Pattern Recognition," in *Proc. First International Joint Conference on Pattern Recognition*, 1973, pp. 3–17.
16. R. S. Michalski and J. B. Larson, "Selection of Most Representative Training Examples and Incremental Generation of VL1 Hypothesis: The Underlying Methodology and the Description of Programs ESEL and AQ11," Technical Report 867, Dept. of Computer Science, University of Illinois, Urbana (1978).
17. R. S. Michalski, I. Mozetic, J. Hong, and N. Lavrac, "The AQ15 Induction Learning System: An Overview and Experiments," in *Proc. American Association for Artificial Intelligence Conference*, Morgan Kaufmann, San Mateo, CA, 1986.
18. J. R. Quinlan, "Discovering Rules by Induction from Large Databases," in *Expert*

*References 6, 9, 7, 11, 12, 37, and 49 are good basic guides to the machine learning field.

Systems in the Micro-Electronic Age, D. Michie (ed.), Edinburgh University Press, Edinburgh, 1979.

19. J. R. Quinlan, "Learning Efficient Classification Procedures and Their Application to Chess End Games," in *Machine Learning: An Artificial Intelligence Approach*, R. S. Michalski, J. G. Carbonell, and T. M. Mitchell (eds.), Tioga Pub. Co., Palo Alto, CA, 1983, pp. 463–482.

20. J. R. Quinlan, "Induction of Decision Trees," *Machine Learn., 1*, 81–106 (1986).

21. J. R. Quinlan, "Probabilistic Decision Trees," in *Machine Learning: An Artificial Intelligence Approach*, Y. Kodratoff and R. S. Michalski (eds.), Morgan Kaufmann, San Mateo, CA, 1990, Vol. 3, pp. 140–152.

22. J. R. Quinlan, "Decision Trees and Decisionmaking," *IEEE Trans. Syst. Man Cyber., SMC-20*, 339–346 (1990).

23. J. R. Quinlan, *C4.5: Programs for Machine Learning*, Morgan Kaufmann, San Mateo, CA, 1992.

24. R. Davis and D. B. Lenat, *Knowledge-Based System in Artificial Intelligence*, McGraw-Hill, New York, 1982.

25. B. G. Buchanan and E. A. Feigenbaum, "DENDRAL and Meta-DENDRAL: Their Applications Dimension," *AI, 11*, 5–24 (1978).

26. S. K. M. Wong and W. Ziarko, "INFER – An Adoptive Decision Support System Based on the Probabilistic Approximate Classification," in *The 6th International Workshop on Expert Systems and Their Applications*, 1986, vol. I, pp. 713–726.

27. S. K. M. Wong and J. H. Wong, "An Inductive Learning System – ILS," in *Proceedings of the Second International Symposium on Methodologies for Intelligent Systems, in Charlotte, North Carolina*, ACM SIGART/North-Holland, Amsterdam, 1987, pp. 370–378.

28. J. W. Grzymala-Busse, "LERS – A System for Learning from Examples Based on Rough Sets," in *Intelligent Decision Support: Handbook of Applications and Advances in Rough Set Theory*, R. Slowinski (ed.), Kluwer Academic, Boston, 1992, pp. 3–18.

29. M. Hadjimichael and A. Wasilewska, "Interactive Inductive Learning," *Int. J. Man-Machine Stud., 38*, 147–167 (1993).

30. Z. Pawlak, "Rough Sets," *Int. J. Inform. Computer Sci., 11*, 344–356 (1982).

31. Y. P. Dubey, "Decision Support Systems: Development and Trends," in *Encyclopedia of Computer Science and Technology*, Marcel Dekker, New York, 1988, Vol. 14.

32. R. Slowinski (ed.), *Intelligent Decision Support: Handbook of Applications and Advances in Rough Set Theory*, Kluwer Academic, Boston, 1992.

33. D. A. Waterman and F. Hayew-Roth (eds.), *Pattern-Directed Inference Systems*, Academic Press, New York, 1978.

34. R. S. Michalski, "A Theory and Methodology of Inductive Learning," in *Machine Learning: An Artificial Intelligence Approach*, R. S. Michalski, J. G. Carbonell, and T. M. Mitchell (eds.), Tioga Pub. Co., Palo Alto, CA, 1983.

35. B. R. Gaines, "Knowledge Acquisition: The Continuum Linking Machine Learning and Expertise Transfer," in *Proc. Third European Workshop on Knowledge Acquisition for Knowledge-Based Systems*, D. Sleeman (ed.), Express-Tirage, Bouns-la-Reine, France, 1989, pp. 90–101.

36. J. L. Maté and J. Pazos, "Knowledge Engineering Design and Construction of Expert Systems," in *Encyclopedia of Computer Science and Technology*, Marcel Dekker, New York, 1990, Vol. 23.

37. M. L. G. Shaw and B. R. Gaines, "Knowledge Acquisition: Some Foundations, Manual Methods, and Future Trends," in *Proc. Third European Workshop on Knowledge Acquisition for Knowledge-Based Systems*, D. Sleeman (ed.), Express-Tirages, Bouns-la-Reine, France, 1989, pp. 3–18.

38. B. W. Wah, "Knowledge and Data Engineering," in *Encyclopedia of Computer Science and Technology*, Marcel Dekker, New York, 1991, Vol. 24.

39. J. H. Boose and B. R. Gaines, "Knowledge Acquisition for Knowledge-based Systems: Notes on the State of the Art," *Machine Learn., 4*, 377–394 (1989).

40. H. Motoda, R. Mizoguchi, J. Boose, and B. Gaines (eds.), *Knowledge Acquisition for Knowledge-Based Systems*, IOS Press, Amsterdam, 1991.

41. W. Nejdl, "Expert Systems in Engineering," in *Encyclopedia of Computer Science and Technology*, Marcel Dekker, New York, 1992, Vol. 26.

42. M. J. Pazzani and C. A. Brunk, "Detecting and Correcting Errors in Rule-based Expert Systems: An Integration of Emphirical and Explanation-Based Learning," *Knowl. Acquisition, 3*, 157–173 (1991).

43. J. H. Boose, J. M. Bradshaw, and D. B. Shema, "Recent Progress in AQUINAS, a Knowledge Acquisition Workbench," in *Proc. Second European Workshop on Knowledge Acquisition for Knowledge-Based Systems*, 1988, pp. 1–15.

44. J. H. Boose, J. M. Bradshaw, C. M. Kitto and D. B. Shema, "From ETS to AQUINAS: Six Years of Knowledge Acquisition Tool Development," in *Proc. Third European Workshop on Knowledge Acquisition for Knowledge-Based Systems*, D. Sleeman (ed.), Express-Tirages, Bouns-la-Reine, France, 1989, pp. 502–516.

45. G. Webb, "Man-Machine Collaboration for Knowledge Acquisition," in *AI '92*, A. Adams and L. Sterling (eds.), World Scientific, Singapore, 1992, pp. 329–334.

46. G. Webb, "Control, Capabilities and Communication: Three Key Issues for Machine-Expert Collaborative Knowledge Acquisition," in *Proc. Seventh European Workshop on Knowledge Acquisition for Knowledge-based Systems, Toulouse, France*, Springer-Verlag, New York, 1993, pp. 263–275.

47. L. deRaedt and M. Bruynooghe, "On Interactive Concept-Learning and Assimilation," in *EWSL-88, Proc. Third European Working Session on Learning*, D. Sleeman (ed.), Pitman, London, 1988, pp. 167–175.

48. W. Clancey, "Heuristic Classification," in *Knowledge-based Problem Solving*, J. Kowalik (ed.), Prentice-Hall, Englewood Cliffs, NJ, 1986.

49. J. H. Boose, "Knowledge Acquisition," in *Encyclopedia of Artificial Intelligence*, 2nd ed., S. C. Shapiro (ed.), John Wiley and Sons, New York, 1990, Vol. 1.

50. T. Arciszewski, M. Mustafa, and W. Ziarko, "A Methodology of Design Knowledge-Acquisition for Use in Learning Expert Systems," *Int. J. Man-Machine Stud., 27*, 23–32 (1987).

51. J. R. Quinlan, "The Effect of Noise on Concept Learning," in *Machine Learning: An Artificial Intelligence Approach*, R. S. Michalski, J. G. Carbonell, and T. M. Mitchell (eds.), Morgan Kaufmann, San Mateo, CA, 1986, Vol. 2.

52. G. Biswas, J. B. Weinberg, and G. Koller, "Data Exploration in Non numeric Databases," in *Advances in Database and Artificial Intelligence*, F. Petry and L. Del Cambre (eds.), JAI Press, Greenwich, CT, 1993.

53. M. Huntbach, "Interactive Program Debugging and Synthesis," Ph.D. dissertation, University of Sussex, Brighton, UK (1990).

54. G. J. Chaitin, "On the Length of Programs for Computing Finite Sequences," *Commun. ACM, 13*, 547–549 (1966).

55. K. K. Obermeier, "Expert Systems," in *Encyclopedia of Computer Science and Technology*, Marcel Dekker, New York, 1987, Vol. 17.

56. R. Abbot, "Knowledge Abstraction," in *Encyclopedia of Computer Science and Technology*, Marcel Dekker, New York, 1987, Vol. 17.

57. J. R. Quinlan, "Generating Production Rules from Decision Trees," in *International Joint Conference on Artificial Intelligence*, Morgan Kaufmann, San Mateo, CA, 1987, pp. 304–307.

58. S. R. Safavian and D. Landgrebe, "A Survey of Decision Tree Classifier Methodology," *IEEE Trans. Syst. Man Cyber., SMC-21*, 660–674 (1991).

59. D. Gerger, A. Paz, and J. Pearl, "Learning Causal Trees from Dependency Information," in *Proc. Eight National Conference of Artificial Intelligence, Boston*, AAAI Press, Menlo Park, CA, 1990, pp. 770–776.

60. J. R. Quinlan, "Simplifying Decision Trees," *Int. J. Man-Machine Stud., 27*, 221–234 (1987).

61. R. A. Pearson, "Tree Simplification Through Test Removal," in *AI '90: Fourth Australian Joint Conference on Artificial Intelligence, Perth*, C. P. Tsang (ed.), World Scientific, Singapore, 1990, pp. 48–61.

62. S. K. M. Wong, W. Ziarko, and R. L. Ye, "Comparison of Rough Set and Statistical Methods in Inductive Learning," *Int. J. Man-Machine Stud., 24*, 53–72 (1986).

63. W. Ziarko, "Variable Perception Rough Sets Model," *J. Computer Syst. Sci., 46*(1), 39–59 (1993).

64. P. E. Utgoff, "Incremental Induction of Decision Trees," *Machine Learn., 4*, 161–186 (1989).

65. M. James, *Classification Algorithms*, John Wiley and Sons, New York, 1985.

66. J. R. Quinlan, "Unknown Attribute Values in Induction," in *International Workshop on Machine Learning*, Morgan Kaufmann, San Mateo, CA, 1989, pp. 164–168.

67. S. M. Weiss and C. A. Kulikowski, *Computer Systems That Learn: Classification and Prediction Methods from Statistics, Neural Nets, Machine Learning, and Expert Systems*, Morgan Kaufmann, San Mateo, CA, 1991.

68. L. G. Valiant, "Learning Disjunctions of Conjunctions," in *Proc. International Joint Conference on Artificial Intelligence-85*, 1985, pp. 560–566.

69. D. Haussler, "Quantifying Inductive Bias: AI Learning Algorithms and Valiant's Learning Framework," *AI, 36*, 177–221 (1988).

70. D. Haussler, "Probably Approximately Correct Learning," in *Proc. American Association for Artificial Conference*, AIII Press, Menlo Park, CA, 1990, pp. 1101–1108.

71. D. Angluin and C. H. Smith, "Inductive Inference: Theory and Methods," *Comput. Surv., 15*(3), 237–269 (1983).

72. L. G. Valiant, "A Theory of the Learnable," *Commun. ACM, 27*(11) (1984) 1134–1142.

73. L. Pitt, "Probabilistic Inductive Inference," *J. Assoc. Comput. Mach., 36*(2), 383–433 (1989).

74. E. Ehrenfeucht and D. Haussler, "Learning Decision Trees from Random Examples," *Inform. Control, 82*, 231–246 (1989).

75. P. Utgoff, *Machine Learning of Inductive Bias*, Kluwer Academic, Norwell, MA, 1986.

76. A. Wasilewska, "Conditional Knowledge Representation System — Model for an Implementation," *Bull. Polish Acad. Sci., 37*(1–6), 63–69 (1990).

77. M. Hadjimichael and A. Wasilewska, "Rule Reduction for Knowledge Representation Systems," *Bull. Polish Acad. Sci., 38*(1–12), 113–120 (1990).

78. Z. Pawlak, S. K. M. Wong, and W. Ziarko, "Rough Sets: Probabilistic versus Deterministic Approach," *Int. J. Man-Machine Stud., 29*, 81–95 (1988).

79. S. K. M. Wong, W. Ziarko, and R. L. Ye, "On Learning and Evaluation of Decision Rules in Context of Rough Sets," in *Proceedings of the First International Symposium on Methodologies for Intelligent Systems, Knoxville, Tenn*, ACM SIGART/National Technical Information Service, U.S. Dept. of Commerce, Springfield, VA, 1986, pp. 308–324.

80. Z. Pawlak (ed.), *Rough Sets (Theoretical Aspects of Reasoning about Data)*, Kluwer Academic, Boston, 1991.

81. R. Yasdi and W. Ziarko, "Conceptual Schema Design: A Machine Learning Approach," in *Proceedings of the Second International Symposium on Methodology for Intelligent Systems, in Charlotte, North Carolina*, ACM SIGART/North-Holland, Amsterdam, 1987, pp. 379–391.

82. A. Pettorossi, Z. Ras, and M. Zemankova, "On Learning with Imperfect Teachers," in *Proceedings of the Second International Symposium in Methodologies for Intelligent Systems*, ACM SIGART/North-Holland, Amsterdam, 1987, pp. 256–263.
83. Z. Ras and M. Zemankova, "Learning in Knowledge Based Systems: A Possibilistic Approach," in *Proceedings of the 1986 'CISS*, Princeton, NJ, 1986, pp. 844–847.
84. M. Hadjimichael and A. Wasilewska, "Application of a Rough Set-based Inductive Learning System," *Fund. Inform., 18*, 209–220 (1993).

MICHAEL HADJIMICHAEL

AN INTRODUCTION TO ASYNCHRONOUS CIRCUIT DESIGN

INTRODUCTION

The intent of this article is to provide an introductory yet comprehensive overview of the field of asynchronous circuit design. The focus on design implies that a number of theoretical aspects of the discipline which do not directly affect the practical design process will be ignored. Given the size of the field and the number of design methods, it is impossible to cover all of the various design methods in depth. On the other hand, little could be learned if all of the methods were just mentioned superficially. The result is that there will be enough depth in this chapter to introduce the basic concepts and to highlight a few of the design styles. Other design methodologies will be covered more cursorily, at the conceptual level. Differences and similarities between methods will be discussed. The many citations and extensive references provide ample direction for an in-depth study of any particular method.

MOTIVATION AND BASIC CONCEPTS

Circuit design styles can be classified into two major categories, namely synchronous and asynchronous. It is worthwhile to note that neither is independent of the other and that there are many designs that have been produced using a hybrid design style which mixes aspects of both categories. Synchronous circuits may be defined simply as circuits which are sequenced by one or more globally distributed periodic timing signals called clocks. Asynchronous circuits are an inherently larger class of circuits, as there are many sequencing options other than global periodic clock signals. It may be difficult to understand the motivation for asynchronous circuit techniques when the bulk of commercial practice and considerable experience, artifact, and momentum exists for the synchronous circuit design style. For some, the motivation to pursue the study of asynchronous circuits is based on the simple fact that they are different. Others find that asynchronous circuits have a particular modular elegance that is amenable to theoretical analysis. However, for those interested in the practical aspects of asynchronous circuit design, the motivation often comes from some concern with the basic nature of synchronous circuits.

Of common concern are the cost issues associated with the global, periodic, and common clock that is the temporal basis for synchronous circuits. The *fixed* clock period of synchronous circuits is chosen as a result of worst-case timing analysis. It is not adaptive and, therefore, does not take advantage of average- or even best-case computational situations. Asynchronous circuit proponents view this as an opportunity to achieve increased performance because asynchronous methods are inherently adaptive. Arithmetic circuits provide a good example. Arithmetic circuit performance is typically dominated by the propagation delay of carry or borrow signals. The worst-case propagation situation rarely occurs, yet synchronous arithmetic circuits must be clocked in a manner that accommodates this rare worst-case condition. Some asynchronous circuit designers have made the mistake of generalizing this observation into a view that the inherent adaptivity of asynchronous circuits implies that they are capable of achieving higher performance in general. However, this is not necessarily the case.

All asynchronous circuits have additional operational constraints when compared to their synchronous counterparts. Ideally, digital signals represent binary values and, therefore, model 2 distinct voltage levels. For convenience, let them be called 0 and 1. These signals then have the possibility of either remaining constant or changing as a result of a circuit action or *event*. When signals change, the change may not be a monotonic transition between one voltage level and the other. Such a nonmonotonic change is often called a *glitch*. A circuit producing an output which may glitch is said to contain a *hazard*. There are many types of hazards which are discussed in the subsection Hazards. A glitch on a clock signal of a synchronous circuit will typically cause the circuit to malfunction. Glitches on nonclock signals do not cause a malfunction as long as the signal is stable at its new value for a certain time before and after a clock signal transition. This glitch issue is both the advantage and the disadvantage of synchronous circuits. It implies that nonclock signals need not be hazard-free, which often times results in smaller circuits. However, the clock must be carefully controlled and, as it must be globally distributed, this often proves to be difficult. All forms of asynchronous circuits are concerned with providing hazard- or *glitch-free* outputs under some timing model.

In order to achieve hazard-free behavior, an asynchronous circuit will often contain more gates than a functionally equivalent synchronous circuit. Therefore, in terms of the number of basic components, asynchronous circuits are often somewhat larger than synchronous circuits. More gates implies more wires, and this may result in slower rather than faster circuit latencies. Furthermore, in order to achieve their inherently adaptive nature, asynchronous circuits must *explicitly* generate sequence control signals such as a request and an acknowledge signal. The request signal can be used to signal initiation of some action and the corresponding acknowledge signal indicates completion of that action. In synchronous circuits, much of this type of control signaling is *implicit* in the common clock signal. The generation of these explicit control signals further exacerbates the complexity of asynchronous circuits and may lead to a further performance degradation.

The adaptive potential remains where the worst-case situation is rare and when the difference between the worst-case and average-case latencies is significant. However, synchronous circuit designers are also well aware of this situation and take considerable care to create a clock model and circuit structure that can take advantage of these differences. The most notable example of this tactic is in the finely grained pipeline structures of modern floating-point units. Yet, for very large circuits, such as microprocessors, balancing all the timing constraints of a large computational space to minimize the difference between the worst-case and average-case timing models is a difficult task. The work by Mark Dean on the STRiP processor (1) provides an interesting example. Dean showed that even a well-balanced and well-designed processor such as the MIPS-X CPU could be sped up if the instruction set were split into three classes and the clock period adjusted appropriately to match the temporal needs of each class.

Dean also demonstrated that an even greater performance enhancement could be achieved due to the tighter margins which are possible with adaptive clocking. Synchronous systems usually rely on an externally generated clock signal which is distributed as the common timing reference to all of the system components. The speed at which integrated circuits operate varies with the circuit fabrication process and fluctuations in operating temperature and supply voltage. In order to achieve a reasonable shield against these variables, the clock period is extended by a certain *margin*. In current practice, these margins are often 100% or more in high-speed systems. Adaptive clocking cannot be generated externally and, therefore, must be provided internally to each device. The fact that the clock generator is affected by the same process, temperature, and supply variations as the rest of the chip permits the safety margin to be reduced significantly.

Clock distribution is becoming an increasingly costly component of large modern designs. Today's microprocessors contain over 10 million transistors and their clock rates are around 200–400 MHz. The clock period is determined by adding the worst-case propagation delay, the margin, and the maximum clock skew. *Clock skew* is simply the maximum difference in the clock arrival as seen by all clocked points in the circuit. The latency of the clock pulse to the reception points is not a concern. With today's large VLSI circuits exceeding 20 mm per side, several nanoseconds of skew is easily possible. However, with a 5-ns clock period, several nanoseconds of skew is a disaster. Clock distribution and deskewing methods are abundant, but they share the common characteristic of being expensive in either power or area and they become more so as clock speeds increase. A common method is to distribute the clock via a balanced H-tree configuration (2) with amplifying buffers placed at the fanout points. The problem with this approach is that as more buffers are added to a clock path, larger skew results. The designers of the DEC Alpha CPU (3) took the opposite approach. The Alpha contains 1.68 million transistors and is fabricated in a 0.75-μm, 3.3-V CMOS process. Even with three layers of metal, the chip is 16.8 mm by 13.9 mm. In order to keep the clock skew to within 300 ps, the Alpha's designers localized the clock buffering to minimize process-induced variations and, therefore, the skew induced by the buffers. Details of the method can be found in Ref. 4, but the result is a clock driver circuit that occupies about 10% of the chip area and consumes over 40% of the 30 W of power dissipated by the chip. The 19 mm^2 of area and over 12 W of power is a very high price to pay for keeping the skew under control. Power concerns, in particular, will limit the use of this technique as circuit speeds and transistor counts increase.

A similar skew problem exists for circuit boards as well as chips. The literature contains an abundance of methods for deskewing clocks (5,6) on a board, but most of them are also costly in either area or complexity, and some will probably not be robust enough for use in commercial circuits. An interesting example is the Monarch (7) processor chip which used active signal selection on each input pad. In this instance, a five-slot delay line was used to skew signals to match the clock skew. The appropriate tap in the delay line was selected based on analyzing the clock versus the incoming signal. Although the technique did work, its cost and complexity are probably more instructive in a pathological sense. The bottom line is that clock management is a difficult problem and solving it in today's high-speed complex designs is costly. Asynchronous circuit proponents advocate a simple solution, namely throw away the whole concept of a global clock. This is not a free solution, because global absolute timing must be replaced with the relative and sequential mechanisms which lie at the heart of asynchronous circuit signaling protocols. Chuck Seitz wrote an excellent introduction to this general topic in his chapter on system timing in the classic VLSI book by Mead and Conway (8). The next section of this article presents some of the more commonly used protocols and terminology.

Another common motivation for using asynchronous circuits is the quest for low-power circuit operation. The consumer market's hunger for powerful yet portable digital systems which run on lightweight battery packs is growing at a rapid rate. Hence, there is a strong commercial interest in low-power design methods which extend the operational life of a particular battery technology. CMOS circuits have a particular appeal, because they consume negligible power when they are idle. This would not be true, however, if the clock of a synchronous circuit were to continue running. Therefore, low-power synchronous circuits usually involve some method of shutting down the clock to subsystems which are not needed at a particular time. Clocks must be continuously supplied to the subcomponent that must monitor the environment for the next call to action. The result is that power must be consumed even during idle periods. Furthermore, these clock switches exacerbate the clock skew issues which limit performance and also reduce the circuit's ability to provide maximum performance when it is needed. Asynchronous circuits have the advantage that they go into idle mode *for free* because, by nature, when there is nothing to do, there are no transitions on any wire in the circuit. Another advantage is that even for an active system, only the subsystems that are required for the computation at hand will dissipate any power. Researchers such as Kees van Berkel (9) and Steve Furber (10) are pursuing asynchronous circuit designs in an attempt to exploit this feature.

The final motivation of asynchronous design is the inherent ease of composing asynchronous subsystems into larger asynchronous systems. Although there is still room for doubt about whether asynchronous circuits can generally achieve their potential advantages in terms of higher-performance or lower-power operation than synchronous circuits, there is little doubt that asynchronous circuits do have a definite advantage with respect to composability. Asynchronous circuits are functional modules in that they contain both their timing and data requirements *explicitly* in their interfaces. In a sense, they "keep time for themselves" — hence the term *self-timed circuits*. Synchronous circuit modules contain only data requirements in their interfaces and *share* the clock. However, important temporal issues, such as when data must be valid to avoid setup and hold-time violations between modules, are *implicit* at best. In contrast, composing asynchronous modules is almost trivial. If the interfaces match and observe the same signaling protocol, then they can simply be connected. The same cannot be said for synchronous circuits with their global timing requirements and clock-based sequencing. The result is that a more detailed knowledge of module internals is required before synchronous subsystems can be connected.

The problem of combining synchronous systems is exacerbated when each module has a separate clock, each running at a different frequency. The effects of this problem are numerous and probabilistically involve some variant of metastability failure (11). It is commonly accepted, although not definitively proven to the authors' knowledge, that it is impossible to build a perfect synchronizer. Many of the subsystems in today's computers run on clocks which are not synchronized with the CPU. A good example is the I/O subsystem. Often, these subsystems are confusingly called asynchronous or are considered to have an asynchronous interface. In reality, they are synchronous systems which use some sort of synchronizing scheme in their interface. Synchronizers, although imperfect, effectively trade increased latency for more reliable synchronization. The reliability is adjusted to meet the MTBF (Mean Time Before Failure) requirements of the system, and the resulting decreased performance is simply viewed as the price that must be paid for the required reliability.

The ease of composing asynchronous subsystems is a clear advantage. It allows components from previous designs to be reused, it allows modification of slower components which may result in incremental performance improvements without impacting the overall design, and it facilitates behavioral analysis by formal methods. However, asynchronous circuits are not presently the mainstay of commercial practice. The definite advantage of composability is not a strong enough factor to counter the significant synchronous circuit momentum, and the promises of improved performance and decreased power consumption remain to be generally realized. There is also a clear gap in the quality of the design infrastructure (e.g., CAD tools, libraries, etc.). In addition, the level of synchronous design experience dwarfs the small experience base in asynchronous circuit design. The subsequent sections on current research are indications that this gap is narrowing. The asynchronous circuit discipline is becoming more viable, even though much work remains to be done before they will be competitive in the commercial sector.

CONTROLLING ASYNCHRONOUS CIRCUITS

Signaling Protocols

Most asynchronous circuit signaling schemes are based on some sort of protocol involving *requests*, which are used to initiate an action, and corresponding *acknowledgments*, used to signal completion of that action. These control signals provide all of the necessary sequence controls for computational events in the system. Strictly speaking, these *handshake* signals are independent of any global system time and are only concerned with the relative temporal relationships between two subsystems sharing a common interface. The resulting computational model is very much like a data-flow model (12,13), where the arrival of the necessary operand data triggers an operation. Similarly, there is a concept of a sender of information and a corresponding receiver. From the circuit perspective, and ignoring data transmission issues for now, these request and acknowledge control signals typically pass between two modules of an asynchronous system. For example, let there be two modules, a sender A and a receiver B. A request is sent from A to B to indicate that A is requesting some action by B. When B is either done with the action or has stored the request, it acknowledges the request by asserting the acknowledge signal, which is sent from B to A. Most asynchronous signaling protocols require a strict alternation of request and acknowledge events. These ideas can be extended to interfaces shared by more than two subsystems, although this is not the common case due to performance and circuit complexity issues.

There are several choices of how these alternating events are encoded onto specific control wires. Two choices have been so pervasive that they will be described

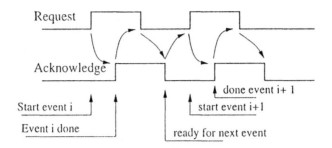

FIGURE 1   Four-cycle asynchronous signaling protocol.

here in detail. One common choice is the *four-cycle* protocol shown in Figure 1. Other names for this protocol are also in common use: *RZ* (return to zero), *four-phase*, and *level signaling*. In Figure 1, the waveforms appear periodic for convenience, but they do not need to be so in practice. The curved arrows indicate the required causal sequence of events. There is no implicit assumption about the delay between successive events. Note that in this protocol typically four transitions (two on the request and two on the acknowledge) required to complete a particular event transaction. Proponents of this scheme argue that four-cycle circuits are typically smaller than they are for two-cycle signaling and that the time required for the falling transitions on the request on acknowledge lines do not usually cause a performance degradation. This is because falling transitions can happen in parallel with other circuit operations or can be used to control the transmission of the answer data back to the requester.

The other common choice is *two-cycle* signaling, as shown in Figure 2, also called *transition, two-phase*, or *NRZ* (nonreturn to zero) signaling. In this case, the waveforms are the same as for four-cycle signaling except that every transition on the request wire, both falling and rising, indicates a new request. The same is true for transitions on the acknowledge wire. Two-cycle signaling is particularly useful for high-speed micropipelines, as pointed out by Ivan Sutherland in his Turing Award paper (14).

Two-cycle proponents argue that that two-cycle signaling is better from both a power and a performance standpoint, as every transition represents a meaningful

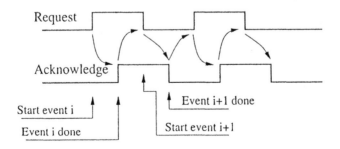

FIGURE 2   Two-cycle asynchronous signaling protocol.

event, and no transitions or power are consumed in returning to zero because there is no resetting of the handshake link. Although, in principle, this is true, it is also the case that most two-cycle interface implementations require more logic than their four-cycle equivalents. The increased logic complexity may consume more power than is saved by the reduced control transitions. This was shown to be the case in the two versions of the low-power asynchronous ARM processor produced by researchers at the University of Manchester. ARM1 (10) was a two-cycle design. The lack of a distinct low-power advantage in ARM1 led to an improved ARM2 (15) four-cycle design which demonstrated both a performance and low-power improvement over the ARM1. Some of this improvement can certainly be attributed to increased design expertise, but the experience provides compelling evidence that power and performance arguments cannot be based solely on counting the number of control transitions per event.

Four-cycle proponents argue that the falling (return to zero) transitions are often easily hidden by overlapping them with other actions in the circuit. Another approach, called *early acknowledge*, is to design four-cycle circuits to indicate event completion with the falling transition on the acknowledge wire rather than by the rising transition. Because the sender can then deassert the request, the implication is that the receiver must latch the incoming transaction prior to completing the requested action. The result is an asynchronous pipeline structure similar to synchronous pipeline circuits. The goal of all pipeline circuits is the increase in throughput performance. Still, most designers would agree that two- and four-cycle protocols each have advantages over the other in particular circuits. Certain design styles (16) and designs (17) show that two- and four-cycle protocols can coexist in the same system, albeit on different interfaces. Numerous two-cycle to four-cycle (and vice versa) conversion circuits exist and can be used for interfaces where performance is not critical, as the circuits do add some latency to the interface operation.

Other interface protocols, based on similar sequencing rules, exist for three or more module interfaces. A particularly common design requirement is to join two or more requests to provide a single outgoing request or, conversely, to provide a conjunction of acknowledge signals. A commonly used asynchronous element is the *C-element*, which can be viewed as a protocol-preserving conjunctive gate. This element is equally useful for both two- and four-cycle protocols. The description here will consider a two-input C-element for simplicity. The common logic symbol and a positive-logic gate-level implementation are shown in Figure 3. In an initial state where inputs x and y are both low, output z is low. When both x and y go high, then the output z will go high. Similarly, when both inputs go low, then the output will go low. The C-element effectively merges two requests into a single request and permits three subsystems to communicate in a protocol-preserving two- or four-cycle manner. Many consider C-elements to be as fundamental as a NAND gate in asynchronous circuits, and they will appear repeatedly in many of the basic circuits that will be subsequently presented here. The feedback signal from the output of the C-element to two of the two-input NAND gates indicates that the C-element is itself a form of latch. It, therefore, acts as a synchronization point which is necessary for protocol preservation. However, excess synchronization reduces performance, and there are numerous asynchronous circuits which have been designed with too many C-elements and their performance has suffered. An AND (or NAND) gate is a conjunction of only the low-to-high input signal trajectories, whereas the C-element

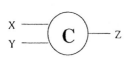

Symbol

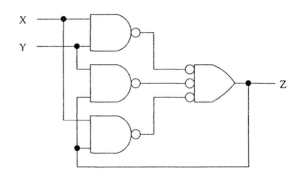

Gate Level Implementation

FIGURE 3   The C-element.

is conjunctive for both rising and falling trajectories. The important point is to
properly understand the conjunction requirements of the given circuits and not to
use C-elements where some form of AND gate will suffice. It is rare that large
asynchronous circuits can be built using no C-elements, but the existence of many
C-elements in a circuit is often an indication that performance will be reduced.

So far, the discussion has only addressed control signals. There are also several
choices for how to encode data. One common choice is the use of a *bundled* protocol with either two- or four-cycle signaling. In this case, for an *n*-bit data value to
be passed from the sender to the receiver, *n* + 2 wires will be required (*n* bits of
data, 1 request bit, and 1 acknowledge bit). Although this choice is conservative in
terms of wires, *it does* contain an implied timing assumption; namely, the assumption is that the propagation times of the control and data lines are either equal or
that the control propagates slower than the data signals. A sending module will
assert the data wires, and when they are valid, it will assert the request. It is
important that the same relationship of data being valid prior to request assertion
be observed at the receiving side. If this were not the case, the receiver could initiate
the requested action with incorrect data values. This requirement is often simply
called a *bundling constraint*. Most asynchronous circuits have been designed with
bundled data protocols because the logic and wires needed to implement bundled
data circuits are significantly less than with nonbundled approaches. However, in
order for bundled data asynchronous circuits to work properly, the bundling constraint must be met. Antagonists of this approach note that these timing assumptions, although local to a particular interface, are similar to those made for synchronous circuit design.

A common alternative to the bundled data approach is *dual-rail* encoding. In
this case, data and control signals are not separated onto distinct wire paths. Instead, a bit of data is encoded with its own request onto two wires. A typical
dual-rail encoding has four states:

1.   00 — Idle, data not valid
2.   10 — Valid 0
3.   01 — Valid 1
4.   11 — Illegal

In this case, for an n-bit data value, the link between sender and receiver must contain $3n$ wires: two wires for each bit of data and the associated request plus one bit for the acknowledge. An improvement on this protocol is possible when n bits of data are considered to be associated in every transaction, as is the case when the circuit operates on bytes or words. In this case, it is convenient to combine all the acknowledges onto a single wire. The resulting wiring complexity is then reduced to $2n + 1$ wires: $2n$ for the data and requests plus one additional acknowledge signal. In a four-cycle variant of this dual-rail protocol, sending a bit requires the transition from the idle state to either the valid 0 or valid 1 state and then, after receiving the acknowledge, it must transition back to the idle state. The acknowledge wire must be reset prior to a subsequent assertion of a valid 0 or 1. The illegal state is not used. If recognized by the receiver, it should cause an error.

A two-cycle dual-rail protocol would signal a valid 0 by a single transition of the left bit, whereas a valid 1 would be signaled by a transition on the right bit. Concurrent transitions on both the left and right bits are illegal. Sending a 0 or a 1 must be followed by a transition on the acknowledge wire before another bit can be transmitted. Alternative encoding schemes have been proposed as well (18,19). Dual-rail signaling is insensitive to the delays on any wire and, therefore, is more robust when assumptions like a bundling constraint cannot be guaranteed. The receiver will need to check for validity of all n bits before using the data or asserting the acknowledge. The downside of the dual-rail approach is often the increased complexity in both wiring and logic.

Completion Signals

One of the added complexities of asynchronous circuits is the need to generate completion signals that directly or indirectly control the acknowledge signal in a signaling protocol. There are many methods, none of which is universally satisfactory. One approach is to design an asynchronous module in a manner that is similar to a synchronous circuit; namely, the arrival of the request starts the modules internal clock generator and after a certain number of internal clocks, the circuit is done, the clock is stopped, and an acknowledge is generated. The idea was originally suggested by Chuck Seitz and was used during the construction of the first data-flow computer, DDM1 (13). This technique works well when the module is large, but when the module is small, the additional logic required for the internal clock generator represents an overhead that is too costly. Also, the technique does not lend itself well to high-performance designs, due to the increased circuit complexity and the delay associated with starting the clock generator. The result is that this approach is seldom used today, as modules represent relatively small pieces of an integrated circuit.

Another choice for completion signal generation is the use of a *model delay*. In this case, conventional synchronous timing analysis of the data path is used to determine how long the circuit will take to compute a valid result after the request has been received. A delay element, such as an inverter chain, is then used to turn the request into the appropriately delayed acknowledge signal. Note that this method works equally well for both two- and four-cycle signaling protocols.

Special functions often have unique opportunities. For example, arithmetic circuits can be built to generate completion signals based on carry propagation patterns (20). Other functions can independently compute both F and $\overline{F}$ and use the exclusive-OR of their outputs to generate the acknowledge signal. Note that this technique will only work directly in a four-cycle signaling protocol. If used with a two-cycle protocol, additional logic such as a T flip-flop will be required.

A novel technique was proposed by Mark Dean (21), in which completion detection was performed by observing the power consumption of the circuit. When activated, the circuit consumes power, and when it is done, the power consumption falls below a particular threshold.

The study of completion signal generation in asynchronous circuits could be the topic of an entire book. For now, it is only necessary to realize that some method must be chosen and that the need for completion signals and related signaling protocols is a necessary overhead of asynchronous circuit design. Many modern memory chips are integrated into synchronous systems using this same technique. For example, memories are not inherently synchronous but do have specified access latencies. These specifications are essentially model delays. Systems which use these chips assume that the access is complete after a certain number of clock cycles which correspond to a delay that is no smaller than the access latency of the device.

DELAY MODELS AND HAZARDS

Delay Models, Circuits, and Environments

There is a wide spectrum of asynchronous designs. One way to distinguish among them is to understand the different underlying models of delay and operation. Every physical circuit has inherent delay. However, because synchronous circuits process inputs between fixed clock ticks, they can often be regarded as instantaneous operators, computing a new result in each clock cycle. On the other hand, because asynchronous circuits have no clock, they are best regarded as computing dynamically through time. Therefore, a delay model is critical in defining the dynamic behavior of an asynchronous circuit.

There are two fundamental models of delay: the *pure delay* model and the *inertial delay* model (22,23). A pure delay can delay the propagation of a waveform but does not otherwise alter it. An inertial delay can alter the shape of a waveform by attenuating short glitches. More formally, an inertial delay has a threshold period, δ. Pulses of duration less than δ are filtered out.

Delays are also characterized by their timing models. In a *fixed delay* model, a delay is assumed to have a fixed value. In a *bounded delay* model, a delay may have any value in a given time interval. In an *unbounded delay* model, a delay may take on any finite value.

An entire circuit's behavior can be modeled on the basis of its component models. In a *simple-gate*, or *gate-level*, model, each gate and primitive component in the circuit has a corresponding delay. In a *complex-gate* model, an entire subnetwork of gates is modeled by a single delay; that is, the network is assumed to behave as a single operator, with no internal delays. Wires between gates are also modeled by delays. A *circuit model* is thus defined in terms of the delay models for the individual wires and components. Typically, the functionality of a gate is modeled by an instantaneous operator with an attached delay.

Given a circuit model, it is also important to characterize the interaction of the circuit with its *environment*. The circuit and environment together form a closed system, called a *complete circuit* (see Muller in Ref. 24). If the environment is allowed to respond to a circuit's outputs without any timing constraints, the two interact in an *input/output mode* (25). Otherwise, environmental timing constraints are assumed. The most common example is the *fundamental mode* (22,26), where the environment must wait for a circuit to stabilize before responding to circuit outputs. Such a requirement can be seen as the hold time for a simple latch or flip-flop (27).

Classes of Asynchronous Circuits

Given these models for a circuit and its environment, asynchronous circuits can be classified into a hierarchy.

A *delay-insensitive* (DI) circuit is one which is designed to operate correctly regardless of the delays on its gates and wires; that is, an unbounded gate and wire delay model is assumed. The concept of a delay-insensitive circuit grows out of work by Clark and Molnar in the 1960s on *Macromodules* (28).* The DI systems have been formalized by Udding (30) and Dill (31). The class of DI circuits built out of simple gates and operators is quite limited. In fact, it has been proven that almost no useful DI circuits can be built if one is restricted to a class of simple gates and operators (32,33). However, many practical DI circuits can be built if one allows more complex components (34,35). A complex component is constructed out of several simple gates. Internal to the component, timing assumptions must be satisfied; externally, the component operates in a delay-insensitive manner. A C-element is such a component, and other examples of DI designs using complex components are described in the subsection Transformation Methods; see Figure 15.

A *quasi-delay-insensitive* (*quasi-DI* or *QDI*) circuit is delay-insensitive, except that "isochronic forks" are required (36). An isochronic fork is a forked wire where all branches have exactly the same delay. In other formulations, a bounded skew is allowed between the different branches of each fork. In contrast, in a DI circuit, delays on the different fork branches are completely independent and may vary considerably. The motivation of QDI circuits is that they are the weakest compromise to pure delay insensitivity needed to build practical circuits using simple gates and operators. C-elements are somewhat problematic because they inherently con-

---

*This article contains numerous references to the work of Charles Molnar. The asynchronous circuit discipline lost one of its brightest lights when Charlie passed away in December 1996. Charlie's influence on the field was profound. He inspired many of the people who are today considered to be pioneers and senior statesmen of the field. His inventions are numerous as both his publications and patents attest. The difficult aspect of Charlie's influence for people to grasp, with the exception of the few who had the privilege to know and work with Charlie over the years, is the depth and creativity of his thinking. Charlie's work has provided both a solid foundation for the field as well as an inspiration to continue. At the time of his death, he was one of the creative leaders of the asynchronous circuits group at Sun Microsystems Laboratories, Inc. (29). His influence will be sorely missed.

tain an output which is fed back internally to the C-element. This case represents the worst form of isochronic fork, as one of the forks is contained within the C-element circuit module while the other is exported to outside modules. Martin (37) and van Berkel (9) have used QDI circuits extensively and have described their advantages and disadvantages (32,38).

A *speed-independent* (SI) circuit is one which operates correctly regardless of gate delays; wires are assumed to have zero or negligible delay. SI circuits were introduced by David Muller in the 1950s (see Ref. 24). Muller's formulation only considered deterministic input and output behavior. This class has recently been extended to include circuits with a limited form of nondeterminism (39,40).

A *self-timed* circuit, described by Seitz (8), contains a group of self-timed "elements." Each element is contained in an "equipotential region," where wires have negligible or well-bounded delay. An element itself may be an SI circuit, or a circuit whose correct operation relies on the use of local timing assumptions. However, no timing assumptions are made on the communication between regions; that is, communication between regions is delay-insensitive.

Each of the above circuits operate in the input/output mode: There are no timing assumptions on when the environment responds to the circuit. The most general category is an *asynchronous circuit* (22). These circuits contain no global clock. However, they may make use of timing assumptions both within the circuit and in the interaction between circuit and environment. Latches and flip-flops, with setup and hold times, belong to this class. Other examples include *timed circuits* (41), where both internal and environmental bounded-delay assumptions are used to optimize the designs.

Hazards

A fundamental difference between synchronous and asynchronous circuits is in their treatment of *hazards*. In a synchronous system, computation occurs between clock ticks. Glitches on wires during a clock cycle are usually not a problem. The system operates correctly as long as a stable and valid result is produced before the next clock tick, when the result is sampled. In contrast, in an asynchronous system, there is no global clock; computation is no longer sampled at discrete intervals. As a result, any glitch may be treated by the system as a real change in value and may cause the system to malfunction.

The potential for a glitch in an asynchronous design is called a *hazard* (22). Hazards were first studied in the context of asynchronous combinational logic. Sequential hazards are also possible in asynchronous-state machines; these are called *critical races* or *essential hazards* and will be discussed later.

Several approaches have been used to eliminate combinational hazards. First, inertial delays may be used to attenuate undesired "spikes"; much of the early work in asynchronous synthesis relied on the use of inertial delays (see Ref. 22). Second, if a bounded delay model is assumed, hazards may be "fixed" by adding appropriate delays to slow down certain paths in a circuit. Third, hazards are sometimes tolerated where they will do no harm; this approach was also used in some early work. Finally, and most importantly, synthesis methods can be used to produce circuits with no hazards (i.e., *hazard-free* circuits).

In the remainder of this section, the basics of hazard-free combinational synthesis are presented. Two traditional classes of combinational hazards are defined: *SIC* and *MIC* hazards. Classic techniques to eliminate both SIC and MIC hazards in two-level circuits are introduced, illustrated by some simple examples. The section concludes with a description of recent work on hazard-free minimization. Throughout this section, a conservative circuit model is used: The combinational circuit is assumed to have unknown gate and wire delays; that is, an unbounded gate and wire delay model is assumed.

SIC Hazards

Hazards are temporal phenomena: They are manifest during the dynamic operation of a circuit. For example, consider the Karnaugh map ("K map") (27) in Figure 4a, defining a Boolean function with three inputs: *A*, *B*, and *C*. A minimum-cost sum-of-products realization, or *cover*, is given by the expression $f = A'B + AC$; the corresponding AND-OR circuit is shown in the figure. Consider the behavior of the circuit during the *single-input change* (SIC) from $ABC = 011$ to $ABC = 111$. In this transition, only one input, *A*, changes value. Initially, AND-gate $A'B$ is 1, AND-gate AC is 0, and the OR-gate has output 1. When *A* changes, AND-gate $A'B$ goes to 0 and AC goes to 1. However, if AND-gate AC is slower than $A'B$, the result is a glitch on the OR-gate output: $1 \rightarrow 0 \rightarrow 1$. Therefore, the circuit has a hazard for the transition.

The Karnaugh map in Figure 4b shows an alternative *hazard-free* realization of the function. A third product, *BC*, has been added to the cover. For the same SIC transition, AND-gate *BC* holds its value at 1, and the OR-gate output remains

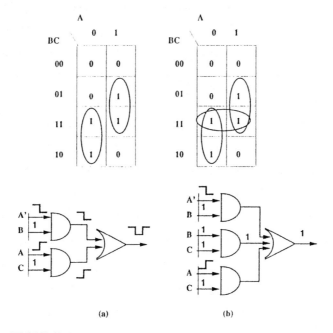

(a) (b)

FIGURE 4 Combinational hazard example: SIC transition.

at 1 without any glitches. Therefore, the new circuit is hazard-free for the transition. This new product, *BC*, is redundant in terms of function *f*, but it is necessary to eliminate the hazard. This product is used to cover the K-map transition, *ABC*: 011 → 111.

The original theory of combinational hazards for SIC transitions was developed by Huffman et al. (see Ref. 22). The above example indicates how to eliminate an SIC *static*-1 hazard, that is, for an input change where the function makes a 1 → 1 transition. In this case, *some* product must cover (i.e., completely contain) the entire transition. There are three remaining types of transitions, where the output makes a 0 → 0, 0 → 1, or 1 → 0 transition. It has been shown that given an arbitrary AND-OR implementation, *no* hazard will occur for any of these three transitions* (22); that is, only static-1 SIC hazards must be avoided during synthesis of an AND-OR circuit; other SIC transitions will be hazard-free.

MIC Hazards

The case of a *multiple-input change* (MIC) is much more complex: Both static and dynamic hazards must be eliminated. An MIC transition has a start input value, *M*, and a destination input value, *N*, where *several* inputs change monotonically between *M* and *N*.

The first problem which arises when considering MIC transitions is that of *function hazards* (22). Consider the Karnaugh map in Figure 5a. An example of an MIC transition has start point *ABCD* = 0010 and end point *ABCD* = 0111, and two changing inputs: *B* and *D*. During this MIC transition, the function itself is not monotonic; that is, it can change value several times. To see this, consider the change in the function's value if input *D* first goes to 1, followed by input *B*. Initially, at *ABCD* = 0010, the function is 1. When *D* goes high, the function changes to 0. When *B* then goes high, the function then changes to 1. Therefore, the function itself changes value more than once. Such an MIC transition is said to have a *function hazard*.

It has been shown that assuming gates and wires may have arbitrary delay, there is no guaranteed method to synthesize a circuit which is hazard-free for a transition with a function hazard (22). Intuitively, a function hazard is a glitch that is inherent in the Karnaugh map specification itself. If input *D* changes much later than input *B*, there is no way to prevent the function output from glitching.†

In summary, function hazards cannot be avoided. Therefore, classic synthesis methods focus only on MIC transitions which are already *function-hazard-free*. Examples of function-hazard-free transitions are shown in Figure 5a. The transition from *ABCD* = 0100 to *ABCD* = 0111 is *static*, because the output remains at a single value (1) throughout the transition. A *dynamic* transition is shown from *ABCD* = 0111 to *ABCD* = 1110; this transition is function-hazard-free, because the output changes *exactly once*, from 1 to 0, on all direct paths from the start point to the end point.

---

*More precisely, these realizations will be hazard-free as long as no AND gate contains a pair of complementary literals.

†Alternatively, even if *B* and *D* change simultaneously, there are always delay values for the given gates to force the function to drop low before going high.

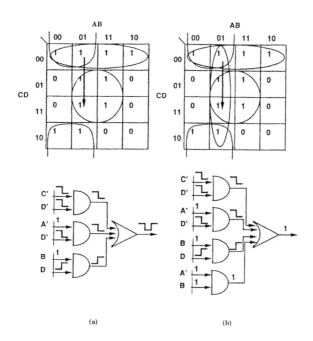

FIGURE 5   Combinational hazard example: static MIC transition.

Given a function-hazard-free MIC transition, a goal of hazard-free synthesis is to produce an AND-OR circuit which is glitch-free for the transition. If a glitch can occur, the transition is said to have a *logic hazard*. If no glitches are possible, the transition is *logic-hazard-free*.

Static-1 logic hazards (i.e., hazards during a $1 \to 1$ transition) can be avoided in an AND-OR implementation by using an approach similar to the SIC case (42). For example, consider the Karnaugh map in Figure 5a. A minimum-cost sum-of-products realization is $f = C'D' + A'D' + BD$. Consider the MIC transition from $ABCD = 0100$ to $ABCD = 0111$, indicated by an arrow. AND-gates $C'D'$ and $A'D'$ each make a $1 \to 0$ transition, and AND-gate BD makes a $0 \to 1$ transition. If BD is slow, the result is a glitch on the OR-gate output: $1 \to 0 \to 1$. Therefore, the implementation has a static logic hazard. An alternative hazard-free implementation is shown in Figure 5b. The hazard is eliminated by adding a fourth product term, $A'B$, which holds its value at 1 throughout the transition. This product covers the entire transition, $ABCD$: $0100 \to 0111$.

The next problem is to eliminate static-0 logic hazards. These hazards are easily handled. In fact, it has been shown that given any MIC $0 \to 0$ transition which is *already* function-hazard-free, the transition is *guaranteed* to be free of logic hazards in any AND-OR implementation (42); that is, no special care need be taken during two-level synthesis to avoid static-0 logic hazards.

The most difficult problem is to eliminate MIC dynamic logic hazards. Figure 6a contains the same Karnaugh map as in Figure 5b but with a new MIC transition: from $ABCD = 0111$ to $ABCD = 1110$. This is a dynamic function-hazard-free transition; the function makes a $1 \to 0$ transition. The implementation has a dy-

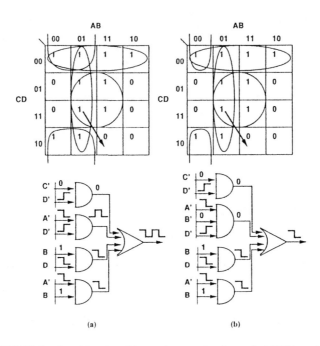

FIGURE 6   Combinational hazard example: dynamic MIC transition.

namic logic hazard. AND-gates BD and $A'B$ each make a $1 \to 0$ transition. At the same time, AND-gate $A'D'$ has inputs changing from 10 to 01 and, therefore, may glitch: $0 \to 1 \to 0$. If $A'D'$ is slow, this glitch will propagate to the OR-gate *after* the other AND-gates have gone to 0, and the OR-gate output will glitch: $1 \to 0 \to 1 \to 0$.

To prevent a dynamic MIC hazard, *no* AND-gate may temporarily turn on during the transition. In the example, $A'D'$ becomes enabled, then disabled, as inputs A and D changed value. This phenomenon is apparent in the Karnaugh map: product $A'D'$ intersects the transition from $ABCD$: $0111 \to 1110$, but intersects *neither* the start point ($ABCD = 0111$) *nor* the end point ($ABCD = 1110$) of the transition (43). A solution to this problem was proposed by Beister (44): Product $A'D'$ is *reduced* to a smaller product $A'B'D'$ which no longer intersects the transition. Note that this product is nonprime. The final cover is shown in Figure 6b. AND-gate $A'B'D$ remains at 0 throughout the transition, and the dynamic MIC transition is hazard-free.

Hazard-Free Minimization

The above examples show how to eliminate hazards for any one MIC transition. Hazard elimination can be viewed as a covering problem on a Karnaugh map. For the $1 \to 1$ case, the entire transition must be covered by some product. For the $1 \to 0$ and $0 \to 1$ cases, every product which intersects the transition must also contain its start or end point. For the remaining case, $0 \to 0$, no hazard will occur in any AND-OR realization (22). These conditions suffice to eliminate any single MIC hazard. Unfortunately, when attempting to eliminate hazards for *several* MIC transitions simultaneously, these covering conditions may be unsatisfiable; that is, for a given set of MIC transitions, a hazard-free cover may not exist (22,45,46).

An exact hazard-free two-level minimization algorithm was developed by Nowick and Dill (46). The algorithm finds an exactly minimum-cost cover which is hazard-free for a set of MIC transitions, if a solution exists. A heuristic hazard-free two-level minimization algorithm has also been developed (47).

There is a rich literature on *multilevel* hazard-free circuits as well, and several synthesis methods have been proposed. One approach is to start with a hazard-free circuit (e.g., a two-level circuit) and apply *hazard-nonincreasing* multilevel transformations (22,48,49). These transformations transform a hazard-free two-level circuit into a hazard-free multilevel circuit. Alternatively, a hazard-free multilevel circuit can be synthesized directly, using binary decision diagrams (BDDs) (50). Other algorithms have been developed for the hazard-free *technology mapping* of circuits to arbitrary cell libraries (51–53).

An Alternative View of Hazards

The above discussion follows a classical framework, focusing on combinational hazards separately from sequential hazards. This distinction has been quite useful for synthesis of asynchronous state-machines. However, for other synthesis styles, a uniform treatment of hazards is more natural. For example, each gate and sequential component may be assigned a specified "legal" behavior describing the correct operation of the component. As components are combined into a circuit, their composite behavior is formally determined. If a component may produce an output which cannot legally be accepted by another component, then a violation occurs. This notion has been formalized, in different contexts, as *computation interference* (34), *stability violation* (37), and *choking* (31).

ARBITRATION

To avoid nondeterministic behavior, asynchronous circuits must be hazard-free under some circuit delay model. As discussed above, certain forms of MIC behavior can be handled, but the most general forms of signal concurrency must be controlled by arbitration in order to avoid unrestricted MIC behaviors that result in circuit hazards. For example, if some circuit is to react one way if it sees a transition on signal A and react differently for a transition on signal B, then some guarantee must be provided that this circuit will see mutually exclusive transitions on inputs A and B. Nondeterministic behavior will occur if this guarantee cannot be provided. Such mutually exclusive signal conditioning is usually provided by *arbitration*.

Latches and flip-flops cannot be used for arbitration due to the inherent possibility that they may enter their metastable regions (16,54). Arbiter circuits are typically constructed to adhere to a particular signaling protocol and therefore vary somewhat. However, all arbiters rely on a *mutual exclusion*, or *ME element*, to separate possible concurrent signal transitions. The ME element is essentially a latch with an analog metastability detector on its outputs. If sufficient signal separation exists between the two inputs, then the first one wins. However, if both inputs occur within a device-specific time, then the latch will go metastable, but the metastability

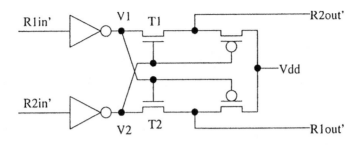

FIGURE 7   The mutual exclusion element.

detector will prevent the outputs of the ME circuit from changing until the metastability condition is resolved. The duration of metastability is unbounded, but normally persists for a very short time. It has been experimentally confirmed (16,54) that the metastability duration is an exponentially-decaying probability which depends somewhat on the particular latch properties. The result is that in the case of a tie, exactly one side will win the arbitration. The additional implication is that the distinction of which side wins does not matter.

Chuck Seitz proposed an ME circuit that is particularly useful for MOS-based designs, shown in Figure 7. The cross-coupled inverters form the usual SR latch. The outputs of the latch are connected to a pair of transistors which form the metastability detector. When the latch is in its metastable region, V1 and V2 will differ by less than the threshold voltage of the N-type transistors. In this case, both T1 and T2 will be off, because the gate-to-source voltage will be less than the threshold. If T1 and T2 are off, then the outputs of the ME circuit will remain high. When V1 and V2 differ by more than the threshold voltage, then the latch will stabilize into either of its stable states. At this point, either T1 or T2 will turn on and the respective output will fall to its asserted level.

Once the mutually exclusive resolution of the input race has been provided by an ME element, constructing the rest of an arbiter circuit to conform to a particular signaling protocol is relatively straightforward. An example of a four-cycle arbiter originally proposed by David Dill and Ed Clarke is shown in Figure 8. Four-cycle

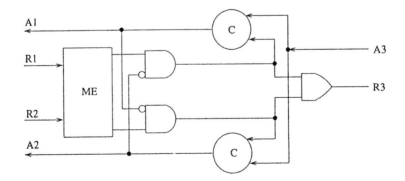

FIGURE 8   A four-cycle arbiter.

arbitration is relatively simple, as the input race must only be detected for both signal trajectories going in the same single direction (typically a low-to-high transition). The use of the C-elements in the arbiter prevents another pending request from passing through the arbiter until after the active request cycle has cleared.

Two-cycle arbitration is somewhat more complex, as the inputs of the arbiter may race in all possible combinations of signal trajectories. Ebergen (25), for example, has reported on a particular two-cycle arbiter known as the RGD (Request, Grant, Done) arbiter.

Another interesting arbitration problem was posed by Davis and Stevens during the development of the Post Office chip (55). One potential performance difficulty with asynchronous signaling protocols is that waiting for the next event is the normal mode of operation. Hence, if two requesters want to share some resource, the loser must wait until the winner is finished before access to that resource can be granted. However, if the loser wants to do something else if it does not win arbitration, then the previously discussed arbitration methods will be insufficient. The need is for a NACKing arbiter which provides the requester with an acknowledge if the resource is available, and a *negative acknowledge* (NACK) if the resource is busy. Several versions of this NACKing arbiter have been designed. The version used in the Post Office design used four ME elements (56). Each ME element resolved one of the four possible race trajectories. The remaining protocol control was provided by an asynchronous finite-state machine.

Arbiters for more than two inputs allow numerous implementation options. The simplest case is to create a binary tree of two-input arbiters of the appropriate size (see Ref. 31). The tree may be balanced or unbalanced. Balanced trees are *fair* in that they give equal priority to all of the leaf inputs. Unbalanced trees inherently provide higher priority for inputs which enter the structure closest to the root (in this case, the output) of the arbitration tree. The problem with tree-structured *N*-way arbiters is that they contain many C-elements and, therefore, suffer from decreased performance. Another approach is to use redundant ME elements to provide mutually exclusive assertion of 1 of the *N* input signals. This approach was also used by Ken Stevens in the design of the Post Office chip (55), and several variants of the multiple ME element theme have been investigated by Charles Molnar at Sun Laboratories for the counterflow pipeline processor (29).

Perhaps some of the best work on cascaded arbiters and nacking arbiters has been performed by Robert Shapiro and Hartmann Genrich (57,58). Sadly, this work has not been published in an available forum. Their work started as a formal effort to prove the cascaded arbiter properties of the arbiter circuits used in the aforementioned Post Office chip after a defect was discovered during testing of an arbiter fragment chip. Shapiro and Genrich used Petri Net-based models to create behavioral traces of both the basic arbitration modules and their properties when cascaded. Their analysis found what turned out to be a simple design flaw which had caused the problem. The more important aspect of their work is that they then found that the arbitration circuits were overconstrained in terms of C-element synchronization. They produced a series of four-cycle designs which contained few C-elements. The C-elements were replaced by NAND gates. Another interesting result of their work is that arbiters can be made to be faster than those containing C-elements in either the forward (requesting) direction or in the backward (acknowledge) direction, but not both.

Another interesting approach to the low-latency cascaded arbitration problem has been taken by Yakovlev et al. (59). Their circuits are speed independent and have an improved response delay at the input request–grant handshake link due to two factors. First, request propagation is performed in parallel with the start of arbitration. The arrival of any request at a stage can trigger an immediate request to the next higher stage, prior to arbitration resolution in the lower stage. Second, resetting the request–grant handshakes is done concurrently in different cascades of the request–grant propagation chain.

The field of arbiter design is as diverse as the circuits for which the arbiters are being designed. Although the methods are diverse, there is little doubt that the design of efficient arbitration structures is a key aspect of any high-performance asynchronous system design. In fact, organizing the system so that the arbitration requirements become minimal is viewed by many designers as the key factor in achieving high performance.

AN OVERVIEW OF PRIOR WORK

Pioneering Efforts

In the mid-1950s, asynchronous circuits were first studied by analyzing the nature of input restrictions on sequential circuits. These efforts were part of the general interest in switching theory. Huffman postulated (60,61) that there must be a *minimum* time between input changes in order for a sequential circuit to be able to recognize them as being distinct. There must then be two critical periods, δ_1 and δ_2 where $\delta_1 < \delta_2$. Signals which occur within a time that is less than or equal to δ_1 cannot be distinguished as being separate events. Signals which are separated by a time of δ_2 or greater are distinguishable as a sequence of separate events. Signal events separated by a time between δ_1 and δ_2 cause nondeterministic sequential circuit behavior. This led to a class of circuits that became known as *Huffman* circuits. This work was extended in the 1950s and 1960s by the fundamental contributions of Unger, McCluskey, and others.

Muller (62,63) proposed a different class of circuits which are more closely related to several modern asynchronous design styles. In particular, he proposed the use of a *ready* signal. Input signals to Muller circuits were only permitted when the ready signal was asserted. In some sense, the concept is similar to that of a simple four-cycle circuit. The unasserted acknowledge serves as a ready indication. When the circuit is not ready to accept additional input, then it can merely hold its acknowledge to indicate that no further requests can be tolerated.

The efforts of Muller and Huffman spurred considerable theoretical debate in the switching circuit literature. The next notable even from a modern perspective was the seminal work by Stephen Unger that resulted in the publication of his classic text (22). In that work, Unger provided a detailed method for synthesizing single-input change asynchronous sequential switching circuits. He also provided a partial view of what would be required for the larger domain of multiple-input change circuits. This book had a significant influence on much of the practical work that followed in the next decade. For example, the subsequent work of both of these authors was heavily influenced by Unger's work. Additionally, several early mainframe computers were constructed as entirely asynchronous systems, notably the MU-5 and Atlas computers.

Another noteworthy effort, the *Macromodule Project* (28), conducted at Washington University in St. Louis, provided an early demonstration of the composition benefits of asynchronous circuit modules. This project created a digital "Lego" kit of modules. These modules could (and were) rapidly used to configure special-purpose computing engines, as well as general-purpose computers. The project took a significant step forward and provided a sound foundation for the numerous macromodular synthesis approaches being investigated today (34,64,65).

Yet another noteworthy pioneer was Chuck Seitz, whose MIT dissertation (66) introduced a Petri Net-like formalism which proved to be extremely useful in the design and analysis of asynchronous circuits. In his subsequent academic career, Seitz taught numerous courses at the University of Utah and then later at CalTech where he infected a large number of students with what proved to be an incurable interest in asynchronous circuits. His influence directly resulted in the asynchronous implementation of the first operational data-flow computer (13) and the first commercial graphics system, the Evans & Sutherland LDS-1. Seitz's role as an educator is also significant in that his courses on asynchronous circuits, starting as early as 1970, inspired many of the field's current researchers.

The influence of these pioneering efforts is still seen in most of the asynchronous circuit work that is in progress today.

Synthesis of Controllers

Asynchronous State Machines

The most traditional approach to specifying and synthesizing asynchronous controllers is to view them as finite-state machines. This view of computation is *state-based*: A machine is in some state, it receives inputs, generates outputs, and moves to a new state. Such specifications are naturally described by a *flow table* or *state table* (22). These tables define the behavior of outputs and next state as a function of the inputs and current state. Current and next states are described symbolically (see Fig. 9).

The earliest asynchronous state machine implementations were *Huffman machines* (see Ref. 22). These machines consist of combinational logic, primary inputs, primary outputs, and fedback state variables. No latches or flip-flops are used: The state is stored on feedback loops, which may have added delay elements. A block diagram of a Huffman machine is shown in Figure 10.

Synthesis methods for asynchronous state machines usually follow the same general outline as synchronous methods (27). A flow table is reduced through *state minimization*. Symbolic states are assigned binary codes using *state assignment*. Finally, the resulting Boolean functions are implemented in combinational logic using *logic minimization*.

There are several possible *operating modes* for an asynchronous state machine. Unger (67) proposed a hierarchy, based on the kinds of input changes that a machine can accept. In a *single-input change* (SIC) machine, only one input may change at a time. Once the input has changed, no further inputs may change until the machine has stabilized. This operating mode is highly restrictive but simplifies

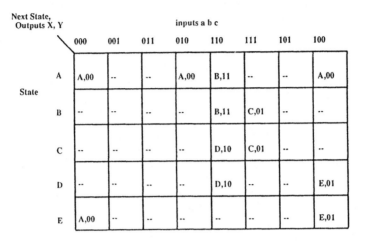

FIGURE 9   An asynchronous flow table.

the elimination of hazards. A summary of SIC asynchronous state machines can be found in Ref. 22.

A *multiple-input change* (MIC) machine allows several inputs to change concurrently. Once the inputs change, no further inputs may change until the machine has stabilized. This approach allows greater concurrency, but it is still quite restricted. In particular, MIC machines have the added constraint that the multiple-input change is *almost simultaneous*. More formally, all inputs must change within some narrow time period, δ. This constraint helps to simplify hazard elimination, which is still more complicated than in the SIC case.

MIC designs were proposed by Friedman and Menon (68) and Mago (69). These designs require the use of delays on inputs or outputs, special "delay boxes,"

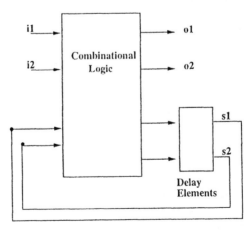

FIGURE 10   Block diagram of a Huffman machine.

and careful timing requirements. The usefulness of these designs in a concurrent environment is limited, since input changes are required to be near-simultaneous.

Finally, an *unrestricted-input change* (UIC) machine allows arbitrary input changes, as long as no one input changes more than once in some given time interval, δ. This behavior is quite general, but hazard elimination is problematic. UIC designs were first proposed by Unger (67). These designs are not currently practical: they require the use of large inertial delays and have not been proven to avoid metastability problems.

In any asynchronous state machine, the problem of hazards must be addressed. First is the problem of combinational hazards. The difficulty of combinational hazard elimination depends on whether the machine operates in the SIC or MIC mode. As indicated earlier, SIC hazards are easier to eliminate. Hazards are eliminated by hazard-free synthesis or by using inertial delays to filter out glitches. Alternatively, many traditional synthesis methods ignore hazards on outputs and only eliminate hazards in the next-state logic. Such machines are called *S-proper* or *properly realizable* (22).

Second, because asynchronous state machines have state, sequential hazards must be addressed. When a state machine goes from one state to another, several state bits may change. If the machine may stabilize incorrectly in a transient state, a *critical race* occurs. Critical races are eliminated using specialized state encodings, such as *one-hot* (22), *one-shot* (22), Liu (70), or Tracey (71) *critical race-free* codes. These codes often require extra bits. A second type of sequential problem is an *essential hazard* (22). Essential hazards arise if a machine has not fully absorbed an input change at the time the next state begins to change. In effect, the machine sees the new state before the combinational logic has stabilized from the input change. Essential hazards are avoided by adding delays to the feedback path or, in some cases, using special logic factoring (72).

Because of the complexity of building correct Huffman machines, an alternative approach was proposed, called *self-synchronized machines*. These machines are similar to Huffman machines but have a local self-synchronization unit which acts like a clock on the machine's latches or flip-flops. Unlike a synchronous design, the clock is *aperiodic*, being generated as needed for the given computations. A block diagram of a self-synchronized machine is shown in Figure 11. Both SIC (73,74) and MIC (75–78) self-synchronized machines have been proposed. In a related approach, the local clock is replaced by an explicit external completion signal (79). Other researchers have developed hybrid *mixed-operation mode* machines (80,81). Self-synchronized machines tend to have a simpler construction but a greater overhead than Huffman machines.

In general, asynchronous state machines offer a number of attractive features. First, input-to-output latency is often low: If no delays are added to inputs or outputs, the delay is combinational. Second, because the machines are state based, many sequential and combinational optimization algorithms can be used, similar to those which have been effective in the synchronous domain. However, asynchronous state machine design is subtle: It is difficult to design hazard-free implementations which (i) allow reasonable concurrency and (ii) have high performance.

Much of the recent work on asynchronous state machines is centered on *burst-mode machines*. These specifications were introduced to allow more much more concurrency than traditional SIC machines and, therefore, to be more effective in

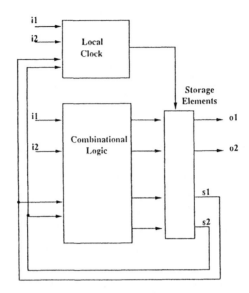

FIGURE 11   Block diagram of self-synchronized machine.

building concurrent systems. At the same time, burst-mode implementations are guaranteed to be hazard-free while maintaining high performance. Burst-mode specifications are based on the work of Davis on the *DDM Machine* (82). In this data-flow machine, Davis used state machines which would wait for a collection of input changes ("input burst") and then respond with a collection of output changes ("output burst"). The key difference between this data-driven style and MIC mode is that, unlike MIC machines, inputs within a burst could be *uncorrelated*: arriving in any order and at any time. As a result, these machines could operate more flexibly in a concurrent environment.

More recently, Davis et al. implemented this approach in the MEAT synthesis system at Hewlett-Packard Laboratories (16). The synthesis method was applied to the design of controllers for the Post Office routing chip for the Mayfly project. However, although it produced high-performance implementations, it relied on a verifier to ensure hazard-free designs. An example of a burst-mode specification is shown in Figure 12. Each transition is labeled with an input burst followed by an output burst. Input and output bursts are separated by a slash, /. A rising transition is indicated by a "+" and a falling transition is indicated by a "−". The specification describes a controller, *pe-send-ifc*, which has been implemented in the Post Office chip.

Nowick and Dill (83,84) made three main contributions. First, they constrained and formalized the specifications used in MEAT into the final form called *burst mode* (83,84). Second, they introduced a new self-synchronized design style called a *locally-clocked state machine* (83,84). This was the first burst-mode synthesis method to guarantee a hazard-free gate-level implementation, given a burst-mode specification. In addition, unlike several previous self-synchronized design methods, this method produces low-latency designs, where the latency of the ma-

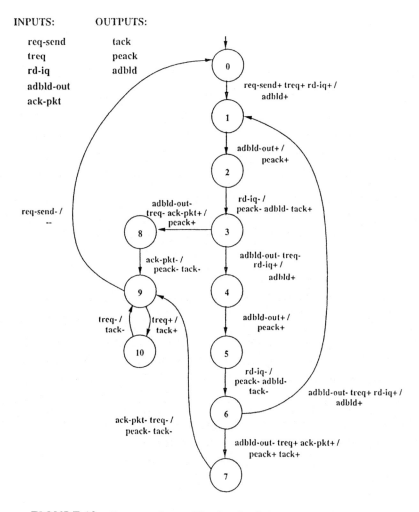

INPUTS: OUTPUTS:

req-send   tack
treq   peack
rd-iq   adbld
adbld-out
ack-pkt

FIGURE 12   Burst-mode specification for HP controller *pe-send-ifc*.

chine is primarily combinational delay. The design method has been automated and applied to a number of significant designs: a high-performance second-level cache controller (85), a DRAM controller and a SCSI controller (86). Finally, they developed a hazard-free two-level minimization algorithm, which produces a minimum-cost hazard-free sum-of-products implementation (46). The minimizer has been refined into a CAD package called *hfmin* (87), which includes multioutput and multivalued minimization and uses highly optimized synchronous tools such as *mincov* (88) to solve substeps. A heuristic hazard-free minimizer, *espresso-hf*, has also been developed (47).

Yun and Dill (89) later proposed an alternative implementation style for burst-mode machines, called a *3D machine*. These machines are named after the three-dimensional flow table used in their synthesis. Unlike locally clocked machines, these are Huffman machines, with no local clock or latches. The synthesis method has been fully automated into a CAD tool and applied to several large designs, including an experimental SCSI controller at AMD Corporation (90). A more recent unclocked burst-mode method, *UCLOCK*, was developed by Nowick and Coates (91).

The burst-mode approach allows greater concurrency than MIC designs, but it still has two main limitations. First, it requires strictly alternating bursts of inputs and outputs: concurrency occurs only within a burst. Second, as in many asynchronous design styles, there is no notion of "sampling" signal levels which may or may not change. Yun et al. (92,93) introduced *extended burst-mode* specifications to eliminate these two restrictions. These generalized specifications allow a limited form of intermingled input and output changes and provide greater concurrency. These designs also allow the sampling of level signals. Yun has modified his 3D synthesis algorithms and tools to handle extended burst-mode specifications (93). His work includes performance-oriented optimizations targeted to multilevel implementations (94). A novelty of Yun's method is that it can be used to synthesize controllers for mixed synchronous/asynchronous systems, where the global clock is one of the controller inputs (93).

A number of CAD optimization algorithms have been developed, which have been used in burst-mode synthesis. These include optimal state assignment (87), hazard-free two-level logic minimization (both exact [*hfmin* (86,87)] and heuristic [*espresso-hf* (47)]), hazard-free multilevel logic optimization (49,50), and hazard nonincreasing technology mapping (51–53), which allows modern standard cell libraries to be utilized.

Marshall et al. (95) have built a CAD framework to incorporate many of the burst-mode synthesis methods. The framework includes tools for simulation and layout as well. Their tools have been applied to several significant designs, including a low-power infrared communications chip for portable communication, developed at Hewlett-Packard Laboratories and Stanford University. An experimental chip has been fabricated; the measured current consumption of the core receiver (without pads) is less than 1 mA at 5 V when the receiver is actually receiving data, and less than 1 μA when it is waiting for data.

Beerel and Yun have recently used burst-mode synthesis tools at Intel Corporation, including *3D* (89,93) and *hfmin* (46,87), to design of an experimental high-performance instruction decoder. Gopalakrishnan et al. have developed a high-level asynchronous synthesis tool, called *ACK* (96), which incorporates burst-mode CAD tools to synthesize controllers.

Petri Net and Graph-Based Methods

Petri Nets and other graphical notations are a widely used alternative to specify and synthesize asynchronous circuits. In this model, an asynchronous system is viewed not as state-based, but rather as a *partially-ordered* sequence of events. A Petri Net (97) is a directed bipartite graph which can describe both concurrency and choice. The net consists of two kinds of vertices: *places* and *transitions*. *Tokens* are assigned to the various places in the net. An assignment of tokens is called a *marking*, which captures the state of the concurrent system. Numerous semantics have been associated with Petri Nets. A useful introductory view is that a marked place is an indication that a condition is true, and a transition specifies an action. When all of the conditions preceding a transition are true, the action may *fire*, which removes the tokens from the preceding places and marks the successor places. Hence, starting from an initial marking, tokens flow through the net, transforming the system from one marking to another. As tokens flow, they fire transitions in their path according to certain *firing rules*. As the firing of a transition in a Petri Net corresponds to the execution of an event, each such simulation or *token game* describes a different possible interleaved execution of the system.

A Petri Net is shown in Figure 13a. Places are drawn as circles, and transitions as bars. The initial marking is indicated by black dots in two of the places. If a place is connected by an arc to a transition, the former is called an *input place* of the transition. Likewise, if a transition is connected by an arc to a place, the latter is called an *output place* of the transition. In this example, transition X has input place 1 and output place 2; transition Y has input place 3 and output place 4.

Two transitions are enabled in the figure: X and Y. Each transition is enabled because there is a token in each input place. An enabled transition may fire at any time, removing a token from each input place and moving one to each output place. The result of firing transition X is shown in Figure 13b. The firing of a transition corresponds to the occurrence of an event. In this example, events X and Y can occur concurrently: Both transitions are enabled and may fire in any order. Figure 13c indicates the result of firing transition Y after X. After both events have fired, transition Z is enabled and may fire.

Patil (98) proposed the synthesis of Petri Nets into *asynchronous logic arrays*. In this approach, the structure of the Petri Net is mapped directly into hardware. In contrast, more modern synthesis methods use a Petri Net as a behavioral specification only, not as a structural specification. Using *reachability analysis*, the Petri Net is typically transformed into a *state graph*, which describes the explicit sequencing behavior of the net. An asynchronous circuit is then derived from the state graph.

Several synthesis methods use a constrained class of Petri Net called a *marked graph* (99). Marked graphs are used to model concurrency, but not choice; that is, a marked graph cannot model that one of several possible inputs (or outputs) may change in some state. Examples include Seitz's *M-Nets* (100) and Rosenblum and

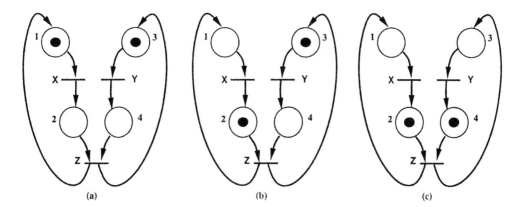

FIGURE 13   Petri Net example.

Yakovlev's Signal Graphs (101). Vanbekbergen et al. (102) introduced the notion of a *lock class* to synthesize designs from marked graphs.

More general classes of Petri Nets include Molnar et al.'s *I-Nets* (103) and Chu's *Signal Transition Graphs* or *STGs* (104,105). These nets allow both concurrency and a limited form of choice. Chu developed a synthesis method which transforms an STG into a speed-independent circuit and applied the method to a number of examples, such as an A-to-D controller and a resource locking module. This work was extended by Meng (106), who produced an automated synthesis tool for speed-independent designs from STGs. Meng also explored design tradeoffs to allow greater concurrency in the resulting circuits.

Recent work on Petri Net and graph-based asynchronous synthesis is proceeding in three major directions: (i) extending specifications; (ii) optimizing synthesis algorithms; and (iii) improving hazard elimination.

Several extensions have been proposed to describe more general behavior than is possible with the original STGs. These include the use of "epsilon" and "dummy" transitions (104), "don't-care" and "toggle" transitions (107), *OR-causality* (108), and semaphore transitions (109). Sutherland and Sproull have introduced a notation for composite Petri Nets called "snippets." Others allow timing constraints for specification and synthesis, using a related *Event–Rule* formalism (41).

In addition, some researchers are using state graphs for specifications, as an alternative to Petri Nets (39,40,110). State graphs allow the direct specification of interleaved behavior, avoiding some of the structural complexity of Petri Nets. The target designs are usually speed-independent gate-level implementations. Originally, this work focused on determinate specifications, having no input or output choice, based on Muller's semimodular lattice formulations (see Ref. 24). More recent research allows generalized behavior with choice.

A number of optimized synthesis algorithms have been developed. Lavagno et al. (111), Vanbekbergen et al. (112), Chu et al. (43), and Puri and Gu (114) have each developed algorithms for state minimization and state assignment from STG specifications. A partitioning algorithm for STG-based specifications was proposed by Puri and Gu (115). Lin and Lin (116) have developed algorithms which avoid expensive intermediate representations during synthesis, instead performing synthesis directly on an STG representation, for a limited class of STGs. More recently, the *theory of regions* has been used as a powerful tool in developing efficient STG algorithms, including state minimization and assignment (see Refs. 117 and 118). A region is a set of states in the state graph corresponding to a place in the associated STG. The theory of regions allows synthesis steps to be performed directly on the STG, without the need to generate a complete state graph.

Recent STG methods are also addressing the problem of gate-level hazards. Early STG synthesis methods typically assumed a *complex-gate model*, where an entire combinational circuit is treated as a monolithic block rather than a collection of separate gates with individual delays. These methods could not be used to synthesize large circuits, where blocks are mapped to a *network* of gates, since the resulting network could have hazards. Several recent methods address this problem, using a *simple-gate model* which can model hazards due to actual delays in a collection of individual gates and wires. Moon et al. (107) and Yu and Subrahmanyam (119) proposed heuristic techniques for gate-level hazard elimination for speed-independent design. Lavagno et al. (120) used logic synthesis algorithms, hazard analysis, and added delays to avoid hazards, assuming bounded-gate delays. Lavagno has developed an influential CAD system for STG synthesis, which has been incorporated into the Berkeley *SIS* tool package (121,122).

Several speed-independent synthesis methods have been developed which ensure hazard freedom at the gate level. Much of this work has been pursued by Kishinevsky et al. (110,123), by Beerel and Meng (39), and by Cortadella et al. and others (40,117). These methods have been effectively applied to a number of designs. The sustained research effort of Kishinevsky et al., pursued over many years in Russia and Japan, has been especially noteworthy, resulting in a collection of algorithms and tools which are making SI design practical. A general asynchronous CAD system, including speed-independent tools, has also been developed at IMEC Laboratory (124). A comprehensive solution to the problem of hazard-free decomposition complex-gates into simpler gates, under a speed-independent model, has been developed by Burns (125).

Transformation Methods

Whereas STG-based methods view computation as partially ordered sequences of events, a different approach is to view an asynchronous system as a collection of *communicating processes*. A system is specified as a program in a high-level language of concurrency. Typically, the program is based on a variant of Hoare's *CSP* (126), such as *occam* or *trace theory* (127). The program is then transformed, by a series of steps, into a low-level program which maps directly to a circuit. Such transformation methods use algebraic or compiler techniques to carry out the translation. Some of these methods treat data path and control uniformly during synthesis.

Ebergen (34) introduced a synthesis method for delay-insensitive circuits using specifications called *commands*. A command is a concise program notation to describe concurrent computation based on trace theory. Several operations are used to construct a complex command from simpler commands, such as *concatenation*, *repetition*, and *weave*.

Figure 14 illustrates commands for several basic DI components. A *wire* is a component with one input, $a?$, and one output, $b!$. The symbol "?" indicates an input to the wire, and "!" indicates an output of the wire. In a delay-insensitive system, a wire may have arbitrary finite delay. As a result, if two successive changes occur on input $a?$, the output behavior is unpredictable: $b!$ may glitch. To ensure correct operation, input and output events must strictly alternate: Once input $a?$ changes value, no further change on $a?$ is permitted until output event $b!$ occurs. A command for *wire* is given in Figure 14a. The notation $a?;b!$ indicates that input event $a?$ must be followed by output event $b!$; ";" is the *concatenation* operator. No distinction is made between a *rising* or *falling* event on a wire; $a?$ simply means a change in value on the wire. An asterisk (*) indicates *repetition*: $a?$ and $b!$ may alternate any number of times. Finally, "pref" is the *prefix-closure* operator, indicating that any prefix of a permitted behavior is also permitted. The final command describes the permitted interaction of a wire and its environment when it is properly used.

Figure 14b illustrates a more complex component called a *toggle*. A toggle has one input, $a?$, and two outputs, $b!$ and $c!$. Each input event, $a?$, results in exactly one output event. Output events alternate or toggle: The first input event $a?$ results

NAME	COMMAND	SCHEMATIC
Wire	**pref*** [a?;b!]	
Toggle	**pref*** [a?;b!;a?c!]	
C-element	**pref*** [a?‖b?;c!]	
Merge	**pref*** [(a?|b?);c!]	

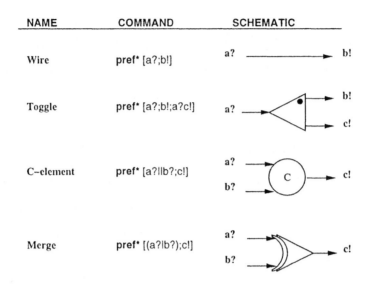

FIGURE 14   Commands for some simple components.

in output event *b*! (as indicated by the black dot); the next input event results in output event *c*!; and so on. The resulting command is shown in the figure.

Another important component is a *C-element*, shown in Figure 14c (also known as a Muller C-element, DI C-element, rendezvous, or join element). The component has two inputs, *a*? and *b*?, and one output, *c*!. The component waits for events on *both* inputs. When both inputs arrive, the component produces a single event on output *c*!. Each input may change only once between output events, but the input events *a*? and *b*? may occur in any order. Such parallel behavior is described in a command by the *weave operator: a*? ‖ *b*?. The final command for a C-element, allowing repeated behavior, is shown in the figure.

A final component, called a *merge*, is shown in Figure 14d. The component is basically an *exclusive-or* gate, but its operation is restricted so that no glitching occurs. The component has two inputs, *a*? and *b*?, and one output, *c*!. The component waits for *exactly one* input event: either *a*? or *b*?. Once an input event occurs, the component responds with output event, *c*!. The component can be thought of as "joining" two input streams to a single output stream, where only one input stream is active at a time. Such an exclusive choice between inputs is described in a command by the *union operator: a*? | *b*?. The final command for a join element, allowing for repeated behavior, is shown in the figure.

A command can also be used to specify a complex circuit or system. The command is then *decomposed* in a series of steps into an equivalent network of components, using a "calculus of decomposition." As an example, a *modulo-3-counter* can be specified by the following command (34):

$$MOD3 = \mathbf{pref}*[a?;q!;a?;q!;a?;p!]$$

This command describes a counter with one input, *a*?, and two outputs, *p*! and *q*!. The counter receives events on input *a*?. Each input event must be acknowledged by one output event before the next input event can occur. The first and second input events are acknowledged on $q!$, whereas the third input event is acknowledged on $p!$. This behavior repeats, hence the command describes a modulo-3-counter. Using techniques for delay-insensitive decomposition, this command can be decomposed into a network of two toggles and one merge which implements equivalent behavior, as shown in Figure 15. Ebergen has applied his decomposition method to a number of designs, including modulo-n counters, stacks, committee schedulers (128), and token ring arbiters.

A related algebraic approach was proposed by Udding and Josephs (30,35). Their method is based on a *delay-insensitive algebra* which formally characterizes a delay-insensitive system. Using axioms and lemmas, a specification is transformed into a provably correct delay-insensitive circuit. An alternative *speed-independent algebra* has also been proposed (129). Proof methods for recursively defined DI specifications have been formally justified (130). The DI synthesis method has been used to design a stack, a routing chip, an up-down counter, and a polynomial divider (131). Lucassen and Udding (132) have used DI algebra to design, and prove correct, a stage in the Counterflow Pipeline Processor developed at Sun Laboratories. In related work, Patra and Fussell (133) have proposed a "basis set" of DI components. They have shown that any DI circuit can be constructed using only components from the set and that the set is minimal.

Whereas the above methods use algebraic calculi to derive asynchronous circuits, other transformation methods rely on compiler-oriented techniques. An elegant and influential method for QDI synthesis has been developed by Martin and his students at Caltech (37,134). Martin specifies an asynchronous system as a set of concurrent processes which communicate on channels, using a CSP-like language. The language uses communication constructs from Hoare's CSP, sequential constructs from Dijkstra's guarded command language, and new constructs such as the *probe* (see Ref. 37). The specification is then translated into a collection of gates and components which communicate on wires.

Martin's translation process is accomplished in several steps: (i) in *process decomposition*, a process is refined into an equivalent collection of interacting simpler processes; (ii) in *handshaking expansion*, each "communication channel" between processes is replaced by a pair of wires, and each atomic "communication action" is replaced by a handshaking protocol on the wires; (iii) in *production-rule expansion*, each handshaking expansion is replaced by a set of "production rules (PRs)," where each rule has a "guard" that ensures it is activated (i.e., "fires") under

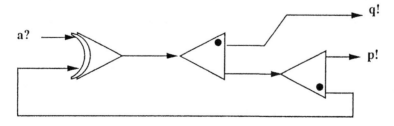

FIGURE 15   Ebergen's modulo-3 counter.

the same semantics as specified by the earlier handshaking expansion; and, finally, (iv) in *operator reduction*, PRs are grouped into clusters, and each cluster is then mapped to a basic hardware component. These steps include several optimizations and substeps, such as reshuffling, in step (ii); and state assignment, guard strengthening, and guard symmetrization, in step (iii). In most designs, a four-phase handshaking protocol is used [step (ii)], although two-phase handshaking can be used as well.

Martin's synthesis method has been automated by Burns (135,136) and applied to many substantial examples, including a distributed mutual exclusion element (136,137), a stack (37), and a multiply-accumulate unit (138). The compiler includes algorithms for optimal transistor sizing (36). (Designs for other datapath components, and for a microprocessor, using this method are described in the next two sections.) Martin's work has been extended by Akella and Gopalakrishnan in a system called *SHILPA* (139). This method allows global shared variables and uses flow analysis techniques to optimize resource allocation.

A different compiler-based approach was developed by van Berkel, Rem, and others (9,65,140,141) at Philips Research Laboratories and Eindhoven University of Technology, using the *Tangram* language. Tangram, based on CSP, is a specification language for concurrent systems. A system is specified by a Tangram program, which is then compiled by syntax-directed translation into an intermediate representation called a *handshake circuit*. A handshake circuit consists of a network of *handshake processes*, or *components*, which communicate asynchronously on channels using handshaking protocols. The circuit is then improved using peephole optimization and, finally, components are mapped to VLSI implementations.

As an example, the following is a Tangram program for a one-place buffer, BUF1:

$$(a?W\&b!W) \cdot | [x : \text{var } W | \#[a?x;b!x]] |$$

The buffer accepts input data on a and produces output data on b. The expression in parentheses is a declaration of the external ports of the module. The buffer has an *input port, a*, and an *output port, b*, handling data of some type, W. The remainder of the program, structured as a block, is called a *command*. A local variable x is defined for internal storage of data. The statement $\#[a?x;b!x]$ indicates that data are received on port a and stored in internal variable x; the data are then sent out on port b. The ";" operator indicates sequencing, and "#" indicates infinite repetition.

This Tangram program is translated into the handshake circuit of Figure 16. Each circle represents a handshake process or component. Each arc represents a channel, which connects an *active port* (indicated by a black dot) to a *passive port* (indicated by a white dot). Communication on a channel is by handshaking: an active port initiates a request and a passive port returns an acknowledgement.

In this example, port ▷ is the top-level port for the circuit, called *go*. The environment activates the buffer by an initial request on this passive port. This port is connected to a *repeater* process, which implements the repetition operator, "#". This process repeatedly initiates handshaking on channel c. Channel c is connected to a *sequencer* process, which implements the ";" operator. The sequencer first performs handshaking on channel d. When handshaking is complete, it then performs handshaking on channel e.

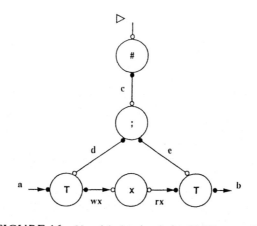

FIGURE 16   Handshake circuit for BUF1 example.

Channels *d* and *e*, in turn, are each connected to *transferrers*, labeled *T*. When the sequencer process initiates a request on channel *d*, the corresponding transferrer actively fetches data on input channel *a* and then transfers it to storage element *x*. Once the transfer is complete, the sequencer initiates a request on channel *e*, causing the second transferrer to fetch the data from *x* and transfer it to output channel *b*.

A more complex example is the two-place buffer, BUF2, which can be described in terms of 2 one-place buffers:

$$(a?W\&c!W) \cdot \mid [b : \text{chan } W \mid \text{BUF}_1\ (a, b) \parallel \text{BUF}_2\ (b, c))] \mid$$

The program defines the buffer by the parallel composition, $\parallel$, of the 2 one-place buffers, which are connected by an internal channel, *b*. The corresponding handshake circuit is shown in Figure 17. A *parallel* component implements the composition operator, $\parallel$. An initial request on its passive *go* port results in parallel communi-

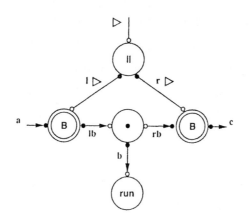

FIGURE 17   Handshake circuit for BUF2 example.

cation on channels *l* and *r*. These channels are both connected to a one-place buffer *B* (indicated by double circles). The two buffers communicate through a *synchronizer* process (indicated by a black dot). If active requests arrive on both of its channels, *lb*, and *rb*, the synchronizer first performs handshaking on channel *b*, then returns parallel acknowledgements on channels *lb* and *rb*. The attached *run* process is used to hide channel *b*; it simply acknowledges every request it receives.

The Tangram compiler has been successfully used at Philips for several experimental DSP designs for portable electronics, including a systolic RSA Converter, counters, decoders, image generators, and an error corrector for a digital compact cassette player (142). A major goal of this work is rapid turnaround time and low-power implementation.

Even though some peephole optimizations have been developed, Tangram is basically a syntax-directed translation method. Recently, two *resynthesis* methods have been proposed, by Pena and Cortadella (143) and Kolks et al. (144), which use aggressive peephole techniques to further optimize the resulting Tangram circuits. In each approach, handshaking components are clustered, formally specified as a single block, then resynthesized using STG techniques. A different approach has been proposed, which uses burst-mode techniques for the resynthesis step (145).

Brunvand and Sproull (146,147) introduced an alternative compiler using occam specifications. Unlike the approaches of Martin and van Berkel, communication between processes is through two-phase handshaking, or transition signaling. In their method, an occam specification is first compiled into an unoptimized circuit using syntax-directed translation. Peephole optimization techniques are then applied to improve the resulting circuits. The circuits are then mapped to a library of transition-signaling components.

Timed Methods

Although all asynchronous synthesis methods make some timing assumptions, much of the discipline is focused on minimizing these timing assumptions or at least localizing them into low-level modules. Myers and Meng (41,148) contends that this approach often leads to additional time and space being spent in the circuit to deal with contingencies which never occur. In his timed state-space method, rather than using timing analysis for post-synthesis-based optimizations to remove unnecessary circuitry, timing information is used *during* synthesis to avoid generating unnecessary circuitry. The method is based on *timed event rule (ER) structures* (149), which can be automatically generated from high-level language representations such as CSP or VHDL. ER structures and Petri Nets use a similar representational semantics, but ER structures have a more concise syntax.

A *rule set* represents a causal dependence between events. It is notated as a 4-tuple, $\langle e, f, l, u \rangle$, consisting of an enabling event *e*, an enabled event *f*, a lower timing bound *l*, and an upper timing bound *u*. The rule is considered to be *satisfied* for the time between *l* and *u* after an enabling event has occurred. The use of this timing bound restricts the possible state space to events which can actually occur. A disjunction operator is used to permit both choice and exclusive-OR causality behaviors, although there is currently no provision for true OR behaviors. Myers' gate-level synthesis method permits larger circuits to be synthesized more efficiently as a result of the state-space reduction.

A new set of timing analysis algorithms, based on a theory of geometric regions (150), allows a large number of discrete timed states to be condensed into a single region. The worst-case complexity of the algorithms is actually worse than discrete methods, but it has been shown that the region-based approach works well in practice (151 – 153). The method is automated in a tool called **ATACS**, which has been used to design a number of practical circuits. The tool has also been used at Intel Corporation in the design of an experimental high-performance instruction decoder.

Results show that, in the best case, circuits can be up to 40% smaller and 50% faster than those synthesized using methods which do not eliminate temporally unreachable states. Perhaps the most interesting aspect of this work is that it treats synchronous circuits as a subset of timed circuits and, therefore, provides a method for treating hybrid circuit structures consisting of both synchronous and asynchronous modules.

Design of Asynchronous Datapaths

As in synchronous design, different techniques and structures are used when designing datapaths and controllers.

Modern datapaths are often built using pipelines. However, the operation of synchronous and asynchronous pipelines are fundamentally different. In a synchronous pipeline, data advances at a fixed clock rate, in lock-step, through the pipe. Because function blocks in the stages may have different delays, the clock cycle must be set to the slowest stage. Furthermore, a stage's latency varies with the actual temperature, voltage, process, and data inputs; therefore, an additional delay margin is typically added to the clock cycle. Finally, the clock speed must be further reduced to avoid clock skew problems. As a result, under typical operating conditions, a synchronous pipeline may operate far slower than its potential performance.

In contrast, an asynchronous pipeline is not globally clocked. Therefore, in principle, each stage may pass data to its neighbor whenever the stage is done and the neighbor is free. Such *elastic* pipelines promise improved performance: Different stages may operate at different speeds, and stages may complete early depending on the actual data. Of course, new overhead may be introduced because each stage must now tell its neighbor when it is ready.

Sutherland introduced an elegant and influential approach to building asynchronous pipelines, he called *micropipelines* (14). A micropipeline has alternating computation stages separated by storage elements and control circuitry. This approach uses transition signaling for control along with bundled data. Sutherland describes several designs for the storage elements, called "event-controlled registers," which respond symmetrically to rising and falling transitions on inputs. Such pipelines have been used by several researchers in the design of asynchronous microprocessors. Sutherland, Sproull, Molnar, and others at Sun Labs have recently designed a "counterflow microprocessor" based on micropipelines (29). Micropipelines also form the basis for the Manchester ARM microprocessors, developed by Furber and the AMULET group (10,154,155).

Figure 18 illustrates the operation of a micropipeline with four stages. For simplicity, only the control is indicated. In practice, a bundled datapath is also used, along with event-controlled registers to store the data as they propagate down the pipe. A control stage of the pipeline consists of a C-element (described above). A

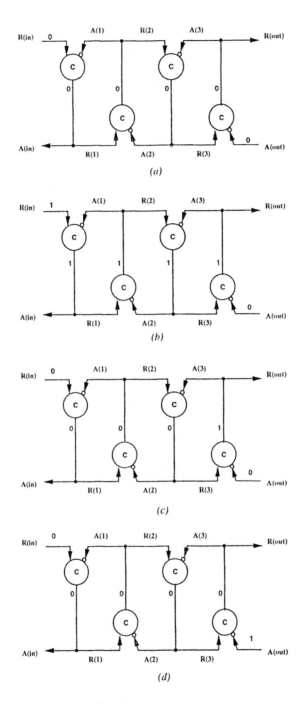

FIGURE 18   Micropipeline example.

C-element with two inputs and one output behaves as follows. If both inputs are 1, the output is 1; if both inputs are 0, the output is 0. Otherwise, if inputs have different values, the output holds its current value. The C-elements in the micropipeline behave similarly, except that each has one inverted input.

Initially, all wires in the micropipeline are at 0, as shown in Figure 18a. When new data arrive, a request $R(in)$ is asserted [$R(in)$ goes to 1]. The first C-element, C_1, becomes enabled, and its output makes a transition (to 1). This event has two consequences: The request is acknowledged on the left interface [transition on $A(in)$], and the request is forwarded to the right interface [transition on $R(1)$]. The same behavior is repeated at the second stage: the request is acknowledged on the left interface [transition on $A(1)$], and the request is forwarded to the right interface [transition on $R(2)$]. This process continues through stages 3 and 4, and a final request appears on the rightmost interface, $R(out)$. Effectively, the initial request propagates to the right through the pipe and acknowledges are generated to the left. The resulting micropipeline configuration is shown in Figure 18b. Note that because transition signaling is used, only one request and one acknowledge are generated between each pair of stages. In contrast, a four-phase (RZ) protocol would have required a second request/acknowledge sequence to reset the wires to their original values.

Because the initial request was acknowledged at the leftmost interface, $A(in)$, new data may now arrive and a second request, $R(in)$, can occur. Because $R(in)$ is currently 1, a request is asserted by changing $R(in)$ to 0. This request propagates through the micropipeline as before. The left interface is acknowledged [$A(in)$ goes to 0], and the request is forwarded to the right interface [$R(1)$ goes to 0]. This process repeats at the second and third stages. However, once the second stage is acknowledged [$A(2)$ goes to 0] and the request is made to the fourth stage [$R(3)$ goes to 0], the propagation halts. Although $R(3)$ made a transition (request from stage 3), stage 4 still contains the earlier data that were entered into the pipe. These data were not removed, as no $A(out)$ transition has occurred. Because $A(out)$ is still 0, no new transition can occur on $R(out)$. Instead, the new data are held in the third stage. The resulting micropipeline configuration is shown in Figure 18c. The micropipeline now contains data in the third and fourth stages.

Finally, the original data in the fourth stage can be removed from the right interface, which then issues an acknowledge [$A(out)$ goes to 1]. At this point, the fourth stage issues a new $R(out)$ transition [because $R(3)$ is 0 and $A(out)$ is 1], as data in stage 3 is moved to stage 4. The third stage is acknowledged as well [$A(3)$ goes to 0]. The resulting configuration is shown in Figure 18d. In practice, more complicated scenarios are possible because data may be added and removed from the pipeline concurrently.

Although micropipelines use transition signaling, other signaling conventions have been used in asynchronous pipelines as well. Williams (156), Martin (157), and van Berkel (9) have used four-phase handshaking (the "return-to-zero" protocol) between stages. An alternative two-phase signaling scheme, called LEDR (level-encoded dual-rail), was introduced to combine advantages of both transition signaling and four-phase (19).

Asynchronous pipelines have been designed for numerous applications: multiplication (14,138), division (158) and DSP (9,159). The Williams and Horowitz self-timed divider (158) is especially impressive: The fabricated chip was twice as fast as comparable synchronous designs.

Research on asynchronous pipelines and datapaths is now proceeding in many directions. Several new asynchronous pipelining schemes have been proposed. Some emphasize low-power (160,161), whereas others emphasize high performance (161–164). In addition, several generalizations to asynchronous pipeline structures have been proposed: *rings* (156), *multirings* (165), and *two-dimensional micropipelines* (166). Techniques to reduce the communication overhead between stages have been developed (21,156,167). Liebchen and Gopalakrishnan have proposed a *reordering pipeline* (168) which allows the freezing and dynamic reordering of data within the pipe using "LockC" elements. Finally, low-power micropipeline structures have been introduced using adaptive scaling of supply voltage (169).

Whereas pipelining is fundamental to high-performance systems, *sequencing* is the basic control operation in lower-performance nonpipelined systems. A number of sequencer designs have been proposed (9,37,140,170–173).

There has been much other recent research on asynchronous datapaths, beyond work on pipelines and sequencers. Much of this work is focused on *low-power design*, including designs for a digital compact cassette (DCC) error corrector (142), an infrared communications chip (95), an FFT (174), a FIR filter bank (175), and cache (176), microprocessor (157,177), and memory designs (178). Others have developed techniques which use novel low-power devices, such as RSFQ (179).

Nowick introduced a method for *high-performance design*, called *speculative completion*, which uses a single-rail bundled data path but also allows early completion (180). The method uses a multi-slotted matched delay, where several of the delays are faster than the worst case. These speculative delays allow early completion and are disabled for worst-case data. The method has been applied to a high-performance Brent–Kung adder (181); SPICE results indicate a 19–29% performance improvement over a comparable synchronous design.

Other data-path research has focused on architectures and protocols for *chip-to-chip communication*, including recent methods by Greenstreet (182) and Roiene (183). An architecture for communication between synchronous and asynchronous chips has been developed by Chappel et al. (184).

Asynchronous Processor Design

Perhaps the greatest challenge in large-scale asynchronous design to date has been to combine the techniques for asynchronous controller and datapath synthesis, and build asynchronous processors. Asynchrony has, in fact, been present in processors from the early days when there was little distinction between synchronous and asynchronous circuits. Some level of persistent asynchrony has always been present, as memory systems have been typically asynchronous. With the advent of virtual memory and cache memory systems, there is significant uncertainty about when a memory access will be resolved. In today's systems, a cache hit takes a few cycles, a cache miss requires approximately 100 cycles, and a page miss takes 500,000 or more cycles to resolve. The result is that the processor–memory interface effectively uses a model delay and a four-cycle protocol where the request is associated with the presentation of an address and a read or write command. The acknowledge is a ready signal, indicating the requested operation has been completed. In a more direct fashion, machines such as the MU-5 and DDM1 (previously cited) have been constructed along more purely asynchronous lines.

However, only recently have asynchronous design techniques have been applied to the design of single-chip asynchronous microprocessors. Probably the very first asynchronous microprocessors were designed in the early 1980s by Chuck Seitz and his students at CalTech as class projects for his courses in asynchronous circuits. These processors were used in a series of parallel computers that spawned significant activity in the parallel-processing industry as well.

The first QDI asynchronous microprocessor was also developed at Caltech, by Martin et al. (157) in the late 1980s. The 16-bit design is almost fully quasi-delay-insensitive except for the memory interface. A 2-μ CMOS version consumed 145 mW at 5 V and 6.7 mW at 2 V. A 1.6-μ CMOS version consumed 200 mW at 5 V and 7.6 mW at 2 V. The architecture was later reimplemented in GaAs. Martin's processor design has had a major impact on the field, and has spurred many subsequent efforts. The processor operated correctly under a wide range of temperature and voltage, and included architectural and logic-level design decisions which grew directly off of the asynchronous methodology.

More recently, Furber and the AMULET group at Manchester University have fabricated two asynchronous implementations of the ARM microprocessor (10,154,155,185). The designs are based on micropipelined datapaths and are part of a large-scale investigation of low-power techniques. The project addresses issues such as caching, exceptions, and architectural optimization which are critical to the development of production-quality asynchronous machines. The Amulet1 used two-cycle protocols and was disappointing in terms of both power and performance in comparison to its synchronous ARM equivalent. This is not surprising because the Amulet1 was the first significant asynchronous design attempted by the Manchester group and the design experience gave them a significant data point for analysis. The result was that, even though two-cycle signaling is conceptually elegant, it resulted in circuits which were too large and slow and which consumed too much power for their intended ARM application.

This Amulet1 results forced the Manchester design team to explore other protocol options for the subsequent Amulet2 effort. A version of the Amulet2 called the Amulet2e (177) has been fabricated. The Amulet2e is an Amulet2 processor core (93,000 transistors) coupled with 4K bytes of memory, in a 128-pin package containing 454,000 transistors. It was fabricated in a 0.5 μ CMOS technology and operates at 3.3 V. The Amulet2e is intended for embedded controller applications. A number of architectural enhancements were made, including a jump target buffer and a flexible external interface called the *funnel*. The funnel permits 8-, 16-, and 32-bit external devices to be attached to the controller, as well as a DRAM-based main memory system. Another key difference is that the Amulet2e uses four-cycle signaling protocols, which results in improved performance, power consumption, and circuit areas. Although the power-consumption data has not yet been released, the performance of the Amulet2e is 38 Dhrystone MIPS, which is faster than the synchronous ARM710 but about half that of the recently announced ARM810, which uses the same process technology.

Sutherland, Sproull, Molnar, and others at Sun Labs have been developing an asynchronous *Counterflow Pipeline Processor* (29). The architecture is based on a novel looped micropipeline, which synchronizes instructions and data flowing in opposite directions. The processor makes careful use of arbiters to regulate the synchronization.

Brunvand developed the *NSR* RISC microprocessor (147) at the University of Utah using transition signaling for control, bundled data, and a micropipelined data path. The NSR was implemented using commercially available FPGA technology. The result of the NSR effort led to a more aggressive architecture called FRED (186,187) which was implemented to the level of structural VHDL and subsequently analyzed. FRED is perhaps the closest attempt to create an equivalent to the modern microprocessor in that it provided speculative execution and precise interrupts while utilizing a novel architecture that was inspired, or perhaps constrained, by asynchronous design techniques. FRED was an architectural study and, therefore, was not actually fabricated. Other micropipelined-based RISC designs have been proposed by David et al. (188) and Ginosar and Michell (189).

A delay-insensitive microprocessor, *TITAC*, has been developed by Nanya et al. at Tokyo Institute of Technology (190). The designers introduce several optimizations to improve performance. A different approach was proposed by Unger at Columbia University (170). His "computers without clocks" use traditional asynchronous state machines for control logic, and a building block approach to design rather than compilation schemes. This approach requires a spectrum of timing assumptions to ensure correct designs.

Finally, Dean's *STRiP* (self-timed RISC) processor at Stanford University combines synchronous and asynchronous features (1). The design uses synchronous functional units in a globally clocked pipeline. However, the clock rate may change dynamically based on the current contents of the pipeline, using a technique called *dynamic clocking*. The clock is also suspended during off-chip operations, such as input/output or access to a second-level cache. Using careful simulation, the design was shown to be almost twice as fast as a comparable synchronous design due solely to its asynchronous features.

Verification, Timing Analysis, and Testing

The above survey indicates an impressive surge of activity in the design of asynchronous controllers, datapaths, and processors. However, design techniques alone cannot make asynchronous circuits commercially viable. In synchronous design, many ancillary technology components are needed to ensure the correctness of designs, including verification, timing analysis, and testing. These techniques are especially critical for asynchronous design because of their inherent subtlety. This section briefly sketches some of the recent work on validation of asynchronous designs.

Formal Verification and Timing Analysis

Due to the large variety of asynchronous design approaches, it is difficult to find a unified approach to the analysis and verification of all asynchronous circuits. For speed-independent and delay-insensitive systems, though, Hoare's *CSP* (126) and Milner's *CCS* (191) have been especially effective as formal underpinnings.

Rem, Snepscheut, and Udding's *trace theory* (127), based on CSP, has been used both for specification and formal verification. In trace theory, the behavior of a concurrent system is described by the set of possible *traces*, or sequences of events, which may be observed. Each trace describes one possible interleaved behavior of the system. The traces are combined into a set, which defines the observable behavior of the system. Dill (31,192) and Ebergen (193) have built effective verification tools for SI and DI circuits based on trace theory. In Dill's theory, an implementation and specification are each modeled by trace sets. These sets are compared using a formal relation called *conformance*, which defines precisely when an implementation meets its specification. Dill has uncovered bugs in published circuits using the verifier. More efficient algorithms for approximate verification (allowing occasional false negatives) have been developed by Beerel et al. (194).

Dill's verifier effectively checks for safety violations (where a design has incorrect behavior) but does not check for liveness violations (where a design has deadlock or livelock). Dill also introduced a theory of *complete trace structures* (31), based on Buchi automata, which can model general liveness properties. Although these general verification algorithms may be too expensive to apply in practice, a verifier has been developed for a constrained class of specifications (195). Other methods use a restricted notion of liveness that can be easily checked (193,196,197). A method which uses Signal Graphs for verification of properties of speed-independent circuits has been proposed by Kishinevsky et al. (198). Another approach, by Kol et al. (199), uses *state charts* to verify both safety and liveness properties.

An alternative verification method based on CCS has been proposed by Birtwistle et al. (195,200). CCS has been successfully used for the specification of several asynchronous designs, including a token-ring arbiter and SCSI controller. Specifications can then be checked for deadlock, safety, and liveness properties using a modal logic. A substantial specification has been developed for the AMULET processor (201) with detailed models for the different instruction classes.

The above verification techniques handle SI and DI circuits and protocols and therefore are not concerned with timing. However, timing is critical for the analysis and verification of many asynchronous systems. A general model for timed systems was introduced by Alur and Dill (202). Timing analysis and verification methods for asynchronous state machines with bounded delays were developed by Devadas et al. (203) and Chakraborty et al. (204,205). Methods using Timed Petri Nets have been developed by Rokicki (150), Semenov et al. (206), and Verlind et al. (207). In addition, Williams (156) and Burns (36) have introduced general methods to analyze the performance of systems. A notion of *timing-reliability* was proposed by Kuwako and Nanya (208). Timing and hazard analysis tools have been developed by Ashkinazy et al. (209). Other recent work has focused on timing analysis to determine minimum and maximum separation of events in a concurrent circuit or system (210–212). Such analysis can aid in both the optimization and verification of asynchronous designs.

Testing and Synthesis-for-Testability

Whereas formal verification is used to validate designs, testing is needed to validate the correctness of fabricated implementations. Testing and synthesis-for-testability play a major role in the industrial production of synchronous chips. However, the testing of asynchronous circuits is complicated by their special design constraints. For example, asynchronous circuits may use redundant logic to eliminate hazards, but redundant logic makes testing more difficult.

Initial results on the testing of speed-independent circuits include work by Beerel and Meng (213) and Martin and Hazewindus (214). These articles indicate that certain classes of speed-independent circuits are "self-testing" with respect to stuck-at faults, where certain faults will cause the circuit to halt. Beerel and Meng generalized their approach to handle stuck-at faults in timed control circuits (215).

A general synthesis-for-testability method which considers both stuck-at and path-delay faults in combinational circuits was proposed by Keutzer et al. (216). The method uses algebraic transformations to produce hazard-free and fully testable multilevel logic. This work was extended by Nowick et al. (217), to include a richer set of transformations and to handle a more general class of hazards.

Subsequent research has focused on testing of handshaking circuits and micropipelines. Roncken et al. (218,219) at Philips Research Laboratories have developed techniques and tools for a partial scan of handshaking circuits. The method is now used in the Tangram synthesis compiler. A novelty of the approach is that testability is ensured at the highest level i.e., by modifying the Tangram program specification. The method was used in the design of a DCC error corrector, where it led to 99.9% stuck-at output fault coverage at an expense of less than 3% additional area (142,219). More realistic fault models, such as for I_{DDQ} testing, have recently been addressed as well (220).

The most prevalent "design-for-test" technique in the synchronous domain has been the use of a serial *scan path* technique, which effectively creates a shift register out of the storage components on the chip. The external interface provides both read and write capability to this shift register. The method works well for synchronous systems, as the concept of state corresponds to the contents of the storage elements in the circuit after a particular clock. However, the inherent *temporally decoupled* nature of asynchronous circuits tends to make the concept of "total system state" counterproductive. The implication is that the design for test methods developed for synchronous circuits are not appropriate for asynchronous systems. However, a surprisingly analogous technique was developed by Khoche (221,222). This technique applies to macromodular, micropipelined self-timed circuits. The key idea is that while the circuits operate asynchronously in normal mode, the scan mode operation is synchronous and the clock propagates in the backward direction along the micropipeline. Khoche demonstrated that the overhead of adding *scanability* to asynchronous circuits is commensurate with the overhead for synchronous circuits. More recent approaches to testing micropipelines have been developed as well (223,224).

An issue related to testing is *initializability*, which is the process of driving a circuit at power-up to a known state. Initializability is also often required by automatic test-pattern generators. Two recent methods for asynchronous initializability have been developed (225,226).

One interesting area of asynchronous circuit testing that is just beginning to be studied is the issue of hazards. Asynchronous circuits by nature often contain redundant logic to prevent hazards. This is a particularly problematic issue with respect to testing; namely, if the circuit contains redundant logic to prevent hazards, then how is this redundancy tested at the chip's external pins? Fundamentally, a solution requires that redundancy path analysis connections be exported to the pad ring of the chip. The increase of area, power consumption, and packaging costs of the device to support this capability directly is a problem. However, integrating this analysis capability within the scan path is an interesting option. The solution and its complexity remain open research issues.

CONCLUSIONS

This article has provided an introduction to the current (1997) state of the art of asynchronous circuit design. The focus has been on motivations, fundamental concepts, design methods, and the physical artifacts and results that have been the result of these design styles.

The current status of asynchronous circuits is that it is a growing research area that has yet to have significant impact on the design of commercial integrated circuits. However, there are significant signs that asynchronous circuits may become more of a mainstream discipline in the future. Serious asynchronous circuit efforts exist in corporate research labs, namely in Sun Microsystems, Philips, and Intel. The goals of these groups vary from increased performance at Sun and Intel, to reduced power consumption at Philips.

Another promising sign is the rapid restructuring of the semiconductor design and electronic design automation (EDA) companies. The industry leaders have joined together to form the **VSI Alliance**. VSI stands for virtual socket interface, and the purpose of the alliance is to create standards for design technology to be exchanged and reused easily. The goal is to prevent the need to redesign circuits that already exist in another company. Rapid changes in the marketplace result in rapidly decreasing design cycle requirements. The result is that companies simply do not have the time to design each new product from scratch. It is becoming more cost-effective to buy macrocells and processor cores and combine them to create a new design. The high level of competition however requires that new products take full advantage of the latest integrated circuit technology. The new technology is faster but creates a new set of timing problems which must be managed carefully in a synchronous design. The inherent ease of asynchronous module composition nicely fits the requirements of this new industry model. The composability advantage is directly due to the fact that asynchronous circuits explicitly export their timing requirements at their interfaces via their signaling protocols.

More fundamental motivations for asynchronous design come from basic integrated circuit technology trends. As transistor sizes shrink and as chips become significantly larger, the cost of distributing increasingly faster clock frequencies with minimal skew becomes too expensive. The expense comes both in terms of reduced performance and increased power consumption. It is highly unlikely that one billion transistor chips will be both cost-effective and synchronous. This article has provided a number of options that may well be the basis for the future.

REFERENCES

1. M. E. Dean, "STRiP: A Self-Timed RISC Processor Architecture," Technical Report, Stanford University (1992).
2. H. B. Bakoglu, *Circuits, Interconnections, and Packaging for VLSI.* Addison-Wesley, Reading, MA, 1990.
3. R. L. Sites, *Alpha Architecture Reference Manual*, Digital Equipment Corporation, 1992.
4. D. W. Dobberpuhl et al., "A 200-MHz 64-Bit Dual-Issue CMOS Microprocessor," *Digital Tech. J., 4*(4), 35–50 (1993).
5. M. Afhahi and C. Svensson, "Performance of Sychronous and Asynchronous Schemes for VLSI Systems," *IEEE Trans. Computers, C-41*(7), 858–872 (1992).
6. V. L. Chi, "Salphasic Distribution of Clock Signals for Synchronous Systems," *IEEE Trans. Computers, C-43*(5), 597–602 (1994).

7. R. D. Rettberg, W. R. Crowther, P. P. Carvey, and R. S. Tomlinson, "The Monarch Parallel Processor Hardware Design," *Computer, 23*(4), 18–30 (1990).

8. C. L. Seitz, "System Timing," in *Introduction to VLSI Systems*, C. Mead and L. Conway (eds.), Addison-Wesley, Reading, MA, 1980.

9. K. van Berkel, *Handshake Circuits. An Asynchronous Architecture for VLSI Programming*, Cambridge University Press, Cambridge, 1993.

10. S. B. Furber, P. Day, J. D. Garside, N. C. Paver, and J. V. Woods, "A Micropipelined ARM," in *Proceedings of VLSI 93*, September 1993, pp. 5.4.1–5.4.10.

11. T. J. Chaney, S. M. Ornstein, and W. M. Littlefield, "Beware the Synchronizer," in *IEEE Sixth International Computer Conference*, 1972, pp. 317–319.

12. W. B. Ackerman and J. B. Dennis, "VAL — A Value-Oriented Algorithmic Language Preliminary Reference Manual," Technical Report LCS/TR-218, Massachusetts Institute Technology, Computer Science Department (1979).

13. A. L. Davis, "The Architecture and System Method of DDM-1: A Recursively-Structured Data Driven Machine," in *Proc. Fifth Annual Symposium on Computer Architecture*, 1978.

14. I. E. Sutherland, "Micropipelines," *Commun. ACM, 32*(6), 720–738 (1989).

15. S. B. Furber and P. Woods, "Four-Phase Micropipeline Latch Control Circuits," *IEEE Trans. VLSI Syst., VS-4*(2), 247–253 (1996).

16. A. Davis, B. Coates, and K. Stevens, "Automatic Synthesis of Fast Compact Self-Timed Control Circuits," in *1993 IFIP Working Conference on Asynchronous Design Methodologies*, 1993.

17. K. S. Stevens, S. V. Robison, and A. L. Davis, "The Post Office — Communication Support for Distributed Ensemble Architectures," in *Sixth International Conference on Distributed Computing Systems*, 1986.

18. T. Verhoeff, "Delay-Insensitive Codes — An Overview," *Distributed Computing, 3*(1), 1–8 (1988).

19. M. E. Dean, T. E. Williams, and D. L. Dill, "Efficient Self-Timing with Level-Encoded 2-Phase Dual-Rail (LEDR)," in *Advanced Research in VLSI: Proceedings of the 1991 University of California Santa Cruz Conference*, Carlo Sequin (ed.), The MIT Press, Cambridge, MA, 1991, pp. 55–70.

20. K. Hwang, *Computer Arithmetic: Principles, Architecture, and Design,* John Wiley and Sons, New York, 1979.

21. M. E. Dean, D. L. Dill, and M. Horowitz, "Self-Timed Logic Using Current-Sensing Completion Detection (CSCD)," in *Proceedings of the IEEE International Conference on Computer Design*, IEEE Computer Society Press, Los Alamitos, CA, 1991.

22. S. H. Unger, *Asynchronous Sequential Switching Circuits*, Wiley-Interscience, New York, 1969.

23. C.-J. Seger, "A Bounded Delay Race Model," in *Proceedings of the IEEE International Conference on Computer-Aided Design*, IEEE Computer Society Press, Los Alamitos, CA, 1989, pp. 130–133.

24. R. E. Miller, *Switching Theory. Volume II: Sequential Circuits and Machines*, John Wiley and Sons, New York, 1965.

25. J. A. Brzozowski and J. C. Ebergen, "Recent Developments in the Design of Asynchronous Circuits," Technical Report CS-89-18, University of Waterloo, Computer Science Department (1989).

26. E. J. McCluskey, *Introduction to the Theory of Switching Circuits*, McGraw-Hill, New York, 1965.

27. E. J. McCluskey, *Logic Design Principles: With Emphasis on Testable Semicustom Circuits*, Prentice-Hall, Englewood Cliffs, NJ, 1986.

28. W. A. Clark, "Macromodular Computer Systems," in *Proceedings of the Spring Joint Computer Conference, AFIPS*, April 1967.

29. R. F. Sproull, I. E. Sutherland, and C. E. Molnar, "The Counterflow Pipeline Processor Architecture," *IEEE Design Test Computers, 11*(3), 48–59 (1994).

30. J. T. Udding, "A Formal Model for Defining and Classifying Delay-Insensitive Circuits and Systems," *Distributed Computing, 1*(4), 197–204 (1986).

31. D. L. Dill, *Trace Theory for Automatic Hierarchical Verification of Speed-Independent Circuits*, MIT Press, Cambridge, MA, 1989.

32. A. J. Martin, "The Limitation to Delay-Insensitivity in Asynchronous Circuits," in *Advanced Research in VLSI: Proceedings of the Sixth MIT Conference*, W. J. Dally (ed.), MIT Press, Cambridge, MA, 1990, pp. 263–278.

33. J. A. Brzozowski and J. C. Ebergen, "On the Delay-Sensitivity of Gate Networks," *IEEE Trans. Computers, C-41*(11), 1349–1360 (1992).

34. J. C. Ebergen, "A Formal Approach to Designing Delay-Insensitive Circuits," *Distributed Computing, 5*(3), 107–119 (1991).

35. M. B. Josephs and J. T. Udding, "An Overview of D-I Algebra," in *Proceedings of the Twenty-Sixth Annual Hawaii International Conference on System Sciences*, IEEE Computer Society Press, Los Alamitos, CA, 1993, Vol. I, pp. 329–338.

36. S. M. Burns, "Performance Analysis and Optimization of Asynchronous Circuits," Technical Report Caltech-CS-TR-91-01, California Institute of Technology (1991).

37. A. J. Martin, "Programming in VLSI: From Communicating Processes to Delay-Insensitive Circuits," in *Developments in Concurrency and Communication*, C. A. R. Hoare (ed.), UT Year of Programming Institute on Concurrent Programming, Addison-Wesley, Reading, MA, 1990, pp. 1–64.

38. K. van Berkel, "Beware the Isochronic Fork," *INTEGRATION, 13*(2), 103–128 (1992).

39. P. A. Beerel and T. Meng, "Automatic Gate-Level Synthesis of Speed-Independent Circuits," in *Proceedings of the IEEE/ACM International Conference on Computer-Aided Design*, IEEE Computer Society Press, Los Alamitos, 1992, pp. 581–586.

40. A. Kondratyev, M. Kishinevsky, B. Lin, P. Vanbekbergen, and A. Yakovlev, "Basic Gate Implementation of Speed-Independent Circuits," in *Proceedings of the 31st ACM/IEEE Design Automation Conference*, ACM, New York, 1994, pp. 56–62.

41. C. Myers and T. Meng, "Synthesis of Timed Asynchronous Circuits," in *Proceedings of the IEEE International Conference on Computer Design*, IEEE Computer Society Press, Los Alamitos, CA, 1992; pp. 279–284.

42. E. B. Eichelberger, "Hazard Detection in Combinational and Sequential Switching Circuits," *IBM J. Res. Devel., 9*(2), 90–99 (1965).

43. J. G. Bredeson and P. T. Hulina, "Elimination of Static and Dynamic Hazards for Multiple Input Changes in Combinational Switching Circuits," *Inform. Control, 20*, 114–224 (1972).

44. J. Beister, "A Unified Approach to Combinational Hazards," *IEEE Trans. Computers, C-23*(6), 566–575 (1974).

45. J. Frackowiak, "Methoden der analyse und synthese von hasardarmen schaltnetzen mit minimalen kosten I. *Elektronische Informationsverarbeitung Kybernetik, 10*(2/3), 149–187 (1974).

46. S. M. Nowick and D. L. Dill, "Exact Two-Level Minimization of Hazard-Free Logic with Multiple-Input Changes," *IEEE Trans. Computer-Aided Design Integrated Circuits Syst., 14*(8), 986–997 (1995).

47. M. Theobald, S. M. Nowick, and T. Wu, "Espresso-HF: A Heuristic Hazard-Free Minimizer for Two-Level Logic," in *33rd ACM/IEEE Design Automation Conference*, June 1996, pp. 71–76.

48. J. G. Bredeson, "Synthesis of Multiple-Input Change Hazard-Free Combinational Switching Circuits Without Feedback," *Int. J. Electron. (GB), 39*(6), 615–624 (1975).

49. D. S. Kung, "Hazard-Non-increasing Gate-Level Optimization Algorithms," in *Pro-*

ceedings of the IEEE/ACM International Conference on Computer-Aided Design, IEEE Computer Society Press, Los Alamitos, CA, 1992, pp. 631–634.

50. B. Lin and S. Devadas, "Synthesis of Hazard-Free Multi-level Logic under Multiple-Input Changes from Binary Decision Diagrams," in *Proceedings of the IEEE/ACM International Conference on Computer-Aided Design*, IEEE Computer Society Press, Los Alamitos, CA, 1994, pp. 542–549.

51. P. Siegel, G. De Micheli, and D. Dill, "Technology Mapping for Generalized Fundamental-Mode Asynchronous Designs," in *Proceedings of the 30th ACM/IEEE Design Automation Conference*, ACM, New York, 1993, pp. 61–67.

52. P. Kudva, G. Gopalakrishnan, H. Jacobson, and S. M. Nowick, "Synthesis of Hazard-Free Customized CMOS Complex-Gate Networks under Multiple-Input Changes," in *33rd ACM/IEEE Design Automation Conference*, June 1996, pp. 77–82.

53. P. A. Beerel, K. Y. Yun, and W. C. Chou, "Optimizing Average-Case Delay in Technology Mapping of Burst-Mode Circuits," in *Proceedings of the International Symposium on Advanced Research in Asynchronous Circuits and Systems (Async96)*, IEEE Computer Society Press, Los Alamitos, CA, 1996, pp. 244–260.

54. T. J. Chaney and C. E. Molnar, "Anomalous Behaviour of Synchronizer and Arbiter Circuits," *IEEE Trans. Computers, C-22*(4), 421–422 (1973).

55. A. L. Davis, B. Coates, and K. Stevens, "The Post Office Experience: Designing a Large Asynchronous Chip," in *Proceedings of the Twenty-Sixth Annual Hawaii International Conference on System Sciences*, IEEE Computer Society Press, Los Alamitos, CA, Vol. I, pp. 409–418.

56. A. L. Davis, "Synthesizing Asynchronous Circuits: Practice and Experience," in *Asynchronous Digital Circuit Design*, 1995, pp. 104–150.

57. R. Shapiro and H. Genrich, "Formal Verification of an Arbiter Cascade," MetaSoftware, Inc. Cambridge, MA, 1992.

58. R. Shapiro and H. Genrich, "A Design of a Cascadable Nacking Arbiter," MetaSoftware, Inc. Cambridge, MA, 1993.

59. A. Yakovlev, A. Petrov, and L. Lavagno, "A Low Latency Asynchronous Arbitration Circuit," *IEEE Trans. VLSI Syst, VS-2*(3), 372–377 (1994).

60. D. A. Huffman, "The Synthesis of Sequential Switching Circuits," *J. Franklin Inst., 257*(3), 161–190 (1954).

61. D. A. Huffman, "The Synthesis of Sequential Switching Circuits," *J. Franklin Inst., 257*(4), 275–303 (1954).

62. D. E. Muller and W. S. Bartky, "A Theory of Asynchronous Circuits I," Digital Computer Laboratory 75, University of Illinois (November 1956).

63. D. E. Muller and W. S. Bartky, "A Theory of Asynchronous Circuits II," Digital Computer Laboratory 78, University of Illinois (March 1957).

64. E. Brunvand and R. F. Sproull, "Translating Concurrent Programs into Delay-Insensitive Circuits," in *Proceedings of the IEEE International Conference on Computer-Aided Design*, IEEE Computer Society Press, Los Alamitos, CA, 1989, pp. 262–265.

65. C. H. van Berkel and R. W. J. J. Saeijs, "Compilation of Communicating Processes into Delay-Insensitive Circuits," in *Proceedings of the IEEE International Conference on Computer Design*, IEEE Computer Society Press, Los Alamitos, CA, 1988, pp. 157–162.

66. C. L. Seitz, "Graph Representations for Logical Machines," Ph.D. thesis, MIT (January 1971).

67. S. H. Unger, Asynchronous Sequential Switching Circuits with Unrestricted Input Changes," *IEEE Trans. Computers, C-20*(12), 1437–1444 (1971).

68. A. D. Friedman and P. R. Menon, "Synthesis of Asynchronous Sequential Circuits with Multiple-Input Changes," *IEEE Trans. Computers, C-17*(6), 559–566 (1968).

69. G. Mago, "Realization Methods for Asynchronous Sequential Circuits," *IEEE Trans. Computers, C-20*(3), 290–297 (1971).

70. C. N. Liu, "A State Variable Assignment Method for Asynchronous Sequential Switching Circuits," *J. ACM, 10,* 209–216 (1963).

71. J. H. Tracey, "Internal State Assignments for Asynchronous Sequential Machines," *IEEE Trans. Electron. Computers, EC-15*, 551–560 (1966).

72. D. B. Armstrong, A. D. Friedman, and P. R. Menon, "Realization of Asynchronous Sequential Circuits Without Inserted Delay Elements," *IEEE Trans. Computers, C-17*(2), 129–134.

73. A. B. Hayes, "Stored State Asynchronous Sequential Circuits," *IEEE Trans. Computers, C-30*(8), 596–600 (1981).

74. M. A. Tapia, "Synthesis of Asynchronous Sequential Systems Using Boolean Calculus," in *14th Asilomar Conference on Circuits, Systems and Computers*, November 1980, pp. 205–209.

75. F. Aghdasi, "Synthesis of Asynchronous Sequential Machines for VLSI Applications," in *Proceedings of the 1991 International Conference on Concurrent Engineering and Electronic Design Automation (CEEDA)*, March 1991, pp. 55–59.

76. H. Y. H. Chuang and S. Das, "Synthesis of Multiple-Input Change Asynchronous Machines Using Controlled Excitation and Flip-Flops," *IEEE Trans. Computers, C-22*(12), 1103–1109 (1973).

77. C. A. Rey and J. Vaucher, "Self-Synchronized Asynchronous Sequential Machines," *IEEE Trans. Computers, C-23*(12), 1306–1311 (1974).

78. S. H. Unger, "Self-Synchronizing Circuits and Nonfundamental Mode Operation," *IEEE Trans. Computers, C-26*(3), 278–281 (1977).

79. M. Ladd and W. P. Birmingham, "Synthesis of Multiple-Input Change Asynchronous Finite State Machines," in *Proceedings of the 28th ACM/IEEE Design Automation Conference*, ACM, New York, 1991, pp. 309–314.

80. O. Yenersoy, "Synthesis of Asynchronous Machines Using Mixed-Operation Mode," *IEEE Trans. Computers, C-28*(4), 325–329 (1979).

81. J.-S. Chiang and D. Radhakrishnan, "Hazard-Free Design of Mixed Operating Mode Asynchronous Sequential Circuits," *Int. J. Electron., 68*(1), 23–37 (1990).

82. A. L. Davis, "A Data-Driven Machine Architecture Suitable for VLSI Implementation," in *Proceedings of the Caltech Conference on Very Large Scale Integration*, C. L. Seitz (ed.), January 1979, pp. 479–494.

83. S. M. Nowick and D. L. Dill, "Synthesis of Asynchronous State Machines Using a Local Clock," in *Proceedings of the IEEE International Conference on Computer Design*, IEEE Computer Society Press, Los Alamitos, CA, 1991, pp. 192–197.

84. S. M. Nowick, "Automatic Synthesis of Burst-Mode Asynchronous Controllers," Technical Report, Stanford University (March 1993). Ph.D. thesis (available as Stanford University Computer Systems Laboratory Technical Report, CSL-TR-95-686, Dec. 95).

85. S. M. Nowick, M. E. Dean, D. L. Dill, and M. Horowitz, "The Design of a High-Performance Cache Controller: A Case Study in Asynchronous Synthesis," *INTEGRATION, 15*(3), 241–262 (1993).

86. S. M. Nowick, K. Y. Yun, and D. L. Dill, "Practical Asynchronous Controller Design," in *Proceedings of the IEEE International Conference on Computer Design*, IEEE Computer Society Press, Los Alamitos, CA, 1992, pp. 341–345.

87. R. M. Fuhrer, B. Lin, and S. M. Nowick, "Symbolic Hazard-Free Minimization and Encoding of Asynchronous Finite State Machines," in *IEEE/ACM International Conference on Computer-Aided Design (ICCAD)*, November 1995, pp. 604–611.

88. R. Rudell and A. Sangiovanni-Vincentelli, "Multiple-Valued Optimization for PLA

Optimization," *IEEE Trans. Computer-Aided Design Integrated Circuits Syst., 6*(5), 727–750 (1987).

89. K. Y. Yun and D. L. Dill, "Automatic Synthesis of 3D Asynchronous Finite-State Machines," in *Proceedings of the IEEE/ACM International Conference on Computer-Aided Design*, IEEE Computer Society Press, Los Alamitos, CA, 1992.

90. K. Y. Yun and D. L. Dill, "A High-Performance Asynchronous SCSI Controller," in *Proceedings of the IEEE International Conference on Computer Design*, IEEE Computer Society Press, Los Alamitos, CA, 1995, pp. 44–49.

91. S. M. Nowick and B. Coates, "UCLOCK: Automated Design of High-Performance Unclocked State Machines," in *Proceedings of the IEEE International Conference on Computer Design*, IEEE Computer Society Press, Los Alamitos, CA, 1994, pp. 434–441.

92. K. Y. Yun, D. L. Dill, and S. M. Nowick, "Practical Generalizations of Asynchronous State Machines," in *The 1993 European Conference on Design Automation*, IEEE Computer Society Press, Los Alamitos, CA, 1993, pp. 525–530.

93. K. Y. Yun and D. L. Dill, "Unifying Synchronous/Asynchronous State Machine Synthesis," in *Proceedings of the IEEE/ACM International Conference on Computer-Aided Design*, IEEE Computer Society Press, Los Alamitos, CA, 1993, pp. 255–260.

94. K. Y. Yun, B. Lin, D. L. Dill, and S. Devadas, "Performance-Driven Synthesis of Asynchronous Controllers," in *IEEE/ACM International Conference on Computer-Aided Design (ICCAD)*, November 1994.

95. A. Marshall, B. Coates, and P. Siegel, "The Design of an Asynchronous Communications Chip," *IEEE Design Test, 11*(2), 8–21 (1994).

96. P. Kudva, G. Gopalakrishnan, and H. Jacobson, "A Technique for Synthesizing Distributed Burst-Mode Circuits," in *33rd ACM/IEEE Design Automation Conference*, June 1996.

97. J. L. Peterson, *Petri Net Theory and the Modeling of Systems*, Prentice-Hall, Englewood Cliffs, NJ, 1981.

98. S. S. Patil, "An Asynchronous Logic Array," Technical Report Technical Memorandom 62, Massachusetts Institute of Technology, Project MAC (1975).

99. F. Commoner, A. Holt, S. Even, and A. Pnueli, "Marked Directed Graphs," *J. Computer Syst. Sci., 5*(5), 511–523 (1971).

100. C. L. Seitz, "Asynchronous Machines Exhibiting Concurrency," in *Conference Record of the Project MAC Conference on Concurrent Systems and Parallel Computation*, 1970.

101. L. Y. Rosenblum and A. V. Yakovlev, "Signal Graphs: From Self-Timed to Timed Ones," in *Proceedings of International Workshop on Timed Petri Nets, Torino, Italy*, IEEE Computer Society Press, Los Alamitos, CA, 1985, pp. 199–207.

102. P. Vanbekbergen, F. Catthoor, G. Goossens, and H. De Man, "Optimized Synthesis of Asynchronous Control Circuits from Graph-Theoretic Specifications," in *Proceedings of the IEEE International Conference on Computer-Aided Design*, IEEE Computer Society Press, Los Alamitos, CA, 1990, pp. 184–187.

103. C. E. Molnar, T.-P. Fang, and F. U. Rosenberger, "Synthesis of Delay-Insensitive Modules," in *Proceedings of the 1985 Chapel Hill Conference on Very Large Scale Integration*, Henry Fuchs (ed.), CSP, Inc., 1985, pp. 67–86.

104. T.-A. Chu, "Synthesis of Self-Timed VLSI Circuits from Graph-Theoretic Specifications," Technical Report MIT-LCS-TR-393, Massachusetts Institute of Technology (1987).

105. T.-A. Chu, "Automatic Synthesis and Verification of Hazard-Free Control Circuits from Asynchronous Finite State Machine Specifications," in *Proceedings of the IEEE International Conference on Computer Design*, IEEE Computer Society Press, Los Alamitos, CA, 1992, pp. 407–413.

106. T. H.-Y. Meng, R. W. Brodersen, and D. G. Messerschmitt, "Automatic Synthesis of Asynchronous Circuits from High-Level Specifications," *IEEE Trans. Computer-Aided Design Integrated Circuits Syst.*, 8(11), 1185-1205 (1989).

107. C. W. Moon, P. R. Stephan, and R. K. Brayton, "Synthesis of Hazard-Free Asynchronous Circuits from Graphical Specifications," in *Proceedings of the IEEE International Conference on Computer-Aided Design*, IEEE Computer Society Press, Los Alamitos, CA, 1991, pp. 322-325.

108. A. V. Yakovlev, "On Limitations and Extensions of STG Model for Designing Asynchronous Control Circuits," in *Proceedings of the IEEE International Conference on Computer Design,* IEEE Computer Society Press, Los Alamitos, CA, 1992, pp. 396-400.

109. J. Cortadella, L. Lavagno, P. Vanbekbergen, and A. Yakovlev, "Designing Asynchronous Circuits from Behavioural Specifications with Internal Conflicts," in *Proceedings of the International Symposium on Advanced Research in Asynchronous Circuits and Systems* (*Async94*), IEEE Computer Society Press, Los Alamitos, CA, 1994, pp. 106-115.

110. V. I. Varshavsky, M. A. Kishinevsky, V. B. Marakhovsky, V.A. Peschansky, L. Y. Rosenblum, A. R. Taubin, and B. S. Tzirlin, *Self-timed Control of Concurrent Processes.* Kluwer Academic Publishers, Boston, 1990 (Russian edition: 1986).

111. L. Lavagno, C. W. Moon, R. K. Brayton, and A. Sangiovanni-Vincentelli, "Solving the State Assignment Problem for Signal Transition Graphs," in *Proceedings of the 29th IEEE/ACM Design Automation Conference*, IEEE Computer Society Press, Los Alamitos, CA, 1992, pp. 568-572.

112. P. Vanbekbergen, B. Lin, G. Goossens, and H. De Man, "A Generalized State Assignment Theory for Transformations on Signal Transition Graphs," in *Proceedings of the IEEE/ACM International Conference on Computer-Aided Design*, IEEE Computer Society, Los Alamitos, CA, 1992, pp. 112-117.

113. T.-A. Chu, N. Mani, and C. K. C. Leung, "An Efficient Critical Race-Free State Assignment Technique for Asynchronous Finite State Machines," in *Proceedings of the 30th ACM/IEEE Design Automation Conference*, ACM, New York, 1993, pp. 2-6.

114. R. Puri and J. Gu, "Area Efficient Synthesis of Asynchronous Interface Circuits," in *Proceedings of the IEEE International Conference on Computer Design*, IEEE Computer Society Press, Los Alamitos, CA, 1994, pp. 212-216.

115. R. Puri and J. Gu, "A Modular Partitioning Approach of Asynchronous Circuit Synthesis," in *Proceedings of the 31st ACM/IEEE Design Automation Conference*, ACM, New York, 1994, pp. 63-69.

116. K.-J. Lin and C.-S. Lin, "Automatic Synthesis of Asynchronous Circuits," in *Proceedings of the 28th ACM/IEEE Design Automation Conference*, ACM, New York, 1991, pp. 296-301.

117. J. Cortadella, M. Kishinevsky, A. Kondratyev, L. Lavagno, and A. Yakovlev, "Complete State Encoding Based on the Theory of Regions," in *Proceedings of the International Symposium on Advanced Research in Asynchronous Circuits and Systems* (*Async96*), IEEE Computer Society Press, Los Alamitos, CA, 1996, pp. 36-47.

118. J. Cortadella, M. Kishinevsky, A. Kondratyev, L. Lavagno, and A. Yakovlev, "Methodology and Tools for State Encoding in Asynchronous Circuit Synthesis," in *33rd ACM/IEEE Design Automation Conference*, June 1996.

119. M. L. Yu and P. A. Subrahmanyam, "A Path-Oriented Approach for Reducing Hazards in Asynchronous Designs," in *Proceedings of the 29th IEEE/ACM Design Automation Conference*, IEEE Computer Society Press, Los Alamitos, CA, 1992, pp. 239-244.

120. L. Lavagno, K. Keutzer, and A. Sangiovanni-Vincentelli, "Algorithms for Synthesis of

Hazard-Free Asynchronous Circuits," in *Proceedings of the 28th ACM/IEEE Design Automation Conference*, New York, 1991, pp. 302–308.

121. L. Lavagno and A. Sangiovanni-Vincentelli. *Algorithms for synthesis and testing of asynchronous circuits*. Kluwer Academic, 1993.

122. E. M. Sentovich, "SIS: A System for Sequential Circuit Synthesis," Technical Report UCB/ERL M92/41, UC Berkeley, Dept. of EECS (May 1992).

123. M. A. Kishinevsky, A. Y. Kondratyev, A. R. Taubin, and V. I. Varshavsky, *Concurrent Hardware: The Theory and Practice of Self-Timed Design*. John Wiley and Sons Ltd., London, 1994.

124. C. Ykman-Couvreur, B. Lin, and H. De Man, "ASSASSIN: A Synthesis System for Asynchronous Control Circuits," Technical report, IMEC Laboratory (September 1994); user and tutorial manual.

125. S. M. Burns, "General Condition for the Decomposition of State Holding Elements," in *Proceedings of the International Symposium on Advanced Research in Asynchronous Circuits and Systems (Async96)*, IEEE Computer Society Press, Los Alamitos, CA, 1996, pp. 48–57.

126. C. A. R. Hoare, "Communicating Sequential Processes," *Commun. ACM, 21*(8), 666–677 (1978).

127. M. Rem, J. L. A. van de Snepscheut, and J. T. Udding, "Trace Theory and the Definition of Hierarchical Components," in *Proceedings of the Third Caltech Conference on Very Large Scale Integration*, R. Bryant (ed.), CSP, Inc., 1983, pp. 225–239.

128. I. Benko and J. C. Ebergen, "Delay-Insensitive Solutions to the Committee Problem," in *Proceedings of the International Symposium on Advanced Research in Asynchronous Circuits and Systems (Async94)*, IEEE Computer Society Press, Los Alamitos, CA, 1994, pp. 228–237.

129. M. B. Josephs, "Receptive Process Theory," *Acta Inform., 29*, 17–31 (1992).

130. W. C. Mallon and J. T. Udding, "Using Metrics for Proof Rules for Recursively Defined Delay-Insensitive Specifications," in *Proceedings of the International Symposium on Advanced Research in Asynchronous Circuits and Systems (Async97)*, IEEE Computer Society Press, Los Alamitos, CA, 1997.

131. M. B. Josephs, P. G. Lucassen, J. T. Udding, and T. Verhoeff, "Formal Design of an Asynchronous DSP Counterflow Pipeline: A Case Study in Handshake Algebra," in *Proccedings of the International Symposium on Advanced Research in Asynchronous Circuits and Systems (Async94)*, IEEE Computer Society Press, Los Alamitos, CA, 1994, pp. 206–215.

132. P. G. Lucassen and J. T. Udding, "On the Correctness of the Sproull Counterflow Pipeline Processor," in *Proceedings of the International Symposium on Advanced Research in Asynchronous Circuits and Systems (Async96)*, IEEE Computer Society Press, Los Alamitos, CA, 1996, pp. 112–120.

133. P. Patra and D. S. Fussell, "Efficient Building Blocks for Delay Insensitive Circuits," in *Proceedings of the International Symposium on Advanced Research in Asynchronous Circuits and Systems (Async94)*, IEEE Computer Society Press, Los Alamitos, CA, 1994, pp. 196–205.

134. A. J. Martin, "Compiling Communicating Processes into Delay-Insensitive VLSI Circuits," *Distributed Computing, 1*, 226–234 (1986).

135. S. M. Burns and A. J. Martin, "Syntax-Directed Translation of Concurrent Programs into Self-Timed Circuits," in *Advanced Research in VLSI: Proceedings of the Fifth MIT Conference*, J. Allen and T. F. Leighton, (eds.), MIT Press, Cambridge, MA, 1988, pp. 35–50.

136. S. M. Burns, "Automated Compilation of Concurrent Programs into Self-Timed Circuits," Technical Report Caltech-CS-TR-88-2, California Institute of Technology (1987).

137. A. J. Martin, "The Design of a Self-Timed Circuit for Distributed Mutual Exclusion," in *Proceedings of the 1985 Chapel Hill Conference on Very Large Scale Integration*, Henry Fuchs (ed.), CSP, Inc., 1985, pp. 245–260.

138. C. D. Nielsen and A. Martin, "The Design of a Delay-Insensitive Multiply-Accumulate Unit," in *Proceedings of the Twenty-Sixth Annual Hawaii International Conference on System Sciences*, IEEE Computer Society Press, Los Alamitos, CA, Vol. I, pp. 379–388.

139. V. Akella and G. Gopalakrishnan, "SHILPA: A High-Level Synthesis System for Self-Timed Circuits," in *Proceedings of the IEEE/ACM International Conference on Computer-Aided Design*, IEEE Computer Society Press, Los Alamitos, CA, 1992, pp. 587–591.

140. A. Peeters, "Single-Rail Handshake Circuits," Technical Report, Eindhoven University of Technology, (June 1996).

141. K. van Berkel and A. Bink, "Single-Track Handshake Signaling with Application to Micropipelines," in *Proceedings of the International Symposium on Advanced Research in Asynchronous Circuits and Systems (Async96)*, IEEE Computer Society Press, Los Alamitos, CA, 1996, pp. 122–133.

142. K. van Berkel, R. Burgess, J. Kessels, A. Peeters, M. Roncken, and F. Schalij, "Asynchronous Circuits for Low Power: A DCC Error Corrector," *IEEE Design Test, 11*(2), 22–32 (1994).

143. M. A. Pena and J. Cortadella, "Combining Process Algebras and Petri Nets for the Specification and Synthesis of Asynchronous Circuits," in *Proceedings of the International Symposium on Advanced Research in Asynchronous Circuits and Systems (Async96)*, IEEE Computer Society Press, Los Alamitos, CA, 1996, pp. 222–232.

144. T. Kolks, S. Vercauteren, and B. Lin, "Control Resynthesis for Control-Dominated Asynchronous Designs," in *Proceedings of the International Symposium on Advanced Research in Asynchronous Circuits and Systems (Async96)*, IEEE Computer Society Press, Los Alamitos, CA, 1996, pp. 233–243.

145. G. Gopalakrishnan, P. Kudva, and E. Brunvand, "Peephole Optimization of Asynchronous Macromodule Networks," in *Proceedings of the IEEE International Conference on Computer Design*, IEEE Computer Society Press, Los Alamitos, CA, 1994, pp. 442–446.

146. E. Brunvand, "Translating Concurrent Communicating Programs into Asynchronous Circuits," Technical Report CMU-CS-91-198, Carnegie Mellon University (1991).

147. E. Brunvand, "The NSR Processor," in *Proceedings of the Twenty-Sixth Annual Hawaii International Conference on System Sciences*, IEEE Computer Society Press, Los Alamitos, CA, 1993, Vol. I, pp. 428–435.

148. C. Myers and T. Meng, "Synthesis of Timed Asynchronous Circuits," *IEEE Trans. VLSI Syst., VS-1*(2), 106–119 (1993).

149. C. Myers, "Computer-Aided Synthesis and Verification of Gate-Level Timed Circuits," Ph.D. thesis, Stanford University (1995).

150. T. Rokicki, "Representing and Modeling Digital Circuits," Technical Report, Stanford University (December 1993).

151. T. Rokicki and C. Myers, "Automatic Verification of Timed Circuits," in *International Conference on Computer-Aided Verification*, Springer-Verlag, New York, 1994, pp. 468–480.

152. C. J. Myers, T. G. Rokicki, and T. H.-Y. Meng, "Automatic Synthesis of Gate-Level Timed Circuits with Choice," in *Advanced Research in VLSI: Proceedings of the 1995 University of North Carolina Conference*, W. J. Dally, J. W. Poulton, and A. T. Ishii (eds.), IEEE Computer Society Press, Los Alamitos, CA, 1995, pp. 42–58.

153. W. Belluomini and C. J. Myers, "Efficient Timing Analysis Algorithms for Timed State Space Exploration," in *Proceedings of the International Symposium on Ad-*

vanced Research in Asynchronous Circuits and Systems (Async97), IEEE Computer Society Press, Los Alamitos, CA, 1997.

154. S. B. Furber, P. Day, J. D. Garside, N. C. Paver, S. Temple, and J. V. Woods, "The Design and Evaluation of an Asynchronous Microprocessor," in *Proceedings of the IEEE International Conference on Computer Design*, IEEE Computer Society Press, Los Alamitos, CA, 1994, pp. 217–229.

155. N. C. Paver, "The Design and Implementation of an Asynchronous Microprocessor," Technical Report, University of Manchester (June 1994).

156. T. E. Williams, "Self-Timed Rings and Their Application to Division," Technical Report CSL-TR-91-482, Computer Systems Laboratory, Stanford University (1991).

157. A. J. Martin, S. M. Burns, T. K. Lee, D. Borkovic, and P. J. Hazewindus, "The Design of an Asynchronous Microprocessor," in *1989 Caltech Conference on Very Large Scale Integration*, 1989.

158. T. E. Williams and M. A. Horowitz, "A Zero-Overhead Self-Timed 54b 160ns CMOS divider," *IEEE J. Solid-State Circuits, SSC-26*(11), 1651–1661 (1991).

159. T. H. Meng, *Synchronization Design for Digital Systems*, Kluwer Academic Publishers, Boston, 1991.

160. C. Farnsworth, D. A. Edwards, and S. S. Sikand, "Utilising Dynamic Logic for Low Power Consumption in Asynchronous Circuits," in *Proceedings of the International Symposium on Advanced Research in Asynchronous Circuits and Systems (Async94)*, IEEE Computer Society Press, Los Alamitos, CA, 1994, pp. 186–194.

161. S. B. Furber and J. Liu, "Dynamic Logic in Four-Phase Micropipelines," in *Proceedings of the International Symposium on Advanced Research in Asynchronous Circuits and Systems (Async96)*, IEEE Computer Society Press, Los Alamitos, CA, 1996, pp. 11–16.

162. P. Day and J. V. Woods, "Investigation into Micropipeline Latch Design Styles," *IEEE Trans. VLSI Syst., VS-3*(2), 264–272 (1995).

163. K. Y. Yun, P. A. Beerel, and J. Arceo, "High-Performance Asynchronous Pipeline Circuits," in *Proceedings of the International Symposium on Advanced Research in Asynchronous Circuits and Systems (Async96)*, IEEE Computer Society Press, Los Alamitos, CA, 1996, pp. 17–28.

164. C. E. Molnar, I. W. Jones, B. Coates, and J. Lexau, "A FIFO Ring Oscillator Performance Experiment," in *Proceedings of the International Symposium on Advanced Research in Asynchronous Circuits and Systems (Async97)*, IEEE Computer Society Press, Los Alamitos, CA, 1997.

165. J. Sparso and J. Staunstrup, "Design and Performance Analysis of Delay Insensitive Multi-ring Structures," in *Proceedings of the Twenty-Sixth Annual Hawaii International Conference on System Sciences*, IEEE Computer Society Press, Los Alamitos, CA, 1993, Vol. I, pp. 349–358.

166. G. Gopalakrishnan, "Micropipeline Wavefront Arbiters Using Lockable C-Elements," *IEEE Design Test, 11*(4), 55–64 (1994).

167. E. Grass, R. C. S. Morling, and I. Kale, "Activity-Monitoring Completion-Detection (AMCD): A New Single Rail Approach to Achieve Self Timing," in *Proceedings of the International Symposium on Advanced Research in Asynchronous Circuits and Systems (Async96)*, IEEE Computer Society Press, Los Alamitos, CA, 1996, pp. 143–149.

168. A. Liebchen and G. Gopalakrishnan, "Dynamic Reordering of High Latency Transactions Using a Modified Micropipeline," in *Proceedings of the IEEE International Conference on Computer Design*, IEEE Computer Society Press, Los Alamitos, CA, 1992, pp. 336–340.

169. L. S. Nielsen, C. Niessen, J. Sparso, and K. van Berkel, "Low-Power Operation Using Self-Timed Circuits and Adaptive Scaling of the Supply Voltage," *IEEE Trans. VLSI, 2*(4), 7 (1994).

170. S. H. Unger, "A Building Block Approach to Unclocked Systems," in *Proceedings of the Twenty-Sixth Annual Hawaii International Conference on System Sciences*, IEEE Computer Society Press, Los Alamitos, CA, 1993, Vol. I, pp. 339–348.

171. A. M. Bailey and M. B. Josephs, "Sequencer Circuits for VLSI Programming," in *Proceedings of the Working Conference on Asynchronous Design Methodologies*, IEEE Computer Society Press, Los Alamitos, CA, 1995, pp. 82–90.

172. C. Farnsworth, D. A. Edwards, J. Liu, and S. S. Sikand, "A Hybrid Asynchronous System Design Environment," in *Proceedings of the Working Conference on Asynchronous Design Methodologies*, IEEE Computer Society Press, Los Alamitos, CA, 1995, pp. 91–98.

173. L. Plana and S. M. Nowick, "Concurrency-Oriented Optimization for Low-Power Asynchronous Systems," in *IEEE International Symposium on Low-Power Electronics and Design*, IEEE Computer Society Press, Los Alamitos, CA, 1996, pp. 151–156.

174. S. V. Morton, S. S. Appleton, and M. J. Liebelt, "An Event Controlled Reconfigurable Multi-chip FFT," in *Proceedings of the International Symposium on Advanced Research in Asynchronous Circuits and Systems (Async94)*, IEEE Computer Society Press, Los Alamitos, CA, 1994, pp. 144–153.

175. L. S. Nielsen and J. Sparso, "A Low-Power Asynchronous Data Path for a Fir Filter Bank," in *Proceedings of the International Symposium on Advanced Research in Asynchronous Circuits and Systems (Async96)*, IEEE Computer Society Press, Los Alamitos, CA, 1996, pp. 197–207.

176. J. D. Garside, S. Temple, and R. Mehra, "The AMULET2e Cache System," in *Proceedings of the International Symposium on Advanced Research in Asynchronous Circuits and Systems (Async96)*, IEEE Computer Society Press, Los Alamitos, CA, 1996, pp. 208–217.

177. S. Furber, P. Day, J. Garside, N. Paver, and S. Temple, "Amulet2e," in *EMSYS96 — OMI Sixth Annual Conference*, IOS Press, 1996.

178. J. A. Tierno and A. J. Martin, "Low-Energy Asynchronous Memory Design," in *Proceedings of the International Symposium on Advanced Research in Asynchronous Circuits and Systems (Async94)*, IEEE Computer Society Press, Los Alamitos, CA, 1994, pp. 176–185.

179. M. Maezawa, I. Kurosawa, Y. Kameda, and T. Nanya, "Pulse-Driven Dual-Rail Logic Gate Family Based on Rapid Single-Flux-Quantum (RSFQ) Devices for Asynchronous Circuits," in *Proceedings of the International Symposium on Advanced Research in Asynchronous Circuits and Systems (Async96)*, IEEE Computer Society Press, Los Alamitos, CA, 1996, pp. 134–142.

180. S. M. Nowick, "Design of a Low-Latency Asynchronous Adder Using Speculative Completion," *IEE Proc. — Computers Digital Tech., 143*(5), 301–307 (1996).

181. S. M. Nowick, K. Y. Yun, P. A. Beerel, and A. E. Dooply, "Speculative Completion for the Design of High-Performance Asynchronous Dynamic Adders," in *Proceedings of the International Symposium on Advanced Research in Asynchronous Circuits and Systems (Async97)*, IEEE Computer Society Press, Los Alamitos, CA, 1997.

182. M. Greenstreet, "Implementing a STARI Chip," in *Proceedings of the IEEE International Conference on Computer Design*, IEEE Computer Society Press, Los Alamitos, CA, 1995, pp. 38–43.

183. P. T. Roeine, "A System for Asynchronous High-Speed Chip to Chip Communication," in *Proceedings of the International Symposium on Advanced Research in Asynchronous Circuits and Systems (Async96)*, IEEE Computer Society Press, Los Alamitos, CA, 1996, pp. 2–10.

184. J. F. Chappel and S. G. Zaky, " A Delay-Controlled Phase-Locked Loop to Reduce Timing Errors in Synchronous/Asynchronous Communication Links," in *Proceedings of the International Symposium on Advanced Research in Asynchronous Circuits and*

Systems (Async94), IEEE Computer Society Press, Los Alamitos, CA, 1994, pp. 156–165.

185. N. C. Paver, P. Day, S. B. Furber, J. D. Garside, and J. V. Woods, "Register Locking in an Asynchronous Microprocessor," in *Proceedings of the IEEE International Conference on Computer Design*, IEEE Computer Society Press, Los Alamitos, CA, 1992, pp. 351–355.

186. W. Richardson and E. Brunvand, "Fred: An Architecture for a Self-Timed Decoupled Computer," in *Advanced Research in Asynchronous Circuits and Systems*, IEEE Computer Society Press, Los Alamitos, CA, 1996, pp. 60–68.

187. W. F. Richardson, "Architectural Considerations for a Self-Timed Decoupled Processor," Ph.D. thesis, University of Utah (March 1996).

188. I. David, R. Ginosar, and M. Yoeli, "Self-Timed Implementation of a Reduced Instruction Set Computer," Technical Report 732, Technion and Israel Institute of Technology (October 1989).

189. R. Ginosar and N. Michell, "On the Potential of Asynchronous Pipelined Processors," Technical Report UUCS-90-015, VLSI Systems Research Group, University of Utah (1990).

190. T. Nanya, Y. Ueno, H. Kagotani, M. Kuwako, and A. Takamura, "TITAC: Design of a Quasi-Delay-Insensitive Microprocessor," *IEEE Design Test, 11*(2), 50–63 (1994).

191. R. Milner, *Communication and Concurrency*, Prentice-Hall, London, 1989.

192. D. L. Dill, S. M. Nowick, and R. F. Sproull, "Specification and Automatic Verification of Self-Timed Queues," *Formal Methods System Design, 1*(1), 29–60 (1992).

193. J. C. Ebergen, "A Verifier for Network Decompositions of Command-Based Specifications," in *Proceedings of the Twenty-Sixth Annual Hawaii International Conference on System Sciences*, IEEE Computer Society Press, Los Alamitos, CA, 1993, Vol. I, pp. 310–318.

194. P. A. Beerel, J. Burch, and T. Meng, "Efficient Verification of Determinate Speed-Independent Circuits," in *Proceedings of the IEEE/ACM International Conference on Computer-Aided Design*, IEEE Computer Society Press, Los Alamitos, CA, 1993, pp. 261–267.

195. K. Stevens, "Practical Verification and Synthesis of Low Latency Asynchronous Systems," Ph.D. Thesis, Computer Science Department, University of Calgary (1994).

196. G. Gopalakrishnan, E. Brunvand, N. Michell, and S. M. Nowick, "A Correctness Criterion for Asynchronous Circuit Validation and Optimization," *IEEE Trans. Computer-Aided Design of Integrated Circuits and Systems, 13*(11), 1309–1318 (1994).

197. T. Yoneda and T. Yoshikawa, "Using Partial Orders for Trace Theoretic Verification of Asynchronous Circuits," in *Proceedings of the International Symposium on Advanced Research in Asynchronous Circuits and Systems (Async96)*, IEEE Computer Society Press, Los Alamitos, CA, 1996, pp. 152–163.

198. M. Kishinevsky, A. Kondratyev, A. Taubin, and V. Varshavsky, "Analysis and Identification of Speed-Independent Circuits on an Event Model," *Formal Methods System Design, 4*(1), 33–75 (1994).

199. R. Kol, R. Ginosar, and G. Samuel, "Statechart Methodology for the Design, Validation, and Synthesis of Large Scale Asynchronous Systems," in *Proceedings of the International Symposium on Advanced Research in Asynchronous Circuits and Systems (Async96)*, IEEE Computer Society Press, Los Alamitos, CA, 1996, pp. 164–174.

200. K. Stevens, J. Aldwinckle, G. Birtwistle, and Y. Liu, "Designing Parallel Specifications in CCS," in *Proceedings of Canadian Conference on Electrical and Computer Engineering*, 1993.

201. G. Birtwistle and Y. Liu, "Specification of the Manchester Amulet 1: Top level Specification," Computer Science Department Technical Report, University of Calgary (December 1994).

202. R. Alur and D. L. Dill, "A Theory of Timed Automata," *Theoret. Computer Sci.*, *1*(126), 183-235.

203. S. Devadas, K. Keutzer, S. Malik, and A. Wang, "Verification of Asynchronous Interface Circuits with Bounded Wire Delays," in *Proceedings of the IEEE/ACM International Conference on Computer-Aided Design*, IEEE Computer Society Press, Los Alamitos, CA, 1992, pp. 188-195.

204. S. Chakraborty and D. L. Dill, "More Accurate Polynomial-Time Min-Max Timing Simulation," in *Proceedings of the International Symposium on Advanced Research in Asynchronous Circuits and Systems (Async97)*, IEEE Computer Society Press, Los Alamitos, CA, 1997.

205. S. Chakraborty, D. L. Dill, K.-Y. Chang, and K. Y. Yun, "Timing Analysis for Extended Burst-Mode Circuits," in *Proceedings of the International Symposium on Advanced Research in Asynchronous Circuits and Systems (Async97)*, IEEE Computer Society Press, Los Alamitos, CA, 1997.

206. A. Semenov and A. Yakovlev, "Verification of Asynchronous Circuits Using Time Petri Net Unfolding," In *33rd ACM/IEEE Design Automation Conference*, June 1996.

207. E. Verlind, G. de Jong, and B. Lin. Efficient partial enumeration for timing analysis of asynchronous systems. In *33rd ACM/IEEE Design Automation Conference*, June 1996.

208. M. Kuwako and T. Nanya, "Timing-Reliability Evaluation of Asynchronous Circuits Based on Different Delay Models," in *Proceedings of the International Symposium on Advanced Research in Asynchronous Circuits and Systems (Async94)*, IEEE Computer Society Press, Los Alamitos, CA, 1994, pp. 22-31.

209. A. Ashkinazy, D. Edwards, C. Farnsworth, G. Gendel, and S. Sikand, "Tools for Validating Asynchronous Digital Circuits," in *Proceedings of the International Symposium on Advanced Research in Asynchronous Circuits and Systems (Async94)*, IEEE Computer Society Press, Los Alamitos, CA, 1994, pp. 12-21.

210. K. McMillan and D. L. Dill, "Algorithms for Interface Timing Verification," in *Proceedings of the IEEE International Conference on Computer Design*, IEEE Computer Society Press, Los Alamitos, CA, 1992, pp. 48-51.

211. H. Hulgaard, S. M. Burns, T. Amon, and G. Borriello, "Practical Applications of an Efficient Time Separation of Events Algorithm," in *Proceedings of the IEEE/ACM International Conference on Computer-Aided Design*, IEEE Computer Society Press, Los Alamitos, CA, 1993, pp. 146-151.

212. H. Hulgaard and S. M. Burns, "Bounded Delay Timing Analysis of a Class of CSP Programs with Choice," in *Proceedings of the International Symposium on Advanced Research in Asynchronous Circuits and Systems (Async94)*, IEEE Computer Society Press, Los Alamitos, CA, 1994, pp. 2-11.

213. P. Beerel and T. Meng, "Semi-Modularity and Self-Diagnostic Asynchronous Control Circuits," in *Proceedings of the 1991 University of California/Santa Cruz Conference*, C. H. Sequin (ed.), The MIT Press, Cambridge, MA, 1991, pp. 103-117.

214. A. J. Martin and P. J. Hazewindus, "Testing Delay-Insensitive Circuits," in *Advanced Research in VLSI: Proceedings of the 1991 UC Santa Cruz Conference*, Carlo H. Séquin (ed.), MIT Press, Cambridge, MA, 1991, pp. 118-132.

215. P. A. Beerel and T. H.-Y. Meng, "Testability of Asynchronous Timed Control Circuits with Delay Assumptions," in *Proceedings of the 28th ACM/IEEE Design Automation Conference*, ACM, New York, 1991, pp. 446-451.

216. K. Keutzer, L. Lavagno, and A. Sangiovanni-Vincentelli, "Synthesis for Testability Techniques for Asynchronous Circuits," in *Proceedings of the IEEE International Conference on Computer-Aided Design*, IEEE Computer Society Press, Los Alamitos, CA, 1991, pp. 326-329.

217. S. M. Nowick, N. K. Jha, and F.-C. Cheng, "Synthesis of Asynchronous Circuits for Stuck-at and Robust Path Delay Fault Testability," in *Proceedings of the Eighth International Conference on VLSI Design* (*VLSI Design 95*), IEEE Computer Society Press, Los Alamitos, CA, 1995.

218. M. Roncken and R. Saeijs, "Linear Test Times for Delay-Insensitive Circuits: A Compilation Strategy," in *Proceedings of the IFIP WG 10.5 Working Conference on Asynchronous Design Methodologies, Manchester*, S. Furber and M. Edwards (eds.), Elsevier Science Publishers B. V., Amsterdam, 1993, pp. 13–27.

219. M. Roncken, "Partial Scan Test for Asynchronous Circuits Illustrated on a DCC Error Corrector," in *Proceedings of the International Symposium on Advanced Research in Asynchronous Circuits and Systems* (*Async94*), IEEE Computer Society Press, Los Alamitos, CA, 1994, pp. 247–256.

220. M. Roncken and E. Bruls, "Test Quality of Asynchronous Circuits: A Defect-Oriented Evaluation," in *Proceedings of the IEEE International Test Conference*, IEEE Computer Society Press, Los Alamitos, CA, 1996.

221. A. Khoche and E. Brunvand, "Testing Micropipelines," in *Proceedings of the International Symposium on Advanced Research in Asynchronous Circuits and Systems* (*Async94*), IEEE Computer Society Press, Los Alamitos, 1994, pp. 239–246.

222. A. Khoche, "Testing Macro-Module Based Self-Timed Circuits," PhD thesis, University of Utah (1996).

223. V. Schoeber and T. Kiel, "An Asynchronous Scan Path Concept for Micropipelines Using the Bundled Data Convention," in *Proceedings of the IEEE International Test Conference*, IEEE Computer Society Press, Los Alamitos, CA, 1996.

224. M. Roncken, E. Aarts, and W. Verhaegh, "Optimal Scan for Pipelined Testing: An Asynchronous Foundation," in *Proceedings of the IEEE International Test Conference*, IEEE Computer Society Press, Los Alamitos, CA, 1996.

225. S. T. Chakradhar, S. Banerjee, R. K. Roy, and D. K. Pradhan, "Synthesis of Initializable Asynchronous Circuits," *IEEE Trans. VLSI Systems, VS-4*(2), 254–262 (1996).

226. M. Singh and S. M. Nowick, "Synthesis-for-Testability of Asynchronous Sequential Machines," in *Proceedings of the IEEE International Test Conference*, IEEE Computer Society Press, Los Alamitos, CA, 1996.

AL DAVIS

STEVEN M. NOWICK

JOB SCHEDULING FOR PARALLEL SUPERCOMPUTERS

INTRODUCTION

Parallel job scheduling schemes enable the expensive, scarce resources of a parallel supercomputer to be shared among a large community of users. Unfortunately, the successful, multiuser scheduling schemes for uniprocessors do not readily translate to address the challenges posed by parallelism. This article surveys many of the commercial and academic attempts at scheduling jobs on a parallel supercomputer.

Although parallel computers are more difficult to use effectively than their sequential counterparts, many programmers are willing to pay the price because their applications need the additional resources. An application executed on a parallel computer can potentially complete in a shorter time and make use of much larger aggregate cache capacity, physical memory size, and I/O bandwidth. Of course, when an application must compete for a share of these resources, the payoff becomes far less attractive. Very few people are willing to wait a month to get one hour's time on a supercomputer; the application usually could be finished sooner on a dedicated workstation.

Literally hundreds of papers have been written about job scheduling in parallel systems (see Ref. 1). However, in many respects, we are at the beginning of the beginning. The large variety of vague goals, parallel programming languages, parallel computer architectures, and parallel operating systems means that there is no one ideal scheduling strategy.

System design is (or, at least, should be) driven by requirements. Thus, one source of disagreement about the merits of different designs is controversy over exactly what are the requirements that need to be satisfied. Some requirements reflect first principles — that the scheduler be aware of the fact that multiple processes belong to the same job (and all should be killed if one terminates abnormally) and that systems where processors have somewhat different configurations have to be supported efficiently (2,3). In addition, it is important to understand the workload that must be supported.

Obviously, the workload is related to the ultimate use of the parallel machine. It seems that parallel supercomputers are used for three main reasons:

- **Short response time.** Parallelism enables a computation to complete in less time, and this may make a qualitative rather than just a quantitative difference. For example, reducing the time to compute a 3-day forecast from a week to a day makes it relevant. At the interactive level, running a circuit simulation in a matter of minutes rather than hours allows an engineer to iteratively tinker with parameters, leading to increased productivity.

- **Large resource requirements.** Parallel supercomputers allow more resources to be harnessed for solving the same problem than other systems. The resources in question can be both compute power and memory. An example is the GF-11, which took about a year to perform a calculation aimed at verifying the theory of quantum chromo-dynamics.
- **Because it's there.** Parallel processing is intriguing and challenging because it is inherently different from the sequential human stream of consciousness (as opposed to the underlying structure of the brain, which is massively parallel). This fascinates and attracts many people. Moreover, in the last few years, it has been the "in" thing to do. This is an important factor, because users are human beings who do not always perform a full cost/benefit analysis before choosing a course of action. The fact that many vendors report that entry-level systems account for a large fraction of their sales, as opposed to large-scale systems, bears testimony to the fact that many parallel systems are not used to solve extremely large or time-sensitive problems, as implied by the previous two categories.

In addition, there are secondary reasons for using a parallel machine. Most notable is its use in the development and debugging of parallel application. These activities are important because their requirements are typically different from those of the application being developed: Fewer and smaller resources are needed, and an interactive response time is crucial.

What does all of this mean for parallel scheduling? Above everything else, it means that arguments to the effect that parallel supercomputers should only be used in batch mode for large problems are wrong. There is a very diverse set of requirements, spanning a spectrum from rather small interactive jobs, through large but time-sensitive jobs, to very large and not-time-sensitive jobs that can be satisfied by a batch system (4). The problem is that these different classes may be present on the same system at the same time, and each must be serviced according to its unique requirements. This wide distribution of requirements implies that some sort of time slicing has to be used (5).

An important aspect of workload requirements that is often overlooked is memory and secondary storage. In fact, many respectable commercial parallel systems (e.g., the CM-5) do not support memory paging: applications are required to fit into physical memory. When a machine is dedicated to executing a very large application for a very long time, the overhead of a fancy scheduler is not worthwhile and, similarly, the overhead of a paging system may not be worthwhile. If the machine is shared among a number of applications, their combined needs are required to fit into memory. Many proposed scheduling schemes make the same assumption, and fall apart once memory considerations are introduced. The simple solution adopted by some recent systems, such as the IBM SP2, is to have independent paging on each node. This has the undesirable side effect that processes can be blocked asynchronously for relatively long periods, preventing fine-grain synchronization and communication from taking place. To quote a somewhat overused phrase, "there must be a better way."

Finally, one should remember that the operating system is there to serve applications, and through them, to serve users, and the client is always right. Thus, the operating system should provide opportunities, not impose restrictions. In the context of scheduling, it does not do to support only certain models of computation, and limit users to their use. It is hard enough to program parallel machines effectively without restricting the available tools and idioms. In addition, it is important to provide consistent and predictable service, including provisions for fairness and control (6).

This article first outlines the range of objects that are to be scheduled. A survey of the scheduling approaches is then presented. The article concludes with several comments about the requirements for job scheduling.

BACKGROUND

A major problem in talking about "scheduling on parallel machines" is that this expression means different things to different people. A good start is to distinguish the different classes of objects that are to be scheduled on parallel systems. The major objects are *jobs* and *threads*. Jobs are autonomous programs that execute in their own protection domain. One job should not be allowed to access the memory of another job nor interfere with the other job's message-space. A job may consist of many threads (i.e., be a parallel job) and may be batch or interactive. We use the term "thread" to specify the thing that can execute in parallel in a parallel program. It is synonymous with terms like "chore" or "activity," as sometimes used by others.

We refrain from using "task," as this term has been used with innumerable conflicting meanings in the literature. Furthermore, we set aside "process" to denote an autonomous execution unit. Thus, in uniprocessors, the terms *job* and *process* are synonymous. In parallel systems, if the operating system is aware of the fact that multiple executing entities are part of the same application, then each execution unit is referred to as a thread and the whole thing together is a job. If, on the other hand, the interacting entities are independent as far as the operating system is concerned, we call them processes and each of these processes is a separate job, whereas, to the user, they collectively represent a single job.

Although a parallel job consists of threads whose execution is specified in a parallel program, there is no single universally agreed-upon parallel programming language. Figure 1 gives a very broad classification of parallel programming styles. The threads can be static or dynamic and the communication between them can be static or dynamic. For example, in a single-program, multiple-data (SPMD) language, the number of threads is fixed and is often equal to the number of processors, but the communication patterns between the threads can change dynamically during the execution.

| | | Communication pattern | |
		Static	*Dynamic*
Thread creation	*Static*	DAG	SPMD, HPF
	Dynamic	Dataflow Functional	Nested parallelism Unix fork-join

FIGURE 1   A simple classification of parallel programming styles. The range is actually much more complex than what is shown here.

Threads can be very lightweight, as in the case of data flow or functional programming with very limited communication—data are passed to the thread upon its creation, and the thread passes on data when it terminates. In this case, there are few restrictions on where the thread can execute. On the other hand, threads can be heavyweight involving lots of computation and many communications with other threads. In a message-passing system, such threads often cannot be moved once begun because most message-passing libraries use physical PE addresses for messages.

The machine architecture, thus, has a serious impact on the scheduler. Figure 2 gives a very coarse classification. In machines in which processors are assembled in a restricted topology such as a mesh or hypercube, jobs are assigned to specific partitions of the machines (e.g., subcubes). In symmetric multiprocessors with uniform access to shared memory, it is easy to stop a thread and reschedule it on any other processor. Some machines offer a mixture: the KSR is billed as an UMA machine, due to the automatic migration of data to wherever needed, but has a clustered structure. The CM-5 offers a complete-network view in terms of message passing, but can only be partitioned according to subtrees of its fat-free network.

The following subsections review some of the classes of scheduling. Each class may have its own goal or be directed at a particular class of machine or language.

Static Scheduling

In order to understand the theoretical limitations of scheduling, a restricted version of parallel programs is considered in which there is nearly complete knowledge of the computation. An application is modeled as a directed acyclic graph (DAG) where each node denotes a task and directed edges or arcs denote dependencies among the tasks: The task at the origin of the arc must complete before the task at its end may commence. These dependencies typically represent data transfers; that is, the task at the sink of a directed arc uses some data values that are generated by the task at the source of the arc. Both nodes and arcs may have weights attached to them. The weight of a node denotes the required amount of computation, whereas the weight of an arc denotes the amount of data that is transferred.

When the system is modeled as a set of homogeneous processors that can each execute one task at a time, the objective is usually to minimize the makespan (7). In

	Shared memory	*Message passing*
Complete network	UMA SMPs SGI Challenge	IBM SP2 NOWs
Mixed	KSR	TMC CM-5
Visible topology	NUMA Cm*, DASH	Intel Paragon Cray T3D Hypercubes

FIGURE 2 A simple classification of parallel machine classes. "Mixed" denotes cases that have characteristics of both complete networks and topological restrictions. (SMP = symmetric multiprocessor; UMA = uniform memory access; NUMA = nonuniform memory access.)

some cases, communication costs are also explicitly modeled. Thus, if two neighboring tasks are assigned to different processors, the second one is delayed by an amount of time proportional to the weight of the arc between them, but if they are assigned to the same processor, there is no such delay.

Many restricted cases of DAG scheduling have been shown to be NP-complete, meaning that it is impractical to look for an optimal schedule. This is true even for very restricted special cases (e.g., when communication is free and all tasks have unit execution times) (8,9).

Many parallel programming styles are close to the DAG model, although with substantially less information. Data flow, functional programming, and other side-effect-free programming models can be viewed as DAGs. Consequently, various heuristics have been developed to approximate good schedules. One approach is to assign priorities to nodes in the DAG according to their distance from the termination node. Another concentrates on the critical path in the DAG. When communication costs are taken into account, the main issue is how to partition the DAG into clusters of nodes, and then schedule these clusters on processors. This is a compromise between two conflicting forces: Keeping nodes separate increases parallelism at the cost of communication, whereas clustering them causes serialization but saves on communication (10,11). If the interconnection network has some specific topology, this can also be taken into account (12).

Scheduling in the Run-Time System

Although DAG scheduling has generated a large body of research, much of it cannot be applied to programming environments that use other representations. In many such environments, the programmer is actually shielded from the details of how the program is mapped onto the machine. The details are then handled by the environment's run-time system.

One example of this approach is the use of thread packages (13). The application is structured as a set of interacting threads. The environment supplies functions for thread creation, synchronization, and termination. The run-time system is responsible for implementing these functions when they are called.

Another example is the use of parallelizing compilers. Parallelizing compilers usually extract parallelism from the loops of sequential programs. At run time, the different loop iterations are scheduled for execution on distinct processors (14). A typical approach is to assign decreasing chunks of iterations to the different processors, so as to balance the load on one hand while avoiding extra coordination on the other. Again, the programmer does not have to worry about how this is done.

Scheduling in the Operating System

Scheduling by the programmer or run-time system aims to satisfy the individual needs of the program in question. But when multiple programs must coexist in the same system, it is necessary to balance the needs of the individual with those of the community in general. Such considerations and mechanisms lie in the realm of the operating system.

The fact that the mechanisms and considerations of scheduling at the operating-system level are sometimes very similar to those applied at the application and run-time level has hindered progress — it is not clear who is in charge of the problem.

Some even claim that all scheduling should be done at the application level, and the operating system should stay out of the way, because interrupts, context switches, and memory swapping are overheads that can be very costly on a parallel supercomputer. However, as parallel systems become more commonly used, there is growing recognition of the need for resource management at the operating-system level. It is this class of scheduling that is addressed in the rest of this article.

Many requirements make scheduling difficult. For example, it is important that different jobs execute in different protection domains; that is, one job cannot access the memory or message space of another job. A second difficulty is that on many machines, partitions have to match the topology of the machine (e.g., only subcubes can be used on a hypercube). Yet another problem is that in many message-passing systems, source and destination addresses are hardwired so that a thread cannot be easily migrated between PEs. Therefore multiple different approaches are used in different systems, as described in the section Current Approaches.

Administrative Scheduling

Finally, some scheduling decisions are made at an administrative rather than at a technical level. For example, the head of a computing facility may decide that a certain project should get exclusive access to a certain machine for 3 weeks, in order to achieve some project goals. Or, it may be the policy to encourage short, massively parallel jobs instead of longer jobs of smaller parallelism. Or, what should be the ratio of batch jobs to interactive ones? Although little research is directed toward this type of activity, it undeniably has a significant effect on many users. Mechanisms that enable such policy control are of interest. Finally, the issue of accounting and how to charge users for the computational resources they consume becomes a major concern.

ASSUMPTIONS ABOUT THE GOALS OF A JOB SCHEDULER

There are many scheduling systems for parallel computers and even more that are being proposed and analyzed. The systems are widely disparate both in what they hope to accomplish and in the ways they hope to accomplish it. This section reviews some of the various, sometimes conflicting goals of schedulers.

Run Jobs

The primary goal of all schedulers is to enable the successful execution of a job, hopefully a parallel one, on a parallel machine. Although obvious, this goal should never be forgotten. In particular, maximizing secondary goals should not starve certain classes of jobs.

Secondary scheduling goals, described in the following subsections, vary and depend on satisfying the needs of the group versus the needs of the individual. These goals can be broadly classified as being system-centric or user-centric. Some are measurable well-defined metrics, whereas others are functional desiderata. They are summarized in Table 1.

TABLE 1 Classification of Scheduler Goals

	User-centric	System-centric
Metric	Response time	Utilization Throughput
Function	Run jobs	
	Emulate dedicated machine	Administrative preferences

Maximize Utilization of the Machine

It might appear obvious that a scheduler should maximize the utilization of the machine. Utilization can be defined in either of two ways: either as the percentage of CPU cycles *actually used* for productive computation, or as the percentage of CPU cycles *allocated* to user jobs that pay for them. The difference is that the first definition integrates the efficiency of user code into the equation, whereas the latter makes a clear distinction between the allocation of resources by the operating system and their use by the user.

The problem with utilization as a metric is that it is largely dependent on system load (Fig. 3). Consider a simple queuing model of an operating system scheduler: Requests to run jobs arrive, and they are serviced by the system. When load is low and all jobs can be serviced, the utilization is equal to the load. When the load is high and the system saturates, utilization is equal to the saturation point. Therefore, the goal of a system designer is not to increase utilization per se but

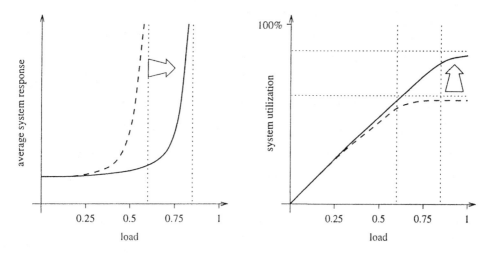

FIGURE 3 Utilization depends on the system load and on how efficiently the system handles it; that is, at what point does it saturate? Arrows indicate improvement in system efficiency.

rather to delay the onset of saturation. In other words, a "good" system will be able to sustain a higher load before becoming saturated, which means that a higher utilization is possible if the load demands it.

Another problem with the utilization metric is that adopting it may lead to starvation of certain jobs. For example, if the job stream includes many jobs that require all the processors in the system, and only a handful of jobs that require fewer processors and cause significant fragmentation, it is best from a utilization point of view to only schedule the jobs that need all the processors.

Maximize Throughput

Throughput is the number of jobs completed per unit time. The throughput metric is similar to the utilization metric in the sense that it is affected by system load and efficiency; but, whereas utilization is maximized when there are mainly massively parallel jobs executing for long time periods, the throughput metric is maximized when there are many small (in parallelism and in CPU usage) jobs.

The rationale behind this metric is that the higher the throughput, the more users are satisfied. In general, maximizing the average throughput also minimizes the average response time for a job. This is true only when there is no knowledge about the execution time of a job. If that is known, then scheduling the shortest jobs first will reduce the average response time without affecting the average throughput rate.

Throughput has the same problem as utilization: By focusing on the average values, the system may undermine the primary goal. A parallel job mix may be difficult to schedule and can cause significant fragmentation (15). For example, a 27-node job on a 32-node parallel machine leaves an awkward 5 nodes free. If one is interested in maximizing the average number of jobs processed by the system, it might be better to ignore jobs that cause fragmentation altogether.

Reduce Average Response Time

Reducing average response time is a very common goal, especially in interactive systems. Although there is some debate about the exact definition of "response time," most researchers use it as a synonym for "turnaround time" (i.e., from job submittal* to job completion time), rather than the time when the first output is produced (16).

One problem with the usual response time metric is its use of absolute values. Consider a job J_a that responds in 1 day and another job J_b that responds in 1 min. If both jobs have the same computational requirement, then there might be something wrong with the scheduler. On the other hand, if job J_a requires 24 h of computation time, then the 1-day response time is pretty good, whereas if job J_b only required 1 μs of computation time, then the 1-min response time may be bad. Jobs can be perceived as having different weights, depending on their run time. A possible solution to this problem is to use the average *slowdown* as a metric instead, where slowdown is the ratio of the time it takes to run the job on a loaded system

---

*We are following Steve Hotovy's campaign to use the term *job submittal* in place of *job submission*, despite the fact that jobs are at the mercy of the scheduler.

divided by the time it takes on a dedicated system [this is sometimes also called the "response ratio" (17)]. This normalizes all jobs to the same scale.

Another problem with this metric is its linearity in regard to time. Actually, response time should be measured as perceived by those who are interested (e.g., human users). For humans, the difference between a response of 1 ms and 100 ms is immeasurable, but the difference between 1 s and 100 s is very annoying (18).

Finally, it should be noted that not all jobs require the same level of service in terms of response time. Interactive jobs require interactive response times, preferably of not more than a couple of seconds. Time-critical jobs require application-dependent response times (e.g., tomorrow's weather forecast should be ready in time to be useful). Some jobs to not have any specific time constraints. In fact, most parallel systems make a distinction between batch jobs and direct jobs, with batch jobs executed only at night or when the machine would otherwise be idle. However, most efforts at modeling do not take this distinction into account.

Fairness Versus Administrative Preferences

Fairness is not often advocated as a requirement on its own accord, but it underlies the requirements for maximizing throughput and minimizing average response time. But, should all jobs be treated the same? For example, we have already noted that batch jobs do not require short response times.

Because all jobs are not created equal, it is often desirable to give preference to certain classes of jobs. For example, is there any preference to schedule two 8-node jobs in place of a single 16-node job? There is no abstract answer to this question; it is dictated by the management personnel of the supercomputer. Due to the high cost of parallel supercomputers and their resulting use as shared resources that are specifically targeted at large computational problems, some installations do, indeed, try to encourage highly parallel jobs at the expense of those with only moderate parallelism.

Encouraging highly parallel jobs can be viewed as "fairness to threads." A job with more threads that exhibits a larger degree of parallelism is assumed to require more computational resources and is, therefore, given better service; that is, administrative preferences may cause the system to be unfair to users or to jobs (i.e., all jobs are not considered equal).

Give the Illusion of a Dedicated Parallel Machine

Multiuser workstations and other nonparallel computers attempt to provide the user with the illusion of a dedicated machine. This is especially true for interactive jobs. When a parallel computer supports multiple users via time slicing or space slicing, it is generally desirable to provide the illusion of a dedicated parallel machine. We define this to mean that if a job receives $1/k$ of the total CPU cycles, then the job should take about k times as long to complete as it would on a dedicated machine, without taking any special actions.

To understand the issue here, consider a job scheduler that allows the individual threads of each parallel job to be time sliced independently. A thread may then waste many CPU cycles waiting for a message to be sent by another thread that is currently not executing. Had the machine been dedicated to the job, this wasted time would not occur. Thus, a user might be charged more CPU time, just because the scheduler decided to execute several jobs in an uncoordinated fashion [a simple solution for this case is, therefore, to use gang scheduling (19)].

Issues That Are Often Ignored

An important observation is that most simple metrics have simple failure modes in which they cause starvation for a class of jobs that do not promote the predefined metric. For example:

- Maximizing utilization may not schedule jobs that cause fragmentation.
- Maximizing throughput may not schedule large jobs.
- Minimizing response time ignores the fact that batch jobs do not need it nor want to pay for it.

A more subtle observation is that a scheduling-centric metric cannot account for interactions with other resources that may become depleted first. For example, memory is a critical resource, and if it is not managed correctly, an application may suffer from thrashing. Consider for a moment a job that consists of two processes: a consumer and a producer. The producer sends messages to the consumer process. If the rate of production is equal to the rate of consumption, and the two processes execute simultaneously in parallel, memory can be used efficiently. On the other hand, if they do not execute simultaneously, each message may need to be buffered. Buffering consumes system resources and could cause other jobs to frequently page fault. Unchecked scheduling of parallel jobs may quickly deplete "swap" disk space. Many large installations provide massive storage systems with latency times measured in minutes. Such time frames must be handled differently from the times involved with a simple page fault.

In the area of functional requirements, the need to support whatever users may want to do is often overlooked. There are a number of examples of oversophisticated schedulers that may end up limiting their users:

- Users sometimes want full control over the number of processors used to run their jobs (e.g., in order to generate speedup curves). A scheduler that sets the number automatically and does not provide an override mechanism makes this impossible to achieve.
- Different applications are easier to write in different programming styles, and users also have their personal preferences. Schedulers that limit the styles that are supported may thus alienate users that would rather use another style. This applies, for example, to schedulers that require all jobs to be able to adapt to changes in resource allocation at run time, something that is difficult to achieve in certain cases.

Finally, in modern complex systems, it is often the case that the scheduler must interact with external agents [e.g., as part of a system for heterogeneous computing (20,21)]. As part of such interactions, the scheduler might need to make reservations for future use. This functionality is often missing, and the performance implications (e.g., loss of resources due to reservations) are usually not included in models and analysis.

ASSUMPTIONS ABOUT THE WORKLOAD

Although there is general agreement that a job is the basic object that is to be scheduled, there is a wide range of opinions as to what information is available to the scheduler about each job. *Parallel jobs*, which are the only ones considered in this article, are jobs composed of independent communicating threads and scheduled to execute on a parallel machine, where there is an underlying assumption that the communication time is fast; for example, the time to communicate a word of information is only about an order of magnitude longer than the time required for a CPU to fetch a word from its memory. We exclude client–server-type jobs and other distributed computing jobs.

The definition of a parallel job from the point of view of a scheduler, unfortunately, is not so clear-cut. There are many styles of parallel programs, and many structures that are imposed by some run-time systems and compilers. Job types may be classified based on the number of processors to be used by the job. The number may be specified by the user, either within the program itself or as part of job submittal specification, or it may be dictated by the scheduler. In addition, the number of processors may be fixed at the start of program execution or may change during the course of the computation. There are, thus, four classes (Table 2). Although one of the problems with the field is that there are too many conflicting terms, we risk adding to the complexity by proposing yet another set of terms. We feel that these terms may help highlight the differences. (See Fig. 4.)

Rigid Jobs

A *rigid job* requires a certain number of processors in order to execute, as specified by the user at job submittal time; there may be other resource requirements as well, such as CPU time and memory, but we will focus on the requirement for processors. A rigid job will not execute with fewer processors and will not make use of any additional processors. The scheduler does not know anything about the job except the number of processors it needs.

From the programmer's perspective, the reasons for using a rigid formulation vary. There are often optimal decompositions based on the problem size. For example, it might be very inefficient to decompose a job with an array of size 100 into 17 processors or the programming language imposes this restriction, as is the case for applications written in High Performance Fortran. In some cases, it is simply what the system interface supports, so even jobs that are written as moldable jobs must be submitted as rigid ones.

TABLE 2 Classification of Job Type Based on Specifying Number of Processors Used

Who decides number	When is it decided	
	At submittal	During execution
User	Rigid	Evolving
System	Moldable	Malleable

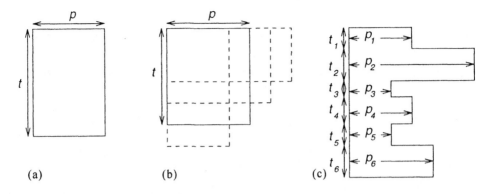

FIGURE 4   (a) Rigid jobs define a rectangle in processor-time space. (b) Moldable jobs use one out of a choice of such rectangles. (c) Evolving and malleable jobs both have a profile with a changing number of processors. The difference is that in evolving jobs the changes are initiated by the job, whereas in malleable ones, they are initiated by the system.

Evolving Jobs

An *evolving job* is one that may change its resource requirements during execution. Note that it is the application itself that initiates the changes. The system must satisfy the requests or the job will not be able to continue its execution. Again, the scheduler knows nothing about the job except for its current requirement for processors.

Although such jobs are not common, there is much activity in the community to define a standard for dynamic processor requests. Such facilities already exist in the PVM interface (22), and they have also been incorporated into the MPI-2 standard.

The reason for the interest in this feature is that many parallel jobs are composed of multiple phases, and each phase has different characteristics. In particular, different phases may contain different degrees of parallelism. By telling the scheduler about these changes, it is possible for jobs to obtain additional resources when needed and to relinquish them when they can be used more profitably elsewhere (thereby reducing the cost of running the job). Also, this type of jobs is commonly modeled by task graphs with changing widths (23).

Moldable Jobs

A job may be flexible in the number of processors that it requires and may allow the system to dictate the allocated number of processors. There are two types of such flexible jobs, which we call *moldable* and *malleable*. With moldable jobs, the number of processors is set at the beginning of execution, and the job initially configures itself to adapt to this number. After it begins execution, the job cannot be reconfigured. It has already conformed to the mold.

If the number of processors is selected by the user and presented to the scheduler as a requirement, the job is actually rigid from the scheduler's point of view. But, given a range of choices, the scheduler can set the number of processors based on knowledge about the system load and competing jobs—knowledge that is typically not available to the user. This has been called "adaptive partitioning" in the literature (24).

A moldable job can be made to execute over a wide range of processors. There is often a minimum number of processors on which it can execute, and above that number, additional processors can be used to improve performance, up to some saturation point. The resource requirement of a minimal number of processors is usually due to memory and response time constraints. From a local efficiency point of view, there is a best number of processors for the job, at the knee of the speedup curve. But because the scheduler cares about maximizing some overall system performance properties, it might be best if the job is executed at another point. In any case, knowledge about application characteristics is typically required (25).

Programs written using the SPMD style (e.g., with the MPI library package) are often moldable. Moreover, workload traces from real parallel systems show that, indeed, the same application may run several times using different partition sizes (4).

Malleable Jobs

The most flexible type of jobs are *malleable* ones that can adapt to changes in the number of processors during execution. The main programming style that permits this flexibility consists of many short independent tasks that access shared data in a very stylized way. For example, if all the tasks have no side effects, then to reduce the number of processors, some tasks are terminated and restarted on the remaining processors later (26).

It is fairly well accepted to call changing the number of processors at run time "dynamic partitioning." We prefer to call the jobs "malleable" rather than "dynamic" because the term "dynamic" does not indicate who is doing the dynamic allocation. On the other hand, the shape of a malleable object can be changed by an outside entity, whereas an evolving object is one that changes of its own accord. However, note that evolving and malleable should usually come together, because one job's evolution will cause others to have to reconfigure.

Analyzing the benefits of dynamic partitioning and malleable jobs has been the subject of much recent research (27–32). This research typically compares the cost of reconfiguration with the resulting improvement in overall performance. But such comparisons do not give a full picture. In many cases, changing the number of processors allocated to a job requires complex interactions between the operating system and the application's run-time system (33). For example, if the thread running on a certain processor holds a lock and then the processor is taken away, there may be no way to free the lock. Implementing the required interfaces to solve such problems naturally complicates the system and makes it harder to implement, which is one reason why malleable jobs are currently not supported on any commercial parallel machine.

An interesting benefit of malleable jobs is that the option for changes can be used to allow the system to collect information about the job at run time, by trying several configurations and checking the resulting performance. This information can later be used to guide allocation decisions (34). This approach has obvious advantages over requiring the information to be available in advance, as is needed for moldable jobs.

CURRENT APPROACHES

In order to multiprogram a parallel machine, the operating system has to decide when to execute each job and on which processors. In general, it is possible to use time slicing (jobs share the use of the same processors), space slicing (each processor is allocated to a specific job until its completion), or a combination of both. An interesting observation is that the two sharing schemes are largely orthogonal, so various combinations can be tried. Indeed, a remarkable variety of approaches have been devised over the years (see Fig. 5) (1).

A scheduler must execute in the environment of an existing operating system and machine architecture. This environment restricts the operations it is allowed to perform. In some machines, the operating system provides a *single system image*; that is, it does not matter on which processor an action is executed, they are all identical. Shared-memory parallel processors (SMPs) often have this feature and it is also being explored in some distributed systems (35). When there is no single system image, it is difficult to migrate tasks. The machine architecture may impose restrictions on the types of processor partitions available and the ability to share access to the communication substrate.

The most limited system has partition sizes of a fixed number of processors and allows only one job to execute from start to finish in a partition at any time. The scheduler simply needs to keep track of empty partitions and map incoming

			time slicing			
			yes			no
			independent PEs		gang scheduling	
			global queue	local queues		
space slicing	yes	flexible	Mach	Meiko/timeshare Paragon/service KSR/interactive transputers Tera/streams Chrysalis	Medusa Butterfly@LLNL Meiko/gang Paragon/gang SGI/gang Tera/PB MAXI/gang	IBM SP2, Victor Meiko/batch Paragon/slice KSR/batch 2-level/bottom TRAC, MICROS Amoeba
		structured		NX/2 on iPSC/2 nCUBE	CM-5 Cedar DHC on SP2 DQT on RWC-1	Cray T3D CM-2 PASM hypercubes
	no		IRIX on SGI NYU Ultra Dynix 2-level/top Hydra/C.mmp	StarOS Psyche Elxsi AP1000	MasPar MP2 Alliant FX/8 Chagori on K2	Illiac IV MPP GF11 Warp

FIGURE 5   Examples of systems that use different combinations of space slicing and time slicing. (Updated from Ref. 1.)

jobs to the appropriate partition. At the extreme, there would be only one partition and so only one job can execute at a time. But most systems allow many more powerful options.

The following subsections survey the four most popular approaches: global queue, variable partitioning, dynamic partitioning with two-level scheduling, and gang scheduling. Of these, two emphasize the use of space slicing (variable and dynamic partitioning) and two the use of time slicing (global queue and gang scheduling). For each, we briefly identify where it is applicable (usually depends on the machine architecture) and highlight its strengths and weaknesses. First, a short overview of mechanisms is in order.

Mechanisms

All scheduling schemes are based on the use of a small number of basic mechanisms, in different combinations. These are different variants of allocation dynamics, reordering of jobs in the queue, and use of preemption and migration.

The variants' allocation dynamics correspond to the different types of job, as discussed earlier. Allocations can be totally inflexible, as required by rigid jobs; they can be somewhat flexible at launch time, as allowed by moldable jobs; or they can be completely flexible even at run time as allowed by malleable jobs.

A scheduler may be able to process jobs in an order different from the job submittal order. Many batch systems have some such flexibility (36–38). Of course, this flexibility is only useful if there is some information as to the resource requirements of the waiting jobs as well as any deadlines or response time requirements.

We mention this option because it easily leads to violation of the primary goal of a scheduler—the execution of every job. Some aging mechanism is required to ensure that jobs are not passed over for arbitrarily long time periods.

Migration refers to the ability of a scheduler to move an executing job or some of its components to other processors. As such, it is an extension of preemption: A task stops running on a certain processor, and it restarts on another processor. Reasons for migration include packing in order to reduce fragmentation (39,40), and the need to withdraw from a workstation when its owner returns (41).

Migration is simple on shared-memory machines, because threads do not have any state that is local to the processor except for their cache and translation lookaside buffer (TLB) footprints. The challenge is to ensure that interacting threads map to distinct processors.

Migration is significantly more problematic in distributed memory machines as it requires migrating the local memory, which can be a very expensive operation. The ability to migrate a task is often hindered by systems whose message-passing libraries specify physical processor numbers as source or destination fields for messages. Note that the elimination of virtual to physical processor mapping increases the speed of a communication. Many systems map the network first-in, first-out (FIFO) queues into user space; disconnecting and reconnecting may also require significant overhead.

Global Queue

Perhaps the simplest way to implement a parallel operating-system scheduler is to run a copy of a uniprocessor system on each node while sharing the main data structures, specifically the run queue. Threads that are ready to run are placed in this queue. Processors pick the first thread from the queue, execute it for a certain time quantum, and then return it to the queue. This approach is especially common on small-scale bus-based UMA shared-memory machines, such as Sequent multiprocessors (42) and Silicon Graphics multiprocessor workstations (43), and is also used in the Mach operating system (44).

The main merit of a global queue is that it provides automatic load sharing. No processor is idle if there is any waiting thread in the system. However, this comes at a price. One problem is contention for the global queue, which grows with the number of processors. Another is that threads will typically execute on different processors each time they are scheduled. As a result, threads cannot stash data in local memory, and their cache state is wiped out with each rescheduling. This effect is countered to a certain degree by *affinity* scheduling, which attempts to reschedule threads on the same processors they used before (45). Alternatively, it is possible to provide global load balance with local queues and occasional migration to overcome any imbalance (46).

A third problem with a global queue is that the threads in a single application are scheduled in an uncoordinated manner. If the threads do not interact with each other, this is okay. But in many parallel programs, the threads do interact and synchronize with each other. If the threads interact at a high rate (i.e., at a fine granularity), the lack of coordination in the scheduling implies that often the interacting partners will not be executing at the same time. Therefore, the interactions will not be able to proceed, inducing extra context switches and overhead (19).

Finally, scheduling from a global queue has the interesting property that the service a job receives is proportional to the number of threads that it spawns. It is subject to debate whether this is good or bad. On one hand, this is a natural way for jobs that require more computation to get the necessary resources. On the other hand, it impairs fairness and might be susceptible to user countermeasures. These problems can probably be solved by suitable accounting practices.

Variable Partitioning

Nowadays, most systems allow the processors to be partitioned on a job-by-job basis. This is sometimes referred to as *space slicing*. The exact number of processors may be forced to match the topology of the machine, as in hypercube topologies in which partitions must also be hypercubes, but of a smaller dimension. However, in many cases, especially when the network topology is hidden from the programmer, there are no such restrictions, and partitions may be formed using arbitrary subsets of processors.

There are different approaches to partitioning, and the following taxonomy is common (see Table 3) (1): *Fixed* partitioning is when the partition sizes are set in advance by the system administrator. Repartitioning requires a reboot. *Variable* is when the set of nodes are partitioned according to user requests when jobs are submitted; that is, a large partition can be divided into smaller partitions to allow several small jobs to execute in parallel. Partitions are fused when the jobs terminate. *Adaptive* is when the partitions are automatically set by the system according to current load when the job is submitted. *Dynamic* is when the size can change at run time to reflect changes in requirements and load. Of these, the most popular are variable and dynamic partitioning.

TABLE 3   A Taxonomy of Partitioning Schemes

| Scheme | Parameters taken into account | | |
	User request	System load	Changes
Fixed	No	No	No
Variable	Yes	No	No
Adaptive	Yes	Yes	No
Dynamic	Yes	Yes	Yes

A rigid job is submitted for execution along with a specification of the number of processors that it requires. The scheduler then creates a partition of that size and schedules the job to execute within that partition (20,36,38,47–50). With moldable jobs, it is the scheduler that selects the partition size (24).

Evolving and malleable jobs require partitions that are not only flexible but can also change dynamically at run time. This places an added burden both on the programmer, who must write application code that requests and adapts to such changes, and on the scheduler, that must handle the reallocation decisions and coordinate them with the applications.

Variable partitioning is popular on distributed-memory machines and is used on Intel and nCUBE hypercubes, on the IBM SP2, on the Intel Paragon, on the Meiko CS-2, and on the Cray T3D. The nonuniform memory access feature or the lack of a shared address space of these machines make the previous global queue approach impractical. The advantages of running a job on a dedicated partition with variable partitioning is that this gives a good approximation of a dedicated machine. It places the needs of individual jobs over that of the system. The program has control over the distribution of data in the memories of the processors on which it runs. There is no cache interference and no operating system overheads. Depending on the system topology, there may also be no network interference (in hypercubes, for example, each subcube uses a disjoint set of links, but in systems that use a multistage network, such as an IBM SP2, some links may be shared by different partitions).

Of course, variable partitioning also has some disadvantages. These disadvantages stem from the possible mismatch between the available processors and the user requests. Two distinct problems may occur. One is fragmentation, which occurs when the available (free) processors are insufficient to satisfy the requests of any submitted jobs, so these processors are left idle. The other problem is that submitted jobs can be queued for a long time until the requested processors become available. Even if allocated processors are momentarily idle due to an I/O operation, they cannot be given to another job. Therefore, variable partitioning is more suitable for batch processing than for interactive work. Indeed, the inability to run a program when desired sometimes causes significant user frustration, especially during the program-development phase. To reduce this effect, sophisticated batch systems are designed (36,37,51).

Dynamic Partitioning with Two-Level Scheduling

One way to reduce the waiting time of queued jobs is to prevent jobs from monopolizing too many processors when the system is heavily loaded. This is done by adaptive partitioning schemes, and several ideas about how to allocate the processors have been proposed (52). The problem with adaptive partitioning, however, is that once a number of processors are allocated to a job, this number is fixed until the job terminates. It does not change in response to load changes and cannot be changed to reflect changes in the degree of parallelism in the job.

Changes in allocation during execution are provided by dynamic partitioning. To support such behavior, applications are required to use a programming model that can both express changes in requirements and handle system-induced changes in allocation. This is typically done by using a workpile model, where the work to be done is represented as an unordered pile of tasks or chores, and the computation is carried out by a set of worker threads, one per processor, that take one chore at a time from the workpile. This decouples the work (the chores) from the agents of computation (the workers) and allows for adjustment to different numbers of processors by changing the number of workers. The result is a two-level scheduling scheme: The operating system deals with the allocation of processors to jobs while the applications handle the scheduling of chores on those processors.

One common heuristic for dynamic partitioning is to strive for equal-sized partitions (usually called "equipartitioning") (53). The problem with this approach is that it might require all jobs to be interrupted whenever something changes. An alternative is to use *folding* (53). With folding, the number of processors allocated to a job can only grow or shrink by factors of 2; that is, the partition size may be halved or doubled. When a partition is halved, the run-time system may choose to simply "fold over" the application, and time-slice two tasks on each processor. Thus, an application that has a balanced workload over a particular partition size is likely to remain balanced after a folding operation. Many speedup curves resemble step functions, with poor speedup values for nonpowers of two number of processors. However, there is some debate over the benefits of folding (29,30).

Dynamic partitioning with two-level scheduling is probably the most studied parallel scheduling scheme and has repeatedly been shown to be superior to other schemes (31,32) either by analytic means or through simulation with synthetic workloads. This is due to a number of factors:

- There is no loss of resources to fragmentation.
- There is no overhead for context switching, except that for redistributing the processors when the load changes. The second level of scheduling within the application is assumed to require less overhead.
- There is no waste of CPU cycles on busy waiting for synchronization, as threads can be blocked inexpensively.
- The degree of parallelism provided to each job is automatically decreased under load conditions, leading to better efficiency. This is often hidden from application programmers by a user-level thread library.

However, dynamic partitioning does have its drawbacks. It does not support popular programming styles such as the SPMD (used by MPI) and dataparallel (used by HPF) models. Moreover, the overheads for repartitioning may negate the benefits that were expected (54). Finally, it could lead to extensive queuing if sufficient processors are not available. It has, therefore, been suggested that dynamic partitioning be combined with gang scheduling (55).

In addition, dynamic partitioning requires extensive coordination between the operating system and the application's internal scheduler, so as to handle the changes in processor allocation efficiently (33). For example, if a processor is taken away from an application, the whole application might deadlock if the thread running on that processor happened to be holding a lock. To prevent such scenarios, the application's run-time system should be notified so it can take appropriate action. This means that the operating system and the programming environment run-time system must be designed together, limiting their portability and ability to work in other environments. A possible solution is to only change the processor allocation at certain points in the program (e.g., at the beginning of a new parallel loop) (56).

As a result of the above shortcomings, dynamic partitioning has so far been used only to a very limited degree, mainly in the context of running parallel jobs on networks of workstations, where the workstation must be returned to its owner when required (26,57).

Gang Scheduling

The only way to guarantee interactive response times is via time slicing. However, this should not be done in an uncoordinated manner, as with a global queue. Rather, the context switching should be coordinated across the processors. Thus, all the threads in the job will execute at the same time, allowing them to interact at a fine granularity. In addition, the threads can be mapped permanently to processors, allowing them to make use of local memory and maybe to benefit from sustained cache state. This solution is completely general, and works for any programming model. In fact, it decouples the application from the operating system. This approach is used by some vendors [e.g., the CM-5 from Thinking Machines (58), the IRIX system on SGI multiprocessors (43), the Intel Paragon (59), and the Meiko CS-2]. It has also been studied in academia and research prototypes (60–63).

It should be noted that gang scheduling is nearly always coupled with some form of partitioning as well—that is, a number of jobs are executed side by side in each time slot. This adds flexibility and reduces the adverse effects of fragmentation. It has also been suggested to improve utilization even further by shortening the time slice in slots that suffer from high fragmentation (15).

An interesting variant of gang scheduling is based on the observation that coordinated scheduling is only needed if the job's threads interact frequently (19). Therefore, the rate of interaction can be used to drive the grouping of threads into gangs (64,65). Other variants include *coscheduling*, which attempts to schedule a large subset of the gang if it is impossible to schedule all the threads at once, and *family scheduling*, which allows more threads than processors and uses a second level of internal time slicing (66). Note that it is desirable to also preempt the network (i.e., to flush any traffic that belongs to the job that is being descheduled) so as to present a clean slate to the new job (67).

Gang scheduling suffers the overhead of context switching and corrupts the cache state, but for a large enough time quantum, these overheads can be made insignificant (32). In addition, there may be some fragmentation. However, due to the time slicing, its effect is less severe than in variable partitioning (68,69). Indeed, most studies find that gang scheduling is nearly as efficient as dynamic partitioning (70). Time slicing, in general, reduces the average response time provided the distribution of execution times has a large variance (5), which, in fact, is typical in practice (4).

RESEARCH CLUSTERS

The spectrum of job schedulers for parallel machines may be expected to span a large part of all the different options for assumptions about goals, metrics, and workloads. In fact, this is not so. Several "clusters" have formed, each with its own set of assumptions and often oblivious of the others. This section identifies and characterizes these "clusters of assumptions." The clusters are summarized in Table 4. The most controversial part is probably our classification of the goals. Mostly, if the scheduling system ensured that jobs run with all their required resources in a timely fashion, response time was considered as a goal. We evaluated the goals of utilization and throughput by considering how the scheduler treats large batch jobs and small interactive jobs.

Rigid Jobs and Variable Partitioning

Maybe the simplest scheduling scheme is to reduce the role of the operating system to that of a processor rental agency. Jobs request a certain number of processors, and the system provides them for exclusive use if they are available. The only goal

TABLE 4   "Clusters" of Common Combinations of Assumptions

	Variable partitioning	Gang scheduling	Shared queue	Adaptive partitioning	Dynamic partitioning
Goals					
Run jobs	Yes	Yes	Yes	Yes	Yes
Utilization	No			Yes	Yes
Throughput	No		Yes	Yes	Yes
Response	No	Yes		No	
Admin					
Dedicated	Yes	Yes	Yes		No
Workloads					
Rigid	Yes	Yes	Yes	Yes	No
Evolving	No	No	Yes	No	Yes
Moldable	Yes	Yes	Yes	Yes	No
Malleable	No	No	No	No	Yes
Actions					
Partitioning	Yes	Yes	No	Yes	Yes
Preemption	No	Yes	Yes	No	Yes
Synchronized	N/A	Yes	No	N/A	No
Migration	No	No	Yes	No	
Ordering	Yes	N/A	N/A		

is to (eventually) run the jobs. No knowledge about job behavior is assumed, and no special actions need be supported, except some measure of partitioning the machine. This scheme has been called "variable partitioning" or "pure space sharing" in the literature.

Despite its simplicity and the resulting drawbacks in terms of responsiveness, fragmentation, and reliability, this scheme is widely used. It is especially common on large distributed-memory machines (20,38,48,49,71). The reason is that it gets the job done, albeit not optimally, but with relatively little investment in system development. In an industry where time-to-market is a crucial element of success, this is a true virtue (47). As a result, users sometimes have to revert to sign-up sheets as the actual processor allocation mechanism.

Because variable partitioning cannot run jobs immediately if the requested number of processors is not available, jobs often have to be queued. As a result, this scheme implies a batch mode of operation. With sufficient backlog, it is then possible to select an execution order that improves system utilization and throughput (36,72). Thus, even this simple scheme has bred some interesting research. In addition, it has prompted research into improvements such as adaptive and dynamic partitioning (see below).

Rigid Jobs and Gang Scheduling

Gang scheduling has been reinvented many times over because it is an intuitive extension of time-sharing on uniprocessors. It supports interactive use and gives the illusion of using a dedicated machine, without placing restrictions on the programming model and without assuming knowledge about the workload. It has, therefore, enjoyed considerable popularity among vendors, at least in the form of "hype" (all vendors claim to support some form of gang scheduling), but good implementations also exist. Moreover, there have been a number of experimental implementations (40,60,61,63,73,74) that demonstrate its usefulness.

Academically speaking, gang scheduling has repeatedly been shown to be inferior to dynamic partitioning (see below) but only by a small margin (32,75). The main drawbacks cited are interference with cache state and possible loss of resources to fragmentation. As the first can be lessened by using long time quanta (32), and recent research suggests that the second is not so severe (40), it seems that the advantages of gang scheduling generally outweigh its drawbacks. Furthermore, time slicing is known to be crucial for achieving low average response times under workloads with high variability (5,55).

However, there are still some unresolved issues. The main one concerns the possible interaction between gang scheduling and overcommitting memory resources. Time slicing between two active jobs requires more memory that executing these jobs sequentially. The direct solution is to provide adequate swapping to disks, but, so far, little research has been done on this issue, and parallel systems are notoriously underpowered in terms of I/O. Another criticism of gang scheduling is the lack of fault tolerance—if a processor fails, many jobs may have to be aborted. Although important, this problem is not unique to gang scheduling: It is also present in other scheduling schemes and in other components of parallel operating systems (e.g., message-passing facilities).

In summary, gang scheduling is a promising policy for general workloads, and not only for jobs that exhibit fine granularity of interaction between threads.

Evolving Jobs and a Shared Queue

Another simple extension of time-sharing on uniprocessors is to use a shared queue. Each processor chooses a process from the head of the centralized ready queue, executes it for a time quantum, and then returns it to the tail of the queue. As processors are not allocated permanently to jobs, the number of processes in a job may change during run time without causing any problems. This scheme is especially suitable for shared-memory multiprocessors, and, indeed, it is used on many bus-based systems (42,43).

Using a shared queue as described above may suffer from three drawbacks: contention for the queue, frequent migration of processes, and lack of coordinated scheduling. The issue of possible contention has led to the design of wait-free queues, where different processes can access the queue simultaneously by using suitable hardware primitives, such as fetch-and-add. Indeed, this was one of the driving forces in the design of the NYU Ultracomputer, and its support for fetch-and-add via a combining multistage network (76). However, the idea of combining networks has not caught on because of their added complexity and design costs.

Migration occurs in this scheme because processes are typically executed on a different processor each time they arrive at the head of the queue. As a result, any state that may be left in a processor's cache is lost. It has been suggested that this effect can be reduced by using affinity scheduling, where an effort is made to reschedule the process on the same processor as used last time (77,78). However, it is not clear to what degree data indeed remain in the cache, and, in any case, affinity scheduling is largely equivalent to just using longer time quanta (45).

The third issue, lack of coordinated scheduling, may cause problems for applications where the processes interact with each other frequently. The only solution is to use gang scheduling. Although gang scheduling and a shared queue seem to be in conflict with each other, a scheme that integrates both has been designed in the context of the IRIX operating system for SGI multiprocessor workstations (43).

Finally, it should be noted that this scheme benefits from similarity with run-time systems and thread packages that run within the confines of a single job.

Moldable Jobs and Adaptive Partitioning

As noted above, variable partitioning is a simple but somewhat inefficient scheduling scheme. The inefficiencies result both from fragmentation, where the remaining processors are insufficient for any queued job, and from the fact that jobs may request more processors than they can use efficiently. It is, therefore, an interesting exercise to assess the degree to which efficiency can be improved by adding flexibility and information about the characteristics of different jobs.

The model adopted for this line of research is that jobs can be molded to run on different numbers of processors, and some information about their average parallelism or execution profile is provided. This allows the system to judiciously choose partition sizes, without significantly affecting the programming model. Thus, when the system is lightly loaded, jobs are allowed to use larger numbers of processors, even if they do not utilize them efficiently, but when system load increases, jobs are cut down to size (24,25,79). It has also been suggested that the system keep some processors idle on the side in anticipation of additional arrivals (52).

In summary, this approach has generated a rather large body of research, but it has yet to lead to any implementations in real systems.

Malleable Jobs and Dynamic Partitioning

A more extreme approach to system optimization calls for sacrificing common programming models along with the illusion of a dedicated machine in order to promote efficiency. In some sense, this approach demonstrates the best performance that can be achieved, given full system flexibility in the allocation of resources, and jobs that are willing to cooperate with the system (and through it, with each other).

The programming model requires each job to accurately inform the system about its resource requirements and be able to adapt to changes in resource allocation that result from fluctuations in system load. The system uses information about the characteristics of the jobs to decide on the optimal allocation: Jobs are only given additional processors if there is nothing better to do with them. When a new job arrives, some processors are taken from existing jobs and given to the new job, so that it will not have to wait. When a job terminates, its processors are distributed among the other jobs, so as not to waste them (31,53,80).

A good implementation requires the codesign of the operating system, the run-time system, and the programming environment (33). Indeed, no production implementation for parallel machines have been reported so far, despite much research that shows the benefits of this approach in terms of efficiency. On the other hand, this approach has the unique advantage that jobs may be able to tolerate system faults: A faulty processor is similar to one that is taken away and given to another job. Likewise, jobs running on a network of workstations will be able to tolerate workstations that drop out of the processor pool when they are reclaimed by their owners. Therefore, this approach has lately become prominent in the context of network computing (26,57).

CONCLUSIONS

The issue of job scheduling has suffered due to the common lack of distinction between job scheduling by the operating system and static or dynamic scheduling within an application by the programmer or run-time system. Nevertheless, hundreds of papers about parallel job scheduling have been published. Despite this large body of work, we seem to be at the beginning of a long road, and much remains to be done. Specific topics that cry out for further research include the following:

- Integration of scheduling with other system services, and most notably, with memory management. This includes requirements that the scheduling subsystem places on the hardware and I/O subsystem, and interactions between the different subsystems.
- Better characterization of the workloads that are found on general-purpose parallel systems. This includes the jobs themselves (how many processors they use, how much memory they need, how long they run) and issues such as the arrival process.

- Evaluation of alternatives that is both fair (i.e., use the best possible implementation of each scheme) and informative (i.e., use the same workloads and metrics, and make it the right metrics).

Of course, there is also ample place for more work on scheduling schemes for both common parallel systems and emerging new types of systems, such as multiheaded architectures (81) and NOWs (26,82). The future will tell which of these survive the ultimate test, that of satisfying real users.

REFERENCES

1. D. G. Feitelson, "A Survey of Scheduling in Multiprogrammed Parallel Systems," Research Report RC 19790 (87657), IBM T. J. Watson Research Center (Oct. 1994).
2. W. Saphir, L. A. Tanner, and B. Traversat, "Job Management Requirements for NAS Parallel Systems and Clusters," in *Job Scheduling Strategies for Parallel Processing*, D. G. Feitelson and L. Rudolph (eds.), Lecture Notes in Computer Science Vol. 949, Springer-Verlag, New York, 1995, pp. 319–336.
3. M. E. Rosenkrantz, D. J. Schneider, R. Leibensperger, M. Shore, and J. Zollweg, "Requirements of the Cornell Theory Center for Resource Management and Process Scheduling," in *Job Scheduling Strategies for Parallel Processing*, D. G. Feitelson and L. Rudolph (eds.), Lecture Notes in Computer Science Vol. 949, Springer-Verlag, New York, 1995, pp. 304–318.
4. D. G. Feitelson and B. Nitzberg, "Job Characteristics of a Production Parallel Scientific Workload on the NASA Ames iPSC/860," in *Job Scheduling Strategies for Parallel Processing*, D. G. Feitelson and L. Rudolph (eds.), Lecture Notes in Computer Science Vol. 949, Springer-Verlag, New York, 1995, pp. 337–360.
5. E. W. Parsons and K. C. Sevcik, "Multiprocessor Scheduling for High-Variability Service Time Distributions," in *Job Scheduling Strategies for Parallel Processing*, D. G. Feitelson and L. Rudolph (eds.), Lecture Notes in Computer Science Vol. 949, Springer-Verlag, New York, 1995, pp. 127–145.
6. I. Stoica, H. Abdel-Wahab, and A. Pothen, "A Microeconomic Scheduler for Parallel Computers," in *Job Scheduling Strategies for Parallel Processing*, D. G. Feitelson and L. Rudolph (eds.), Lecture Notes in Computer Science Vol. 949, Springer-Verlag, New York, 1995, pp. 200–218.
7. M. G. Norman and P. Thanisch, "Models of Machines and Computation for Mapping in Multicomputers," *ACM Comput. Surv.*, 25(3), 263–302 (1993).
8. J. D. Ullman, "Complexity of Sequencing Problems," in *Computer and Job-Shop Scheduling Theory*, E. G. Coffman, Jr. (ed.), John Wiley and Sons, New York, 1976.
9. M. J. Gonzalez, Jr., "Deterministic Processor Scheduling," *ACM Comput. Surv.*, 9(3), 173–204 (1977).
10. V. M. Lo, "Heuristic Algorithms for Task Assignment in Distributed Systems," *IEEE Trans. Computers*, C-37(11), 1384–1397 (1988).
11. C. H. Papadimitriou and M. Yannakakis, "Towards an Architecture-Independent Analysis of Parallel Algorithms," *SIAM J. Comput.*, 19(2), 322–328 (1990).
12. S. H. Bokhari, "On the Mapping Problem," *IEEE Trans. Computers*, C-30(3), 207–214 (1981).
13. C. M. Pancake, "Multithreaded Languages for Scientific and Technical Computing," *Proc. IEEE*, 81(2), 288–304 (1993).
14. D. J. Lilja, "Exploiting the Parallelism Available in Loops," *Computer*, 27(2), 13–26 (1994).
15. D. G. Feitelson and L. Rudolph, "Evaluation of Design Choices for Gang Scheduling Using Distributed Hierarchical Control," *J. Parallel Distributed Comput.*, 35(1), 18–34 (1996).

16. J. Peterson and A. Silberschatz, *Operating System Concepts*, Addison-Wesley, Reading, MA, 1983.

17. P. Brinch Hansen, "An Analysis of Response Ratio Scheduling," in *IFIP Congress*, Ljubljana, August, 1971, pp. TA-3 150-154.

18. D. G. Feitelson and L. Rudolph, "Parallel Job Scheduling: Issues and Approaches," in *Job Scheduling Strategies for Parallel Processing*, D. G. Feitelson and L. Rudolph (eds.), Lecture Notes in Computer Science Vol. 949, Springer-Verlag, New York, 1995, pp. 1-18.

19. D. G. Feitelson and L. Rudolph, "Gang Scheduling Performance Benefits for Fine-Grain Synchronization," *J. Parallel Distributed Comput.*, *16*(4), 306-318 (1992).

20. J. Gehring and F. Ramme, "Architecture-Independent Request-Scheduling with Tight Waiting-Time Estimations," in *Job Scheduling Strategies for Parallel Processing*, D. G. Feitelson and L. Rudolph (eds.), Lecture Notes in Computer Science Vol. 1162, Springer-Verlag, New York, 1996, pp. 65-88.

21. A. A. Khokhar, V. K. Prasanna, M. E. Shaaban, and C-L. Wang, "Heterogeneous Computing: Challenges and Opportunities," *Computer*, *26*(6), 18-27 (1993).

22. A. Geist, A. Beguelin, J. Dongarra, W. Jiang, R. Manchek, and V. Sunderam, "PVM 3 User's Guide and Reference Manual," Technical Report ORNL/TM-12187, Oak Ridge National Laboratory (May 1994).

23. J. Zahorjan and C. McCann, "Processor Scheduling in Shared Memory Multiprocessors," in *SIGMETRICS Conf. Measurement & Modeling of Comput. Syst.*, May 1990, pp. 214-225.

24. E. Rosti, E. Smirni, L. W. Dowdy, G. Serazzi, and B. M. Carlson, "Robust Partitioning Schemes of Multiprocessor Systems," *Perform. Eval.*, *19*(2-3), 141-165 (1994).

25. K. C. Sevcik, "Application Scheduling and Processor Allocation in Multiprogrammed Parallel Processing Systems," *Perform. Eval.*, *19*(2-3), 107-140 (1994).

26. J. Pruyne and M. Livny, "Parallel Processing on Dynamic Resources with CARMI," in *Job Scheduling Strategies for Parallel Processing*, D. G. Feitelson and L. Rudolph (eds.), Lecture Notes in Computer Science Vol. 949, Springer-Verlag, New York, 1995, pp. 259-278.

27. T. D. Nguyen, R. Vaswani, and J. Zahorjan, "Parallel Application Characterization for Multiprocessor Scheduling Policy Design," in *Job Scheduling Strategies for Parallel Processing*, D. G. Feitelson and L. Rudolph (eds.), Lecture Notes in Computer Science Vol. 1162, Springer-Verlag, New York, 1996, pp. 175-199.

28. S-H. Chiang and M. Vernon, "Dynamic vs. Static Quantum-Based Parallel Processor Allocation," in *Job Scheduling Strategies for Parallel Processing*, D. G. Feitelson and L. Rudolph (eds.), Springer-Verlag, Lecture Notes in Computer Science Vol. 1162, Springer-Verlag, New York, 1996, pp. 200-223.

29. N. Islam, A. Prodromidis, and M. Squillante, "Dynamic Partitioning in Different Distributed-Memory Environments," in *Job Scheduling Strategies for Parallel Processing*, D. G. Feitelson and L. Rudolph (eds.), Lecture Notes in Computer Science Vol. 1162, Springer-Verlag, New York, 1996, pp. 244-270.

30. J. D. Padhye and L. W. Dowdy, "Dynamic Versus Adoptive Processor Allocation Policies for Message Passing Parallel Computers: An Empirical Comparison," in *Job Scheduling Strategies for Parallel Processing*, D. G. Feitelson and L. Rudolph (eds.), Lecture Notes in Computer Science Vol. 1162, Springer-Verlag, New York, 1996, pp. 224-243.

31. C. McCann, R. Vaswani, and J. Zahorjan, "A Dynamic Processor Allocation Policy for Multiprogrammed Shared-Memory Multiprocessors," *ACM Trans. Comput. Syst.*, *11*(2), 146-178 (1993).

32. A. Gupta, A. Tucker, and S. Urushibara, "The Impact of Operating System Scheduling Policies and Synchronization Methods on the Performance of Parallel Applications," in *SIGMETRICS Conf. Measurement & Modeling of Comput. Syst.*, May 1991, pp. 120-132.

33. T. E. Anderson, B. N. Bershad, E. D. Lazowska, and H. M. Levy, "Scheduler Activations: Effective Kernel Support for the User-Level Management of Parallelism," *ACM Trans. Comput. Syst.*, *10*(1), 53–79 (1992).

34. T. D. Nguyen, R. Vaswani, and J. Zahorjan, "Using Runtime Measured Workload Characteristics in Parallel Processor Scheduling," in *Job Scheduling Strategies for Parallel Processing*, D. G. Feitelson and L. Rudolph (eds.), Lecture Notes in Computer Science Vol. 1162, Springer-Verlag, New York, 1996, pp. 155–174.

35. Y. A. Khalidi, J. Bernabeu, V. Matena, K. Shirriff, and M. Thadani, "Solaris MC: A Multi Computer OS," in *Proc. USENIX Conf.*, January 1996, pp. 191–203.

36. D. Lifka, "The ANL/IBM SP Scheduling System," in *Job Scheduling Strategies for Parallel Processing*, D. G. Feitelson and L. Rudolph (eds.), Lecture Notes in Computer Science Vol. 949, Springer-Verlag, New York, 1995, pp. 295–303.

37. R. L. Henderson, "Job Scheduling Under the Portable Batch System," in *Job Scheduling Strategies for Parallel Processing*, D. G. Feitelson and L. Rudolph (eds.), Lecture Notes in Computer Science Vol. 949, Springer-Verlag, New York, 1995, pp. 279–294.

38. M. Wan, R. Moore, G. Kremenek, and K. Steube, "A Batch Scheduler for the Intel Paragon MPP System with a Non-contiguous Node Allocation Algorithm," in *Job Scheduling Strategies for Parallel Processing*, D. G. Feitelson and L. Rudolph (eds.), Lecture Notes in Computer Science Vol. 1162, Springer-Verlag, New York, 1996, pp. 48–64.

39. M-S. Chen and K. G. Shin, "Subcube Allocation and Task Migration in Hypercube Multiprocessors," *IEEE Trans. Computers*, *39*(9), 1146–1155 (1990).

40. D. G. Feitelson, "Packing Schemes for Gang Scheduling," in *Job Scheduling Strategies for Parallel Processing*, D. G. Feitelson and L. Rudolph (eds.), Lecture Notes in Computer Science Vol. 1162, Springer-Verlag, New York, 1996, pp. 89–110.

41. J. Pruyne and M. Livny, "Managing Checkpoints for Parallel Programs," in *Job Scheduling Strategies for Parallel Processing*, D. G. Feitelson and L. Rudolph (eds.), Lecture Notes in Computer Science Vol. 1162, Springer-Verlag, New York, 1996, pp. 140–154.

42. S. Thakkar, P. Gifford, and G. Fielland, "Balance: A Shared Memory Multiprocessor System," in *2nd Intl. Conf. Supercomputing*, 1987, Vol. I, pp. 93–101.

43. J. M. Barton and N. Bitar, "A Scalable Multi-discipline, Multiple-Processor Scheduling Framework for IRIX," in *Job Scheduling Strategies for Parallel Processing*, D. G. Feitelson and L. Rudolph (eds.), Lecture Notes in Computer Science Vol. 949, Springer-Verlag, New York, 1995, pp. 45–69.

44. D. L. Black, "Scheduling Support for Concurrency and Parallelism in the Mach Operating System," *Computer*, *23*(5), 35–43 (1990).

45. J. Torrellas, A. Tucker, and A. Gupta, "Evaluating the Performance of Cache-Affinity Scheduling in Shared-Memory Multiprocessors," *J. Parallel Distributed Comput.*, *24*(2), 139–151 (1995).

46. L. Rudolph, M. Slivkin-Allalouf, and E. Upfal, "A Simple Load Balancing Scheme for Task Allocation in Parallel Machines," in *3rd Symp. Parallel Algorithms & Architectures*, July 1991, pp. 237–245.

47. T. Agerwala, J. L. Martin, J. H. Mirza, D. C. Sadler, D. M. Dias, and M. Snir, "SP2 System Architecture," *IBM Syst. J.*, *34*(2), 152–184 (1995).

48. D. Das Sharma and D. K. Pradhan, "A Fast and Efficient Strategy for Submesh Allocation in Mesh-Connected Parallel Computers," in *IEEE Symp. Parallel & Distributed Processing*, December 1993, pp. 682–689.

49. P. Krueger, T-H. Lai, and V. A. Dixit-Radiya, "Job Scheduling Is More Important Than Processor Allocation for Hypercube Computers," *IEEE Trans. Parallel Distributed Syst.*, *5*(5), 488–497 (1994).

50. W. Liu, V. Lo, K. Windisch, and B. Nitzberg, "Non-contiguous Processor Allocation Algorithms for Distributed Memory Multicomputers," in *Supercomputing '94*, November 1994, pp. 227–236.

51. O. Kipersztok and J. C. Patterson, "Intelligent Fuzzy Control to Augment the Schedul-

ing Capabilities of Network Queueing Systems," in *Job Scheduling Strategies for Parallel Processing*, D. G. Feitelson and L. Rudolph (eds.), Lecture Notes in Computer Science Vol. 949, Springer-Verlag, New York, 1995, pp. 239–258.

52. E. Rosti, E. Smirni, G. Serazzi, and L. W. Dowdy, "Analysis of Non-work-Conserving Processor Partitioning Policies," in *Job Scheduling Strategies for Parallel Processing*, D. G. Feitelson and L. Rudolph (eds.), Lecture Notes in Computer Science Vol. 949, Springer-Verlag, New York, 1995, pp. 165–181.

53. C. McCann and J. Zahorjan, "Processor Allocation Policies for Message Passing Parallel Computers," in *SIGMETRICS Conf. Measurement & Modeling of Comput. Syst.*, May 1994, pp. 19–32.

54. M. S. Squillante, "On the Benefits and Limitations of Dynamic Partitioning in Parallel Computer Systems," in *Job Scheduling Strategies for Parallel Processing*, D. G. Feitelson and L. Rudolph (eds.), Lecture Notes in Computer Science Vol. 949, Springer-Verlag, New York, 1995, pp. 219–238.

55. C. McCann and J. Zahorjan, "Scheduling Memory Constrained Jobs on Distributed Memory Parallel Computers," in *SIGMETRICS Conf. Measurement & Modeling of Comput. Syst.*, May 1995, pp. 208–219.

56. K. K. Yue and D. J. Lilja, "Loop-Level Process Control: An Effective Processor Allocation Policy for Multiprogrammed Shared-Memory Multiprocessors," in *Job Scheduling Strategies for Parallel Processing*, D. G. Feitelson and L. Rudolph (eds.), Lecture Notes in Computer Science Vol. 949, Springer-Verlag, New York, 1995, pp. 182–199.

57. N. Carriero, E. Freedman, D. Gelernter, and D. Kaminsky, "Adaptive Parallelism and Piranha," *Computer*, 28(1), 40–49 (1995).

58. C. E. Leiserson, Z. S. Abuhamdeh, D. C. Douglas, C. R. Feynman, M. N. Ganmukhi, J. V. Hill, W. D. Hillis, B. C. Kuszmaul, M. A. St. Pierre, D. S. Wells, M. C. Wong, S-W. Yang, and R. Zak, "The Network Architecture of the Connection Machine CM-5," in *4th Symp. Parallel Algorithms & Architectures*, June 1992, pp. 272–285.

59. Intel Supercomputer Systems Division, *Paragon User's Guide*, Intel, Beaverton, OR, 1994.

60. J. K. Ousterhout, "Scheduling Techniques for Concurrent Systems," in *3rd Intl. Conf. Distributed Comput. Syst.*, October 1982, pp. 22–30.

61. D. G. Feitelson and L. Rudolph, "Distributed Hierarchical Control for Parallel Processing," *Computer*, 23(5), 65–77 (1990).

62. B. C. Gorda and E. D. Brooks III, "Gang Scheduling a Parallel Machine," Technical Report UCRL-JC-107020, Lawrence Livermore National Laboratory (Dec. 1991).

63. A. Hori, T. Yokota, Y. Ishikawa, S. Sakai, H. Konaka, M. Maeda, T. Tomokiyo, J. Nolte, H. Matsuoka, K. Okamoto, and H. Hirono, "Time Space Sharing Scheduling and Architectural Support," in *Job Scheduling Strategies for Parallel Processing*, D. G. Feitelson and L. Rudolph (eds.), Lecture Notes in Computer Science Vol. 949, Springer-Verlag, New York, 1995, pp. 92–105.

64. D. G. Feitelson and L. Rudolph, "Coscheduling Based on Runtime Identification of Activity Working Sets," *Intl. J. Parallel Programming*, 23(2), 135–160 (1995).

65. P. G. Sobalvarro and W. E. Weihl, "Demand-Based Coscheduling of Parallel Jobs on Multiprogrammed Multiprocessors," in *Job Scheduling Strategies for Parallel Processing*, D. G. Feitelson and L. Rudolph (eds.), Lecture Notes in Computer Science Vol. 949, Springer-Verlag, New York, 1995, pp. 106–126.

66. R. M. Bryant, H-Y. Chang, and B. S. Rosenburg, "Operating System Support for Parallel Programming on RP3," *IBM J. Res. Devel.*, 35(5/6), 617–634 (1991).

67. A. Hori, H. Tezuka, Y. Ishikawa, N. Soda, H. Konaka, and M. Maeda, "Implementation of Gang-Scheduling on Workstation Cluster," in *Job Scheduling Strategies for Parallel Processing*, D. G. Feitelson and L. Rudolph (eds.), Lecture Notes in Computer Science Vol. 1162, Springer-Verlag, New York, 1996, pp. 126–139.

68. D. G. Feitelson and L. Rudolph, "Mapping and Scheduling in a Shared Parallel Environment Using Distributed Hierarchical Control," in *Intl. Conf. Parallel Processing*, August 1990, Vol. I, pp. 1–8.

69. D. G. Feitelson and L. Rudolph, "Wasted Resources in Gang Scheduling," in *5th Jerusalem Conf. Information Technology*, IEEE Computer Society Press, Los Alamitos, CA, 1990, pp. 127–136.

70. R. Chandra, S. Devine, B. Verghese, A. Gupta, and M. Rosenblum, "Scheduling and Page Migration for Multiprocessor Compute Servers," in *6th Intl. Conf. Architect. Support for Prog. Lang. & Operating Syst.*, November 1994, pp. 12–24.

71. S. Hotovy, "Workload Evolution on the Cornell Theory Center IBM SP2," in *Job Scheduling Strategies for Parallel Processing*, D. G. Feitelson and L. Rudolph (eds.), Lecture Notes in Computer Science Vol. 1162, Springer-Verlag, New York, 1996, pp. 27–40.

72. J. Skovira, W. Chan, H. Zhou, and D. Lifka, "The EASY–LoadLeveler API Project," in *Job Scheduling Strategies for Parallel Processing*, D. G. Feitelson and L. Rudolph (eds.), Lecture Notes in Computer Science Vol. 1162, Springer-Verlag, New York, 1996, pp. 41–47.

73. F. Wang, H. Franke, M. Papaefthymiou, P. Pattnaik, L. Rudolph, and M. Squillante, "A Gang Scheduling Design for Multiprogrammed Parallel Computing Environments," in *Job Scheduling Strategies for Parallel Processing*, D. G. Feitelson and L. Rudolph (eds.), Lecture Notes in Computer Science Vol. 1162, Springer-Verlag, New York, 1996, pp. 111–125.

74. B. Gorda and R. Wolski, "Time Sharing Massively Parallel Machines," in *Intl. Conf. Parallel Processing*, August 1995, Vol. II, pp. 214–217.

75. M. Crovella, P. Das, C. Dubnicki, T. LeBlanc, and E. Markatos, "Multiprogramming on Multiprocessors," in *3rd IEEE Symp. Parallel & Distributed Processing*, 1991, pp. 590–597.

76. J. Edler, A. Gottlieb, C. P. Kruskal, K. P. McAuliffe, L. Rudolph, M. Snir, P. J. Teller, and J. Wilson, "Issues Related to MIMD Shared-Memory Computers: The NYU Ultracomputer Approach," in *12th Ann. Intl. Symp. Computer Architecture Conf. Proc.*, 1985, pp. 126–135.

77. M. S. Squillante and E. D. Lazowska, "Using Processor-Cache Affinity Information in Shared-Memory Multiprocessor Scheduling," *IEEE Trans. Parallel Distributed Syst.*, 4(2), 131–143 (1993).

78. M. Devarakonda and A. Mukherjee, "Issues in Implementation of Cache-Affinity Scheduling," in *Proc. Winter USENIX Technical Conf.*, January 1992, pp. 345–357.

79. K. C. Sevcik, "Characterization of Parallelism in Applications and Their Use in Scheduling," in *SIGMETRICS Conf. Measurement & Modeling of Comput. Syst.*, May 1989, pp. 171–180.

80. A. Tucker and A. Gupta, "Process Control and Scheduling Issues for Multiprogrammed Shared-Memory Multiprocessors," in *12th Symp. Operating Systems Principles*, December 1989, pp.159–166.

81. G. Alverson, S. Kahan, R. Korry, C. McCann, and B. Smith, "Scheduling on the Tera MTA," in *Job Scheduling Strategies for Parallel Processing*, D. G. Feitelson and L. Rudolph (eds.), Lecture Notes in Computer Science Vol. 949, Springer-Verlag, New York, 1995, pp. 19–44.

82. A. Dusseau, R. H. Arpaci, and D. E. Culler, "Effective Distributed Scheduling of Parallel Workloads," in *SIGMETRICS Conf. Measurement & Modeling of Comput. Syst.*, May 1996, pp. 25–36.

DROR G. FEITELSON

LARRY RUDOLPH

THE LOOKINGGLASS DISTRIBUTED SHARED WORKSPACE

INTRODUCTION

Recently, a number of researchers have addressed the problem of providing computer-supported cooperative work systems for remote synchronous work. Analysis of workspace activity in face-to-face settings (e.g., around a table, using pen and paper) has been the starting point for much of this work. The studies have elicited many of the actions and functions occurring in such settings, which have subsequently been respecified as computer system requirements for Computer Supported Co-operative Work (CSCW) systems.

Typically, each of these systems provides a subset of workspace features identified in face-to-face studies. In this article, a novel shared workspace system — called the LookingGlass — is described and its application in synchronous person-to-person design work discussed. The novelty of this computerized workspace is that it integrates a view of one's remote partner with the shared worksurface, allowing eye-to-eye contact to be achieved, and gestures and direction of gaze in relation to the workspace to be observed.

In what follows, previous work on shared workspace systems is first described in order to place the LookingGlass in context and to draw out the novel aspects of the system. The architecture of the system is then described in the third section, whereas the fourth section details a number of studies conducted during the development of the LookingGlass to determine the display conditions for the integrated worker/workspace visualisation, before proceeding in the fifth section to consider the system as a tool for collaborative design.

SHARED DRAWING ACTIVITY AND SHARED DRAWING SURFACES

Face-to-face collaborative work often involves the use of a shared drawing surface, be it a scrap of paper, a sketchpad, or a whiteboard. Indeed, in some fields, such as graphic or architectural design, drawings are a primary means of communicating ideas between co-workers. Recently, a growing community of researchers has investigated "shared drawing activity" among geographically separated groups. Much of this work has used observational techniques to establish the scope of face-to-face shared drawing activity prior to the construction of computer or video-based shared drawing surfaces for use by dispersed groups.

Observational studies by Tang and Leifer (1) and Bly (2) at Xerox PARC have shown that, in group settings, the activity of creating and using the marks on a drawing surface is as important as the marks themselves. Hence, the need to build tools which let groups interact with drawings as well as simply create and present them is now well understood.

Existing Shared Drawing Surfaces

The *Commune* system (3) features a PC-based multiuser drawing package which can be used by two or three geographically separated users. Each user operates the package via the stylus of a transparent digitizing tablet which is placed over a horizontally positioned monitor. By pressing down with the stylus nib, each user can draw or write on their own screen. The monitors are "daisy-chained" together so that the same image appears on each.

In studies, which also provided users with a separate audio and video link, Commune was found to support designers working remotely in ways similar to face-to-face drawing interaction (3,4).

VideoDraw and *VideoWhiteboard* (5,6) use video-based technology to create shared drawing surfaces which support the use of hand and body gestures in the collaborative drawing process. VideoDraw is a desktop system which can be used by two designers working in different locations. They are able to sketch on individual drawing surfaces using ordinary marker pens. Video images of each surface are combined and displayed in such a way that there is the illusion of sharing a single drawing surface. VideoWhiteboard uses similar techniques, enabling two geographically separated groups to share a large "virtual whiteboard."

The *ROCOCO Station* is a computer-mediated shared workspace that features a high-quality audio link, a separate eye-to-eye video link, and a computer-based shared drawing surface, called the *ROCOCO Sketchpad* (7). This system was developed to support an extensive study of the workspace activity of pairs of product designers (see Refs. 8 and 9).

GroupSketch and *GroupDraw* (10) are computer-based drawing tools intended for use in group design settings. GroupSketch is a simple sketching tool which allows an arbitrary number of people to draw on a "virtual piece of paper" — the screen — using the mouse. All users can interact with the system simultaneously. GroupDraw is an object-oriented drawing program, allowing users to create, move, resize, and delete drawing objects (rectangles, lines, circles, etc.) as well as sketch.

Ishii and Miyake (11) note that even in a heavily computerized individual workplace, people continue to use a physical desktop. They believe that, when using a distributed shared workspace, individuals should be able to freely choose either computers or desktops as the medium of interaction. They call such an environment the "open shared workspace."

TeamWorkStation (TWS) is an attempt to establish an open shared workspace by "fusing" individual group members' workspaces (11,12). It provides geographically separated work groups, of two to four members, with live video and audio communication links and a "shared screen." The shared screen can work in the "computer-sharing" mode or "overlay" mode. The overlay mode uses a technique described as "a translucent overlay of individual workspace images." This allows live video images of group members' computer screens and physical desktop surfaces to be combined and a single shared workspace to be displayed on the shared screen. This forms an "open" shared workspace within which users can choose to use either computers or desktops during a conferencing session. For example, TeamWorkStation can be used to form a shared drawing surface in which one user interacts via a computer drawing package and the other uses a pad of paper positioned on the desk.

Supporting Awareness of Gaze Direction

Designers working face-to-face frequently direct their gaze around the workspace. Scrivener et al. (9) found that pairs of designers working on a predefined brief while seated across a table, using pen and paper, gazed at the brief, at each other, at their own drawings and their partner's drawings, and established eye-to-eye contact. The range of gaze activity possible in this setting allows the gazer to obtain information about the task (e.g., from the brief and the drawings), about their partner's focus of attention in relation to the workspace (e.g., attending to the gazer or to a particular drawing), and about their partner's state of attention (i.e., engrossed in drawing, or thinking, or listening).

At the time of the study which is the subject of this article, computer-mediated shared drawing systems only partially supported the range of gaze activity possible in face-to-face working; in particular, none supported awareness of one's partner's gaze in relation to the drawing surface. The LookingGlass system was devised principally to investigate this aspect of workspace activity in the context of computer-mediate person-to-person interaction.

Since the development of the LookingGlass (see Ref. 13), a system known as ClearBoard (14,15) has been reported which also supports "gaze awareness" (14) between users of a drawing surface. The similarities between the two systems are discussed later.

ARCHITECTURE OF THE LOOKINGGLASS SYSTEM

The LookingGlass allows two persons located at different computer workstations to see each other via an eye-to-eye video link, to speak to each other via a high-quality audio link, and to draw together on a shared drawing surface. As noted earlier, a number of systems have been constructed which offer a similar basic functionality. The LookingGlass is unusual in that the shared drawing surface is displayed over the video image of the remote partner on a single computer screen. When using the system, the visual effect is that of viewing your remote partner through the drawing surface. Subjectively, the workspace is like a window through which the user can see the space occupied by one's partner, and vice versa; to a user, the work surface appears to visually link the two workspaces on either side of it. Clearly, as users sketch on the drawing surface, their view of each other becomes progressively obscured. However, because the multiuser drawing package used offers a number of pages, it is possible to switch to a blank page at any time and see a complete video image of one's remote partner.

LookingGlass Workstation

Each LookingGlass workstation (shown in Fig. 1) consists of an Apple Macintosh II computer fitted with a VideoLogic DVA4000 video-card (16), a CCD video camera, a mirror arrangement for eye-to-eye contact, an audio headset, and a digitizing tablet and stylus. In initial trials of the system (reported below), resources only permitted the use of a mouse for drawing. The software packages used are a commercially available Macintosh X Window System server and the ROCOCO

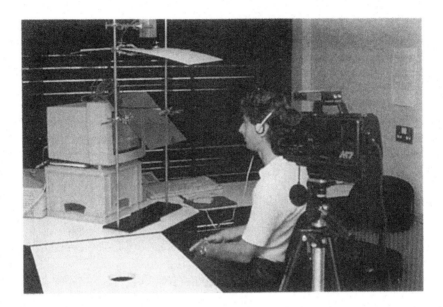

FIGURE 1   The LookingGlass workstation (the camcorder on the right is used for recording purposes only).

Sketchpad X-based multiuser drawing package. Computer communication is via 10 Mb EtherNet and audio and video communication via co-axial cables.

ROCOCO Sketchpad Shared Drawing Surface

The ROCOCO Sketchpad (7) is a computer application which allows two or more geographically separated persons to share a "virtual sketchpad." The drawing surface is a large shared window which is displayed on each user's workstation screen. Users are able to sketch in the window using a variety of pen colors and pen thicknesses. All users can sketch at the same time, and the marks made at any one workstation appear almost instantly at the others. As well as being able to sketch, users can direct remote colleagues' attention to a particular area on the surface via a continuously displayed telepointer.

The system was developed following detailed observation of six pairs of product designers working in a face-to-face environment using the conventional medium of pen and paper (8,9). The sketchpad application was written using the X Window System (17).

Eye-to-Eye Contact over the Video Link

An important feature of the LookingGlass is that its users are able to make eye-to-eye contact over the video link. The effect is achieved by positioning the CCD video camera directly above a sheet of half-silvered glass placed at an angle of 45° in front of each workstation screen (see Figs. 2 and 3). This arrangement results in each camera's viewpoint being "placed" at the center of the local computer screen. Hence,

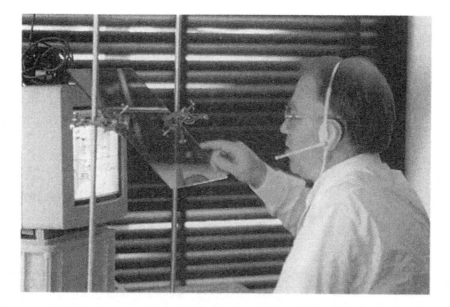

FIGURE 2   The half-silvered glass positioned in front of the Macintosh screen.

when both users are in front of the screen and look directly at each others' video image, there is the appearance of eye-to-eye contact. The configuration is similar to the "VideoTunnel" device developed at EuroPARC by Smith et al. (18) and the more recent "Drafter-mirror" architecture developed by Ishii and Kobayashi (14).

Generation of the Video Overlay

The video-overlay effect is achieved with the VideoLogic DVA4000 video card. The DVA4000 allows an external PAL or NTSC video source to be mixed with a Macintosh display in a variety of ways.

In the LookingGlass, both Macintosh computers are configured to act as X Window System servers. A ROCOCO Sketchpad X client, running on a SPARC station 1 + workstation and connected to the Macintoshes via a local-area network, displays a shared drawing surface window on each. The drawing surface occupies the entire Macintosh screen (13 in. screens were used). A full-screen video image of the remote partner's head and shoulders is then mixed with the image of the drawing surface to provide a display consisting of a full-screen shared drawing surface and a full-screen video image. For development purposes, video and graphics combinations were explored empirically. The results of these investigations are reported in the following section. The way in which the components of the LookingGlass workstations are connected is illustrated in Figure 4.

Features of the LookingGlass

The combination of the video-overlay technique together with the eye-to-eye video link gives rise to a number of interesting features. First, it is possible for a user to ascertain approximately where on the computer screen their remote partner is look-

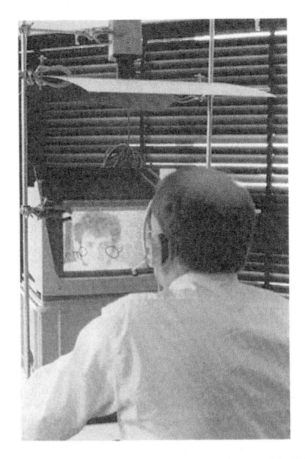

FIGURE 3   The CCD video camera positioned directly above the half silvered glass.

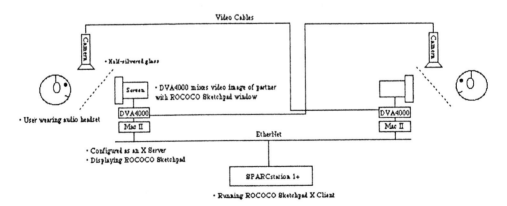

FIGURE 4   The connections between the LookingGlass workstations.

ing. If a user is looking at, say, the bottom left of their screen, their video image will appear to look at the same area of the remote partner's screen. Second, it is possible for a user to use hand gestures when referring to areas of the computer screen. For example, when a user points at a drawing on the shared drawing surface, their video image appears to point at the same drawing on the remote partner's screen.

The LookingGlass system was designed to support synchronous competitive speech, eye-to-eye contact and traceable gaze between partners, and simple gestures (using hand movements) viewed in relation to the work surface, and to provide a fully shared work surface, with simultaneous access for each user, offering facilities for writing, drawing, and telepointer gesturing.

STUDIES INTO THE USE OF VIDEO OVERLAY IN THE LOOKINGGLASS

A number of preliminary studies were performed in order to investigate the ease of use of different combinations of video and graphics overlay. The studies were carried out using a single LookingGlass workstation and focused on establishing any fundamental problems arising as a result of combining the video and graphics images.

Two trials were performed: The first compared three different methods of combining video and graphics images on a single screen, and the second compared different levels of video and graphics image strength. The trials were designed to provide initial insights into the ease of use of each overlay method and to ascertain individual preferences, as a basis for the selection of a video/graphics combination.

Studying the Effect of Transparent, Washed, and Translucent Video

This trial had two aims: the first to assist in deciding which kind of overlay effect to exploit in the system; the second to find out whether individuals had a preference for any one particular video background.

The VideoLogic DVA4000 video card allows the video and graphics layers to be combined in a variety of ways, enabling a number of different effects to be produced. For example, parts of the graphics layer can be made completely "transparent" to allow the full-strength video image to "show through," or the strength of the graphics layer can be faded to produce a composite image that combines the video and graphics images in inverse proportion to each other (i.e., as the strength of one increases, the strength of the other decreases). Figure 5 provides a conceptual model of how the video and graphics layers relate. The graphics layer is viewed as being in front of the video layer. The graphics layer consists of "figure" (i.e., text/drawing) and "ground" (i.e., the graphics drawing surface) components; the figure being "on top" of the ground.

A number of the parameters in this model can be altered to modify the appearance of the display. First, the strength of the graphics ground can be continuously varied; for example, at zero strength the full video image shows through, at half-strength the video appears faded, and at full strength the video image is completely blocked out. Similarly, and independently of the graphics ground, the strength of

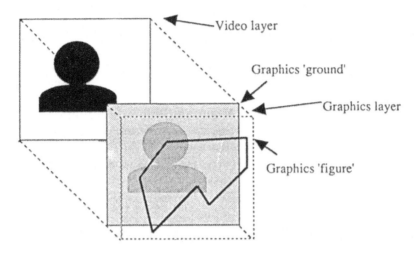

FIGURE 5   Relationship between the video and graphics layers.

the graphics figure can be altered. In this study, three graphics figure and ground display combinations were tested. These are shown in Table 1.

Considering the graphics layer as a sheet of glass and the writing or graphics as marks made on the glass using pens, then the "transparent" condition is like drawing on plain glass with opaque inks, whereas the washed condition is like drawing in opaque inks on ground glass, and finally the 'translucent' condition is like drawing in translucent inks on ground glass.

Test Procedure

A text-based selection test was chosen, where participants, six in all, were required to read through a word processor document "overlaid" on a video image. The

TABLE 1   Graphics Ground and Figure Combinations Tested in the First Study

	Graphics ground	Graphics figure
Transparent	The ground of the graphics layer was cleared, allowing a complete video image to show "through."	The full-strength graphics figure consisted of solid writing, and hence appeared to be overlaid on the video image.
Washed	The graphics layer was reduced to 50% of its maximum strength to produce a "faded" video image.	The full-strength graphics figure consisted of solid writing, and hence appeared to be overlaid on the video image.
Translucent	The graphics layer was reduced to 50% of its maximum strength to produce a "faded" video image.	The graphics figure was also reduced to 50% of its maximum to produce an overall "translucent" screen.

subjects were timed performing two tasks in each of the three display conditions; in the first task, aimed at discovering the readability of the text, the participants were asked to find and highlight a particular phrase from several pages of prose; in the second task, users were asked to move the phrase to a new position. The participants were subjected to each of the conditions in a different order, so as to reduce the possibility of unrepresentative results arising through task familiarity.

The passages involved in the tests were all selected from one book to ensure that they were of comparable difficulty. Care was taken to ensure that they were all of similar length and that all key phrases appeared in similar positions within the text so that results could be compared between the conditions.

Results and Discussion

Appendix 1 shows the times for each subject under each condition. From the average performance time under each condition (see Fig. 6), it can be concluded that subjects generally performed both tasks faster when using the washed graphics ground with graphics figure consisting of solid writing.

Only two subjects expressed a preference for any of the three display conditions, and both of these preferred the washed background. Other participants claimed that they could not tell the difference between conditions, although, on average, performance was improved using the washed condition.

Studying the Effect of Altering the Strength of the Graphics Ground on Task Performance

The first test established that the washed display produced the fastest task performance times and, where a preference was expressed, also proved to be the preferred condition. This study was followed by a further study having two aims: the first to discover what level of graphics ground wash was most suitable for task perfor-

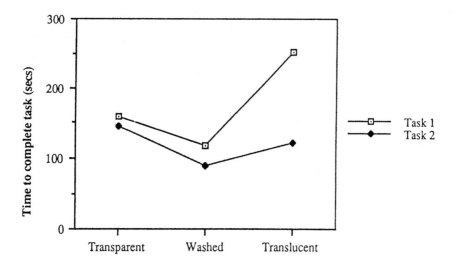

FIGURE 6   Average task performance times for the three display conditions studied.

mance, where the task involved the division of attention between the work surface and the video image; the second to discover subjects preference regarding the level of graphics ground wash. Five display conditions were tested during this study, each condition using a different graphics ground strength. The percentage graphics ground strength used for each test is shown in Table 2.

Test Procedure

Six subjects took part in the study. Subjects were required to scan a grid of large letters overlaid on a video image. Each subject was merely required to locate a specified letter, but to ensure that they took note of changes in the "background" video image during their search, they also had to record a shape which was displayed for 2 seconds. Different grids were randomly used with different display conditions to ensure that all results were independent.

Results and Discussion

Subjects' performance times were slower (found from the mean performance times) when using display condition 3 (graphics ground strength reduced to 45% of the maximum) than they were for any other condition (this can be seen in Fig. 7 and Appendix 2). Although initially this result appears to be surprising, there is an explanation.

When the graphics ground strength is reduced to only 60% or 75% of the maximum (i.e., when the strength of video image is low), the video layer image is less likely to interfere with the task and, hence, the task can be performed more quickly. This may explain why two subjects failed to notice or correctly identify shapes which appeared in the background video image during these two experiments.

When the graphics ground strength is reduced to 15% or 30% of the maximum (i.e., when the strength of the video image is high), intuition would suggest that task performance times would be high. However, Figure 7 shows that times are not very different to these involving low video image strength. One explanation for this might be that subjects are required to concentrate far more to view the grid and, as a result, actually improve their performance times (compared to the 45% condition). This hypothesis is supported by the fact that one subject failed to view either of the shapes that appeared during the tests involving display conditions 1 and 2 even though the strength of the video image was high.

TABLE 2   Values of the Graphics Ground Strength Tested in the Second Study

Condition	Ground strength (percent of maximum)
1	15
2	30
3	45
4	60
5	75

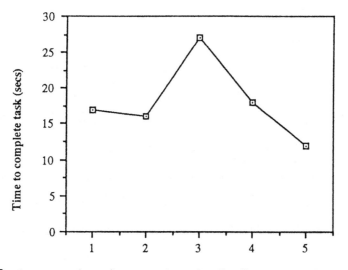

FIGURE 7   Average task performance times for the five washed display conditions studied.

When the graphics ground is around half-strength, resulting in a video image of half-strength (as is the case in display condition 3), the subjects would not be able to ignore one layer entirely (i.e., the graphics figure or the video layer). This explains why task performance was slower when this display condition was involved and also why no errors in video image shape detection were made by any subject during the test involving display condition 3.

Over half the subjects believed display condition 3 to be the easiest to use when required to take note of events occurring in both the graphics figure and video layers. Two of the six subjects preferred to use display condition 5, where the video strength was at its minimum. However, this preference may be explained by the fact that both candidates performed the searching task particularly quickly while using this condition.

Summary and Conclusions

The studies carried out to investigate the effect of varying the type and strength of the screen image, using the DVA4000 video card, produced some interesting results. The trial involving graphics ground and figure combinations revealed that a washed graphics ground, where a "faded" video image appears "through" the graphics ground, produced the highest rate of subject performance when compared to other backgrounds. All subjects who expressed a preference also stated that this display condition was the easiest to use.

When studying the effect of varying the strength of the graphics ground component (and, hence, the strength of the video image), subjects were found to perform faster when either the video image was very strong or very weak. However, these conditions resulted in more errors when recording shapes which appeared in the background. From this, it can be concluded that although subjects appear to be able to perform tasks quickly under these conditions, they are unable to divide their attention between both images. Task performance is slower when the strength of the video image is around 50%; however, few mistakes are made and subjects can readily perceive changes in both layers (i.e., the graphics figure and the video layer).

It is important that a task is not made unnecessarily difficult or time-consuming for computer users to perform. However, when users are involved in shared drawing activity, the ability to divide attention between communication with a partner and the drawing task is more important than sheer speed. For this reason, the washed graphics ground, at 45% strength, was selected as being the most suitable display condition for the LookingGlass system because users are able to divide their attention between their partner and the task in hand.

INVESTIGATING THE LOOKINGGLASS SHARED WORKSPACE

The preliminary studies, described above, focused on establishing the display settings to be used in the LookingGlass system. The objectives of the pilot investigation described below was to explore the potential of the complete workspace in design tasks involving drawing.

As stated previously, the aims of the LookingGlass system were to support synchronous competitive speech, eye-to-eye contact and traceable gaze between partners, and gesture (using hand movements) enabling hand gestures to be viewed in relation to the work surface, and to provide a fully shared worksurface with simultaneous access for each user, offering facilities for writing, drawing, and telepointer gesturing.

Test Procedure

Three pairs of subjects, from different fields of design, carried out a design task. A pair of product designers were asked to design a barbecue, a pair of artists to design the layout of a garden, and a pair of graphic designers a logo for a ski resort. The tasks were selected to suit the needs of the subjects, as the aim was to determine the effectiveness of the system, not their ability to design. The subjects were given 55 minutes to complete the task, enabling them to use the system fully without feeling pressured to produce anything more than a concept design.

A questionnaire was used to obtain a subjective view of the LookingGlass' effectiveness. The questions were designed to yield information relevant to the aims of the LookingGlass. Appendix 3 contains the complete results of the questionnaire.

Results and Discussion

To analyze the overall perceived performance of the LookingGlass system, the questions were grouped into seven categories. To establish how positive the users were about the system in terms of these categories, each was assigned a percentage effectiveness value, by calculating the number of user responses which were positive toward the system. For example, if a user replied "yes" to the question, "Was the headset comfortable?" this was taken to be a positive response; however, if they replied "yes" to the question, "Did you find the video link awkward to use?" this was taken to be a negative response. The percentage of positive replies was then calculated, using the total, to give an overall value for that category. Figure 8 shows the percentage of positive responses for each of the seven categories employed. The questionnaire data was treated in this way merely to give an indication as to which aspects of the systems required the most immediate improvements.

Utterance, Drawing, and Task

From Figure 8, it can be seen that the utterance, drawing, and task categories were acceptable. This means that the responses from users were positive in these three areas; that is, the users found that spoken communication was well supported by the system; they were able to draw cooperatively with their partner, and the task they were required to perform was appropriate.

Hardware

The response value for the questions in the hardware category was 74%. As was anticipated, the figure for hardware was greatly affected by the use of the mouse as the drawing tool, with all users finding it difficult to draw and write using this tool. This has since been overcome by using a digitizing tablet with stylus. The most interesting result is that users did not find the video link awkward to use, nor did it interfere with the task.

Vision

In the vision category, users found that they were able to alter their attention from partner to the work surface, as the preliminary studies had indicated. They also believed the image of their partner to be a natural one, not noticing that, in fact, the image had been inverted. However, responses to questions concerning eye contact and line of sight were not so positive, with only 40% of users able to maintain eye contact with their partners, or able to see where their partner was looking.

Eye contact is, however, a subtle form of gesture which is used very selectively

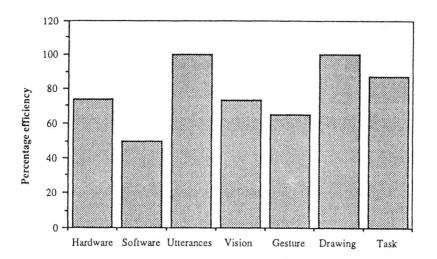

FIGURE 8   Percentage positive response values for the questionnaire categories.

and possibly subconsciously during communication; hence, the direct question, "Were you able to maintain eye contact with your partner?" might not have encouraged users to think about this form of communication. In experiments with the ClearBoard system, Ishii et al. (15) were able to show that users gazed at each other simultaneously, suggesting that the users of the similar LookingGlass system utilized this feature without being aware of it. However, further investigation is required to establish whether this is the case.

The opinions of users regarding the line of sight of their partners appear to challenge the results of an investigation of users' ability to judge their collaborating partner's line of sight (13). This study concluded that a subject's line of sight was distinguishable when objects on the screen were between 6 and 9 cm apart. Furthermore, Ishii et al. (15) were able to show experimentally that users of the ClearBoard system were able to detect their partner's direction of gaze. A possible explanation for the different results is that the extensive amount of drawing on the screen may have obscured the video image to the point where direction of gaze could not be accurately detected. Again, like eye-to-eye contact, the detection and use of line of sight may occur unconsciously. Hence, users may be making use of this information without realizing it. It is encouraging that those users who reported an awareness of their partner's direction of gaze found this feature of the LookingGlass useful. However, the results indicate that further, and more subtle, investigation is required in order to establish whether line of sight is detected and effectively utilized in the LookingGlass shared workspace, and, if so, how its effectiveness is impaired by the volume and complexity of the material in the shared work surface.

Software

The final two categories, gesture and software, produced the least positive responses. Although subjects generally found the software easy to use, all would like to have seen additional features added to the package. These features varied depending on the type of user; for example, the artists and product designers requested an eraser and more colors, whereas the graphic designers wanted enlargement, cut-and-paste facilities, and text.

The ROCOCO Sketchpad software used in the study was designed to provide only those features which are essential to drawing. For designers who regularly use more elaborate software, any unfamiliar package is unlikely to meet with approval; hence, it would be better to allow designers to use their own familiar packages within the LookingGlass system. Currently some "view sharing" packages are available, such as Timbuktu (19), which allow any single-user application to be shared across a network. This type of package could enable designers to use any familiar drawing package within the LookingGlass system.

Gesture

The gesture category yielded only a 65% positive response. Users were able to gesture naturally using hands and head and, in general, were aware of their partner's body language/movements. However, most subjects stated that they were unable or unwilling to point at specific parts of the screen. This was a disappointing result, particularly as direct trials showed that an object on the screen could be detected to within 2 cm by means of pointing (13). There are two possible reasons for subject's reluctance to point to the screen: first, the obtrusive nature of the half-silvered glass and, second, the height of the screen, which was necessary to centralize the video "face" displays. Keen (13) proposed a method for overcoming these problems which, by coincidence, is the same as that employed the ClearBoard-2 (15), although Clear-Board-2 additionally supports direct drawing onto the shared drawing surface.

Subjects

One additional section of the questionnaire concerned the professions of subjects. This was used to establish whether the subjects would have reason to use the system within their area of work. Three of the six subjects claimed to work remotely with other designers, with two of these being over long distances. These two were very enthusiastic about the system, believing it to have great potential in their field of work, provided that the software was matched to their needs. This suggests that the system could be valuable within the design profession. However, research is required to establish the requirements of potential users to ensure that the Looking-Glass is developed to suit those needs.

CONCLUSIONS

This article has described the development and use of a shared workspace system, called the LookingGlass, that integrates many of the features provided by previous systems, and additionally provides features that support eye-to-eye contact, awareness of one's partner's direction of gaze in relation to oneself and the work surface, and hand and body gestures occurring either "freely" or directed "over" or "at" the work surface, including direct pointing.

Generally, the results indicate that the LookingGlass provides an effective environment for shared drawing tasks. However, a number of aspects of the workspace require further investigation. First, although the unusual arrangement of overlaid work surface and partner image appeared natural and users were able to switch attention between the two "layers," the potential for eye-to-eye contact and awareness of a partner's gaze [or simply "gaze awareness' as it has been referred to by Ishii and Kobayashi (14)] provided by the system was not fully recognized. Several explanations for this result can be suggested: One possibility is that these activities occur unconsciously and therefore cannot be reported; another possibility is that the marks made in the drawing surface make it impossible to maintain eye-to-eye contact and gaze awareness; a third possibility, of course, is that eye-to-eye contact and gaze awareness do not fulfill any useful function in the tasks studied and therefore were not exploited by users. However, evidence suggests that this last explanation is unlikely. From analysis of video recordings, Scrivener et al. (9) found that designers, working face-to-face on tasks similar to those used in the Looking-Glass study, regularly established eye-to-eye contact and gazed at their partner. Further studies need to be undertaken in order to clarify these matters.

The lack of value attached to direct pointing at the screen surface is a second area that requires further study. It is known that in face-to-face working, direct pointing at objects in the workspace occurs frequently (see, e.g., Ref. 9). In the LookingGlass, although direct pointing was possible, users did not seem to make use of it. However, indirect pointing was possible using a telepointer, and user reports show that this facility was useful. The configuration of the LookingGlass system is the likely explanation for the lack of direct pointing; it simply makes pointing too difficult and effortful compared to telepointing, thus limiting its use. The ClearBoard system (14,15) appears to support direct pointing effectively.

In the LookingGlass study, a different art and design domain was represented in each pair. The questionnaire results indicate that each design domain will require domain-specific shared drawing surface functionality. Thus, for example, the graphic designers required improved facilities for text and image manipulation, characteristic of existing single-user graphic design systems. This of itself is not very surprising; however, it does raise the issue of how much domain-specific requirements are likely to impact on the general applicability and configuration of the LookingGlass system as a whole, rather than just the functionality of the shared application. For example, in page layout design, the spatial properties of elements, and relationships between them, are important design variables, and designers go to great lengths to achieve a balance between, say, text and white space that communicates the effect they desire. The background video in the LookingGlass shared workspace may interfer with designer' ability to make visual judgments, thus impairing the designer's task performance. Even given shared work surface applications that match users's task demands, it remains a matter of speculation as to how effective the LookingGlass arrangement will prove to be in such a circumstance. Finally, as noted in the fourth section, the speed at which the task is completed may not be the most important criterion to consider when designing multilayer systems such as the LookingGlass.

ACKNOWLEDGMENTS

Thanks to our colleagues on the ROCOCO project—Tony Clarke, John Connolly, Steve Garner, Hilary Palmén, André Schappo, and Michael Smyth—for their helpful comments during the development and evaluation of the LookingGlass system. Thanks also to the subjects who took part in our experiments. DVA4000 is a trademark of VideoLogic Ltd. Apple and Macintosh are trademarks of Apple Computer Inc.

APPENDICES

Appendix 1.   Table Showing Time Taken to Perform Each Task in the First Study

Task 1

Subject	Transparent	Washed	Translucent
a	162	176	194
b	129	111	566
c	38	62	44
d	315	109	410
e	89	68	154
f	219	181	143

Task 2

Subject	Transparent	Washed	Translucent
a	197	170	54
b	136	104	119
c	109	44	43
d	173	104	78
e	88	75	127
f	165	160	192

Appendix 2. Table Showing Time Taken to Perform Each Task in the Second Study

Subject	Display 1	Display 2	Display 3	Display 4	Display 5
a	12	7	4	8	12
b	31	8	21	28	7
c	20	12	33	21	12
d	9	26	27	11	7
e	14	12	40	19	3
f	14	31	39	20	28

Appendix 3. Responses to Questionnaire Used in the Pilot Investigation

	Yes	No	Don't know
1 — Hardware			
Was the headset comfortable?	6	—	—
Did you find the VideoTunnel awkward to use?	—	6	—
Did the VideoTunnel arrangement interfere with your task?	—	6	—
Did you find it easy to draw with the mouse?	—	6	—
Could you write using the mouse?	2	3	1
Did you find it easy working with the vertical drawing surface?	6	—	—
2 — Software			
Did you find the drawing package features easy to understand?	6	—	—
Did any problems arise when using the vertical drawing surface?	1	5	—
Did you have a wide enough selection of pens and colors?	1	5	—
Would you like to see any extra features added to the package?	6	—	—
3 — Utterance			
Were you able to hear your partner's speech clearly?	6	—	—
Were you and your partner able to speak naturally?	6	—	—

Did your partner's lip movements match the speech you heard?	2	—	4

4 – Vision

Did the orientation of your partner's image appear to be natural?	6	—	—
Could you see where your partner was looking?	2	3	1
If yes, did you find this useful to your task?	2	—	—
Were you able to maintain eye contact with your partner?	2	3	1
Did you find it easy to switch your attention between the work surface and your partner?	6	—	—

5 – Gesture

Were you able to gesture naturally using your arms and head?	—	6	—
Did your partner use body language/body movements?	4	—	2
Could you see the gestures of your partner clearly?	5	1	—
Were you and your partner able to point to specific parts of the screen without confusion?	—	5	1

6 – Drawing

Did you and your partner draw at the same time?	2	—	4
Did you find the telepointer useful in locating your partner's activity in relation to the worksurface?	6	—	—

7 – Task

Did you understand exactly what the brief entailed?	6	—	—
Did you have sufficient time to complete the task?	5	—	1
Did the LookingGlass tool aid you in completing your task?	4	—	2

REFERENCES

1. J. Tang and L. Leifer, "A Framework for Understanding the Workspace Activity of Design Teams," in *Proceedings of the Conference on Computer-Supported Co-operative Work (CSCW '88)*, ACM Press, New York, 1988, pp. 244–249.

2. S. Bly, "A Use of Drawing Surfaces in Different Collaborative Settings," In *Proceedings of the Conference on Computer-Supported Co-operative Work (CSCW '88)*, ACM Press, New York, 1988, pp. 250–256.

3. S. Bly and S. Minneman, "Commune: A Shared Drawing Surface," in *Proceedings of the Conference on Office Information Systems (OIS '90)*, ACM Press, New York, 1990, pp. 184–192.

4. S. Minneman and S. Bly, "Managing a Trois: A Study of a Multi-user Drawing Tool in Distributed Design Work," in *Proceedings of the ACM/SIGCHI Conference on Human Factors in Computing (CHI '91)*, ACM Press, New York, 1991, pp. 217–224.

5. J. Tang and S. Minneman, "VideoDraw: A Video Interface for Collaborative Drawing," in *Proceedings of the ACM/SIGCHI Conference on Human Factors in Computing (CHI '90)*, ACM Press, New York, 1990, pp. 313–320.

6. J. Tang and S. Minneman, "VideoWhiteboard: Video Shadows to Support Remote

Collaboration," in *Proceedings of the ACM/SIGCHI Conference on Human Factors in Computing (CHI '91)*, ACM Press, New York, 1991, pp. 315–322.

7. C. Clark and S. A. R. Scrivener, "The ROCOCO Sketchpad Distributed Shared Drawing Surface," Report 92/C/LUTCHI/0150, LUTCHI Research Centre, Loughborough University of Technology, Loughborough, UK (1992).

8. S. W. Garner, S. A. R. Scrivener, A. A. Clarke et al., "The Use of Design Activity for Research into Computer-Supported Co-operative Work (CSCW), in *Proceedings of DATER '91*, 1991, pp.84–96.

9. S. A. R. Scrivener, A. A. Clarke, J. H. Connolly et al., "The ROCOCO Project Phase 1 Report," LUTCHI Research Centre, Loughborough University of Technology, Loughborough, UK (1992).

10. S. Greenberg and R. Bohnet "GroupSketch: A Multi-user Sketchpad for Geographically Separated Small Groups," in *Proceedings of Graphics Interface '91*, 1991.

11. H. Ishii and N. Miyake, "Towards an Open-Shared Workspace: Computer and Video Fusion Approach of TeamWorkStation," *Commun. ACM*, 34(12), 37–50 (1991).

12. H. Ishii, "TeamWorkStation: Towards a Seamless Shared Space," in *Proceedings of the Conference on Computer-Supported Co-operative Work (CSCW '90)*, ACM Press, New York, 1990, pp. 13–26.

13. N. Keen, "The LookingGlass Distributed Shared Workspace," M.Sc. dissertation, LUTCHI Research Centre, Loughborough University of Technology, Loughborough, UK (1991).

14. H. Ishii and M. Kobayashi, "ClearBoard: A Seamless Medium for Shared Drawing and Conversation with Eye Contact," in *Proceedings of the ACM/SIGCHI Conference on Human Factors in Computing (CHI '92)*, ACM Press, New York, 1992, pp. 525–532.

15. H. Ishii, M. Kobayashi, and J. Grudin, "Integration of Inter-personal Space and Shared Workspace: ClearBoard Design and Experiments," in *Proceedings of the Conference on Computer Supported Co-operative Work (CSCW '92)*, ACM Press, New York, 1992.

16. VideoLogic, *DVA4000/Macintosh User Guide*, VideoLogic Limited, Kings Langley, UK, 1990.

17. R. W. Scheifler and J. Gettys, "The X Window System," *ACM Trans. Graphics*, 5(2), 29–109 (1986).

18. R. B. Smith, T. O'Shea, C. O'Malley et al., "Preliminary Experiments with a Distributed Multi-media Problem Solving Environment," in *Proceedings of the European Conference on Computer Supported Co-operative Work*, 1989, pp. 19–34.

19. Farallon, *Timbuktu User's Guide*, Farallon Computing Inc., Berkeley, CA, 1988.

STEPHEN A. R. SCRIVENER

S. M. CLARK

N. KEEN

A PRACTICAL METHODOLOGY FOR APPLYING NEURAL NETWORKS TO BUSINESS DECISION PROBLEMS

INTRODUCTION

The term "artificial neural network" (ANN) can mean different things to different people. *Artificial neural networks* (or just *neural networks*) are popularly perceived as descriptive models, designed to emulate low-level operations in the human brain. Yet, most computer scientists view the similarity of artificial neural architectures to the brain circuitry as no more than a useful analogy. This is because neural networks have proven to be powerful computational models in their own right, regardless of their biological justification.

Since the inception of artificial neural networks in the mid-1940s, the area has attracted researchers from computer science, psychology, neurology, mathematics, physics, and statistics. During the past decade, in particular, numerous neural-network-based decision models have been developed to carry out a wide variety of computational tasks, from scientific and engineering applications to banking and marketing.

Several software vendors now offer off-the-shelf products that enable end users to develop and test neural networks with minimal programming (3–5), and shells that originated from academic institutions, like the Rochester Connectionist Simulator [6], can be also obtained (by other universities) for nominal fees. Is it possible that these programs will eventually become as popular as other business tools, like statistical packages and spreadsheet programs? The answer seems to go far beyond user interface and performance considerations; it is related to deeper issues regarding the appropriateness of neural computing to the special nature of business applications, in general, and decision support systems, in particular. In this article, we wish to systematically explore the limitations and potential of this technology to decision support applications as well as to discuss successful applications in industry.

By and large, there are three ways to think about neural networks: from the *descriptive* perspective, from the *normative* perspective, and from the *computational* perspective.

The *descriptive* line of thought, popular among neuroscientists and psychologists, provided much of the early motivation for research on artificial neural networks (7–9). This line of thought is concerned with the proximity of the artificial model to biological systems. Indeed, the "hardware" of neural networks was much inspired by the architecture and behavior of the brain circuitry, to the extent that we presently understand it. For example, some types of real neurons tend to become

---

This article was based, in part, on material developed in Refs. 1 and 2, with kind permission from Elsevier Science, Amsterdam, The Netherlands and Prentice-Hall, New York, New York.

activated or *fire* only when their combined (electrochemical) input exceeds a certain threshold value. This nonlinear firing pattern is simulated in some artificial neuron models by a sigmoid activation function which behaves in a similar way.

The *normative* view of neural networks examines the mathematical and statistical backdrop of neural architectures and "learning" algorithms. This approach attempts to cut through the esoteric terminology of the field and elucidate what neural networks really do in the way of data analysis. The normative interpretation of neural networks is critically important; it shows where neural networks are isomorphic to related techniques like linear regression and cluster analysis and, conversely, where neural networks either violate or extend what can be already done with other, more traditional models.

Finally, the *pragmatic* approach to neural networks, popular among computer scientists, views this model as a novel computational paradigm, akin to a von Neumann or a Turing machine. Over the last decade, numerous experiments have indicated that neural networks can efficiently solve many problems that defeat standard sequential algorithms. This led to the pragmatic conclusion that neural networks have an important computational merit *independent of their biological interpretation*. Hence, the computational approach to neural networks focuses more on the functionality and limitations of the model, and less on its cognitive plausibility.

In this article, we adopt this last view of the field, perceiving neural networks as a resource that can be used develop decision support systems. We find this view to be most in line with the way in which many neural network applications are developed and used in business settings. With this pragmatic perspective, we wish to answer such questions as: What kind of decision problems lend themselves to neural networks? What are the contingent relationships between the structure of the underlying decision problem and the behavior of a neural-network-based decision support system?

To answer these questions in a comprehensive fashion, we have adopted a systemic framework, proposed by Dhar and Stein (2) for mapping tasks to problems from a business perspective. Using this framework, users and developers consider the nature of the problem, the resources (human and fixed) available to the organization, the organization's needs, and the characteristics of the technique.

The remainder of this article is organized as follows. The second section provides a brief overview of key neural network concepts; the third section presents a sampling of applications that have seen neural networks fit successfully into a business decision environment; the fourth section provides a framework and thumbnail analysis of neural computing for decision support, following Dhar and Stein (2). The fifth section provides concluding remarks. To avoid clutter, we have located the bulk of the more technical material describing neural networks in the Appendix. The Appendix discusses the mechanics of training a multilayer perceptron neural network and how complex networks are developed from simple single-unit models. The Appendix is not essential to understanding the material in the body of the article.

AN OVERVIEW OF NEURAL NETWORKS

The computer science literature offers several comprehensive reviews of neural networks, and the interested reader is referred to Refs. 10–14 for a sample of good surveys/tutorials of the subject.

There are many excellent neural networks survey/tutorial books. In this rapidly developing field, *Parallel Distributed Processing* by Rumelhart et al. (15), a 1986 publication, is now considered a classic. This two-volume book gives a comprehensive review of all the key ideas that led to the development of feedforward networks and back-propagation algorithms, along with a series of articles on theory and applications written by some of the top researchers in the field. Haykin's *Neural Networks: A Comprehensive Foundation* (16) also provides a thorough treatment of the foundations as well as providing detailed discussions of the more recent developments in the field. In addition, there are several introductory books that have managed to give an accurate and compact view of the field without getting into too much technical detail; Wasserman's *Neural Computing: Theory and Practice* (17), Alexander and Morton's *Introduction to Neural Computing* (18), Claudill and Butler's *Understanding Neural Networks* (19), and Freeman and Skapura's *Neural Networks: Algorithms, Applications, and Programming Techniques* (20) are good examples.

In the remainder of this section and in the Appendix, we attempt to pack the essence of some of the survey articles into a few pages, with the objective of equipping the reader with some essential terminology and conceptual understanding of how neural networks are constructed, trained, and used in the field. In particular, we will focus on feed-forward neural architectures and associated learning algorithms, as they unfold in the context of typical business classification and prediction problems.

Feed-Forward Artificial Neural Networks

A feed-forward neural network is a collection of many independent processing elements, also called *neurons* or *units*. The units are usually organized into *layers*. The units in each layer are linked to a set of inputs, from one end, and to a set of outputs, on the other (Fig. 1). The interunit *connections* (shown as lines in the

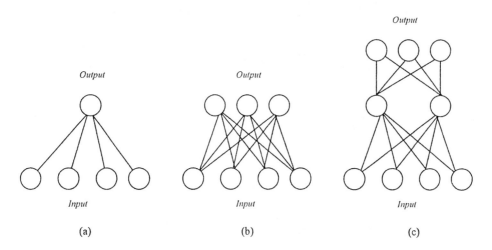

FIGURE 1   Three successive architectures of feed-forward networks. The basic neural network architecture (a) contains only an input layer and a single unit output layer. This architecture is extended by adding additional output nodes (b) and more layers (c).

figure) each represent a numeric *weight* that controls the intensity of the signals that go through the network. When a unit receives a set of messages via its incoming connections, it multiplies them by their respective weights, sums up the result, and passes it to an *activation* or *transfer* function which determines the unit's output (Fig. 2).

The simplest activation function is a linear one that simply passes the weighted sum of the inputs and the weights on without changing its value. In such a case, the reader will note that the single-unit neural network is activated in the same manner as a linear model, such as a fitted-regression equation.

However, in practice it is usually more convenient to use a nonlinear activation function. The simplest of these, the signum function, acts by setting the unit's output to 1 if the weighted sum exceeds a set threshold, and setting the output to −1 if the weighted sum is below the threshold. This nonlinear transformation serves to either cancel out a weak signal (if it falls short of the threshold) or amplify it to an upper bound (if it exceeds the threshold). The resulting signal is transmitted via the unit's outgoing connection to another unit, and so on.

The output of a neural network depends, in large part, on the values assigned to its weights. This raises the question of how these weights are determined. Typically (but not always), a *training* algorithm is used to adjust the weights of a neural network in response to some sample data set.

In the typical case, records from this data set (the *training set*) are presented to the neural network, which processes the data as described above. The actual output of the neural network is then compared to the desired output (the "right" answer), and in cases where the two differ, the training algorithm makes adjustments to the network weights in an attempt to reduce the error (Fig. 2). This is repeated for each record in the training set, often more than once, until the performance of the network is deemed sufficiently high. This process is often likened to the network "learning" from the data.

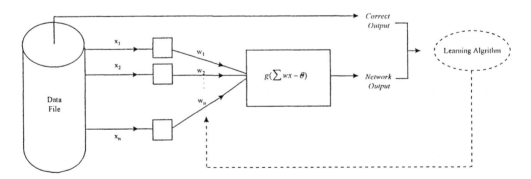

FIGURE 2 The generic structure and training of a single neuron neural network. Data are presented to the input nodes of the neural network. The input is attenuated by the weights between each of the input nodes and the output node. A weighted sum is calculated in the output node. This sum is then transformed using the transfer function with threshold Θ. The output represents the neural network's assessment of the input. The learning algorithm compares the output of the neural network with the actual correct output and uses this information to adjust the weights in order to reduce future errors.

A description of neural network architecture and training is found in the Appendix.

Variations and Enhancements

Despite the recent attention being given neural networks by the popular press, artificial neural networks (ANNs) are an old emerging technology. Versions of the basic model — also called the *perception machine* — were first articulated by McCulloch and Pitts (8) and by Widrow and Hoff (21). Rosenblatt developed the first perceptron learning algorithm (22), and Minsky and Pappert provided a thorough analysis of their mathematical properties (23), showing, among other things, that a simple perceptron model could not model the elementary "exclusive or" (XOR) problem. This negative finding may well have been responsible for the lack of development in the field that followed for some time after Minsky and Pappert's publication (16). It was not until the 1980s that some of the limitations of early neural networks were overcome to a sufficient degree to make ANNs practical for real-world applications.

Over the years, the early work evolved into a variety of neural network "subspecies" including back-propagation networks (15), counterpropagation networks (24,25), Hopfield networks (26), associative memories (27), adaptive resonance networks (28), radial-basis functions (29,30), generalized regression neural networks (31), recirculation neural networks (32), and so on. These models differ from each other in terms of their connectivity pattern (e.g., full or partial), topology (free form or layered), data flow (cyclical or acyclical), data type (discrete, binary, or real), output representation (localized or distributed), learning paradigms (autonomous or feedback), and training methods (iterative or single pass).

In spite of these differences, though, most neural models are basically variations on the same theme: a connected collection of many independent processors, working in tandem to carry out a global computational task. With that in mind, it is important to understand that different neural models do not necessarily compete with each other; rather, they represent different specializations designed to solve different types of problems.

Fifty or so years of research notwithstanding, there are still many open issues relating to the theory and application of ANNs. It has been proven mathematically that almost any classification problem, no matter how complex (barring some exceptions that generally do not inhibit practical applications), can be simulated by a neural network with only one hidden layer of neurons (33,34). Yet the mathematical proofs are strictly existential: They do not describe how many neurons the hidden layer should include, what learning parameters will be most effective, or when convergence to a stable set of weights should occur. These issues are most commonly determined using heuristics and experimentation. Although the construction of an effective topology is still more of an art than a science, network construction guidelines are beginning to emerge (35–38).

Ambiguity also surrounds the *meaning* of the network. Given that a certain network topology is indeed a successful classifier, how can we credibly justify the network's operations, short of pointing to empirical results? If a network is supposed to serve as a component of a decision support system, it may need to offer a certain degree of intuitive face validity and analytic accountability; yet, neural networks are generally difficult to interpret analytically. Although some advances in neural network interpretation have been made (39–41), this area is still in its infancy. As a result, even though we can confirm empirically that a particular neural network performs well on a large training set, we often cannot explain this success analytically. Therefore, we cannot guarantee that a network will not make freak decisions at some point in the future, and we cannot justify its analytic rational. We will return to this point in the fourth section.

A PARTIAL SURVEY OF ORGANIZATIONS APPLYING ANNs TO BUSINESS DECISION PROBLEMS

In the previous section, we presented a sketch of how neural networks function from an operational perspective. In this section, we present a sampling of how these tools are used for decision support in business organizations.

A recent U.S. Commmerce Department survey reported that 70% of America's top 500 companies are using some form of "artificial intelligence" (42). Many of these applications involve neural networks. Any contemporary survey of applications of neural networks is necessarily incomplete. This is due not only to space constraints but also to the large number of proprietary systems developed in business and industry. Nonetheless, we will attempt to give the reader a flavor of the business applications of ANNs by highlighting some of these projects.

Because the focus of this article is the use of neural networks as decision-making tools, we will not discuss such applications as automatic control, character recognition, and signal processing, although there are many ANN systems in these areas.

Before we go on to describe applications of neural networks, two points bear noting. First, in gathering much of the information regarding the systems described in this section, we relied heavily on popular press accounts and third-hand reports. As a result, the scope and efficacy of some of these systems may have been inflated by enthusiastic reporters or interviewees. Second, the reader is cautioned that many of the organizations described, particularly those in the financial domain, have only a few years of experience in using their systems. As with any technology, early positive results may not be indicative of the long-run viability of these systems.

Having said this, we, nonetheless, feel it useful to present examples of organizations that are using ANNs as components of their decision support system (DSS) processes.

Banking and Finance

The financial industry has long pursued proprietary quantitative methods for conducting analysis. Neural networks often fill that need nicely for certain problems with high degrees of nonlinearity or nonstationarity. In general, financial firms are reticent to discuss their methods or their results. Nonetheless, some interesting cases have been documented.

Market prediction is probably the most active area of development in the financial sector. The British firm Econostat, Ltd. trains neural networks using fundamental economic data and uses the models to control loss risk associated with its investments in the long-term bonds of G7 nations. The fund doubled the market's performance over 2 years (43). Similarly, Nikko Securities developed a trading system to predict the future value of the TOPIX, an index of the Tokyo Stock exchange. Nikko's system incorporates technical indicators as well as fundamental economic variables. The system achieved a successful prediction rate of more than 62% over a 2½-year period (44–46). Mellon Equity Associates (a subsidiary of Mellon Bank) has developed a system for various types of market prediction using neural network technology (47), as has the Dia-Ichi Kangyo Bank (44).

Several financial firms have explored the use of neural networks for managing portfolios of assets. Fidelity Investments developed a system that selects the top 200 equity issues out of a universe of 2000 U.S. stocks using financial ratios and fundamental and technical indicators. The firm uses the system to manage a $150 million portfolio (43,48). LBS Capital Management Inc. trains a suite of over 3000 neural networks on a weekly basis, one for each mid-cap equity the firm follows. Rigorous testing procedures are used to determine the few models that are predictive at any point in time (2,49). John Deere and Co. uses a similar strategy to manage a $100 million portfolio, achieving about 30% returns, considerably higher than industry benchmarks (43).

Bankers have also begun to adopt decision systems based on neural networks for a wide variety of industry-specific applications such as loan approval and fraud detection (50). HNC Software, for example, produces a suite of credit-card-related neural network products. Falcon, the most noted of these, develops customized profiles of each cardholder's buying patterns. The system then identifies anomalous, and potentially fraudulent, card activity. Banks using the system include, BankAmerica, Wells Fargo, and MBNA (51–53). American Express, as well as other banks use their own versions of neural network fraud-detection systems on their credit-card portfolios (53). VISA International has also developed a system that cost $2 million to build and saved the bank an estimated $4.4 million in just over a year (54).

Marketing and Retail

Due to their ability to identify and predict high-dimensional patterns in data, neural networks have found a number of applications in market segmentation and consumer behavior analysis. For example, neural nets have been used by some firms to predict the impact of advertising campaigns. Kmart, one of the world's largest mass-merchandise retailers, uses a system that combines an expert system and a neural network. The expert system identifies the sectors that should be advertised and the neural network predicts the impact of advertisements based on such attributes as page location, competitors activities, and so forth (55). The London-based ad agency of McCann-Erickson has been using an ANN to forecast the impact of various ad campaigns and to help the firm schedule advertisements (56).

Another common marketing application is segmentation of customer bases. Sun Alliance, the U.K. insurance firm, uses a neural-network-based analysis system to determine to which clients to send direct mailings. Using the system, the firm was able to reduce mailings by 20% while only reducing responses by 3% (54). Thomas Cook Holidays also used neural network technology to target to which clients to send direct mail offers (56), as does First Commerce Corp. (57). Software giant

Microsoft has developed a neural network for its direct marketing campaigns. The system reportedly increases the response rate from 4.9% to 8.2% which translates into about a 35% reduction in costs (58).

Neural networks are also used by some firms for higher-level marketing applications. Fleet Financial Group, Inc., for example, uses a neural-network-based system to enhance the bank's cross-selling efforts, tailor products to specific client types, and help the bank form its marketing strategy (59). The British soft drink producer Britvic uses an ANN to predict future sales volumes based on consumer demand (56). Kay-Bee Toy Stores uses an ANN-based analysis to identify sales trends in outlet performance analysis (60).

Health Care and Medicine

In the medical field, neural networks are used for a variety of diagnosis problems. Due to the often conflicting nature of symptoms and vital signs, diagnosis is a subtle science. The ability of neural networks to manipulate high-dimensional data spaces makes them good candidates for solving such problems.

PapNet, for example, was developed for cervical cancer screening. The system is used to rescreen Pap smears that have been determined to be negative (no cancer). The system is sensitive enough to detect cancerous cells that human experts may miss. In some cases, the accuracy of the conventional methods was almost 50% lower than with the system (61). At the time of this writing, the system was available in 138 U.S. labs and in 21 other countries (62).

Florida Hospital uses a neural-network-based system for heart attack diagnosis (60).

A system has also been developed for monitoring the vital signs of premature infants. This system is trained on the individual pattern for each infant for about 10 minutes and then notifies medical staff if there is a deviation from the baby's expected pattern. The system has resulted in a reduction in false alarms that are more common with less sophisticated threshold trigger systems (63).

Another application area is illness prediction and determination of hospital-stay requirements. Anderson Memorial Hospital in South Carolina uses individually trained neural networks to analyze the severity of illnesses and expected length of hospital stay. The system saved the hospital $500,000 in its first 15 months of limited usage (64).

Neural networks have also proven useful in drug development. Vysis, Inc., a wholly owned subsidiary of a division of Amoco Corporation, uses a system that combines advances in database technology with neural networks to expedite the identification of candidate protein molecules for drug development (65). Alanex Corp. uses an artificial neural net to analyze molecular structures to help search for new drugs as well (66).

Other Domains

In addition to the more general classes of applications discussed in the sections above, neural networks have been applied to solve more domain-specific problems.

Mercury Communications, the U.K.'s second largest telecommunications operator, for example, uses an ANN-based solution to predict the staffing demands at the firm's Customer Call Center. The center, which handles about 13,000 calls a day, realized a 5% savings by using the system (63).

Several manufacturing firms use neural networks to inspect their products during the production process. Nippon Steel uses ANNs to detect "break-out" which occurs when chips that form on the surface of hot steel damage the production line (45). Colgate-Palmolive has developed an inspection system to evaluate the packaging of its products. The system led to a reduction in errors and relieved employees of a tedious part of their jobs (67).

Neural networks have also been used to "sniff out" criminal activity. The Chicago Police Department's personnel department uses a neural-network-based system to analyze the behavior of police officers and identify those who may be corrupt (60,68). The London Stock Exchange uses a neural network to spot patterns of insider trading (69,70). Similarly, The State of Texas has commissioned a neural-network-based Medicaid fraud-detection system. Nationally, Medicaid fraud costs $31 billion annually, but in almost 20 years, Texas's current (simple trigger based) fraud-detection system has not resulted in a single prosecutable case (71).

Arco and Texaco use a neural-network-based system to analyze geological data to determine which sites have the highest probability of containing petroleum deposits (72).

Finally, a Japanese firm called Earth Weather, Inc. uses a neural network to produce highly accurate localized weather forecasts. The system uses basic meteorological data such as air movements and water-vapor content to predict the weather for areas as small as 100 m^2 for companies that conduct weather-sensitive operations such as ocean-based loading and unloading operations (73).

CONSIDERATIONS IN APPLYING ANNs TO BUSINESS DECISION PROBLEMS

In the previous section, we tried to give a flavor of how neural networks have been used successfully in industry. But not all neural network stories are successes. Many organizations have developed neural network systems only to see them not provide any benefit, or, worse, increase costs due to wasted development time and inaccurate DSS-based decisions. How can an organization determine when a neural network will provide a useful solution for a particular decision problem?

The DSS Stretch Plot

Many frameworks exist for exploring the fit between decision support technologies and decision problems. In this article, we adopt a framework presented to Dhar and Stein (2). The framework proposes that business problems and potential solutions to them be considered with respect to the organizational constraints of the environment, the limitations of various competing options, and the dynamics of the problem. In this section, we present a thumbnail analysis of how these issues bear on neural networks for decision support problems. Interested readers can see Ref. 2 for a more detailed analysis.

Stein and Dhar present a framework for intelligent decision support based on a plot of attributes or dimensions called a *Stretch Plot*. The dimensions of a problem represent either attributes of a particular solution (e.g., neural network), the constraints of a problem or organization, or an interaction of the two.

The dimensions of the problem space are mapped onto a 2 × 2 plot. In understanding how the dimensions are positioned on the Stretch Plot, it is useful to consider how the plot divides them up both along horizontal and vertical axes. Dividing the plot first horizontally, the dimensions in the top half of the Stretch Plot relate to the proposed system itself (in this case, an ANN) and characterize the requirements of the DSS. Those in the bottom half of the plot represent the business environment in which the DSS will be developed and used.

Looking now at the plot along the vertical axis, the right half of the plot contains dimensions that specify constraints imposed on the DSS, whereas the left half contains dimensions that represent the quality of the actual inputs and outputs to the DSS.

So, for example, the dimension of *accuracy* is located in the Model/Quality quadrant because it deals with characteristics of the DSS model and the quality of

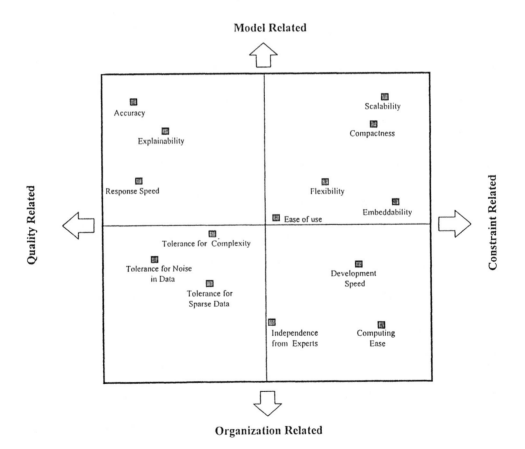

FIGURE 3   A Stretch Plot of DSS dimensions for intelligent systems. (Adapted from Ref. 2.)

its output. *Development speed* is in the Organization/Constraints quadrant because the development time restrictions are constraints that are imposed by the organization in which a particular DSS is being developed.

The dimensions of the Stretch Plot are designed so that, *ceteris paribus*, a DSS that can provide high values for the attributes is more desirable than one that provides low values. For example, if two alternative DSS solutions are competing, all things being equal, decision-makers would prefer the one that had higher accuracy. Similarly, an organization would prefer a solution that had a faster development time (high development speed) to one that was slower.

It turns out, however, that there is no magic bullet, single DSS technique that optimizes all of the dimensions. Rather, decision support options tend to excel at certain dimensions, and muddle by or fail on others. For example, it is often very clear how a rule-based expert system arrives at a particular decision recommendation. A user can obtain an "audit trail" of the rules that were fired and follow the logic. This dimension is called *explainability* and it relates to how easily the rationale for a particular decision is understood. Rule-based systems generally have high explainability.

TABLE 1   Summary of the Dimensions of the Stretch Plot

Dimension	Attribute measured
Accuracy	How close the outputs of a system are to the correct or best decision
Compactness	How small the system can be made
Ease of use	How complicated the system is to use for business people
Embeddability	How easily a system can be incorporated into the existing infrastructure of an organization
Explainability	How easy it is to understand the process by which a conclusion was reached
Flexibility	How easily the relationships among the variables can be changed, or the goals of the system modified
Independence from experts	The degree to which the system can be designed, built, and tested without requiring the developers to consult with business experts
Response speed	The time it takes for a system to complete its analysis at the desired level of accuracy
Scalability	How easily more variables can be added to a problem or the range of variables can be increased
Tolerance for complexity	How dramatically the quality of a system is affected by interactions among the various components of the process being modeled or in the knowledge used to model a process
Tolerance for Data sparseness	How dramatically the quality of a system is affected by incompleteness or lack of development data
Tolerance for noise in data	The degree to which the quality of a system, most notably its accuracy, is affected by noise in the data

To continue the example, we note that, again, in general, rule-based systems do not scale well from a small domain to a much larger domain, because the knowledge required to feed the system and the interactions between these pieces of knowledge often grows exponentially. Thus, with respect to the dimension *scalability*, rule-based expert systems tend to perform poorly.

We find similar dichotomies of performance with respect to the Stretch Plot among other DSS candidate solutions. Furthermore, the characteristics of some organizational contexts act to "level the playing field" along certain dimensions. For example, the dimension *tolerance for sparse data* refers to the ease with which developers can implement a particular modeling technique in the absence of large volumes of data about the process being modeled. Techniques like neural networks and recursive partitioning algorithms tend to require large volumes of data, whereas others like fuzzy systems or rule-based systems do not. If, however, an organization has plenty of high-quality data available, then all four of these techniques will compete equally along the *tolerance for sparse data* dimension, as those techniques that require data will be able to use it and those that do not require data will be no worse off for having it.

A similar line of reasoning shows that some problem domain-specific attributes (*tolerance for complexity* or *explainability*) can similarly drop out of the analysis if the problem being considered does not require high levels of these attributes. For example, a problem which did not require the output of a DSS to be produced quickly would cause the *response speed* dimension to be dropped from analysis.

The Stretch Plot allows DSS developers to first analyze the nature of the organizational problem and context that they are dealing with and then evaluate candidate solutions with respect to how they satisfy the problem requirements.

A Stretch Plot Analysis of ANNs

Pros

When might an organization wish to use a neural network solution? A primary advantage recommending neural networks over some other approaches to decision support is the relative independence of the developer from so-called domain experts who have expertise about the business problem. Because neural networks abstract problem structure from sample data, much less expert guidance is needed for training.

This independence can be useful for three reasons. First, some processes (e.g., some financial markets) are very complex and often defy simple codification. Second, experts are not always able to articulate their knowledge, making it difficult to map relationships based on their feedback. Third, experts are usually busy, expensive resources. Because neural networks avoid the "knowledge acquisition bottleneck" of interviewing experts and encoding their heuristics, neural networks can also be attractive in situations where a particular process may change frequently (e.g., consumer preferences, financial markets, etc.). Neural network models can be refit by retraining on up-to-date data sets. Finally, even experts can suffer from tunnel vision and lack of consistency in describing their thought processes. Fortunately, well-trained neural networks can learn from data rather than experts.

Neural networks have been dubbed "universal approximators," as they have been found to excel at interpolation problems. In particular, ANNs fit "prediction surfaces" to training data sets, by interpolating along the data.* ANNs store the "shape" of the data and, as result, exhibit very high accuracy with respect to interpolation tasks. Furthermore, these models can, depending on their architecture, model very complex surfaces for these interpolation tasks.

From an operational standpoint, most applications that use neural networks in business take advantage of trained networks, preferring to train the neural net off-line and use the fitted model on-line in their posttraining mode. Most neural networks reduce to simple sets of equations, usually composed of arithmetic operations and transcendental functions. Such models offer two distinct advantages. First, the models are very compact, requiring only a small amount of memory overhead to encode. This also makes it easier to embed them in larger applications. Second, the small size means that this type of model performs quite quickly in practice, requiring minimal computing operations to evaluate input.

Cons

However attractive the *Pros* section may make neural networks appear, they are not panaceas for modeling decision problems. Because neural networks rely heavily on data to develop their representations of the problem domain, developers must pay a fair amount of attention to ensuring that the data used are plentiful and of fairly good quality. A large portion of the development time for most neural network systems centers around identifying and preprocessing data; a range of techniques has developed for doing this (74,75).

Determining a neural network topology and training processes is still considered by many to be more of an art than a science. The number of hidden nodes, learning parameter values, and so forth all affect the likelihood that the net will converge to a useful solution. In general, the more complicated the network becomes, the less likely it is to find good solutions. This is due to the fact that as the number of neurons increases, the number of parameters in the form of connection weights also increases, but at a faster rate. As in most numerical and statistical problems, as the number of parameters increases, both the likelihood of over fitting and the need for more data increase. Because the neural network discovers and exploits useful relationships in data, it may, at times, find patterns in the *noise* rather than patterns in the *data*.

This also highlights what is probably the most often bemoaned drawback of neural networks. The results of processing inputs are opaque and the model derived by the net uses are not easily understood. This stems in part from the fact that the original knowledge is not coded in an explicit form. Even though each component of a neural network is made up of a relatively simple equation, these simple equations interact with each other in such a way as to create higher-order nonlinear functional equations and mappings. The result is that it is difficult to isolate which variables caused what behavior in a neural network. This situation has begun to change due to some recent research, as discussed in the subsection but these efforts are still relatively undeveloped.

---

*With two variables, this interpolated surface is a curve or closed area; with three variables, it is a (possibly deformed) plane; and so forth.

Summary

Whereas neural networks offer much in the way of hands-off robust modeling, there are significant drawbacks as well. Thus, in practice, the decision to use or pass over a neural network for a decision problem becomes an analysis of how the organization and the problem at hand relate to the inherent strengths and weaknesses of neural network technology. A summary of this thumbnail analysis, taken from Ref. 2, is shown in Table 2.

An Example of Applying the Stretch Plot

In this section, we present a simplified example of how an organization can use the Stretch Plot to make decisions about various technology options for implementing a DSS. The case, as well as many others, is developed more fully in Ref. 2.

Earlier, we mention that LBS Capital Management Inc., an asset management and investment firm, uses a sophisticated system of ANNs to select and trade securities. LBS manages about $600 million in assets, primarily in stocks and mutual funds, for both institutional and individual investors. This includes a Fortune 100 pension fund and a large international bank. Why is an ANN approach a good choice for LBS? What other options did the firm have?

LBS's objective in developing a DSS was to maximize the return on the assets it invests for its clients while minimizing their risk exposure. LBS, like many other asset-management enterprises, believes that a key ingredient to successful investing is *timing*. LBS tries to determine whether the market is providing any *signals* about how it is likely to behave in the intermediate term and *when* to buy and sell *which* of the securities. Initially, LBS experimented with a variety of objectives for their models. Over time, however, the objective became more focused: to have a system provide recommendations on individual stocks.

But it is extremely difficult to find consistent tools that model financial markets well. These markets are complex and only partially understood. Prediction, even in the short term, is a very difficult exercise. The problem of developing a system to estimate future prices is daunting because financial processes are generally characterized by high levels of nonlinearity and complexity, making them hard to

TABLE 2   Summary of Thumbnail Analysis

Dimension	Neural network
Accuracy	High
Explainability	Low
Response speed	High
Compactness	High
Flexibility	High
Embeddability	High
Tolerance for complexity	High
Tolerance for sparse data	Low
Independence from experts	High

Source: Adapted from Ref. 2.

model. The amount of data available to an analyst is overwhelming. Furthermore, financial markets are constantly evolving so models must adapt to these changes.

LBS's DSS system needed to reflect these factors:

- The system needed to be able to quickly incorporate knowledge about a domain which often defies explicit definition. It is not unusual to have widely varying interpretations of the data from different experts even *after* the fact.
- The system needed to be able to deal with and analyze complex data.
- The system needed to be able to deal with the *large amounts* of economic and financial data that are generated daily.
- The system needed to be able to adapt quickly over time. Financial markets are highly nonstationary: They often change rapidly over time. Even a strategy that worked well in *last year's* bear market might not do so well in *this year's* bear market.

In essence, LBS wanted models to sift through the volumes of data the firm has and to highlight the more interesting relationships. The data that LBS would be using were plentiful, although not necessarily clean. Errors entered the data as a result of a number problems during downloading, recording at the source, and so forth.

LBS needed to be able to integrate the results of the analysis into their then-current analytic processes and produce results in reasonable time. To do this, the system needed to interface smoothly with the financial databases where the firm's market data are stored. This was necessary both for reading data into the model and for determining the "goodness" or a particular model.

Goodness would be measured by the accuracy and consistency of a system. In order to make this realistic, though, LBS would use simulated trading systems to test the models. Models were then tested (or *validated*) by back testing over several historical years to determine how they would have performed.

Because a decision-maker (typically a portfolio manager) would be interpreting the results of a prediction, it would be useful if the model were able offer some insight into its analysis. It was also important that the system fit smoothly into the LBS's work flow and current modeling tools.

The system also needed to be able to be expanded to accommodate additional securities and input factors which are expected to be added over time. To be practical, the model would also need to be flexible enough to accommodate new market trends, new types of data, and portfolio objectives. In addition, LBS needed to be able to update its model's "view of the world" frequently and easily. Furthermore, as there would be thousands of securities to analyze, the DSS needed to be able to perform the analysis on each individual security in a reasonable amount of time.

In summary, each of the DSS options that LBS would consider needed be compared on at least the Stretch Plot dimensions outlined in Table 3.

What options did LBS have?

The mainstays of many asset-management firms are statistical analysis, charting, and visualization techniques. LBS also makes use of these techniques to try to understand trends within the financial markets better.

In the mid-1980s, LBS began to pursue expert-systems technology as a way of supporting investment decisions. By the late 1980s, the firm had begun to build a rule-based expert system for assisting in *market timing* decisions. A system, based

TABLE 3   Stretch Plot Dimensions

Dimension	Target solution
Accuracy	Moderate
Explainability	Moderate
Response speed	Moderate
Scalability	Moderate
Flexibility	High
Embeddability	High
Tolerance for complexity	High
Tolerance for noise in data	High
Independence from experts	High

on the reasoning processes and trading practices of one of its expert traders, was designed to combine various pieces of market data and to evaluate the direction of the market (as characterized by the S&P 500).

By the early 1990s, LBS also began to focus on other intelligent systems technologies such as neural networks and also undertook the task of modeling individual securities.

Each of the three approaches, traditional statistics, rule-based systems, and neural networks, offers a potential method for making sense out of the huge volumes of data that LBS has available to assist in its decision making.

Although a detailed discussion of the strengths and weaknesses of statistical methods and rule-based systems vis-à-vis LBS's problem are beyond the scope of this article, we present the summarized results of the Stretch Plot analysis in Table 4. From examining Table 4, it becomes very clear that approaches like traditional statistical methods, by themselves, suffer along some crucial attributes, whereas the RBS approach also has a fair share of flaws with respect to LBS's problem. Interestingly, even the ANN approach, in this example the clearly dominant approach, suffers in that it does not offer the explainability that the firm wanted. If this dimension were crucial to LBS's operations, an ANN-based DSS would not be

TABLE 4   Results of the Stretch Plot Analysis

Dimension	Target solution	RBS	STATS	ANN
Accuracy	Moderate	✔	✔	✔
Explainability	Moderate	✔	✔	
Response time	Moderate	✔	✔	✔
Scalability	Moderate	✔	✔	✔
Flexibility	High			✔
Embeddability	High		✔	✔
Tolerance for complexity	High			✔
Tolerance for noise in data	High			✔
Independence from experts	High		✔	✔

a viable option. For LBS, however, this turned out to be "negotiable," and the firm went on to implement a DSS based on neural network technology. As we described earlier, the asset manager's favorable results support the validity of their decision.

In this section, we have tried to briefly present a methodological framework for mapping DSS problems onto potential solutions. Although we have focused exclusively on the application of the framework to neural networks, it should be evident that the methodology is general enough to apply to a wide range of DSS problems and solution options.

CONCLUSION

Decision support system designers and practitioners often find it difficult to determine when a particular decision problem might be treated effectively with a neural network. During the last decade, neural networks have proliferated in so many directions that it is no longer simple to define what the term "neural network" represents. In order to keep track of the field, researchers and practitioners must monitor several journals in neuroscience, computer science, psychology, mathematics, physics, and statistics. The situation is exasturbated by the numerous hyperbolic articles on neural networks which appear at an alarming rate in journals, conference proceedings and, as the reference section of this article demonstrates, the popular press. Potential adopters of the technology often become confused by the overwhelming gamut and esoteric terminology of neural computing.

With that in mind, we have taken a different stance—one that assumes that the acceptability (or the lack of it) of any new DSS resource must be examined with respect to the organizational issues associated with its use.

By presenting a partial survey of decision problems that have been solved using ANNs, we have highlighted the many instances in which these models have demonstrated their applicability and effectiveness for business DSS. We have chosen these examples from a wide variety of fields to highlight the versatility of the paradigm, as well as to provide insight into the types of applications that have been successfully developed.

Yet, rather than casting neural networks as panaceas for *all* decision support applications, we present an analysis of the technology for individual problems using the framework suggested in Ref. 2. This analysis provides practitioners with guidelines for evaluating when a particular business problem might be treated with neural networks, given a particular organizational setting, and, as importantly, when a particular situation rules out ANNs.

We believe that this balanced view will help researchers and practitioners realize the exciting possibilities that neural networks entail, without losing sight of the limitations that still inhibit their use in decision support.

APPENDIX: THE ARCHITECTURE AND TRAINING OF A FEED-FORWARD ANN

Here, we focus on one specific model which lurks behind many business applications of neural computing: *feed-forward back-propagation networks*. This model, which resulted from the seminal work of the PDP Research Group (14), is widely used in practice for a number of reasons.

First, the training algorithm of feed-forward networks, known as back-propagation (BP) learning, is relatively well established and well understood. There exists a large body of theoretical research on the properties and behavior of back-propagation training paradigms. BP is very general in its behavior and can be used to optimize the weight space of a wide variety of networks. To this end, numerous extensions have been added to the basic BP algorithm (e.g., Delta-Bar-Delta (76), Extended Delta-Bar-Delta (77), etc.). Finally, and perhaps most importantly, BP is fairly simple to implement and there exist many software shells that enable users to build and train feed-forward networks with minimal programming.

The extension of feed-forward networks from a single-neuron machine to a multilayered architecture is outlined in Figure 1. The simplest model consists of a single neuron designed to classify n-dimensional objects into two classes. This basic model can be extended in two different ways. First, in order to classify objects into $m > 2$ classes, one adds more neurons to the network, each representing a different class (Fig. 1b). Second, in order to classify objects which are not linearly separable, one adds more layers of neurons between the n-ary input layer and the m-ary output layer (Fig. 1c). The "hidden layers" are designed to model nonlinear boundaries in the objects space, as will be explained shortly.

Hence, feed-forward networks represent an elegant ascent from simple to complex architectures. The extensions from one architecture to another are straightforward, a complex network being a union of simpler networks, all the way down to the level of individual neurons. In other words, all feed-forward networks are made up of the same atomic material — independent neurons — arranged in different patterns of connectivity.

The Single-Neuron Model*

For the sake of clarity, we will begin with the simplest neural model — consisting of a single neuron — and gradually extend it to a multilayered, feed-forward network of neurons. This later model is by far the most widely used neural architecture in business applications.

Consider the following problem, taken from the domain of direct-mail marketing. A consumer-products company plans to promote a new product through a fancy (and expensive) mailing kit. In order to cut cost and maximize yield, the company seeks to approach only those customers who are likely to purchase the new product. Strictly speaking, the company wishes to partition its customer base into two categories: "targets" (c_1) and "nontargets" (c_2). This, of course, is a generic classification problem: The objective is to sort n-dimensional entities (customers) into m classes (here, $m = 2$).

We assume that the company maintains a customers file and a transactions file. The first file keeps track of n customer attributes, denoted $x_1, \ldots, x_n$ (e.g., age, income, zip–code, etc.). With this notation, the universe of all possible customers is the cartesian product $X = x_1 \times \cdots \times x_n$, a specific customer is denoted $x \in X$, and the company's customers file is denoted $X_f \subset X$.

The transactions file specifies which of the customers purchased what prod-

---

*Throughout this section, italic letters (x), boldface letters ($\mathbf{x}$), and italicized uppercase letters (X) represent scalar, vector, and set variables, respectively.

uct in the past, and when. A customer may either purchase the product or not. We also assume that there is a certain metric or a domain expert who can partition the company's products into two sets: products that are "related" to the promoted product and products that are "unrelated."

Based on these assumptions, the company's files can be reprocessed to generate two data sets, as follows: $X_1 = \{x \mid x \in X_f \text{ purchased a related product}\}$, and $X_2 = X_f \setminus X_1$. The first set contains examples of customers who might be interested in the promoted product, whereas the second set contains all the other customers. To complete the problem's setting, suppose now that the company has access to a mailing list, denoted $X_3 \subset X$, consisting of potential adopters of the product whose buying behavior is unknown.

Can we use X_1 and X_2 and a neural network to predict which X_3 customers are likely to purchase the new product? In other words, can the network learn to take as input X_p and classify each of its members?

We begin with a simple network, consisting on n input units and a single processing unit (Fig. 2). The input units are connected to the processing unit by n "wires" whose "widths" are represented by a set of numeric weights, denoted w_1, . . . , w_n, or $\mathbf{w}$. The input units store the descriptor values (customer attributes), denoted x_1, . . . , x_n, or $\mathbf{x}$.

The processing unit is characterized by two mathematical operations: a fixed weighted-sum operator which computes the inner product $\mathbf{wx} = \Sigma w_i x_i$, and a fixed activation function, denoted $g(\cdot)$, which maps $\mathbf{wx}$ on $[-1, 1]$ (the role of the threshold θ will be discussed shortly). If the network "thinks" that the customer in question should be classified as "target," it will output 1. Otherwise, it will output -1.

The training data consists of the sets X_1 and X_2, whose member vectors are known ex post to be targets and non targets, respectively. Initially, the network's weight values are set to small random values.

The training phase is a cyclical process in which a "teacher," the network's training program, repetitively samples objects, $\mathbf{x}$, from X_1 and X_2 and passes them to the network for classification. After comparing the network's response with the actual correct classification, an error-minimizing procedure adjusts the network's weights in a direction and magnitude to reduce the overall error associated with a wrong classification decision. Next, the network is fed another object, and the process continues. The details are as follows:

1. Initialize $\mathbf{w}$ and θ to small random values.
2. Select at random one of the training sets X_1 or X_2 and sample an object x from it. If $x \in X_1$, set $d = 1$. If not, set $d = -1$.
3. Compute the classification of $\mathbf{x}_i$ as follows:
   If $g(\mathbf{wx} - \theta) > 0$, set $y = 1$.
   Otherwise, set $y = -1$.
4. If $\mathbf{x}_i$ was misclassified, compute a new set of weights $\mathbf{w}'$ as follows: $w_j' = w_j + \eta \cdot (y_i - y) \cdot x$.
5. Set $\mathbf{w} = \mathbf{w}'$ and go to Step 2.

The output of the model, which is determined in Step 3, is denoted y. The parameter η in Step 4 is a gain factor between 0 and 1 which determines the rate at which the model converges to a stable set of weights.

The threshold value θ appears to be fixed in Steps 1-5, but this is done only for the sake of clear exposition. In most models the threshold is made a learnable parameter through the following modification of Steps 1–5:

(a) Add a new input unit x_0 to the model, but instead of drawing it from the data, clamp its value to -1

(b) Replace $g(\mathbf{wx} - \theta)$ in Step 3 with $g(\mathbf{wx})$ [$\mathbf{w}$ and $\mathbf{x}$ are now $(n + 1)$-ary vectors]

This way, θ becomes yet another weight (w_0) which is adjusted by Steps 1–5 like all the other weights in the model. By convention, x_0 is called a *bias* term and can also be thought of as similar to the intercept in an additive linear model.

In general, the model is a symmetric implementation of Hebb's rule of learning (78): *A connection between two neurons should be strengthened whenever both neurons fire.* In the present model, when $\mathbf{x}$ is misclassified, Step 4 serves to either increment, or decrement, the weights along the active connections (where $x_i \neq 0$), according to the direction of the classification error. Hence, the weights are continuously modified to promote improved network performance. In fact, the data-driven weights constitute the only "moving parts" of the network's machinery; All the other features of the network, namely the units topology and the functions $\mathbf{w} \cdot \mathbf{x}$ and $g(\cdot)$, remain constant throughout the network's operations.

The termination condition of Steps 1–5 is pragmatic. If the object's space X is linearly separable, the procedure is guaranteed to converge to a stable set of weights (this result is known as Rosenblatt's theorem). In other cases, the process is halted when all the examples have been exhausted, or when the error term is sufficiently small.

The above procedure is the computational reality behind the popular claim that neural networks can "train themselves" or "learn from experience." We see that these anthropomorphic phrases should not be taken at face value: Neural learning algorithms are based on simple error-minimizing procedures which are far removed from what we normally construe as human learning. It is possible that human learning at its lowest level, namely at the neuron's level, is somewhat similar to Steps 1–5, but biological evidence that this is indeed the case is wanting (79).

First Extension: More Neurons

Suppose now that instead of classifying the customers into two categories, the company wishes to discern three categories, as follows: prime targets, secondary-targets, and nontargets, denoted c_1, c_2, and c_3, respectively. (This would make sense if, for example, the company had two types of mailing kits which vary in production and mailing cost.)

In order to represent the three categories, we extend the single processing-unit model as follows. First, the input layer of the network remains the same, with n input units, one for each customer attribute. This layer, however, will be connected not to a single processing unit, as before, but rather to three processing units, denoted y_j, $j = 1, 2, 3$. Each of these units will be connected to the same n input lines by a separate weight vector $\mathbf{w}_j = \langle w_{1,j}, \ldots, w_{n,j} \rangle$, $j = 1, 2, 3$ (see Fig. 1b, and note that for $j = 1$, the model reduces to the single-unite model depicted in Fig. 1a).

When a new customer's profile $\mathbf{x} = \langle x_1, \ldots, x_n \rangle$ is fed to the network, the three processing units compute (in parallel) the three inner products $\mathbf{w}_j\mathbf{x}$, $j = 1, 2,$ 3. The output unit with the largest inner product is then selected as the most promising category of the classified object. The rationale behind this procedure is as follows.

As the network sees more and more examples, the learning algorithm continuously adjusts the three weight vectors. If learning is successful, the weight vector $\mathbf{w}_j$ will eventually store the "average" characteristics (features) of the vectors that are known to belong to the class c_j. With that in mind, the inner products $\mathbf{w}_j\mathbf{x}$, $j = 1,$ 2, 3, measure the three vectorial similarities (akin to correlations) between the new vector, $\mathbf{x}$, and the up-to-date average characteristics of the three classes c_j, $j = 1, 2,$ 3. Leaving the question of whether or not this procedure will work to the next section, we note that the extension of a single processing unit to a layer of multiple units is straightforward. A single unit is a binary classifier. A layer of m units acts as a slab of m competing classifiers, each measuring the vectorial similarity between its own set of weights and the input vector.

Second Extension: More Layers

The network described in the previous section will probably not work in realistic settings. This is because the objects space (the world of customer characteristics) is probably not linearly separable, but the network, in its present form, can carry out only linear classification. In order to visualize this limitation, picture a two-dimensional objects space in which each object (customer) is represented by a fixed point in the (x_1, x_2) plane (e.g., income and age values). Furthermore, assume that the customers are partitioned into three classes [i.e., that some points in the (x_1, x_2) plane are labeled A, others B, yet others C]. Finally, assume that even though the points exist, you still do not get to see them. At that point, you are staring at an empty (x_1, x_2) plane on which three lines are randomly drawn.

Suppose now that you are provided with a ruler and a pencil and you are asked to go through the following iterative exercise: in each step, one point (x_1, x_2) will be exposed, along with its label (one of A, B, or C). Your job (in each iteration) is to separate the three sets of already visible points by adjusting the three straight lines (Fig. 3a–3d). If at some step you fail to separate the points correctly, so would the network. To complete the analogy, denote the slopes and offsets of the three lines in step k by the three pairs $(\langle w_1/w_2, \theta\rangle_j, j = 1, 2, 3)_k$. Note that the entire setting corresponds exactly to the network's learning procedure, in which the set of weights and threshold values are continuously adjusted to achieve better classification. If the objects space is not linearly separable, the network will fail to converge to a stable set of weights: The rulers will continue to oscillate, indefinitely (Fig. 3d).

As it turns out, most interesting classification problems are not linearly separable. For example, consider the customers space spanned by the attributes $X_1, \ldots,$ X_n. In general, it would be naive to assume that the factors that determine a purchase likelihood of a new product are simple linear functions of customer attributes. To make matters worse, it might be that the boundaries of a certain class (e.g., A) in the object space cannot be expressed in mathematics. In other words, in the worst case (which is unfortunately quite common) we are facing an opaque classification problem $f : X_1 \times \cdots \times X_n \rightarrow \{c_1, \ldots, c_m\}$ in which f may not only be unknown but also nonanalytical.

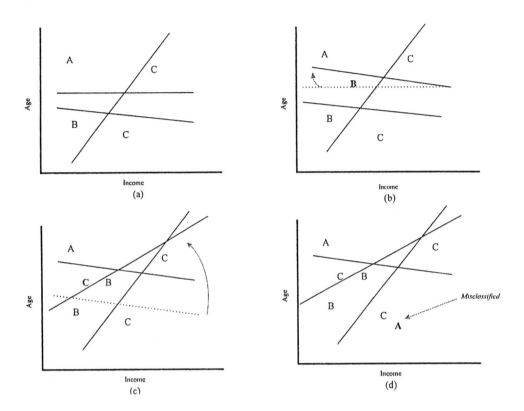

FIGURE 4   Nonlinearly separable classes. Starting with three lines and a data point from each of three classes (a), the lines are used to separate the classes. As more data items are revealed, the lines are adjusted to preserve the separation of classes (b, c). Finally, a point is revealed that violates the linear separability of the classes and at least one point will be misclassified using the line shifting method, regardless of how the lines are shifted (d).

However, although we may never know the underlying structure of the elusive f, we still may have access to many examples of its "operation," namely to vectors x and their correct classifications $f(x)$. Can we use this raw information to build a machine that simulates f without making any assumptions on its underlying structure?

This is precisely what *multilayered* feed-forward networks attempt to do. In a multilayered network architecture, the input and the output layers are separated by one or more "hidden" layers of intermediate neurons (see Fig. 1c). If the network's topology is well constructed, some hidden neurons will "learn" to recognize subtle (read: nonlinear) interaction effects among the input neurons (the object attributes) and the target classes. In doing so, the boundaries separating the classes will cease to be lines and become curves and/or closed regions.

As mentioned earlier, it has been proven mathematically that almost any classification problem can be simulated by a neural network with only one hidden layer of neurons (32,33).

REFERENCES

1. S. Schocken and G. Ariav, "Neural Networks for Decision Support: Problems and Opportunities," *Decision Support Syst., 11*, 393–414 (1994).
2. V. Dhar and R. Stein, *Seven Methods for Transforming Corporate Data into Business Intelligence*, Prentice-Hall, Englewood Cliffs, NJ, 1997.
3. MathWorks, *Neural Network Toolbox, ver. 2.0b*, The Math Works, Inc., 1994.
4. NeuralWare, *NeuralWorks Professional II/PLUS*, ver. 5.2, NeuralWare, Inc., 1995.
5. CalSci, BrainMaker, ver. 3.1, California Scientific Software, 1996.
6. N. H. Goddard, K. J. Lynne, and T. Mintz, "Rochester Connectionist Simulator, Technical Report" Computer Science Department, University of Rochester, Rochester, Technical Report 233 (1988).
7. M. L. Minsky, "Theory of Neural-Analog Reinforcement Systems and Its Application to the Brain-Model Problem," Princeton University, Princeton, NJ, 1954.
8. W. W. McCulloch and W. Pitts, "A Logical Calculus of the Ideas Imminent in Nervous Activity," *Bull. Math. Biophys, 5*, 115–133 (1943).
9. N. Rochester, J. H. Holland, L. H. Haibit, and W. L. Duda, "Tests on a Cell Assembly Theory of the Action of the Brain, Using a Large Digital Computer," *IRE Trans. Inform. Theory, IT-2*, 80–93 (1956).
10. R. P. Lippmann, "An Introduction to Computing with Neural Nets," *IEEE ASSP Mag.* (1987).
11. P. D. Wasserman and T. Schwartz, "Neural Networks: Part 1," *IEEE Expert* (1987).
12. P. D. Wasserman and T. Schwartz, "Neural Networks: Part 2," *IEEE Expert* (1987).
13. G. E. Hinton, "How Neural Networks Learn from Experience," *Sci. Am.* (September 1992).
14. J. A. Feldman, M. A. Fanty, N. H. Goddard, and K. J. Lynne, "Computing with Structured Connectionist Networks," *Commun. ACM, 31*, 170–187 (1988).
15. D. E. Rumelhart and J. L. McClelland, *Parallel Distributed Processing: Exploring the Microstructure of Cognition*, MIT Press, Cambridge, MA, 1986.
16. S. Haykin, *Neural Networks: A Comprehensive Foundation*, Macmillan College Publishing Company, New York, 1994.
17. P. D. Wasserman, *Neural Computing: Theory and Practice*, Van Nostrand Reinhold, New York, 1989.
18. I. Alexander and M. Morton, *An Introduction to Neural Computing*, Chapman & Hall, London, 1990.
19. M. Caudill and C. Butler, *Understanding Neural Networks: Computer Explorations*, MIT Press, Cambridge, MA, 1992.
20. J. A. Freeman and D. M. Skapura, *Neural Networks: Algorithms, Applications, and Programming Techniques*, Addison-Wesley, Reading, MA, 1992.
21. B. Widrow and M. E. Hoff, "Adaptive Switching Circuits," *IRE WESCON Convention Record, Part 4*, Institute of Radio Engineers, 1960, pp. 96–104.
22. F. Rosenblatt, *Principles of Neurodynamics*, Spartan Books, New York, 1962.
23. M. Minsky and S. Pappert, *Perceptrons: An Introduction to Computational Geometry*, MIT Press, Cambridge, MA, 1969.
24. T. Kohonen, *Self-Organization and Associative Memory*, Springer-Verlag, New York, 1988.
25. R. Hecht-Nielsen, "Counterpropagation Networks," *Appl. Opt., 26*, 4979–4984 (1987).
26. J. J. Hopfield and D. W. Tank, "Neural Computations of Decisions in Optimization Problems," *Biol. Cybern, 52*, 141–152 (1985).
27. B. Kosko, "Bi-directional Associative Memories," *IEEE Trans. Systems Man Cybern, SMC-18*, 49–60 (1987).
28. G. Carpenter and S. Grossberg, "A Massively Parallel Architecture for a Self-

Organizing Neural Pattern Recognition Machine," *Comput. Vision Graphics, Image Process, 37*, 54–115 (1987).

29. J. E. Moody and C. J. Darkin, "Fast Learning Networks of Locally-Tuned Processing Units," *Neural Comput, 1* (1989).

30. T. Poggio and F. Girosi, "Networks for Approximation and Learning," *Proc. IEEE, 78* (1990).

31. D. F. Specht, "A General Regression Neural Network," *IEEE Trans. Neural Networks, 2* (1991).

32. G. E. Hinton and J. L. McClelland, "Learning Representations by Recirculation," in IEEE Conference on Neural Information Processing Systems, 1988.

33. M. Leshno, V. Lin, A. Piukus, and S. Schocken, "Multi-layer feedforward Networks with Non-polynomial Activation Functions Can Approximate Any Continuous Function," *J. Neural Networks, 6* (1993).

34. K. Hornik, "Approximation Capabilities of Multilayer Feed Forward Networks," *J. Neural Networks, 4*, 251–257 (1991).

35. R. P. Gorman and T. J. Sejnowski, "Analysis of Hidden Units in a Layered Network Trained to Classify Sonar Targets," *Neural Networks, 1*, 75–90 (1988).

36. E. B. Baum and D. Haussler, "What Size Net Gives Valid Generalizations?," *Neural Comput., 1*, 151–160 (1988).

37. C. Ho, "On Multi-layered Connectionist Models: Adding Layers vs Increasing Width," in 11th International Joint Conf on Artificial Intelligence, 1989.

38. J. Utans and J. Moody, "Selecting Neural Network Architectures via the Prediction Risk: Application to Corporate Bond Rating Prediction," in 1st International Conference on Artificial Intelligence Applications on Wall Street, 1991.

39. S. Galant, "Connectionist Expert Systems," *Commun. ACM, 31*, 152–169 (1988).

40. L. M. Fu, "Rule Learning by Searching Adapted Nets," in Ninth National Conference on Artificial Intelligence, 1991.

41. L. M. Fu, "Rule Generalization from Neural Networks," *IEEE Trans. Systems, Man, Cybern., SMC-28*, 1114–1124 (1994).

42. O. Port, "Computers That Think Are Here," *Business Week*, July 17, 1995.

43. P. Refenes, "Neural Computing in Finance," *Neural Edge* (Spring 1995).

44. Bondweek, "Japanese Bank Improves Futures Forcasting with Neurocomputer," *Bondweek*, 1990.

45. Y. Inoue, "From Bond Rates to Exams, 'Neuros' Right on the Money," *Nikkei Weekly*, August 3.

46. M. Yoda, "Predicting the Tokyo Stock Market," in *Trading on the Edge: Neural Genetic and Fuzzy Systems for Chaotic Financial Markets* (G. Deboeck, ed.), John Wiley and Sons, New York, 1994.

47. P. Enrado, "Banking on Neural Networks," *AI Expert* (June 1994).

48. R. McGough, "Fidelity's Bradford Lewis Takes Aim at Indexes with his 'Neural Network' Computer Program," *Wall Street Journal*, October 27, 1992.

49. D. S. Barr and G. Mani, "Neural Nets in Investment Management: Multiple Uses," in 2nd International Conference on Artificial Intelligence Applications on Wall Street, 1993.

50. A. Mandelman, "The Computer's Bullish! A Money Manager's Love Affair with Neural Network Programs," *Barron's*, December 14.

51. HNC, "Bank of America Selects HNC's Falcon to Fight Credit Card Fraud," HNC Software, Press release February 28, 1994.

52. M. Barthel, "First USA's Card-Fraud Weapon: A Neural Network," *Am. Banker*, November 30, 1992.

53. D. Sullivan, "Secret Weapon Stymies Card Fraud: Neural Networks Can Spot Alarming Loss Patterns," *Am. Banker*, February 10.

54. BT, "Neural Networks—Brainwaves in Fraud Busting," *Banking Technol.*, December 15, 1995.

55. G. Robins, "Neural Networks: Automatic Data Analysis Finds Retail Applications," *Stores* (1993).

56. V. Houlder, "Measures of Success—Advertisers Are Looking to Neural Networks to Evaluate Effectiveness," *Financial Times*, May 25, 1995.

57. BM, "Database Marketing Solution: First Commerce Corporation," *Bank Manag.*, Jan/Feb. 1996.

58. CalSci, "BrainMaker Maximizes Returns on Direct Mail," *http://www.calsci.com/micro.html*, September 9, 1996.

59. S. Marjanovic, "Fleet Using Neural Networks to Focus Sales Effort," *Am. Banker*, May 30, 1995.

60. E. B. Baatz, "Making Brain Waves," *CIO Mag.*, January 15, 1996.

61. NMS, "Clinical Benefit of Papnet Confirmed in Long-Term Trial," Neuromedical Systems, Inc., Press release, July 9, 1996.

62. DJNS, "Neuromedical Sys Papnet Tests Used in 138 U.S. Labs," *Dow Jones News Service*, July 7.

63. A. Macdermid, "Smart Microwave as Neural Network Gets Cooking," *The Herald*, September 8, 1994.

64. CalSci, "BrainMaker Improves Hospital Treatment and Reduces Expenses," *http://www.calsci.com/micro.html*, September 9, 1996.

65. K. Quakenbush and M. N. Liebman, "Developing an Integrated Computer Network for Drug Discovery," *Sci. Computing Autom.*

66. H. Goldner, "Molecular Design Software Speeds Discovery of Peptoidomitic Drugs," *R&D, 36* (1994).

67. J. R. Coleman, "Headache-Free Quality," *Quality, 33* (1994).

68. E. Helmore, "Neural Nets Make Chicago Blues See Red," *The Independent*, July 8.

69. P. Gosling, "Software to Challenge the Insider Dealers; Artificial Intelligence Can Detect Doggy Deals, Says Paul Gosling," *The Independent*, July 3.

70. J. Gapper, "Stock Exchange Steps Up Insider Dealing Offensive: Artificial Intelligence Techniques Will Identify Suspicious Trading Patterns," *Financial Times*, May 20, 1996.

71. R. Bryce, "Texas Drops a Smart Bomb on Medicaid Fraud," *The Christian Science Monitor*, February 1.

72. E. I. Schwartz and J. B. Treece, "Smart Programs Go to Work," *Business Week*, March 2, 1992.

73. H. Takita, "Pennies from Heaven: Selling Accurate Weather Predictions," *Tokyo Business Today*, July 1995.

74. R. M. Stein, "Preprocessing Data for Neural Networks," *AI Expert* (March 1993).

75. R. M. Stein, "Selecting Data for Neural Networks," *AI Expert* (February 1993).

76. R. A. Jacobs, "Increased Rates of Convergence Through Learning Rate Adaption," *Neural Networks, 1* (1988).

77. A. A. Minia and R. D. Williams, "Acceleration of Back-Propagation Through Learning Rate and Momentum Adaptation," in International Joint Conference on Neural Networks, 1990.

78. D. O. Hebb, *The Organization of Behavior*, John Wiley and Sons, New York, 1849.

79. F. Crick, *What Mad Pursuit*, Basic Books, New York, 1988.

ROGER M. STEIN

SHIMON SCHOCKEN

VASANT DHAR

TRANSACTION MODELS AND ARCHITECTURES

INTRODUCTION

A database management system (DBMS) is a hardware/software system able to handle, in an organized and uniform way, large volumes of data representing information from real-world application environments. DBMSs are a mature yet still evolving technology, whose application scope continuously widens. Today, a DBMS supports a large variety of applications, from financial and administrative applications to medical and scientific applications as well as manufacturing applications. New applications arise every day, often demanding extensions to current DBMS technology.

The main tasks of a DBMS are to provide an efficient and suitable environment for accessing and storing data items, to protect data from failures and attempts of unauthorized accesses, and to ensure data quality. Failures may arise because of errors in the application programs or in the DBMS itself, or because of hardware crashes, such as disk crashes. If no proper mechanism is in place, failures may undermine data correctness and cause serious data losses. Another source of potential errors is in the concurrent executions of applications programs. Because of performance requirements and the high volume of operations typical of most applications, DBMSs allow application programs to be concurrently executed. Because different programs may access the same data, accesses to data must be properly synchronized.

Because of the importance of data protection and correctness, a large effort in DBMS research and development has been devoted to devising proper techniques to deal with errors and failures. A key notion, underlying all those techniques, is represented by the notion of a *transaction*. A transaction can be defined as a set of data operations representing a meaningful unit of work from the application point of view.* The execution of a transaction is in general characterized by a set of properties, known as *ACID* properties. Those properties are the key elements in ensuring data protection against errors and failures.† The development of algorithms, techniques, and systems implementing those properties together with their theoretical formalization has characterized a large part of database research in both academic institutions and industrial laboratories.

Historically, transaction processing systems were first developed to support on-line applications. Those applications are characterized by short programs that

---

*We elaborate more on different perspectives in the section Basic Concepts.
†For completeness, it is important to note that data protection also involves preventing data accesses from unauthorized users and application programs; we do not deal with those issues here and refer the reader to Ref. 1.

are activated by users from possibly remote terminals. In general, such applications have large numbers of terminals (hundreds or thousands) and data are often concurrently accessed. Examples of those applications are airline reservation systems. Earlier transaction processing systems included IBM's Customer Information and Control Systems (CICS) and Transaction Processing Facility (TPF) (2). More modern transaction processing systems have been developed for Unix platforms. They include Encina and Tuxedo (2). Transaction processing systems were developed in parallel as part of a DBMS. The most fundamental advancements in transaction processing for DBMSs have been in the framework of relational systems, such as System R, System R*, and Ingres. Basic concepts concerning transaction synchronization and recovery were developed within those systems. However, the continuing evolution of database technology has always demanded extensions and innovations to transaction processing techniques. This makes the area of transaction systems an important research area with a strong impact on commercial developments.

The objective of this article is the formal definition of the concept of transaction, together with a survey of models and architectures supporting such concept. In particular, in the second section, the basic concepts underlying transactions are introduced, whereas a simple transaction model is presented in the third section. The next three sections deal with several aspects related to transaction processing systems. Problems related to concurrency control are surveyed in the fourth section, introducing several protocols ensuring database consistency when concurrent accesses to data are allowed. The fifth section deals with recovery, whose aim is to detect failures and restore the database to a consistent state. Isolation allows a system to give the illusion that each transaction is executed alone, even if transactions are executed concurrently. This topic is dealt with in the sixth section. The seventh section presents a brief survey of transaction processing monitors, allowing the integration of different systems and the management of resources, so that applications spanning several systems and sources are executed accordingly to the transactional model. A brief outline of the most well-known extensions to the flat transaction model is then presented in the eighth section. Finally, the last section presents some conclusions.

BASIC CONCEPTS

In general, users interact with a database system through special application programs called *transactions*. The term *transaction* is used in the database literature with different meanings:

1. A transaction is the request or input message activating the execution of a set of operation(s) on the database.
2. A transaction represents all the effects of the execution of a set of operation(s) on the database.
3. A transaction is the program executing a set of operations on the database.

Those different interpretations arise because of the different perspectives of users involved in transaction execution and management. End users only see the request and the reply and, consequently, think of transactions in these terms. Operators see the effects of the requested execution, so they take that view. System administrators deal with naming, security, installation, and maintenance of transaction programs. They, therefore, often think of the transaction as the program source rather than the program execution. In this article, we adopt the second definition: *A transaction is a partially ordered set of read/write operations; it represents the effect on the database of the processing of programs executing functions required by the users.*

Transaction processing systems pioneered many concepts in distributed computing and fault-tolerant computing. They introduced the notion of transaction ACID properties—atomicity, consistency, isolation, and durability—as unifying concepts for fault-tolerant and correct computations in both centralized and distributed settings. A transaction can be considered as a collection of operations with the following properties:

1. *Atomicity* (also called all-or-nothing property): It refers to the fact that all the operations of a transaction must be treated as a single unit; therefore, either all operations are executed or none are.
2. *Consistency*: It deals with the correctness of concurrently executing transactions. If executed alone, a transaction transforms a database from one consistent state to another consistent state. When transactions are executed concurrently, the DBMS must assure that the database consistency is preserved as if each transaction were executed alone.
3. *Isolation*: It requires each transaction to observe a consistent database, that is, not to read intermediate results of other transactions.
4. *Durability*: It requires the results of a committed transaction be made permanent in the database in spite of possible system failures.

Example 1. Consider a banking debit transaction on Mr. Money's current account. Such a transaction would consist of releasing money and updating the account. It is atomic if it never happens that only one operation is performed; for instance, the money is released but the account is not updated. It is consistent if the amount of money released is the same as the amount debited to the account. It is isolated if the transaction program need not worry about other programs concurrently reading and/or updating the account (e.g., Mrs. Money making a concurrent deposit). It is durable if, once the transaction has completed, the account balance exactly reflects the withdrawal. □

The ACIDity properties of transactions are ensured by two classes of algorithms or *protocols*. The first class of protocols deals with *concurrency*, whereas the second deals with *recovery*. Those protocols are implemented by specific subsystems within the DBMS. Concurrency control protocols are used to synchronize concurrent transactions. Thus, they ensure the C-property. Recovery protocols support the abstraction of failure atomicity; that is, they make sure that no incomplete transaction executions arise because of failures. In the event of a crash, a recovery protocol typically (1) *undoes* the effects of the transactions that were executing, but had not yet completed, at the time of the crash or (2) *redoes* the transactions that had completed, but possibly had not yet installed their changes into the database, at the time of the crash. Therefore, recovery protocols ensure both the A-property and the D-property. Finally, the I-property is jointly ensured by the concurrency control and the recovery protocols. The concurrency protocol must make sure that no other transaction accesses a data item being modified by a transaction. The recovery subsystem must notify the concurrency control subsystem of when the transaction has completed, so that access to the data items modified by the completed transaction can be given to waiting transactions.

Note, however, that the recovery subsystem uses the services provided by concurrency control, for example, when performing undoing and redoing activities. We have simplified the above discussion for the sake of clarity.

A SIMPLE TRANSACTION MODEL

A large number of transaction models have been proposed and implemented. Most of them are extensions of a basic transaction model; transactions handled by the basic model are usually referred to as *flat transactions*.

Flat transactions represent the simplest kind of transaction model. They have been used in all commercially available DBMS and are now being introduced in operating systems and communication systems. The implementation techniques are well known, and so are the limitations.

Flat Transactions

A flat transaction is the basic block in organizing an application into atomic actions. The operations part of the same transaction are delimited by two special operations. The BeginWork operation starts a (flat) transaction. The CommitWork operation indicates to the DBMS that the transaction has completed its execution and wishes to install its updates into the database. If the Commit call successfully completes, the DBMS guarantees that all operations enclosed between BeginWork and CommitWork are executed according to the ACID properties. Durability, in particular, guarantees that nothing* can cause the performed updates to be lost. Alternatively, a transaction can terminate by issuing an Abort operation to indicate that some errors occurred during the execution and therefore all (partial) updates performed by the transaction must be removed from the database. Note that an application program may contain several transactions.

The above transaction model is called *flat* because there is only one layer of control by the application. Everything inside the pair BeginWork/CommitWork or BeginWork/Abort is at the same level; that is, the transaction will either survive (commit) or it will be rolled back (abort).

A good characteristic of flat transactions is that they cover not only database operations but also that the ACID properties hold for everything executed between BeginWork and CommitWork.† This is particularly important when handling messages. As an example, consider the message sent from a transaction to an automated teller machine — ATM. The ACID properties make sure that either the message will

---

*That is, nothing within the specification of the system. If more errors than the system was designed for occur at the same time, this guarantee does not hold.

†A popular misunderstanding is that transactions are bound to databases. Although it is true that, historically, transactions have evolved from the database field, it must be clearly understood that they establish a general execution paradigm that ideally covers all the subsystems involved in their execution.

be sent (the cash will be dispensed), which means that the entire transaction will be successfully completed, or the transaction will fail, in which case no money will be dispensed. This general notion of transactions involving several subsystems, not necessarily only DBMS, is supported by specialized systems known as Transaction Processing (TP) Monitors, which we discuss in the section Transaction Processing Monitors.

In the following, a formal definition of flat transaction is proposed to the reader.

Definition 1. A flat transaction T_i is a set on which is defined a partial order $<_i$ where

- $T_i \subseteq \mathcal{I} \cup \{a_i, c_i\}$, where
  1. $\mathcal{I}$ is the power set of $\{\text{read}_i[x], \text{write}_i[x]/x \text{ is a data item}\}$.
  2. a_i indicates that the transaction was not successfully completed (i.e. it has been aborted).
  3. c_i indicates that the transaction was successfully completed (i.e. it has been committed).
- $a_i \in T_i \text{ iff } c_i \notin T_i$.
- If $t = a_i \text{ or } t = c_i$, then $\forall$ other operation $p \in T_i, p <_i t$.
- If $\text{read}_i[x], \text{write}_i[x] \in T_i$, then either $\text{read}_i[x] <_i \text{write}_i[x]$ *or* $\text{write}_i[x] <_i \text{read}_i[x]$.

Flat Transactions and SQL

Structured query language (SQL) is the most well-known query language for relational databases. It was initially developed for System R.* It is also usually known with its former name, Sequel. Many SQL implementations allow SQL queries to be submitted from a program written in a general-purpose language, such as Pascal, C, COBOL, PL/1, or Fortran. This extends the programmer's ability to manipulate the database. Embedded SQL is a slightly modified form of SQL than can be used within a host programming language. There are many available commercial database systems that use embedded SQL to interact with the database; among them are SQL/Data System (SQL/DS), DB2, ORACLE, and Ingres.

When a programmer writes Embedded SQL code in a host language source file, any SQL statement must be preceded by the *exec sql* statement. To support transactions, specific SQL statements are provided by the various DBMS. Such statements are invoked from within application programs and allow the application programmers to denote the start and ending of a transaction as well as to abort a transaction. In the following example, a very simple Embedded SQL program in C hosted by Oracle taken from Ref. 3 is presented, showing how a transaction is programmed at application level.

---

*The System R research project began at the IBM San Jose Research Laboratory in 1974. The goal of the project was to demonstrate the practicality of the newly proposed relational data model. A great number of fundamental concepts were established by this research, and several commercial products were derived from System R research.

Example 2.   Consider the Embedded SQL program illustrated in Figure 1. The program repeatedly prompts a user for a customer identifier cid and replies by printing the customer name and discount, halting when the user inputs an empty string. An Embedded SQL program must be able to use normal program variables, usually referred to as host variables. In Figure 1, cust–name, cust–discnt, and cust–id variables are declared to contain retrieved values for, respectively, customer name cname, discount discnt, and cid, a value written by the user. In order to use these host variables in an Embedded SQL statement, they must first be declared to the precompiler. This is accomplished declaring variables between exec sql begin declare section and exec sql end declare section parenthesis.

Obviously, it is essential that host language variables used in Embedded SQL code have data type known to the database system.

```
#include <stdio.h>                        /* header for ORACLE datatypes */
#include <ctype.h>

exec sql include sqlca;                   /* communication area */
int promptl(char[ ], char[ ], int);
char prompt[ ] = "Please enter customer identifier"

main()
{ exec sql begin declare section;         /*declare SQL host variables */

    VARCHAR cust_id[5], cust_name[14];    /* ORACLE character strings */
    float cust_discnt;                    /* host var for discnt value */
    VARCHAR user_name[20], user_pwd[10];
  exec sql end declare section;

  exec sql whenever sqlerror stop;        /* error trap condition */
  strcpy(user_name, arr, "poneilsql");
  user_name.len = strlen(cust_id, arr);
  strcpy(user_pwd, arr, "XXXX"); user_pwd.len = strlen("XXXX");
  exec sql connect :user_name
      identified by :user_pwd;            /* ORACLE format: connect */
  while((promptl(prompt, cust_id, arr, 4)) >= 0)  /* main loop: cid */
      {cust_id.len = strlen(cust_id.arr);  /* set lenght of cust_id */
       exec sql select cname,
             discnt into :cust_name, :cust_discnt  /* retrieve cname, discnt */
                 from customers where cid = :cust_id;
       cust_name.arr[cust_name.len] = '\0';   /* null terminated string */
       exec sql commit work;

       printf("Customer = %s; discount = %f\n", cust_name.arr, cust_discnt); }

  exec sql disconnect; }                   /* disconnect from database */
```

FIGURE 1   An example of Oracle Embedded SQL program.

At the beginning, an Embedded SQL program has to connect with the SQL DBMS and to the right database. This is possible through the exec sql connect :user-name identified by :user-pwd statement. Note that colons are used to identify the host variables as arguments for SQL syntax. In particular, the connect statement has the effect of starting the transaction, thus implementing the Begin-Work primitive. To disconnect from the database, the exec sql disconnect statement is used. Note that the statement at the end of main loop of main( ), exec sql commit work, is used after a sequence of reads from a table, before any user interaction such as printing results. In the example program, potential errors in executing Embedded SQL are dealt with. At the beginning of the program, potential errors in executing Embedded SQL are dealt with. At the beginning of the program, exec sql include sqlca allocates space for certain errors and statistics to be communicated by the database system monitor. The statement exec sql whenever sqlerror stop sets up an error trap condition to capture simple default behavior in dealing with erroneous calls. The effect of these statements is to stop the program if an error arises at run-time execution. □

Limitations of Flat Transactions

The major restriction of flat transactions is that there is no way to either commit of abort parts of such transactions, or committing results in several steps. For a simple state transformation, such as debiting or crediting an account, an atomic unit of work is certainly appropriate. Those are the applications for which flat transactions were originally designed. However, many other applications exist, for which this model is too restrictive. Flat transactions have a simple structure which is not able to model more complex application structures. To support such applications, it is desirable to provide the transaction model with more expressive power. This may lead to the risk of losing one of the major virtues of flat transactions — simplicity — which makes ACID transactions so successful. Examples 3 and 4 show a fairly simple application structure that is not supported well by flat transactions. Example 3 refers to trip planning; Example 4 refers to bulk updates executed by a banking transaction.

Example 3. Suppose that Mr. Money wants to go from Pittsburgh, USA, to Finale Ligure, Italy. Because there are no direct flights between the two places, a number of connecting flights must be booked, perhaps some trains, and so on. The travel agent, using a transaction system, tries to find a good travel plan for Mr. Money. The produced transaction is the following:

- BeginWork
- Book flight from Pittsburgh to London
- Book flight from London to Milan, same day
- Book flight from Milan to Genoa, same day

Problem: There is no way to reach Finale Ligure from Genoa in the same day, except by a rental car. Mr. Money, however, prefers to travel at a lower cost.

What can the travel agent do in that situation? One solution might be to have Mr. Money go from Milan to Nice (France) and then go by train from there. Or the situation might require Mr. Money to fly from Milan to Torino, or perhaps somewhere else.

The point is that, given a flat transaction model, the travel agent has only two choices: (1) Issue RollBackWork. This gives up much more of the previous work than needed. In particular, there is no need for undoing the reservation on the flight to London. (2) Explicitly cancel all reservations that are no longer useful. This solution might be very expensive if the amount of work is larger than that in the example above.   □

What is needed in such an application is a *selective* rollback. Rather than aborting the whole transaction, it should be possible to roll back only the last two reservations, maintaining the first. If such a feature is not available, the application designer is forced to use a programming style where updates no longer needed must be reversed by the application.

Example 4.   Consider that, in our simplified banking system, at the end of a month a bank wants to modify one million of its accounts by crediting or debiting the interest. Suppose now that the whole work was done by only one flat transaction, whose code was approximately the following:

    UpdateAccounts( )
      BeginWork;
      for each account A:
        Update A;
      CommitWork.

If all goes right, then all updates will be permanently stored at commit time. On the contrary, if, for example, 999,999 accounts have been modified and after that a system crash occurs; 999,999 updates have to be rolled back, according to the atomicity property. Of course, this is not desirable because the updates performed are not invalid in any sense and, moreover, rolling back 999,999 updates takes about as long as it took to do them the first time. On the other hand, it has to be guaranteed that each account tuple is updated exactly once. With flat transactions, the only way to assure this guarantee is the "bulk" transaction shown above. The solution of making each tuple a transaction in order to minimize the loss in case of system crash is not good, because, in this case, the system will have no information about which account was updated last before the crash (i.e., where it has to pick up work again after recovery*).   □

To overcome the limitations of the flat transaction model, several extensions to this model have been proposed for expanding its scope, generalizing its semantics, and making it more powerful. We will discuss such extensions in the section Extended Transaction Models.

---

*In terms of concepts that are rigorously defined in the section Commit Protocols and Recovery, the system has information about which was the last successful update because it writes that update to the log. For the moment, it is sufficient to note that this is a "dirty" solution because the log is not part of a data model such as SQL. Using this dirty solution means exceeding the capabilities of a simple flat transaction environment. But this is exactly what new and extended transaction models are all about.

CONCURRENCY CONTROL

Concurrency control is an important functionality that each multiuser DBMS should provide. The aim of a concurrency control mechanism is to ensure database consistency when there are concurrent accesses to data by several users; it uses synchronization techniques to handle concurrent transactions. The following example explains the extreme importance of concurrency control in a database system.

Example 5. Consider a database organizing some information about a bank clients's account. Suppose now that Mr. Money owns two accounts: a checking account and a deposit account, whose balances are $100 and $1000, respectively; the checking account is also owned by Mrs. Money. Mr. Money wants to transfer some funds from one account to the other. A bank employee therefore invokes a transaction T which transfers $150 from the deposit account to the checking account. At the same time, Mrs. Money performs a deposit, at another branch of the same bank, of the amount of $500 on the checking account. Let T' be the transaction invoked on behalf of Mrs. Money. The concurrent execution of those transactions may cause several problems.

Execution 1

T	T'
Read dep__acct	
dep__acct = dep__acct − 150	
	Read check__acct
Write dep__acct	
	check__acct = check__acct + 500
Read check__acct	
	Write check__acct
	Commit T'
check__acct = check__acct	
Write check__acct	
Commit T	

In the above concurrent execution, because of an interference between T and T', T' has succeeded in its execution, but it does not produce any effect on the database, because the amount of money deposited by T' has been lost. Such concurrent execution is not correct and it should not be allowed by the database management system. Note, in particular, that the updates performed by T' do not have any effect on the database state. Such an anomaly is called a lost update.

Serializability

How should a valid concurrency control mechanism handle the situation illustrated in Example 5? The interleaving, in such example, produces an incorrect database state. Each transaction would produce a correct state when executed alone. In other words, this problem would not arise if T and T' were executed one after the other; such an execution is called a *serial execution*. In general, it is not necessary to impose such restrictive conditions.

Example 6. The following execution, although not serial, does not cause any anomaly.

Execution 2

T	T'
Read dep__acct	
	Read check__acct
dep__acct = dep__acct − 150	
	check__acct = check__acct + 500
Write dep__acct	
	Write check__acct
	Commit T'
Read check__acct	
check__acct = check__acct + 150	
Write check__acct	
Commit T	

The above execution shows that, even though operations from different transactions interleave, the effect on the database is the same that would have been obtained executing T and T' sequentially.   □

Executions proved to be equivalent to a serial execution are called *serializable*.

Concurrency Control Protocols

Different protocols have been proposed to ensure the serializability property for concurrent transactions. Among the proposed protocols, the most well known are *two-phase locking* and *time-stamp ordering* protocols. Time-stamping-based protocols assign a unique time stamp to each transaction. Each data item is associated with the time stamp of the last transaction reading/writing it. In the following, both protocols are surveyed.

Lock-Based Protocols

Lock-based protocols delay executions of conflicting operations, by locking on data items before performing read/write operations. In other words, a transaction can access a data item only if it has obtained the appropriate lock on that data item.

There are various modes in which a data item can be locked. The basic ones are the following:

1. *Shared.* If a transaction T has obtained a shared mode lock on item Q, then T can read, but not write, Q.
2. *Exclusive.* If a transaction T has obtained an exclusive mode lock on item Q, then T can both read and write Q.

Thus, each transaction must acquire a lock in an appropriate mode on data item Q, depending on the type of operations it will perform on Q.

Given a set of lock modes, one can define a *compatibility function* on them as follows. Let A and B represent arbitrary lock modes. Suppose that a transaction T_i requests a lock mode A on item Q on which transaction T_j ($T_i \neq T_j$) currently holds a lock of mode B. If transaction T_i can be granted a lock on Q immediately, in spite of the presence of the mode B lock, then mode A is said *compatible* with mode B. Such functions can be represented by a matrix M, where $M(i, j)$ = true if lock mode i is compatible with lock mode j; $M(i, j)$ = false otherwise. Figure 2 shows the compatibility matrix M just described.

Compatibility matrix	Shared	Exclusive
Shared	true	false
Exclusive	false	false

FIGURE 2   Lock compatibility matrix M. $M(i, j)$ = true if lock mode i is compatible with lock mode j.

A transaction requires a shared lock on data item Q by an Ls(Q) statement. In a similar way, an exclusive lock is required using an Lx(Q) statement. A data item Q is unlocked through an Un(Q) statement.

The *two-phase locking protocol* demands that each transaction requires locks and unlocks on data items in two different phases:

1. *Increasing phase*. A transaction, during this phase, can only obtain new locks, but it cannot release any lock.
2. *Decreasing phase*. A transaction, during this phase, can only release locks, but it cannot obtain additional new locks.

Initially, a transaction performs an increasing phase, during which it acquires all locks necessary for its operations. When the transaction releases one lock, it enters into a decreasing phase, and new lock requests will not be granted.

As previously stated, the two-phase locking protocol ensures serializability. It is, however, deadlock-sensitive.*

Example 7.   Let T_i and T_j be two transaction acting on data items a, b and c as follows:

Execution 3

        T

        Read(a)
        Read(b)
        Read(c)
        Write(a)
        Commit T

---

*A system is said to be in *deadlock* if there exists a set of transactions such that each transaction in the set is waiting for another transaction, belonging to the set, to continue its execution (see the subsection Deadlock Detection and Resolution).

T'

Read(a)
Read(b)
Commit T'

If the two-phase protocol is used, then T_i must lock a in exclusive mode. Therefore, no concurrent execution of the two transactions is possible. The only possible processing is the serial one. Notice, however, that T_i needs an exclusive lock on data item a only at the end of its execution, when it writes a. Thus, if T_i could initially lock data item a in a shared mode, changing it into exclusive later, it could allow more parallelism, as T_i and T_j could access data item a and b simultaneously.   □

The above observation leads to a modification to the basic two-phase locking, allowing *lock conversion*; that is, a particular mechanism is provided to *promote* a shared lock into an exclusive lock and to *regress* an exclusive lock into a shared lock. Conversion cannot occur arbitrarily. It can only occur during the increasing phase; a lock can be regressed only during the decreasing phase.

Time-Stamp Ordering Protocol

In the above-described locking protocols, the order among conflicting transactions is determined during the increasing phase, when two transactions lock the first data item they have in common, in incompatible mode. Another way to establish the serializability order is by selecting an order in advance, between each pair of transactions. The most common approach to implement such scheme is the use of a *time-stamp ordering*.

Each transaction T_i, in the system, is assigned a unique time stamp, denoted by $TS(T_i)$. This label is assigned by the database system before the transaction T_i starts its execution. If a time stamp has been assigned to T_i and a new transaction T_j enters the system, then $TS(T_i) < TS(T_j)$. Two simple methods are used to implement such a scheme:

1. Using the system clock as a time stamp. The transaction time stamp is the value the clock has when the transaction enters the system.
2. Using a logic counter that is increased after the assignment of a new time stamp. The transaction time stamp is the value of the counter when the transaction enters the system.

Transaction time-stamps establish a serializability order. Thus, if $TS(T_i) < TS(T_j)$, the system must ensure that the produced schedule* is equivalent to a serial schedule in which T_i appears before T_j. To implement this scheme, two time-stamp values are associated with each data item Q:

1. *W-time-stamp(Q)* denotes the greatest time stamp among the time stamps of all transactions that succeeded in executing a write(Q) operation.
2. *R-time-stamp(Q)* denotes the greatest time stamp among all transactions that succeeded in executing a read(Q) operation.

---

*A schedule represents the order in which operations are executed in the system, according to the chronological order.

These values are updated whenever a new write(Q) or read(Q) operation is performed.

The time-stamp ordering protocol ensures that all conflicting read/write operations are executed in the time-stamping order. The protocol is organized as follows:

1. Suppose that a transaction T_i is required to perform a read(Q) operation:
   (a) If $TS(T_i) <$ W-time-stamp(Q), this means that T_i needs to read a value of Q that has already been overwritten. Then the read operation must be rejected and T_i must be rolled back.
   (b) If $TS(T_i) \geq$ W-time-stamp(Q), it follows that the reading may be executed, and R-time-stamp(Q) is set to the maximum value between R-time-stamp(Q) and $TS(T_i)$.
2. Suppose that transaction T_i is required to perform a write(Q) operation:
   (a) If $TS(T_i) <$ R-time-stamp(Q), this means that the value of data item Q, which T_i is modifying, has previously been read by some other transaction and then is not possible to perform any update.
   (b) If $TS(T_i) <$ W-time-stamp(Q), this means that T_i is trying to write an obsolete value of Q. The write operation is therefore simply ignored.
   (c) Otherwise, the write operation is performed, and W-time-stamp(Q) is set to the maximum value between W-time-stamp(Q) and $TS(T_i)$.

Each transaction that is rolled back, due to the concurrency control, is assigned a new time stamp and it is restarted. The time-stamp ordering protocol ensures serializability. This follows from the fact that conflicting operations are processed in time-stamp order. Such protocol ensures also the absence of deadlocks, as transactions never wait.

The above time-stamp ordering protocol may, however, result in cascading rollbacks. To overcome this problem, one must ensure that a transaction can read only those values modified by transactions successfully completed. This can be achieved by associating a *commit bit* with each transaction T_i, and a pointer to that bit from each data item written by T_i. Initially, the commit bit is set to "false." It will be set to "true" only after the commit of the transaction. Therefore, a transaction wishing to read a data item can do it immediately if the commit bit is set to "true"; otherwise, it must wait until this happens.

Multiversioning

The concurrency control approaches discussed so far ensure serializability, by delaying an operation or aborting the transaction that requested the execution of the operation.

In multiversioning protocols, each write(Q) operation generates a new version of Q. When a read(Q) operation is issued, the system selects one of the Q versions. The concurrency control protocol must ensure that the selection of the version guarantees serializability. Moreover, it is crucial, for performance reasons, that a transaction can easily and quickly determine which data version must be read.

The most common technique used for multiversion schemes is time stamping. Each transaction T_i is assigned a unique static label, denoted by $TS(T_i)$. This label is assigned as in the time-stamp ordering protocol.

Each data item Q has a sequence of versions $<Q_1, Q_2, \ldots, Q_m>$. Each version contains three components:

1. *Content*: It is the value of version Q_k.
2. *W-time-stamp*(Q_k): It denotes the time stamp of the transaction that created version Q_k.
3. *R-time-stamp*(Q_k): It denotes the greatest time stamp among the time stamps of all transactions that successfully read version Q_k.

A transaction T_i creates a new version Q_k of a data item Q, requiring the execution of a write(Q) operation. The content field of the version stores the value written by T_i. The W-time-stamp and the R-time-stamp are initialized with the TS(T_i) value. The R-time-stamp is updated whenever a transaction T_j reads the content of Q_k and R-time-stamp(Q_k) < TS(T_j).

The scheme works as follows. Suppose that a transaction T_i wishes to execute a read(Q) or write(Q) operation. Let Q_k be a version of Q such that W-time-stamp(Q_k) is the time stamp lower or equal to TS(T_i).

1. If T_i performs read(Q), the returned value is content of version Q_k.
2. If T_i performs write(Q) and if TS(T_i) < R-time-stamp(Q_k), T_i is rolled back; otherwise, a new version Q_k is created.

The motivation for the first condition is clear: A transaction always reads the most recent version. The latter condition forces a transaction to abort if it is "too late" performing a write. More precisely, if T_i tries to write a version that some other transaction could have read, it is not correct to allow the execution of such write.

The multiversioning protocol has the nice feature that a read request never fails and never waits. In real database systems, where reading is more frequent than writing, this advantage can be very significant. It has, however, three drawbacks. First, reading a data item requires updating the R-time-stamp field, and this may require two disk accesses rather than one. Second, transaction conflicts are solved through rollbacks rather than waits. This could be very expensive. Finally, cascading rollbacks may arise. To avoid cascading rollbacks, the same techniques of the time-stamping concurrency control protocol can be adopted.

Deadlock Detection and Resolution

As already mentioned, a system is in deadlock if a set of transactions exist such that each transaction in the set waits on another transaction in the same set to continue its own processing. More precisely, a set of waiting transactions $\{T_0, T_1, \ldots, T_n\}$ exists such that T_0 waits for a data item that is currently held by T_1; T_1 waits for a data item that is currently held by T_2; $\ldots T_{n-1}$ waits for a data item that is currently held by T_n, and T_n waits for a data item that is currently held by T_0. The only solution to this undesirable situation is some drastic action, as, for example, rolling back one of the transactions involved in the deadlock.

There are two main solutions to the deadlock problem. A deadlock prevention protocol can be used to ensure that the system never enters a deadlock state. Alternatively, one may allow the system to enter a deadlock state, and then recover from the deadlock using a deadlock detection and resolution scheme. Although the prevention protocols were conceptually very simple, it is not actually used in any real system, as it may result in useless rollbacks. The interested reader can find a description of the most well-known prevention protocols in Ref. 4.

In the following subsections, deadlock detection and deadlock resolution algorithms are surveyed.

Deadlock Detection

An algorithm analyzing the system state is periodically invoked to detect if any deadlock has occurred. The algorithm has to perform two main tasks:

1. Maintaining information about the current data allocation to the transactions and about pending data requests.
2. Solving the deadlock when it is actually found.

Deadlocks can be precisely characterized with a direct graph, called a *wait-for graph*. This graph consists of a pair G = (V, E), where V is a set of vertices and E is a set of edges. Each element belonging to E is an ordered pair (T_i, T_j). If $(T_i, T_j) \in$ E, then there is a direct edge from T_i to T_j, and this means that T_i needs, to continue doing its work, for T_j to release a certain data item.

When T_i requires a data item currently held by a transaction T_j, an edge (T_i, T_j) is inserted in the wait-for graph. This edge is removed only when T_j releases the data item requested by T_j.

A deadlock occurs in the system if and only if the wait-for graph contains a cycle. Each transaction involved in the cycle is blocked. To detect deadlocks, the system maintains the wait-for graph and periodically invokes an algorithm looking for cycles in the graph. Figure 3 illustrates two examples of cyclic and acyclic wait-for graph. Whereas the wait-for graph on the left side contains a cycle, emphasized with bold arrows, and therefore a deadlock occurs, the wait-for graph on the right side does not contain any cycle. Thus, in any case, no deadlock is detected.

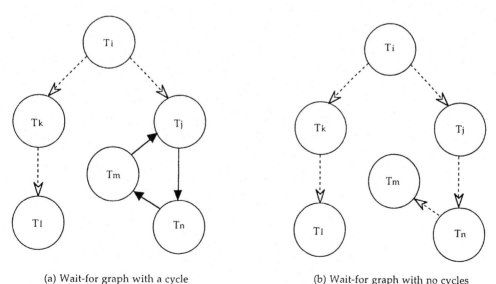

(a) Wait-for graph with a cycle   (b) Wait-for graph with no cycles

FIGURE 3 Example of cyclic and acyclic graphs.

Deadlock Resolution

If the detection algorithm signals a deadlock, the system must solve the blocking situation. The most common solution is to roll back one or more transactions. To do so, three different issues need to be addressed:

1. *Selection of a victim.* Given a set of blocked transactions, one must determine which transactions have to roll back in order to break the deadlock. Transactions to roll back are those with the minimum cost. Unfortunately, the term "minimum cost" is not precise. Several factors are involved in the rollback cost of a transaction:

   (a) How many computations the transaction has already performed, and how much longer the transaction will compute, before completing.

   (b) How many data items the transaction has used.

   (c) How many data items the transaction still needs, before completing.

   (d) How many transactions would be involved in the transaction rollback.

2. *Rollback.* Once the transaction victim is identified, one must determine how far the transaction should be rolled back. The simplest solution is to perform a total rollback; that is, rolling back the transaction at its beginning and restarting it. It would be better, however, to roll back only the part of the transaction which is sufficient to break the deadlock. This method requires the system to maintain additional information about the state of the executing transactions (see the section Extended Transaction Models).

3. *Starvation.* If the choice of the victim is cost based, it may happen that the same transaction is always selected as victim. This means that the transaction can never complete its execution. Clearly, it must be ensured that a transaction is selected as victim only a small number of times. The most common solution is including in the cost the number of times the transaction has been rolled back.

COMMIT PROTOCOLS AND RECOVERY

Faults

A computer system, as other electrical or mechanical devices, is subject to failures. Techniques for preventing errors and recovering from them have been widely investigated in areas such as distributed systems and telecommunication systems. The specific technique to adopt depends on the type of foreseen failures. When discussing such techniques in the database context, it is useful to distinguish three common causes of failures:

1. *Disk crash.* Information residing on disks is lost. The most common types of such failure are head crashing and errors occurring during a data transfer operation.

2. *Power failure.* Information stored in main memory and registers is lost.

3. *Software errors.* Some results generated while processing the transaction can be incorrect and can return erroneous results to the user; moreover, the database could enter an inconsistent state. The most common types of

such failure are logical errors (the program cannot continue its normal execution because of certain internal conditions, such as an erroneous input, data not found, overflow, etc.) and system errors (the system has entered in a undesirable state, so the program cannot continue its normal execution, but it can be, however, reexecuted later.)

Several kinds of failure can occur in a system, each of which needs to be handled in a different way. The simplest failures to handle are those that do not result in information loss. Obviously, the more difficult to handle are the ones resulting in information loss.

A fundamental component of any database system is the *recovery subsystem*, responsible for detecting failures and restoring the database to the (consistent) state existing before the failure. Recovering a database means avoiding data loss and inconsistency. It is useful to classify the various storage media with respect to how the information they store is affected by the various types of failure:

1. *Volatile storage.* Information residing in volatile storage is lost on system crashes. Examples of such types of storage are main memory and cache memory.
2. *Nonvolatile storage.* Information residing in nonvolatile storage usually survives system crashes. Examples of such type of storage are disk and magnetic tape. However, both media are subject to media failures (for example head crashes), that can result in a loss of information.
3. *Stable storage.* Information residing in stable storage is never lost. To implement an approximation of this kind of media, information is duplicated in several nonvolatile storage media having independent probability of failure.

An Abstract Model of Transaction Executions

In order to discuss recovery techniques, it is necessary to specify, in a more appropriate way, what "successful completion" of a transaction means. To do this, one establishes a simple abstract model. According to this model, a transaction is always in one of the following states:

1. *Active*, the initial state
2. *Partially committed*, after the execution of the last instruction
3. *Failed*, after discovering that the transaction cannot normally continue
4. *Aborted*, after rolling back the transaction and recovering the database to the state that existed before the transaction started
5. *Committed*, after "successful" completion

Figure 4, adapted from Ref. 4, shows the state diagram. A transaction starts in the *active* state. After executing the last instruction, it enters the *partially committed* state. Now, the transaction has completed its processing, but a failure is still possible, because its actual output cannot yet be permanently installed on nonvolatile storage; thus, a hardware failure could hamper the successful completion.

Particular care is necessary if *external observable writes* occurs; these are not erasable writes (e.g., those on terminals or on printers). Several systems force these writes to be executed only after the transaction enters a *commit* state. One way to

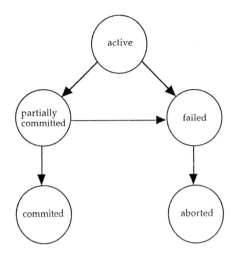

FIGURE 4   State diagram of a transaction. (Adapted from Ref. 4.)

implement this approach is to temporarily store values associated with external write in a nonvolatile storage, and execute actual writes only at commit confirmation. A committed transaction will always be able to complete external writes, except when a disk failure occurs. If one wants to assure that a disk failure does not prevent a succeeding external observable write, stable storage could be used.

A transaction enters into the *failed* state after it is determined that the transaction cannot continue its normal processing. Such a transaction has to be eliminated by a rollback operation. Once the rollback is performed, the transaction enters the *aborted* state. Now, the system has two options:

1. *Reexecute the transaction.* This can take place only if the transaction is aborted because of some software or hardware errors not produced by the transaction internal logic. A reexecuted transaction is considered a new transaction.
2. *Eliminate the transaction.* This usually takes place if there are internal errors that can only be corrected by rewriting the application program.

A transaction enters the *commit* state if it is *partially committed* and it is guaranteed that it will never be aborted.

Example 8.   Consider the usual simplified banking system and be *T* a transaction transferring $100 from account A to account B, whose balance are $1000 and $15,000, respectively; during *T* processing, after A modification, and before B modification, a system crash occurs. Memory contents are lost, and it is not possible to determine what happened to the transaction. Possible actions are the following:

1. Reexecuting *T*. In this way, a state will be produced in which A assumes the value $800, and B assumes the value $15,100.
2. Not reexecuting *T*. In the current state, A assumes the value $900, and B still has the value $15,000.

In both cases, the crash causes an inconsistent database state; this trivial recovery scheme is not working properly. □

The problem is in having modified the database without having the assurance that the transaction will indeed commit.

The next subsection will introduce a recovery scheme widely used to handle logical errors, system errors, and system crashes.

Log-Based Mechanisms

The idea of recovery with a log is very simple: During a transaction processing, all write operations are stored in a particular file managed by the system, called *log file*. Log information is used if failures occur before the transaction completion. If a system crash occurs before a transaction completes, or if the transaction fails, log information is simply ignored. Conceptually, the log can be thought of as a sequential file. The actual implementation uses multiple physical files to make record storage easy. Each record inserted in the log is assigned a unique identifier [called the log sequence number (LSN)]. LSNs are generated as an increasing sequence. Typically, they are logical addresses of the pertinent log record.

The nonvolatile version of the log is stored in stable storage (e.g., on disk); two identical copies of the log are usually kept on different devices.

Whenever log records are written, they are placed only on log file buffers in volatile memory. At commit time, all log records, up to LSN, are written in sequences of log pages, on stable storage. This operation is said to be "forcing" the log up to LSN. The system, besides forcing the log because of activities of buffer and transaction management, can periodically force log buffer pages as they fill up.

The most well-known recovery mechanisms with a log are the *incremental log with deferred updates* and the *incremental log with immediate updates*.

Incremental Log with Deferred Updates

During a transaction processing, all writing operations are deferred until the transaction enters the *partially committed* state. All updates are stored in the log file.

The execution of a transaction T_i proceeds as follows: Before T_i starts its execution, a record $< T_i$, starts$>$ is written on the log. During the processing, any *write*[x] operation results in a new log record. Such record consists of the following fields:

1. The transaction name (i.e., T_i)
2. The data item name (i.e., x)
3. The new data value

Finally, when T_i enters the *partially committed* state, the record $< T_i$, commits$>$ is written on the log. The record associated with a transaction, in the log, are used to perform deferred writes.

Because a failure can occur while the updates are actually executed, all log records are written on stable storage. Once done, updates can take place. At this point, the transaction enters the *committed* state.

By using the log, the system can handle any failure involving the loss of information on volatile memory. The recovery scheme uses the redo(T_i) procedure, which sets all data items updated by T_i to the new values.

The redo operation must be *idempotent*; that is, multiple executions of the operation are equivalent to a single execution. This is required to guarantee correct behavior even if a failure occurs during the recovery procedure.

After a failure, the recovery subsystem analyzes the log to determine which transactions have to be reexecuted. A transaction T_i needs to be reexecuted if the log contains both $< T_i$, starts$>$ and $< T_i$, commits$>$ records. Therefore, if a system crash occurs after the transaction completion, the information stored on the log is used to recover the database state to a consistent state.

Consider, finally, the case in which a second system crash occurs while the system is performing the recovery procedure that restores the state after the first crash. Some changes would have been made in the database, because of the redo operation, or no changes would have been made. When the system comes up after the second crash, the recovery procedure proceeds exactly like the first one. For each $< T_i$, commits$>$ found in the log, a redo operation in performed. In other words, the recovery actions restart from the beginning. Because redo writes values on the database that are independent of the values currently on the database, the result of a second attempt of redo is the same as if redo had succeeded the first time.

Incremental Log with Immediate Updates

Another recovery technique is based on the application of all updates directly to the database and the use of an *incremental log* with all changes performed by the database. If a failure occurs, the log information is used to recover the system state to a consistent state.

Before a transaction T_i starts, all *write*[x] operations must be preceded by the writing of a new log record. Each of the records consists of the following fields:

1. The transaction name (i.e., T_i)
2. The data item name (i.e., x)
3. The data item old value
4. The data item new value

When T_i enters the *partially committed* state, a $< T_i$, commits$>$ record is written on the log.

Because the log information is used to rebuild the database state, the actual update on the database cannot be allowed before the pertinent log record is written on stable storage.

With this approach, the system can manage any failure not resulting in loss of information from nonvolatile memory. The recovery scheme uses two recovery procedures:

- undo(T_i), which restores the values of all data items updated by T_i to the old values
- redo(T_i), which sets the values of all data items updated by T_i to new values

The set of data items updated by T_i and its old and new values can be found in the log. Redo and undo operations must be idempotent to guarantee a correct behavior even if a failure occurs during the recovery process.

After a failure, the recovery scheme consults the log to determine which transactions needs to be reexecuted and which must be rolled back. The procedure is the following:

1. The transaction T_i needs to be rolled back if the log contains the $< T_i$, starts $>$ record, but it does not contain the $< T_i$, commits $>$ record;
2. The transaction T_i needs to be reexecuted if the log contains both the $< T_i$, starts $>$ and $< T_i$, commits $>$ records.

Checkpoints

When a crash system occurs, it is necessary to consult the log to determine which transactions must be reexecuted and which must be rolled back. In general, the entire log file must be scanned. This leads to two problems:

1. The search time is high, and it impacts system performance.
2. Many transactions needing to be reexecuted have already written their updates on the database and they do not *really* need to be reexecuted.

To overcome this drawback, the *checkpoints* mechanism is used. During execution, the system maintains the log according to one of the above approaches. Besides, the system periodically performs the following sequence of actions:

1. It forces all log records resident in main memory to stable storage.
2. It forces all buffer blocks to disk.
3. It forces the $<$ checkpoint $>$ record to stable storage.

With the checkpoint mechanism, one can refine the recovery scheme. After a failure occurs, the recovery scheme scans the log to find the last transaction T_i that started its execution before the last checkpoint took place. Such a transaction can be found by searching backward in the log for the first $<$ checkpoint $>$ record and then, going on, the subsequent $< T_i$, starts $>$ record.

As the transaction T_i is identified, redo and undo (only in the case of an incremental log with immediate updates) operations must be applied to T_i and to all transactions T_j that started their execution after T_i. The following steps are required:

1. For each transaction T_k such that the $< T_k$, commits $>$ appears in the log, redo(T_k) must be executed.
2. For each transaction T_k such that the $< T_k$, commits $>$ does not appear in the log, undo(T_k) must be executed.

ARIES

A particularly simple and efficient recovery method was introduced by Mohan et al. (5): ARIES (Algorithm for Recovery and Isolation Exploiting Semantics). To ensure data and transaction recovery, ARIES stores the progresses of each transaction in a log, and all actions determining changes in data.

It is a recovery method based on an incremental log with an immediate update approach. More specifically, ARIES uses a widely accepted log protocol, known as the *Write Ahead Logging* (WAL) protocol. In WAL-based systems, an updated page is written on the same nonvolatile memory location from where it was read. This means that an "update on place" is performed on nonvolatile memory.

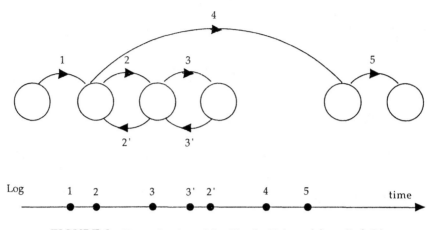

FIGURE 5   Example of partial rollback. (Adapted from Ref. 5.)

The WAL protocol enforces the fact that the log records representing changes to data must already be in stable storage before the modified data replace the previous version on nonvolatile storage; that is, the system does not write an updated page on nonvolatile memory until the undo portions of the log records describing the updates to the page are written on stable storage. To increase the reliability of this protocol, systems using WAL recovery store, in each page, the log sequence number (LSN) of the log record describing the most recent update executed on that page. In many WAL-based systems, updates executed during a rollback are kept on the log by means of *Compensation Log Records* (CLR). The eventuality of never rolling back a CLR's update depends on the particular system. As shown later, in ARIES a CLR update is never rolled back — CLR records are only redo log records; that is, they contain only redo information.

ARIES also stores, typically using CLR records, all updates performed during total (and partial) rollbacks under normal and restarting processing. Figure 5, adapted from Ref. 5, gives an example of partial rollback where a transaction, having executed three updates (respectively 1, 2 and 3), rolls back two of them (updates 2 and 3), and then goes on. Because of the undo of the two updates, 2′ and 3′, CLR records are written. At the bottom of Figure 5, the execution order of updates is depicted.

By properly chaining CLRs to log records written during forward processing, a limited amount of logging activity needs to be executed during rollbacks, also in the case of repeated failures during restarting or within nested rollback.*

The reader may note in Figure 6 (adapted from Ref. 5) that rolling back a log record results in a new CLR record. Such a record, besides containing a description of the compensating action (for redo purposes), contains a pointer (UndoNxtLSN) to the just rolled back log record predecessor. Predecessor information is quickly available, because each log record, including CLRs, contains a pointer (PrevLSN)

---

*A nested rollback takes place if a total rollback occurs after a partial one, whose termination point is a point in the transaction preceding the termination point of the first rollback.

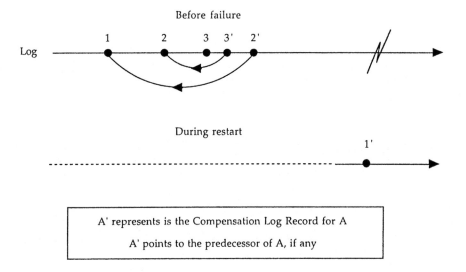

FIGURE 6   ARIES technique to avoid compensating compensations and duplicated compensations. (Adapted from Ref. 5.)

to the most recent previous log record written by the same transaction. Undo-NxtLSN allows the precise determination of how much of the transaction has not been undone so far. In Figure 6, log record 3′, which is the CLR for log record 3, points to log record 2, which is the predecessor of log record 3. Therefore, during transaction rollback, the UndoNxtLSN field of the most recently written CLR keeps track of rollback progresses. It tells the system from which point to continue if a system failure were to interrupt the completion of rollback or if a nested rollback were executed. It allows the system to bypass log records that have already been rolled back. Because CLRs are available to describe which actions are actually performed during the original action undoing, the undo action does not need to be the exact reverse of the original action. Therefore, a form of logical undo is possible, supporting a high degree of concurrency.

ARIES uses a single LSN on each page to track the page state. Whenever a page is updated and a log record is written, the LSN of the log record is placed on the page–LSN field of the updated page. By tagging this page with the LSN allows ARIES, for restart and recovery purposes, to precisely track the page state with respect to the logged updates for that page. This allows ARIES to support innovative locking modes, using which, before confirming an update on a record field on behalf of a transaction, another transaction may be authorized to modify the same data item.

Periodically, during normal processing, ARIES performs checkpoints. Checkpoint records identify active transactions, their states, and the most recently written LSNs. Moreover, they identify updated data items in the buffer. The last information is needed to determine from where the redo step must start its processing. During recovery, ARIES first scans the log, starting from the last checkpoint, until the end of the log. During this *analysis step*, information on updated pages and on transactions that were executing when the checkpoint was performed are collected. The analysis step uses information on updated pages to find the starting point to scan the log for the immediately subsequent redo step. The analysis step, moreover, determines all transactions that must be rolled back during the undo phase. For each active transaction, the most recently written LSN log record is also determined. Then, during the redo step, ARIES "replays the history" with respect to updates logged on stable storage, but whose effects on the database pages were not reflected on nonvolatile storage before the failure occurred. This simply reestablishes the database state existing when the failure occurred. A log record update is performed if page–LSN field in the affected page is lower that LSN log record.

The next step is the undo step, during which all updates are undone in reverse chronological order in a single log scanning. This is done, keeping the maximum of the LSNs of the next log record to be processed, for each of the transactions yet to be completely undone until no transaction remains to be undone. Unlike what happens during the redo step, the undo processing is not a conditional operation; that is, ARIES does not compare page–LSN fields of the affected page with the LSN log record to decide whether to perform the undo operation or not. When it finds a non-CLR record during the undo step and if it is a undo–redo log record or a only-undo, then the updates in the record must be performed. In any case, the next record to process for such transaction is determined by examining PrevLSN field of the non-CLR record. As CLRs are never undone, when a CLR is encountered during undo it is used to determine the next log record to process using the CLR UndoNxtLSN field.

Finally, in the case of transactions that were already being undone at time of failure, ARIES will only undo the actions not yet undone. This is possible because for such transaction, history has been replayed and because the last CLR written for each transaction points (directly or indirectly) to the next non-CLR record to be undone.

ISOLATION LEVELS

One of the key properties that transactions must preserve is *isolation*. In a shared database, a completely isolated system gives the illusion to each transaction that it is being executed alone, even though other transactions are executed concurrently. Providing strict isolation may, however, reduce performance. There are many applications for which it is acceptable to read not completely consistent data. To this purpose, many DBMS offer different degrees – 0, 1, 2, or 3 – of isolation to transactions. Degree 0 isolation, also known as *chaos*, is least restrictive. This degree of isolation does not allow more than one transaction to simultaneously update a data item. However, a transaction may read dirty data; that is, data which is being modified by another transaction and not yet committed by this transaction. Moreover, this degree of isolation does not prevent the updates performed by a transaction from being overwritten by another transaction before the completion of the first transaction. Degree 1 isolation, also called *browse*, does not allow data updated by uncommitted transactions to be overwritten. However, a transaction may still perform dirty reads. Degree 2 isolation, known also as *cursor stability*, in addition to providing degree 1 isolation, restricts transactions to read only committed data.

Degree 3 isolation, also called *repeatable reads*, is the most restrictive and provides complete isolation. With degree 3 isolation, a transaction that wants to read/write a data item must wait for the completion of all other transactions that previously wrote/read such data item. By allowing transactions to specify a low degree of isolation, a system can improve the response time, although at the expense of consistency.

In the remainder of this section, we first formally define the various isolation degrees. Then we show how they can be achieved by using the lock-based concurrency control protocols. Although a transaction may perform either commit or abort operations, the analysis in this section is limited to those executions containing only committed transactions. Isolation degrees may be described with histories that can be defined as follows.

Definition 2. A history H on $T = \{T_0, \ldots, T_n\}$, where $\forall T_i$, $i = 0, \ldots, n$, is a flat transaction, is a partial order with ordering relation $<_H$, where

- $H = \bigcup_{i=0}^{n} T_i$
- $<_H \supseteq \bigcup_{i=0}^{n} <_i$.

With degree 0 isolation, a transaction is not allowed to update a data item while another transaction is updating the same data item. In terms of the history, any two write operations on the same data item by two different transactions must be ordered. Formally:

Definition 3. A history H is a degree 0 isolation history if $\forall w_i[x], w_j[x] \in H$, either $w_i[x] <_H w_j[x]$ or $w_j[x] <_H w_i[x]$.

In similar manner, other isolation levels can be defined:

Definition 4. A history H is a degree 1 isolation history if

1. $\forall w_i[x], w_j[x] \in H$, either $w_i[x] <_H w_j[x]$ or $w_j[x] <_H w_i[x]$
2. $\forall w_i[x] <_H w_j[x], c_i <_H w_j[x]$.

Definition 5. A history H is a degree 2 isolation history if

1. $\forall o_i[x], o_j[x] \in H$, two conflicting operations, either $o_i[x] <_H o_j[x]$ or $o_j[x] <_H o_i[x]$
2. $\forall w_i[x] <_H o_j[x], c_i <_H o_j[x]$.

Definition 6. A history H is a degree 3 isolation history if

1. H is serializable (as defined in Ref. 6)
2. $\forall w_i[x] <_H o_j[x], c_i <_H o_j[x]$.

The most well-known protocols for achieving different isolation degrees are based on the lock. Time-stamp-based protocols have also been defined. In the following, we only present lock-based protocols. Interested readers are referred to Ref. 7 for a detailed explanation of lock-based and time-stamp-based protocols.

Degree 0 *Locking Protocol*: A transaction T_i observes degree 0 isolation if it acquires an exclusive lock on a data item x before writing it and T_i releases this lock after performing the write operation.

Degree 1 *Locking Protocol*: A transaction T_i observes degree 1 isolation if

1. T_i acquires an exclusive lock on a data item x before writing it and T_i releases this lock only at its commit time.
2. T_i does not acquire any more exclusive lock once it releases an exclusive lock on a data item.

Degree 2 *Locking Protocol*: A transaction T_i observes degree 2 isolation if

1. T_i acquires a shared lock on a data item x before reading it and acquires an exclusive lock before writing it and T_i releases its shared locks after performing the read operation but holds all its exclusive locks until its commit time.
2. T_i does not acquire any more exclusive locks once it releases an exclusive lock on a data item.

Degree 3 *Locking Protocol*: A transaction T_i observes degree 3 isolation if

1. T_i acquires a shared lock on a data item x before reading it and acquires an exclusive lock before writing it and T_i holds all its exclusive locks until its commit time.
2. T_i does not acquire any more locks on a data item.

TRANSACTION PROCESSING MONITORS

The main function of a Transaction Processing (TP) monitor is the *integration* of different systems and the management of resources, so that applications spanning several systems and resources are executed according to the transactional model. As Figure 7 suggests, a TP monitor interfaces different software systems, and its main goal is to make these systems able to work together in a particular mode, known as *transaction-oriented processing*. Consequently, a TP monitor model is not a mono-lithic piece of software; integration functions are distributed on an arbitrary number of separated system components, generally executed through several processes and, depending on the environment, on different nodes. Note that TP monitors are different from DBMSs. A DBMS, in addition to providing transactional services, provides a number of functions, such as query processing, data dictionaries, and views. By contrast, a TP monitor is focused on transactional services. Very often, a TP monitor coordinates several DBMSs, which are thus seen very much as the other resources. It is important to note, however, that not every DBMS can be managed as a resource by any TP monitor. For a DBMS to be managed by a given TP monitor, it must support the specific transaction protocol of the TP monitor. Trans-action protocols are, however, being currently standardized. Such standardization efforts open the way to improving interoperability among DBMSs and, in general, among software systems. In the following subsections, we define what transaction-oriented processing means and which services must be provided by a transaction processing system.

Transaction-Oriented Processing

Transaction-oriented processing can be characterized by several properties:

1. *Sharing*. In a transaction-oriented system, reads and writes are allowed on databases shared by several users.

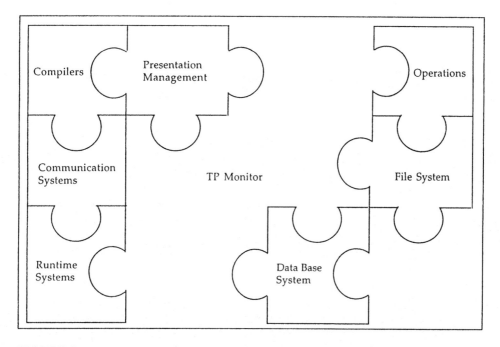

FIGURE 7   Integration function of the TP monitor with respect to different system components.

2. *Variable requests.* Requests performed by users are random; they may be distributed according to some statistics, but individual requests cannot be foreseen.

3. *Repetitive workload.* Users do not perform arbitrary programs, but they require the system to execute some functions belonging to a predefined set. Each function is an instance of a type of transaction; that is, it invokes a transaction program implementing the required function. Typical transaction processing systems provide hundreds of different functions.

4. *Mainly simple function.* Most functions are limited in size and have the duration of typical batch jobs. They are quite similar to classical batch computation, except that they respect ACID properties, have no recoverable output, and allow some degree of data sharing.

5. *Multiple terminals.* In very large On-Line Transaction Processing (OLTP) systems, there are 1000 to 100,000 terminals (clients).

6. *Intelligent clients.* OLTP terminals are often intelligent clients (workstations) which can execute their own processing, keeping some of their data items, execute window management applications, and so on.

7. *High reliability.* Because of the large number of users, the system must be available and reliable.

8. *The system performs recovery procedures.* Because data sharing is in use, there must be a formal assurance of consistency. After a failure occurs, all users must be informed about the current state of their environment,

about which functions have been executed and which have not been executed, and so on. The guiding principle in this case is based on the ACID properties of transactions.

9. *Automatic load balance*. The system should have a high throughput, assuring at the same time a short response time to the majority of user requests.

Transaction Processing System Services

A transaction processing system must allow the application programmer to take advantage of a programming environment, which provides transactional services. For data sharing, applications can use the services provided by a database manager. Database systems provide most of the mechanisms required to synchronize concurrent accesses to shared data, and to restore these data to a consistent state upon either a failure or a program error. DBMSs, however, are not able to handle functions according to request/response style, which is characteristic of on-line transaction processing (OLTP) systems. DBMSs are designed to process dynamic or precompiled SQL functions able to support batch transactions and ad hoc queries that are executed by a process per user (terminal). This approach is not adequate to the general case of transaction-oriented processing, where requests are presented with a most general client–server style, requiring some predefined services, and where a transaction can include multiple interactions among different clients and servers.

Apart from data sharing access techniques, several other system services are required to support transaction-oriented processing. Services that a transaction-oriented system must provide, possibly by cooperation with a DBMS, are the following:

1. *Handling heterogeneity*. If the application function requires access to different (heterogeneous) databases or to different resource devices (e.g., different subsystems for vendors), local mechanisms are not sufficient to ensure ACID properties for the entire function. Services must link all operations on autonomous systems into a single function.

2. *Communications control*. If the application function (or some resource manager invoked by the application) establishes communications with a remote process, the state of such communications must be controlled on behalf of the transaction services. Naturally, this requires adequate support from the underlying communication mechanism. This mechanism is called Transactional Remote Procedure Call (TRPC).

3. *Terminal management*. Functions are invoked by users through terminals of different types (workstations, conventional terminals, automated teller machines, bar code readers, etc.). Programs implementing functions must then communicate with these terminals by messages. Because ACID properties of a transaction must be perceived by the user, in addition to the program, sending and receiving messages must be part of transactions. This control must be performed by the TP monitor. In particular, the TP monitor must handle the problem arising when a response message is actually sent by the user, in case a failure occurs at the time the message has been sent.

4. *Presentation services*. If the terminal uses sophisticated presentation ser-

vices (such as a X-window system), recovery of the window environment, the cursor position, and so on must be ensured if a workstation failure occurs. This means that in a transactional environment, a X-client must act as a resource manager, implementing ACID properties for its objects (windows) in cooperation with other system resource managers.

5. *Context management.* After a transaction has been executed on behalf of a user, next function invocation (a user's input) often needs to have available the context* of the previous transaction executed by that user, terminal, or application. Some types of context are bound at only the terminal or the user, independent of any previous execution. Maintaining different types of context management is one of the duties of a TP monitor.

6. *Start/restart.* Because services are responsible for all components the application needs for its execution, the TP monitor must also manage the restart phase after any failure. By doing that, all subsystems reach a state which is consistent with respect to the ACID properties.

Note that the above list of services is not complete. We have discussed only those services which have a more or less immediate impact on the way programs are written in a transactional environment.

To summarize, we can say that a TP monitor offers the application programmer an environment providing the following features: all local executions are performed under a transaction protection; the program does not have to worry about concurrency, failures, erasing, and so on. This is all managed by underlying transaction services. All external services of the above-mentioned types automatically participate in the client's transaction. Therefore, the program does not have to worry about matters such as recovering broken connections and context rebuilding.

EXTENDED TRANSACTION MODELS

In the section A Simple Transaction Model, we have discussed the limitations of the flat transaction model. Several efforts have been made to solve each of such limitations. These researches led to the definition of new proposals extending the standard model. For example, complex updates (see Example 3) are supported by savepoints or by nested transactions; bulk updates (see Example 4) are supported by chained transactions, and so on. A new type of application results in a new, specialized, transaction model.

In the remainder of this section, the most well-known extensions to the flat transaction model are presented. The interest reader should refer to Refs. 2 and 8 for other kinds of extended model.

Flat Transactions with Savepoints

The "all-or-nothing" characteristic of the flat transaction model is both a virtue and a vice. It gives the simplest of all possible failure semantics, but in order to face possible errors during the execution, the application programmer has only two

---

*A context is the set of values of local variables, registers, and data obtained by the transaction execution.

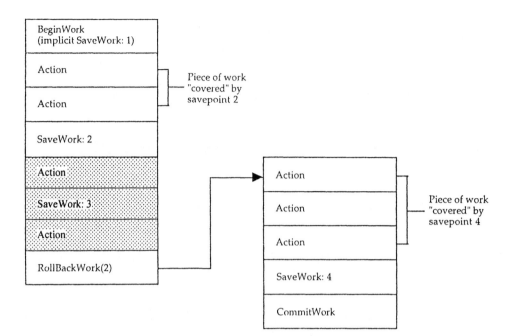

FIGURE 8   Example of the use of savepoints inside a transaction.

possibilities: He can insert into the application some special logic to recover from errors (the conventional method), or insert a RollBackWork command, giving up everything that would have been executed up to the error occurrence.

The latter approach is simpler and is appropriate for very short applications. There are, however, situations in which a substantial amount of work has been done and not all the work is invalidated by a single error in the transaction execution. If this happens, giving up the entire work is both undesirable and expensive. Having the option of stepping back to an earlier state inside the same transaction, the application can return to a proper state after an error occurs. Savepoints are used for this type of occurrence.

A *savepoint* is established by invoking a function, usually called SaveWork, which causes the system to record the current state of execution.* The application program is given a label that can be subsequently used to refer to that savepoint. Typically, the label is a monotonically increasing number. To reestablish a savepoint, the application invokes the RollBackWork function and, rather than requesting the entire transaction to be aborted, it passes the number of the savepoint it wants to restore. This approach is illustrated in Figure 8, in which shadowed actions are those rolled back due to the invocation of the RollBackWork(2) statement; the arrow points to pieces of work performed after the execution of such a statement.

A closer inspection of Figure 8 shows some interesting aspects about save-

---

*By state of execution, computer literature means the actual value of local variables, registers, and shared data.

points. First, the successful execution of the BeginWork statement establishes the first savepoint of the transaction. Second, there is a substantial difference between rolling a transaction back completely (aborting it) and rolling back to savepoint 1. In the first case, the transaction disappears from the system, is disconnected from the program that was running it, and loses all its resources. When rolling back to savepoint 1, the transaction stays alive, keeps its resources, and simply returns to an "empty state" where it has not yet done anything.

Chained Transactions

Chained transactions are a variation of savepoints. They try to achieve a compromise between rollback and the amount of lost work. This requires, however, a careful programming by the application developer.

The basic idea of a chained transaction is that, rather than taking savepoints, the application program commits what it has done so far, thereby giving up its rights to perform a rollback. At the same time, however, it is required to stay within the same transaction scope. In particular, the data items the program has acquired during the previous processing are not released. This special commit operation is called ChainWork operation. It is a combination of CommitWork and BeginWork operations. Note that this is not the same as calling CommitWork and then starting a new transaction. The combination of both statements keeps the database context bound to the application, whereas a normal commit gives up all the context. Note that using a normal commit/begin sequence, with the next transaction reestablishing the previous context, would not work. The commit and the begin are separate statements; therefore, between their executions, some other transaction could have changed the database. The next transaction in the sequence would, thus, find the database state to be very different from what it expects.

According to the transaction chaining model, one can commit one transaction, release all data items that are no longer needed, and pass on the processing context that is required for the next transaction that is started. Note that the commitment of the first transaction and the beginning of the next one are executed as one atomic operation. This means that no other transaction can have seen (or changed) any of the data that are passed from one transaction to the other. Apart from the commit/ begin sequence, each transaction behaves like a flat transaction.

We note the following differences between a transaction in the chain and one savepoint interval. First, because the chaining step irrevocably completes a transaction, rollback is limited to the currently active transaction. This corresponds to restoring the previous savepoint only, rather than selecting an arbitrary savepoint. Second, the commit allows the application to free locks that it does not need later. This provides a higher degree of concurrency than using a savepoint, which does not free any locks acquired so far. Finally, savepoints allow for a more flexible state restoration than flat transactions. After a crash, the entire chain of transactions is rolled back, irrespective of any savepoints taken so far.

Nested Transactions

Nested transactions are a generalization of savepoints. Whereas savepoints allow organizing a transaction into a *sequence* of actions that can be rolled back individually, nested transactions form a *hierarchy* of pieces of work. A nested transaction consists of a top-level transaction, controlling the activity of lower-level transactions, called *subtransactions*. Each of these subtransactions becomes a self-contained but dependent action (with the A-, C-, and I-properties of ACID), which can be completed or rolled back individually. Nesting has as many levels as the abstract layers in the application, without limitations.

The most popular definition of nested transaction is that developed by Moss (9), which can be summarized as follows:

1. A nested transaction is a tree of transactions; the subtrees are either nested or flat transactions.
2. Transactions at the leaf level are flat transactions. The distance from the root to the leaves is arbitrary.
3. The transaction at the root of the tree is called the *top-level transaction*; all the others are called *subtransactions*. A transaction predecessor in the tree is called a *parent*; a subtransaction at the next lower level is also called a *child*.
4. A subtransaction can either commit or roll back; its commit takes effect only if the parent transaction commits. By induction, therefore, any subtransaction can finally commit only if the root transaction commits.
5. Rolling back a transaction in the tree causes all its subtransactions to roll back. This condition, together with the previous one, is the reason why subtransactions have only A-, C-, and I-properties, but not the D-property.

In Moss's model, the actual work can only be performed by the leaf transactions. Only these transactions can access the database, send messages, and acquire other types of resource. The aim of higher-level transactions is to organize the processing flow and determine when to invoke subtransactions.

The rules establishing the behavior of nested transactions are the following:

1. *Commit rule.* The commit of a subtransaction makes its results accessible only to the parent transaction. The subtransaction will release its results to the outside world only if it has committed itself locally and all its ancestors up to the root have committed.
2. *Rollback rule.* If a (sub)transaction is rolled back, all its subtransactions are also rolled back, regardless of what they have done. This rule is applied recursively down the nesting hierarchy. The immediate consequence is that if the root transaction is rolled back, all its subtransactions are also rolled back.
3. *Visibility rule.* All changes made by a subtransaction become visible to the parent transaction at subtransaction commitment. All data items held by a parent transaction can be made accessible to its subtransactions. Changes made by a subtransaction are not visible to its siblings, in case they execute concurrently.

It is important to note that subtransactions are not exactly equivalent to flat transactions. Subtransactions are valid only within the confines of the surrounding higher-level transaction. They are *atomic* from the point of view of the parent transaction; they are *consistency-preserving* with respect to the local function they implement; they are *isolated* from all other activities inside and outside the parent transaction; they are *not durable* because of the commit rule.

Distributed Transactions

A distributed transaction consists of a flat transaction that runs in a distributed environment and, therefore, has to visit several nodes in the network, depending on where the data are located. There exist several differences between distributed transactions and nested transactions.

Nested transactions are structured by the functional decomposition of the application (i.e., by what the application views). The structure of a distributed transaction depends on the distribution of data in a network. The invocation structure of a distributed transaction is, however, exactly the same of a nested transaction.

As mentioned, the decomposition into subtransactions does not reflect a hierarchical structure in the programs to be executed but is induced by the position of the data in the network. Simple flat transactions (from the application perspective) may be executed as distributed transactions if they run in a distributed database system and the data they access are scattered across multiple nodes. If a subtransaction issues CommitWork, this signals the commit of the entire transaction, which forces all other subtransactions to commit. By comparison, in a nested transaction this is simply a local commit of that subtransaction. Distributed transactions normally cannot roll back independently; their decision to abort also affects the entire transaction. This all means that the connection between subtransactions and their parents is much stronger in the distributed transaction model than those existing in the nested transaction model.

Multilevel Transactions

Multilevel transactions are a generalized and more liberal version of nested transactions. They allow a premature commitment of a subtransaction (also called precommit). However, rather than just letting the subtransaction disappear, they assume the existence of a compensating transaction, able to semantically reverse the actions performed by the original subtransaction in case the parent transaction decides (or is forced) to roll back. This compensating transaction can, of course, be another nested or multilevel transaction.

Note, again, the important differences in techniques used to achieve atomicity: As long as strict commitment control can be exercised over the modified data, it is possible at any point in time to decide to roll back, which then can be performed by just reestablishing the old value.

Open-Nested Transactions

Open-nested transactions are the "anarchic" version of multilevel transactions. Subtransactions can either abort or commit independently to the status of the parent transaction. There are no restrictions with respect to the semantic relationships of parent and child transactions. In particular, no data hierarchy, or anything like it, is assumed.

Another way to describe open-nested transactions is to say that they are a means for firing off other top-level transactions without exercising any further control over them.

Work-Flow Transactions

An important application area has recently entered the database management systems world: managing all activities that belong to the business sphere of a given company. The goal is to better support business processes of companies and organizations.

Today, companies must face several problems, such as competition with other companies practicing the same activity and reduction of business management costs, assuring at the same time a fast development of new services/products. To do this, they must constantly optimize business procedures and make existing information systems and applications more flexible.

Initially, business procedures were entirely handled by humans. As a result of introducing information technology, processes have been partially or totally automated by programs executed by computers able to perform procedures and to enforce rules previously handled by humans.

The *work-flow technology* plays a fundamental role in automating business procedures. It provides software to support business processes, modeling them through *work-flow specifications*.

There is no work-flow definition commonly adopted. The term work-flow is used to denote a business process, a process specification, the software implementing and automating a process, and the software supporting coordination and cooperation among people who implement a process.

Following the definition adopted in Ref. 10, *a work flow is a collection of tasks* organized in such a way to perform business processes (for instance, telephonic purchase orders and insurance claims processing). A process can be performed by one or more software systems, one or more groups of people, or a combination of them. Besides being a collection of tasks, *a work flow defines processes invocation order* and *processes invocation conditions*; moreover, it handles *processes synchronization* and *information flow*.

Work-Flow Management (WFM) is a technology which supports reengineering of business processes. It deals with defining work flow or describing those aspects of a process that can be relevant for establishing the control and the coordination of the various tasks constituting it. Moreover, a WFM system must support (re)design and (re)implementation of processes because of changes in information and business processing systems.

To efficiently support WFM, existing processing environments must be extended to achieve new distributed environments that exhibit the following:

1. Are *component oriented*, which means supporting integration and interoperability among system components
2. Support *work-flow applications*, corresponding to implementations of information or business processes accessing to heterogeneous, autonomous, and distributed (HAD) systems

3. Assure application correctness and reliability* in case of concurrent executions and failures
4. Support evolution, addition, and elimination of work-flow applications and system components when reengineering is necessary

Several commercial systems have been developed to support WFM. Nowadays, WFM systems for office automation can support document management, application management, and/or human coordination, collaboration, and codecision. Although many such WFM systems meet the above requirements, they only support a limited interoperability (in terms of HAD system types they can integrate and tasks they can support). Moreover, they are not able to ensure correctness and reliability of applications when concurrently executing and in spite of failures, and they also suffer from low performance.

To meet the above requirements, as pointed out in Ref. 10, two technologies need to be combined with those supplied by commercial WFM systems:

- Distributed Object Management (DOM)
- Customized Transaction Management (CTM)

DOM supports interoperability and integration among HAD systems and applications implementing information and business processes. DOM also allows a WFM system to deal with problems such as replacement, migration, and evolution of HAD systems and modifications in their functions. Moreover, DOM technology provides an object model that makes managing complexity easy, by means of functionalities that are typical of object-oriented systems, such as abstraction, inheritance, and polymorphism.

CTM technology assures correctness and reliability of applications that implement information and business processes, also fulfilling some important requirements, such as isolation, coordination, and collaboration among tasks. Moreover, CTM handles changes in correctness and reliability requirements of a process, and guarantees correctness and reliability.

In the following, the generic term *process* is used to refer to business processes, information processes, or both business processes and their corresponding information processes. WFM includes everything from modeling processes to synchronization of activities among systems and people performing processes. In particular, work-flow management involves the following:

1. *Modeling processes and work-flow specifications*: This requires designing work-flow models and methodologies to represent processes as work-flow specifications.
2. *Processes reengineering*: This requires ad hoc methodologies to optimize business processes.
3. *Work-flow implementation and automation*: This requires methodologies/technologies for using information systems, and people to implement, perform, and control tasks according to work-flow specifications.

---

*When multiple objects (databases, files, document, etc.) are accessed by a work-flow execution, several consistency problems may arise because of concurrent execution and failures. This leads to the requirement for concurrency control, recovery, and transactions coordination mechanisms.

The modeling phase of a process starts with a request for information from people having expert knowledge about the process. When a sufficient amount of information is collected, work-flow specifications are produced to formally model the process. On the other hand, executing work-flow specifications requires a *work-flow model*. This model typically includes a set of useful concepts to describe processes, their tasks, dependencies among tasks, and roles of specified tasks.

Work-flow specifications are usually expressed by a *specification language*. Work-flow specification languages of commercial WFM systems use rules, constraints, and/or graphical constructs to describe ordering and synchronization among tasks of a work flow, and use tasks attributes to describe tasks and their roles.

The aim of reengineering methodologies is optimizing business processes. Process optimization strategies depend on reengineering objectives (for instance, reducing business costs and introducing new products/services).

Work-flow implementation deals with all problems about realizing a work flow, using computers, software, information systems, and WFM systems. Work-flow automation deals, instead, with scheduling and controlling the work-flow execution.

Transaction mechanisms for work-flow applications require several extensions that we discuss in the following subsection.

Customized Transaction Management

A customized transaction management (CTM) system can specifically support correctness, reliability, and functional requirements for work-flow applications. To ensure work-flow correctness and reliability, each work-flow application must be associated with a *transactional model*. DBMS and TP monitors provide an ACID transactional model as a default for every application that uses their transaction processing services. The basic transaction model must verify all ACID properties; this allows applications to interleave only if their concurrent execution is equivalent to a serial execution. The basic transaction model is not appropriate for many work-flow applications. For instance, the basic model ensures process isolation, but it does not permit any cooperation among processes. This is too restrictive for work-flows requesting process interaction.

CTM is the technology satisfying work-flow requirements. CTM supports the definition of extended transactional models. *Transactional work flow* enables the coordinated execution of several processes, can involve human resources, and support the use of ACID properties for any process or for the entire work flow. Transactional work-flow is supported by an extended transactional model defining correctness and reliability criteria for work flows. Work-flow requirements are typically so different that a single extended model is not sufficient to satisfy work-flow necessities.

The need to introduce extended models to extend the traditional transaction model in order to provide further functionalities requested by applications and to improve system performance has been recognized a long time ago. Several extended models have been proposed; however, many of these extensions resulted in new models offering correctness guarantees that are appropriate for an application but do not assure correctness for other applications. Moreover, an extended model can impose restrictions not acceptable for an application, although required by others.

If no extended models satisfy an application requirement, a new model must be defined, and so on.

Transactional work-flow specification involves the specification of customized models by defining work-flow structures and correctness criteria. A customized model specification is based on the fact that a transaction consists of a set of component transactions (corresponding to processes constituting a work flow) and a set of transactional dependencies among them (corresponding to the work-flow structure and correctness criteria). If a transactional work flow allows nested levels, the constituent transactions may contain, in turn, component transactions. Each transactional work flow T has two types of dependency:

- Intratransaction dependencies, defining relations among the component transactions of T
- Intertransaction dependencies, defining relations among T and all other transactional work flow.

A first category of intratransactions consists of *state dependencies*. Dependencies in this category are conditions on transaction states. Defining intratransaction state dependencies involves the use of transaction semantics (e.g., BeginWork, Abort-Work and CommitWork) to specify the work-flow processes ordering. Such specifications are more precise than those achieved by work-flow specification languages of WFM systems.

The second category of intratransaction dependencies consists of *correctness dependencies*, which specify which concurrent executions of transactional work flows preserve consistency and produce correct results, thereby defining correctness criteria.

Commercial DBMSs, TP monitors, and multidatabases currently support only a small set of extended models. For example, a CORBA transaction service (see Ref. 11 for more explanations) is essentially a TP monitor. Therefore, it has the same limitations of other TP monitors. The CTM concept and the research to develop CTM technologies are quite recent. The Transaction Specification and Management Environment (TSME) is an example of a research effort to develop a CTM technology (12). To support specifications of an extended model and the configuration of the corresponding transaction management mechanism, TSME provides a transaction dependencies specification facility and a programmable mechanism for managing transactions.

CONCLUDING REMARKS

In this article, we have presented the main concepts underlying the notion of transaction as well as techniques giving a concrete implementation of these concepts. Before concluding the article, we would like to take a look at other developments in the transaction area. Because of its relevance to database technology, the transaction processing area has been and still is a very active area of research and development. Roughly speaking, developments can be categorized along three directions: extensions arising from new data models; extensions arising from developments in system architectures; and extensions arising from new applications. In the remainder, we briefly discuss such directions.

The database area has been characterized by intense research in the area of data models with the goal of developing models semantically richer than the relational model. Very well-known models include the object-oriented data model, the deductive data model, the active data model, and the most recent object-relational model. The semantic expressivity of those models has required extensions to transaction models in several respects. Modeling notions such as inheritance hierarchies, composite objects, and versions required the introduction of new locking modes (13). Triggers, typical of active database systems, have required investigating different *coupling modes* for processing updates generated by trigger executions; for example, such updates can be executed during the transaction which generated them or as a separate transaction. Moreover, the fact that more semantics about the data is represented by those models makes it possible to exploit the semantics for more efficient concurrency control algorithms, thus resulting in *semantics-based* algorithms.

Among the developments in system architectures that have an impact on transaction processing techniques, we would like to mention main-memory systems and parallel systems. In main-memory systems, the entire database resides in main memory with backup copies on secondary storage. Such an architecture has required revisiting recovery techniques to ensure that information needed to recover the database can be saved on secondary storage without performance penalty on the normal main-memory operations. An approach proposed in Ref. 14 is based on the use of two independent processors: a main processor and a recovery processor. Parallel architectures are crucial in database systems because of their role in substantially improving performance. In such architectures, data sets are often partitioned across multiple nodes. Such an approach allows the same operation to be performed in parallel on all data belonging to the same set. It requires, however, maintaining consistency among the various partitions and in all related access structures (see, for example, the locking protocol for the two-level indices presented in Ref. 15).

Database management systems are being used in many different environments; many of them require substantial extensions to transaction models and architectures. Among the application environments, we would like to recall the following: design applications, highly secure systems, real-time systems, mobile computing systems, and WWW applications. Design applications are characterized by the fact that change to the data may require days or weeks or even months, unlike conventional transactions that last a few milliseconds. Often, in such applications, data are extracted from a common database, cached at the user workstations, and modified by the users through specialized editors (e.g., CAD editors). To support such applications, notions such as long-duration transactions, check-in/check-out mechanisms, and versions have been introduced. Highly secure systems require transactions accessing highly sensitive data be executed in complete isolation from other transactions. This requires the use of special concurrency control techniques to prevent any interference among transactions accessing data of different sensitivity. Today, commercial products are available using such techniques. Real-time systems represent an important and difficult area. Such systems have transactions with stringent deadlines; each transaction must complete with a certain time. In general, a transaction in such a system is assigned a priority denoting the "urgency" that the transaction has in completing its execution. Because of this requirement, a transaction with high priority may not be able to wait for a lock to be released; therefore, special approaches must be used in scheduling transactions. Mobile computing systems are characterized by the fact that users perform their tasks on mobile computing devices — called mobile hosts. Mobile hosts are connected via wireless networks to fixed hosts. Mobile hosts interact with the fixed hosts to retrieve and store data. Mobile hosts may, however, become disconnected from the fixed hosts. The main problem is that users may continue working on their mobile hosts, even when being disconnected from the network. This situation requires extending recovery and concurrency control techniques, developed for distributed systems, to this new environment. Finally, WWW applications and Java-like systems will raise new requirements toward transaction managements. Research to identify those requirements and related approaches is just at its beginning (16).

REFERENCES

1. E. Bertino, S. Jajodia, and P. Samarati, "Database Security: Research and Practice," *Inform. Syst.*, *20*(7), 537–556 (1995).
2. J. Gray and A. Reuter, *Transaction Processing: Concepts and Techniques*, Morgan Kaufmann, San Mateo, CA, 1993.
3. P. O'Neil, *Database — Principles, Programming, Performance*, Morgan Kaufmann, San Mateo, CA, 1994.
4. H. F. Korth and A. Silberschatz, *Database System Concepts*, McGraw-Hill, Singapore, 1986.
5. C. Mohan, D. Haderle, B. Lindsay, H. Pirahesh, and P. Schwarz, "ARIES: A Transaction Recovery Method Supporting Fine-Granularity Locking and Partial Rollbacks Using Write-Ahead Logging," *ACM Trans. Database Syst.*, *17*(1), 94–162 (1992).
6. P. A. Bernstein, V. Hadzilacos, and N. Goodman, *Concurrency Control and Recovery in Database Systems*, Addison-Wesley, Reading, MA, 1987.
7. V. Atluri, E. Bertino, and S. Jajodia, "A Theoretical Formulation for Degrees of Isolation in Databases," *Inform. Software Technol, 39*(1), 47–53 (1997).
8. A. K. Elmagarmid, *Database Transaction Models for Advanced Applications*, Morgan Kaufmann, San Mateo, CA, 1990.
9. J. E. B. Moss, "Nested Transaction: An Approach to Reliable Distributed Computing," Technical Report MIT, LCS-TR-260 (1981).
10. D. Georgakopolous, M. Hornik, and A. Sheth, "An Overview of Workflow Management: From Process Modeling to Workflow Automation Infrastructure," *Distrib. Parallel Databases*, *3*, 119–153 (1995).
11. *Object Transaction Service.* OMG TC Document 92.11.1 (1992).
12. D. Georgakopolous, M. Hornik, P. Krychniak, and F. Manola, "Specification and Management of Extended Transactions in a Programmable Transaction Environment," in *Proc. of the 10th Int. Conference on Data Engineering*, February 1994.
13. W. Kim, E. Bertino, and J. Garza, "Composite Objects Revisited," in *Proc. of the Int. ACM–SIGMOD Conference on Management of Data*, May 1989.
14. T. Lehman and M. Carey, "A Recovery Algorithm for a High-Performance Memory-Resident Database Systems," in *Proc. of the Int. ACM–SIGMOD Conference on Management of Data*, May 27–29, 1987.
15. D. M. Choy and C. Mohan, "Locking Protocols for Two-Tier Indexing of Partitioned Data," in *Proc. of the Int. Workshop on Advanced Transaction Models and Architectures (ATMA)*, August 31–September 2, 1996.

16. L. Daynes, M. Atkinson, and P. Valduriez, "Efficient Support for Customizing Concurrency Control in Persistent Java," in *Proc. of the Int. Workshop on Advanced Transaction Models and Architectures (ATMA)*, August 31–September 2, 1996.

ELISA BERTINO

BARBARA CATANIA

ALESSIA VINAI